THE Java™ Tutorial *Continued*

The Rest of the JDK™

The Java™ Series

Lisa Friendly, Series Editor
Tim Lindholm, Technical Editor
Please see our web site (http://www.awl.com /cseng/javaseries) for more information on these titles.

Ken Arnold and James Gosling, *The Java™ Programming Language, Second Edition*
ISBN 0-201-31006-6

Mary Campione and Kathy Walrath, *The Java™ Tutorial, Second Edition: Object-Oriented Programming for the Internet* (Book/CD)
ISBN 0-201-31007-4

Mary Campione, Kathy Walrath, Alison Huml, and the Tutorial Team, *The Java™ Tutorial Continued: The Rest of the JDK™* (Book/CD)
ISBN 0-201-48558-3

Patrick Chan, *The Java™ Developers Almanac 1999*
ISBN 0-201-43298-6

Patrick Chan and Rosanna Lee, *The Java™ Class Libraries, Second Edition, Volume 2: java.applet, java.awt, java.beans*
ISBN 0-201-31003-1

Patrick Chan, Rosanna Lee, and Doug Kramer, *The Java™ Class Libraries, Second Edition, Volume 1: java.io, java.lang, java.math, java.net, java.text, java.util*
ISBN 0-201-31002-3

Patrick Chan, Rosanna Lee, and Doug Kramer, *The Java™ Class Libraries, Second Edition, Volume 1: 1.2 Supplement*
ISBN 0-201-48552-4

James Gosling, Bill Joy, and Guy Steele, *The Java™ Language Specification*
ISBN 0-201-63451-1

James Gosling, Frank Yellin, and The Java Team, *The Java™ Application Programming Interface, Volume 1: Core Packages*
ISBN 0-201-63453-8

James Gosling, Frank Yellin, and The Java Team, *The Java™ Application Programming Interface, Volume 2: Window Toolkit and Applets*
ISBN 0-201-63459-7

Graham Hamilton, Rick Cattell, and Maydene Fisher, *JDBC™ Database Access with Java™: A Tutorial and Annotated Reference*
ISBN 0-201-30995-5

Jonni Kanerva, *The Java™ FAQ*
ISBN 0-201-63456-2

Doug Lea, *Concurrent Programming in Java™: Design Principles and Patterns*
ISBN 0-201-69581-2

Tim Lindholm and Frank Yellin, *The Java™ Virtual Machine Specification*
ISBN 0-201-63452-X

Henry Sowizral, Kevin Rushforth, and Michael Deering, *The Java™ 3D API Specification*
ISBN 0-201-32576-4

THE Java™ Tutorial *Continued*

The Rest of the JDK™

Mary Campione
Kathy Walrath
Alison Huml
and the
Tutorial Team

ADDISON-WESLEY
An imprint of Addison Wesley Longman, Inc.
Reading, Massachusetts • Harlow, England • Menlo Park, California
Berkeley, California • Don Mills, Ontario • Sydney
Bonn • Amsterdam • Tokyo • Mexico City

Library of Congress Cataloging-in-Publication Data

Campione, Mary.

The Java tutorial continued: the rest of the JDK/ Mary Campione, Kathy Walrath, Alison Huml, the tutorial team.

p. cm. -- (The Java series)

Includes bibliographical references and index.

ISBN 0-201-48558-3

1. Object-oriented programming (Computer science) 2. Java (Computer program language) 3. Internet programming I. Walrath, Kathy. II. Huml, Alison. III. Title.

TS1925.K5413 1998

005.1'7--dc21 98-37595

CIP

The publisher offers discounts on this book when ordered in quantity for special sales.
For more information, please contact: Corporate, Government and Special Sales; Addison Wesley Longman, Inc.; One Jacob Way; Reading, Massachusetts 01867.

ISBN 0-201-48558-3
1 2 3 4 5 6 7 8 9-CRS-0201009998
First Printing, December 1998

Contents

Preface

As the title implies, this volume of *The Java Tutorial* starts where the first ends. The first book covers API present in the Java platform's first release. This book covers API subsequently added to the Java platform.

This book is a collection of tutorials written by Java team members. Each author who contributed to this book is an authority in his or her area of the Java platform. Some authors are the creators of the API they describe.

The content of this book, along with the content of the other tutorial books,[1] is available online here:

```
http://java.sun.com/docs/books/tutorial/index.html
```

From the online tutorial to the first book, and from the first book to this one, our intent has always been to create a fun, easy-to-read, task-oriented programmer's guide with lots of practical examples to help people learn to program using the Java platform.

The hyperlinked origins of this book will be evident as you read it. For instance, underlined phrases throughout this book mimic online links. A link to material within this book is followed by the appropriate page number. A link to material outside this book, such as to the JDK API documentation, is accompanied by a footnote that contains a URL. Other evidence of this book's online origin can be found on the first page of each trail/lesson, which provides the URL where the trail/lesson can be found in the online tutorial.

You might be wondering why we use the terms "trails" and "lessons." We know that people don't learn linearly. People learn by posing a problem, solving it, uncovering other problems, solving them, and learning information as the need

[1] *The Java Tutorial, Second Edition* and *The JFC Swing Tutorial*

arises. Our original vision for the online tutorial was to encourage and enable this type of thinking and learning. We envisioned a mountain of ski trails, where at any junction, a reader could choose the most interesting or appropriate path at that time. But we also needed some sort of structure and organization, so we created a two-tiered hierarchy: trails at the top level and lessons within them. We also use a high level of linking to help you pick and choose where you go and when.

What You Need

This book documents the Java Development Kit™ (JDK) 1.1 and 1.2 versions of the Java platform. To compile and run the examples in this book you need a development environment that is compatible with JDK 1.1 or 1.2. You can use a commercially-available development environment or the JDK itself. The CD-ROM that accompanies this book includes copies of the latest available release of each JDK version. Or you might want to visit the Java Web site to download the latest JDK release:

```
http://java.sun.com/products/jdk/
```

If you are using the JDK provided by Sun Microsystems, you will need one of the following systems:

- Microsoft Windows 95/NT 4.0 running on Intel (or compatible) x86
- Solaris 2.4 or 2.5 running on SPARC
- Solaris 2.5 running on x86

If you are developing applets, you either need a browser that supports the JDK 1.1 or 1.2 API, or you need to install the Java Plug-in. The Java Plug-in ensures that your browser uses the latest Java Runtime Environment compatible with JDK 1.1 or 1.2. The Java Plug-in is included on the CD-ROM that accompanies this book and is also available online.[1] For testing applets, you can also use a special, limited browser called the Applet Viewer that ships with the JDK.

Finally, you need an editor that can save files in ASCII format with a `.java` extension. Also, the editor must allow you to specify both uppercase and lowercase letters in the filename.

---

[1] http://java.sun.com/products/plugin/

Editor Acknowledgments

The editors would like to thank the authors who contributed to this volume. Their work on this book was in addition to their normal, crazy workload. We appreciate their hard work and enthusiasm for this project.

Our reviewers include a patient group of readers at Sun Microsystems and our diligent and patient Internet readers, who send us email to point out our errors and help us revise our awkward sentences. In particular, we'd like to thank Jennifer Ball, Pat Chan, Lisa Friendly, Doug Kramer, and Tim Lindholm for helping to review the trails in this book.

Our team managers, Lisa Friendly, Rick Levenson, and Stans Kleijnen, create a supportive work environment that helps us get our job done. Lisa Friendly is also a helpful source of advice, consolation, encouragement, and stories. Mike Hendrickson, our editorial advisor at Addison-Wesley, is patient, motivating, and full of inspiring ideas for the next thing. Sarah Weaver was the wonderful production manager on the book who kept us on schedule. Evelyn Pyle was our attentive copy editor. Marina Lang and the rest of the team at Addison-Wesley have been a pleasure to work with and continually strive for excellence on this and the other books in the series.

For acknowledgments from the contributing authors, see "About the Author" at the end of each trail.

About the Editors

Mary Campione is a senior technical writer at Sun Microsystems, where she's been writing about the Java platform since 1995. Mary graduated from Cal Poly, San Luis Obispo, with a B.S. in Computer Science and has been a technical writer and programmer for 13 years. In addition to the tutorial books, she is the co-author of *PostScript by Example* (Addison-Wesley, 1992). Mary and her family enjoy summer weekends at the beach and winter weekends on the slopes.

Kathy Walrath is a senior technical writer on the Swing team at Sun Microsystems. After graduating from UC Berkeley with a B.S. in Electrical Engineering and Computer Science, Kathy wrote extensively about UNIX, Mach, and NEXTSTEP. Since 1993, Kathy has been writing specifications and how-to guides for the Java platform. She and her family spend their free hours spelunking for books, coffee, and used furniture in San Francisco.

Alison Huml is a technical writer at Sun Microsystems. Alison graduated from UC Berkeley and is currently pursuing a master's degree in Interdisciplinary Computer Science at Mills College. Prior to joining Sun, Alison worked as a technical writer at various start-ups, including Black Sun Interactive. She specializes in documentation designed for the Web. When not sitting in front of her computer, Alison enjoys carving, hiking, and getting coffee with her husband.

For biographies of authors who contributed to this volume, see the section "About the Author" at the end of each trail.

Before You Start

PLEASE read one or both of the following sections, according to your experience with the Java platform.

Getting Started (page 1) is for Java newbies. Skip this if you're comfortable writing and running programs in the Java language.

Finding the Information You Want (page 2) is for all readers. It lists the navigational aids that can help you find your path through this book.

Getting Started

If you haven't written and run programs in the Java language, then please close this book and go to the Getting Started trail of *The Java Tutorial*. That trail introduces you to the Java language and platform, and then leads you through writing and running a basic application and applet. You can find it either at the beginning of the first tutorial book, *The Java Tutorial, Second Edition*, or online at this URL:

```
http://java.sun.com/docs/books/tutorial/getStarted/index.html
```

At various points, the Getting Started trail suggests other sections that you might want to read. For example, it introduces you to objects and classes, and then tells you where you can find detailed information about them. Once you feel comfortable with the Java language and confident that you know your way around *The Java Tutorial*, please return to this book.

Finding the Information You Want

We try to make it easy for you to skip around this book, choosing exactly which trails and lessons you want to read. That's why this book is heavily cross-referenced and why we provide self-contained trails and lessons. We also provide the following navigational aids:

- Contents (page v) lists all of the trails and lessons in this book.
- The Trail Map (page 3) describes each trail in this book and also shows trail groups. For example, security, RMI, and IDL all are related to connectivity, so those trails are in one group.
- The Overview (page 5) describes each topic covered by this book and summarizes the evolution of the Java platform. Each mention of a feature is accompanied by a link to the trail, lesson, or online resource in which the API is covered.
- The beginning of each trail is a mini-preface—it provides a description of the trail, its audience, alternatives to the trail, and so on. Additionally, each trail has its own miniature table of contents that lists each lesson and major section in the trail.
- The beginning of each lesson is similar to the beginning of each trail. You will find there a list of sections in the lesson and a description of what you can expect to learn.
- Within each lesson, you can expect to find links to related information whenever appropriate.
- The Code Examples (page 717) contains full source code listings, along with links to where in this book each program is discussed.
- The Index (page 923) is a traditional book index.

Trail Map

Trail	Description
Overview	Find brief descriptions of the topics covered in this book.
Collections	Use Java's collection framework to store and manipulate groups of related objects. Collections can make your programs smaller, faster, and more reusable.
Internationalization	Write programs for the global market. After internationalization, your software can support new languages and cultures without changes to the source code.
2D Graphics	Enhance the appearance of your GUI with shapes, color, stylized text, foreign-language text, and image processing. Also, learn how to add printing capability to your programs.
Sound	Play sounds in AIFF, AU, WAV, MIDI, or RAF formats in your applets and applications.
JavaBeans	Learn how to develop platform-independent components in the Java programming language. This trail covers JavaBeans basics, the BeanBox, and Beans Development Kit.
JDBC Database Access	Use the JDBC to connect to a database, send SQL statements, and process the results. The JDBC provides uniform access to a wide range of relational databases and provides a common base on which database tools can be built
Remote Method Invocation	Call methods on an object running in another VM. RMI is often used to implement client/server applications.
Java IDL	Java IDL provides CORBA-compliant interoperability for programs written in Java.
Servlets	Learn how to use the Servlet API to extend the functionality of your server.
Security	Learn how built-in security features protect you from malevolent programs. See how to use tools for controlling access to resources, generating and checking digital signatures, and creating and managing keys needed for signature generation and checking. See how to incorporate security checks and cryptography services into your programs.
JAR File Format	Bundle a Java program and its resources into an easily downloadable, secure archive.
Java Extension Mechanism	Expand the functionality of the Java platform by using a standard, scalable way to make custom APIs available to all applications running on the Java platform.
Java Native Interface	Use the Java Native Interface API to retain your investment in code written in other languages. The JNI lets you integrate native methods written in C or C++ with Java programs.
Reflection	Learn how to dynamically create objects, invoke methods, access fields, and examine classes.

Overview

Essential Classes

Advanced GUI Building

Networking and Connectivity

Packaging Your Programs

Advanced Language Topics

Overview

by Monica Pawlan

IN general, this book covers core API that was added to the Java™ Development Kit (JDK™) for the 1.1 or 1.2 release. It also covers one standard extension—servlets. Most of the topics that are not in this book are covered in the online tutorial[1] and in the other tutorial books.[2]

To help you sort out which features were added in which release, we provide two tables. Table 1, "Features Added to JDK 1.1 and Enhanced in JDK 1.2," on page 13 summarizes the features added to JDK 1.1, with notes about any JDK 1.2 enhancements. Table 2, "Summary of Features Added to JDK 1.2," on page 15 summarizes the features introduced in JDK 1.2. The tables include references to trails in this book or online where you can find information about each topic.

Because the list of features covered in this book is long, we've grouped related features together as follows:

- **Essential Classes**—Collections and Internationalization
- **Advanced GUI Building**—2D Graphics, Sound, and JavaBeans™
- **Networking and Connectivity**—JDBC™, RMI, IDL, Servlets, and Security
- **Packaging**—JAR and the Extension Mechanism
- **Advanced Language Topics**—Java Native Interface and Reflection

---

1 *The Java Tutorial* in its entirety is included on the CD-ROM that accompanies this book and can also be found online here: http://java.sun.com/docs/books/tutorial/index.html

2 *The Java Tutorial, Second Edition*, and *The JFC Swing Tutorial: A Guide to Constructing GUIs*.

Essential Classes

The collections and internationalization APIs are essential to most enterprise applications.

Collections

A collection, or container, consists of multiple objects grouped into a single object. Normally collections represent data items that form a natural group, such as names and addresses or resumes.

The collections API includes a framework, which is a unified architecture for representing and manipulating collections of objects independent of their representation details. Collections enable interoperability between unrelated API, encourage software reuse, and make it easier to design, implement, or learn a new API.

Collections were added in JDK 1.2.

Internationalization

Internationalization lets you design an application so it can be adapted to many languages and regions without recompiling. The textual data, such as messages and GUI component labels, and other culturally dependent data, such as dates and currencies, are isolated from the rest of the application in sets of files, with one set containing the text for a given language and region. For example, a single application might have a set of files for French and another set for Canadian French; because the language code is specified at runtime, the same application can be distributed to Canada and to France with no modifications to the executable code. By isolating the text to be translated, you also save translation costs.

In JDK 1.2 changes to the internationalization API include the addition of the input method framework and a number of surface changes that involved renaming and moving methods and changing the order of method parameters for simplification.

Advanced GUI Building

The Java 2D API, JavaBeans, and the Sound engine provide advanced functionality for building interesting, modular, and more usable user interfaces.

2D Graphics

The Java 2D API, introduced in JDK 1.2, gives you everything you need to enhance the appearance of your GUI with shapes, color, stylized text, foreign-language text, and image processing. The Java 2D API also introduces a printing model that gives you more control, power, and flexibility in application-level printing.

The `java.awt` and the `java.awt.image` packages are enhanced. New packages are `java.awt.color`, `java.awt.font`, `java.awt.geom`, and `java.awt.print`.

- The `java.awt` package includes the new `Graphics2D` class for better geometry, transformation, color, and text rendering, and has enhanced color and font capabilities. The `Color` class supports a full range of color spaces, and the `Font` class supports any font on the system. You also get more texture map and fill pattern options; image compositing and transparency capabilities; more line widths, end caps, line styles, and dash patterns; and a flexible device model.
- The `java.awt.color` package supports high-quality color output, using profiles and a full array of color spaces for defining device-dependent and device-independent color attributes.
- The `java.awt.font` package supports *glyphs* and text with multiple fonts that can be transformed and drawn into a graphics context.
- The `java.awt.geom` package lets you create a wide range of shapes, including arbitrary and point-by-point paths; perform *affine* transformations (transformations that maintain parallel lines); and use float and/or double precision in most cases.
- The `java.awt.image` package supports a full range of image-processing capabilities, including affine transformation, amplitude scaling, lookup-table modification, color conversions, and convolutions. The `BufferedImage` class describes an image with an accessible buffer of image data consisting of color model and data layout information.
- The `java.awt.print` package introduces for the Win32 and Solaris platforms a printing model whereby the printing system drives the printing process to give you more control, power, and flexibility in application-level printing. The Java 2D printing system can print all Java 2D regular and composite graphics, and supports soft collating, reverse-order printing, and booklet printing.

Sound

Before JDK 1.2, only applets could play sound and only one sound format was supported. JDK 1.2 adds an `Applet` class method, `newAudioClip`, that enables all kinds of programs to load and play sounds. The Sound engine in JDK 1.2 adds support for several sound formats, including AIFF, WAV, MIDI, and RMF.

JavaBeans

Introduced in JDK 1.1, JavaBeans let you build reusable and interchangeable software components that can be visually constructed and manipulated in builder tools. JavaBeans can be simple, such as pushbuttons or dialog boxes, or more complex, such as spreadsheets and calendars. Individual JavaBeans vary in functionality, but most have the following features in common:

- Introspection, which allows a builder tool to analyze how a Bean works.
- Customization, which allows a user to alter the appearance and the behavior of a Bean.
- Events, which allow Beans to fire events and to inform builder tools about events.
- Properties, which allow Beans to be manipulated programmatically and to support customization.
- Persistence, which allows customized Beans in an application builder to have their states saved and restored. Typically persistence is used with an application builder's Save and Load menu commands to restore any work that has gone into constructing an application.

In JDK 1.2 JavaBeans includes an extensible and standard runtime containment and services protocol, as well as drag-and-drop support. When a Bean is introduced to its environment, it knows it is running inside the Java Virtual Machine (JVM) and has access to the core Java API. The protocol provides a standard way to nest Beans within other Beans and to have the nested Bean be able to access additional runtime services from its environment. Also, the environment or containing Bean can extend its capabilities directly to the nested Bean.

Drag-and-drop support means that Java and non-Java applications can readily share data. JavaBeans Drag and Drop works with the JFC accessibility API and can be extended to support diverse input devices.

Networking and Connectivity

Various Java APIs let you safely interact with resources on the Internet, on the network, and in databases.

JDBC Database Access

Introduced in JDK 1.1, JDBC makes it possible to send SQL statements to a database and to process the results that are returned. JDBC provides uniform access to a wide range of relational databases and provides a common base on which database tools can be built.

The JDBC implementation includes a driver manager to support multiple drivers that mediate the connections between JDBC and various databases. A driver can be written either entirely in the Java programming language so it can be downloaded as part of an applet or in a mixture of the Java programming language and native methods if it needs to bridge to existing database access libraries.

In JDK 1.2 the `java.sql` package builds on the existing SQL functionality to include

- Result sets that scroll forward and backward
- Batch updates so an application can submit multiple update statements (insert/update/delete) in one request
- Additional support for persistent storage of objects in the Java programming language
- SQL3 data types, such as binary large object (BLOB) and character large object (CLOB)
- Structured types
- User-defined types (UDTs)
- Character stream support so character data can be retrieved and sent to the database as a stream of internationalized Unicode characters
- New methods to allow `java.math.BigDecimal` values to be returned with full precision

Remote Method Invocation

Remote method invocation (RMI) first appeared in JDK 1.1 and lets Java applications use remote method calls (rather than sockets and streams) to communicate across a network. The communicating applications can be running on different computers on opposite sides of the planet. This higher-level, method-based approach to network communications allows access to a remote object as easily as to a local object.

JDK 1.2 RMI enhancements include remote object activation, downloadable socket factories, and other minor enhancements, including

- Remote object activation introduces support for persistent references to remote objects and automatic object activation by way of these references.
- Downloadable socket factories allow a remote object to specify the custom socket factory that RMI will use for remote calls to that object. RMI over a secure transport, such as SSL, can be supported by using downloadable socket factories.
- Other minor enhancements allow unexporting a remote object, obtaining the stub for an object implementation, and exporting an object on a specific port.

Java IDL

Java IDL adds CORBA (Common Object Request Broker Architecture) capability to the Java platform to provide standards-based interoperability and connectivity. Java IDL is new with JDK 1.2, so distributed Web-enabled Java applications can transparently invoke operations on remote network services, using the industry-standard Object Management Group (OMG) interface definition language (IDL) and Internet Inter-ORB Protocol (IIOP) defined by the OMG. Runtime components include a fully compliant Java ORB for distributed computing using IIOP communication.

The two main Java IDL packages are `org.omg.CORBA` and `org.omg.CosNaming`. The `org.omg.CORBA` package supplies the mapping of OMG CORBA 1.0 to the Java programming language. An implementation of the ORB class is included so a programmer can use it as a fully functional object request broker (ORB). An ORB object handles, or brokers, method invocations between a client and the method implementation on the server. Because the client and the server can be anywhere on a network and the invocation and implementation can be in different languages, an ORB object does a lot of behind-the-scenes work to enable the communication.

The `org.omg.CosNaming` package specifies the naming service for Java IDL. The package and all of its classes and interfaces were generated by running the `idltojava` compiler on the file `nameservice.idl`, which is a module written in OMG IDL.

Servlets

Servlets let you extend server functionality. Servlets can be implemented to extend a Web server's functionality in the same way that Common Gateway Interface (CGI) scripts do. For example, a servlet can process data entered into a form on an HTML page and can store it in a database. Unlike CGI scripts, however, servlets use fewer resources, are faster, and because they are coded entirely in the Java programming language, work seamlessly across multiple hardware, software, and server platforms.

The Java servlets API is a standard extension included in the Servlet Development Kit; it is not part of the JDK.

Security Architecture

JDK releases continue to enhance the security features inherent in the Java programming language and built into the Java platform. JDK 1.0.2 restricts applets to a secure environment, or *sandbox*, so they cannot access local system resources outside their sandbox. JDK 1.1 provides digitally signed Java ARchive (JAR) files to sign and to verify the signature on applet and application files.

JDK 1.2 introduces a strong security model and accompanying tools so end users and system administrators can extend the security policy to applications and can determine how much access to system resources an applet or a Java application can have. The JDK 1.2 security policy is easy to configure, provides fine-grain access control, and applies to all Java applets and applications. The JDK 1.2 security tools are `JavaKey`, for creating a database of keys; JAR Signer, for signing JAR files; andPolicy Tool, for granting access to system resources.

Packaging

The JAR file format and the Java extension mechanism give you convenient and efficient ways to package and to install programs written in the Java programming language.

Java ARchive (JAR) File Format

Introduced in JDK 1.1, the JAR file format lets you bundle multiple class files and the associated resources into a single archive file that can be easily downloaded, e-mailed, or stored in one convenient package. In JDK 1.2 the JAR file format has new functionality for updating JAR files, provides new standard API for reading and writing JAR files, and supports the use of JAR files in the extension mechanism.

Java Extension Mechanism

JDK 1.2 supports extensions, which are packages of Java classes (and any associated native code) that application developers can use to extend the functionality of the core platform. The extension mechanism allows the Java Virtual Machine to use the extension classes in much the same way as the Java VM uses the system classes. The extension mechanism also provides a way to retrieve extensions from URLs when they are not available as part of the JDK or the Java Runtime Environment (JRE).

Extensions are packaged as JAR files and are installed in the `/lib/ext` directory of the JDK or the JRE. When installed in the `/lib/ext` directory, extensions can be used by applets and applications without being explicitly included in the class path.

Advanced Language Topics

The Java platform provides the JNI and reflection API to provide a way to invoke native methods and to get information on loaded classes.

Java Native Interface

The ability to interface to code written in other programming languages has been with the Java programming language since its inception. However, for JDK 1.1 the API was completely rewritten and ceremoniously renamed the JNI.

The JNI defines a standard naming and calling convention so the Java VM can locate and invoke native methods. JNI also offers a set of standard interface functions to call from native code to do such things as access, manipulate, release, or create objects or to call methods in the Java programming language. Finally, the JNI supports an invocation to load, initialize, and invoke the Java VM. In JDK 1.2 a number of new methods add functionality in the areas of library and version management, local reference management, weak global references, array operations, string operations, reflection support, and the invocation API.

Reflection

Introduced in JDK 1.1, reflection lets a program written in the Java programming language access information about the fields, methods, and constructors of loaded classes and use reflected field, method, and constructor objects to operate within security restrictions on the fields, methods, and constructors in other objects. The reflection API accommodates applications that need access to either the public members of a target object (based on its runtime class) or the members declared by a given class.

Some clients, such as the serialization service, development tools, and debuggers, need to bypass the default access controls built into the Java programming language when they use reflected members or constructors. These controls govern how method and constructor reflectives can access fields, invoke members, and create new class instances according to whether the field, method, or class is public, private, or protected.

In JDK 1.2 reflected field, method and constructor objects extend a new base class (`AccessibleObject`) with a flag field that can be set to bypass the default access controls. Flag values for this field are either `True` or `False`, and the default flag value is `False`. If the flag is `True`, access checks are bypassed, and the requested operation proceeds. If the flag is `False`, normal access checks are in force.

Setting the flag is under the control of the JDK 1.2 security architecture. In addition to the `AccessibleObject` instance, which has the necessary state and methods to set the flag to `True`, a `ReflectPermission` object is needed. The `ReflectPermission` object has methods to grant the necessary permission in the policy file to allow the reflective access.

Tables of JDK Features

The following table summarizes features added to JDK 1.1 and enhanced in JDK 1.2. The first column in the table identifies the trails in this book or online in which you can find more information.

Table 1 Features Added to JDK 1.1 and Enhanced in JDK 1.2

Trail	Package	JDK 1.1	JDK 1.2 Enhancements
Internationalization (page 95)	`java.text` `java.io`	Handles international languages and scripts	Input method framework and minor API changes
Sound (page 219)	`java.applet`	Same as for 1.0.	Support for non-applet sound; more sound formats.

Table 1 Features Added to JDK 1.1 and Enhanced in JDK 1.2

Trail	Package	JDK 1.1	JDK 1.2 Enhancements
JavaBeans (page 229)	`java.beans`	Reusable software components that can be manipulated in a GUI	Runtime containment and services protocol; drag-and-drop support
Security (page 477)	`java.security`	Digital signature and message digest API. Applets confined to secure environment and digitally signed JAR files	Policy-oriented architecture; API to support cryptographic services and key management; fine-grain access control for applets and applications
JDBC Database Access (page 291)	`java.sql`	Standard API to issue and process SQL statements	Result sets that scroll forward and backward, batch updates, persistent object storage, character stream support, and full precision `java.math.BigDecimal` values
Remote Method Invocation (page 359)	`java.rmi`	Method-based standard API for network communications	Remote object activation, downloadable socket factories, and minor enhancements
JAR File Format (page 565)	`java.util.jar`	Mechanism to bundle and to sign Java program files	Enhanced command line JAR tool, new API for reading and writing JAR files, ability to reference JAR files at a specified URL
Java Native Interface (page 625)	NA	Standard naming and calling conventions for native method invocation	New methods for library and version management, local reference management, weak global references, array operations, string operations, reflection support, and the invocation API
Reflection (page 681)	`java.lang.reflect`	Accesses information on fields, methods, and constructors of loaded classes	Ability to bypass JDK 1.2 access controls

Table 2 summarizes features added to JDK 1.2. The first column in the table identifies the trails in this book or online in which you can find more information.

Table 2 Summary of Features Added to JDK 1.2

Trail	Package	JDK 1.2
Collections (page 17)	`java.util`	Groups and manipulates objects of different types

2D Graphics (page 173)	`java.awt`
	`java.awt.color`
	`java.awt.geom`
	`java.awt.image`
	`java.awt.print`
		API for designing more interesting and user-friendly interfaces, handling color, processing images, addressing multilingual requirements, using stylized text, and printing

Swing Components[a]	`javax.swing`
	`javax.swing.*`
	`javax.swing.*.*`
		Provides a rich set of GUI components; features include model-UI separation and a pluggable look and feel

Java IDL (page 397)	`org.omg.CORBA` `org.omg.CosNaming`	Invokes a transparent remote operation
Java Extension Mechanism (page 607)	NA	Adds extensions to core platform
Reference Objects[b]	`java.lang.ref`	Creates a reference to an object so a program can maintain a reference to that object after it is eligible for garbage collection

a. `http://java.sun.com/docs/books/tutorial/ui/index.html`
b. `http://java.sun.com/products/jdk/1.2/docs/api/java/lang/ref/package-summary.html`

Because servlets are a standard extension, not part of the JDK, they aren't mentioned in either table. To read more about servlets, see the trail Servlets (page 427).

About the Author

MONICA PAWLAN is a staff writer for the Java Developer Connection (JDC), and contributing author for the Java Tutorial. She has a background in 2D and 3D graphics, security, and database products, and loves to study and write about emerging technologies. When not writing, she spends her spare time gardening, studying classical piano, and dreaming of far away places—some of which she occasionally visits.

Acknowledgments

The author would like to thank Pat Chan and Doug Kramer for their thoughtful reviews.

Collections

by Joshua Bloch

THIS trail introduces the Java™ Collections Framework and consists of the following lessons.

Introduction (page 21) tells you what collections are and how they'll make your job easier and your programs better. You'll learn about the core elements that compose the Collections Framework: interfaces, implementations, and algorithms.

Interfaces (page 25) describes the core collection interfaces, which are the heart and soul of the Java Collections Framework. You'll learn general guidelines for effective use of these interfaces, including when to use which interface. You'll also learn idioms for each interface to help you get the most out of the interfaces.

Implementations (page 67) describes the general-purpose collection implementations provided by the Java Development Kit (JDK™) and tells you when to use which implementation. You'll also learn about the wrapper implementations, which add functionality to general-purpose implementations.

Algorithms (page 77) describes the polymorphic algorithms the JDK provides to operate on collections. With any luck you'll never have to write your own sort routine again!

Custom Implementations (page 83) explains why you might want to write your own collection implementation (instead of using one of the general-purpose implementations provided by the JDK) and how you'd go about it. It's easy with the JDK's abstract collection implementations.

Interoperability (page 89) tells you how the Collections Framework interoperates with older APIs that predate the addition of collections to the JDK. This lesson also tells you how to design new APIs so that they'll interoperate seamlessly with other new APIs.

1 Introduction

A collection (sometimes called a *container*) is simply an object that groups multiple elements into a single unit. Collections are used to store, to retrieve, and to manipulate data and to transmit data from one method to another. Collections typically represent data items that form a natural group, such as a poker hand (a collection of cards), a mail folder (a collection of letters), or a telephone directory (a mapping of names to phone numbers).

If you've used the Java programming language—or just about any other programming language—you're already familiar with collections. Collection implementations in earlier versions of the Java platform included `Vector`, `Hashtable`, and `array`. Although earlier versions of the Java platform contained these implementations, they did not contain a *Collections Framework*.

What Is a Collections Framework?

A Collections Framework is a unified architecture for representing and manipulating collections. All collections frameworks contain three things:

- **Interfaces:** abstract data types representing collections. Interfaces allow collections to be manipulated independently of the details of their representation. In object-oriented languages, these interfaces generally form a hierarchy.
- **Implementations:** concrete implementations of the collection interfaces. In essence these are *reusable data structures*.
- **Algorithms:** methods that perform useful computations, such as searching and sorting, on objects that implement collection interfaces. These algo-

rithms are said to be *polymorphic*; the same method can be used on many different implementations of the appropriate collection interface. In essence algorithms are *reusable functionality*.

The best-known examples of collections frameworks are the C++ Standard Template Library (STL) and Smalltalk's collection hierarchy.

Benefits

The Collections Framework provides the following benefits.

- **Reduces programming effort:** By providing useful data structures and algorithms, the Collections Framework frees you to concentrate on the important parts of your program rather than on the low-level plumbing required to make it work. By facilitating interoperability among unrelated APIs, the Collections Framework frees you from writing oodles of adapter objects or conversion code to connect APIs.
- **Increases program speed and quality:** The Collections Framework does this primarily by providing high-performance, high-quality implementations of useful data structures and algorithms. Also, because the various implementations of each interface are interchangeable, programs can be easily tuned by switching collection implementations. Finally, because you're freed from the drudgery of writing your own data structures, you'll have more time to devote to improving the quality and the performance of the rest of the program.
- **Allows interoperability among unrelated APIs:** The collection interfaces will become the vernacular by which APIs pass collections back and forth. If my network administration API furnishes a `Collection` of node names and if your GUI toolkit expects a `Collection` of column headings, our APIs will interoperate seamlessly, even though they were written independently.
- **Reduces effort to learn and use new APIs:** Many APIs naturally take collections on input and output. In the past each such API had a little "sub-API" devoted to manipulating its collections. There was little consistency among these ad-hoc collections sub-APIs, so you had to learn each one from scratch, and it was easy to make mistakes when using them. With the advent of standard collection interfaces, the problem goes away.
- **Reduces effort to design new APIs:** This is the flip side of the previous advantage: Designers and implementers don't have to reinvent the wheel

each time they create an API that relies on collections. They just use the standard collection interfaces.

- **Fosters software reuse:** New data structures that conform to the standard collection interfaces are by nature reusable. The same goes for new algorithms that operate on objects that implement these interfaces.

Drawbacks of the Collections Framework

Historically collections frameworks have been quite complex, which gave them a reputation for having a steep learning curve. We believe that Java's new Collections Framework breaks with this tradition, as you will learn for yourself in the following lessons.

Interfaces

THE *core collection interfaces* are used to manipulate collections and to pass them from one method to another. The basic purpose of these interfaces is to allow collections to be manipulated independently of the details of their representation. The core collection interfaces are the heart and soul of the Collections Framework. When you understand how to use these interfaces, you know most of what there is to know about the framework. The core collection interfaces are shown in the following figure.

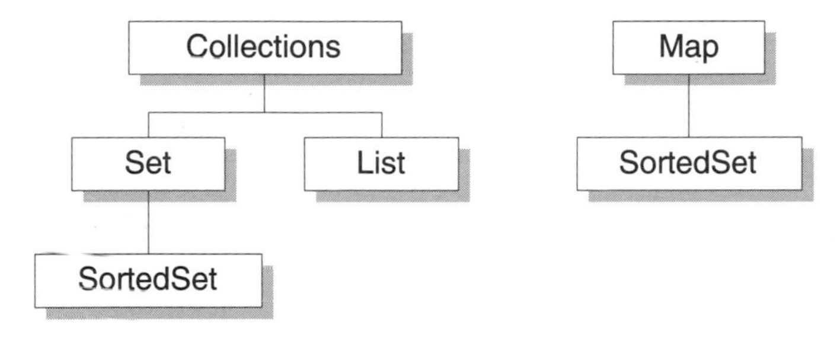

Figure 1 The core collection interfaces.

The core collection interfaces form a *hierarchy*: A `Set` is a special kind of `Collection`, a `SortedSet` is a special kind of `Set`, and so forth. Note also that the hierarchy consists of two distinct trees: A `Map` is not a true `Collection`.

To keep the number of core collection interfaces manageable, the JDK doesn't provide separate interfaces for each variant of each collection type. (Possible variants include immutable, fixed-size, and append-only.) Instead the modification operations in each interface are designated *optional*: A given implementation may not support some of these operations. If an unsupported operation is invoked, a collection throws an `UnsupportedOperationException`. Implementations are responsible for documenting which of the optional operations they support. All of the JDK's general-purpose implementations support all of the optional operations.

The four basic core collection interfaces are as follows:

- The `Collection` interface, the root of the collection hierarchy, represents a group of objects, known as its *elements*. Some `Collection` implementations allow duplicate elements, and others do not. Some are ordered and others unordered. The JDK doesn't provide any direct implementations of this interface but does provide implementations of more specific subinterfaces, such as `Set` and `List`. This interface is the least common denominator that all collections implement and is used to pass collections around and to manipulate them when maximum generality is desired. See the section Collection Interface (page 27).
- A `Set` is a collection that cannot contain duplicate elements. As you might expect, this interface models the mathematical *set* abstraction and is used to represent sets, such as the cards in a poker hand, the courses making up a student's schedule, or the processes running on a machine. See the section Set Interface (page 30).
- A `List` is an ordered collection (sometimes called a *sequence*). Lists can contain duplicate elements. The user of a `List` generally has precise control over where in the `List` each element is inserted. The user can access elements by their integer index (position). If you've used `Vector`, you're familiar with the general flavor of `List`. See the section List Interface (page 35).
- A `Map` is an object that maps keys to values. Maps cannot contain duplicate keys: Each key can map to at most one value. If you've used `Hashtable`, you're already familiar with the general flavor of `Map`. See the section Map Interface (page 45).

The last two core collection interfaces (`SortedSet` and `SortedMap`) are merely sorted versions of `Set` and `Map`. To understand these interfaces, you have to know how order is maintained among objects.

There are two ways to order objects: The `Comparable` interface provides automatic *natural order* on classes that implement it; the `Comparator` interface gives the programmer complete control over object ordering. Note that these are *not* core collection interfaces but rather underlying infrastructure. See the section Object Ordering (page 54).

The last two core collection interfaces are as follows:

- A SortedSet is a Set that maintains its elements in ascending order. Several additional operations are provided to take advantage of the ordering. Sorted sets are used for naturally ordered sets such as word lists and membership rolls. See the section SortedSet Interface (page 61).
- A SortedMap is a Map that maintains its mappings in ascending key order. It is the Map analog of SortedSet. Sorted maps are used for naturally ordered collections of key/value pairs such as dictionaries and telephone directories. See the section SortedMap Interface (page 65).

Collection Interface

A Collection represents a group of objects, known as its *elements*. The primary use of the Collection interface is to pass around collections of objects where maximum generality is desired. For example, by convention all general-purpose collection implementations, which typically implement a subinterface of Collection such as Set or List, have a constructor that takes a Collection argument. This constructor initializes the new Collection to contain all of the elements in the specified Collection. This constructor allows the caller to create a Collection of a desired implementation type, initially containing all of the elements in any given Collection, whatever its subinterface or implementation type. Suppose, for example, that you have a Collection, c, which may be a List, a Set, or another kind of Collection. The following idiom creates a new ArrayList (an implementation of the List interface), initially containing all of the elements in c:

```
List l = new ArrayList(c);
```

The Collection interface follows.

```
public interface Collection {
    // Basic Operations
    int size();
    boolean isEmpty();
    boolean contains(Object element);
    boolean add(Object element);    // Optional
    boolean remove(Object element); // Optional
    Iterator iterator();

    // Bulk Operations
    boolean containsAll(Collection c);
    boolean addAll(Collection c);    // Optional
    boolean removeAll(Collection c); // Optional
    boolean retainAll(Collection c); // Optional
    void clear();                    // Optional
```

```
        // Array Operations
        Object[] toArray();
        Object[] toArray(Object a[]);
    }
```

The interface does about what you'd expect, given that a `Collection` represents a group of objects. It has methods to tell you how many elements are in the collection (`size`, `isEmpty`), to check whether a given object is in the collection (`contains`), to add and to remove an element from the collection (`add`, `remove`), and to provide an iterator over the collection (`iterator`).

The `add` method is defined generally enough so that it makes sense for both collections that allow duplicates and those that don't. It guarantees that the `Collection` will contain the specified element after the call completes and returns `true` if the `Collection` changes as a result of the call. Similarly the `remove` method is defined to remove *a single instance* of the specified element from the `Collection`, assuming that it contains the element, and to return `true` if the `Collection` was modified as a result.

Iterators

The object returned by the `iterator` method deserves special mention. It is an `Iterator`, which is very similar to an `Enumeration`, but differs in two respects.

- `Iterator` allows the caller to remove elements from the underlying collection during the iteration, with well-defined semantics.
- Method names have been improved.

The first point is important: There was *no* safe way to remove elements from a collection while traversing it with an `Enumeration`. The semantics of this operation were ill-defined and differed from implementation to implementation.

The `Iterator` interface follows.

```
    public interface Iterator {
        boolean hasNext();
        Object next();
        void remove();     // Optional
    }
```

The `hasNext` method is identical in function to `Enumeration.hasMoreElements`, and the `next` method is identical in function to `Enumeration.nextElement`. The `remove` method removes from the underlying `Collection` the last element that was returned by `next`. The `remove` method may be called only once per call to `next` and throws an exception if this rule is violated. Note that `Iterator.remove` is the *only* safe way to modify a collection during iteration; the behavior is unspecified if the underlying collection is modified in any other way while the iteration is in progress.

The following snippet shows you how to use an `Iterator` to *filter* a `Collection`, that is, to traverse the collection, removing every element that does not satisfy some condition:

```
static void filter(Collection c) {
    for (Iterator i = c.iterator(); i.hasNext(); )
        if (!cond(i.next()))
            i.remove();
}
```

You should keep two things in mind when looking at this simple piece of code.

- The code is *polymorphic*: It works for *any* `Collection` that supports element removal, regardless of implementation. That's how easy it is to write a polymorphic algorithm under the Collections Framework!
- It would have been impossible to write this using `Enumeration` instead of `Iterator`, because there's no safe way to remove an element from a collection while traversing it with an `Enumeration`.

Bulk Operations

The *bulk operations* perform an operation on an entire `Collection` in a single shot. These shorthand operations can be simulated, perhaps less efficiently, by using the basic operations described previously. The bulk operations follow.

- `c1.containsAll(c2)`: Returns `true` if `c1` contains all of the elements in `c2`.
- `c1.addAll(c2)`: Adds all of the elements in `c2` to `c1`.
- `c1.removeAll(c2)`: Removes from `c1` all of its elements that are also contained in `c2`.
- `c1.retainAll(c2)`: Removes from `c1` all of its elements that are *not* also contained in `c2`. That is, it retains in `c1` only those elements that are also contained in `c2`.
- `c.clear()`: Removes all elements from `c`.

The addAll, removeAll, and retainAll methods all return true if the Collection was modified in the process of executing the operation.

As a simple example of the power of the bulk operations, consider the following idiom to remove *all* instances of a specified element, e, from a Collection, c:

```
c.removeAll(Collections.singleton(e));
```

More specifically, suppose that you want to remove all of the null elements from a Collection:

```
c.removeAll(Collections.singleton(null));
```

This idiom uses Collections.singleton, which is a static factory method that returns an immutable Set containing only the specified element.

Array Operations

The toArray methods are provided as a bridge between collections and older APIs that expect arrays on input. These methods allow the contents of a Collection to be translated into an array. The simple form with no arguments creates a new array of Object. The more complex form allows the caller to provide an array or to choose the runtime type of the output array.

For example, suppose that c is a Collection. The following snippet dumps the contents of c into a newly allocated array of Object whose length is identical to the number of elements in c:

```
Object[] a = c.toArray();
```

Suppose c is known to contain only strings. The following snippet dumps the contents of c into a newly allocated array of String whose length is identical to the number of elements in c:

```
String[] a = (String[]) c.toArray(new String[0]);
```

Set Interface

A Set is a Collection that cannot contain duplicate elements. Set models the mathematical *set* abstraction. The Set interface contains *no* methods other than those inherited from Collection. Set adds the restriction that duplicate elements are prohibited. Set also adds a stronger contract on the behavior of the equals and hashCode operations, allowing Set objects to be compared meaningfully, even if their implementation types differ. Two Set objects are equal if they contain the same elements. The Set interface follows.

```
public interface Set {
    // Basic Operations
    int size();
    boolean isEmpty();
    boolean contains(Object element);
    boolean add(Object element);    // Optional
    boolean remove(Object element); // Optional
    Iterator iterator();

    // Bulk Operations
    boolean containsAll(Collection c);
    boolean addAll(Collection c);    // Optional
    boolean removeAll(Collection c); // Optional
    boolean retainAll(Collection c); // Optional
    void clear();                    // Optional

    // Array Operations
    Object[] toArray();
    Object[] toArray(Object a[]);
}
```

The JDK contains two general-purpose Set implementations. HashSet, which stores its elements in a hash table, is the best-performing implementation. TreeSet, which stores its elements in a red-black tree,[1] guarantees the order of iteration. For more information on implementations, see the next lesson, Implementations (page 67).

Here's a simple but useful Set idiom. Suppose that you have a Collection, c, and that you want to create another Collection containing the same elements but with all duplicates eliminated. The following one-liner does the trick:

```
Collection noDups = new HashSet(c);
```

It works by creating a Set (which by definition cannot contain duplicates) initially containing all of the elements in c. It uses the standard Collection constructor described in the section Collection Interface (page 27).

[1] A red-black tree is a data structure, a kind of balanced binary tree generally regarded to be among the best. The red-black tree offers guaranteed log(n) performance for all basic operations (lookup, insert, delete) and, empirically speaking, is just plain fast.

Basic Operations

The `size` operation returns the number of elements in the `Set` (its *cardinality*). The `isEmpty` method does exactly what you think it does. The `add` method adds the specified element to the `Set` if it's not already present and returns a boolean indicating whether the element was added. Similarly the `remove` method removes the specified element from the `Set` if it's present and returns a boolean indicating whether the element was present. The `iterator` method returns an `Iterator` over the `Set`.

Here's a little program that takes the words in its argument list and prints out any duplicate words, the number of distinct words, and a list of the words with duplicates eliminated.

```
import java.util.*;

public class FindDups {
    public static void main(String args[]) {
        Set s = new HashSet();
        for (int i=0; i<args.length; i++)
            if (!s.add(args[i]))
                System.out.println("Duplicate: "+ args[i]);

        System.out.println(s.size()+" distinct words: "+s);
    }
}
```

Now let's run the program.

```
% java FindDups i came i saw i left
```

The following output is produced.

```
Duplicate: i
Duplicate: i
4 distinct words: [came, left, saw, i]
```

Note that the code always refers to the collection by its interface type (`Set`) rather than by its implementation type (`HashSet`). This is a *strongly* recommended programming practice, as it gives you the flexibility to change implementations merely by changing the constructor. If either the variables used to store a collection or the parameters used to pass it around are declared to be of the collection's implementation type rather than of its interface type, *all* such variables and parameters must be changed to change the collection's implementation type. Furthermore there's no guarantee that the resulting program will work; if the program uses any nonstandard operations that are present in the original implementation type but not in the new one, the program will fail. Referring to collections only by their interface keeps you honest, preventing you from using any nonstandard operations.

The implementation type of the `Set` in the preceding example is `HashSet`, which makes no guarantees as to the order of the elements in the `Set`. If you want the program to print the word list in alphabetical order, merely change the set's implementation type from `HashSet` to `TreeSet`. Making this trivial one-line change causes the command line in the previous example to generate the following output:

```
% java FindDups i came i saw i left
Duplicate word: i
Duplicate word: i
4 distinct words: [came, i, left, saw]
```

Bulk Operations

The bulk operations are particularly well suited to `Sets`; when applied to sets they perform standard set-algebraic operations. Suppose that `s1` and `s2` are `Sets`. Here's what the bulk operations do:

- `s1.containsAll(s2)`: Returns `true` if `s2` is a *subset* of `s1`. (Set `s2` is a subset of set `s1` if set `s1` contains all of the elements in `s2`.)
- `s1.addAll(s2)`: Transforms `s1` into the *union* of `s1` and `s2`. (The union of two sets is the set containing all of the elements contained in either set.)
- `s1.retainAll(s2)`: Transforms `s1` into the *intersection* of `s1` and `s2`. (The intersection of two sets is the set containing only the elements that are common to both sets.)
- `s1.removeAll(s2)`: Transforms `s1` into the (asymmetric) *set difference* of `s1` and `s2`. (For example, the set difference of `s1` and `s2` is the set containing all of the elements found in `s1` but not in `s2`.)

To calculate the union, intersection, or set difference of two sets *nondestructively* (without modifying either set), the caller must copy one set before calling the appropriate bulk operation. The resulting idioms follow.

```
Set union = new HashSet(s1);
union.addAll(s2);

Set intersection = new HashSet(s1);
intersection.retainAll(s2);
Set difference = new HashSet(s1);
difference.removeAll(s2);
```

The implementation type of the result `Set` in the preceding idioms is `HashSet`, which is, as already mentioned, the best all-around `Set` implementation. However, any general-purpose `Set` implementation could be substituted.

Let's revisit the `FindDups` program. Suppose that you want to know which words in the argument list occur only once and which occur more than once, but that you do not want duplicates printed out repeatedly. This effect can be achieved by generating two sets, one containing every word in the argument list and the other containing only the duplicates. The words that occur only once are the set difference of these two sets, which we know how to compute. Here's how the resulting program looks.

```
import java.util.*;

public class FindDups2 {
    public static void main(String args[]) {
        Set uniques = new HashSet();
        Set dups = new HashSet();

        for (int i = 0; i < args.length; i++)
            if (!uniques.add(args[i]))
                dups.add(args[i]);
        uniques.removeAll(dups); // Destructive set-difference

        System.out.println("Unique words:    " + uniques);
        System.out.println("Duplicate words: " + dups);
    }
}
```

When run with the same argument list used earlier ("`i came i saw i left`"), this program yields the output:

```
Unique words:    [came, left, saw]
Duplicate words: [i]
```

A less common set-algebraic operation is the *symmetric set difference*: the set of elements contained in either of two specified sets but not in both. The following code calculates the symmetric set difference of two sets nondestructively.

```
Set symmetricDiff = new HashSet(s1);
symmetricDiff.addAll(s2);
Set tmp = new HashSet(s1);
tmp.retainAll(s2));
symmetricDiff.removeAll(tmp);
```

Array Operations

The array operations don't do anything special for Sets beyond what they do for any other Collection. These operations are described in the section Collection Interface (page 27).

List Interface

A List is an ordered Collection, sometimes called a *sequence*. Lists may contain duplicate elements. In addition to the operations inherited from Collection, the List interface includes operations for the following.

- **Positional access:** Manipulate elements based on their numerical position in the list.
- **Search:** Search for a specified object in the list and return its numerical position.
- **List iteration:** Extend Iterator semantics to take advantage of the list's sequential nature.
- **Range-view:** Perform arbitrary *range operations* on the list.

The List interface follows.

```
public interface List extends Collection {
    // Positional Access
    Object get(int index);
    Object set(int index, Object element);          //Optional
    void add(int index, Object element);            //Optional
    Object remove(int index);                       //Optional
   abstract boolean addAll(int index, Collection c); //Optional

    // Search
    int indexOf(Object o);
    int lastIndexOf(Object o);

    // Iteration
    ListIterator listIterator();
    ListIterator listIterator(int index);

    // Range-view
    List subList(int from, int to);
}
```

The JDK contains two general-purpose `List` implementations: `ArrayList`, which is generally the best-performing implementation, and `LinkedList`, which offers better performance under certain circumstances. Also, `Vector` has been retrofitted to implement `List`. For more information on implementations, see the lesson Implementations (page 67).

Comparison to Vector

If you've used `Vector`, you're already familiar with the general flavor of `List`. (Of course, `List` is an interface and `Vector` is a concrete implementation.) `List` fixes several minor API deficiencies in `Vector`. Commonly used `Vector` operations, such as `elementAt` and `setElementAt`, have been given much shorter names. When you consider that these two operations are the `List` analogue of brackets for arrays, it becomes apparent that shorter names are highly desirable. Consider the following assignment statement:

```
a[i] = a[j].times(a[k]);
```

The `Vector` equivalent is:

```
v.setElementAt(v.elementAt(j).times(v.elementAt(k)), i);
```

The `List` equivalent is:

```
v.set(i, v.get(j).times(v.get(k)));
```

You may already have noticed that the `set` method, which replaces the `Vector` method `setElementAt`, reverses the order of the arguments so that they match the corresponding array operation. Consider this assignment statement:

```
beatle[5] = "Billy Preston";
```

The `Vector` equivalent is:

```
beatle.setElementAt("Billy Preston", 5);
```

The `List` equivalent is:

```
beatle.set(5, "Billy Preston");
```

For consistency's sake, the `add(int, Object)` method, which replaces the method `insertElementAt(Object, int)`, also reverses the order of the arguments.

The various range operations in `Vector` (`indexOf`, `lastIndexOf(setSize)`) have been replaced by a single *range-view* operation (`subList`), which is far more powerful and consistent.

Collection Operations

The operations inherited from `Collection` all do about what you'd expect them to do, assuming that you're already familiar with them from `Collection`. If you're not familiar with them, now would be a good time to read the section Collection Interface (page 27). The `remove` operation always removes the *first* occurrence of the specified element from the list. The `add` and `addAll` operations always append the new element(s) to the *end* of the list. Thus the following idiom concatenates one list to another:

```
list1.addAll(list2);
```

Here's a nondestructive form of this idiom, which produces a third `List` consisting of the second list appended to the first:

```
List list3 = new ArrayList(list1);
list3.addAll(list2);
```

Note that the idiom, in its nondestructive form, takes advantage of `ArrayList`'s standard `Collection` constructor.

Like the `Set` interface, `List` strengthens the requirements on the `equals` and `hashCode` methods so that two `List` objects can be compared for logical equality without regard to their implementation classes. Two `List` objects are equal if they contain the same elements in the same order.

Positional Access and Search Operations

The basic positional access operations (`get`, `set`, `add`, and `remove`) behave just like their longer-named counterparts in `Vector` (`elementAt`, `setElementAt`, `insertElementAt`, and `removeElementAt`), with one noteworthy exception. The `set` and the `remove` operations return the old value that is being overwritten or removed; the counterparts in `Vector` (`setElementAt` and `removeElementAt`) return nothing (`void`). The search operations `indexOf` and `lastIndexOf` behave exactly like the identically named operations in `Vector`.

The `addAll(int, Collection)` operation inserts all of the elements of the specified `Collection`, starting at the specified position in the list. The elements are inserted in the order they are returned by the specified `Collection`'s `iterator`. This call is the positional access analog of `Collection`'s `addAll` operation.

Here's a little function to swap two indexed values in a `List`. It should look familiar from Programming 101 (assuming you stayed awake):

```
private static void swap(List a, int i, int j) {
    Object tmp = a.get(i);
    a.set(i, a.get(j));
    a.set(j, tmp);
}
```

Of course there's one big difference. This is a *polymorphic* algorithm: It swaps two elements in *any* `List`, regardless of its implementation type. "Big deal," you say, "What's it good for?" Funny you should ask. Take a look at this:

```
public static void shuffle(List list, Random rnd) {
    for (int i=list.size(); i>1; i--)
        swap(list, i-1, rnd.nextInt(i));
}
```

This algorithm, which is included in the JDK's `Collections` class, randomly permutes the specified `List`, using the specified source of randomness. It's a bit subtle: It runs up the list from the bottom, repeatedly swapping a randomly selected element into the current position. Unlike most naive attempts at shuffling, it's *fair* (all permutations occur with equal likelihood, assuming an unbiased source of randomness) and *fast* (requiring exactly `list.size()-1` iterations). The following short program uses this algorithm to print the words in its argument list in random order.

```
import java.util.*;

public class Shuffle {
    public static void main(String args[]) {
        List l = new ArrayList();
        for (int i=0; i<args.length; i++)
            l.add(args[i]);
        Collections.shuffle(l, new Random());
        System.out.println(l);
    }
}
```

In fact, we can make this program even shorter and faster. The `Arrays` class has a static factory method, `asList`, that allows an array to be *viewed* as a `List`. This method does not copy the array; changes in the `List` write through to the array, and vice versa. The resulting List is not a general-purpose List implementation in that it doesn't implement the (optional) add and remove operations: Arrays are not resizable. Taking advantage of Arrays.asList and calling an alternative form of shuffle that uses a default source of randomness, you get the following tiny program, whose behavior is identical to that of the previous program.

```
import java.util.*;

public class Shuffle {
    public static void main(String args[]) {
        List l = Arrays.asList(args);
        Collections.shuffle(l);
        System.out.println(l);
    }
}
```

Iterators

As you'd expect, the Iterator returned by List's iterator operation returns the elements of the list in proper sequence. List also provides a richer iterator, called a ListIterator, that allows you to traverse the list in either direction, to modify the list during iteration, and to obtain the current position of the iterator. The ListIterator interface follows, including the three methods it inherits from Iterator.

```
public interface ListIterator extends Iterator {
    boolean hasNext();
    Object next();

    boolean hasPrevious();
    Object previous();

    int nextIndex();
    int previousIndex();

    void remove();        // Optional
    void set(Object o); // Optional
    void add(Object o); // Optional
}
```

The three methods that ListIterator inherits from Iterator (hasNext, next, and remove) are intended to do exactly the same thing in both interfaces. The hasPrevious and the previous operations are exact analogs of hasNext and next. The former operations refer to the element before the (implicit) cursor, whereas the latter refer to the element after the cursor. The `previous` operation moves the cursor backward whereas `next` moves it forward.

Here's the standard idiom for iterating backward through a list:

```
for(ListIterator i=l.listIterator(l.size());l.hasPrevious();){
    Foo f = (Foo) l.previous();
    ...
}
```

Note the argument to `listIterator` in the preceding idiom. The `List` interface has two forms of the `listIterator` method. The form with no arguments returns a `ListIterator` positioned at the beginning of the list; the form with an `int` argument returns a `ListIterator` positioned at the specified index. The index refers to the element that would be returned by an initial call to `next`. An initial call to `previous` would return the element whose index was `index-1`. In a list of length `n`, there are `n+1` valid values for `index`, from `0` to `n`, inclusive.

Intuitively speaking the cursor is always between two elements: the one that would be returned by a call to `previous` and the one that would be returned by a call to `next`. The `n+1` valid `index` values correspond to the `n+1` gaps between elements, from the gap before the first element to the gap after the last one. The following diagram shows the five possible cursor positions in a list containing four elements.

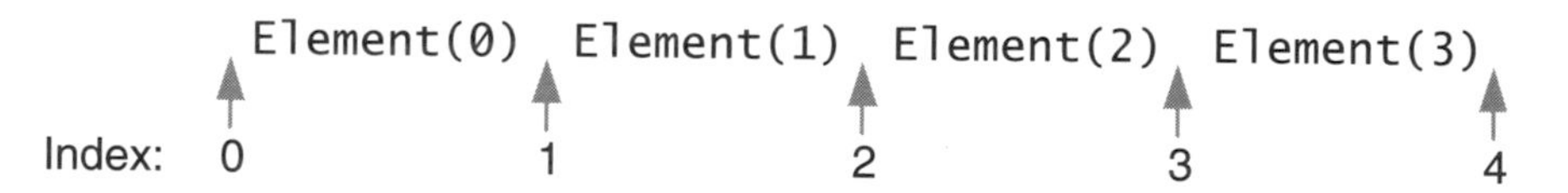

Figure 2 Five possible cursor positions in a list with four elements.

Calls to `next` and `previous` can be intermixed, but you have to be a bit careful. After a sequence of calls to `next`, the first call to `previous` returns the same element as the last call to `next`. Similarly, after a sequence of calls to `previous`, the first call to `next` returns the same element as the last call to `previous`.

It should come as no surprise that the `nextIndex` method returns the index of the element that would be returned by a subsequent call to `next` and that `previousIndex` returns the index of the element that would be returned by a subsequent call to `previous`. These calls are typically used either to report the position where something was found or to record the position of the `ListIterator` so that another `ListIterator` with identical position can be created.

It should also come as no surprise that the number returned by `nextIndex` is always one greater than the number returned by `previousIndex`. This implies the behavior of the two boundary cases: a call to `previousIndex` when the cursor is before the initial element returns `-1` and a call to `nextIndex` when the cursor is after the final element returns `list.size()`. To make all of this concrete, here's a possible implementation of `List.indexOf`:

```
public int indexOf(Object o) {
    for (ListIterator i = listIterator(); i.hasNext(); )
        if (o==null ? i.next()==null : o.equals(i.next()))
            return i.previousIndex();

    return -1; // Object not found
}
```

Note that the `indexOf` method returns `i.previousIndex()` although it is traversing the list in the forward direction. The reason is that `i.nextIndex()` would return the index of the element that we are about to examine, and we want to return the index of the element we just examined.

Another bit of trickiness in this example is the equality test between 0 and `i.next`. We have to special-case a 0 value of `null` in order to prevent a `NullPointerException`.

The `Iterator` interface provides the `remove` operation to remove from the `Collection` the last element returned by `next`. For `ListIterator`, this operation removes the last element returned by `next` or `previous`. The `ListIterator` interface provides two additional operations to modify the list: `set` and `add`. The `set` method overwrites the last element returned by `next` or `previous` with the specified element. The following polymorphic algorithm uses `set` to replace all occurrences of one specified value with another.

```
public void replace(List l, Object val, Object newVal) {
    for (ListIterator i = l.listIterator(); i.hasNext(); )
        if (val==null ? i.next()==null : val.equals(i.next()))
            i.set(newVal);
}
```

The `add` method inserts a new element into the list, immediately before the current cursor position. This method is illustrated in the following polymorphic algorithm to replace all occurrences of a specified value with the sequence of values contained in the specified list:

```
public static void replace(List l, Object val, List newVals) {
    for (ListIterator i = l.listIterator(); i.hasNext(); ) {
        if (val==null ? i.next()==null : val.equals(i.next())) {
            i.remove();
            for (Iterator j=newVals.iterator(); j.hasNext(); )
                i.add(j.next());
        }
    }
}
```

Range-View Operation

The range-view operation, `subList(int fromIndex, int toIndex)`, returns a `List` *view* of the portion of this list whose indices range from `fromIndex`, inclusive, to `toIndex`, exclusive. This *half-open range* mirrors the typical `for` loop:

```
for (int i=fromIndex; i<toIndex; i++) {
    ...
}
```

As the term *view* implies, the returned `List` is backed by the `List` on which `subList` was called, so changes in the former `List` are reflected in the latter.

This method eliminates the need for explicit range operations (of the sort that commonly exist for arrays). Any operation that expects a `List` can be used as a range operation by passing a `subList` view instead of a whole `List`. For example, the following idiom removes a range of elements from a list:

```
list.subList(fromIndex, toIndex).clear();
```

Similar idioms may be constructed to search for an element in a range.

```
int i = list.subList(fromIndex, toIndex).indexOf(o);
int j = list.subList(fromIndex, toIndex).lastIndexOf(o);
```

Note that the preceding idioms return the index of the found element in the `subList`, not the index in the backing `List`.

Any polymorphic algorithm that operates on a `List`, such as the `replace` and `shuffle` examples, works with the `List` returned by `subList`.

Here's a polymorphic algorithm whose implementation uses `subList` to deal a hand from a deck. That is to say, it returns a new `List` (the "hand") containing the specified number of elements taken from the end of the specified `List` (the "deck"). The elements returned in the hand are removed from the deck.

```
public static List dealHand(List deck, int n) {
    int deckSize = deck.size();
    List handView = deck.subList(deckSize-n, deckSize);
    List hand = new ArrayList(handView);
    handView.clear();
    return hand;
}
```

Note that this algorithm removes the hand from the *end* of the deck. For many common `List` implementations, such as `ArrayList`, the performance of removing elements from the end of the list is substantially better than that of removing elements from the beginning.[1]

Here's a program using the `dealHand` method in combination with `Collections.shuffle` to generate hands from a normal 52-card deck. The program takes two command line arguments: the number of hands to deal and the number of cards in each hand. The full code for `Deal.java` (page 719) is in the Appendix.

```
import java.util.*;
class Deal {
    public static void main(String args[]) {
        int numHands = Integer.parseInt(args[0]);
        int cardsPerHand = Integer.parseInt(args[1]);

        // Make a normal 52-card deck
        String[] suit = new String[]
                  {"spades", "hearts", "diamonds", "clubs"};
        String[] rank = new String[]
                  {"ace","2","3","4","5","6","7",
                   "8","9","10","jack","queen","king"};
        List deck = new ArrayList();
        for (int i=0; i<suit.length; i++)
            for (int j=0; j<rank.length; j++)
                deck.add(rank[j] + " of " + suit[i]);

        Collections.shuffle(deck);

        for (int i=0; i<numHands; i++)
            System.out.println(dealHand(deck, cardsPerHand));
    }
}
```

[1] The literal-minded might say that this program deals from the bottom of the deck, but I prefer to think that the computer is holding the deck upside down.

Let's run the program:

```
% java Deal 4 5

[8 of hearts, jack of spades, 3 of spades, 4 of spades,
   king of diamonds]
[4 of diamonds, ace of clubs, 6 of clubs, jack of
   hearts, queen of hearts]
[7 of spades, 5 of spades, 2 of diamonds,
   queen of diamonds, 9 of clubs]
[8 of spades, 6 of diamonds, ace of spades, 3 of hearts,
   ace of hearts]
```

Although the `subList` operation is extremely powerful, some care must be exercised when using it. The semantics of the `List` returned by `subList` become undefined if elements are added to or removed from the backing `List` in any way other than via the returned `List`. Thus it's highly recommended that you use the `List` returned by `subList` only as a transient object, to perform one or a sequence of range operations on the backing `List`. The longer you use the `subList` object, the greater the probability that you'll compromise it by modifying the backing `List` directly or through another `subList` object. Note that it is legal to modify a sublist of a sublist, and then continue using the original sublist.

Algorithms

Most of the polymorphic algorithms in the `Collections` class apply specifically to `List`. Having all of these algorithms at your disposal makes it very easy to manipulate lists. Here's a summary of these algorithms, which are described in more detail in the lesson Algorithms (page 77).

- `sort(List)`: Sorts a `List` using a merge sort algorithm.
- `shuffle(List)`: Randomly permutes the elements in a `List`.
- `reverse(List)`: Reverses the order of the elements in a `List`.
- `fill(List, Object)`: Overwrites every element in a `List` with the specified value.
- `copy(List dest, List src)`: Copies the source `List` into the destination `List`.
- `binarySearch(List, Object)`: Searches for an element in an ordered `List`, using the binary search algorithm.

Map Interface

A `Map` is an object that maps keys to values. A map cannot contain duplicate keys: Each key can map to at most one value. The `Map` interface follows.

```
public interface Map {
    // Basic Operations
    Object put(Object key, Object value);
    Object get(Object key);
    Object remove(Object key);
    boolean containsKey(Object key);
    boolean containsValue(Object value);
    int size();
    boolean isEmpty();

    // Bulk Operations
    void putAll(Map t);
    void clear();

    // Collection Views
    public Set keySet();
    public Collection values();
    public Set entrySet();

    // Interface for entrySet elements
    public interface Entry {
        Object getKey();
        Object getValue();
        Object setValue(Object value);
    }
}
```

The JDK contains two new general-purpose `Map` implementations. `HashMap`, which stores its entries in a hash table, is the best-performing implementation. `TreeMap`, which stores its entries in a red-black tree, guarantees the order of iteration. Also, `Hashtable` has been retrofitted to implement `Map`. For more information, see the next lesson, Implementations (page 67).

Comparison to Hashtable

If you've used `Hashtable`, you're already familiar with the general flavor of `Map`. (Of course, `Map` is an interface, whereas `Hashtable` is a concrete implementation.) Here are the major differences.

- Map provides Collection-views instead of direct support for iteration via Enumeration objects. Collection-views greatly enhance the expressiveness of the interface, as discussed later in this lesson.
- Map allows you to iterate over keys, values, or key-value pairs; Hashtable does not provide the third option.
- Map provides a safe way to remove entries in the midst of iteration; Hashtable does not.

Further, Map fixes a minor deficiency in the Hashtable interface. Hashtable has a method called contains, which returns true if the Hashtable contains a given *value*. Given its name, you'd expect this method to return true if the Hashtable contained a given *key*, as the key is the primary access mechanism for a Hashtable. The Map interface eliminates this source of confusion by renaming the method containsValue. Also, this improves the consistency of the interface: containsValue parallels containsKey nicely.

Basic Operations

The basic operations (put, get, remove, containsKey, containsValue, size, and isEmpty) behave exactly like their counterparts in Hashtable. Here's a simple program to generate a frequency table of the words found in its argument list. The frequency table maps each word to the number of times it occurs in the argument list.

```
import java.util.*;

public class Freq {
    private static final Integer ONE = new Integer(1);

    public static void main(String args[]) {
        Map m = new HashMap();

        // Initialize frequency table from command line
        for (int i=0; i<args.length; i++) {
            Integer freq = (Integer) m.get(args[i]);
            m.put(args[i], (freq==null ? ONE :
                            new Integer(freq.intValue() + 1)));
        }
        System.out.println(m.size() + " distinct words:");
        System.out.println(m);
    }
}
```

The only thing even slightly tricky about this program is the second argument of the put statement. That argument is a conditional expression that has the effect of setting the frequency to one if the word has never been seen before or one more than its current value if the word has already been seen. Try running this program with the command:

```
% java Freq if it is to be it is up to me to delegate
```

The program yields the following output.

```
8 distinct words:
{to=3, me=1, delegate=1, it=2, is=2, if=1, be=1, up=1}
```

Suppose you'd prefer to see the frequency table in alphabetical order. All you have to do is change the implementation type of the Map from HashMap to TreeMap. Making this four-character change causes the program to generate the following output from the same command line:

```
8 distinct words:
{be=1, delegate=1, if=1, is=2, it=2, me=1, to=3, up=1}
```

Are interfaces cool, or what?

Like the Set and List interfaces, Map strengthens the requirements on the equals and hashCode methods so that two Map objects can be compared for logical equality without regard to their implementation types. Two Map objects are equal if they represent the same key-value mappings.

By convention all Map implementations provide constructors that take a Map object and initialize the new Map to contain all of the key-value mappings in the specified Map. This standard Map constructor is entirely analogous to the standard collection constructor for Collection implementations. The caller can create a Map of a desired implementation type that initially contains all of the mappings in another Map, regardless of the other Map's implementation type. For example, suppose that you have a Map named m. The following one-liner creates a new HashMap initially containing all of the same key-value mappings as m:

```
Map copy = new HashMap(m);
```

Bulk Operations

The clear operation does exactly what you think it does: It removes all of the mappings from the Map. The putAll operation is the Map analog of the Collection interface's addAll operation. In addition to its obvious use of dumping one Map into another, it has a second, more subtle use. Suppose that a Map is used to represent a collection of attribute-value pairs; the putAll operation, in combination with the standard Map constructor, provides a neat way to implement attribute map creation with default values. Here's a static factory method demonstrating this technique:

```
Map newAttributeMap(Map defaults, Map overrides) {
    Map result = new HashMap(defaults);
    result.putAll(overrides);
    return result;
}
```

Collection Views

The Collection-view methods allow a Map to be viewed as a Collection in three ways:

- keySet: The Set of keys contained in the Map.
- values: The Collection of values contained in the Map. This Collection is not a Set, as multiple keys can map to the same value.
- entrySet: The Set of key-value pairs contained in the Map. The Map interface provides a small nested interface called Map.Entry, the type of the elements in this Set.

The Collection-views provide the *only* means to iterate over a Map. Here's an example illustrating the standard idiom for iterating over the keys in a Map:

```
for (Iterator i=m.keySet().iterator(); i.hasNext(); ) {
    System.out.println(i.next());
}
```

The idiom for iterating over values is analogous. Here's the idiom for iterating over key-value pairs:

```
for (Iterator i=m.entrySet().iterator(); i.hasNext(); )
    Map.Entry e = (Map.Entry) i.next();
    System.out.println(e.getKey() + ": " + e.getValue());
```

At first many people worry that these idioms might be slow because the Map has to create a new Collection object each time a Collection-view operation is called. Rest easy: There's no reason that a Map can't always return the same object each time it is asked for a given `Collection` view. This is precisely what all of the JDK's `Map` implementations do.

With all three `Collection`-views, calling an `Iterator`'s `remove` operation removes the associated entry from the backing `Map`, assuming that the backing map supports element removal to begin with. With the `entrySet` view, it is also possible to change the value associated with a key, by calling a `Map.Entry`'s `setValue` method during iteration, again assuming that the `Map` supports value modification to begin with. Note that these are the *only* safe ways to modify a `Map` during iteration; the behavior is unspecified if the underlying `Map` is modified in any other way while the iteration is in progress.

The `Collection`-views support element removal in all its many forms: the `remove`, `removeAll`, `retainAll`, and `clear` operations, as well as the `Iterator.remove` operation. (Yet again this assumes that the backing `Map` supports element removal.)

The `Collection`-views do *not* support element addition under any circumstances. It would make no sense for the `keySet` and the `values` views, and it's unnecessary for the `entrySet` view, as the backing `Map`'s `put` and `putAll` provide the same functionality.

Fancy Uses of Collection-Views: Map Algebra

When applied to the `Collection`-views, the bulk operations (`containsAll`, `removeAll`, and `retainAll`) are a surprisingly potent tool. Suppose that you want to know whether one `Map` is a submap of another, that is, whether the first `Map` contains all of the key-value mappings in the second. The following idiom does the trick:

```
if (m1.entrySet().containsAll(m2.entrySet())) {
    ...
}
```

Along similar lines, suppose that you want to know whether two `Map` objects contain mappings for all the same keys:

```
if (m1.keySet().equals(m2.keySet())) {
    ...
}
```

Suppose that you have a map representing a collection of attribute-value pairs and two sets representing required attributes and permissible attributes. (The permissible attributes include the required attributes.) The following snippet determines whether the attribute map conforms to these constraints and prints a detailed error message if it doesn't:

```
boolean valid = true;
Set attributes = attributeMap.keySet();
if (!attributes.containsAll(requiredAttributes)) {
    Set missing = new HashSet(requiredAttributes);
    missing.removeAll(attributes);
    System.out.println("Missing attributes: " + missing);
    valid = false;
}

if (!permissibleAttributes.containsAll(attributes)) {
    illegal = new HashSet(attributes);
    illegal.removeAll(permissibleAttributes));
    System.out.println(Illegal attributes: " + illegal);
    valid = false;
}

if (valid)
    System.out.println("OK");
```

Suppose that you want to know all of the keys common to two `Map` objects.

```
Set commonKeys = new HashSet(a.keySet());
commonKeys.retainAll(b.keySet);
```

A similar idiom gets you the common values and the common key-value pairs. Extra care is needed if you get the common key-value pairs, as the elements of the resulting `Set`, which are `Map.Entry` objects, may become invalid if the `Map` is modified.

All of the idioms presented thus far have been nondestructive; that is, they don't modify the backing `Map`. Here are a few that do. Suppose that you want to remove all of the key-value pairs that one `Map` has in common with another:

```
m1.entrySet().removeAll(m2.entrySet());
```

Suppose that you want to remove from one `Map` all of the keys that have mappings in another:

```
m1.keySet().removeAll(m2.keySet());
```

What happens when you start mixing keys and values in the same bulk operation? Suppose that you have a `Map`, `managers`, that maps each employee in a company to the employee's manager. We'll be deliberately vague about the types of the key and the value objects. It doesn't matter, so long as they're the same. Now suppose that you want to know who all the individual contributors are. (This is corporate-speak for employees who are not managers.) The following two-liner tells you exactly what you want to know:

```
Set individualContributors = new HashSet(managers.keySet());
individualContributors.removeAll(managers.values());
```

Suppose that you want to fire all of the employees who report directly to a particular manager, Herbert:

```
Employee herbert = ... ;
managers.values().removeAll(Collections.singleton(herbert));
```

Note that this idiom makes use of `Collections.singleton`, a static factory method that returns an immutable `Set` with the single, specified element.

Once you've done this, you may have a bunch of employees whose managers no longer work for the company (if any of Herbert's direct-reports were themselves managers). The following code tells you all of the employees whose manager no longer works for the company:

```
Map m = new HashMap(managers);
m.values().removeAll(managers.keySet());
Set slackers = m.keySet();
```

This example is a bit tricky. First, it makes a temporary copy of the `Map`, and it removes from the temporary copy all entries whose (manager) value is a key in the original `Map`. Remember that the original `Map` has an entry for each employee. Thus the remaining entries in the temporary `Map` comprise all of the entries from the original `Map` whose (manager) values are no longer employees. The keys in the temporary copy, then, represent precisely the employees we're looking for.

There are many, many more idioms like the ones contained in this section, but it would be impractical and tedious to list them all. Once you get the hang of it, it's not that difficult to come up with the right one when you need it.

Multimaps

A *multimap* is like a map but can map each key to multiple values. The Collections Framework doesn't include an interface for multimaps, because they aren't used all that commonly. It's a fairly simple matter to use a `Map` whose values are `List` objects as a multimap. This technique is demonstrated in the next code example, which reads a dictionary containing one word per line (all lowercase) and prints out all of the *permutation groups* that meet a size criterion. A *permutation group* is a bunch of words all of which contain exactly the same letters but in a different order. The program takes two arguments on the command line: the name of the dictionary file and the minimum size of permutation group to print out. Permutation groups containing fewer words than the specified minimum are not printed.

There is a standard trick for finding permutation groups: For each word in the dictionary, alphabetize the letters in the word (that is, reorder the word's letters into alphabetical order) and put an entry into a multimap, mapping the alphabetized word to the original word. For example, the word "bad" causes an entry mapping "abd" into "bad" to be put into the multimap. A moment's reflection will show that all of the words to which any given key maps form a permutation group. It's a simple matter to iterate over the keys in the multimap, printing out each permutation group that meets the size constraint.

The following program is a straightforward implementation of this technique. The only tricky part is the `alphabetize` method, which returns a string containing the same characters as its argument, in alphabetical order. This routine (which has nothing to do with the Collections Framework) implements a slick *bucket sort*. It assumes that the word being alphabetized consists entirely of lowercase alphabetic characters.

```
import java.util.*;
import java.io.*;

public class Perm {
    public static void main(String[] args) {
        int minGroupSize = Integer.parseInt(args[1]);

        // Read words from file and put into simulated multimap
        Map m = new HashMap();
        try {
            BufferedReader in =
                 new BufferedReader(new FileReader(args[0]));
            String word;
            while((word = in.readLine()) != null) {
                String alpha = alphabetize(word);
                List l = (List) m.get(alpha);
                if (l==null)
                    m.put(alpha, l=new ArrayList());
                l.add(word);
            }
```

```
        } catch(IOException e) {
            System.err.println(e);
            System.exit(1);
        }

        // Print all permutation groups above size threshold
        for (Iterator i = m.values().iterator(); i.hasNext(); ) {
            List l = (List) i.next();
            if (l.size() >= minGroupSize)
                System.out.println(l.size() + ": " + l);
        }
    }

    private static String alphabetize(String s) {
        int count[] = new int[256];
        int len = s.length();
        StringBuffer result = new StringBuffer(len);
        for (int i=0; i<len; i++)
            count[s.charAt(i)]++;
        for (char c='a'; c<='z'; c++)
            for (int i=0; i<count[c]; i++)
                result.append(c);
        return result.toString();
    }
}
```

Running the program on an 80,000-word dictionary takes about 16 seconds on an aging UltraSparc 1. With a minimum permutation group size of eight, it produces the following output:

```
 9: [estrin, inerts, insert, inters, niters, nitres, sinter,
    triens, trines]

 8: [carets, cartes, caster, caters, crates, reacts, recast,
    traces]

 9: [capers, crapes, escarp, pacers, parsec, recaps, scrape,
    secpar, spacer]

 8: [ates, east, eats, etas, sate, seat, seta, teas]

12: [apers, apres, asper, pares, parse, pears, prase, presa,
    rapes, reaps, spare, spear]

 9: [anestri, antsier, nastier, ratines, retains, retinas,
    retsina, stainer, stearin]
```

```
10: [least, setal, slate, stale, steal, stela, taels, tales,
    teals, tesla]

 8: [arles, earls, lares, laser, lears, rales, reals, seral]

 8: [lapse, leaps, pales, peals, pleas, salep, sepal, spale]

 8: [aspers, parses, passer, prases, repass, spares, sparse,
    spears]

 8: [earings, erasing, gainers, reagins, regains, reginas,
    searing, seringa]

11: [alerts, alters, artels, estral, laster, ratels, salter,
    slater, staler, stelar, talers]

 9: [palest, palets, pastel, petals, plates, pleats, septal,
    staple, tepals]

 8: [enters, nester, renest, rentes, resent, tenser, ternes,
    treens]

 8: [peris, piers, pries, prise, ripes, speir, spier, spire]
```

Many of these words seem a bit bogus, but that's not the program's fault; they're in the dictionary file.

Object Ordering

A `List l` may be sorted as follows:

```
Collections.sort(l);
```

If the `list` consists of `String` elements, it will be sorted into alphabetical order. If it consists of `Date` elements, it will be sorted into chronological order. How can this be? It's magic. Well, no. Actually `String` and `Date` both implement the `Comparable` interface, which provides a *natural ordering* for a class, allowing objects of that class to be sorted automatically. Table 3 summarizes the JDK classes that implement `Comparable`.

If you try to sort a list whose elements do not implement `Comparable`, `Collections.sort(list)` will throw a `ClassCastException`. Similarly if you try to sort a list whose elements cannot be compared *to one another*, `Collections.sort` will throw a `ClassCastException`. Elements that can be compared to one another are called *mutually comparable*. Although elements of different types can be mutually comparable, none of the JDK types listed here permit interclass comparison.

Table 3 JDK Classes Implementing `Comparable`

Class	Natural Ordering
`Byte`	Signed numerical
`Character`	Unsigned numerical
`Long`	Signed numerical
`Integer`	Signed numerical
`Short`	Signed numerical
`Double`	Signed numerical
`Float`	Signed numerical
`BigInteger`	Signed numerical
`BigDecimal`	Signed numerical
`File`	System-dependent lexicographic on pathname
`String`	Lexicographic
`Date`	Chronological
`CollationKey`	Locale-specific lexicographic

This is all you really need to know about the `Comparable` interface if you just want to sort lists of comparable elements or to create sorted collections of them. The next section will be of interest to you if you want to implement your own `Comparable` type.

Writing Your Own Comparable Types

The `Comparable` interface consists of a single method:

```
public interface Comparable {
    public int compareTo(Object o);
}
```

The `compareTo` method compares the receiving object with the specified object and returns a negative integer, zero, or a positive integer as the receiving object is less than, equal to, or greater than the specified object. If the specified object cannot be compared to the receiving object, the method throws a `ClassCastException`.

The following class, representing a person's name, implements `Comparable`.

```
import java.util.*;

public class Name implements Comparable {
    private String firstName, lastName;

    public Name(String firstName, String lastName) {
        if (firstName==null || lastName==null)
            throw new NullPointerException();
        this.firstName = firstName;
        this.lastName = lastName;
    }

    public String firstName() {return firstName;}

    public String lastName()  {return lastName;}

    public boolean equals(Object o) {
        if (!(o instanceof Name))
            return false;
        Name n = (Name)o;
        return n.firstName.equals(firstName) &&
               n.lastName.equals(lastName);
    }

    public int hashCode() {
        return 31*firstName.hashCode() + lastName.hashCode();
    }

    public String toString() {
        return firstName + " " + lastName;
    }

    public int compareTo(Object o) {
        Name n = (Name)o;
        int lastCmp = lastName.compareTo(n.lastName);
        return (lastCmp !=0 ? lastCmp :
                firstName.compareTo(n.firstName));
    }
}
```

To keep the example short, the class is somewhat limited: It doesn't support middle names, it demands both a first and a last name, and it is not internationalized in any way. Nonetheless, it illustrates several important points.

- `Name` objects are *immutable*. All other things being equal, immutable types are the way to go, especially for objects that will be used as elements in `Sets` or as keys in `Maps`. These collections will break if you modify their elements or keys while they're in the collection.
- The constructor checks its arguments for `null`. This ensures that all `Name` objects are well formed, so that none of the other methods will ever throw a `NullPointerException`.
- The `hashCode` method is redefined. This is *essential* for any class that redefines the `equals` method. (Equal objects must have equal hash codes.)
- The `equals` method returns `false` if the specified object is `null` or of an inappropriate type. The `compareTo` method throws a runtime exception under these circumstances. Both of these behaviors are *required* by the general contracts of the respective methods.
- The `toString` method has been redefined to print the name in human-readable form. This is always a good idea, especially for objects that will be put into collections. The various collection types' `toString` methods depend on the `toString` methods of their elements, keys, and values.

Since this section is about element ordering, let's talk more about `Name`'s `compareTo` method. It implements the standard name-ordering algorithm, where last names take precedence over first names. This is exactly what you want in a *natural ordering*. It would be confusing if the natural ordering were unnatural!

Take a look at how `compareTo` is implemented, because it's quite typical. First, you cast the `Object` argument to the appropriate type. This throws the appropriate exception (`ClassCastException`) if the argument's type is inappropriate. Then you compare the most significant part of the object (in this case, the last name). Often, you can just use the natural ordering of the part's type. In this case the part is a `String`, and the natural (lexicographic) ordering is exactly what's called for. If the comparison results in anything other than zero, which represents equality, you're done: You just return the result. If the most significant parts are equal, you go on to compare the next-most-significant parts. In this case there are only two parts, first name and last name. If there were more parts, you'd proceed in the obvious fashion, comparing parts until you found two that weren't equal or you were comparing the least-significant parts, at which point you'd return the result of the comparison.

Just to show that it all works, here's a little program that builds a list of names and sorts them.

```
import java.util.*;

class NameSort {
    public static void main(String args[]) {
        Name n[] = {
            new Name("John", "Lennon"),
            new Name("Karl", "Marx"),
            new Name("Groucho", "Marx"),
            new Name("Oscar", "Grouch")
        };
        List l = Arrays.asList(n);
        Collections.sort(l);
        System.out.println(l);
    }
}
```

If you run this program, here's what it prints:

```
[Oscar Grouch, John Lennon, Groucho Marx, Karl Marx]
```

There are four restrictions on the behavior of the `compareTo` method, which we won't go over now because they're fairly technical and boring and are better left in the API documentation. It's really important that all classes that implement `Comparable` obey these restrictions, so read the documentation for `Comparable` if you're writing a class that implements it. Attempting to sort a list of objects that violate these restrictions has undefined behavior. Technically speaking, these restrictions ensure that the natural ordering is a *total order* on the objects of a class that implements it; this is necessary to ensure that sorting is well-defined.

Comparators

What if you want to sort some objects in an order other than their natural order? Or what if you want to sort some objects that don't implement `Comparable`? To do either of these things, you'll need to provide a `Comparator`, an object that encapsulates an ordering. Like the `Comparable` interface, the `Comparator` interface consists of a single method.

```
public interface Comparator {
   int compare(Object o1, Object o2);
}
```

The compare method compares its two arguments and returns a negative integer, zero, or a positive integer according to whether the first argument is less than, equal to, or greater than the second. If either of the arguments has an inappropriate type for the Comparator, the compare method throws a ClassCastException.

Much of what was said about Comparable applies to Comparator as well. Writing a compare method is nearly identical to writing a compareTo method, except that the former gets both objects passed in as arguments. The compare method has to obey the same four technical restrictions as Comparable's compareTo method, for the same reason: A Comparator must induce a *total order* on the objects it compares.

Suppose that you have a class called EmployeeRecord:

```
public class EmployeeRecord implements Comparable {
    public Name name();
    public int empNumber();
    public Date hireDate();
             ...
}
```

Let's assume that the natural ordering of EmployeeRecord objects is Name ordering (as defined in the previous example) on employee name. Unfortunately the boss has asked us for a list of employees in order of seniority. This means that we have to do some work, but not much. Here's a program that will produce the required list.

```
import java.util.*;

class EmpSort {
   static final Comparator SENIORITY_ORDER = new Comparator() {
        public int compare(Object o1, Object o2) {
            EmployeeRecord r1 = (EmployeeRecord) o1;
            EmployeeRecord r2 = (EmployeeRecord) o2;
            return r2.hireDate().compareTo(r1.hireDate());
        }
    };

    // Employee Database
    static final Collection employees = ... ;

    public static void main(String args[]) {
        List emp = new ArrayList(employees);
```

```
            Collections.sort(emp, SENIORITY_ORDER);
            System.out.println(emp);
        }
    }
```

The Comparator in the program is reasonably straightforward. It casts its arguments to EmployeeRecord and relies on the natural ordering of Date applied to the results of hireDate accessor method. Note that the Comparator passes the hire date of its second argument to that of its first, rather than vice-versa. This is because the employee who was hired most recently is least senior: Sorting in order of hire date would put the list in *reverse* seniority order. Another way to achieve the same effect would be to maintain the argument order but to negate the result of the comparison:

```
return -r1.hireDate().compareTo(r2.hireDate());
```

The two techniques are equally preferable. Use whichever looks best to you.

The Comparator in the preceding program works fine for sorting a List, but it does have one deficiency: It cannot be used to order a sorted collection, such as TreeSet, because it generates an ordering that is *not compatible with equals*. This means that this comparator equates objects that the equals method does not. In particular, any two employees who were hired on the same date will compare as equal. When you're sorting a List, this doesn't matter, but when you're using the Comparator to maintain order in a sorted collection, it's fatal. If you use this Comparator to insert multiple employees hired on the same date into a TreeSet, only the first one will be added to the set. The second will be seen as a duplicate element and will be ignored.

To fix this problem, simply tweak the Comparator so that it produces an ordering that *is compatible with equals*. In other words, tweak it so that the only elements that are seen as equal when using compare are those that are also seen as equal when compared using equals. The way to do this is to do a two-part comparison (like we did for Name), where the first part is the one that we're interested in (in this case the hire date), and the second part is an attribute that uniquely identifies the object. In this case the employee number is the obvious attribute. Here's the Comparator that results:

```
static final Comparator SENIORITY_ORDER = new Comparator() {
    public int compare(Object o1, Object o2) {
        FmployeeRecord r1 = (EmployeeRecord) o1;
        EmployeeRecord r2 = (EmployeeRecord) o2;
        int dateCmp = r2.hireDate().compareTo(r1.hireDate());
        if (dateCmp != 0)
```

```
                return dateCmp;
            return (r1.empNumber() < r2.empNumber() ? -1 :
                    (r1.empNumber() == r2.empNumber() ? 0 : 1));
        }
    };
```

One last note: You might be tempted to replace the final `return` statement in the `Comparator` with the simpler:

```
    return r1.empNumber() - r2.empNumber();
```

Don't do it unless you're *absolutely sure* that no one will ever have a negative employee number! This trick does not work in general, as the signed integer type is not big enough to represent the difference of two arbitrary signed integers. If `i` is a large positive integer and `j` is a large negative integer, `i-j` will overflow and will return a negative integer. The resulting `Comparator` violates one of the four technical restrictions that we keep talking about (transitivity) and produces horrible, subtle bugs. This is not a purely theoretical concern; people get burned by it.

SortedSet Interface

A `SortedSet` is a `Set` that maintains its elements in ascending order, sorted according to the elements' *natural order* or according to a `Comparator` provided at `SortedSet` creation time. In addition to the normal `Set` operations, the `Set` interface provides operations for:

- Range-view: Performs arbitrary *range operations* on the sorted set.
- Endpoints: Returns the first or the last element in the sorted set.
- Comparator access: Returns the `Comparator`, if any, used to sort the set.

The `SortedSet` interface follows:

```
public interface SortedSet extends Set {
    // Range-view
    SortedSet subSet(Object fromElement, Object toElement);
    SortedSet headSet(Object toElement);
    SortedSet tailSet(Object fromElement);

    // Endpoints
    Object first();
    Object last();

    // Comparator access
    Comparator comparator();
}
```

Set Operations

The operations that `SortedSet` inherits from `Set` behave identically on sorted sets and normal sets, with two exceptions.

- The `Iterator` returned by the `iterator` operation traverses the sorted set in order.
- The array returned by `toArray` contains the sorted set's elements in order.

Although the interface doesn't guarantee it, the `toString` method of the JDK's `SortedSet` implementations returns a string containing all of the elements of the sorted set, in order.

Standard Constructors

By convention all `Collection` implementations provide a standard constructor that takes a `Collection`, and `SortedSet` implementations are no exception. This constructor creates a `SortedSet` object that orders its elements according to their natural order. In addition, `SortedSet` implementations provide, by convention, two other standard constructors.

- One takes a `Comparator` and returns a new (empty) `SortedSet` sorted according to the specified `Comparator`.
- One takes a `SortedSet` and returns a new `SortedSet` containing the same elements as the given `SortedSet`, *sorted according to the same `Comparator`* (or using the elements' natural ordering, if the specified `SortedSet` did too). Note that the compile-time type of the argument determines whether this constructor is invoked in preference to the ordinary `Set` constructor and not the runtime type!

The first of these standard constructors is the normal way to create an empty `SortedSet` with an explicit `Comparator`. The second is similar in spirit to the standard `Collection` constructor: It creates a copy of a `SortedSet` with the same ordering but with a programmer-specified implementation type.

Range-View Operations

The range-view operations are somewhat analogous to those provided by the `List` interface, but there is one big difference. Range-views of a sorted set remain valid even if the backing sorted set is modified directly. This is feasible because the endpoints of a range view of a sorted set are absolute points in the element space rather than specific elements in the backing collection, as is the case for lists. A range-view of a sorted set is really just a window onto whatever portion of the set lies in the designated part of the element space. Changes to the range-view write back to the backing sorted set, *and vice-versa*. Thus it's OK to use range-views on sorted sets for long periods of time, unlike range-views on lists.

Sorted sets provide three range-view operations. The first, `subSet`, takes two endpoints, like `subList`. Rather than indices, the endpoints are objects. They must be comparable to the elements in the sorted set, using the set's `Comparator` or the natural ordering of its elements, whichever the set uses to order itself. Like `subList` the range is *half-open*, including its low endpoint but excluding the high one.

Thus the following example tells you how many words between "doorbell" and "pickle," including "doorbell" but excluding "pickle," are contained in a `SortedSet` of strings called `dictionary`:

```
int count = dictionary.subSet("doorbell", "pickle").size();
```

Similarly the following one-liner removes all of the elements beginning with the letter "f":[1]

```
dictionary.subSet("f", "g").clear();
```

A similar trick can be used to print a table telling you how many words begin with each letter.

```
for (char ch='a'; ch<='z'; ch++) {
    String from = new String(new char[] {ch});
    String to = new String(new char[] {(char)(ch+1)});
    SortedSet section = dictionary.subSet(from, to);
    System.out.println(from + ": " + section.size());
}
```

Suppose that you want to view a *closed interval*, which contains both its endpoints, instead of an open interval. If the element type allows for the calculation of the successor of a given value in the element space, merely request the `subSet` from `lowEndpoint` to `successor(highEndpoint)`. Although it isn't entirely obvious, the successor of a string `s` in `String`'s natural ordering is `s+"\0"` (that is, `s` with a null character appended).

---

[1] A rather heavy-handed approach to censorship?

Thus the following one-liner tells you how many words between "doorbell" and "pickle," including "doorbell" *and* "pickle," are contained in the dictionary:

```
int count = dictionary.subSet("doorbell", "pickle\0").size();
```

A similar technique can be used to view an *open interval*, which contains neither endpoint. The open-interval view from `lowEndpoint` to `highEndpoint` is the half-open interval from `successor(lowEndpoint)` to `highEndpoint`. To calculate the number of words between "doorbell" and "pickle," excluding both:

```
int count = dictionary.subSet("doorbell\0", "pickle").size();
```

The `SortedSet` interface contains two more range-view operations, `headSet` and `tailSet`, both of which take a single `Object` argument. The former returns a view of the initial portion of the backing `SortedSet`, up to but not including the specified object. The latter returns a view of the final portion of the backing `SortedSet`, beginning with the specified object and continuing to the end of the backing `SortedSet`. Thus the following code allows you to view the dictionary as two disjoint "volumes" (a–m and n–z):

```
SortedSet volume1 = dictionary.headSet("n");
SortedSet volume2 = dictionary.tailSet("n");
```

Endpoint Operations

The `SortedSet` interface contains operations to return the first and the last elements in the sorted set, called (not surprisingly) `first` and `last`. In addition to their obvious uses, `last` allows a workaround for a deficiency in the `SortedSet` interface. One thing you'd like to do with a `SortedSet` is to go into the interior of the set and to iterate forward or backward. It's easy enough to go forward from the interior: Just get a `tailSet` and iterate over it. Unfortunately there's no easy way to go backward.

The following idiom obtains the first element in a sorted set that is less than a specified object `o` in the element space:

```
Object predecessor = dictionary.headSet(o).last();
```

This is a fine way to go one element backward from a point in the interior of a sorted set. It could be applied repeatedly to iterate backward, but this is very inefficient, requiring a lookup for each element returned.

Comparator Accessor

The `SortedSet` interface contains an accessor method, called `comparator` that returns the `Comparator` used to sort the set or `null` if the set is sorted according to the *natural order* of its elements. This method is provided so that sorted sets can be copied into new sorted sets with the same ordering. This method is used by the standard `SortedSet` constructor, described previously.

SortedMap Interface

A `SortedMap` is a `Map` that maintains its entries in ascending order, sorted according to the keys' *natural order*, or according to a `Comparator` provided at the creation time of the `SortedMap`. Natural order and `Comparators` are discussed in the section Object Ordering (page 54). The `SortedMap` interface provides operations for the normal `Map` operations as well as for:

- **Range-view:** Performs arbitrary *range operations* on the sorted map
- **Endpoints:** Returns the first or the last key in the sorted map
- **Comparator access:** Returns the `Comparator`, if any, used to sort the map

This interface is the `Map` analogue of `SortedSet`.

```
public interface SortedMap extends Map {
    Comparator comparator();

    SortedMap subMap(Object fromKey, Object toKey);
    SortedMap headMap(Object toKey);
    SortedMap tailMap(Object fromKey);

    Object first();
    Object last();
}
```

Map Operations

The operations that `SortedMap` inherits from `Map` behave identically on sorted maps and normal maps, with two exceptions.

- The `Iterator` returned by the `iterator` operation on any of the sorted map's `Collection`-views traverse the collections in order.
- The arrays returned by the `Collection`-views' `toArray` operations contain the keys, values, or entries in order.

Although it isn't guaranteed by the interface, the `toString` method of the JDK's `SortedMap` implementations returns a string containing all of the mappings in the map, in key-order. The `toString` method behaves similarly when applied to the collection views.

Standard Constructors

By convention, all `Map` implementations provide a standard constructor that takes a `Map`, and `SortedMap` implementations are no exception. This constructor creates a `SortedMap` object that orders its entries according to their keys' natural order. Additionally, `SortedMap` implementations, by convention, provide two other standard constructors.

- One takes a `Comparator` and returns a new (empty) `SortedMap` sorted according to the specified `Comparator`.
- One takes a `SortedMap` and returns a new `SortedMap` containing the same mappings as the given `SortedMap`, *sorted according to the same `Comparator`* (or using the elements' natural ordering, if the specified `SortedMap` did too). Note that it is the compile-time type of the argument that determines whether this constructor is invoked in preference to the ordinary `Map` constructor, and not its runtime type!

The first of these standard constructors is the normal way to create an empty `SortedMap` with an explicit `Comparator`. The second is similar in spirit to the standard `Map` constructor, creating a copy of a `SortedMap` with the same ordering but with a programmer-specified implementation type.

Comparison to SortedSet

Because this interface is a precise `Map` analog of `SortedSet`, all of the idioms and code examples in the section SortedSet Interface (page 61) apply to `SortedMap`, with only trivial modifications.

Implementations

IMPLEMENTATIONS are the data objects used to store collections; they implement the *core collection interfaces* described in the previous lesson, Interfaces (page 25). The sections in this lesson describe three kinds of implementations:

General-Purpose Implementations (page 67)
: General-purpose implementations are the classes that provide the primary implementations of the core collection interfaces.

Wrapper Implementations (page 71)
: Wrapper implementations are used in combination with other types of implementations (often the general-purpose implementations) to provide added functionality.

Convenience Implementations (page 73)
: Convenience implementations are mini-implementations, typically made available via *static factory methods*, provide convenient, efficient alternatives to the general-purpose implementations for special collections (such as *singleton* sets).

Additionally, you can build your own implementations, based on the JDK's *abstract implementations*. This topic is described in a separate lesson, Custom Implementations (page 83), because it's an advanced topic. It's not particularly difficult, but relatively few people will need to do it.

General-Purpose Implementations

The general-purpose implementations are summarized in the following table. The table highlights their regular naming pattern: Names are all of the form `<Implementation> <Interface>`, where `<Interface>` is the core collection interface implemented by the class, and <Implementation> signifies the data structure underlying the implementation.

Table 4 Naming Patterns of the General-Purpose Implementations

	Implementations				
Interfaces		**Hash Table**	**Resizable Array**	**Balanced Tree**	**Linked List**
	Set	`HashSet`		`TreeSet`	
	List		`ArrayList`		`LinkedList`
	Map	`HashMap`		`TreeMap`	

JDK 1.2 provides two implementations of each interface (with the exception of `Collection`, which has no direct implementations but serves as a least common denominator for the other collection interfaces). In each case one implementation is clearly the primary implementation: the one to use, all other things being equal. The primary implementations are `HashSet`, `ArrayList`, and `HashMap`. Note that the `SortedSet` and the `SortedMap` interfaces do not have rows in the table. Each of those interfaces has one implementation, `TreeSet` and `TreeMap`, which are listed in the `Set` and the `Map` rows.

The implementations have not only consistent names, but also consistent behavior. They implement all of the *optional operations* contained in their interfaces. All permit `null` elements, keys, and values. Each one is not synchronized. All have fail-fast iterators, which detect illegal concurrent modification during iteration and fail quickly and cleanly, rather than risking arbitrary, nondeterministic behavior at an undetermined time in the future. All are `Serializable`, and all support a public `clone` method.

The fact that the new implementations are unsynchronized represents a break with the past: `Vector` and `Hashtable` are synchronized. The new approach was taken because collections are frequently used when the synchronization is of no benefit. Such uses include single-threaded use, read-only use, and use as part of a larger data object that does its own synchronization. In general it is good API design practice not to make users pay for a feature that they don't use. Further, unnecessary synchronization can result in deadlock under certain circumstances.

If you need a synchronized collection, the *synchronization wrappers*, described in the section Wrapper Implementations (page 71), allow *any* collection to be transformed into a synchronized collection. Thus synchronization is optional for the new collection implementations where it was mandatory for the old.

As a rule of thumb you should be thinking about the interfaces, not the implementations. That is why there are no programming examples in this lesson. For the most part the choice of implementation affects only performance. The preferred style, as mentioned in the lesson Interfaces (page 25), is to choose an implementation when a collection is created and to immediately assign the new collection to a variable of the corresponding interface type (or to pass the collection to a method expecting an argument of the interface type). In this way the program does not become dependent on any added methods in a given implementation, leaving the programmer free to change implementations at the drop of a hat, if performance concerns so warrant.

The general-purpose implementations are briefly discussed here. The performance of the implementations is described with such words as *constant*, *log*, *linear*, *n log(n)*, and *quadratic*. These words refer to the *asymptotic upper bound* on the *time complexity* of performing the operation. All of this is quite a mouthful, and it doesn't matter much if you don't know what it means. If you're interested, refer to any good algorithms textbook. One thing to keep in mind is that this sort of performance metric has its limitations. Sometimes the nominally slower implementation may be faster for your application. When in doubt, measure the performance.

Set

The two general-purpose `Set` implementations are `HashSet` and `TreeSet`. It's very straightforward to decide which of these two to use. `HashSet` is much faster (constant time versus log time for most operations) but offers no ordering guarantees. If you need to use the operations in the `SortedSet` interface or if in-order iteration is important to you, use `TreeSet`. Otherwise use `HashSet`. It's a fair bet that you'll end up using `HashSet` most of the time.

One thing worth keeping in mind about `HashSet` is that iteration cost is linear in the sum of the number of entries and the number of buckets (the *capacity*). Thus it's important to choose an appropriate initial capacity if iteration performance is important. Choosing a capacity that's too high can waste both space and time. The default initial capacity is 101, and that's often more than you need. The initial capacity may be specified by using the `int` constructor. The following line of code allocates a `HashSet` whose initial capacity is 17.

```
Set s = new HashSet(17);
```

HashSets have one other tuning parameter, called the *load factor*. If you care deeply about the space consumption of your HashSet, read the HashSet documentation[1] for more information. Otherwise just live with the default. If you accept the default load factor but want to specify an initial capacity, pick a number that's about twice the size that you expect the Set to grow to. If your guess is way off, the capacity may have to grow or you may waste a bit of space, but either way it's no big problem. If you know a prime number of about the right size, use it. If not, use an odd number. Or use an even number. It doesn't really matter much; these things might make the HashSet perform a wee bit better, but nothing to write home about.

TreeSet has no tuning parameters. With the exception of clone, neither HashSet nor TreeSet has any operations other than those required by their respective interfaces (Set and TreeSet).

List

The two general-purpose List implementations are ArrayList and LinkedList. Most of the time you'll probably use ArrayList. It offers constant time positional access and is just plain fast, because it does not have to allocate a node object for each element in the List, and it can take advantage of the native method System.arraycopy when it has to move multiple elements at once. Think of ArrayList as Vector without the synchronization overhead.

If you frequently add elements to the beginning of the List or iterate over the List to delete elements from its interior, you should consider using LinkedList. These operations are constant time in a LinkedList but linear time in an ArrayList. But you pay a big price! Positional access is linear time in a LinkedList and constant time in an ArrayList. Furthermore, the constant factor for LinkedList is much worse. If you think that you want to use a LinkedList, measure the performance with both LinkedList and ArrayList. You may be surprised.

ArrayList has one tuning parameter, the *initial capacity*. It refers to the number of elements the ArrayList can hold before it has to grow. There's not much to say about it. The only ArrayList operations that are not required by List are ensureCapacity and trimToSize (which alter the excess capacity) and clone.

LinkedList has no tuning parameters and seven optional operations, one of which is clone. The other six are addFirst, getFirst, removeFirst, addLast, getLast, and removeLast. They make it a bit more convenient to use a

---

[1] The API documentation for HashSet is available on the CD-ROM that accompanies this book and online here: http://java.sun.com/products/jdk/1.2/docs/api/java/util/HashSet.html

LinkedList as a queue or as a double-ended queue (*dequeue*), but they also prevent you from easily switching representations when you discover that ArrayList is faster.

If you need synchronization, a Vector will be slightly faster than an ArrayList synchronized with Collections.synchronizedList. But Vector has loads of legacy operations, so be extra careful to always manipulate the Vector with the List interface, or you'll be stuck with it for life.

If your List is fixed in size (that is, you'll never use remove, add, or any of the bulk operations other than containsAll), you have a third option that's definitely worth considering. See Arrays.asList in the section Convenience Implementations (page 73) for more information.

Map

The two general-purpose Map implementations are HashMap and TreeMap. The situation for Map is *exactly* analogous to Set. If you need SortedMap operations or in-order Collection-view iteration, go for TreeMap; otherwise, go for HashMap. Everything else in the section Set (page 69) also applies to Map.

Completeness requires that we mention Hashtable. As with Vector and ArrayList, if you need synchronization, a Hashtable will be slightly faster than a HashMap synchronized with Collections.synchronizedMap. Again, Hashtable has loads of legacy operations, so be extra careful always to manipulate it with the Map interface, or you'll be stuck with it for life.

Wrapper Implementations

Wrapper implementations delegate all of their real work to a specified collection but add extra functionality on top of what this collection offers. For *design patterns* fans, this is an example of the *decorator* pattern. Although it may seem a bit exotic, it's really pretty straightforward.

These implementations are *anonymous:* Rather than providing a public class, the JDK provides a *static factory method.* All of these implementations are found in the Collections class, which consists solely of static methods.

Synchronization Wrappers

The synchronization wrappers add automatic synchronization (thread safety) to an arbitrary collection. Each of the six core collection interfaces has one static factory method:

```
public static Collection synchronizedCollection(Collection c);
public static Set synchronizedSet(Set s);
public static List synchronizedList(List list);
public static Map synchronizedMap(Map m);
public static SortedSet synchronizedSortedSet(SortedSet s);
public static SortedMap synchronizedSortedMap(SortedMap m);
```

Each of these methods returns a synchronized (thread-safe) `Collection` backed by the specified collection. In order to guarantee serial access, all access to the backing collection must be accomplished through the returned collection. The easy way to guarantee this is not to keep a reference to the backing collection. Creating the synchronized collection like this does the trick:

```
List list = Collections.synchronizedList(new ArrayList());
```

A collection created in this fashion is every bit as thread-safe as a normally synchronized collection, such as a `Vector`.

In the face of concurrent access, it is imperative that the user manually synchronize on the returned collection when iterating over it. The reason is that iteration is accomplished via multiple calls into the collection, which must be composed into a single atomic operation. The idiom to iterate over a wrapper-synchronized collection is:

```
Collection sc = Collections.synchronizedCollection(c);
synchronized(sc) {
    Iterator i = sc.iterator(); // Must be in synchronized block
    while (i.hasNext())
        foo(i.next());
}
```

Failure to follow this advice may result in nondeterministic behavior.

The idiom for iterating over a `Collection`-view of a synchronized `Map` is similar; however, it is imperative that the user manually synchronize on the synchronized `Map` when iterating over any of its `Collection`-views, rather than synchronizing on the `Collection`-view itself.

```
Map m = Collections.synchronizedMap(new HashMap());
    ...
Set s = m.keySet();  // Needn't be in synchronized block
    ...
synchronized(m) {   // Synchronizing on m, not s!
    Iterator i = s.iterator(); // Must be in synchronized block
    while (i.hasNext())
        foo(i.next();
}
```

One minor downside of using wrapper implementations is that you do not have the ability to execute any noninterface operations of a wrapped implementation. So, for instance, in the preceding `List` example, one cannot call `ArrayList`'s `ensureCapacity` operation on the wrapped `ArrayList`.

Unmodifiable Wrappers

The unmodifiable wrappers are conceptually similar to the synchronization wrappers but simpler. Rather than adding functionality to the wrapped collection, they take it away. In particular, they take away the ability to modify the collection, by intercepting all of the operations that would modify the collection and throwing an `UnsupportedOperationException`. The unmodifiable wrappers have two main uses:

- To make a collection immutable once it has been built. In this case it's good practice not to maintain a reference to the backing collection. This absolutely guarantees immutability.
- To allow "second-class citizens" read-only access to your data structures. You keep a reference to the backing collection but hand out a reference to the wrapper. In this way the second-class citizens can look but not touch, while you maintain full access.

Like the synchronization wrappers, each of the six core collection interfaces has one static factory method.

```
public static Collection unmodifiableCollection(Collection c);
public static Set unmodifiableSet(Set s);
public static List unmodifiableList(List list);
public static Map unmodifiableMap(Map m);
public static SortedSet unmodifiableSortedSet(SortedSet s);
public static SortedMap unmodifiableSortedMap(SortedMap m);
```

Convenience Implementations

This section describes several mini-implementations that can be more convenient and more efficient than the general-purpose implementations when you don't need their full power. All of the implementations in this section are made available via static factory methods or exported constants, rather than public classes.

List-View of an Array

The `Arrays.asList` method returns a `List`-view of its array argument. Changes to the `List` write through to the array and vice-versa. The size of the collection is that of the array and cannot be changed. If the add or the remove method is called on the List, an UnsupportedOperationException will result.

The normal use of this implementation is as a bridge between array-based and collection-based APIs. It allows you to pass an array to a method expecting a Collection or a List. However, this implementation also has another use. If you need a fixed-size List, it's more efficient than any general-purpose List implementation. Here's the idiom:

```
List l = Arrays.asList(new Object[size]);
```

Note that a reference to the backing array is not retained.

Immutable Multiple-Copy List

Occasionally you'll need an immutable List consisting of multiple copies of the same element. The Collections.nCopies method returns such a List. This implementation has two main uses. The first is to initialize a newly created List. For example, suppose that you want an ArrayList initially consisting of 1,000 null elements. The following incantation does the trick:

```
List l = new ArrayList(Collections.nCopies(1000, null));
```

Of course, the initial value of each element does not need to be null. The second main use is to grow an existing List. For example, suppose that you want to add 69 copies of the string "fruit bat" to the end of a List. It's not clear why you'd want to do such a thing, but let's just suppose you did. Here's how you'd do it:

```
lovablePets.addAll(Collections.nCopies(69, "fruit bat"));
```

By using the form of addAll that takes both an index and a Collection, you can add the new elements to the middle of a List instead of at the end.

Immutable Singleton Set

Sometimes you'll need an immutable *singleton* Set, which consists of a single specified element. The Collections.singleton method returns such a Set. One use of this implementation is to remove all occurrences of a specified element from a Collection:

```
c.removeAll(Collections.singleton(e));
```

A related idiom removes from a `Map` all elements that map to a specified value. For example, suppose that you have a `Map`, `profession`, that maps people to their line of work. Suppose that you want to eliminate all of the lawyers. This one-liner will do the deed:

```
profession.values().removeAll(Collections.singleton(LAWYER));
```

One more use of this implementation is to provide a single input value to a method that is written to accept a `Collection` of values.

Empty Set and Empty List Constants

The `Collections` class provides two constants, representing the empty `Set` and the empty `List`, `Collections.EMPTY_SET` and `Collections.EMPTY_LIST`. The main use of these constants is as input to methods that take a `Collection` of values, when you don't want to provide any values at all.

4 Algorithms

THE *polymorphic algorithms* described in this lesson are pieces of reusable functionality provided by the JDK. All of them come from the `Collections` class, and all take the form of static methods whose first argument is the collection on which the operation is to be performed. The great majority of the algorithms provided by the Java platform operate on `List` objects, but a couple of them (`min` and `max`) operate on arbitrary `Collection` objects. The sections in this lesson describe the following algorithms:

Sorting

The `sort` algorithm reorders a `List` so that its elements are in ascending order according to an ordering relation. Two forms of the operation are provided. The simple form takes a `List` and sorts it according to its elements' *natural ordering*. If you're unfamiliar with the concept of natural ordering, read the section Object Ordering (page 54).

The `sort` operation uses a slightly optimized *merge sort* algorithm. This algorithm is:

- **Fast:** This algorithm is guaranteed to run in `n log(n)` time and runs substantially faster on nearly sorted lists. Empirical trials showed it to be as fast as a highly optimized quicksort. Quicksort is generally regarded to be faster than merge sort but isn't *stable* and doesn't *guarantee* `n log(n)` performance.
- **Stable:** That is to say, it doesn't reorder equal elements. This is important if you sort the same list repeatedly on different attributes. If a user of a mail program sorts the in-box by mailing date and then sorts it by sender, the user naturally expects that the now contiguous list of messages from a given sender will (still) be sorted by mailing date. This is guaranteed only if the second sort was stable.

Here's a trivial program that prints out its arguments in lexicographic (alphabetical) order.

```
import java.util.*;

public class Sort {
    public static void main(String args[]) {
        List l = Arrays.asList(args);
        Collections.sort(l);
        System.out.println(l);
    }
}
```

Let's run the program.

```
% java Sort i walk the line
```

The following output is produced:

```
[i, line, the, walk]
```

The program was included only to show you that algorithms really are as easy to use as they appear to be.

The second form of `sort` takes a `Comparator` in addition to a `List` and sorts the elements with the `Comparator`. Suppose that you wanted to print out the permutation groups from the example shown in the section Map Interface (page 45) in reverse order of size, largest permutation group first. The following example shows you how to achieve this with the help of the second form of the `sort` method.

Recall that the permutation groups are stored as values in a `Map`, in the form of `List` objects. The revised printing code iterates through the `Map`'s `values`-view, putting every `List` that passes the minimum-size test into a `List` of `Lists`. Then the code sorts this `List`, using a `Comparator` that expects `List` objects, and implements reverse-size ordering. Finally, the code iterates through the sorted `List`, printing its elements (the permutation groups). The following code replaces the printing code at the end of `Perm`'s `main` method:

```
// Make a List of permutation groups above size threshold
List winners = new ArrayList();
for (Iterator i = m.values().iterator(); i.hasNext(); ) {
    List l = (List) i.next();
    if (l.size() >= minGroupSize)
        winners.add(l);
}

// Sort permutation groups according to size
Collections.sort(winners, new Comparator() {
    public int compare(Object o1, Object o2) {
        return ((List)o2).size() - ((List)o1).size();
    }
});

// Print permutation groups
for (Iterator i=winners.iterator(); i.hasNext(); ) {
    List l = (List) i.next();
    System.out.println(l.size() + ": " + l);
}
```

Running the program on the same dictionary in the section Map Interface (page 45), with the same minimum permutation group size (eight), produces the following output:

```
12: [apers, apres, asper, pares, parse, pears, prase, presa,
     rapes, reaps, spare, spear]

11: [alerts, alters, artels, estral, laster, ratels, salter,
     slater, staler, stelar, talers]

10: [least, setal, slate, stale, steal, stela, taels, tales,
     teals, tesla]

 9: [estrin, inerts, insert, inters, niters, nitres, sinter,
     triens, trines]
```

```
9: [capers, crapes, escarp, pacers, parsec, recaps, scrape,
    secpar, spacer]

9: [anestri, antsier, nastier, ratines, retains, retinas,
    retsina, stainer, stearin]

9: [palest, palets, pastel, petals, plates, pleats, septal,
    staple, tepals]

8: [carets, cartes, caster, caters, crates, reacts, recast,
    traces]

8: [ates, east, eats, etas, sate, seat, seta, teas]

8: [arles, earls, lares, laser, lears, rales, reals, seral]

8: [lapse, leaps, pales, peals, pleas, salep, sepal, spale]

8: [aspers, parses, passer, prases, repass, spares, sparse,
    spears]

8: [earings, erasing, gainers, reagins, regains, reginas,
    searing, seringa]

8: [enters, nester, renest, rentes, resent, tenser, ternes,
    treens]

8: [peris, piers, pries, prise, ripes, speir, spier, spire]
```

Shuffling

The `shuffle` algorithm does the opposite of what `sort` does, destroying any trace of order that may have been present in a `List`. That is to say, this algorithm reorders the `List`, based on input from a source of randomness, such that all possible permutations occur with equal likelihood (assuming a fair source of randomness). This algorithm is useful in implementing games of chance. For example, it could be used to shuffle a `List` of `Card` objects representing a deck. Also, it's useful for generating test cases.

This operation has two forms. The first takes a `List` and uses a default source of randomness. The second also requires the caller to provide a `Random` object to use as a source of randomness. The code for this algorithm is used as an example in the section List Interface (page 35).

Routine Data Manipulation

The `Collections` class provides three algorithms for doing routine data manipulation on `List` objects. All of these algorithms are pretty straightforward:

- `reverse`: Reverses the order of the elements in a List.
- `fill`: Overwrites every element in a `List` with the specified value. This operation is useful for reinitializing a `List`.
- `copy`: Takes two arguments, a destination `List` and a source `List`, and copies the elements of the source into the destination, overwriting its contents. The destination `List` must be at least as long as the source. If it is longer, the remaining elements in the destination `List` are unaffected.

Searching

The `binary search` algorithm searches for a specified element in a sorted `List`. This algorithm has two forms. The first takes a `List` and an element to search for (the "search key"). This form assumes that the `List` is sorted into ascending order according to the natural ordering of its elements. The second form of the call takes a `Comparator` in addition to the `List` and the search key and assumes that the `List` is sorted into ascending order according to the specified `Comparator`. The `sort` algorithm can be used to sort the `List` prior to calling `binarySearch`.

The return value is the same for both forms. If the `List` contains the search key, its index is returned. If not, the return value is `(-(`*`insertion point`*`) - 1)`, where the *insertion point* is the point at which the value would be inserted into the List: the index of the first element greater than the value or `list.size()` if all elements in the `List` are less than the specified value. This admittedly ugly formula guarantees that the return value will be `>= 0` if and only if the search key is found. It's basically a hack to combine a boolean (`found`) and an integer (`index`) into a single `int` return value.

The following idiom, usable with both forms of the `binarySearch` operation, looks for the specified search key and inserts it at the appropriate position if it's not already present:

```
int pos = Collections.binarySearch(l, key);
if (pos < 0)
    l.add(-pos-1);
```

Finding Extreme Values

The `min` and the `max` algorithms return, respectively, the minimum and maximum element contained in a specified `Collection`. Both of these operations come in two forms. The simple form takes only a `Collection` and returns the minimum (or maximum) element according to the elements' natural ordering. The second form takes a `Comparator` in addition to the `Collection` and returns the minimum (or maximum) element according to the specified `Comparator`.

These are the only algorithms provided by the Java platform that work on arbitrary `Collection` objects, as opposed to `List` objects. Like the `fill` algorithm, these algorithms are quite straightforward to implement and are included in the Java platform solely as a convenience to programmers.

http://java.sun.com/docs/books/tutorial/collections/custom-implementations/index.html

5 Custom Implementations

MANY programmers will never need to implement their own collections classes. You can go pretty far using the implementations described in the previous lessons of this trail. Someday, however, you might want to write your own implementation of a core collection interface. It's easy to do with the *abstract implementations* provided by the Java platform. Both sections in this lesson will tell you all about writing custom implementations:

Reasons to Write Your Own Implementation

The following list enumerates several kinds of collections you might implement. It is not intended to be exhaustive.

- **Persistent:** All of the built-in collection implementations reside in main memory and vanish when the VM exits. If you want a collection that will still be present the next time the VM starts, you can implement it by building a veneer over an external database. Such a collection might conceivably be concurrently accessible by multiple VMs, since it resides outside the VM.
- **Application specific:** This is a very broad category. One example is an unmodifiable `Map` containing real-time telemetry data. The keys might represent locations, and the values could be read from sensors at these locations in response to the `get` operation.

- **Highly concurrent:** The built-in collections are not designed to support high concurrency. The synchronization wrappers (and the legacy implementations) lock the *entire* collection every time it's accessed. Suppose that you're building a server and need a `Map` implementation that can be accessed by many threads concurrently. It is reasonably straightforward to build a hash table that locks each bucket separately, allowing multiple threads to access the table concurrently (assuming that they're accessing keys that hash to different buckets).
- **High-performance, special-purpose:** Many data structures take advantage of restricted usage to offer better performance than is possible with general-purpose implementations. For example, consider a `Set` whose elements are restricted to a small, fixed universe. Such a `Set` can be represented as a *bit-vector*, which offers blindingly fast performance as well as low memory usage. Another example concerns a `List` containing long runs of identical element values. Such lists, which occur frequently in text processing, can be *run-length encoded*; runs can be represented as a single object containing the repeated element and the number of consecutive repetitions. This example is interesting because it trades off two aspects of performance: It requires far less space than an `ArrayList` but more time.
- **High-performance, general-purpose:** The engineers who designed the Collections Framework tried to provide the best general-purpose implementations for each interface, but many, many data structures could have been used, and new ones are invented every day. Maybe you can come up with something faster!
- **Enhanced functionality:** Suppose that you need a `Map` (or a `Set`) implementation that offers constant time access, as well as insertion-order iteration. This combination can be achieved with a hash table, all of whose elements are further joined, in insertion order, into a doubly linked list. Alternatively suppose that you need an efficient *bag* implementation (also known as a *multiset*): a `Collection` that offers constant time access while allowing duplicate elements. It's reasonably straightforward to implement such a collection atop a `HashMap`.
- **Convenience:** You may want additional convenience implementations beyond those offered by the Java platform. For instance, you may have a frequent need for immutable `Map` objects representing a single key-value mapping or `List` objects representing a contiguous range of `Integer`s.
- **Adapter:** Suppose that you are using a legacy API that has its own ad hoc collections API. You can write an *adapter* implementation that permits these collections to operate in the Java Collections Framework. An adapter

implementation is a thin veneer that wraps objects of one type and makes them behave like objects of another type by translating operations on the latter type into operations on the former.

How to Write a Custom Implementation

Writing a custom implementation is surprisingly easy with the aid of the *abstract implementations* furnished by the Java platform. Abstract implementations are skeletal implementations of the core collection interfaces that are designed expressly to facilitate custom implementations. We'll start with an example, an implementation of `Arrays.asList`.

```
public static List asList(Object[] a) {
   return new ArrayList(a);
}

private static class ArrayList extends AbstractList
                             implements java.io.Serializable {
   private Object[] a;

   ArrayList(Object[] array) {
       a = array;
   }

   public Object get(int index) {
       return a[index];
   }

   public Object set(int index, Object element) {
       Object oldValue = a[index];
       a[index] = element;
       return oldValue;
   }

   public int size() {
       return a.length;
   }
}
```

Believe it or not, this is almost exactly the implementation contained in the JDK. It's that simple! You provide a constructor and the `get`, `set`, and `size` methods, and `AbstractList` does all the rest. You get the `ListIterator`, bulk operations, search operations, hash code computation, comparison, and string representation for free.

Suppose that you want to make the implementation a bit faster. The API documentation for the abstract implementations describes precisely how each method is implemented so you'll know which methods to override in order to get the performance you want. The performance of the preceding implementation is fine, but it can be improved a bit. In particular the `toArray` method iterates over the `List`, copying one element at a time. Given the internal representation, it's a lot faster and more sensible just to clone the array:

```
public Object[] toArray() {
    return (Object[]) a.clone();
}
```

With the addition of this override and a similar one for `toArray(Object[])`, this implementation is *exactly* the one found in the JDK. In the interests of full disclosure, it's a bit tougher to use the other abstract implementations, because they require you to write your own iterator, but it's still not that difficult.

The abstract implementations are summarized as follows:

- `AbstractCollection`: A `Collection` that is neither a `Set` nor a `List`, such as a *bag*. At a minimum you must provide the `iterator` and the `size` method.
- `AbstractSet`: A `Set`. Its use is identical to `AbstractCollection`.
- `AbstractList`: A `List` backed by a random-access data store (such as an array). At a minimum you must provide the positional access methods (`get(int)` and, optionally, `set(int)`, `remove(int)`, and `add(int)`) and the `size` method. The abstract class takes care of `listIterator` (and `iterator`).
- `AbstractSequentialList`: A `List` backed by a sequential-access data store (such as a linked list). At a minimum you must provide the `listIterator` and `size` methods. The abstract class takes care of the positional access methods. (This is the opposite of `AbstractList`.)
- `AbstractMap`: A `Map`. At a minimum you must provide the `entrySet` view. This is typically implemented with the `AbstractSet` class. If the `Map` is modifiable, you must also provide the `put` method.

The process of writing a custom implementation follows.

1. Choose the appropriate abstract implementation class from the preceding list.
2. Provide implementations for all of the class's abstract methods. If your custom collection is to be modifiable, you'll have to override one or more

concrete methods as well. The API documentation for the abstract implementation class tells you which methods to override.

3. Test and, if necessary, debug the implementation. You now have a working custom collection implementation!
4. If you're concerned about performance, read the abstract implementation class's API documentation for all of the methods whose implementations you're inheriting. If any of them seem too slow, override them. If you override any methods, be sure to measure the performance of the method before and after the override! How much effort you put into tweaking the performance should be a function of how much use the implementation will get and how performance-critical the use. (Often this step is best omitted.)

http://java.sun.com/docs/books/tutorial/collections/interoperability/index.html 6

Interoperability

IN this lesson, you'll learn about two aspects of interoperability:

This section shows you how collections can be made to work with older APIs that predate the addition of collections to the Java platform.

This section teaches you how to design new APIs so that they'll interoperate seamlessly.

Compatibility

The Collections Framework was designed to ensure complete interoperability between the new `collection` interfaces and the types that have traditionally been used to represent collections: `Vector`, `Hashtable`, `array`, and `Enumeration`. In this section you'll learn how to transform traditional collections to new collections and vice versa.

Upward Compatibility

Suppose that you're using an API that returns traditional collections in tandem with another API that requires objects implementing the collection interfaces introduced in JDK 1.2. To make the two APIs interoperate smoothly, you'll have to transform the traditional collections into new collections. Luckily the Collections Framework makes this easy.

Suppose that the old API returns an array of objects and that the new API requires a `Collection`. As discussed in the lesson Implementations (page 67), the Collections Framework has a convenience implementation that allows an array of objects to be *viewed* as a `List`. You use `Arrays.asList` to pass an array to any method requiring a `Collection` or a `List`.

```
Foo[] result = oldMethod(arg);
newMethod(Arrays.asList(result));
```

If the old API returns a `Vector` or a `Hashtable`, you have no work to do at all, since `Vector` has been retrofitted to implement the `List` interface, and `Hashtable` has been retrofitted to implement `Map`. A `Vector` may be passed directly to any method calling for a `Collection` or a `List`.

```
Vector result = oldMethod(arg);
newMethod(result);
```

Similarly a `Hashtable` may be passed directly to any method calling for a `Map`.

```
Hashtable result = oldMethod(arg);
newMethod(result);
```

Less frequently an API may return an `Enumeration` that represents a collection of objects. Although there is no direct support for translating an `Enumeration` into a `Collection`, it's a simple matter to create a `Collection` containing all of the elements returned by an `Enumeration`.

```
Enumeration e = oldMethod(arg);
List l = new ArrayList;
while (e.hasMoreElements())
    l.add(e.nextElement());
newMethod(l);
```

Backward Compatibility

Suppose that you're using an API that returns new collections in tandem with another API that requires you to pass in traditional collections. To make the two APIs interoperate smoothly, you have to transform the new collections into traditional collections. Again the Collection Framework makes this easy.

Suppose that the new API returns a `Collection` and that the old API requires an array of `Object`. As you're probably aware, the `Collection` interface contains a `toArray` method, designed expressly for this situation.

```
Collection c = newMethod();
oldMethod(c.toArray());
```

What if the old API requires an array of `String` (or another type) instead of an array of `Object`? You just use the other form of `toArray`, the one that takes an array on input.

```
Collection c = newMethod();
oldMethod((String[]) (c.toArray(new String[0])));
```

If the old API requires a `Vector`, the standard collection constructor comes in handy.

```
Collection c = newMethod();
oldMethod(new Vector(c));
```

The case in which the old API requires a `Hashtable` is handled analogously.

```
Map m = newMethod();
oldMethod(new Hashtable(m));
```

Finally, what do you do if the old API requires an `Enumeration`? This case isn't common, but it does happen from time to time, and the `Collections.enumeration` method was provided to handle it. This static factory method takes a `Collection` and returns an `Enumeration` over the elements of the `Collection`.

```
Collection c = newMethod();
oldMethod(Collections.enumeration(c));
```

API Design

In this short but important section, you'll learn a few simple guidelines that will allow your API to interoperate seamlessly with all the other fine APIs that follow these guidelines. In essence these rules define what it takes to be a good citizen in the brave new world of collections.

In-Parameters

If your API contains a method that requires a collection on input, it is of paramount importance that you declare the relevant parameter type to be one of the collection interface types. See the lesson Interfaces (page 25) for more information on interface types. Never use an `implementation` type, as this defeats the purpose of an interface-based collections framework, which is to allow collections to be manipulated without regard to implementation details.

Further you should always use the least specific type that makes sense. For example, don't require a `List` or a `Set` if a `Collection` would do. It's not that you should never require a `List` or a `Set` on input; it is correct to do so if a method depends on a property of one of these interfaces. For example, many of the `algorithms` provided by the Java platform require a `List` on input because they depend on the fact that lists are ordered. As a general rule, however, the best types to use on input are the most general: `Collection` and `Map`.

Caution: Never, ever define your own ad hoc collection class and require objects of this class on input. By doing this, you'd lose all the benefits provided by the Collections Framework.

Return Values

You can afford to be much more flexible with return values than input parameters. It's fine to return an object of any type that implements or that extends one of the collection interfaces. This can be one of the interfaces, or a special-purpose type that implements or that extends one of these interfaces.

For example, one could imagine an image-processing package that returned objects of a new class that implements `List`, called `ImageList`. In addition to the `List` operations, `ImageList` could support any application-specific operations that seemed desirable. It might provide an `indexImage` operation that returned an image containing thumbnail images of each graphic in the `ImageList`. It's critical to note that even if the API furnishes `ImageList` objects on output, it should accept arbitrary `Collection` (or perhaps `List`) objects on input.

In one sense return values should have the opposite behavior of input parameters: It's best to return the most specific applicable collection interface rather than the most general. For example, if you're sure that you'll always return a `SortedMap`, you should give the relevant method the return type of `SortedMap` rather than `Map`. `SortedMap` objects are both more time consuming to build than ordinary `Map` objects and more powerful. Given that your module has already invested the time to build a `SortedMap`, it makes good sense to give the user access to its increased power. Furthermore the user will be able to pass the returned object to methods that demand a `SortedMap`, as well as those that accept any `Map`.

Again, never, ever define your own ad hoc collection class and furnish an object of this class as a return value. By doing this, you'd lose all of the benefits provided by the Collections Framework.

Legacy APIs

Currently plenty of APIs out there define their own ad hoc collection types. This is unfortunate, but a fact of life, given that there was no Collections Framework in the first two major releases of the Java platform. Suppose that you own one of these APIs. Here's what you can do about it.

If possible, retrofit your legacy collection type to implement one of the standard collection interfaces. Then all of the collections that you return will interoperate smoothly with other collection-based APIs. If this is impossible (for example, because one or more of the preexisting type signatures conflict with the standard collection interfaces), define an *adapter class* that wraps one of your legacy collections objects, allowing it to function as a standard collection.

Note: The adapter class is an example of a custom implementation. See the lesson Custom Implementations (page 83) for more information.

If possible, retrofit your API with new calls that follow the preceding input guidelines, accepting objects of a standard collection interface. Such calls can coexist with the calls that take the legacy collection type. If this is impossible, provide for your legacy type a constructor or static factory method that takes an object of one of the standard interfaces and returns a legacy collection containing the same elements (or mappings). Either of these approaches will allow users to pass arbitrary collections into your API.

About the Author

JOSHUA BLOCH is a Senior Staff Engineer at Sun Microsystems' Java Software division, where he works as an architect in the Java Language Group. He designed and implemented the Collections Framework and `java.math`, and contributed to other parts of the JDK. Previously, he was a Senior Systems Designer at Transarc Corporation, where he designed and implemented many parts of the Encina distributed transaction processing system. He holds a Ph.D. in Computer Science from Carnegie-Mellon University and a B.S. in Computer Science from Columbia University.

Acknowledgments

The author would like to thank Cindy Bloch, Beth Bottos, Doug Lea, and David Karr for reviewing drafts of this chapter.

Internationalization

by Dale Green

THE lessons in this trail teach you how to internationalize Java™ applications. Internationalized applications are easy to tailor to the customs and languages of end users around the world.

Introduction (page 99) defines the term internationalization, gives a quick sample program, and provides a checklist you can use to internationalize an existing program.

Setting the Locale (page 109) explains how to create and how to use `Locale` objects.

Isolating Locale-Specific Data (page 115) shows how to dynamically access objects that vary with `Locale`.

Formatting (page 127) explains how to format numbers, dates, and text messages according to `Locale` and how to create customized formats with patterns.

Working with Text (page 149) provides techniques for manipulating text in a locale-independent manner.

http://java.sun.com/docs/books/tutorial/i18n/intro/index.html

7 Introduction

INTERNATIONALIZATION is the process of designing an application so that it can be adapted to various languages and regions without engineering changes. Sometimes the term internationalization is abbreviated as i18n, because there are 18 letters between the first "i" and the last "n."

An internationalized program has the following characteristics:

- With the addition of localized data, the same executable can run worldwide.
- Textual elements, such as status messages and the GUI component labels, are not hardcoded in the program. Instead they are stored outside the source code and retrieved dynamically.
- Support for new languages does not require recompilation.
- Culturally-dependent data, such as dates and currencies, appear in formats that conform to the end user's region and language.
- It can be localized quickly.

Localization is the process of adapting software for a specific region or language by adding locale-specific components and translating text. The term localization is often abbreviated as l10n, because there are 10 letters between the "l" and the "n." Usually, the most time-consuming portion of the localization phase is the translation of text. Other types of data, such as sounds and images, may require localization if they are culturally sensitive. Localizers also verify that the formatting of dates, numbers, and currencies conforms to local requirements.

Internationalization may seem a bit daunting at first. Reading the following sections will help ease you into the subject.

A Quick Example

If you're new to internationalizing software, this lesson is for you. This lesson uses a simple example to demonstrate how to internationalize a program so that it displays text messages in the appropriate language. You'll learn how `Locale` and `ResourceBundle` objects work together and how to use properties files.

Before Internationalization

Suppose that you've written a program that displays three messages, as follows:

```
public class NotI18N {

    static public void main(String[] args) {

        System.out.println("Hello.");
        System.out.println("How are you?");
        System.out.println("Goodbye.");
    }
}
```

You've decided that this program needs to display these same messages for people living in France and Germany. Unfortunately your programming staff is not multilingual, so you'll need help translating the messages into French and German. Since the translators aren't programmers, you'll have to move the messages out of the source code and into text files that the translators can edit. Also, the program must be flexible enough so that it can display the messages in other languages, but right now no one knows what those languages will be.

It looks like the program needs to be internationalized.

After Internationalization

The source code for the internationalized program follows. Notice that the text of the messages is not hardcoded.

```
import java.util.*;

public class I18NSample {

    static public void main(String[] args) {

        String language;
        String country;

        if (args.length != 2) {
            language = new String("en");
            country = new String("US");
        } else {
            language = new String(args[0]);
            country = new String(args[1]);
        }

        Locale currentLocale;
        ResourceBundle messages;

        currentLocale = new Locale(language, country);

        messages = ResourceBundle.getBundle("MessagesBundle",
                                           currentLocale);

        System.out.println(messages.getString("greetings"));
        System.out.println(messages.getString("inquiry"));
        System.out.println(messages.getString("farewell"));
    }
}
```

Running the Sample Program

The internationalized program is flexible; it allows the end user to specify a language and a country on the command line. In the following example the language code is `fr` (French) and the country code is `FR` (France), so the program displays the messages in French:

```
% java I18NSample fr FR
Bonjour.
Comment allez-vous?
Au revoir.
```

In the next example the language code is en (English) and the country code is US (United States) so the program displays the messages in English:

```
% java I18NSample en US
Hello.
How are you?
Goodbye.
```

Internationalizing the Sample Program

If you look at the internationalized source code, you'll notice that the hardcoded English messages have been removed. Because the messages are no longer hardcoded and because the language code is specified at run time, the same executable can be distributed worldwide. No recompilation is required for localization. The program has been internationalized.

You may be wondering what happened to the text of the messages or what the language and country codes mean. Don't worry. You'll learn about these concepts as you step through the process of internationalizing the sample program.

1. Create the Properties Files

A properties file stores information about the characteristics of a program or environment. A properties file is in plain-text format. You can create the file with just about any text editor.

In the example the properties files store the translatable text of the messages to be displayed. Before the program was internationalized, the English version of this text was hardcoded in the System.out.println statements. The default properties file, which is called MessagesBundle.properties, contains the following lines:

```
greetings = Hello
farewell = Goodbye
inquiry = How are you?
```

Now that the messages are in a properties file, they can be translated into various languages. No changes to the source code are required. The French translator has created a properties file called MessagesBundle_fr_FR.properties, which contains these lines:

```
greetings = Bonjour.
farewell = Au revoir.
inquiry = Comment allez-vous?
```

Notice that the values to the right side of the equal sign have been translated but that the keys on the left side have not been changed. These keys must not change, because they will be referenced when your program fetches the translated text.

The name of the properties file is important. For example, the name of the `MessagesBundle_fr_FR.properties` file contains the `fr` language code and the `FR` country code. These codes are also used when creating a `Locale` object.

2. Define the Locale

The `Locale` object identifies a particular language and country. The following statement defines a `Locale` for which the language is English and the country is the United States:

```
aLocale = new Locale("en","US");
```

The next example creates `Locale` objects for the French language in Canada and in France:

```
caLocale = new Locale("fr","CA");
frLocale = new Locale("fr","FR");
```

The program is flexible. Instead of using hardcoded language and country codes, the program gets them from the command line at run time:

```
String language = new String(args[0]);
String country = new String(args[1]);
currentLocale = new Locale(language, country);
```

`Locale` objects are only identifiers. After defining a `Locale`, you pass it to other objects that perform useful tasks, such as formatting dates and numbers. These objects are *locale-sensitive* because their behavior varies according to `Locale`. A `ResourceBundle` is an example of a locale-sensitive object.

3. Create a ResourceBundle

`ResourceBundle` objects contain locale-specific objects. You use `ResourceBundle` objects to isolate locale-sensitive data, such as translatable text. In the sample program the `ResourceBundle` is backed by the properties files that contain the message text we want to display.

The `ResourceBundle` is created as follows:

```
message =

ResourceBundle.getBundle("MessagesBundle",currentLocale);
```

The arguments passed to the `getBundle` method identify which properties file will be accessed. The first argument, `MessagesBundle`, refers to this family of properties files:

```
MessagesBundle_en_US.properties
MessagesBundle_fr_FR.properties
MessagesBundle_de_DE.properties
```

The `Locale`, which is the second argument of `getBundle`, specifies which of the `MessagesBundle` files is chosen. When the `Locale` was created, the language code and the country code were passed to its constructor. Note that the language and country codes follow `MessagesBundle` in the names of the properties files.

Now all you have to do is get the translated messages from the `ResourceBundle`.

4. Fetch the Text from the ResourceBundle

The properties files contain key-value pairs. The values consist of the translated text that the program will display. You specify the keys when fetching the translated messages from the `ResourceBundle` with the `getString` method. For example, to retrieve the message identified by the greetings key, you invoke `getString` as follows:

```
String msg1 = messages.getString("greetings");
```

The sample program uses the key `greetings` because it reflects the content of the message, but it could have used another `String`, such as `s1` or `msg1`. Just remember that the key is hardcoded in the program and it must be present in the properties files. If your translators accidentally modify the keys in the properties files, `getString` won't be able to find the messages.

Conclusion

That's it. As you can see, internationalizing a program isn't too difficult. It requires some planning and a little extra coding, but the benefits are enormous. To provide you with an overview of the internationalization process, the sample program in this lesson was intentionally kept simple. As you read the lessons that follow, you'll learn about the more advanced internationalization features of the Java programming language.

Checklist

Many programs are not internationalized when first written. These programs may have started as prototypes, or perhaps they were not intended for international distribution. If you must internationalize an existing program, take the following steps:

Identify Culturally Dependent Data

Text messages are the most obvious form of data that varies with culture. However, other types of data may vary with region or language. The following list contains examples of culturally dependent data:

- Messages
- Labels on GUI components
- Online help
- Sounds
- Colors
- Graphics
- Icons
- Dates
- Times
- Numbers
- Currencies
- Measurements
- Phone numbers
- Honorifics and personal titles
- Postal addresses
- Page layouts

Isolate Translatable Text in Resource Bundles

Translation is costly. You can help reduce costs by isolating the text that must be translated in `ResourceBundle` objects. Translatable text includes status messages, error messages, log file entries, and GUI component labels. This text is hardcoded into programs that haven't been internationalized. You need to locate all occurrences of hardcoded text that is displayed to end users. For example, you should clean up code like this:

```
String buttonLabel = "OK";
...
JButton okButton = new JButton(buttonLabel);
```

See the section Isolating Locale-Specific Data (page 115) for details.

Deal with Compound Messages

Compound messages contain variable data. In the message "The disk contains 1100 files." the integer 1100 may vary. This message is difficult to translate because the position of the integer in the sentence is not the same in all languages. The following message is not translatable, because the order of the sentence elements is hardcoded by concatenation:

```
Integer fileCount;
...
String diskStatus = "The disk contains " + fileCount.toString()
                    + " files.";
```

Whenever possible, you should avoid constructing compound messages, because they are difficult to translate. However, if your application requires compound messages, you can handle them with the techniques described in the section Messages (page 139).

Format Numbers and Currencies

If your application displays numbers and currencies, you must format them in a locale-independent manner. The following code is not yet internationalized, because it will not display the number correctly in all countries:

```
Double amount;
TextField amountField;
...
String displayAmount = amount.toString();
amountField.setText(displayAmount);
```

You should replace the preceding code with a routine that formats the number correctly. The Java programming language provides several classes that format numbers and currencies. These classes are discussed in the section Numbers and Currencies (page 127).

Format Dates and Times

Date and time formats differ with region and language. If your code contains statements like the following, you need to change it:

```
Date currentDate = new Date();
TextField dateField;
...
String dateString = currentDate.toString();
dateField.setText(dateString);
```

If you use the date-formatting classes, your application can display dates and times correctly around the world. For examples and instructions, see the section Dates and Times (page 132).

Use Unicode Character Properties

The following code tries to verify that a character is a letter:

```
char ch;
...
if ((ch >= 'a' && ch <= 'z') ||
    (ch >= 'A' && ch <= 'Z'))         // WRONG!
```

Watch out for code like this, because it won't work with languages other than English. For example, the `if` statement misses the character ü in the German word Grün.

The `Character` comparison methods use the Unicode standard to identify character properties. Thus you should replace the previous code with the following:

```
char ch;
...
if (Character.isLetter(ch))
```

For more information on the `Character` comparison methods, see the section Checking Character Properties (page 149).

Compare Strings Properly

When sorting text you often compare strings. If the text is displayed, you shouldn't use the comparison methods of the `String` class. A program that hasn't been internationalized might compare strings as follows:

```
String target;
String candidate;
...

if (target.equals(candidate)) {
...
if (target.compareTo(candidate) < 0) {
...
```

The `String.equals` and `String.compareTo` methods perform binary comparisons, which are ineffective when sorting in most languages. Instead you should use the `Collator` class, which is described in the section Comparing Strings (page 151).

Convert Non-Unicode Text

Characters in the Java programming language are encoded in Unicode. If your application handles non-Unicode text, you might need to translate it into Unicode. For more information, see the section Converting Non-Unicode Text (page 166).

8 Setting the Locale

AN internationalized program can display information differently throughout the world. For example, the program will display different messages in Paris, Tokyo, and New York. If the localization process has been fine-tuned, the program will display different messages in New York and London to account for the differences between American and British English. How does an internationalized program identify the appropriate language and region of its end users? Easy. It references a `Locale` object.

A `Locale` object is an identifier for a particular combination of language and region. If a class varies its behavior according to `Locale`, it is said to be *locale-sensitive*. For example, the `NumberFormat` class is locale-sensitive; the format of the number it returns depends on the `Locale`. Thus `NumberFormat` may return a number as 902 300 (France), or 902.300 (Germany), or 902,300 (United States). `Locale` objects are only identifiers. The real work, such as formatting and detecting word boundaries, is performed by the methods of the locale-sensitive classes.

The following sections explain how to work with `Locale` objects:

: When creating a `Locale` object, you usually specify a language code and a country code. A third parameter, the variant, is optional.

: Locale-sensitive classes support only certain `Locale` definitions. This section shows you how to determine which `Locale` definitions are supported.

: On the Java platform you do not specify a global `Locale` by setting an environment variable before running the application. Instead you either rely on the default `Locale` or assign a `Locale` to each locale-sensitive object.

Creating a Locale

To create a `Locale` object, you typically specify the language code and the country code. For example, to specify the French language and the country of Canada, you would invoke the constructor as follows:

```
aLocale = new Locale("fr","CA");
```

The next example creates `Locale` objects for the English language in the United States and Great Britain:

```
bLocale = new Locale("en","US");
cLocale = new Locale("en","GB");
```

The first argument is the language code, a pair of lowercase letters that conform to ISO-639. You can find a full list of the ISO-639 codes at

```
http://www.ics.uci.edu/pub/ietf/http/related/iso639.txt
```

The following table lists just a few of the language codes.

Table 5 Sample Language Codes

Language Code	Description
de	German
en	English
fr	French
ja	Japanese
jw	Javanese
ko	Korean
zh	Chinese

The second argument of the `Locale` constructor is the country code. It consists of two uppercase letters and conforms to ISO-3166. A copy of ISO-3166 can be found at:

```
http://www.chemie.fu-berlin.de/diverse/doc/ISO_3166.html
```

Table 6 contains several sample country codes.

Table 6 Sample Country Codes

Country Code	Description
CN	China
DE	Germany
FR	France
IN	India
US	United States

If you need to distinguish your `Locale` further, you can specify a third parameter, called the variant code. Usually you specify variant codes to identify differences caused by the computing platform. For example, font differences may force you to use different characters on Windows and UNIX. You could then define the `Locale` objects with the variant codes WINDOWS and UNIX as follows:

```
xLocale = new Locale("de", "DE" ,"UNIX");
yLocale = new Locale("de", "DE", "WINDOWS");
```

The variant codes conform to no standard. They are arbitrary and specific to your application. If you create `Locale` objects with variant codes only your application will know how to deal with them.

The country and variant codes are optional. When omitting the country code, you specify a null `String`. You may create a `Locale` for the English language as follows:

```
enLocale = new Locale("en", "");
```

For your convenience the `Locale` class provides constants for some languages and countries. For example, you can create `Locale` objects by specifying the `JAPANESE` or `JAPAN` constants. The `Locale` objects created by the following two statements are equivalent:

```
j1Locale = Locale.JAPAN;
j2Locale = new Locale("ja", "JP");
```

When you specify a language constant, the country portion of the `Locale` is undefined. The next two statements create equivalent `Locale` objects:

```
j3Locale = Locale.JAPANESE;
j4Locale = new Locale("ja", "");
```

Identifying Available Locales

You can create a `Locale` with any combination of valid language and country codes, but that doesn't mean that you can use it. Remember, a `Locale` object is only an identifier. You pass the `Locale` object to other objects, which then do the real work. These other objects, which we call locale-sensitive, do not know how to deal with all possible `Locale` definitions.

To find out which types of `Locale` definitions a locale-sensitive class recognizes, you invoke the `getAvailableLocales` method. For example, to find out which `Locale` definitions are supported by the `DateFormat` class, you could write a routine such as the following:

```
import java.util.*;
import java.text.*;

public class Available {
    static public void main(String[] args) {
        Locale list[] = DateFormat.getAvailableLocales();
        for (int i = 0; i < list.length; i++) {
            System.out.println(list[i].toString());
        }
    }
}
```

The output of the previous program follows. Note that the `String` returned by `toString` contains the language and country codes, delimited by an underscore:

```
ar_EG
be_BY
bg_BG
ca_ES
cs_CZ
da_DK
de_DE
.
.
.
```

If you want to display a list of `Locale` names to end users, you should show them something easier to understand than the language and country codes returned by `getString`. Instead you can invoke the `Locale.getDisplayName` method, which retrieves a localized `String` of a `Locale` object. For example, when `toString` is replaced by `getDisplayName` in the preceding code, the program prints the following lines:

```
Arabic (Egypt)
Byelorussian (Belarus)
Bulgarian (Bulgaria)
Catalan (Spain)
Czech (Czech Republic)
Danish (Denmark)
German (Germany)
.
.
.
```

The Scope of a Locale

The Java platform does not require you to use the same `Locale` throughout your program. If you wish, you can assign a different `Locale` to every locale-sensitive object in your program. This flexibility allows you to develop multilingual applications, which can display information in multiple languages.

However, most applications are not multi-lingual and their locale-sensitive objects rely on the default `Locale`. Set by the Java Virtual Machine when it starts up, the default `Locale` corresponds to the locale of the host platform. To determine the default `Locale` of your Java Virtual Machine, invoke the `Locale.getDefault` method. You should not set the default `Locale` programmatically because it is shared by all locale-sensitive classes.

Distributed computing raises some interesting issues. For example, suppose you are designing an application server that will receive requests from clients in various countries. If the `Locale` for each client is different, what should be the `Locale` of the server? Perhaps the server is multithreaded, with each thread set to the `Locale` of the client it services. Or perhaps all data passed between the server and the clients should be locale-independent.

Which design approach should you take? If possible, the data passed between the server and the clients should be locale-independent. This simplifies the design of the server by making the clients responsible for displaying the data in a locale-sensitive manner. However, this approach won't work if the server must store the data in a locale-specific form. For example, the server might store Spanish, English, and French versions of the same data in different database columns. In this case, the server might want to query the client for its `Locale`, since the `Locale` may have changed since the last request.

http://java.sun.com/docs/books/tutorial/i18n/resbundle/index.html 9

Isolating Locale-Specific Data

LOCALE-SPECIFIC data must be tailored according to the conventions of the end user's language and region. The text displayed by a user interface is the most obvious example of locale-specific data. For example, an application with a Cancel button in the U.S. will have an Abbrechen button in Germany. In other countries this button will have other labels. Obviously you don't want to hardcode this button label. Wouldn't it be nice if you could automatically get the correct label for a given `Locale`? Fortunately you can, provided that you isolate the locale-specific objects in a `ResourceBundle`.

In this lesson you'll learn how to create and access `ResourceBundle` objects. If you're in a hurry to examine some coding examples, go ahead and check out the last two sections in this lesson. Then you can come back to the first two sections to get some conceptual information about `ResourceBundle` objects.

: `ResourceBundle` objects contain locale-specific objects. When you need a locale-specific object, you fetch it from a `ResourceBundle`, which returns the object that matches the end user's `Locale`. This section explains how a `ResourceBundle` is related to a `Locale`, and describes the `ResourceBundle` subclasses.

: Before you create your `ResourceBundle` objects, you should do a little planning. First, identify the locale-specific objects in your program. Then organize them into categories and store them in different `ResourceBundle` objects accordingly.

Backing a ResourceBundle with Properties Files (page 120)

If your application contains `String` objects that need to be translated into various languages, you can store these `String` objects in a `PropertyResourceBundle`, which is backed up by a set of properties files. Since the properties files are simple text files, they can be created and maintained by your translators. You don't have to change the source code. In this section you'll learn how to set up the properties files that back up a `PropertyResourceBundle`.

Using a ListResource Bundle (page 123)

The `ListResourceBundle` class, which is a subclass of `ResourceBundle`, manages locale-specific objects with a list. A `ListResourceBundle` is backed by a class file, which means that you must code and compile a new source file each time support for an additional `Locale` is needed. However, `ListResourceBundle` objects are useful because unlike properties files, they can store any type of locale-specific object. By stepping through a sample program, this section demonstrates how to use a `ListResourceBundle`.

About the ResourceBundle Class

How a ResourceBundle is Related to a Locale

Conceptually each `ResourceBundle` is a set of related subclasses that share the same base name. The list that follows shows a set of related subclasses. `ButtonLabel` is the base name. The characters following the base name indicate the language code, country code, and variant of a `Locale`. `ButtonLabel_en_GB`, for example, matches the `Locale` specified by the language code for English (`en`) and the country code for Great Britain (`GB`).

```
ButtonLabel
ButtonLabel_de
ButtonLabel_en_GB
ButtonLabel_fr_CA_UNIX
```

To select the appropriate `ResourceBundle`, invoke the `ResourceBundle.getBundle` method. The following example selects the `ButtonLabel` `ResourceBundle` for the `Locale` that matches the French language, the country of Canada, and the UNIX platform.

```
Locale currentLocale = new Locale("fr", "CA", "UNIX");
ResourceBundle introLabels =
      ResourceBundle.getBundle("ButtonLabel", currentLocale);
```

If a `ResourceBundle` class for the specified `Locale` does not exist, `getBundle` tries to find the closest match. For example, if `ButtonLabel_fr_CA_UNIX` is the desired class and the default `Locale` is `en_US`, `getBundle` will look for classes in the following order:

```
ButtonLabel_fr_CA_UNIX
ButtonLabel_fr_CA
ButtonLabel_fr
ButtonLabel_en_US
ButtonLabel_en
ButtonLabel
```

Note that `getBundle` looks for classes based on the default `Locale` before it selects the base class (`ButtonLabel`). If `getBundle` fails to find a match in the preceding list of classes, it throws a `MissingResourceException`. To avoid throwing this exception, you should always provide a base class with no suffixes.

The ListResourceBundle and PropertyResourceBundle Subclasses

The abstract class `ResourceBundle` has two subclasses: `PropertyResourceBundle` and `ListResourceBundle`.

A `PropertyResourceBundle` is backed by a properties file. A properties file is a plain-text file that contains translatable text. Properties files are not part of the Java source code, and they can contain values for `String` objects only. If you need to store other types of objects, use a `ListResourceBundle` instead. The section Backing a ResourceBundle with Properties Files (page 120) shows you how to use a `PropertyResourceBundle`.

The `ListResourceBundle` class manages resources with a convenient list. Each `ListResourceBundle` is backed by a class file. You can store any locale-specific object in a `ListResourceBundle`. To add support for an additional `Locale`, you create another source file and compile it into a class file. The section Using a ListResource Bundle (page 123) has a coding example you may find helpful.

The `ResourceBundle` class is flexible. If you first put your locale-specific `String` objects in a `PropertyResourceBundle` and then later decided to use `ListResourceBundle` instead, there is no impact on your code. For example, the following call to `getBundle` will retrieve a `ResourceBundle` for the appropriate `Locale`, whether `ButtonLabel` is backed up by a class or by a properties file:

```
ResourceBundle introLabels =
        ResourceBundle.getBundle("ButtonLabel", currentLocale);
```

Key-Value Pairs

`ResourceBundle` objects contain an array of key-value pairs. You specify the key, which must be a `String`, when you want to retrieve the value from the `ResourceBundle`. The value is the locale-specific object. The keys in the following example are the `OkKey` and `CancelKey` strings:

```
class ButtonLabel_en extends ListResourceBundle {
    // English version
    public Object[][] getContents() {
        return contents;
    }
    static final Object[][] contents = {
        {"OkKey", "OK"},
        {"CancelKey", "Cancel"},
    };
}
```

To retrieve the `OK` `String` from the `ResourceBundle`, you would specify the appropriate key when invoking `getString`:

```
String okLabel = ButtonLabel.getString("OkKey");
```

A properties file contains key-value pairs. The key is on the left side of the equal sign, and the value is on the right. Each pair is on a separate line. The values may represent `String` objects only. The following example shows the contents of a properties file named `ButtonLabel.properties`:

```
OkKey = OK
CancelKey = Cancel
```

Preparing to Use a ResourceBundle

Identifying the Locale-Specific Objects

If your application has a user interface, it contains many locale-specific objects. To get started, you should go through your source code and look for objects that vary with `Locale`. Your list might include objects instantiated from the following classes:

- `String`
- `Image`
- `Color`
- `AudioClip`

You'll notice that this list doesn't contain objects representing numbers, dates, times, or currencies. The display format of these objects varies with `Locale`, but the objects themselves do not. For example, you format a `Date` according to `Locale`, but you use the same `Date` object regardless of `Locale`. Instead of isolating these objects in a `ResourceBundle`, you format them with special locale-sensitive formatting classes. You'll learn how to do this in the Dates and Times (page 132) section of the Formatting (page 127) lesson.

In general, the objects stored in a `ResourceBundle` are predefined and ship with the product. These objects are not modified while the program is running. For instance, you should store a `Menu` label in a `ResourceBundle` because it is locale-specific and will not change during the program session. However, you should not isolate in a `ResourceBundle` a `String` object the end user enters in a `TextField`. Data such as this `String` may vary from day to day. It is specific to the program session, not to the `Locale` in which the program runs.

Usually most of the objects you need to isolate in a `ResourceBundle` are `String` objects. However, not all `String` objects are locale-specific. For example, if a `String` is a protocol element used by interprocess communication, it doesn't need to be localized, because the end users never see it.

The decision whether to localize some `String` objects is not always clear. Log files are a good example. If a log file is written by one program and read by another, both programs are using the log file as a buffer for communication. Suppose that end users occasionally check the contents of this log file. Shouldn't the log file be localized? On the other hand, if end users rarely check the log file, the cost of translation may not be worthwhile. Your decision to localize this log file depends on a number of factors: program design, ease of use, cost of translation, and supportability.

Organizing ResourceBundle Objects

You can organize your `ResourceBundle` objects according to the category of objects they contain. For example, you might want to load all of the GUI labels for an order entry window into a `ResourceBundle` called `OrderLabelsBundle`. Using multiple `ResourceBundle` objects offers several advantages:

- Your code is easier to read and to maintain.
- You'll avoid huge ResourceBundle objects, which may take too long to load into memory.
- You can reduce memory usage by loading each ResourceBundle only when needed.

Backing a ResourceBundle with Properties Files

This section steps through a sample program named PropertiesDemo. The program's source code is in PropertiesDemo.java (page 726) in the Appendix.

1. Create the Default Properties File

A properties file is a simple text file. You can create and maintain a properties file with just about any text editor.

You should always create a default properties file. The name of this file begins with the base name of your ResourceBundle and ends with the .properties suffix. In the PropertiesDemo program the base name is LabelsBundle. Therefore the default properties file is called LabelsBundle.properties. This file contains the following lines:

```
# This is the default LabelsBundle.properties file
s1 = computer
s2 = disk
s3 = monitor
s4 = keyboard
```

Note that in the preceding file the comment lines begin with a pound sign (#). The other lines contain key-value pairs. The key is on the left side of the equal sign and the value is on the right. For instance, s2 is the key that corresponds to the value disk. The key is arbitrary. We could have called s2 something else, like msg5 or diskID. Once defined, however, the key should not change because it is referenced in the source code. The values may be changed. In fact, when your localizers create new properties files to accommodate additional languages, they will translate the values into various languages.

2. Create Additional Properties Files as Needed

To support an additional Locale, your localizers will create a new properties file that contains the translated values. No changes to your source code are required, because your program references the keys, not the values.

For example, to add support for the German language, your localizers would translate the values in `LabelsBundle.properties` and place them in a file named `LabelsBundle_de.properties`. Notice that the name of this file, like that of the default file, begins with the base name `LabelsBundle` and ends with the `.properties` suffix. However, since this file is intended for a specific `Locale`, the base name is followed by the language code (`de`). The contents of `LabelsBundle_de.properties` are as follows:

```
# This is the LabelsBundle_de.properties file
s1 = Computer
s2 = Platte
s3 = Monitor
s4 = Tastatur
```

The `PropertiesDemo` sample program ships with three properties files:

```
LabelsBundle.properties
LabelsBundle_de.properties
LabelsBundle_fr.properties
```

3. Specify the Locale

The `PropertiesDemo` program creates the `Locale` objects as follows:

```
Locale[] supportedLocales = {
    Locale.FRENCH,
    Locale.GERMAN,
    Locale.ENGLISH
};
```

These `Locale` objects should match the properties files created in the previous two steps. For example, the `Locale.FRENCH` object corresponds to the `LabelsBundle_fr.properties` file. The `Locale.ENGLISH` has no matching `LabelsBundle_en.properties` file, so the default file will be used.

4. Create the ResourceBundle

This step shows how the `Locale`, the properties files, and the `ResourceBundle` are related. To create the `ResourceBundle`, invoke the `getBundle` method, specifying the base name and `Locale`:

```
ResourceBundle labels =
    ResourceBundle.getBundle("LabelsBundle", currentLocale);
```

The `getBundle` method first looks for a class file that matches the base name and the `Locale`. If it can't find a class file, it then checks for properties files. In the `PropertiesDemo` program we're backing the `ResourceBundle` with properties files instead of class files. When the `getBundle` method locates the correct properties file, it returns a `PropertyResourceBundle` object containing the key-value pairs from the properties file.

5. Fetch the Localized Text

To retrieve the translated value from the `ResourceBundle`, invoke the `getString` method as follows:

```
String value = labels.getString(key);
```

The `String` returned by `getString` corresponds to the key specified. The `String` is in the proper language, provided that a properties file exists for the specified `Locale`.

6. Iterate through All the Keys

This step is optional. When debugging your program, you might want to fetch values for all of the keys in a `ResourceBundle`. The `getKeys` method returns an `Enumeration` of all the keys in a `ResourceBundle`. You can iterate through the `Enumeration` and fetch each value with the `getString` method. The following lines of code, which are from the `PropertiesDemo` program, show how this is done:

```
ResourceBundle labels =
    ResourceBundle.getBundle("LabelsBundle", currentLocale);

Enumeration bundleKeys = labels.getKeys();

while (bundleKeys.hasMoreElements()) {
    String key = (String)bundleKeys.nextElement();
    String value = labels.getString(key);
    System.out.println("key = " + key + ", " +
                       "value = " + value);
}
```

7. Run the Demo Program

Running the `PropertiesDemo` program generates the following output. The first three lines show the values returned by `getString` for various `Locale` objects. The program displays the last four lines when iterating through the keys with the `getKeys` method.

```
Locale = fr, key = s2, value = Disque dur
Locale = de, key = s2, value = Platte
Locale = en, key = s2, value = disk

key = s4, value = Clavier
key = s3, value = Moniteur
key = s2, value = Disque dur
key = s1, value = Ordinateur
```

Using a ListResource Bundle

This section illustrates the use of a `ListResourceBundle` object with a sample program called `ListDemo`. The text that follows explains each step involved in creating the `ListDemo` program, along with the `ListResourceBundle` subclasses that support it. The source code for the program is `ListDemo.java` (page 728) in the Appendix.

1. Create the ListResourceBundle Subclasses

A `ListResourceBundle` is backed up by a class file. Therefore the first step is to create a class file for every supported `Locale`. In the `ListDemo` program the base name of the `ListResourceBundle` is `StatsBundle`. Since `ListDemo` supports three `Locale` objects, it requires the following three class files:

```
StatsBundle_en_CA.class
StatsBundle_fr_FR.class
StatsBundle_ja_JP.class
```

The `StatsBundle` class for Japan is defined in the source code that follows. Note that the class name is constructed by appending the language and country codes to the base name of the `ListResourceBundle`. Inside the class the two-dimensional `contents` array is initialized with the key-value pairs. The keys are the first element in each pair: `GDP`, `Population`, and `Literacy`. The keys must be `String` objects and they must be the same in every class in the `StatsBundle` set. The values can be any type of object. In this example the values are two `Integer` objects and a `Double` object.

```
import java.util.*;

public class StatsBundle_ja_JP extends ListResourceBundle {

    public Object[][] getContents() {
        return contents;
    }
```

```
        private Object[][] contents = {
            { "GDP", new Integer(21300) },
            { "Population", new Integer(125449703) },
            { "Literacy", new Double(0.99) },
        };
    }
```

2. Specify the Locale

The `ListDemo` program defines the `Locale` objects as follows:

```
Locale[] supportedLocales = {
    new Locale("en", "CA"),
    new Locale("ja", "JP"),
    new Locale("fr", "FR")
};
```

Each `Locale` object corresponds to one of the `StatsBundle` classes. For example, the Japanese `Locale`, which was defined with the `ja` and `JP` codes, matches `StatsBundle_ja_JP.class`.

3. Create the ResourceBundle

To create the `ListResourceBundle`, invoke the `getBundle` method. The following line of code specifies the base name of the class (`StatsBundle`) and the `Locale`:

```
ResourceBundle stats =
    ResourceBundle.getBundle("StatsBundle", currentLocale);
```

The `getBundle` method searches for a class whose name begins with `StatsBundle` and is followed by the language and country codes of the specified `Locale`. If the `currentLocale` is created with the `ja` and `JP` codes, `getBundle` returns a `ListResourceBundle` corresponding to the class `StatsBundle_ja_JP`, for example.

4. Fetch the Localized Objects

Now that the program has a `ListResourceBundle` for the appropriate `Locale`, it can fetch the localized objects by their keys. The following line of code retrieves the literacy rate by invoking `getObject` with the `Literacy` key parameter. Since `getObject` returns an object, cast it to a `Double`:

```
Double lit = (Double)stats.getObject("Literacy");
```

5. Run the Demo Program

`ListDemo` program prints the data it fetched with the `getBundle` method:

```
Locale = en_CA
GDP = 24400
Population = 28802671
Literacy = 0.97

Locale = ja_JP
GDP = 21300
Population = 125449703
Literacy = 0.99

Locale = fr_FR
GDP = 20200
Population = 58317450
Literacy = 0.99
```

http://java.sun.com/docs/books/tutorial/i18n/format/index.html

10 Formatting

THIS lesson explains how to format numbers, currencies, dates, times, and text messages. Because end users can see these data elements, their format must conform to various cultural conventions. Following the examples in this lesson will teach you how to:

- Format data elements in a locale-sensitive manner
- Keep your code locale-independent
- Avoid the need to write formatting routines for specific locales

This section explains how to use the `NumberFormat`, `DecimalFormat`, and `DecimalFormatSymbols` classes.

This section focuses on the `DateFormat`, `SimpleDateFormat`, and `DateFormatSymbols` classes.

This section shows how the `MessageFormat` and `ChoiceFormat` classes can help you solve some of the problems you might encounter when formatting text messages.

Numbers and Currencies

Programs store and operate on numbers in a locale-independent way. Before displaying or printing a number, a program must convert it to a `String` that is in a locale-sensitive format. For example, in France the number 123456.78 should be formatted as 123 456,78, and in Germany it should appear as 123.456,78. In this section, you will learn how to make your programs independent of the locale conventions for decimal points, thousands-separators, and other formatting properties.

Using Predefined Formats

By invoking the methods provided by the `NumberFormat`[1] class, you can format numbers, currencies, and percentages according to `Locale`. The material that follows demonstrates formatting techniques with a sample program called `NumberFormatDemo.java` (page 730) found in its entirety in the Appendix.

Numbers

You can use the `NumberFormat` methods to format primitive-type numbers, such as `double`, and their corresponding wrapper objects, such as `Double`.

The following code example formats a `Double` according to `Locale`. Invoking the `getNumberInstance` method returns a locale-specific instance of `NumberFormat`. The `format` method accepts the `Double` as an argument and returns the formatted number in a `String`.

```
Double amount = new Double(345987.246);
NumberFormat numberFormatter;
String amountOut;

numberFormatter =
            NumberFormat.getNumberInstance(currentLocale);

amountOut = numberFormatter.format(amount);

System.out.println(amountOut + " " +
                   currentLocale.toString());
```

The output from this example shows how the format of the same number varies with `Locale`:

```
345 987,246 fr_FR

345.987,246 de_DE

345,987.246 en_US
```

---

[1] The API documentation is available on the CD-ROM that accompanies this book and online at: http://java.sun.com/products/jdk/1.2/docs/api/java.text.NumberFormat.html

Currencies

If you're writing business applications, you'll probably need to format and to display currencies. You format currencies in the same manner as numbers, except that you call `getCurrencyInstance` to create a formatter. When you invoke the `format` method, it returns a `String` that includes the formatted number and the appropriate currency sign.

This code example shows how to format currency in a locale-specific manner:

```
Double currency = new Double(9876543.21);
NumberFormat currencyFormatter;
String currencyOut;

currencyFormatter =
            NumberFormat.getCurrencyInstance(currentLocale);
currencyOut = currencyFormatter.format(currency);
System.out.println(currencyOut + " " +
                   currentLocale.toString());
```

The output generated by the preceding lines of code is as follows:

```
9 876 543,21 F fr_FR
9.876.543,21 DM de_DE
$9,876,543.21 en_US
```

At first glance this output may look wrong to you, because the numeric values are all the same. Of course, 9 876 543,21 F is not equivalent to 9.876.543,21 DM. However, bear in mind that the `NumberFormat` class is unaware of exchange rates. The methods belonging to the `NumberFormat` class format currencies but do not convert them.

Percentages

You can also use the methods of the `NumberFormat` class to format percentages. To get the locale-specific formatter, invoke the `getPercentInstance` method. With this formatter, a decimal fraction such as 0.75 is displayed as 75%.

The following code sample shows how to format a percentage.

```
Double percent = new Double(0.75);
NumberFormat percentFormatter;
String percentOut;

percentFormatter =
            NumberFormat.getPercentInstance(currentLocale);
percentOut = percentFormatter.format(percent);
```

Customizing Formats

You can use the DecimalFormat class to format decimal numbers into locale-specific strings. This class allows you to control the display of leading and trailing zeros, prefixes and suffixes, grouping (thousands) separators, and the decimal separator. If you want to change formatting symbols, such as the decimal separator, you can use the DecimalFormatSymbols in conjunction with the DecimalFormat class. These classes offer a great deal of flexibility in the formatting of numbers, but they can make your code more complex.

The text that follows uses examples that demonstrate the DecimalFormat and DecimalFormatSymbols classes. The code examples in this material are from a sample program called DecimalFormatDemo.java (page 732) in the Appendix.

Constructing Patterns

You specify the formatting properties of DecimalFormat with a pattern String. The pattern determines what the formatted number looks like. For a full description of the pattern syntax, see Number Format Pattern Syntax (page 905) in the Reference Appendix.

The example that follows creates a formatter by passing a pattern String to the DecimalFormat constructor. The format method accepts a double value as an argument and returns the formatted number in a String:

```
DecimalFormat myFormatter = new DecimalFormat(pattern);
String output = myFormatter.format(value);
System.out.println(value + " " + pattern + " " + output);
```

The output for the preceding lines of code is described in the following table. The value is the number, a double, that is to be formatted. The pattern is the String that specifies the formatting properties. The output, which is a String, represents the formatted number.

Table 7 Output from DecimalFormatDemo Program

value	pattern	output	Explanation
123456.789	###,###.###	123,456.789	The pound sign (#) denotes a digit, the comma is a placeholder for the grouping separator, and the period is a placeholder for the decimal separator.

Table 7 Output from `DecimalFormatDemo` Program

`value`	`pattern`	`output`	**Explanation**
123456.789	###.##	123456.79	The `value` has three digits to the right of the decimal point, but the `pattern` has only two. The `format` method handles this by rounding up.
123.78	000000.000	000123.780	The `pattern` specifies leading and trailing zeros, because the 0 character is used instead of the pound sign (#).
12345.67	$###,###.###	$12,345.67	The first character in the `pattern` is the dollar sign ($). Note that it immediately precedes the leftmost digit in the formatted `output`.
12345.67	\u00A5###,###.###	¥12,345.67	The `pattern` specifies the currency sign for Japanese yen (¥) with the Unicode value 00A5.

Locale-Sensitive Formatting

The preceding example created a `DecimalFormat` object for the default `Locale`. If you want a `DecimalFormat` object for a nondefault `Locale`, you instantiate a `NumberFormat` and then cast it to `DecimalFormat`. Here's an example:

```
NumberFormat nf = NumberFormat.getNumberInstance(loc);
DecimalFormat df = (DecimalFormat)nf;
df.applyPattern(pattern);
String output = df.format(value);
System.out.println(pattern + " " + output + " " +
                   loc.toString());
```

Running the previous code example results in the output that follows. The formatted number, which is in the second column, varies with `Locale`:

```
###,###.### 123,456.789 en_US
###,###.### 123.456,789 de_DE
###,###.### 123 456,789 fr_FR
```

So far the formatting patterns discussed here follow the conventions of U.S. English. For example, in the pattern ###,###.## the comma is the thousands-separator and the period represents the decimal point. This convention is fine, provided that your end users aren't exposed to it. However, some applications, such as spreadsheets and report generators, allow the end users to define their own formatting patterns. For these applications the formatting patterns specified by the end users should use localized notation. In these cases you'll want to invoke the `applyLocalizedPattern` method on the `DecimalFormat` object.

Altering the Formatting Symbols

You can use the `DecimalFormatSymbols`[1] class to change the symbols that appear in the formatted numbers produced by the `format` method. These symbols include the decimal separator, the grouping separator, the minus sign, and the percent sign, among others.

The next example demonstrates the `DecimalFormatSymbols` class by applying a strange format to a number. The unusual format is the result of the calls to the `setDecimalSeparator`, `setGroupingSeparator`, and `setGroupingSize` methods.

```
DecimalFormatSymbols unusualSymbols =
                new DecimalFormatSymbols(currentLocale);
unusualSymbols.setDecimalSeparator('|');
unusualSymbols.setGroupingSeparator('^');

String strange = "#,##0.###";
DecimalFormat weirdFormatter =
               new DecimalFormat(strange unusualSymbols);
weirdFormatter.setGroupingSize(4);

String bizarre = weirdFormatter.format(12345.678);
System.out.println(bizarre);
```

When run, this example prints the number in a bizarre format:

```
1^2345|678
```

Dates and Times

`Date` objects represent dates and times. You cannot display or print a `Date` object without first converting it to a `String` that is in the proper format. Just what is

[1] The API documentation is available on the CD-ROM that accompanies this book and online at: http://java.sun.com/products/jdk/1.2/docs/api/java.text.DecimalFormatSymbols.html

the “proper” format? First, the format should conform to the conventions of the end user’s Locale. For example, Germans recognize 20.4.98 as a valid date, but Americans expect that same date to appear as 4/20/98. Second, the format should include the necessary information. For instance, a program that measures network performance may report on elapsed milliseconds. An online appointment calendar probably won’t display milliseconds, but it will show the days of the week.

This section explains how to format dates and times in various ways and in a locale-sensitive manner. If you follow these techniques your programs will display dates and times in the appropriate Locale, but your source code will remain independent of any specific Locale.

Using Predefined Formats

The DateFormat[1] class allows you to format dates and times with predefined styles in a locale-sensitive manner. The sections that follow demonstrate how to use the DateFormat class with a program called DateFormatDemo.java (page 733) found in its entirety in the Appendix.

Dates

Formatting dates with the DateFormat class is a two-step process. First, you create a formatter with the getDateInstance method. Second, you invoke the format method, which returns a String containing the formatted date. The following example formats today’s date by calling these two methods:

```
Date today;
String dateOut;
DateFormat dateFormatter;

dateFormatter = DateFormat.getDateInstance(DateFormat.DEFAULT,
                                           currentLocale);
today = new Date();
dateOut = dateFormatter.format(today);

System.out.println(dateOut + " " + currentLocale.toString());
```

The output generated by this code follows. Notice that the formats of the dates vary with Locale. Since DateFormat is locale-sensitive, it takes care of the formatting details for each Locale.

---

1 The API documentation is available on the CD-ROM that accompanies this book and online at: http://java.sun.com/products/jdk/1.2/docs/api/java.text.DateFormat.html

```
9 avr 98 fr_FR
9.4.1998 de_DE
09-Apr-98 en_US
```

The preceding code example specified the `DEFAULT` formatting style. The `DEFAULT` style is just one of the predefined formatting styles that the `DateFormat` class provides, as follows:

- DEFAULT
- SHORT
- MEDIUM
- LONG
- FULL

The following table shows how dates are formatted for each style with the U.S. and French locales:

Table 8 Sample Date Formats

Style	U.S. Locale	French Locale
`DEFAULT`	10-Apr-98	10 avr 98
`SHORT`	4/10/98	10/04/98
`MEDIUM`	10-Apr-98	10 avr 98
`LONG`	April 10, 1998	10 avril 1998
`FULL`	Friday, April 10, 1998	vendredi, 10 avril 1998

Times

`Date` objects represent both dates and times. Formatting times with the `DateFormat` class is similar to formatting dates, except that you create the formatter with the `getTimeInstance` method, as follows:

```
DateFormat timeFormatter = DateFormat.getTimeInstance(
                              DateFormat.DEFAULT, currentLocale);
```

The table that follows shows the various predefined format styles for the U.S. and German locales:

Table 9 Sample Time Formats

Style	U.S. Locale	German Locale
`DEFAULT`	3:58:45 PM	15:58:45
`SHORT`	3:58 PM	15:58
`MEDIUM`	3:58:45 PM	15:58:45
`LONG`	3:58:45 PM PDT	15:58:45 GMT+02:00
`FULL`	3:58:45 oclock PM PDT	15.58 Uhr GMT+02:00

Both Dates and Times

To display a date and time in the same `String`, create the formatter with the `getDateTimeInstance` method. The first parameter is the date style, and the second is the time style. The third parameter is the `Locale`. Here's a quick example:

```
DateFormat formatter = DateFormat.getDateTimeInstance(
        DateFormat.LONG, DateFormat.LONG, currentLocale);
```

The following table shows the date and time formatting styles for the U.S. and French locales:

Table 10 Sample Date and Time Formats

Style	U.S. Locale	French Locale
`DEFAULT`	25-Jun-98 1:32:19 PM	25 jun 98 22:32:20
`SHORT`	6/25/98 1:32 PM	25/06/98 22:32
`MEDIUM`	25-Jun-98 1:32:19 PM	25 jun 98 22:32:20
`LONG`	June 25, 1998 1:32:19 PM PDT	25 juin 1998 22:32:20 GMT+02:00
`FULL`	Thursday, June 25, 1998 1:32:19 o'clock PM PDT	jeudi, 25 juin 1998 22 h 32 GMT+02:00

Customizing Formats

The previous section, Using Predefined Formats (page 133), described the formatting styles provided by the `DateFormat` class. In most cases these predefined formats are adequate. However, if you want to create your own customized formats, you can use the `SimpleDateFormat` class.[1]

---

[1] The API documentation is available on the CD-ROM that accompanies this book and online at: http://java.sun.com/products/jdk/1.2/docs/api/java.text.SimpleDateFormat.html

The code examples that follow demonstrate the methods of the `SimpleDateFormat` class. You can find the full source code for the examples in the file named `SimpleDateFormatDemo.java` (page 736) in the Appendix.

About Patterns

When you create a `SimpleDateFormat` object, you specify a pattern `String`. The contents of the pattern `String` determine the format of the date and time. For a full description of the pattern's syntax, see the tables in Date Format Pattern Syntax (page 906) in the Reference Appendix.

The following code formats a date and time according to the pattern `String` passed to the `SimpleDateFormat` constructor. The `String` returned by the `format` method contains the formatted date and time that are to be displayed.

```
Date today;
String output;
SimpleDateFormat formatter;
formatter = new SimpleDateFormat(pattern, currentLocale);
today = new Date();
output = formatter.format(today);
System.out.println(pattern + " " + output);
```

The following table shows the output generated by the previous code example when the U.S. `Locale` is specified:

Table 11 Customized Date and Time Formats

Pattern	Output
dd.MM.yy	09.04.98
yyyy.MM.dd G 'at' hh:mm:ss z	1998.04.09 AD at 06:15:55 PDT
EEE, MMM d, ''yy	Thu, Apr 9, '98
h:mm a	6:15 PM
H:mm	18:15
H:mm:ss:SSS	18:15:55:624
K:mm a,z	6:15 PM,PDT
yyyy.MMMMM.dd GGG hh:mm aaa	1998.April.09 AD 06:15 PM

Patterns and Locale

The `SimpleDateFormat` class is locale-sensitive. If you instantiate `SimpleDateFormat` without a `Locale` parameter, it will format the date and time according to the default `Locale`. Both the pattern and the `Locale` determine the format. For the same pattern, `SimpleDateFormat` may format a date and time differently if the `Locale` varies.

In the example code that follows, the pattern is hardcoded in the statement that creates the `SimpleDateFormat` object:

```
Date today;
String result;
SimpleDateFormat formatter;

formatter = new SimpleDateFormat("EEE d MMM yy",
                                  currentLocale);
today = new Date();
result = formatter.format(today);

System.out.println("Locale: " + currentLocale.toString());
System.out.println("Result: " + result);
```

When the `currentLocale` is set to different values, the preceding code example generates this output:

```
Locale: fr_FR
Result: ven 10 avr 98
Locale: de_DE
Result: Fr 10 Apr 98
Locale: en_US
Result: Thu 9 Apr 98
```

Changing Date Format Symbols

The `format` method of the `SimpleDateFormat` class returns a `String` composed of digits and symbols. For example, in the `String` "Friday, April 10, 1998," the symbols are "Friday" and "April." If the symbols encapsulated in `SimpleDateFormat` don't meet your needs, you can change them with the `DateFormatSymbols` class.[1] You can change symbols that represent names for months, days of the week, and time zones, among others. The following table lists the `DateFormatSymbols` methods that allow you to modify the symbols:

---

[1] The API documentation is available on the CD-ROM that accompanies this book and online at: http://java.sun.com/products/jdk/1.2/docs/api/java.text.DateFormatSymbols.html

Table 12 DateFormatSymbol Methods

Setter Method	Example of a Symbol the Method Modifies
setAmPmStrings	PM
setEras	AD
setMonths	December
setShortMonths	Dec
setShortWeekdays	Tue
setWeekdays	Tuesday
setZoneStrings	PST

The following example invokes `setShortWeekdays` to change the short names of the days of the week from lowercase to uppercase characters. The full source code for this example is in DateFormatSymbolsDemo.java (page 737) in the Appendix. The first element in the array argument of `setShortWeekdays` is a null `String`. Therefore the array is one-based rather than zero-based. The `SimpleDateFormat` constructor accepts the modified `DateFormatSymbols` object as an argument. Here is the source code:

```
Date today;
String result;
SimpleDateFormat formatter;
DateFormatSymbols symbols;
String[] defaultDays;
String[] modifiedDays;

symbols = new DateFormatSymbols(new Locale("en","US"));
defaultDays = symbols.getShortWeekdays();

for (int i = 0; i < defaultDays.length; i++) {
    System.out.print(defaultDays[i] + " ");
}
System.out.println();

String[] capitalDays = {
        "", "SUN", "MON", "TUE", "WED", "THU", "FRI", "SAT"};
symbols.setShortWeekdays(capitalDays);

modifiedDays = symbols.getShortWeekdays();
for (int i = 0; i < modifiedDays.length; i++) {
    System.out.print(modifiedDays[i] + " ");
}
```

```
System.out.println();
System.out.println();

formatter = new SimpleDateFormat("E", symbols);
today = new Date();
result = formatter.format(today);
System.out.println(result);
```

The preceding code generates this output:

```
Sun Mon Tue Wed Thu Fri Sat

SUN MON TUE WED THU FRI SAT

WED
```

Messages

We all like to use programs that let us know what's going on. Programs that keep us informed often do so by displaying status and error messages. Of course, these messages need to be translated so they can be understood by end users around the world. The section Isolating Locale-Specific Data (page 115) discusses translatable text messages. Usually, you're done after you move a message `String` into a `ResourceBundle`. However, if you've embedded variable data in a message, you'll have to take some extra steps to prepare it for translation.

A *compound message* contains variable data. In the following list of compound messages, the variable data is underlined:

```
The disk named MyDisk contains 300 files.
The current balance of account #34-98-222 is $2,745.72.
405,390 people have visited your website since January 1, 1998.
Delete all files older than 120 days.
```

You might be tempted to construct the last message in the preceding list by concatenating phrases and variables as follows:

```
double numDays;
ResourceBundle msgBundle;
.
.
```

```
.
String message = msgBundle.getString("deleteolder")
                 + numDays.toString()
                 + msgBundle.getString("days");
```

This approach works fine in English, but it won't work for languages in which the verb appears at the end of the sentence. Because the word order of this message is hardcoded, your localizers won't be able to create grammatically correct translations for all languages.

How can you make your program localizable if you need to use compound messages? You can do so by using the `MessageFormat` class, which is the topic of this section.

Caution: Compound messages are difficult to translate because the message text is fragmented. If you use compound messages, localization will take longer and cost more. Therefore you should use compound messages only when necessary.

Dealing with Compound Messages

A compound message may contain several kinds of variables: dates, times, strings, numbers, currencies, and percentages. To format a compound message in a locale-independent manner, you construct a pattern that you apply to a `MessageFormat` object, and store this pattern in a `ResourceBundle`.

By stepping through a sample program, this section demonstrates how to internationalize a compound message. The sample program makes use of the `MessageFormat` class.[1] The full source code for this program is in the file called `MessageFormatDemo.java` (page 738) in the Appendix.

---

[1] The API documentation is available on the CD-ROM that accompanies this book and online at: http://java.sun.com/products/jdk/1.2/docs/api/java.text.MessageFormat.html

1. Identify the Variables in the Message

Suppose that you want to internationalize the following message:

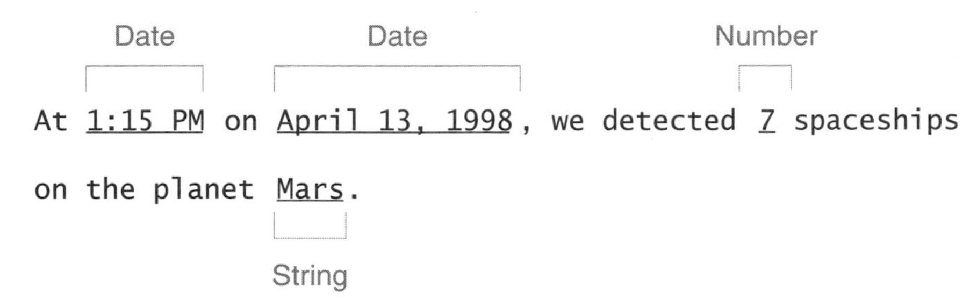

Figure 3 A sample message that needs internationalization.

Notice that we've underlined the variable data and have identified what kind of objects will represent this data.

2. Isolate the Message Pattern in a ResourceBundle

Store the message in a `ResourceBundle` named `MessageBundle`, as follows:

```
ResourceBundle messages =
   ResourceBundle.getBundle("MessageBundle", currentLocale);
```

This `ResourceBundle` is backed by a properties file for each `Locale`. Since the `ResourceBundle` is called `MessageBundle`, the properties file for U.S. English is named `MessageBundle_en_US.properties`. The contents of this file is as follows:

```
template = At {2,time,short} on {2,date,long}, we detected \
           {1,number,integer} spaceships on the planet {0}.
planet = Mars
```

The first line of the properties file contains the message pattern. If you compare this pattern with the message text shown in step 1, you'll see that an argument enclosed in braces replaces each variable in the message text. Each argument starts with a digit called the argument number, which matches the index of an element in an `Object` array that holds the argument values. Note that in the pattern the argument numbers are not in any particular order. You can place the arguments anywhere in the pattern. The only requirement is that the argument number have a matching element in the array of argument values.

The next step discusses the argument value array, but first let's look at each of the arguments in the pattern. The following table provides some details about the arguments:

Table 13 Arguments for `template` in `MessageBundle_en_US.properties`

Argument	Description
`{2,time,short}`	The time portion of a `Date` object. The `short` style specifies the `DateFormat.SHORT` formatting style.
`{2,date,long}`	The date portion of a `Date` object. The same `Date` object is used for both the date and time variables. In the `Object` array of arguments the index of the element holding the `Date` object is 2. (This is described in the next step.)
`{1,number,integer}`	A `Number` object, further qualified with the `integer` number style.
`{0}`	The `String` in the `ResourceBundle` that corresponds to the `planet` key.

For a full description of the argument syntax, see the API documentation for the `MessageFormat` class.[1]

3. Set the Message Arguments

The following lines of code assign values to each argument in the pattern. The indexes of the elements in the `messageArguments` array match the argument numbers in the pattern. For example, the `Integer` element at index 1 corresponds to the `{1,number,integer}` argument in the pattern. Because it must be translated, the `String` object at element 0 will be fetched from the `ResourceBundle` with the `getString` method. Here is the code that defines the array of message arguments:

```
Object[] messageArguments = {
    messages.getString("planet"),
    new Integer(7),
    new Date()
};
```

---

[1] The API documentation is available on the CD-ROM that accompanies this book and online at: http://java.sun.com/products/jdk/1.2/docs/api/java.text.MessageFormat.html

4. Create the Formatter

Next, create a `MessageFormat` object. You set the `Locale` because the message contains `Date` and `Number` objects, which should be formatted in a locale-sensitive manner.

```
MessageFormat formatter = new MessageFormat("");
formatter.setLocale(currentLocale);
```

5. Format the Message Using the Pattern and the Arguments

This step shows how the pattern, message arguments, and formatter all work together. First, fetch the pattern `String` from the `ResourceBundle` with the `getString` method. The key to the pattern is `template`. Pass the pattern `String` to the formatter with the `applyPattern` method. Then format the message using the array of message arguments, by invoking the `format` method. The `String` returned by the `format` method is ready to be displayed. All of this is accomplished with just two lines of code:

```
formatter.applyPattern(messages.getString("template"));
String output = formatter.format(messageArguments);
```

6. Run the Demo Program

The demo program prints the translated messages for the English and German locales and properly formats the date and time variables. Note that the English and German verbs ("detected" and "entdeckt") are in different locations relative to the variables:

```
currentLocale = en_US

At 1:15 PM on April 13, 1998, we detected 7 spaceships on the
planet Mars.

currentLocale = de_DE

Um 13.15 Uhr am 13. April 1998 haben wir 7 Raumschiffe auf dem
Planeten Mars entdeckt.
```

Handling Plurals

The words in a message may vary if both plural and singular word forms are possible. With the `ChoiceFormat` class, you can map a number to a word or a phrase, allowing you to construct grammatically correct messages.

In English the plural and singular forms of a word are usually different. This can present a problem when you are constructing messages that refer to quantities. For example, if your message reports the number of files on a disk, the following variations are possible:

```
There are no files on XDisk.
There is one file on XDisk.
There are 2 files on XDisk.
```

The fastest way to solve this problem is to create a `MessageFormat` pattern like this:

```
There are {0,number} file(s) on {1}.
```

Unfortunately the preceding pattern results in incorrect grammar:

```
There are 1 file(s) on XDisk.
```

You can do better than that, provided that you use the `ChoiceFormat` class.[1] In this section you'll learn how to deal with plurals in a message by stepping through a sample program called `ChoiceFormatDemo.java` (page 739), shown in full in the Appendix. This program also uses the `MessageFormat` class, which is discussed in the previous section, Dealing with Compound Messages (page 140).

1. Define the Message Pattern

First, identify the variables in the message:

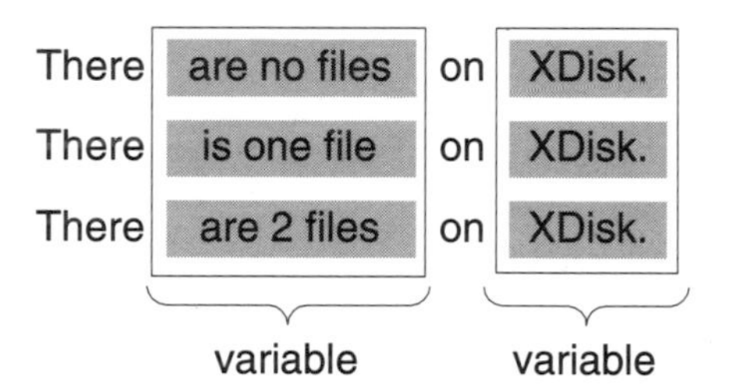

Figure 4 Identifying the variables in a message.

Next, replace the variables in the message with arguments, creating a pattern that can be applied to a `MessageFormat` object:

```
There {0} on {1}.
```

[1] The API documentation is available on the CD-ROM that accompanies this book and online at: http://java.sun.com/products/jdk/1.2/docs/api/java.text.ChoiceFormat.html

The argument for the disk name, which is represented by {1}, is easy enough to deal with. You just treat it like any other String variable in a MessageFormat pattern. This argument matches the element at index 1 in the array of argument values. (See step 7.)

Dealing with argument {0} is more complex, for a couple of reasons:

- The phrase that this argument replaces varies with the number of files. To construct this phrase at run time, you need to map the number of files to a particular String. For example, the number 1 will map to the String containing the phrase is one file. The ChoiceFormat class allows you to perform the necessary mapping.
- If the disk contains multiple files, the phrase includes an integer. The MessageFormat class lets you insert a number into a phrase.

2. Create a ResourceBundle

Because the message text must be translated, isolate it in a ResourceBundle:

```
ResourceBundle bundle =
   ResourceBundle.getBundle("ChoiceBundle", currentLocale);
```

The sample program backs the ResourceBundle with properties files. The ChoiceBundle_en_US.properties file contains the following lines:

```
pattern = There {0} on {1}.
noFiles = are no files
oneFile = is one file
multipleFiles = are {2} files
```

The contents of this properties file show how the message will be constructed and formatted. The first line contains the pattern for MessageFormat. (See step 1.) The other lines contain phrases that will replace argument {0} in the pattern. The phrase for the multipleFiles key contains the argument {2}, which will be replaced by a number.

Here is the French version of the properties file, ChoiceBundle_fr_FR.properties:

```
pattern = Il {0} sur {1}.
noFiles = n'y a pas des fichiers
oneFile = y a un fichier
multipleFiles = y a {2} fichiers
```

3. Create a Message Formatter

In this step you instantiate `MessageFormat` and set its `Locale`:

```
MessageFormat messageForm = new MessageFormat("");
messageForm.setLocale(currentLocale);
```

4. Create a Choice Formatter

The `ChoiceFormat` object allows you to choose, based on a `double` number, a particular `String`. The range of `double` numbers, and the `String` objects to which they map, are specified in arrays:

```
double[] fileLimits = {0,1,2};
String [] fileStrings = {
    bundle.getString("noFiles"),
    bundle.getString("oneFile"),
    bundle.getString("multipleFiles")
};
```

`ChoiceFormat` maps each element in the `double` array to the element in the `String` array that has the same index. In the sample code the 0 maps to the `String` returned by calling `bundle.getString("noFiles")`. By coincidence the index is the same as the value in the `fileLimits` array. If the code had set `fileLimits[0]` to seven, `ChoiceFormat` would map the number 7 to `fileStrings[0]`.

You specify the `double` and `String` arrays when instantiating `ChoiceFormat`:

```
ChoiceFormat choiceForm =
                    new ChoiceFormat(fileLimits, fileStrings);
```

5. Apply the Pattern

Remember the pattern you constructed in step 1? It's time to retrieve the pattern from the `ResourceBundle` and apply it to the `MessageFormat` object:

```
String pattern = bundle.getString("pattern");
messageForm.applyPattern(pattern);
```

6. Assign the Formats

In this step you assign to the `MessageFormat` object the `ChoiceFormat` object created in step 4:

```
Format[] formats =
              {choiceForm, null, NumberFormat.getInstance()};
messageForm.setFormats(formats);
```

The `setFormats` method assigns `Format` objects to the arguments in the message pattern. You must invoke the `applyPattern` method before you call the `setFormats` method. The following table shows how the elements of the `Format` array correspond to the arguments in the message pattern:

Table 14 The `Format` Array of the `ChoiceFormatDemo` Program

Array Element	Pattern Argument
`choiceForm`	`{0}`
`null`	`{1}`
`NumberFormat.getInstance()`	`{2}`

7. Set the Arguments and Format the Message

At run time the program assigns the variables to the array of arguments it passes to the `MessageFormat` object. The elements in the array correspond to the arguments in the pattern. For example, `messageArgument[1]` maps to pattern argument `{1}`, which is a `String` containing the name of the disk. In the previous step the program assigned a `ChoiceFormat` object to argument `{0}` of the pattern. Therefore the number assigned to `messageArgument[0]` determines which `String` the `ChoiceFormat` object selects. If `messageArgument[0]` is greater than or equal to 2, the `String` containing the phrase `are {2} files` replaces argument `{0}` in the pattern. The number assigned to `messageArgument[2]` will be substituted in place of pattern argument `{2}`. Here's the code that tries this out:

```
Object[] messageArguments = {null, "XDisk", null};
for (int numFiles = 0; numFiles < 4; numFiles++) {
    messageArguments[0] = new Integer(numFiles);
    messageArguments[2] = new Integer(numFiles);
    String result = messageForm.format(messageArguments);
    System.out.println(result);
}
```

8. Run the Demo Program

Compare the messages displayed by the program with the phrases in the `ResourceBundle` of step 2. Notice that the `ChoiceFormat` object selects the correct phrase, which the `MessageFormat` object uses to construct the proper message. The output of the `ChoiceFormatDemo` program is as follows:

```
currentLocale = en_US

There are no files on XDisk.
There is one file on XDisk.
There are 2 files on XDisk.
There are 3 files on XDisk.

currentLocale = fr_FR

Il n'y a pas des fichiers sur XDisk.
Il y a un fichier sur XDisk.
Il y a 2 fichiers sur XDisk.
Il y a 3 fichiers sur XDisk.
```

11 Working with Text

NEARLY all programs with user interfaces manipulate text. In an international market the text your programs display must conform to the rules of languages from around the world. The Java programming language provides a number of classes that help you handle text in a locale-independent manner.

Checking Character Properties

You can categorize characters according to their properties. For instance, X is an uppercase letter and 4 is a decimal digit. Checking character properties is a common way to verify the data entered by end users. If you are selling books online, for example, your order entry screen should verify that the characters in the quantity field are all digits.

Developers who aren't used to writing global software might determine a character's properties by comparing it with character constants. For instance, they might write code like this:

```
char ch;
...

// This code is WRONG!

if ((ch >= 'a' && ch <= 'z') || (ch >= 'A' && ch <= 'Z'))
  // ch is a letter
...
if (ch >= '0' && ch <= '9')
  // ch is a digit
...
if ((ch == ' ') || (ch =='\n') || (ch == '\t'))
  // ch is a whitespace
```

The preceding code is *wrong* because it works only with English and a few other languages. To internationalize the previous example, replace it with the following statements:

```
char ch;
...

// This code is OK!

if (Character.isLetter(ch))
...
if (Character.isDigit(ch))
...
if (Character.isSpaceChar(ch))
```

The `Character`[1] methods rely on the Unicode Standard for determining the properties of a character. Unicode is a 16-bit character encoding that supports the world's major languages. In the Java programming language `char` values represent Unicode characters. If you check the properties of a `char` with the appropriate `Character` method, your code will work with all major languages. For example, the `Character.isLetter` method returns `true` if the character is a letter in Chinese, German, Arabic, or another language.

---

[1] The API documentation is available on the CD-ROM that accompanies this book and online at: http://java.sun.com/products/jdk/1.2/docs/api/java.lang.Character.html

The following list gives some of the most useful `Character` comparison methods. The `Character` API documentation fully specifies the methods.

- `isDigit`
- `isLetter`
- `isLetterOrDigit`
- `isLowerCase`
- `isUpperCase`
- `isSpaceChar`
- `isDefined`

The `Character.getType` method returns the Unicode category of a character. Each category corresponds to a constant defined in the `Character` class. For instance, `getType` returns the `Character.UPPERCASE_LETTER` constant for the character A. For a complete list of the category constants returned by `getType`, see the `Character` API documentation.[1] The following example shows how to use `getType` and the `Character` category constants. All of the expressions in these `if` statements are `true`:

```
if (Character.getType('a') == Character.LOWERCASE_LETTER)
...
if (Character.getType('R') == Character.UPPERCASE_LETTER)
...
if (Character.getType('>') == Character.MATH_SYMBOL)
...
if (Character.getType('_') == Character.CONNECTOR_PUNCTUATION)
```

Comparing Strings

Applications that sort through text perform frequent string comparisons. For example, a report generator performs string comparisons when sorting a list of strings in alphabetical order.

If your application audience is limited to people who speak English, you can probably perform string comparisons with the `String.compareTo` method. The `String.compareTo` method performs a binary comparison of the Unicode characters within the two strings. For most languages, however, this binary comparison cannot be relied on to sort strings, because the Unicode values do not correspond to the relative order of the characters.

Fortunately the `Collator`[1] class allows your application to perform string comparisons for different languages. In this section, you'll learn how to use the `Collator` class when sorting text.

Performing Locale-Independent Comparisons

Collation rules define the sort sequence of strings. These rules vary with locale, because various natural languages sort words differently. You can use the predefined collation rules provided by the `Collator` class to sort strings in a locale-independent manner.

To instantiate the `Collator` class invoke the `getInstance` method. Usually, you create a `Collator` for the default `Locale`, as in the following example:

```
Collator myDefaultCollator = Collator.getInstance();
```

You can also specify a particular `Locale` when you create a `Collator`, as follows:

```
Collator myFrenchCollator =
   Collator.getInstance(Locale.FRENCH);
```

The `getInstance` method returns a `RuleBasedCollator`, which is a concrete subclass of `Collator`. The `RuleBasedCollator` contains a set of rules that determine the sort order of strings for the locale you specify. These rules are predefined for each locale. Because the rules are encapsulated within the `RuleBasedCollator`, your program won't need special routines to deal with the way collation rules vary with language.

You invoke the `Collator.compare` method to perform a locale-independent string comparison. The `compare` method returns an integer less than, equal to, or greater than zero when the first string argument is less than, equal to, or greater than the second string argument. The following table contains some sample calls to `Collator.compare`:

Table 15 `Collator.compare` Examples

Example	Return Value	Explanation
`myCollator.compare("abc", "def")`	`-1`	"abc" is less than "def"
`myCollator.compare("rtf", "rtf")`	`0`	the two strings are equal
`myCollator.compare("xyz", "abc")`	`1`	"xyz" is greater than "abc"

[1] The API documentation is available on the CD-ROM that accompanies this book and online at: http://java.sun.com/products/jdk/1.2/docs/api/java.text.Collator.html

You use the `compare` method when performing sort operations. The sample program called `CollatorDemo.java` (page 740) uses the `compare` method to sort an array of English and French words. This program shows what can happen when you sort the same list of words with two different collators:

```
Collator fr_FRCollator =
    Collator.getInstance(new Locale("fr","FR"));

Collator en_USCollator =
    Collator.getInstance(new Locale("en","US"));
```

The method for sorting, called `sortStrings`, can be used with any `Collator`. Notice that the `sortStrings` method invokes the `compare` method:

```
public static void sortStrings(Collator collator,
                               String[] words) {
    String tmp;
    for (int i = 0; i < words.length; i++) {
        for (int j = i + 1; j < words.length; j++) {
            if (collator.compare(words[i], words[j]) > 0) {
                tmp = words[i];
                words[i] = words[j];
                words[j] = tmp;
            }
        }
    }
}
```

The English `Collator` sorts the words as follows:

```
peach
péché
pêche
sin
```

According to the collation rules of the French language, the preceding list is in the wrong order. In French péché should follow pêche in a sorted list. The French `Collator` sorts the array of words correctly, as follows:

```
peach
pêche
péché
sin
```

Customizing Collation Rules

The previous section discussed how to use the predefined rules for a locale to compare strings. These collation rules determine the sort order of strings. If the predefined collation rules do not meet your needs, you can design your own rules and assign them to a `RuleBasedCollator` object.

Customized collation rules are contained in a `String` object that is passed to the `RuleBasedCollator` constructor. Here's a simple example:

```
String simpleRule = "< a < b < c < d";
RuleBasedCollator simpleCollator =
   new RuleBasedCollator(simpleRule);
```

For the `simpleCollator` object in the previous example, `a` is less than `b`, which is less that `c`, and so forth. The `simpleCollator.compare` method references these rules when comparing strings. The full syntax used to construct a collation rule is more flexible and complex than this simple example. For a full description of the syntax, refer to the API documentation for the `RuleBasedCollator` class.[1]

The example that follows sorts a list of Spanish words with two collators. Full source code for this example is in `RulesDemo.java` (page 742) in the Appendix.

The `RulesDemo` program starts by defining collation rules for English and Spanish. The program will sort the Spanish words in the traditional manner. When sorting by the traditional rules, the letters ch and ll and their uppercase equivalents each have their own positions in the sort order. These character pairs compare as if they were one character. For example, ch sorts as a single letter, following cz in the sort order. Note how the rules for the two collators differ:

```
String englishRules =
       ("< a,A < b,B < c,C < d,D < e,E < f,F " +
        "< g,G < h,H < i,I < j,J < k,K < l,L " +
        "< m,M < n,N < o,O < p,P < q,Q < r,R " +
        "< s,S < t,T < u,U < v,V < w,W < x,X " +
        "< y,Y < z,Z");

String smallnTilde = new String("\u00F1"); // ñ
String capitalNTilde = new String("\u00D1"); // Ñ
```

---

[1] The API documentation is available on the CD-ROM that accompanies this book and online at: http://java.sun.com/products/jdk/1.2/docs/api/java.text.RuleBasedCollator.html

```
String traditionalSpanishRules =
    ("< a,A < b,B < c,C " +
     "< ch, cH, Ch, CH " +
     "< d,D < e,E < f,F " +
     "< g,G < h,H < i,I < j,J < k,K < l,L " +
     "< ll, lL, Ll, LL " +
     "< m,M < n,N " +
     "< " + smallnTilde + "," + capitalNTilde + " " +
     "< o,O < p,P < q,Q < r,R " +
     "< s,S < t,T < u,U < v,V < w,W < x,X " +
     "< y,Y < z,Z");
```

The following lines of code create the collators and invoke the sort routine:

```
try {
    RuleBasedCollator enCollator =
            new RuleBasedCollator(englishRules);
    RuleBasedCollator spCollator =
            new RuleBasedCollator(traditionalSpanishRules);

    sortStrings(enCollator, words);
    printStrings(words);

    System.out.println();

    sortStrings(spCollator, words);
    printStrings(words);
} catch (ParseException pe) {
    System.out.println("Parse exception for rules");
}
```

The sort routine, called `sortStrings`, is generic. It will sort any array of words according to the rules of any `Collator` object:

```
public static void sortStrings(Collator collator,
                               String[] words) {
    String tmp;
    for (int i = 0; i < words.length; i++) {
        for (int j = i + 1; j < words.length; j++) {
            if (collator.compare(words[i], words[j]) > 0) {
                tmp = words[i];
                words[i] = words[j];
                words[j] = tmp;
            }
        }
    }
}
```

When sorted with the English collation rules, the array of words is as follows:

```
chalina
curioso
llama
luz
```

Compare the preceding list with the following, which is sorted according to the traditional Spanish rules of collation:

```
curioso
chalina
luz
llama
```

Improving Collation Performance

Sorting long lists of strings is often time consuming. If your sort algorithm compares strings repeatedly, you can speed up the process by using the `CollationKey` class.

A `CollationKey`[1] object represents a sort key for a given `String` and `Collator`. Comparing two `CollationKey` objects involves a bitwise comparison of sort keys and is faster than comparing `String` objects with the `Collator.compare` method. However, generating `CollationKey` objects requires time. Therefore if a `String` is to be compared just once, `Collator.compare` offers better performance.

The example that follows uses a `CollationKey` object to sort an array of words. Source code for this example is in `KeysDemo.java` (page 744) in the Appendix.

The `KeysDemo` program creates an array of `CollationKey` objects in the `main` method. To create a `CollationKey`, you invoke the `getCollationKey` method on a `Collator` object. You cannot compare two `CollationKey` objects unless they originate from the same `Collator`. The `main` method is as follows:

```
static public void main(String[] args) {
    Collator enUSCollator =
             Collator.getInstance (new Locale("en","US"));
    String [] words = {
        "peach",
```

---

[1] The API documentation is available on the CD-ROM that accompanies this book and online at: http://java.sun.com/products/jdk/1.2/docs/api/java.text.CollationKey.html

```
            "apricot",
            "grape",
            "lemon"
        };

        CollationKey[] keys = new CollationKey[words.length];

        for (int k = 0; k < keys.length; k ++) {
            keys[k] = enUSCollator.getCollationKey(words[k]);
        }

        sortArray(keys);
        printArray(keys);
    }
```

The `sortArray` method invokes the `CollationKey.compareTo` method. The `compareTo` method returns an integer less than, equal to, or greater than zero if the `keys[i]` object is less than, equal to, or greater than the `keys[j]` object. Note that the program compares the `CollationKey` objects, not the `String` objects from the original array of words. Here is the code for the `sortArray` method:

```
    public static void sortArray(CollationKey[] keys) {

        CollationKey tmp;
        for (int i = 0; i < keys.length; i++) {
            for (int j = i + 1; j < keys.length; j++) {
                if (keys[i].compareTo(keys[j]) > 0) {
                    tmp = keys[i];
                    keys[i] = keys[j];
                    keys[j] = tmp;
                }
            }
        }
    }
```

The `KeysDemo` program sorts an array of `CollationKey` objects, but the original goal was to sort an array of `String` objects. To retrieve the `String` representation of each `CollationKey`, the program invokes `getSourceString` in the `displayWords` method, as follows:

```
    static void displayWords(CollationKey[] keys) {

        for (int i = 0; i < keys.length; i++) {
            System.out.println(keys[i].getSourceString());
        }
    }
```

The displayWords method prints the following lines:

```
apricot
grape
lemon
peach
```

Detecting Text Boundaries

Applications that manipulate text need to locate boundaries within the text. For example, consider some of the common functions of a word processor: highlighting a character, cutting a word, moving the cursor to the next sentence, and wrapping a word at a line ending. To perform each of these functions, the word processor must be able to detect the logical boundaries in the text. Fortunately you don't have to write your own routines to perform boundary analysis. Instead, you can take advantage of the methods provided by the BreakIterator class.[1]

About the BreakIterator Class

The BreakIterator class is locale-sensitive, because text boundaries vary with language. For example, the syntax rules for line breaks are not the same for all languages. To determine which locales the BreakIterator class supports, invoke the getAvailableLocales method, as follows:

```
Locale[] locales = BreakIterator.getAvailableLocales();
```

You can analyze four kinds of boundaries with the BreakIteratorclass: character, word, sentence, and potential line break. When instantiating a BreakIterator, you invoke the appropriate factory method:

- getCharacterInstance
- getWordInstance
- getSentenceInstance
- getLineInstance

Each instance of BreakIterator can detect just one type of boundary. If you want to locate both character and word boundaries, for example, you create two separate instances.

---

[1] The API documentation is available on the CD-ROM that accompanies this book and online at: http://java.sun.com/products/jdk/1.2/docs/api/java.text.BreakIterator.html

A `BreakIterator` has an imaginary cursor that points to the current boundary in a string of text. You can move this cursor within the text with the `previous` and the `next` methods. For example, if you've created a `BreakIterator` with `getWordInstance`, the cursor moves to the next word boundary in the text every time you invoke the `next` method. The cursor-movement methods return an integer indicating the position of the boundary. This position is the index of the character in the text string that would follow the boundary. Like string indexes, the boundaries are zero-based. The first boundary is at 0, and the last boundary is the length of the string. The following figure shows the word boundaries detected by the `next` and `previous` methods in a line of text:

```
|Hope| |is| |the| |thing| |with| |feathers|
0    4 5  7 8   11 12   17 18  22 23      31
```

Figure 5 Word boundaries.

You should use the `BreakIterator` class only with natural-language text. To tokenize a programming language, use the `StreamTokenizer` class.

The sections that follow give examples for each type of boundary analysis. The coding examples are from the source code file named BreakIteratorDemo.java (page 745).

Character Boundaries

You need to locate character boundaries if your application allows the end user to highlight individual characters or to move a cursor through text one character at a time. To create a `BreakIterator` that locates character boundaries, you invoke the `getCharacterInstance` method, as follows:

```
BreakIterator characterIterator =
        BreakIterator.getCharacterInstance(currentLocale);
```

This type of `BreakIterator` detects boundaries between user characters, not just Unicode characters.

A user character may be composed of more than one Unicode character. For example, the user character ü can be composed by combining the Unicode characters \u0075 (u) and \u00a8 (¨). This isn't the best example, however, because the character ü may also be represented by the single Unicode character \u00fc. We'll draw on the Arabic language for a more realistic example.

In Arabic the word for house is:

Figure 6 The Arabic word for house.

This word contains three user characters, but it is composed of the following six Unicode characters:

```
String house = "\u0628" + "\u064e" + "\u064a" +
               "\u0652" + "\u067a" + "\u064f";
```

The Unicode characters at positions 1, 3, and 5 in the `house` string are diacritics. Arabic requires diacritics because they can alter the meanings of words. The diacritics in the example are nonspacing characters, since they appear above the base characters. In an Arabic word processor you cannot move the cursor on the screen once for every Unicode character in the string. Instead you must move it once for every user character, which may be composed by more than one Unicode character. Therefore you must use a `BreakIterator` to scan the user characters in the string.

The sample program BreakIteratorDemo.java (page 745) creates a `BreakIterator` to scan Arabic characters. The program passes this `BreakIterator`, along with the `String` object created previously, to a method named `listPositions`:

```
BreakIterator arCharIterator =
    BreakIterator.getCharacterInstance(new Locale
("ar","SA"));

listPositions (house, arCharIterator);
```

The `listPositions` method uses a `BreakIterator` to locate the character boundaries in the string. Note that the `BreakIteratorDemo` assigns a particular string to the `BreakIterator` with the `setText` method. The program retrieves the first character boundary with the `first` method and then invokes the `next` method until the constant `BreakIterator.DONE` is returned. The code for this routine is as follows:

```
static void listPositions(String target,
                          BreakIterator iterator) {

    iterator.setText(target);
    int boundary = iterator.first();

    while (boundary != BreakIterator.DONE) {
        System.out.println (boundary);
        boundary = iterator.next();
    }
}
```

The `listPositions` method prints out the following boundary positions for the user characters in the string `house`. Note that the positions of the diacritics (1, 3, 5) are not listed:

```
0
2
4
6
```

Word Boundaries

You invoke the `getWordIterator` method to instantiate a `BreakIterator` that detects word boundaries:

```
BreakIterator wordIterator =
            BreakIterator.getWordInstance(currentLocale);
```

You'll want to create such a `BreakIterator` when your application needs to perform operations on individual words. These operations might be common word-processing functions, such as selecting, cutting, pasting, and copying. Or, your application may search for words, and it must be able to distinguish entire words from simple strings.

When a `BreakIterator` analyzes word boundaries, it differentiates between words and characters that are not part of words. These characters, which include spaces, tabs, punctuation marks, and most symbols, have word boundaries on both sides.

The example that follows, which is from the program `BreakIteratorDemo.java` (page 745), marks the word boundaries in some text. The program creates the `BreakIterator` and then calls the `markBoundaries` method:

```
Locale currentLocale = new Locale ("en","US");

BreakIterator wordIterator =
        BreakIterator.getWordInstance(currentLocale);

String someText = "She stopped.  " +
                "She said, \"Hello there,\" and then went on.";

markBoundaries(someText, wordIterator);
```

The markBoundaries method is defined in BreakIteratorDemo.java. This method marks boundaries by printing carets (^) beneath the target string. In the code that follows, notice the while loop where markBoundaries scans the string by calling the next method:

```
static void markBoundaries(String target,
                           BreakIterator iterator) {

    StringBuffer markers = new StringBuffer();
    markers.setLength(target.length() + 1);
    for (int k = 0; k < markers.length(); k++) {
        markers.setCharAt(k,' ');
    }

    iterator.setText(target);
    int boundary = iterator.first();

    while (boundary != BreakIterator.DONE) {
        markers.setCharAt(boundary,'^');
        boundary = iterator.next();
    }

    System.out.println(target);
    System.out.println(markers);
}
```

The output of the markBoundaries method follows. Note where the carets (^) occur in relation to the punctuation marks and spaces:

```
She stopped.  She said, "Hello there," and then went on.
^  ^^      ^^ ^  ^^   ^^^^    ^^    ^^^^  ^^   ^^   ^^ ^^
```

The BreakIterator class makes it easy to select words from within text. You don't have to write your own routines to handle the punctuation rules of various languages; the BreakIterator class does this for you.

The `extractWords` method in the following example extracts and prints words for a given string. Note that this method uses `Character.isLetterOrDigit` to avoid printing "words" that contain space characters.

```
static void extractWords(String target,
                         BreakIterator wordIterator) {

    wordIterator.setText(target);
    int start = wordIterator.first();
    int end = wordIterator.next();

    while (end != BreakIterator.DONE) {
        String word = target.substring(start,end);
        if (Character.isLetterOrDigit(word.charAt(0))) {
            System.out.println(word);
        }
        start = end;
        end = wordIterator.next();
    }
}
```

The `BreakIteratorDemo` program invokes `extractWords`, passing it the same target string used in the previous example. The `extractWords` method prints out the following list of words:

```
She
stopped
She
said
Hello
there
and
then
went
on
```

Sentence Boundaries

You can use a `BreakIterator` to determine sentence boundaries. You start by creating a `BreakIterator` with the `getSentenceInstance` method:

```
BreakIterator sentenceIterator =
    BreakIterator.getSentenceInstance(currentLocale);
```

To show the sentence boundaries, the program uses the `markBoundaries` method, which is discussed in the section Word Boundaries (page 161). The markBoundaries method prints carets (^) beneath a string to indicate boundary positions. Here are some examples:

```
She stopped.  She said, "Hello there," and then went on.
^             ^                                         ^

He's vanished!  What will we do?  It's up to us.
^               ^                 ^             ^

Please add 1.5 liters to the tank.
^                                 ^
```

Line Boundaries

Applications that format text or that perform line wrapping must locate potential line breaks. You can find these line breaks, or boundaries, with a `BreakIterator` that has been created with the `getLineInstance` method:

```
BreakIterator lineIterator =
    BreakIterator.getLineInstance(currentLocale);
```

This `BreakIterator` determines the positions in a string where text can break to continue on the next line. The positions detected by the `BreakIterator` are potential line breaks. The actual line breaks displayed on the screen may not be the same.

The two examples that follow use the `markBoundaries` method of `BreakIteratorDemo.java` (page 745) to show the line boundaries detected by a `BreakIterator`. The `markBoundaries` method indicates line boundaries by printing carets (^) beneath the target string.

According to a `BreakIterator`, a line boundary occurs after the termination of a sequence of whitespace characters (space, tab, new line). In the following example, note that you can break the line at any of the boundaries detected:

```
She stopped.  She said, "Hello there," and then went on.
^   ^         ^   ^     ^      ^     ^ ^   ^    ^    ^  ^
```

Potential line breaks also occur immediately after a hyphen:

```
There are twenty-four hours in a day.
^     ^   ^      ^    ^     ^  ^ ^   ^
```

The next example breaks a long string of text into fixed-length lines with a method called `formatLines`. This method uses a `BreakIterator` to locate the potential line breaks. The `formatLines` method is short, simple, and, thanks to the `BreakIterator`, locale-independent. Here is the source code:

```
static void formatLines(String target, int maxLength,
                        Locale currentLocale) {

    BreakIterator boundary =
        BreakIterator.getLineInstance(currentLocale);
    boundary.setText(target);
    int start = boundary.first();
    int end = boundary.next();
    int lineLength = 0;

    while (end != BreakIterator.DONE) {
        String word = target.substring(start,end);
        lineLength = lineLength + word.length();
        if (lineLength >= maxLength) {
            System.out.println();
            lineLength = word.length();
        }
    System.out.print(word);
    start = end;
    end = boundary.next();
    }
}
```

The `BreakIteratorDemo` program invokes the `formatLines` method as follows:

```
String moreText = "She said, \"Hello there,\" and then " +
            "went on down the street. When she stopped " +
            "to look at the fur coats in a shop window, " +
            "her dog growled._ \"Sorry Jake,\" she said. " +
            " \"I didn't know you would take it personally.\"";

formatLines(moreText, 30, currentLocale);
```

The output from this call to `formatLines` is:

```
She said, "Hello there," and
then went on down the
street. When she stopped to
look at the fur coats in a
shop window, her dog
growled. "Sorry Jake," she
said. "I didn't know you
would take it personally."
```

Converting Non-Unicode Text

In the Java programming language `char` values represent Unicode characters. Unicode is a 16-bit character encoding that supports the world's major languages. You can learn more about the Unicode standard at the Unicode Consortium Web site found here:

```
http://www.unicode.org/index.html
```

Few text editors currently support Unicode text entry. The text editor we used to write this section's code examples supports only ASCII characters, which are limited to 7 bits. To indicate Unicode characters that cannot be represented in ASCII, such as ö, we used the `\uXXXX` escape sequence. Each `X` in the escape sequence is a hexadecimal digit. The following example shows how to indicate the ö character with an escape sequence:

```
String str = "\u00F6";
char c = '\u00F6';
Character letter = new Character('\u00F6');
```

A variety of character encodings are used by systems around the world. Currently few of these encodings conform to Unicode. Because your program expects characters in Unicode, the text data it gets from the system must be converted into Unicode, and vice versa. Data in text files is automatically converted to Unicode when its encoding matches the default file encoding of the Java Virtual Machine. You can identify the default file encoding by checking the `System` property named `file.properties`, as follows:

```
System.out.println(System.getProperty("file.encoding"));
```

If the `file.encoding` property differs from the encoding of the text data you want to process, then you must perform the conversion yourself. You might need to do this when processing text from another country or computing platform.

This section discusses the APIs you use to translate non-Unicode text into Unicode. Before using these APIs, you should verify that the character encoding you wish to convert into Unicode is supported. The list of supported character encodings is not part of the Java programming language specification. Therefore the character encodings supported by the APIs may vary with platform. To see which encodings the Java Development Kit supports, see the "Supported Encodings" section in the Internationalization Overview document.[1]

---

[1] The API documentation is available on the CD-ROM that accompanies this book and online at: http://java.sun.com/products/jdk/1.2/docs/guide/intl/intlTOC.doc.html

The material that follows describes two techniques for converting non-Unicode text to Unicode. You can convert non-Unicode byte arrays into `String` objects, and vice versa. Or you can translate between streams of Unicode characters and byte streams of non-Unicode text.

Byte Encodings and Strings

If a byte array contains non-Unicode text, you can convert the text to Unicode with one of the `String` constructor methods. Conversely, you can convert a `String` object into a byte array of non-Unicode characters with the `String.getBytes` method. When invoking either of these methods, you specify the encoding identifier as one of the parameters.

The example that follows converts characters between UTF-8 and Unicode. UTF-8 is a transmission format for Unicode that is safe for UNIX file systems. The full source code for the example is in the file `StringConverter.java` (page 749).

The `StringConverter` program starts by creating a `String` containing Unicode characters:

```
String original = new String("A" + "\u00ea" + "\u00f1" +
                             "\u00fc" + "C");
```

When printed, the `String` named `original` appears as:

```
AêñüC
```

To convert the `String` object to UTF-8, invoke the `getBytes` method and specify the appropriate encoding identifier as a parameter. The `getBytes` method returns an array of bytes in UTF-8 format. To create a `String` object from an array of non-Unicode bytes, invoke the `String` constructor with the encoding parameter. The code that makes these calls is enclosed in a `try` block, in case the specified encoding is unsupported:

```
try {
    byte[] utf8Bytes = original.getBytes("UTF8");
    byte[] defaultBytes = original.getBytes();

    String roundTrip = new String(utf8Bytes, "UTF8");
    System.out.println("roundTrip = " + roundTrip);
```

```
        System.out.println();
        printBytes(utf8Bytes, "utf8Bytes");
        System.out.println();
        printBytes(defaultBytes, "defaultBytes");
    } catch (UnsupportedEncodingException e) {
        e.printStackTrace();
    }
```

The `StringConverter` program prints out the values in the `utf8Bytes` and `defaultBytes` arrays to demonstrate an important point: The length of the converted text might not be the same as the length of the source text. Some Unicode characters translate into single bytes, others into pairs or triplets of bytes.

The `printBytes` method displays the byte arrays by invoking the `byteToHex` method, which is defined in the source file, `UnicodeFormatter.java` (page 750) in the Appendix. Here is the `printBytes` method:

```
public static void printBytes(byte[] array, String name) {
    for (int k = 0; k < array.length; k++) {
        System.out.println(name + "[" + k + "] = " + "0x" +
                      UnicodeFormatter.byteToHex(array[k]));
    }
}
```

The output of the `printBytes` method follows. Note that only the first and last bytes, the A and C characters, are the same in both arrays:

```
utf8Bytes[0] = 0x41
utf8Bytes[1] = 0xc3
utf8Bytes[2] = 0xaa
utf8Bytes[3] = 0xc3
utf8Bytes[4] = 0xb1
utf8Bytes[5] = 0xc3
utf8Bytes[6] = 0xbc
utf8Bytes[7] = 0x43
defaultBytes[0] = 0x41
defaultBytes[1] = 0xea
defaultBytes[2] = 0xf1
defaultBytes[3] = 0xfc
defaultBytes[4] = 0x43
```

Character and Byte Streams

The `java.io` package provides classes that allow you to convert between Unicode character streams and byte streams of non-Unicode text. With the `Input-`

StreamReader[1] class, you can convert byte streams to character streams. You use the OutputStreamWriter[2] class to translate character streams into byte streams. The following figure illustrates the conversion process:

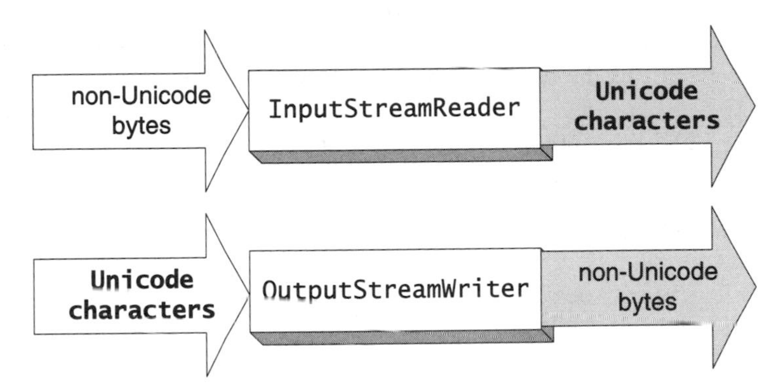

Figure 7 Converting Unicode characters.

When you create InputStreamReader and OutputStreamWriter objects, you specify the byte encoding that you want to convert. For example, to translate a text file in the UTF-8 encoding into Unicode, you create an InputStreamReader as follows:

```
FileInputStream fis = new FileInputStream("test.txt");
InputStreamReader isr = new InputStreamReader(fis, "UTF8");
```

If you omit the encoding identifier, InputStreamReader and OutputStreamWriter rely on the default encoding. You can determine which encoding an InputStreamReader or OutputStreamWriter uses by invoking the getEncoding method, as follows:

```
InputStreamReader defaultReader = new InputStreamReader(fis);
String defaultEncoding = defaultReader.getEncoding();
```

The example that follows shows you how to perform character-set conversions with the InputStreamReader and OutputStreamWriter classes. The full source code for this example is in StreamConverter.java (page 750) in the Appendix. This program displays Japanese characters. Before trying it out, verify that the

---

1 The API documentation is available on the CD-ROM that accompanies this book and online at: http://java.sun.com/products/jdk/1.2/docs/api/java.io.InputStreamReader.html

2 The API documentation is available on the CD-ROM that accompanies this book and online at: http://java.sun.com/products/jdk/1.2/docs/api/java.io.OutputStreamWriter.html

appropriate fonts have been installed on your system. If you are using the JDK software that is compatible with version 1.1, make a copy of the `font.properties` file and then replace it with the `font.properties.ja` file.

The `StreamConverter` program converts a sequence of Unicode characters from a `String` object into a `FileOutputStream` of bytes encoded in UTF-8. The method that performs the conversion is called `writeOutput`:

```
static void writeOutput(String str) {

    try {
        FileOutputStream fos =
                              new FileOutputStream("test.txt");
        Writer out = new OutputStreamWriter(fos, "UTF8");
        out.write(str);
        out.close();
    } catch (IOException e) {
        e.printStackTrace();
    }
}
```

The `readInput` method reads the bytes encoded in UTF-8 from the file created by the `writeOutput` method. An `InputStreamReader` object converts the bytes from UTF-8 into Unicode and returns the result in a `String`. The `readInput` method is as follows:

```
static String readInput() {

    StringBuffer buffer = new StringBuffer();
    try {
        FileInputStream fis = new FileInputStream("test.txt");
        InputStreamReader isr = new InputStreamReader(fis,
                                                          "UTF8");
        Reader in = new BufferedReader(isr);
        int ch;
        while ((ch = in.read()) > -1) {
            buffer.append((char)ch);
        }
        in.close();
        return buffer.toString();
    } catch (IOException e) {
        e.printStackTrace();
        return null;
    }
}
```

The `main` method of the `StreamConverter` program invokes the `writeOutput` method to create a file of bytes encoded in UTF-8. The `readInput` method reads the same file, converting the bytes back into Unicode. Here is the source code for the `main` method:

```
public static void main(String[] args) {

    String jaString =
        new String("\u65e5\u672c\u8a9e\u6587\u5b57\u5217");

    writeOutput(jaString);
    String inputString = readInput();
    String displayString = jaString + " " + inputString;
    new ShowString(displayString, "Conversion Demo");
}
```

The original string (`jaString`) should be identical to the newly created string (`inputString`). To show that the two strings are the same, the program concatenates them and displays them with a `ShowString` object. The `ShowString` class displays a string with the `Graphics.drawString` method. The source code for this class is in <u>`ShowString.java`</u> (page 751) in the Appendix. When the `StreamConverter` program instantiates `ShowString`, the following window appears. The repetition of the characters displayed verifies that the two strings are identical:

Figure 8 The output of the `StreamConverter` program.

About the Author

DALE GREEN is a staff writer with Sun Microsystems, where he documents APIs for the Java programming language. In previous lives he programmed business applications, designed databases, taught technical classes, and documented RDBMS products. In his current incarnation he writes about internationalization and reflection APIs for the Java Tutorial.

Acknowledgments

I'd like to thank the following engineers for their help with foreign languages: AJ Alhait (Arabic), Gilad Bracha (Hebrew), Norbert Lidenberg (German), and Benjamin Renaud (French). The following people provided thoughtful and detailed reviews: Richard Gillam, Waleed Hosny, Doug Kramer, Norbert Lindenberg, and Laura Werner. In their book, *The Java Class Libraries*, *Volume 1*, Patrick Chan and Doug Kramer wrote some terrific code examples that I just had to borrow. And finally, I'm grateful for the suggestions made by our readers on the Internet. It's always a good idea to get advice from the real world.

2D Graphics

by Deborah Adair

THIS trail introduces you to the Java™ 2D API and shows you how to display and print 2D graphics in your Java programs. The Java 2D API enables you to easily

- Draw lines of any thickness
- Fill shapes with gradients and textures
- Move, rotate, scale, and shear text and graphics
- Composite overlapping text and graphics

For example, you could use the Java 2D API to display complex charts and graphs that use various line and fill styles to distinguish sets of data, like those shown in the following figure.

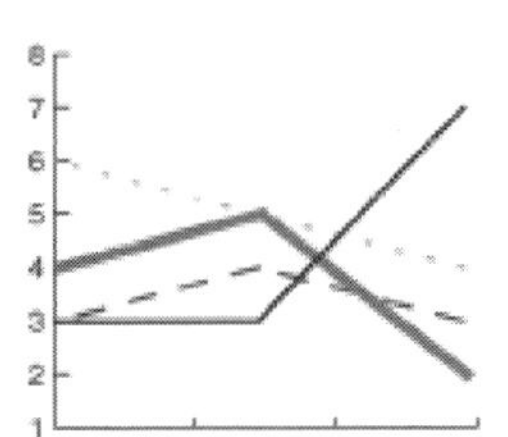

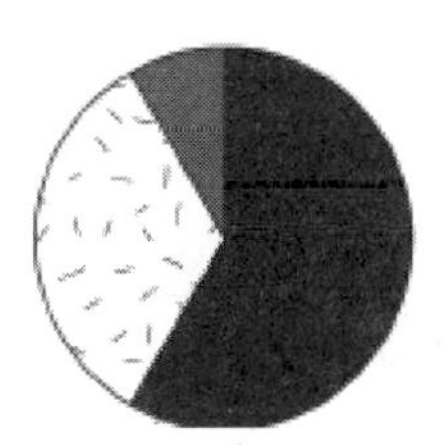

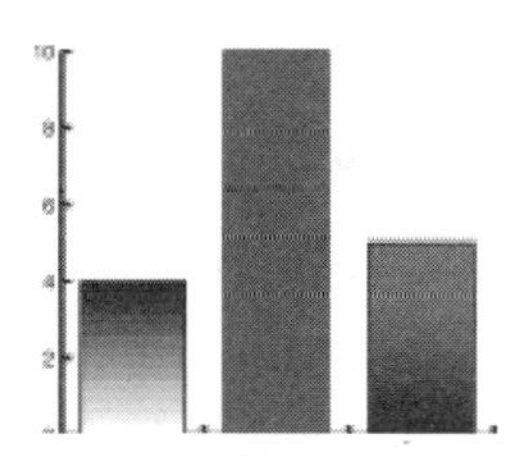

The Java 2D API also enables you to store and to manipulate image data—for example, you can easily perform image-filter operations, such as blur and sharpen, as shown in the following figure.

Image

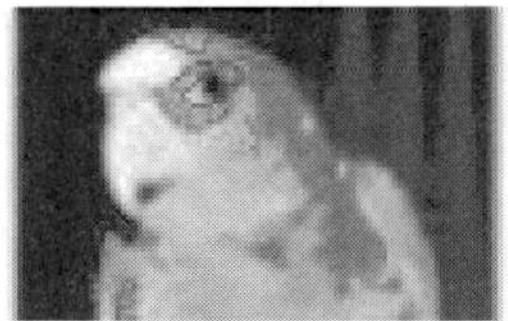

Blur

Sharpen

This trail covers the most common uses of the Java 2D APIs and briefly describes some of the more advanced features. For additional information about using the Java 2D APIs, see the Java 2D Programmer's Guide.[1] Additional sample programs illustrating the Java 2D API features are also available online.[2]

Note: The sample applets in this trail can be run with the JDK™ 1.2 Applet Viewer, a browser with Java Plug-in 1.2 installed, or a JDK 1.2 compatible browser.

The Java 2D APIs are closely integrated with the Abstract Windowing Toolkit (AWT). If you are not familiar with AWT, you might find it useful to review the AWT documentation[3] before reading this trail.

This trail contains the following lessons:

Overview of the Java 2D API (page 177) This lesson introduces the key Java 2D concepts and describes the Java 2D rendering model.

Displaying Graphics with Graphics2D (page 187) In this lesson you learn how to set up the `Graphics2D` rendering context to use fancy stroke and fill styles, perform transformations, clip the drawing region, composite overlapping graphics, and specify rendering preferences.

Manipulating and Displaying Images (page 205) This lesson explains how to implement double buffering and how to perform image-filter operations with `BufferedImage` objects.

Printing (page 211) This last lesson teaches you how to render 2D graphics to a printer and how to print complex documents.

---

[1] http://java.sun.com/products/jdk/1.2/docs/guide/2d/spec/j2d-title.fm.html
[2] http://java.sun.com/products/java-media/2D/samples/index.html
[3] http://java.sun.com/docs/books/tutorial/ui/index.html

http://java.sun.com/docs/books/tutorial/2d/overview/index.html

12 Overview of the Java 2D API

THE Java 2D API introduced in JDK 1.2 provides enhanced two-dimensional graphics, text, and imaging capabilities for Java programs through extensions to the Abstract Windowing Toolkit (AWT). This comprehensive rendering package supports line art, text, and images in a flexible, full-featured framework for developing richer user interfaces, sophisticated drawing programs and image editors.

The Java 2D API provides

- A uniform rendering model for display devices and printers
- A wide range of geometric primitives, such as curves, rectangles, and ellipses and a mechanism for rendering virtually any geometric shape
- Mechanisms for performing hit detection on shapes, text, and images
- A compositing model that provides control over how overlapping objects are rendered
- Enhanced color support that facilitates color management
- Support for printing complex documents

These topics are discussed in the following sections:

Java 2D Rendering

The basic rendering mechanism is the same as in previous versions of the JDK—the drawing system controls when and how programs can draw. When a component needs to be displayed, its `paint` or `update` method is automatically invoked with an appropriate `Graphics` context.

The Java 2D API introduces `java.awt.Graphics2D`,[1] a new type of `Graphics` object. `Graphics2D` extends the `Graphics`[2] class to provide access to the enhanced graphics and rendering features of the Java 2D API.

To use Java 2D API features, you cast the `Graphics` object passed into a component's rendering method to a `Graphics2D` object.

```
public void Paint (Graphics g) {
    Graphics2D g2 = (Graphics2D) g;
    ...
}
```

Graphics2D Rendering Context

The collection of state attributes associated with a `Graphics2D` object is referred to as the `Graphics2D` *rendering context*. To display text, shapes, or images, you set up the `Graphics2D` rendering context and then call one of the `Graphics2D` rendering methods, such as `draw` or `fill`. As the following figure shows, the `Graphics2D` rendering context contains several attributes.

The *pen style* that is applied to the outline of a shape. This *stroke* attribute enables you to draw lines with any point size and dashing pattern and to apply end-cap and join decorations to a line.

The *fill style* that is applied to a shape's interior. This *paint* attribute enables you to fill shapes with solid colors, gradients, and patterns.

---

1 http://java.sun.com/products/jdk/1.2/docs/api/java/awt/Graphics2D.html
2 http://java.sun.com/products/jdk/1.2/docs/api/java/awt/Graphics.html

The *compositing style* that is used when rendered objects overlap existing objects.

The *transform* that is applied during rendering to convert the rendered object from user space to device-space coordinates. Optional translation, rotation, scaling, or shearing transforms can also be applied through this attribute.

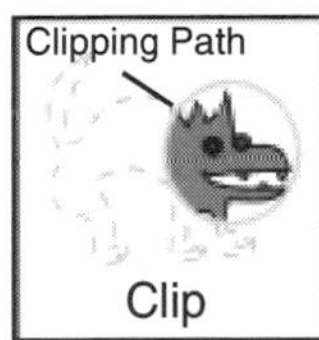

The *clip*, which restricts rendering to the area within the outline of the `Shape` used to define the clipping path. Any `Shape` can be used to define the clip.

Aa
Bb

The *font* used to convert text strings to glyphs.

Rendering hints that specify preferences in the trade-offs between speed and quality. For example, you can specify whether antialiasing should be used, if it's available.

To set an attribute in the `Graphics2D` rendering context, you use the `set`*`Attribute`* methods:

- `setStroke`
- `setPaint`
- `setComposite`
- `setTransform`
- `setClip`
- `setFont`
- `setRenderingHints`

When you set an attribute, you pass in the appropriate attribute object. For example, to change the paint attribute to a blue-green gradient fill, you would construct a `GradientPaint` object and then call `setPaint`.

```
gp = new GradientPaint(0f,0f,blue,0f,30f,green);
g2.setPaint(gp);
```

`Graphics2D` holds *references* to its attribute objects—they are not cloned. If you alter an attribute object that is part of the `Graphics2D` context, you need to call the appropriate `set` method to notify the context. Modifying an attribute object during rendering causes unpredictable behavior.

Graphics2D Rendering Methods

`Graphics2D` provides the following general rendering methods that can be used to draw any geometry primitive, text, or image:

- `draw`—renders the outline of any geometry primitive, using the stroke and paint attributes.
- `fill`—renders any geometry primitive by filling its interior with the color or pattern specified by the paint attribute.
- `drawString`—renders any text string. The font attribute is used to convert the string to glyphs, which are then filled with the color or pattern specified by the paint attribute.
- `drawImage`—renders the specified image.

In addition, `Graphics2D` supports the `Graphics` rendering methods for particular shapes, such as `drawOval` and `fillRect`.

Coordinate Systems

The Java 2D system maintains two coordinate spaces.

- *User space* is the space in which graphics primitives are specified.
- *Device spac*e is the coordinate system of an output device, such as a screen, window, or a printer.

User space is a device-independent logical coordinate system: the coordinate space that your program uses. All geometries passed into Java 2D rendering routines are specified in user-space coordinates.

When the default transformation from user space to device space is used, the origin of user space is the upper-left corner of the component's drawing area. The *x* coordinate increases to the right, and the *y* coordinate increases downward, as shown in the following figure.

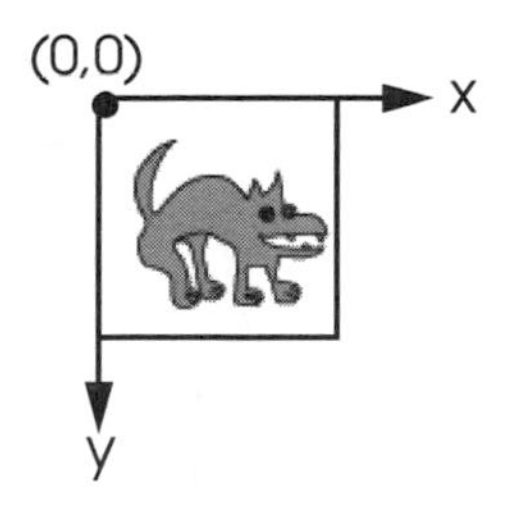

Figure 9 User space.

Device space is a device-dependent coordinate system that varies according to the target rendering device. Although the coordinate system for a window or the screen might be very different from that of a printer, these differences are invisible to Java programs. The necessary conversions between user space and device space are performed automatically during rendering.

Shapes

The classes in the `java.awt.geom` package define common graphics primitives, such as points, lines, curves, arcs, rectangles, and ellipses.

Table 16 Classes in the `java.awt.geom` Package

`Arc2D`	`Ellipse2D`	`QuadCurve2D`
`Area`	`GeneralPath`	`Rectangle2D`
`CubicCurve2D`	`Line2D`	`RectangularShape`
`Dimension2D`	`Point2D`	`RoundRectangle2D`

Except for `Point2D` and `Dimension2D`, each of the geometry classes (*geometries*) implements the `Shape` interface, which provides a common set of methods for describing and inspecting two-dimensional geometric objects.

With these classes you can create virtually any geometric shape and render it through `Graphics2D` by calling the `draw` method or the `fill` method. For example, the geometric shapes in the following `ShapesDemo2D` applet are defined by using basic Java 2D geometries as shown in Figure 10.

If you're curious, the code for this program, `ShapesDemo2D.java` (page 753), is in the Appendix. How to draw and fill shapes is described in the next lesson, Displaying Graphics with Graphics2D (page 187).

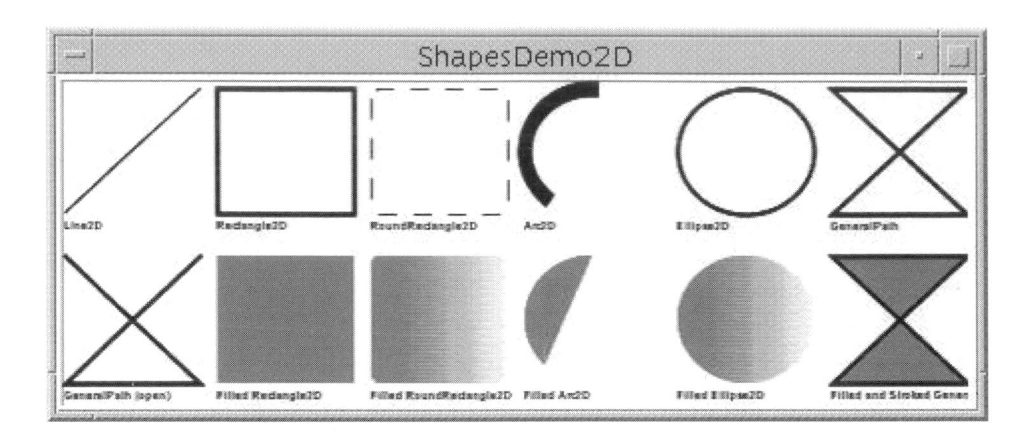

Figure 10 The `ShapesDemo2D` applet.

Rectangular Shapes

The `Rectangle2D`, `RoundRectangle2D`, `Arc2D`, and `Ellipse2D` primitives are all derived from `RectangularShape`, which defines methods for `Shape` objects that can be described by a rectangular bounding box. The geometry of a `RectangularShape` can be extrapolated from a rectangle that completely encloses the outline of the `Shape`.

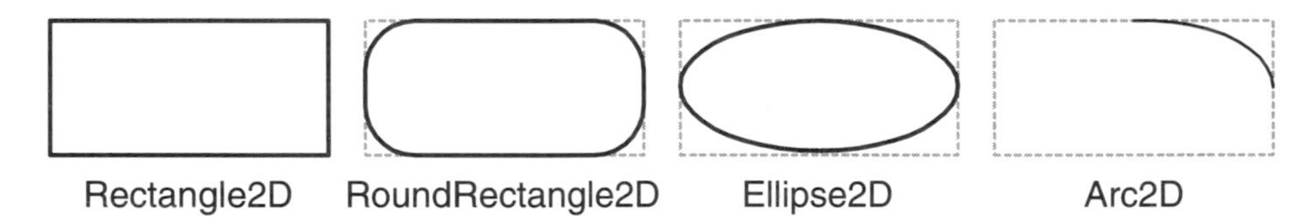

Figure 11 Primitives derived from `RectangularShape`.

GeneralPath

The `GeneralPath` class enables you to construct an arbitrary shape by specifying a series of positions along the shape's boundary. These positions can be connected by line segments, quadratic curves, or cubic (Bézier) curves.

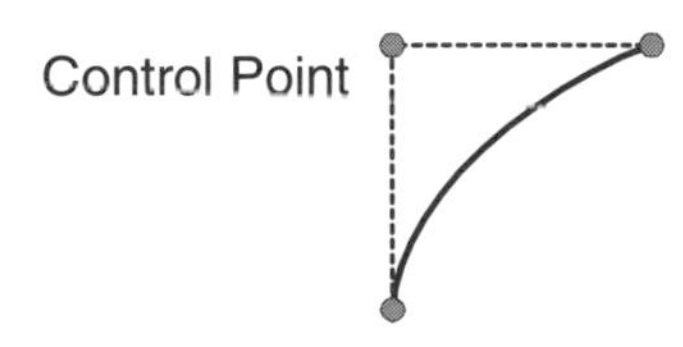

Figure 12 A *quadratic curve* can be defined by two end points and one control point.

Figure 13 A *cubic (Bezier) curve* is defined by four points: two end points, and two control points.

Areas

With the `Area` class you can perform boolean operations, such as union, intersection, and subtraction, on any two `Shape` objects. This technique, often referred to as constructive area geometry, enables you to quickly create complex `Shape` objects without having to describe each line segment or curve.

Text

When you need to display text, you can use one of the text-oriented components, such as the Swing label[1] or text[2] components. When you use a text component, a lot of the work is done for you—for example, `JTextComponent` objects provide built-in support for hit testing and displaying international text.

If you just want to draw a static text string, you can render it directly through `Graphics2D` by using the `drawString` method. To specify the font, you use the `Graphics2D` `setFont` method.

If you want to implement your own text-editing routines or need more control over the layout of the text than the text components provide, you can use the Java 2D text layout classes in `java.awt.font`.

Fonts

The shapes that a font uses to represent the characters in a string are called *glyphs*. A particular character or combination of characters might be represented as one or more glyphs. For example, *á* might be represented by two glyphs, whereas the ligature *fi* might be represented by a single glyph.

---

1 http://java.sun.com/docs/books/tutorial/ui/swing/label.html
2 http://java.sun.com/docs/books/tutorialui/swing/text.html

A *font* can be thought of as a collection of glyphs. A single font might have many *faces*, such as heavy, medium, oblique, gothic, and regular. All of the faces in a font have similar typographic features and can be recognized as members of the same *family*. In other words, a collection of glyphs with a particular style form a *font face*; a collection of font faces forms a *font family*; and the collection of font families forms the set fonts available on the system.

When you're using the Java 2D API, you specify fonts by using an instance of `Font`. You can determine what fonts are available by calling the static method `GraphicsEnvironment.getLocalGraphicsEnvironment` and then querying the returned `GraphicsEnvironment`. The `getAllFonts` method returns an array that contains `Font` instances for all of the fonts available on the system; `getAvailableFontFamilyNames` returns a list of the available font families.

The `GraphicsEnvironment` also describes the collection of platform rendering devices, such as screens and printers, that a Java program can use. This information is used when the system performs the conversion from user space to device space during rendering.

Note: In JDK 1.1 fonts were described by logical names that mapped onto different font faces, depending on the fonts that were available on a particular platform. For backward compatibility, `Graphics2D` also supports the specification of fonts by logical name. To get a list of the logical font names, call `java.awt.Toolkit.getFontList`.

Text Layout

Before text can be displayed, it must be laid out so that the characters are represented by the appropriate glyphs in the proper positions. If you are using Swing, you can let `JLabel` or `JTextComponent` manage text layout for you. `JTextComponent` supports bidirectional text and is designed to handle the needs of most international applications. For more information about using Swing text components, see How to Use Text Components.[1]

If you are not using a Swing text component to automatically display text, you can use one of two Java 2D mechanisms for managing text layout.

- If you want to implement your own text-editing routines, you can use the `TextLayout` class to manage text layout, highlighting, and hit detection. The facilities provided by `TextLayout` handle most common cases, including strings with mixed fonts, mixed languages, and bidirectional text. For

---

[1] http://java.sun.com/docs/books/tutorial/ui/swing/text.html

more information about `TextLayout`, see Managing Text Layout[1] in the *Java 2D Programmer's Guide*.

- If you want total control over how text is shaped and positioned, you can construct your own `GlyphVector` objects by using `Font` and then render each `GlyphVector` through `Graphics2D`. For more information about implementing your own text layout mechanisms, see Implementing a Custom Text Layout Mechanism[2] in the *Java 2D Programmer's Guide*.

Images

The Java 2D API implements a new imaging model that supports the manipulation of fixed-resolution images stored in memory. A new `Image` class in the `java.awt.image` package, `BufferedImage`, can be used to hold and to manipulate image data retrieved from a file or a URL. For example, a `BufferedImage` can be used to implement double buffering—the graphic elements are rendered off-screen to the `BufferedImage` and are then copied to the screen through a call to `Graphics2D drawImage`. The classes `BufferedImage` and `BufferedImageOp` also enable you to perform a variety of image-filtering operations, such as blur and sharpen. The producer/consumer imaging model provided in previous versions of the JDK is supported for backward compatibility.

Printing

All of the AWT and Java 2D graphics, including composited graphics and images, can be rendered to a printer by using the Java 2D Printing API. This API also provides document composition features that enable you to perform such operations as changing the order in which pages are printed.

Rendering to a printer is like rendering to the screen. The printing system controls when pages are rendered, just like the drawing system controls when a component is painted on the screen.

Your application provides the printing system with information about the document to be printed, and the printing system determines when each page needs to be imaged. When pages need to be imaged, the printing system calls your application's `print` method with an appropriate `Graphics` context. To use Java 2D API features when you print, you cast the `Graphics` object to a `Graphics2D`, just like you do when you're rendering to the screen.

---

[1] http://java.sun.com/products/jdk/1.2/docs/guide/2d/spec/j2d-fonts.fm4.html

[2] http://java.sun.com/products/jdk/1.2/docs/guide/2d/spec/j2d-fonts.fm5.html

http://java.sun.com/docs/books/tutorial/2d/display/index.html

13 Displaying Graphics with Graphics2D

THIS lesson shows you how to use `Graphics2D` to display graphics with fancy outline and fill styles, transform graphics when they are rendered, constrain rendering to a particular area, and generally control the way graphics look when they are rendered. You'll also learn how to create complex `Shape` objects by combining simple ones and how to detect when the user clicks on a displayed graphics primitive. These topics are discussed in the following sections:

Supporting User Interaction (page 202)
This section shows you how to perform hit detection on graphics primitives.

Stroking and Filling Graphics Primitives

By changing the stroke and paint attributes in the `Graphics2D` context before rendering, you can easily apply fancy line styles and fill patterns to graphics primitives. For example, you can draw a dashed line by creating an appropriate `Stroke` object and calling `setStroke` to add it to the `Graphics2D` context before you render the line. Similarly, you can apply a gradient fill to a `Shape` by creating a `GradientPaint` object and adding it to the `Graphics2D` context by calling `setPaint` before you render the `Shape`.

The `ShapesDemo2D` applet introduced in the lesson Overview of the Java 2D API (page 177) demonstrates how you can render basic geometries by using the `Graphics2D` `draw` and `fill` methods. Each of the shapes is constructed from one of the geometries and is then rendered through `Graphics2D`. The `rectHeight` and `rectWidth` variables in this example define the dimensions of the space where each shape is drawn, in pixels. The *x* and *y* variables change for each shape so that they are drawn in a grid formation.

```
// draw Line2D.Double
g2.draw(new Line2D.Double(x, y+rectHeight-1,
                          x + rectWidth, y));
```

```
// draw Rectangle2D.Double
g2.setStroke(stroke);
g2.draw(new Rectangle2D.Double(x, y,
                               rectWidth,
                                 rectHeight));
```

```
// draw RoundRectangle2D.Double
g2.setStroke(dashed);
g2.draw(new RoundRectangle2D.Double(x, y,
                                    rectWidth,
                                  rectHeight,
                                    10, 10));
```

```
// draw Arc2D.Double
g2.setStroke(wideStroke);
g2.draw(new Arc2D.Double(x, y,
                         rectWidth,
                         rectHeight,
                         90, 135,
                           Arc2D.OPEN));
```

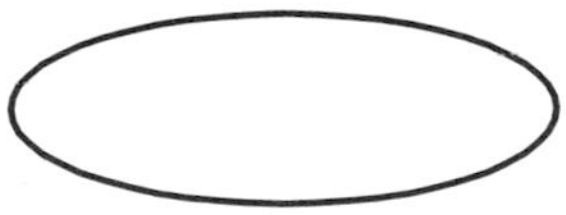

```
// draw Ellipse2D.Double
g2.setStroke(stroke);
g2.draw(new Ellipse2D.Double(x, y,
                             rectWidth,
                               rectHeight));
```

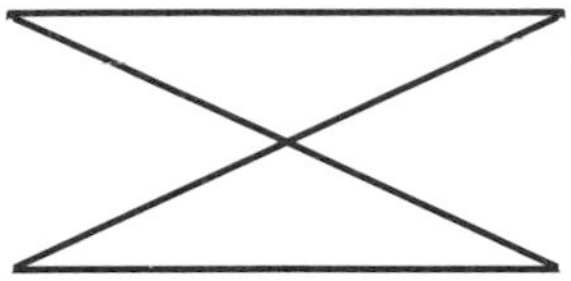

```
// draw GeneralPath (polygon)
int x1Points[] = {x, x+rectWidth,
                  x, x+rectWidth};
int y1Points[] = {y, y+rectHeight,
                  y+rectHeight, y};
GeneralPath polygon = new
        GeneralPath(GeneralPath.WIND_EVEN_ODD,
                    x1Points.length);
polygon.moveTo(x1Points[0], y1Points[0]);
for (int index = 1;
     index < x1Points.length;
     index++) {
        polygon.lineTo(x1Points[index],
                       y1Points[index]);
};
polygon.closePath();
g2.draw(polygon);
```

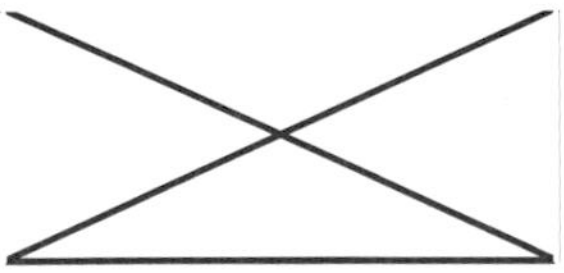

```
// draw GeneralPath (polyline)
int x2Points[] = {x, x+rectWidth, x,
                  x+rectWidth};
int y2Points[] = {y, y+rectHeight,
                  y+rectHeight, y};
GeneralPath polyline = new
        GeneralPath(GeneralPath.WIND_EVEN_ODD,
                    x2Points.length);
polyline.moveTo (x2Points[0], y2Points[0]);
for (int index = 1;
     index < x2Points.length;
      index++) {
        polyline.lineTo(x2Points[index],
         y2Points[index]);
};
g2.draw(polyline);
```

```
// fill Rectangle2D.Double (red)
g2.setPaint(red);
g2.fill(new Rectangle2D.Double(x, y,
        rectWidth, rectHeight));
```

```
// fill RoundRectangle2D.Double
g2.setPaint(redtowhite);
g2.fill(new RoundRectangle2D.Double(x, y,
                                    rectWidth,
                                  rectHeight,
                                    10, 10));
```

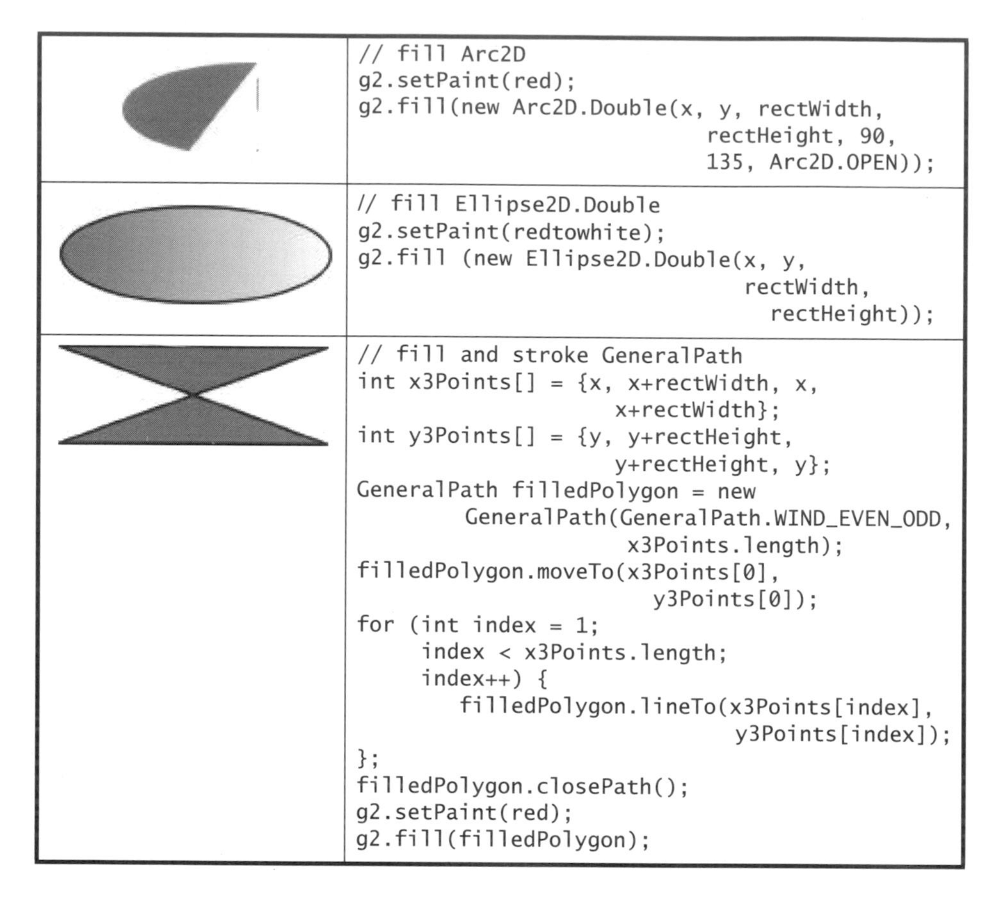

```
// fill Arc2D
g2.setPaint(red);
g2.fill(new Arc2D.Double(x, y, rectWidth,
                         rectHeight, 90,
                         135, Arc2D.OPEN));
```

```
// fill Ellipse2D.Double
g2.setPaint(redtowhite);
g2.fill (new Ellipse2D.Double(x, y,
                              rectWidth,
                                rectHeight));
```

```
// fill and stroke GeneralPath
int x3Points[] = {x, x+rectWidth, x,
                    x+rectWidth};
int y3Points[] = {y, y+rectHeight,
                    y+rectHeight, y};
GeneralPath filledPolygon = new
        GeneralPath(GeneralPath.WIND_EVEN_ODD,
                    x3Points.length);
filledPolygon.moveTo(x3Points[0],
                      y3Points[0]);
for (int index = 1;
     index < x3Points.length;
     index++) {
        filledPolygon.lineTo(x3Points[index],
                             y3Points[index]);
};
filledPolygon.closePath();
g2.setPaint(red);
g2.fill(filledPolygon);
```

Note that this example uses the double-precision implementations of the geometries classes. Where applicable, float and double-precision implementations of each of the geometries are provided as inner classes.

The complete code for `ShapesDemo2D.java` (page 753) is in the Appendix.

Defining Fancy Line Styles and Fill Patterns

You probably noticed that in the previous example some of the shapes have thicker outlines or are filled with a two-color gradient. Using the Java 2D `Stroke` and `Paint` classes, you can easily define fancy line styles and fill patterns.

Line Styles

Line styles are defined by the stroke attribute in the `Graphics2D` rendering context. To set the stroke attribute, you create a `BasicStroke` object and pass it into the `Graphics2D` `setStroke` method.

A `BasicStroke` object holds information about the line width, join style, end-cap style, and dash style. This information is used when a `Shape` is rendered with the `draw` method.

The *line width* is the thickness of the line measured perpendicular to its trajectory. The line width is specified as a `float` value in user coordinate units, which are roughly equivalent to 1/72 inch when the default transform is used.

The *join style* is the decoration that is applied where two line segments meet. `BasicStroke` supports three join styles:

`JOIN_BEVEL`

`JOIN_MITER`

`JOIN_ROUND`

The *end-cap style* is the decoration that is applied where a line segment ends. `BasicStroke` supports three end-cap styles:

`CAP_BUTT`

`CAP_ROUND`

`CAP_SQUARE`

The *dash style* defines the pattern of opaque and transparent sections applied along the length of the line. The dash style is defined by a dash array and a dash phase. The *dash array* defines the dash pattern. Alternating elements in the array represent the dash length and the length of the space between dashes in user coordinate units. Element 0 represents the first dash, element 1 the first space, and so on. The *dash phase* is an offset into the dash pattern, also specified in user coordinate units. The dash phase indicates what part of the dash pattern is applied to the beginning of the line.

Fill Patterns

Fill patterns are defined by the paint attribute in the `Graphics2D` rendering context. To set the paint attribute, you create an instance of an object that implements the `Paint` interface and pass it into the `Graphics2D setPaint` method.

Three classes implement the `Paint` interface: `Color`, `GradientPaint`, and `TexturePaint`. `GradientPaint` and `TexturePaint` are new in JDK 1.2.

To create a `GradientPaint`, you specify a beginning position and color and an ending position and color. The gradient changes proportionally from one color to the other along the line connecting the two positions.

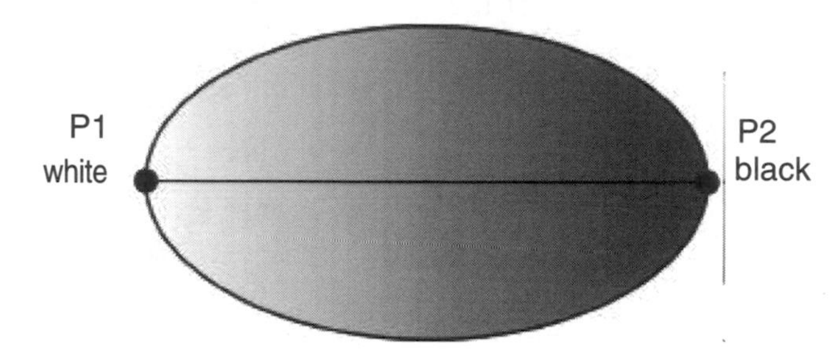

Figure 14 Using `GradientPaint`, the color gradually changes from black at point P2 to white at point P1.

The pattern for a `TexturePaint` is defined by a `BufferedImage`. To create a `TexturePaint`, you specify the image that contains the pattern and a rectangle that is used to replicate and anchor the pattern.

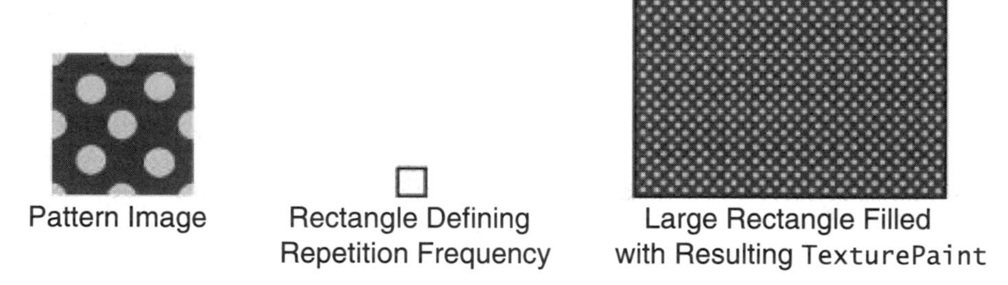

Figure 15 An example demonstrating the use of `TexturePaint`.

Example: StrokeAndFill

The `StrokeAndFill` program allows the user to select a graphics primitive, a line style, and a paint style and to either stroke the object's outline, fill it with the selected paint, or stroke the object in black and then fill it with the selected paint. You can see the applet in action on the CD-ROM that accompanies this book and online here:

```
http://java.sun.com/docs/books/tutorial/2d/display/
example-1dot2/StrokeAndFill.html
```

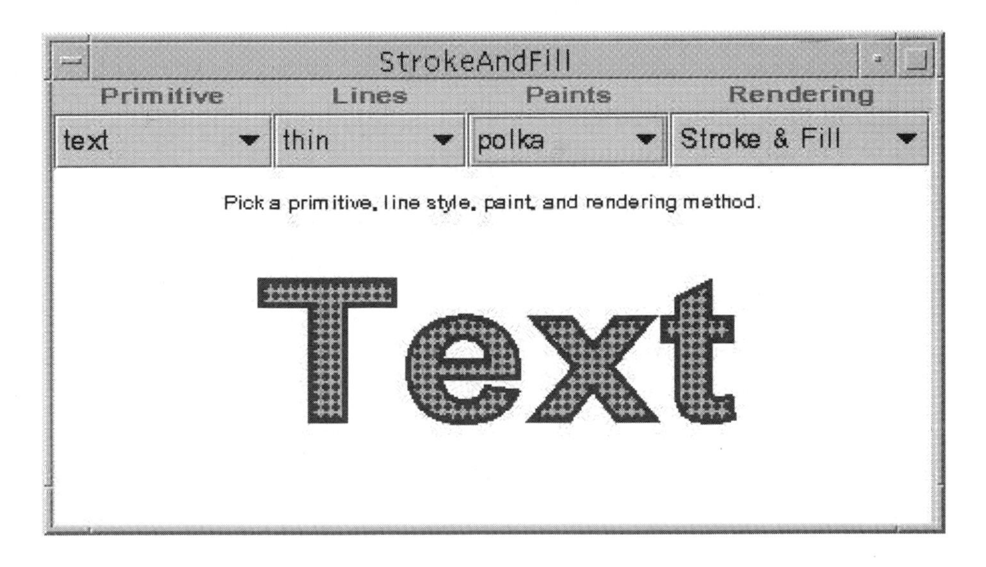

Figure 16 The `StrokeAndFill` applet.

How rendering is performed depends on which rendering option is chosen.

- When the user chooses *stroke*, `Graphics2D.draw` is called to perform the rendering. If *text* is chosen as the primitive, the glyph outlines are retrieved and then rendered with the `draw` method.
- When the user chooses *fill*, `Graphics2D.fill` or `Graphics2D.drawString` is called to perform the rendering.
- When the user chooses *stroke and fill*, `fill` or `drawString` is called to fill the `Shape`, and then `draw` is called to stroke its outline.

Note: To both fill and stroke a graphics primitive, you need to make two separate method calls: `fill` or `drawString` to fill its interior and `draw` to stroke its outline.

The three line styles used in this example—thin, thick, and dashed—are instances of `BasicStroke`.

```
// Sets the Stroke.
...
case 0 : g2.setStroke(new BasicStroke(3.0f)); break;
case 1 : g2.setStroke(new BasicStroke(8.0f)); break;
case 2 : float dash[] = {10.0f};
         g2.setStroke(newBasicStroke(3.0f,BasicStroke.CAP_BUTT,
            BasicStroke.JOIN_MITER, 10.0f, dash, 0.0f)); break;
```

The dash style in this example has 10 unit dashes alternating with 10 unit spaces. The beginning of the dash pattern is applied to the beginning of the line—the dash phase is set to 0.0.

Three paint styles are used in this example—solid, gradient, and polka. The solid-color paint style is an instance of `Color`, the gradient an instance of `GradientPaint`, and the pattern an instance of `TexturePaint`.

```
// Sets the Paint.
...
case 0 : g2.setPaint(Color.blue); break;
case 1 : g2.setPaint(new GradientPaint(0, 0, Color.lightGray,
                            w-250, h, Color.blue, false));
         break;
case 2 : BufferedImage bi = new BufferedImage(5, 5,
                                   BufferedImage.TYPE_INT_RGB);
         Graphics2D big = bi.createGraphics();
         big.setColor(Color.blue);
         big.fillRect(0, 0, 5, 5);
         big.setColor(Color.lightGray);
         big.fillOval(0, 0, 5, 5);
         Rectangle r = new Rectangle(0,0,5,5);
         g2.setPaint(new TexturePaint(bi, r));
         break;
```

You can find the full code for `StrokeAndFill.java` (page 759) in the Appendix.

Transforming Shapes, Text, and Images

You can modify the transform attribute in the `Graphics2D` context to move, rotate, scale, and shear graphics primitives when they are rendered. The transform attribute is defined by an instance of `AffineTransform`. (An affine transform is a transformation such as translate, rotate, scale, or shear in which parallel lines remain parallel even after being transformed.)

`Graphics2D` provides several methods for changing the transform attribute. You can construct a new `AffineTransform` and change the `Graphics2D` transform attribute by calling `setTransform`.

`AffineTransform` defines the following factory methods to make it easier to construct new transforms:

- `getRotateInstance`
- `getScaleInstance`

- `getShearInstance`
- `getTranslateInstance`

Alternatively you can use one of the `Graphics2D` transformation methods to modify the current transform. When you call one of these convenience methods, the resulting transform is concatenated with the current transform and is applied during rendering:

- `rotate`—to specify an angle of rotation in radians
- `scale`—to specify a scaling factor in the *x* and *y* directions
- `shear`—to specify a shearing factor in the *x* and *y* directions
- `translate`—to specify a translation offset in the *x* and *y* directions

You can also construct an `AffineTransform` directly and concatenate it with the current transform by calling the `transform` method.

The `drawImage` method is also overloaded to allow you to specify an `AffineTransform` that is applied to the image as it is rendered. Specifying a transform when you call `drawImage` does not affect the `Graphics2D` transform attribute.

Example: Transform

The following program is the same as `StrokeandFill`, but also allows the user to choose a transformation to apply to the selected object when it is rendered.

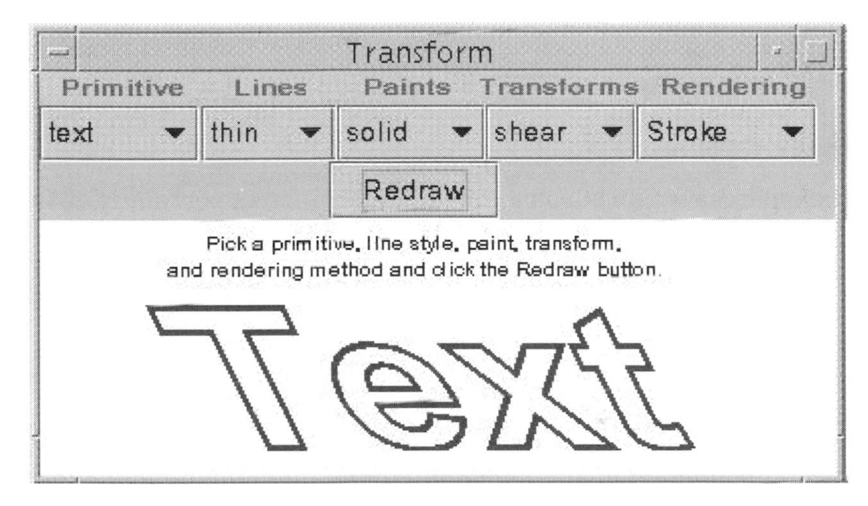

Figure 17 The `Transform` applet can be see in action on the CD-ROM that accompanies this book and online here: `http://java.sun.com/docs/books/tutorial/2d/display/example-1dot2/Transform.html`.

When a transform option is chosen, an instance of `AffineTransform` *at* is modified and is then concatenated with a translation transform that moves the `Shape` to the center of the window. The resulting transform is then passed to the `setTransform` method to set the `Graphics2D` transform attribute.

```
switch (Transform.trans.getSelectedIndex()){
case 0 : at.setToIdentity();
at.translate(w/2, h/2); break;
case 1 : at.rotate(Math.toRadians(45)); break;
case 2 : at.scale(0.5, 0.5); break;
case 3 : at.shear(0.5, 0.0); break;
...
AffineTransform toCenterAt = new AffineTransform();
toCenterAt.concatenate(at);
toCenterAt.translate(-(r.width/2), -(r.height/2));
g2.setTransform(toCenterAt);
```

You can find the full code for Transform.java (page 764) in the Appendix.

Clipping the Drawing Region

Any `Shape` can be used as a clipping path that restricts the portion of the drawing area that will rendered. The clipping path is part of the `Graphics2D` context; to set the clip attribute, you call `Graphics2D.setClip` and pass in the `Shape` that defines the clipping path you want to use. You can shrink the clipping path by calling the `clip` method and passing in another `Shape`; the clip is set to the intersection of the current clip and the specified `Shape`.

Example: ClipImage

This example animates a clipping path to reveal different portions of an image.

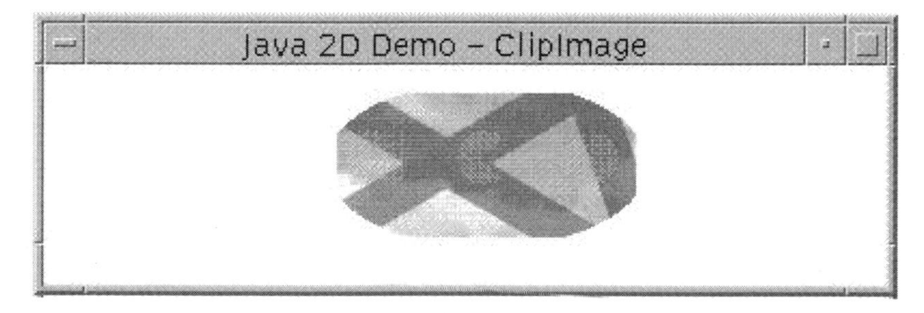

Figure 18 The `ClipImage` applet can be see in action on the CD-ROM that accompanies this book and online here: `http://java.sun.com/docs/books/tutorial/2d/display/example-1dot2/ClipImage.html`.

The clipping path is defined by the intersection of an ellipse and a rectangle whose dimensions are set randomly. The ellipse is passed to the `setClip` method, and then `clip` is called to set the clipping path to the intersection of the ellipse and the rectangle.

```
private Ellipse2D ellipse = new Ellipse2D.Float();
private Rectangle2D rect = new Rectangle2D.Float();
...
ellipse.setFrame(x, y, ew, eh);
g2.setClip(ellipse);
rect.setRect(x+5, y+5, ew-10, eh-10);
g2.clip(rect);
```

The complete code for this program, ClipImage.java (page 771), can be found in the Appendix.

Compositing Graphics

The `AlphaComposite` class encapsulates various compositing styles, which determine how overlapping objects are rendered. An `AlphaComposite` can also have an alpha value that specifies the degree of transparency: alpha = 1.0 is totally opaque, alpha = 0.0 totally transparent (clear). `AlphaComposite` supports most of the standard Porter-Duff compositing rules shown in the following table.

Source-over (`SRC_OVER`) Source Destination	If pixels in the object being rendered (the source) have the same location as previously rendered pixels (the destination), the source pixels are rendered over the destination pixels.
Source-in (`SRC_IN`)	If pixels in the source and the destination overlap, only the source pixels in the overlapping area are rendered.
Source-out (`SRC_OUT`) Source Destination	If pixels in the source and the destination overlap, only the source pixels outside of the overlapping area are rendered. The pixels in the overlapping area are cleared.
Destination-over (`DST_OVER`) Source Destination	If pixels in the source and the destination overlap, only the source pixels outside of the overlapping area are rendered. The pixels in the overlapping area are not changed.
Destination-in (`DST_IN`)	If pixels in the source and the destination overlap, the alpha from the source is applied to the destination pixels in the overlapping area. If the alpha = 1.0, the pixels in the overlapping area are unchanged; if the alpha is 0.0, pixels in the overlapping area are cleared.

Destination-out (DST_OUT)	If pixels in the source and the destination overlap, the alpha from the source is applied to the destination pixels in the overlapping area. If the alpha = 1.0, the pixels in the overlapping area are cleared; if the alpha is 0.0, the pixels in the overlapping area are unchanged.
Clear (CLEAR)	If the pixels in the source and the destination overlap, the pixels in the overlapping area are cleared.

To change the compositing style used by `Graphics2D`, you create an `AlphaComposite` object and pass it into the `setComposite` method.

Example: Composite

This program illustrates the effects of various compositing style and alpha combinations.

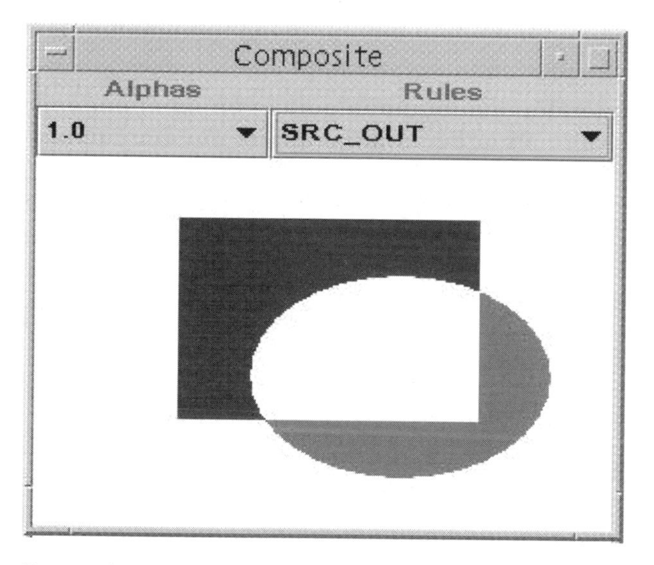

Figure 19 The Composite applet can be found on this book's CD-ROM and online here: `http://java.sun.com/docs/books/tutorial/2d/display/example-1dot2/Composite.html`.

A new `AlphaComposite` object *ac* is constructed by calling `AlphaComposite.getInstance` and specifying the desired compositing rule.

```
AlphaComposite ac =
                AlphaComposite.getInstance(AlphaComposite.SRC);
```

When a different compositing rule or alpha value is selected, AlphaComposite.getInstance is called again, and the new AlphaComposite is assigned to *ac*. The selected alpha is applied in addition to the per-pixel alpha value and is passed as a second parameter to AlphaComposite.getInstance.

```
ac = AlphaComposite.getInstance(getRule(rule), alpha);
```

The composite attribute is modified by passing the AlphaComposite object to Graphics 2D setComposite. The objects are rendered into a BufferedImage and are later copied to the screen, so the composite attribute is set on the Graphics2D context for the BufferedImage:

```
BufferedImage buffImg = new BufferedImage(w, h,
                              BufferedImage.TYPE_INT_ARGB);
Graphics2D gbi = buffImg.createGraphics();
...
gbi.setComposite(ac);
```

You can find the full code for Composite.java (page 775) in the Appendix.

Controlling Rendering Quality

You can use the Graphics2D rendering hints attribute to specify whether you want objects to be rendered as quickly as possible or whether you prefer that the rendering quality be as high as possible.

To set or change the rendering hints attribute in the Graphics2D context, you can construct a RenderingHints object and pass it into Graphics2D setRenderingHints. If you just want to set one hint, you can call Graphics2D setRenderingHint and specify the key-value pair for the hint you want to set. (The key-value pairs are defined in the RenderingHints class.)

For example, to set a preference for antialiasing to be used if possible, you could use setRenderingHint:

```
g2.setRenderingHint(RenderingHints.KEY_ANTIALIASING,aliasing);
```

Note: Not all platforms support modification of the rendering mode, so specifying rendering hints does not guarantee that they will be used.

RenderingHints supports the following types of hints:

- Alpha interpolation—default, quality, or speed
- Antialiasing—default, on, or off

- Color rendering–default, quality, or speed
- Dithering—default, disable, or enable
- Fractional metrics—default, on, or off
- Interpolation—nearest-neighbor, bilinear, or bicubic
- Rendering—default, quality, or speed
- Text antialiasing—default, on, or off

When a hint is set to default, the platform rendering default is used is used.

Constructing Complex Shapes from Geometry Primitives

Constructive area geometry (CAG) is the process of creating new geometric shapes by performing boolean operations on existing ones. In the Java 2D API a special type of `Shape` called an `Area` supports boolean operations. You can construct an `Area` from any `Shape`.

`Areas` support the following boolean operations:

Example: Areas

In this example `Area` objects construct a pear shape from several ellipses.

Figure 20 The Pear applet is available on this book's CD-ROM and online here: `http://java.sun.com/docs/books/tutorial/2d/display/example-1dot2/Pear.html`

The leaves are each created by performing an intersection on two overlapping circles.

```
leaf = new Ellipse2D.Double();
...
leaf1 = new Area(leaf);
leaf2 = new Area(leaf);
...
leaf.setFrame(ew-16, eh-29, 15.0, 15.0);
leaf1 = new Area(leaf);
leaf.setFrame(ew-14, eh-47, 30.0, 30.0);
leaf2 = new Area(leaf);
leaf1.intersect(leaf2);
g2.fill(leaf1);
...
leaf.setFrame(ew+1, eh-29, 15.0, 15.0);
leaf1 = new Area(leaf);
leaf2.intersect(leaf1);
g2.fill(leaf2);
```

Overlapping circles are also used to construct the stem through a subtraction operation.

```
stem = new Ellipse2D.Double();
...
stem.setFrame(ew, eh-42, 40.0, 40.0);
st1 = new Area(stem);
stem.setFrame(ew+3, eh-47, 50.0, 50.0);
st2 = new Area(stem);
st1.subtract(st2);
g2.fill(st1);
```

The body of the pear is constructed by performing a union operation on a circle and an oval.

```
circle = new Ellipse2D.Double();
oval = new Ellipse2D.Double();
circ = new Area(circle);
ov = new Area(oval);
...
circle.setFrame(ew-25, eh, 50.0, 50.0);
oval.setFrame(ew-19, eh-20, 40.0, 70.0);
circ = new Area(circle);
ov = new Area(oval);
circ.add(ov);
g2.fill(circ);
```

You can find the complete code for `Pear.java` (page 779) in the Appendix.

Supporting User Interaction

To allow the user to interact with the graphics you display, you need to be able to determine when the user clicks on one of them. The `Graphics2D` `hit` method provides a way for you to easily determine whether a mouse click occurred over a particular `Shape`. Alternatively you can get the location of the mouse click and call `contains` on the `Shape` to determine whether the click was within the bounds of the `Shape`.

If you are using primitive text, you can perform simple hit testing by getting the outline `Shape` that corresponds to the text and then calling `hit` or `contains` with that `Shape`. Supporting text editing requires much more sophisticated hit testing. If you want to allow the user to edit text, you should generally use one of the Swing editable text components. If you are working with primitive text and are using `TextLayout` to manage the shaping and positioning of the text, you can also use `TextLayout` to perform hit testing for text editing. For more information see the chapter Text and Fonts in the *Java 2D Programmer's Guide*.[1]

Example: ShapeMover

This applet allows the user to drag a `Shape` around within the applet window. The `Shape` is redrawn at every mouse location to provide feedback as the user drags it.

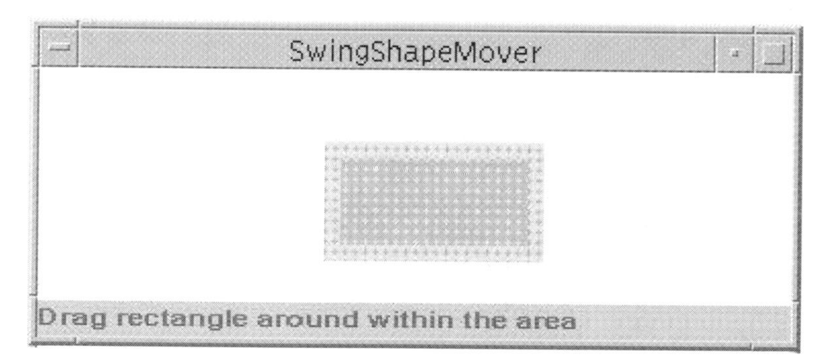

Figure 21 The SwingShapeMover applet is available on this book's CD-ROM and online:
`http://java.sun.com/docs/books/tutorial/2d/display/example-1dot2/SwingShapeMover.html`.

[1] http://java.sun.com/products/jdk/1.2/docs/guide/2d/spec/j2d-fonts.fm.html

The `contains` method is called to determine whether the cursor is within the bounds of the rectangle when the mouse is pressed. If it is, the location of the rectangle is updated.

```
public void mousePressed(MouseEvent e){
    last_x = rect.x - e.getX();
    last_y = rect.y - e.getY();
    if(rect.contains(e.getX(), e.getY())) updateLocation(e);
...

public void updateLocation(MouseEvent e){
    rect.setLocation(last_x + e.getX(), last_y + e.getY());
    ...
    repaint();
```

You can see the complete code for this program, `ShapeMover.java` (page 782), in the Appendix.

You might notice that redrawing the `Shape` at every mouse location is slow, because the filled rectangle is rerendered every time it is moved. Using double buffering can eliminate this problem. If you use Swing, the drawing will be double buffered automatically; you don't have to change the rendering code at all. The code for a Swing version of this program is `SwingShapeMover.java` (page 786) in the Appendix.

If you're not using Swing, the Example: BufferedShapeMover (page 209) section in the next lesson shows how you can implement double buffering by using a `BufferedImage`. You render into the `BufferedImage` and then copy the image to the screen.

http://java.sun.com/docs/books/tutorial/2d/images/index.html

14 Manipulating and Displaying Images

THIS lesson shows you how to perform filter operations on `BufferedImages` and how to use a `BufferedImage` as an off-screen buffer. This lesson contains the following sections.

Immediate-Mode Imaging with BufferedImage

The immediate-mode imaging model enables you to manipulate and display pixel-mapped images whose data is stored in memory. You can access image data in a variety of formats and use several types of filtering operations to manipulate the data.

BufferedImage is the key class in the immediate-mode imaging API. This class manages an image in memory and provides methods for storing, interpreting, and rendering the pixel data. A BufferedImage can be rendered through either a Graphics or a Graphics2D rendering context.

A BufferedImage is essentially an Image with an accessible data buffer. A BufferedImage has a ColorModel and a Raster of image data.

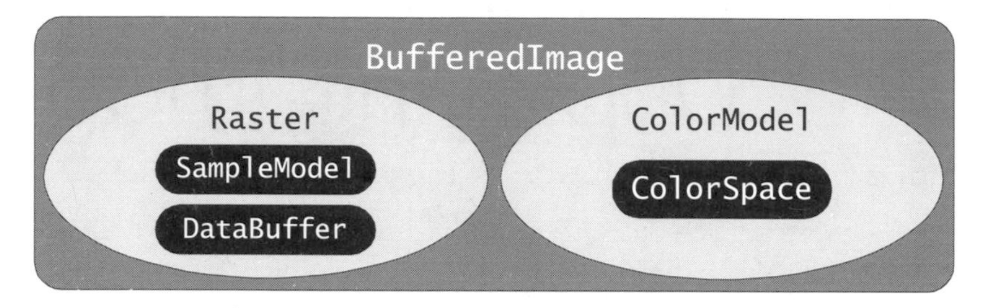

Figure 22 BufferedImage.

The ColorModel provides a color interpretation of the image's pixel data. The Raster represents the rectangular coordinates of the image, maintains image data in memory, and provides a mechanism for creating multiple subimages from a single image data buffer. The Raster also provides methods for accessing specific pixels within the image. For information about directly manipulating pixel data and writing filters for BufferedImage objects, see the chapter Imaging in the *Java 2D Programmer's Guide*.[1]

Filtering a BufferedImage

The Java 2D API defines several filtering operations for BufferedImage objects. Each image-processing operation is embodied in a class that implements the BufferedImageOp interface. The image manipulation is performed in the image operation's filter method. The BufferedImageOp classes in the Java 2D API support

- Affine transformation
- Amplitude scaling
- Lookup-table modification
- Linear combination of bands

[1] http://java.sun.com/products/jdk/1.2/docs/guide/2d/spec/j2d-image.fm.html

- Color conversion
- Convolution

To filter a `BufferedImage` using one of the image operation classes, you

5. Construct an instance of one of the `BufferedImageOp` classes: `Affine-TransformOp`, `BandCombineOp`, `ColorConvertOp`, `ConvolveOp`, `Look-upOp`, or `RescaleOp`.
6. Call the image operation's `filter` method, passing in the `BufferedImage` that you want to filter and the `BufferedImage` where you want to store the results.

Example: ImageOps

This program illustrates the use of four image-filter operations: low-pass, sharpen, lookup, and rescale.

Figure 23 The `ImageOps` applet is available on this book's CD-ROM and online here: `http://java.sun.com/docs/books/tutorial/2d/images/example-1dot2/ImageOps.html`.

You can see the complete code for this program, ImageOps.java (page 791), in the Appendix. The sharpen filter is performed by using a ConvolveOp. Convolution is the process of weighting or averaging the value of each pixel in an image with the values of neighboring pixels. Most spatial-filtering algorithms are based on convolution operations.

To construct and apply the sharpen filter to the BufferedImage, this sample uses code similar to the following snippet.

```
public static final float[] SHARPEN3x3 = {
                            0.f, -1.f, 0.f,
                            -1.f, 5.0f, -1.f,
                            0.f, -1.f, 0.f};
BufferedImage dstbimg = new
              BufferedImage(iw,ih,BufferedImage.TYPE_INT_RGB);
Kernel kernel = new Kernel(3,3,SHARPEN3x3);
ConvolveOp cop = new ConvolveOp(kernel,
                                ConvolveOp.EDGE_NO_OP,
                                null);
cop.filter(srcbimg,dstbimg);
```

The Kernel object mathematically defines how each output pixel is affected by pixels in its immediate area.The definition of the Kernel determines the results of the filter. For more information about how kernels work with ConvolveOp, see the Image Processing and Enhancement[1] section in the *Java 2D Programmer's Guide*.

Using a BufferedImage for Double Buffering

When a graphic is complex or is used repeatedly, you can reduce the time it takes to display it by first rendering it to an off-screen buffer and then copying the buffer to the screen. This technique, called *double buffering*, is often used for animations.

Note: When you are rendering into a Swing component, Swing automatically double-buffers the display.

A BufferedImage can easily be used as an off-screen buffer. To create a BufferedImage whose color space, depth, and pixel layout exactly match the window into which you're drawing, call the Component createImage method. If you

[1] http://java.sun.com/products/jdk/1.2/docs/guide/2d/spec/j2d-image.fm8.html

need control over the off-screen image's type or transparency, you can construct a `BufferedImage` object directly and use it as an off-screen buffer.

To draw into the buffered image, you call the `BufferedImage createGraphics` method to get a `Graphics2D` object; then you call the appropriate rendering methods on the `Graphics2D`. All of the Java 2D API rendering features can be used when you're rendering to a `BufferedImage` that's being used as an off-screen buffer.

When you're ready to copy the `BufferedImage` to the screen, you simply call `drawImage` on your component's `Graphics2D` and pass in the `BufferedImage`.

Example: BufferedShapeMover

This program allows the user to drag a rectangle around within the applet window. Instead of rendering the rectangle at every mouse location to provide feedback as the user drags it, a `BufferedImage` is used as an off-screen buffer. As the rectangle is dragged, it is re-rendered into the `BufferedImage` at each new location and the `BufferedImage` is blitted to the screen.

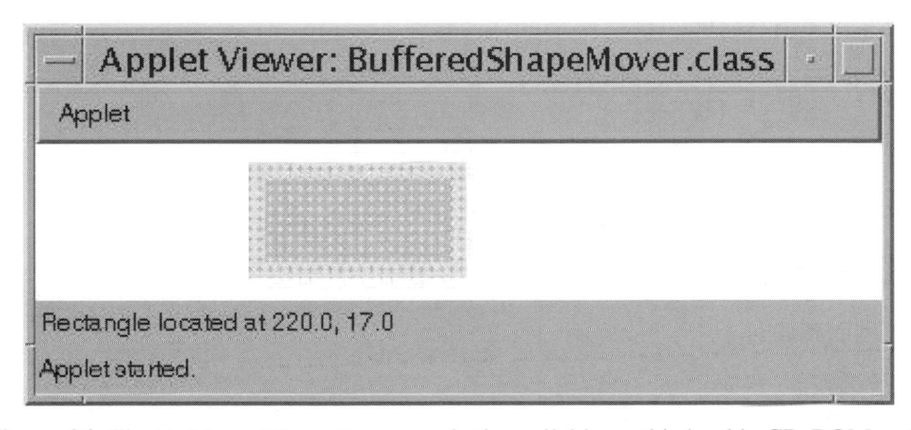

Figure 24 The `BufferedShapeMover` applet is available on this book's CD-ROM and online here: `http://java.sun.com/docs/books/tutorial/2d/images/example-1dot2/BufferedShapeMover.html`

You can see the complete program, <u>`BufferedShapeMover.java`</u> (page 794), in the Appendix. Here is the code used to render into the `BufferedImage` and display the image on the screen:

```
public void updateLocation(MouseEvent e){
    rect.setLocation(last_x + e.getX(),
                     last_y + e.getY());
    ...
```

```
        repaint();
        ...

        // In the update method...
        if(firstTime) {
            Dimension dim = getSize();
            int w = dim.width;
            int h = dim.height;
            area = new Rectangle(dim);
            bi = (BufferedImage)createImage(w, h);
            big = bi.createGraphics();
            rect.setLocation(w/2-50, h/2-25);
            big.setStroke(new BasicStroke(8.0f));
            firstTime = false;
        }

        // Clears the rectangle that was previously drawn.
        big.setColor(Color.white);
        big.clearRect(0, 0, area.width, area.height);

        // Draws and fills the newly positioned rectangle
        // to the buffer.
        big.setPaint(strokePolka);
        big.draw(rect);
        big.setPaint(fillPolka);
        big.fill(rect);

        // Draws the buffered image to the screen.
        g2.drawImage(bi, 0, 0, this);
    }
```

http://java.sun.com/docs/books/tutorial/2d/printing/index.html.

15 Printing

THIS lesson teaches you how to use the Java Printing API to print from your Java applications. You'll learn how to render the contents of your components to a printer instead of a display device and how to compose and print multipage documents. This lesson assumes that you've read the first lesson in this trail, Overview of the Java 2D API (page 177), and that you are familiar with using a `Graphics2D` rendering context. This lesson contains the following sections.

Overview of Printing in Java (page 211)
: This section gives you an overview of the support for printing AWT and Java 2D graphics and describes the Java printing model.

Printing the Contents of a Component (page 213)
: This section teaches you how to create a `PrinterJob` and how to use a `Printable` to print the contents of a component.

Displaying a Page Setup Dialog (page 215)
: This section describes the standard page setup dialog and teaches you how to use it to allow a user to set up a print job.

Printing a Collection of Pages (page 216)
: This section teaches you how to set up a `Book` to print a collection of pages that do not all have the same size or orientation.

Overview of Printing in Java

The system controls the overall printing process, just like it controls when and how a program can draw. Your application provides information about the document to be printed, and the printing system determines when each page needs to be rendered.

This *callback printing model* enables printing to be supported on a wide range of printer and systems. It even allows users to print to a bitmap printer from a computer that doesn't have enough memory or disk space to hold the bitmap of an entire page. In this situation the printing system will ask your application to render the page repeatedly so that it can be printed as a series of smaller images. (These smaller images are typically referred to as *bands,* and this process is commonly called *banded printing*.)

To support printing, an application needs to perform two tasks:

- Job control—managing the print job
- Imaging—rendering the pages to be printed

Job Control

Although the system controls the overall printing process, your application has to get the ball rolling by setting up a `PrinterJob`. The `PrinterJob`, the key point of control for the printing process, stores the print job properties, controls the display of print dialogs, and is used to initiate printing.

To steer the `PrinterJob` through the printing process, your application needs to

1. Get a `PrinterJob` by calling `PrinterJob.getPrinterJob`
2. Tell the `PrinterJob` where the rendering code is by calling `setPrintable` or `setPageable`
3. If desired, display the Page Setup and Print dialogs by calling `pageDialog` and `printDialog`
4. Initiate printing by calling `print`

The rendering of pages is controlled by the printing system through calls to the application's imaging code.

Imaging

Your application must be able to render any page when the printing system requests it. This rendering code is contained in the `print` method of a *page painter*—a class that implements the `Printable` interface. You implement `print` to render page contents by using a `Graphics` or a `Graphics2D` rendering context. You can use either one page painter to render all of the pages in a print job or different page painters for different types of pages. When the printing system needs to render a page, it calls `print` on the appropriate page painter.

When you use a single page painter, the print job is called a *printable job*. Using a printable job is the simplest way to support printing. More complex printing operations that use multiple page painters are referred to as *pageable jobs*. In a pageable job an instance of a class that implements the `Pageable` interface is used to manage the page painters.

Printable Jobs

In a printable job all pages use the same page painter and `PageFormat`, which defines the size and orientation of the page to be printed. The page painter is asked to render each page in indexed order, starting the page at index 0. The page painter might be asked to render a page multiple times before the next page is requested, but no pages are skipped. For example, if a user prints pages 2 and 3 of a document, the page painter is asked to render the pages at indices 0, 1, and 2 even though the page at index 0 will not be printed.

If a print dialog is presented, it will not display the number of pages, because that information is not available to the printing system. The page painter informs the printing system when the end of the document is reached.

Pageable Jobs

Pageable jobs are useful if your application builds an explicit representation of a document, page by page. In a pageable job different pages can use different page painters and `PageFormats`. The printing system can ask the page painters to render pages in any order, and pages can be skipped. For example, if a user prints pages 2 and 3 of a document, the page painter will be asked to render only the pages at indices 1 and 2.

The multiple page painters in a pageable job are coordinated by a class that implements the `Pageable` interface, such as `Book`. A `Book` represents a collection of pages that can use different page painters and that can vary in size and orientation. You can also use your own implementation of the `Pageable` interface if `Book` does not meet your application's needs.

Printing the Contents of a Component

Anything that you render to the screen can also be printed. You can easily use a Printable job to print the contents of a component.

Example: ShapesPrint

In this example we use the same rendering code to both display and print the contents of a component. When the user clicks the Print button, a print job is created, and `printDialog` is called to display the print dialog. If the user continues with the job, the printing process is initiated, and the printing system calls `print` as necessary to render the job to the printer.

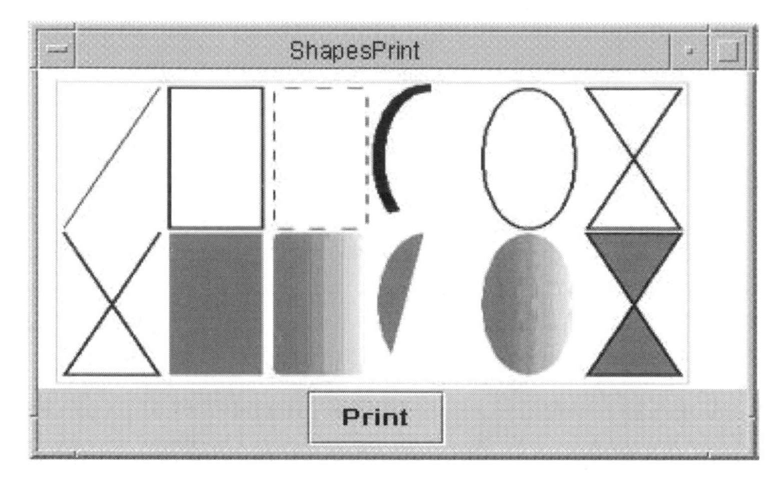

Figure 25 The `ShapesPrint` applet is available on this book's CD-ROM and online here: `http://java.sun.com/docs/books/tutorial/2d/printing/example-1dot2/ShapesPrint.html`

`ShapesPrint` is the page painter. Its `print` method calls `drawShapes` to perform the imaging for the print job. (The `drawShapes` method is also called by `paintComponent` to render to the screen.)

```
public class ShapesPrint extends JPanel
                         implements Printable, ActionListener {
...
public int print(Graphics g, PageFormat pf, int pi)
                          throws PrinterException {
    if (pi >= 1) {
        return Printable.NO_SUCH_PAGE;
    }
    drawShapes((Graphics2D) g);
    return Printable.PAGE_EXISTS;
}
...
public void drawShapes(Graphics2D g2) {
    Dimension d = getSize();
    int gridWidth = 400/6;
    int gridHeight = 300/2;
    int rowspacing = 5;
    int columnspacing = 7;
    int rectWidth = gridWidth - columnspacing;
    int rectHeight = gridHeight - rowspacing;
    ...
```

```
    int x = 85;
    int y = 87;
    ...
    g2.draw(new Rectangle2D.Double(x,y,rectWidth,rectHeight));
    ...
```

The job control code is in the `ShapesPrint` `actionPerformed` method.

```
public void actionPerformed(ActionEvent e) {

    if (e.getSource() instanceof JButton) {
        PrinterJob printJob = PrinterJob.getPrinterJob();
        printJob.setPrintable(this);
        if (printJob.printDialog()) {
            try {
                printJob.print();
            } catch (Exception ex) {
                ex.printStackTrace();
            }
        }
    }
}
```

You can find the complete code for this program, ShapesPrint.java (page 798), in the Appendix.

Displaying a Page Setup Dialog

You can allow the user to specify page characteristics, such as the paper size and orientation, by displaying a Page Setup dialog. The page information is stored in a `PageFormat` object. Like the Print dialog, the Page Setup dialog is displayed by calling a method on the `PrinterJob` object, `pageDialog`.

The Page Setup dialog is initialized by using the `PageFormat` passed to the `pageDialog` method. If the user clicks the OK button in the dialog, the `PageFormat` is cloned, altered to reflect the user's selections, and then returned. If the user cancels the dialog, `pageDialog` returns the original, unaltered `PageFormat`.

`ShapesPrint` could easily be modified to display a Page Setup dialog by adding a call to `pageDialog` after you get the `PrinterJob`.

```
// Get a PrinterJob
PrinterJob job = PrinterJob.getPrinterJob();

// Ask user for page format (e.g., portrait/landscape)
```

```
PageFormat pf = job.pageDialog(job.defaultPage());
```

Printing a Collection of Pages

When you need more control over the individual pages in a print job, you can use a pageable job instead of a printable job. The simplest way to manage a pageable job is to use the Book class, which represents a collection of pages.

Example: SimpleBook

The SimpleBook program uses a Book to manage two page painters: PaintCover is used for the cover page, and PaintContent is used for the content page. The cover page is printed in landscape mode, whereas the content page is printed in portrait mode.

Once the Book is created, pages are added to it with the append method. When you add a page to a Book, you need to specify the Printable and PageFormat to use for that page.

```
// In the program's job control code...
// Get a PrinterJob
PrinterJob job = PrinterJob.getPrinterJob();

// Create a landscape page format
PageFormat landscape = job.defaultPage();
landscape.setOrientation(PageFormat.LANDSCAPE);

// Set up a book
Book bk = new Book();
bk.append(new PaintCover(), job.defaultPage());
bk.append(new PaintContent(), landscape);

// Pass the book to the PrinterJob
job.setPageable(bk);
```

The setPageable method is called on the PrinterJob to tell the printing system to use the Book to locate the appropriate rendering code.

You can find the full program, SimpleBook.java (page 803), in the Appendix.

About the Author

DEBORAH ADAIR, the technical writer for the Java Media group at Sun Microsystems, specializes in designing and writing documentation for software developers and other highly technical readers. She has a degree in Scientific and Technical Communication from the University of Washington and has been writing for the computer industry for the past nine years.

Acknowledgments

The Java 2D and Java Sound trails could not have been completed without the help of Jennifer Ball, a summer intern in the Java Software Technical Publications group. With little assistance or direction and a lot of hard work and persistence, Jennifer single-handedly wrote most of the samples used in these trails. The Java Software engineers who took time out of their own crazy schedules to answer questions and review these trails also played a major role: Kara Kytle, Brent Browning, Jerry Evans, Jim Graham, Jeannette Hung, Brian Lichtenwalter, and Thanh Nguyen. My sincere thanks also go out to Tom Santos, who donated several hours of his own time to the cause. Not only did he answer technical questions and help get the samples running under Swing, he patiently endured living with a stressed-out writer throughout the entire process.

Sound

by Deborah Adair

THIS trail shows you how to use the Java™ Sound engine in JDK™ 1.2 to play audio data from both applications and applets. Java Sound enables you to play many types of audio clips, including AIFF, AU, WAV, MIDI, and RMF files.

Overview (page 221) This lesson describes the features provided by the Java Sound engine and how it is integrated with JDK 1.2 and the other Java Media technologies.

Playing Sounds (page 223) This final lesson shows you how you can play consistent, reliable, high-quality audio from your Java programs.

http://java.sun.com/docs/books/tutorial/sound/overview/index.html

16 Overview

JAVA Sound provides a very high-quality 64-channel audio rendering and MIDI sound synthesis engine that

- Enables consistent, reliable, high-quality audio on all Java platforms
- Minimizes the impact of audio-rich Web pages on computing resources
- Reduces the need for high-cost sound cards by providing a software-only solution that requires only a digital-to-analog converter (DAC)
- Supports a wide range of audio formats

The new sound engine is integrated into the Java Virtual Machine as a core library.

This overview lesson contains the following sections:

Using the Java Sound Engine

JDK 1.2 enables you to create and play `AudioClips` from both applets and applications. The clips can be any of the following audio file formats:

- AIFF
- AU
- WAV

- MIDI (type 0 and type 1 files)
- RMF

The sound engine can handle 8- and 16-bit audio data at virtually any sample rate. In JDK 1.2 audio files are rendered at a sample rate of 22 kHz in 16-bit stereo. If the hardware doesn't support 16-bit data or stereo playback, 8-bit or mono audio is output.

There's no need to worry about the impact of audio-rich Web pages on computing resources. The Java Sound engine minimizes the use of a system's CPU to process sound files. For example, a 24-voice MIDI file uses only 20 percent of the CPU on a Pentium 90 MHz system.

Accessing the Java Sound Engine

A full-featured Java Sound API is under development. This API will provide access to the underlying synthesis and rendering engine and will enable the creation of high-quality telephony and video conferencing applications. With the Java Sound API, professional musicians and sound designers will be able to develop new sounds that can be delivered over the Internet and used seamlessly with Java Sound.

Java Sound and Java Media

Java Sound is part of the Java Media family, which addresses the increasing demand for multimedia in the enterprise by providing a unified, nonproprietary, platform-neutral solution for incorporating time-based media, 2D fonts, graphics and images, speech input and output, 3D models, and telephony in Java programs. By providing standard players and integrating these supporting technologies, the Java Media APIs enable developers to produce and to distribute compelling, media-rich content.

Java Sound provides uniform access to underlying platform sound capabilities, enabling Java programs to read and write sampled and synthesized audio data. Higher-level services, such as compression, decompression, synchronization, streaming, container read/write, and network transport, are handled by the Java Media Framework (JMF). JMF provides a simple, unified way for Java programs to synchronize and display time-based data, such as audio and video. Sun's implementation of JMF uses the Java Sound engine to render audio data.[1]

---

[1] For more information about JMF and the other Java Media technologies, visit the Java Media & Communications pages on the Sun Website: http://java.sun.com/products/java-media

Playing Sounds

WITH JDK 1.2 you can play many different types of audio files from both applets and applications. This lesson contains three sections that show you how.

Playing Sounds from an Applet

The mechanism for playing sounds from an applet is unchanged in JDK 1.2. To play a sound file, you can load the clip by using `Applet.getAudioClip` and control playback through the `AudioClip` `play`, `loop`, and `stop` methods. For example, to play a WAV file from an applet, you could

1. Call `Applet.getAudio` clip and pass in the URL where the `.wav` file is located.
2. Call `play` or `loop` on the `AudioClip`.

The audio data is loaded when the `AudioClip` is constructed. It is not loaded asynchronously.

You can also use `Applet.play` to play any of the supported types of audio files. However, when you use `Applet.play`, the audio data is not preloaded. The first time the user initiates playback of a particular sound, your applet's drawing and event handling will freeze while the audio data is loaded.

Example: SoundApplet

This applet plays several types of audio clips: an AU file, an AIFF file, a WAV file, and a MIDI file.[1]

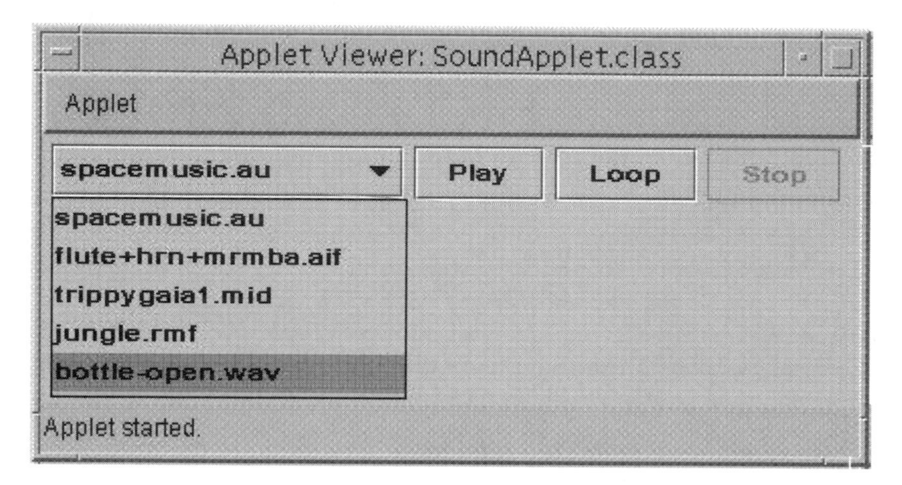

Figure 26 You can see `SoundApplet` on this book's CD-ROM and online here: `http://java.sun.com/docs/books/tutorial/sound/playing/SoundApplet.html`.

Regardless of the type of sound file used, the code for loading and playing the file is the same. This example provides a framework for loading and playing multiple audio clips and loads the audio clips asynchronously, but the code for loading and playing the clips essentially boils down to

```
AudioClip onceClip, loopClip;
onceClip = soundList.getClip(chosenFile);
loopClip = soundList.getClip(chosenFile);
AudioClip audioClip = Applet.getAudioClip(baseURL, relativeURL);
onceClip.play();     //Play it once.
loopClip.loop();     //Start the sound loop.
loopClip.stop();     //Stop the sound loop.
```

This applet stops playing a looping sound when the user leaves the page and resumes playback when the user comes back. This is done through the applet's `start` and `stop` methods.

```
public void stop() {
    onceClip.stop();        //Cut short the one-time sound.
```

[1] The AIFF and WAV files used in this trail's examples were provided by Headspace, Inc.

```
        if (looping) {
            loopClip.stop();    //Stop the sound loop.
        }
    }

    public void start() {
        if (looping) {
            loopClip.loop();    //Restart the sound loop.
        }
    }
```

To reduce the amount of time that the user has to wait before interacting with the applet, the sounds are preloaded in a background thread instead of in the applet's `init` method. If the user initiates playback before a sound has finished loading, the applet can respond appropriately. The loading of the sounds is done in the `SoundLoader` `run` method.

```
    public void run() {
        AudioClip audioClip = Applet.getAudioClip(baseURL,
                                                  relativeURL);
        soundList.putClip(audioClip, relativeURL);
    }
```

You can find the complete code for this program, `SoundApplet.java` (page 809). To run this applet, you will also need the files `AppletSoundList.java` (page 812) and `AppletSoundLoader.java` (page 813), and several sound files.[1]

Playing Sounds from an Application

In JDK 1.2, applications as well as applets can play sounds. A new static method has been added to `java.applet.Applet` to enable applications to create `AudioClips` from a URL.

```
    public static final AudioClip newAudioClip(URL r)
```

To play a sound from an applet, you call `Applet.newAudioClip` to load the sound and then use the `AudioClip` `play`, `loop`, and `stop` methods to control playback. For example, to play a WAV file from an application, you could

---

[1] The sound files are included on the CD-ROM that accompanies this book. You can also download these files from: http://java.sun.com/docs/books/tutorial/sound/playing.html

1. Call `Applet.newAudioClip` and pass in the URL where the `.wav` file is located.
2. Call `play` or `loop` on the `AudioClip`.

Example: SoundApplication

The sound player in the previous example can easily be implemented as an application. The main difference is that `Applet.newAudioClip` is called to load the sounds.

```
AudioClip onceClip, loopClip;
onceClip = soundList.getClip(chosenFile);
loopClip = soundList.getClip(chosenFile);
AudioClip audioClip = Applet.newAudioClip(completeURL);
```

You can find the complete code for this application, `SoundApplication.java` (page 814), in the Appendix. To run this application, you will also need the files `SoundList.java` (page 817) and `AppletSoundLoader.java` (page 813), and several sound files.[1]

Common Problems (and Their Solutions)

Here are solutions to two of the most common problems you might encounter when playing audio files.

Problem: *8 kHz audio files do not sound as good as they did before I switched to JDK 1.2.*

Solution: The Java Sound engine up-samples 8 kHz audio data to 22 kHz, which can result in added noise during playback. If you find that the audio quality is not acceptable, start with a higher-quality audio clip to avoid the up-sampling.

Problem: *Some of my audio files won't play.*

Solution: You cannot play WAV, AU, AIFF, or AU files compressed using ADPCM or other compression schemes. The Java Sound engine supports only linear PCM audio files.

---

[1] The sound files are included on the CD-ROM that accompanies this book. You can also download these files from: http://java.sun.com/docs/books/tutorial/sound/playing.html

About the Author

DEBORAH ADAIR, the technical writer for the Java Media group at Sun Microsystems, specializes in designing and writing documentation for software developers and other highly technical readers. She has a degree in Scientific and Technical Communication from the University of Washington and has been writing for the computer industry for the past nine years.

Acknowledgments

The Java 2D and Java Sound trails could not have been completed without the help of Jennifer Ball, a summer intern in the Java Software Technical Publications group. With little assistance or direction and a lot of hard work and persistence, Jennifer single-handedly wrote most of the samples used in these trails. The Java Software engineers who took time out of their own crazy schedules to answer questions and review these trails also played a major role: Kara Kytle, Brent Browning, Jerry Evans, Jim Graham, Jeannette Hung, Brian Lichtenwalter, and Thanh Nguyen. My sincere thanks also go out to Tom Santos, who donated several hours of his own time to the cause. Not only did he answer technical questions and help get the samples running under Swing, he patiently endured living with a stressed-out writer throughout the entire process.

JavaBeans

by Andy Quinn

JAVABEANS™ brings component technology to the Java™ platform. The JavaBeans API enables you to create reusable, platform-independent components. You can use JavaBeans-compliant application builder tools to combine components into applets, applications, or composite components. JavaBean components are known as *Beans*.

This trail is a hands-on guide to learning JavaBeans and the Beans Development Kit™ (BDK). In addition to the BDK, you will need the Java Development Kit (JDK™). Both the BDK[1] and the JDK are included on the CD-ROM that accompanies this book.

JavaBeans constitutes a core capability of JDK 1.1 and 1.2. Thus, any browser or tool compliant with JDK 1.1 or 1.2 implicitly supports JavaBeans.

This trail includes the following eight lessons:

JavaBeans Concepts and Development Kit (page 233) describes Beans and the Beans Development Kit.

Using the BeanBox (page 237) describes basic BeanBox operation and explains the BeanBox menus.

Writing a SimpleBean (page 245) walks you through the steps of creating a rudimentary Bean, saving the Bean, adding the Bean to the ToolBox, placing the Bean in the BeanBox, inspecting the Bean's properties and events, and generating a Bean introspection report.

---

[1] http://java.sun.com/beans/software/bdk_download.html

Properties (page 251) explains how to give your Beans appearance and behavior characteristics *customizable at design time*.

Manipulating Events in the BeanBox (page 267) describes the BeanBox's event-manipulating capabilities. If you are not familiar with event handling, you might want to read up on JDK 1.1 event mechanism[1] to prepare for this material.

The BeanInfo Interface (page 273) explains how to write Bean information classes: separate classes you can use to explicitly advertise your Bean's properties, methods, and events to builder tools.

Bean Customization (page 279) introduces you to property editors and to the `Customizer` interface.

Bean Persistence (page 285) explains how to save and to restore your Beans and their customized states.

Additional Documentation

The BDK's `beans/docs` directory contains documentation for

- The Beans API
- The BeanBox API
- The demo Beans
- The `java.util` API
- Java Archive (JAR) files and manifests
- Makefiles for `gnumake` (UNIX) and `nmake` (Win32)

A good starting point is the `beans/README.html` file.

The JavaBeans Documentation page[2] contains current JavaBeans API definitions, upcoming JavaBeans feature descriptions, and related Java documentation, such as the Java core reflection API, object serialization, remote method invocation (RMI), and a third-party JavaBeans book list.

---

1 The JDK 1.1 event mechanism is explained in *The Java Tutorial, Second Edition,* and online at http://java.sun.com/docs/books/tutorial/ui/swingOverview/event.html

2 http://java.sun.com/beans/docs/index.html

JavaBeans Concepts and Development Kit

THIS lesson has two sections:

JavaBeans Concepts (page 233)
This section briefly explains the concepts and capabilities that define a Bean. You'll learn about introspection, properties, events, and persistence.

BDK Contents (page 235)
This section gives a brief description of what you get with the BDK.

JavaBeans Concepts

The JavaBeans API makes it possible to write component software in the Java programming language. Components are self-contained, reusable software units that can be visually composed into composite components, applets, applications, and servlets, using visual application builder tools. JavaBean components are known as *Beans*. Although Beans are designed to be understood by builder tools, all key APIs, including support for events, properties, and persistence, have been designed to be easily read and understood by human programmers as well.

Components expose their features, such as public methods and events, to builder tools for visual manipulation. A Bean's features are exposed because feature names adhere to specific *design patterns*. A JavaBeans-enabled builder tool can then examine the Bean's patterns, discern its features, and expose them for visual manipulation. A builder tool maintains Beans in a palette, or toolbox. You can select a Bean from the toolbox, drop the Bean into a form, modify its appearance and behavior, define its interaction with other Beans, and compose it and other Beans into an applet, an application, or a new Bean. You can do all this without writing a line of code.

The following list briefly describes key Bean concepts and indicates where you can read a complete description. Builder tools discover a Bean's features (that is, its properties, methods, and events) by a process known as *introspection*. Beans support introspection in two ways:

- By adhering to specific rules, known as *design patterns*, when naming Bean features. The `java.beans.Introspector`[1] class examines Beans for these design patterns to discover Bean features. The `Introspector` class relies on the *core reflection* API. See Reflection (page 681) trail to learn about reflection.
- By explicitly providing property, method, and event information with a related *Bean information* class. A Bean information class implements the `BeanInfo` interface. A `BeanInfo`[2] class explicitly lists those Bean features that are to be exposed to application builder tools.

Properties, a Bean's appearance and behavior characteristics, can be changed at design time. Builder tools introspect on a Bean to discover its properties and to expose them for manipulation.

Beans expose properties so that they can be *customized* at design time. Customization is supported in two ways: by using property editors or by using more sophisticated Bean customizers.

Beans use *events* to communicate with other Beans. A Bean that wants to receive events (a listener Bean) registers its interest with the Bean that fires the event (a source Bean). Builder tools can examine a Bean and determine which events that Bean can fire (send) and handle (receive).

Persistence enables a Bean to save and restore its state. Once you've changed a Bean's properties, you can save the state of the Bean and can restore that Bean later, property changes intact. JavaBeans use Java object serialization to support persistence.

A Bean's *methods* are no different from Java methods and can be called from other Beans or a scripting environment. By default all public methods are exported.

---

[1] The API documentation is available on the CD-ROM that accompanies this book and online here: http://java.sun.com/products/jdk/1.2/docs/api/java/beans/Introspector.html

[2] The API documentation is available on the CD-ROM that accompanies this book and online here: http://java.sun.com/products/jdk/1.2/docs/api/java/beans/BeanInfo.html

BDK Contents

The BDK is delivered separately from the JDK. You can download the BDK freely from the JavaBeans Web site, which contains instructions for installing the BDK on your system. Following is a general description of the BDK files and directories.

- `README.html` contains an entry point to the BDK documentation.
- `LICENSE.html` contains the BDK license agreement.
- `GNUmakefile` and `Makefile` are UNIX and Win32 makefiles (`.gmk` and `.mk` suffixes) for building the demos and the BeanBox and for running the BeanBox.
- The `beans/apis` directory contains a `java` directory that contains JavaBeans source files and a `sun` directory that contains property editor source files.
- The `beans/beanbox` directory contains makefiles for building the BeanBox, scripts for running the BeanBox, a `classes` directory of BeanBox class files, a `lib` directory containing a BeanBox-support JAR file used by `MakeApplet`'s produced code, `sun` and `sunw` directories containing BeanBox source (`.java`) files, and a `tmp` directory containing automatically generated event adapter source and class files, `.ser` files, and applet files automatically generated by `MakeApplet`.
- The `beans/demos` directory contains makefiles for building the demo Beans; an HTML directory containing an applet wrapper demonstration that must be run in `appletviewer`, HotJava, or JDK 1.1–compliant browsers; a `sunw` directory with two subdirectories: a `wrapper` directory containing a Bean applet wrapper and a `demos` directory containing demo source files.
- The `beans/doc` directory contains demos documentation and a `javadoc` directory containing JavaBeans and JavaBeans-related class and interface documentation.
- The `beans/jars` directory contains JAR files for demo Beans.

Now that we've explored the contents of the BDK, we're ready to learn more about the BeanBox in the next lesson.

http://java.sun.com/docs/books/tutorial/javabeans/beanbox/index.html

19 Using the BeanBox

THE BeanBox is a simple tool you can use to test your JavaBeans and to learn how to visually manipulate their properties and events. The BeanBox is not a builder tool. You'll use the BeanBox to learn about Beans in each section.

This section explains how to start the BeanBox and describes the BeanBox window, the ToolBox, and the Properties sheet.

This section explains each item in the BeanBox File, Edit, and View menus.

This section demonstrates the BeanBox's applet-generating facility.

Starting and Using the BeanBox

This section gives you a brief, introductory look at the BeanBox and its basic operation. The `beans/beanbox` directory contains Win32 (`run.bat`) and UNIX (`run.sh`) scripts that start the BeanBox. You can use the commands in the following table to start the BeanBox. Or you can use a `make` utility.

Table 17 Commands to Start BeanBox

Platform	Command
UNIX	`gmake run`
Win32	`nmake run`

See the BDK files `beans/doc/makefiles.html` and `beans/doc/gnu.txt` for information about getting copies of `gnumake` and `nmake`.

When started, the BeanBox displays three windows: the ToolBox, the BeanBox window, and the Properties sheet.

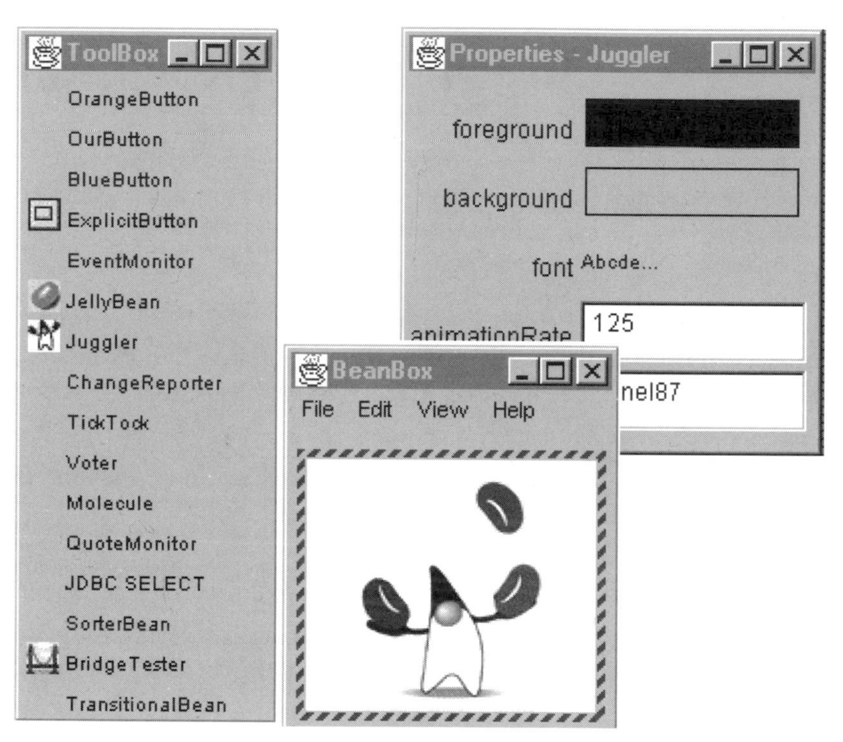

Figure 27 BeanBox initial windows: the ToolBox, the BeanBox window, and the Properties sheet.

Here are brief descriptions of each window.

- The *ToolBox* contains the Beans available for use by the BeanBox. To work on a Bean, you choose it from the ToolBox and drop it on the BeanBox window.
- The *BeanBox* window is the area where you visually "wire" Beans together, defining how Beans appear, and interact with other Beans. The BeanBox window is itself an instance of a BeanBox Bean. The preceding figure shows the BeanBox window with a `Juggler` Bean instance dropped in it. Later you'll see how to wire the `Juggler` to two button Beans that start and stop him juggling. To choose among Beans in the BeanBox window, simply click on the Bean. The selected Bean will have a hatched bor-

der, as the `Juggler` Bean does in the figure. Which Bean is selected has significance for the Properties sheet.

- The Properties sheet displays the properties for the Bean currently selected within the BeanBox window. In the figure, the Properties sheet displays the `Juggler` Bean's properties. If you drop another Bean in the BeanBox window, the Properties sheet will display that Bean's properties.

Adding a Bean to the ToolBox

When the BeanBox is started, it automatically loads the ToolBox with all of the Beans it finds within the JAR files contained in the `beans/jars` directory. Move your JAR files into that directory to have them automatically loaded at BeanBox startup. You can load Beans from JAR files located elsewhere by using the File > LoadJar... BeanBox menu item.

Dropping a Bean on the BeanBox

Clicking on a Bean name within the ToolBox chooses that Bean for placement within the BeanBox. To drop a `JellyBean` instance onto the BeanBox, for example,

1. Click on the word `JellyBean` in the ToolBox. The cursor will change to a crosshair when flying over the BeanBox windows.
2. Click within the BeanBox. The `JellyBean` instance will appear and will be selected.

Note the change in the Properties sheet when you put the `JellyBean` in the BeanBox. Before you placed the `JellyBean` in the BeanBox, the BeanBox's properties were displayed. After placing the `JellyBean` in the BeanBox, the `JellyBean` properties are displayed. If you missed the change, click within the BeanBox, away from the `JellyBean`, to choose the BeanBox rather than the `JellyBean`. The Properties sheet will then display the BeanBox's properties.

After dropping a `JellyBean` instance on the BeanBox, the Properties sheet displays the `JellyBean` properties: `color`, `foreground`, `priceInCents`, `background`, and `font`.

Editing Bean Properties

The Properties sheet displays each property's name and current value. Values are displayed in an editable text field (strings and numbers), a choice menu (Booleans), or as painted values (colors and fonts). Each property has an associated *property editor.* Clicking on a property within the Properties sheet activates the property's editor. Properties displayed in text fields or choice menus are edited within the Properties sheet. Because editing their values requires a more sophisticated user interface, `Color` and `Font` property types use a *custom property editor.* When you click on a color or a font property, a separate panel will pop up to do the editing. Try clicking on each of the `JellyBean` properties.

Saving and Restoring Beans

You can save the state of a Bean that you are customizing and can restore the Bean and its saved state at a later time. The BeanBox uses Java object serialization to save and to restore Beans and their states, as follows.

1. Drop a `JellyBean` on the BeanBox.
2. Change the `color` property to anything you want.
3. Select the File > Save menu item. Use the browser that pops up to save the Bean to a file.
4. Select the File > Clear menu item.
5. Select the File > Load menu item. The file browser will again pop up; use it to retrieve the serialized Bean. The `JellyBean` will be the color you chose.

The BeanBox Menus

The following tables explain each item in the BeanBox File, Edit, and View menus, respectively.

Table 18 File Menu

Menu Item	Action
Save	Saves the Beans currently in the BeanBox, including each Bean's size, position, and internal state. The saved file can be loaded via File > Load.
SerializeComponent...	Saves the Beans in the BeanBox to a serialized (`.ser`) file. This file must be put in a `.jar` file to be usable by the BeanBox.
MakeApplet...	Generates an applet from the BeanBox contents.
Load...	Loads saved files into the BeanBox. This command will not load `.ser` files.

Table 18 File Menu

Menu Item	Action
LoadJar...	Loads a JAR file's contents into the ToolBox.
Print	Prints an image of the BeanBox contents.
Clear	Removes the BeanBox contents.
Exit	Quits the BeanBox *without offering to save.*

Table 19 Edit Menu

Menu Item	Action
Cut	Removes the Bean selected in the BeanBox. The cut Bean is serialized and can then be pasted.
Copy	Copies the Bean selected in the BeanBox. The copied Bean is serialized and can then be pasted.
Paste	Drops the last cut or copied Bean into the BeanBox.
Report...	Generates an introspection report for the selected Bean.
Events	Lists the selected Bean's event-firing methods, grouped by the Java interface that declares the methods.
Bind property...	Lists all of the selected Bean's bound property methods, if any.

Table 20 View Menu

Menu Item	Action
Disable Design Mode/Enable Design Mode	Removes the ToolBox and the Properties sheet from the screen. Eliminates all BeanBox design and test behavior (selected Bean, and so on) and makes the BeanBox behave like an application.
Hide Invisible Beans/Show Invisible Beans	Hides or shows Beans with no GUI.

Using the BeanBox to Generate Applets

You can use the BeanBox's File > MakeApplet... menu item to generate an applet from the BeanBox contents. Making an applet from the BeanBox creates

- A JAR file containing class files and serialized data
- A test HTML file that uses the JAR file (and any other JAR files needed)
- A subdirectory with Java sources and `makefile`
- A `readme` file with complete information about the generated applet and all files involved

Take the following steps to generate an applet from the BeanBox

1. Use the Juggler example that you made in Starting and Using the BeanBox (page 237). If you saved that example to a file, load it into the BeanBox, using the File > Load menu item. If you didn't save the example, repeat the steps to build the example. The generated applet will have the same size as the BeanBox frame, so you might want to adjust the BeanBox size to the size of the applet you want.
2. Choose File > Make Applet to bring up the MakeApplet dialog (Figure 28).

   Use the default JAR file and applet name for this example. Press the OK button.

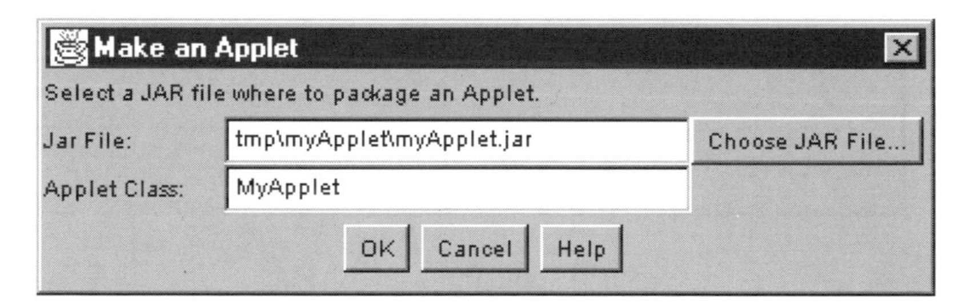

Figure 28 The MakeApplet dialog.

That's it. The generated files were placed in the `beanbox/tmp/myApplet` directory. You can inspect your handiwork by bringing up the applet viewer in the following way:

```
appletviewer BDKInstallation/beanbox/tmp/myApplet.html
```

You can see the result in Figure 29. Don't forget to look at the generated `myApplet_readme` file and the other files generated.

Generated applets can be used in any JDK 1.1– or 1.2–compliant browser. The applet viewer is a good test platform. Another fully compliant browser is the HotJava browser.[1]

[1] The HotJava browser is available on the CD-ROM that accompanies this book and online here: http://java.sun.com/products/hotjava/

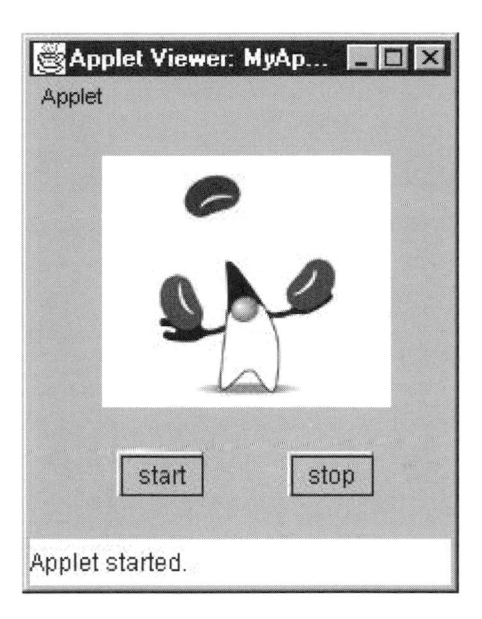

Figure 29 Completed juggler applet.

20 Writing a SimpleBean

IN this lesson you will learn more about Beans and the BeanBox by following steps to

- Create a simple Bean
- Compile and save the Bean into a Java Archive (JAR) file
- Load the Bean into the ToolBox
- Drop a Bean instance into the BeanBox
- Inspect the Bean's properties, methods, and events
- Generate an introspection report

This lesson contains the following sections:

Steps to Writing a Bean

Your Bean will be named `SimpleBean`. Here are the steps to create it and to view it in the BeanBox.

1. Write the SimpleBean code. Put it in a file named `SimpleBean.java`, in the directory of your choice. Here's the code:

```
import java.awt.*;
import java.io.Serializable;

public class SimpleBean extends Canvas
                        implements Serializable {

    //Constructor sets inherited properties
    public SimpleBean() {
        setSize(60,40);
        setBackground(Color.red);
    }
}
```

SimpleBean extends the java.awt.Canvas[1] component and also implements the java.io.Serializable[2] interface, a requirement for all Beans. SimpleBean sets the background color and component size.

2. Compile the Bean.[3] This command generates the file SimpleBean.class:

```
javac SimpleBean.java
```

3. Create a manifest file. Use your favorite text editor to create a file and name it manifest.tmp, that contains the following text:

```
Name: SimpleBean.class
Java-Bean: True
```

4. Create the JAR file. The JAR file will contain the manifest and the SimpleBean class file

```
jar cfm SimpleBean.jar manifest.tmp SimpleBean.class
```

See the trail JAR File Format (page 565) for complete information on JAR files.

5. Load the JAR file into the ToolBox. Select the File > LoadJar menu item. This will bring up a file browser. Navigate to the SimpleBean.jar location and choose it. SimpleBean will appear at the bottom of the ToolBox.

Note: When the BeanBox is started, all Beans in JAR files in the beans/jars directory are automatically loaded into the ToolBox.

---

6. Drop a SimpleBean instance into the BeanBox. In the ToolBox click on the word SimpleBean. The cursor will change to a crosshair. Move the cursor

---

[1] The API documentation is available on the CD-ROM that accompanies this book and online here: http://java.sun.com/products/jdk/1.2/docs/api/java/awt/Canvas.html

[2] http://java.sun.com/products/jdk/1.2/docs/api/java.io.Serializable.html

[3] The -classpath option is treated differently in JDK 1.1 and JDK 1.2. For detailed information on CLASSPATH, refer to http://java.sun.com/products/jdk/1.2/docs/install.html.

to a spot within the BeanBox and click. `SimpleBean` will appear as a painted rectangle with a hatched border indicating that `SimpleBean` is selected. The `SimpleBean` properties will appear in the Properties sheet.

You can resize `SimpleBean`, because it inherits from `Canvas`, by dragging a corner. You will see the cursor change to a right angle when over a corner. You can also reposition `SimpleBean` within the BeanBox by dragging on any noncorner portion of the hatched border. You will see the cursor change to crossed arrows when in position to move the Bean.

SimpleBean Makefiles

Following are two makefiles (UNIX and Win32) set up to create `SimpleBean`. Here is the UNIX version:

```
# gnumake file

CLASSFILES= SimpleBean.class

JARFILE= SimpleBean.jar

all: $(JARFILE)

# Create a JAR file with a suitable manifest.
$(JARFILE): $(CLASSFILES) $(DATAFILES)
        echo "Name: SimpleBean.class" || manifest.tmp
        echo "Java-Bean: True" || manifest.tmp
        jar cfm $(JARFILE) manifest.tmp *.class
        @/bin/rm manifest.tmp

# Compile the sources
%.class: %.java
        export CLASSPATH; CLASSPATH=. ; \
        javac $<

# make clean
clean:
        /bin/rm -f *.class
        /bin/rm -f $(JARFILE)
```

Here is the Win32 nmake version:

```
# nmake file
CLASSFILES= simplebean.class

JARFILE= simplebean.jar
```

```
all: $(JARFILE)

# Create a JAR file with a suitable manifest.

$(JARFILE): $(CLASSFILES) $(DATAFILES)
        jar cfm $(JARFILE) <<manifest.tmp *.class
Name: SimpleBean.class
Java-Bean: True
<<

.SUFFIXES: .java .class

{sunw}.java{sunw}.class :
        set CLASSPATH=.
        javac $<

clean:
        -del sunw.class
        -del $(JARFILE)
```

You can use these makefiles as templates for creating your own Bean makefiles. The sample Bean makefiles, in the `beans/demo` directory, also show you how to use makefiles to build and to maintain your Beans.

Inspecting SimpleBean Properties and Events

The Properties sheet displays the selected Bean's properties. With `SimpleBean` selected, the Properties sheet displays four properties: `foreground`, `background`, `font`, and `name`. We declared no properties in `SimpleBean`, so these are properties inherited from `Canvas`. See the next lesson, Properties (page 251), to learn how to declare properties. Clicking on each property brings up a property editor. The BeanBox provides default property editors for the primitive types, as well as `Font` and `Color` types. You can find the sources for these property editors in `beans/apis/sun/beans/editors`.

Beans communicate with other Beans by sending and receiving event notifications. To see which events `SimpleBean` can send, click on the Edit > Events BeanBox menu item. A list of events, grouped by the Java interface in which the event method is declared, will be displayed. Under each interface group is a list of event methods. These are all inherited from `Canvas`.

Generating Bean Introspection Reports

Introspection is the process of discovering a Bean's design-time features by one of two methods:

- Low-level reflection, which uses design patterns to discover your Bean's features
- Examination of an associated Bean information class that explicitly describes your Bean's features

You can generate a Bean introspection report by clicking on the Edit > Report menu item. The report lists Bean events, properties, and methods and their characteristics.

By default Bean reports are sent to the `java` interpreter's standard output, which is the window in which you started the BeanBox. You can redirect the report to a file by changing the `java` interpreter command in `beanbox/run.sh` or `run.bat` to

```
java sun.beanbox.BeanBoxFrame > beanreport.txt
```

http://java.sun.com/docs/books/tutorial/javabeans/properties/index.html

21 Properties

THE sections in this lesson teach you how to implement Bean properties. Bean appearance and behavior characteristics are customizable at design time in builder tools.

Simple Properties

Properties are aspects of a Bean's appearance and behavior that are changeable at design time. Properties are `private` values accessed through *getter* and *setter* methods. Property getter and setter method names follow specific rules, called *design patterns*. By using these design pattern–based method names, JavaBeans-enabled builder tools (and the BeanBox) can

- Discover a Bean's properties
- Determine the properties' read/write attributes and types
- Locate an appropriate property editor for each property type

- Display the properties (usually in a Properties sheet)
- Alter those properties (at design time)

For example, suppose that a builder tool, on introspecting your Bean, discovers two methods:

```
public Color getColor() { ... }
public void setColor(Color c) { ... }
```

From this the builder tool infers that a property named `color` exists, that it is readable and writable, and that its type is `Color`. Further, the builder tool can attempt to locate a property editor for that type and to display the property (usually in a Properties sheet) so that the property can be edited.

Adding a Color Property to SimpleBean

Make the following changes to `SimpleBean.java` to add a color property.

1. Create and initialize a private instance variable.

```
private Color color = Color.green;
```

2. Write a `public` getter method.

```
public Color getColor() {
    return color;
}
```

3. Write a `public` setter method.

```
public void setColor(Color newColor) {
    color = newColor;
    repaint();
}
```

4. Override the `paint` method inherited from `Canvas`.

```
public void paint(Graphics g) {
    g.setColor(color);
    g.fillRect(20,5, 20, 30);
}
```

5. Compile the Bean, load it into the ToolBox, and create an instance in the BeanBox.

The results: `SimpleBean` will be displayed with a green centered rectangle.

The Properties sheet will contain a new `Color` property. The introspection mechanism will also search for a `Color` property editor. A `Color` property editor is one of the default editors supplied with the BeanBox and is assigned as `Simple-`

Bean's Color property editor. Click on the Color property in the Properties sheet to run this editor. The following figure shows the revised SimpleBean instance within the BeanBox, SimpleBean's new Color property within the Properties sheet, and the Color property editor shipped with the BeanBox.

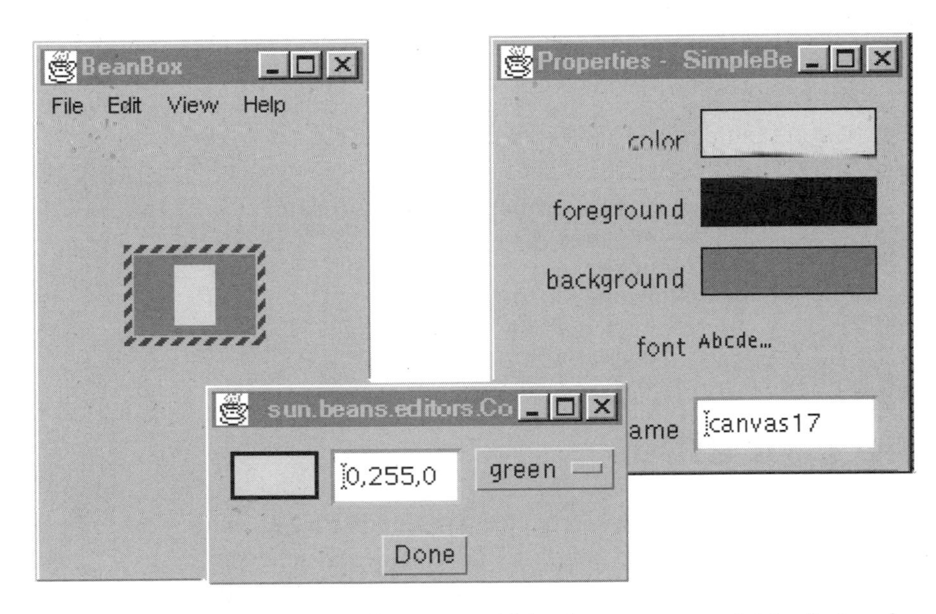

Figure 30 Revised SimpleBean instance within the BeanBox and SimpleBean's new Color property.

You can change the color property by menu or by RGB value. Try changing colors.

Here is the complete SimpleBean source code, revised to add a color property.

```
package sunw.demo.simple;

import java.awt.*;
import java.io.Serializable;

public class SimpleBean extends Canvas implements Serializable{

    private Color color = Color.green;

    //property getter method
    public Color getColor() {
        return color;
    }
```

```
        //property setter method. Sets new SimpleBean
        //color and repaints.
        public void setColor(Color newColor) {
            color = newColor;
            repaint();
        }

        public void paint(Graphics g) {
            g.setColor(color);
            g.fillRect(20, 5, 20, 30);
        }

        //Constructor sets inherited properties
        public SimpleBean() {
            setSize(60,40);
            setBackground(Color.red);
        }
    }
```

Bound Properties

Sometimes when a Bean property changes, another object may want to be notified of the change and to react to the change. Whenever a *bound property* changes, notification of the change is sent to interested listeners.

A Bean containing a bound property must maintain a list of property change listeners and alert them when the bound property changes. The convenience class `PropertyChangeSupport` first implements methods that add and remove `PropertyChangeListener` objects from a list and then fires `PropertyChangeEvent` objects at those listeners when the bound property changes. Your Beans can inherit from this class or use it as an inner class.

An object that wants to listen for property changes must be able to add and to remove itself from the listener list on the Bean containing the bound property, as well as respond to the event notification method that signals a property change. By implementing the `PropertyChangeListener` interface, the listener can be added to the list maintained by the bound property Bean. Because it implements the `PropertyChangeListener.propertyChange` method, the listener can respond to property change notifications.

The `PropertyChangeEvent` class encapsulates property change information and is sent from the property change event source to each object in the property change listener list via the `propertyChange` method. The following sections provide the details of implementing bound properties.

Implementing Bound Property Support Within a Bean

To implement a bound property, take the following steps:

1. Import the `java.beans` package. This gives you access to the `PropertyChangeSupport` class.
2. Instantiate a PropertyChangeSupport object.

```
private PropertyChangeSupport changes =
                        new PropertyChangeSupport(this);
```

   This object maintains the property change listener list and fires property change events. You can also make your class a `PropertyChangeSupport` subclass.

3. Implement methods to maintain the property change listener list. Since `PropertyChangeSupport` implements these methods, you merely wrap calls to the property change support object's methods.

```
public void addPropertyChangeListener(
                            PropertyChangeListener l) {
    changes.addPropertyChangeListener(l);
}
public void removePropertyChangeListener(
                            PropertyChangeListener l) {
    changes.removePropertyChangeListener(l);
}
```

4. Modify a property's setter method to fire a property change event when the property is changed. OurButton's `setLabel` method looks like this:

```
public void setLabel(String newLabel) {
    String oldLabel = label;
    label = newLabel; sizeToFit();
    changes.firePropertyChange("label", oldLabel,
                                newLabel);
}
```

   Note that `setLabel` stores the old `label` value, because both the old and new labels must be passed to `firePropertyChange`.

```
public void firePropertyChange(String propertyName,
                        Object oldValue, Object newValue)
```

   The `firePropertyChange` method bundles its parameters into a `PropertyChangeEvent` object and calls `propertyChange(PropertyChangeEvent pce)` on each registered listener. The old and new values are treated as `Object` values. If your property values are primitive types, you must use the object wrapper version, such as `java.lang.Integer`. Also, property change events are fired *after* the property has changed.

When the BeanBox (or Beans-aware builder tool) recognizes the design patterns for bound properties within your Bean, you will see a `propertyChange` interface item when you choose the Edit > Events menu.

Now that you have given your Bean the ability to broadcast events when a bound property has changed, the next step is to create a listener.

Implementing Bound Property Listeners

To listen for property change events, your listener Bean must implement the `PropertyChangeListener` interface. This interface contains one method:

```
public abstract void propertyChange(PropertyChangeEvent evt)
```

This is the notification method that the source Bean calls on all property change listeners in its property change listener list.

To make your class able to listen and to respond to property change events, you must

- Implement the `PropertyChangeListener` interface.

```
public class MyClass implements
        java.beans.PropertyChangeListener,
        java.io.Serializable {
```

- Implement the `propertyChange` method in the listener. This method needs to contain the code that handles what you need to do when the listener receives property change events. Very often, for example, this is a call to a setter method in the listener class: A property change in the source Bean propagates a change to a property in a listener Bean.

To register interest in receiving notification about a Bean property change, the listener Bean calls the listener registration method on the source Bean.

```
button.addPropertyChangeListener(aButtonListener);
```

Or you can use an adapter class to catch the property change event and subsequently call the correct method within the listener object. The following example is taken from comments in the `beans/demo/sunw/demo/misc/ChangeReporter.java` file.

```
OurButton button = new OurButton();
...
PropertyChangeAdapter adapter = new PropertyChangeAdapter();
...
button.addPropertyChangeListener(adapter);
```

```
...
class PropertyChangeAdapter implements PropertyChangeListener{
    public void propertyChange(PropertyChangeEvent e) {
        reporter.reportChange(e);
    }
}
```

Bound Properties in the BeanBox

The BeanBox handles bound property events just as it handles all events: by using an event hookup adapter. Event hookup adapter classes are generated by builder tools when you connect an event source Bean to an event listener Bean. These objects interpose between event sources and event listeners to provide control and filtering over event delivery. Since an event listener can register with multiple listeners that fire the same event type, event hookup adapters can be used to intercept an event from a particular event source and to forward it to the correct event listener. This saves the event listener from implementing code that would examine each event to determine whether it were from the correct source.

The `OurButton` and `ChangeReporter` Beans can be used to illustrate this technique. To see how this works, take the following steps.

1. Drop `OurButton` and `ChangeReporter` instances on the BeanBox.
2. Select the `OurButton` instance and choose the Edit > Events > propertyChange > propertyChange menu item.
3. Connect the rubber band line to the `ChangeReporter` instance. The `EventTargetDialog` will be displayed.
4. Choose `reportChange` from the `EventTargetDialog`. The event hookup adapter source will be generated and compiled.
5. Select `OurButton` and change some of its properties. You will see change reports in `ChangeReporter`.

Behind the scenes the BeanBox generated the event hookup adapter. This adapter implements the `PropertyChangeListener` interface and also generates a `propertyChange` method implementation that calls `ChangeReporter`'s `reportChange` method. Here's the generated adapter source code.

```
// Automatically generated event hookup file.
package tmp.sunw.beanbox;

import sunw.demo.misc.ChangeReporter;
import java.beans.PropertyChangeListener;
import java.beans.PropertyChangeEvent;
```

```
public class ___Hookup_14636f1560 implements
    java.beans.PropertyChangeListener, java.io.Serializable {

    public void setTarget(sunw.demo.misc.ChangeReporter t) {
        target = t;
    }

    public void propertyChange(java.beans.PropertyChangeEvent
                                    arg0) {
        target.reportChange(arg0);
    }

    private sunw.demo.misc.ChangeReporter target;
}
```

The `ChangeReporter` Bean need not implement the `PropertyChangeListener` interface; instead the BeanBox-generated adapter class implements `PropertyChangeListener`, and the adapter's `propertyChange` method calls the appropriate method in the target object (`ChangeReporter`).

The BeanBox puts the event adapter classes in the `beans/beanbox/tmp/sunw/beanbox` directory. When an adapter class is generated, you can view the adapter source in that directory.

Constrained Properties

A Bean property is constrained when any change to that property can be vetoed. Usually an outside object exercises the right to veto, but the Bean itself can also veto a property change.

The JavaBeans API provides an event mechanism, very similar to the bound property mechanism, that allows objects to veto a Bean's property changes.

Constrained property implementations have three parts:

- A *source* Bean containing one or more constrained properties.
- *Listener* objects that implement the `VetoableChangeListener` interface. A listener object accepts or rejects proposed changes to a constrained property in the source Bean.
- A `PropertyChangeEvent` object containing the property name and its old and new values. This is the same class used for bound properties.

Implementing Constrained Property Support within a Bean

A Bean containing constrained properties must

- Allow `VetoableChangeListener` objects to register and to unregister their interest in receiving notification that a property change is *proposed.*
- Fire property change events at those interested listeners when a property change is proposed. The event should be fired *before* the property change takes place. This gives each listener a chance to veto the proposed change. The `PropertyChangeEvent` is fired by a call to each listener's `vetoableChange` method.
- If a listener vetoes, make sure that any other listeners can revert to the old value. This means reissuing the `vetoableChange` call to all of the listeners, with a `PropertyChangeEvent` containing the old value.

The `VetoableChangeSupport` utility class is provided to implement these capabilities. This class implements methods to add and to remove `VetoableChangeListener` objects to a listener list, as well as a method that fires property change events at each listener in that list when a property change is proposed. This method will also catch any vetoes and will resend the property change event with the original property value. Your Bean can either inherit from `VetoableChangeSupport` or use an instance of it.

Note that constrained properties should generally also be bound properties. When a constrained property change does occur, a `PropertyChangeEvent` can be sent via `PropertyChangeListener.propertyChange` to signal all `VetoableChangeListener` Beans that the change has taken effect. This lets all of the vetoable change listeners know that the change was not vetoed by any listener.

The `JellyBean` demo Bean has a constrained property. We will use its code to illustrate the steps in implementing constrained properties. The following steps implement constrained properties in your Beans.

1. Import the `java.beans` package. This gives you access to the `VetoableChangeSupport` class.
2. Instantiate a `VetoableChangeSupport` object within your Bean.

   ```
   private VetoableChangeSupport vetos =
                              new VetoableChangeSupport(this);
   ```

   `VetoableChangeSupport` manages a list of `VetoableChangeListener` objects and fires property change events at each object in the list when a change occurs to a constrained property.

3. Implement methods to maintain the property change listener list. These merely wrap calls to the `VetoableChangeSupport` object's methods.

```
public void addVetoableChangeListener(
                              VetoableChangeListener l) {
    vetos.addVetoableChangeListener(l);
}
public void removeVetoableChangeListener(
                              VetoableChangeListener l) {
    vetos.removeVetoableChangeListener(l);
}
```

4. Write a property's setter method to fire a property change event when the property is changed. This includes adding a throws clause to the setter method's signature. `JellyBean`'s `setPriceInCents` method looks like this:

```
public void setPriceInCents(int newPriceInCents)
            throws PropertyVetoException {
   int oldPriceInCents = ourPriceInCents;

   // First tell the vetoers about the change. If anyone
   // objects, we don't catch the exception but just let
   // it pass on to our caller.
   vetos.fireVetoableChange("priceInCents",
                        new Integer(oldPriceInCents),
                        new Integer(newPriceInCents));
   // No one vetoed, so go ahead and make the change.
   ourPriceInCents = newPriceInCents;
   changes.firePropertyChange("priceInCents",
                        new Integer(oldPriceInCents),
                        new Integer(newPriceInCents));
}
```

Note that `setPriceInCents` stores the old `price`, because both the old and new prices must be passed to `fireVetoableChange`. Also note that the primitive `int` prices are converted to `Integer` objects.

```
public void fireVetoableChange(String propertyName,
                               Object oldValue,
                               Object newValue)
            throws PropertyVetoException
```

These values are then bundled into a `PropertyChangeEvent` object sent to each listener. The old and new values are treated as `Object` values, so if they are primitive types, such as `int`, you must use the object version, such as `java.lang.Integer`.

Now you are ready to implement a Bean that listens for constrained property changes.

Implementing Constrained Property Listeners

To listen for property change events, your listener Bean must implement the `VetoableChangeListener` interface. This interface contains one method:

```
void vetoableChange(PropertyChangeEvent evt)
                        throws PropertyVetoException;
```

So to make your class able to listen and to respond to property change events, your listener class must

- Implement the `VetoableChangeListener` interface.
- Implement the `vetoableChange` method. This is the method that will be called by the source Bean on each object in the listener list (maintained by the `VetoableChangeSupport` object). This is also the method that exercises veto power. A property change is vetoed by throwing the `PropertyVetoException`.

Note that the `VetoableChangeListener` object is often an adapter class. The adapter class implements the `VetoableChangeListener` interface and the `vetoableChange` method. This adapter is added to the constrained Bean's listener list, intercepts the `vetoableChange` call, and calls the target Bean method that exercises veto power. You'll see an example of this in the next section.

Constrained Properties in the BeanBox

When the BeanBox recognizes the design patterns for constrained properties within your Bean, you will see a `vetoableChange` interface item when you pull down the Edit > Events menu. As with any event hookup, the BeanBox generates an adapter class when you hook up a Bean with a constrained property to another Bean. To see how this works, take the following steps.

1. Drop `Voter` and `JellyBean` instances into the BeanBox.
2. Select the `JellyBean` instance, and choose the Edit > Events > vetoableChange > vetoableChange menu item.
3. Connect the rubber band line to the `Voter` Bean. This brings up the `EventTargetDialog` panel.
4. Choose the `Voter` Bean's `vetoableChange` method, and click on the OK button. This generates an event adapter. You can view this adapter in the `beans/beanbox/tmp/sunw/beanbox` directory.
5. Test the constrained property. Select the `JellyBean` and edit its `priceInCents` property in the Properties sheet. A `PropertyVetoException` is thrown, and an error dialog pops up.

Behind the scenes the BeanBox generated the event hookup adapter. This adapter implements the `VetoableChangeListener` interface and also generates a `vetoableChange` method implementation that calls the `Voter.vetoableChange` method. Here's the generated adapter source code.

```
// Automatically generated event hookup file.

package tmp.sunw.beanbox;

import sunw.demo.misc.Voter;
import java.beans.VetoableChangeListener;
import java.beans.PropertyChangeEvent;

public class ___Hookup_1475dd3cb5 implements
      java.beans.VetoableChangeListener, java.io.Serializable {

    public void setTarget(sunw.demo.misc.Voter t) {
        target = t;
    }

    public void vetoableChange(java.beans.PropertyChangeEvent
                               arg0)
                      throws java.beans.PropertyVeto Exception {
        target.vetoableChange(arg0);
    }

    private sunw.demo.misc.Voter target;
}
```

The `Voter` Bean need not implement the `VetoableChangeListener` interface; instead the generated adapter class implements `VetoableChangeListener`. The adapter's `vetoableChange` method calls the appropriate method in the target object (`Voter`).

Per Property Constraint

As with bound property support, JavaBeans has design pattern support for adding and removing `VetoableChangeListener` objects that are tied to a specific named property.

```
void addVetoableChangeListener(String propertyName,
                               VetoableChangeListener listener);

void removeVetoableChangeListener(String propertyName,
                               VetoableChangeListener listener);
```

As an alternative, a Bean can provide for each constrained property methods with the following signature to register and to unregister vetoable change listeners on a per property basis:

```
void add PropertyName Listener(VetoableChangeListener p);
void remove PropertyName Listener(VetoableChangeListener p);
```

Indexed Properties

Indexed properties represent collections of values accessed, like an array, by index. The indexed property design patterns are

```
//Methods to access the entire indexed property array
public PropertyType[] getPropertyName();
public void setPropertyName(PropertyType[] value);

//Methods to access individual values
public PropertyType getPropertyName(int index);
public void setPropertyName(int index, PropertyType value);
```

Conforming to these patterns lets builder tools know that your Bean contains an indexed property.

The `OurListBox` demo Bean illustrates how to use an indexed property. `OurListBox` extends the `List` class to provide a Bean that presents the user with a list of choices: choices that you can provide and change at design time. Here's an illustration of an `OurListBox` instance.

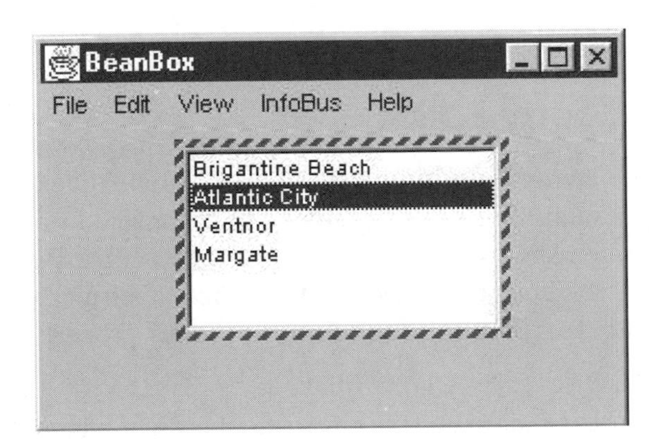

Figure 31 Instance of `OurListBox`.

OurListBox exposes the item indexed property with the following accessor methods:

```
public void setItems(String[] indexprop) {
    String[] oldValue=fieldIndexprop;
    fieldIndexprop=indexprop;
    populateListBox();
    support.firePropertyChange("items",oldValue, indexprop);
}

public void setItems(int index, String indexprop) {
    String[] oldValue=fieldIndexprop;
    fieldIndexprop[index]=indexprop;
    populateListBox();
    support.firePropertyChange("Items",oldValue,
                               fieldIndexprop);
}

public String[] getItems() {
    return fieldIndexprop;
}

public String getItems(int index) {
    return getItems()[index];
}
```

When an item is set by one of the setItems methods, OurListBox is populated with the contents of a String array.

Indexed properties are almost as easily exposed to builder tools as are simple properties. When you write an indexed property editor, however, you need to write a custom property editor.

Indexed Property Editors

The OurListBox demo Bean provides an associated IndexPropertyEditor, which is a good example of how to implement an indexed property editor. The following illustration shows an OurListBox instance in the BeanBox, the Properties sheet that contains an entry for the indexed property items, and the IndexPropertyEditor that pops up when the items property entry is clicked. See Figure 32.

Implementing IndexPropertyEditor is the same as implementing any custom property editor.

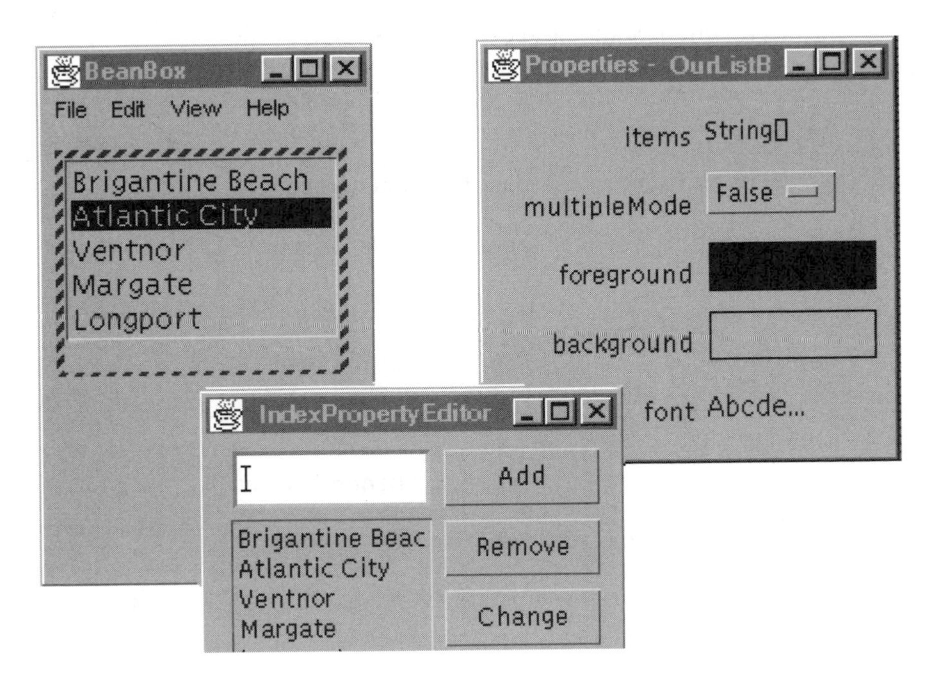

Figure 32 The `ImagePropertyEditor`, an indexed property editor.

1. Implement the `PropertyEditor` interface:

   ```
   public class IndexPropertyEditor extends Panel
                   implements PropertyEditor, Action Listener {
   ```

   You can use the `PropertyEditorSupport` class either by subclassing or using it as an inner class.

2. Denote the custom editor in a related `BeanInfo` class. `OurListBox` has a related `OurListBoxBeanInfo` class that contains the following code:

   ```
   itemsprop.setPropertyEditorClass
      (IndexPropertyEditor.class);
   ```

3. Make the property editor a source for bound property events. The property editor will register property listeners and will fire property change events at those listeners. This is how the property changes are propagated back to the Bean (via the Properties sheet). So `IndexPropertyEditor` instantiates an inner `PropertyChangeSupport` class.

   ```
   private PropertyChangeSupport support =
                               new PropertyChangeSupport(this);
   ```

4. Provide the ability for objects to register their interest in being notified when a property is edited.

```
public void addPropertyChangeListener(
                                PropertyChangeListener l) {
    support.addPropertyChangeListener(l);
}

public void removePropertyChangeListener(
                                PropertyChangeListener l) {
    support.removePropertyChangeListener(l);
}
```

Also fire property change events at those listeners.

```
public void actionPerformed(ActionEvent evt) {
    if (evt.getSource() == addButton) {
        listBox.addItem(textBox.getText());
        textBox.setText("");
        support.firePropertyChange("", null, null);
    } else if (evt.getSource()== textBox) {
        listBox.addItem(textBox.getText());
        textBox.setText("");
        support.firePropertyChange("",null,null);
    }
    ...
}
```

`IndexPropertyEditor` maintains `listbox` as a proxy for `OurListBox`. When a change is made to `listbox`, a property change event is fired to all listeners.

When the Properties sheet, which is registered as an `IndexPropertyEditor` listener, receives a property change event from `IndexPropertyEditor`, the Properties sheet calls `IndexPropertyEditor.getValue` to retrieve the new or changed items and to update the Bean.

http://java.sun.com/docs/books/tutorial/javabeans/events/index.html

22 Manipulating Events in the BeanBox

JAVABEANS use the new event mechanism implemented in JDK 1.1, so implementing Bean events is the same as implementing events in any JDK 1.1 or 1.2 component. This lesson explains how Beans and the BeanBox use this event mechanism. This lesson has the following sections:

Discovering Events

The BeanBox has two ways of discovering what events a bean can fire: design pattern introspection or a `BeanInfo` class.

Using Introspection

JavaBeans provide event-oriented design patterns to give introspecting tools the ability to discover what events a Bean can fire. In order to be the source of an event, a Bean must implement methods that add and remove listener objects for that type of event. The design patterns for these methods are

```
public void add EventListenerType(EventListenerType a)
public void remove EventListenerType(EventListenerType a)
```

These methods let a source Bean know where to fire events. The source Bean then fires events at those listener Beans, using the methods for those particular interfaces. For example, if a source Bean registers `ActionListener` objects, it will fire events at those objects by calling the `actionPerformed` method on those listeners.

To see events discovered using design patterns, drop an instance of `OurButton` into the BeanBox and pull down the Edit > Events menu, which displays a list of event interfaces to which `OurButton` can fire events. Note that `OurButton` itself only adds and removes two of these interfaces; the rest are inherited from the base class.

Using BeanInfo

You can explicitly "publish" the events a Bean fires by using a class that implements the `BeanInfo` interface. The `ExplicitButton` demo Bean is a subclass of `OurButton` and provides an associated `ExplicitButtonBeanInfo` class. `ExplicitButtonBeanInfo` implements the following method to explicitly define interfaces to which `ExplicitButton` fires events.

```
public EventSetDescriptor[] getEventSetDescriptors() {
    try {
        EventSetDescriptor push =
                            new EventSetDescriptor(beanClass,
                            "actionPerformed",
                            java.awt.event.ActionListener.class,
                            "actionPerformed");

        EventSetDescriptor changed =
              new EventSetDescriptor(beanClass,
              "propertyChange",
              java.beans.PropertyChangeListener.class,
              "propertyChange");
              push.setDisplayName("button push");
              changed.setDisplayName("bound property change");

        EventSetDescriptor[] rv = {push, changed};
        return rv;
    } catch (IntrospectionException e) {
        throw new Error(e.toString());
    }
}
```

Drop an `ExplicitButton` instance into the BeanBox, and pull down the Edit > Events menu. Notice that only those interfaces explicitly exposed in the `ExplicitButtonBeanInfo` class are listed. No inherited capabilities are exposed. See the next lesson, The BeanInfo Interface (page 273), for more information.

Viewing Events

If you select an `OurButton` Bean in the BeanBox and then pull down the Edit > Events menu, you will see a list of interfaces that `OurButton` can fire events at. Each interface item will, when chosen, display the methods that fire various events at those interfaces. Each method corresponds to all of the events that `OurButton` can fire.

Hooking Up Events in the BeanBox

In this example you will use two `OurButton` Bean instances to stop and to start an instance of the animated `Juggler` Bean. You will label the buttons Start and Stop; you will make the Start button, when chosen, invoke the `Juggler` Bean's `startJuggling` method; you will make the Stop button, when chosen, invoke the `Juggler` Bean's `stopJuggling` method.

1. Start the BeanBox.
2. Drop a `Juggler` Bean and two `OurButton` Bean instances into the BeanBox.
3. Select an `OurButton` instance. On the Properties sheet change the label property to `Start`. Select the second `OurButton` instance and change its label to `Stop`.
4. Choose the Start button. Choose the Edit > Events > action > actionPerformed menu item. This causes a rubber band line to track between the start button and the cursor. Click on the `Juggler` instance. This brings up the `EventTargetDialog`. See Figure 33.

   This list contains `Juggler` methods that take no arguments or arguments of type `actionPerformed`.
5. Select the `startJuggling` method and click on OK. You will see a message that the BeanBox is generating adapter classes.
6. Do steps 4 and 5 on the Stop button, but choose the `stopJuggling` method in the `EventTargetDialog`.

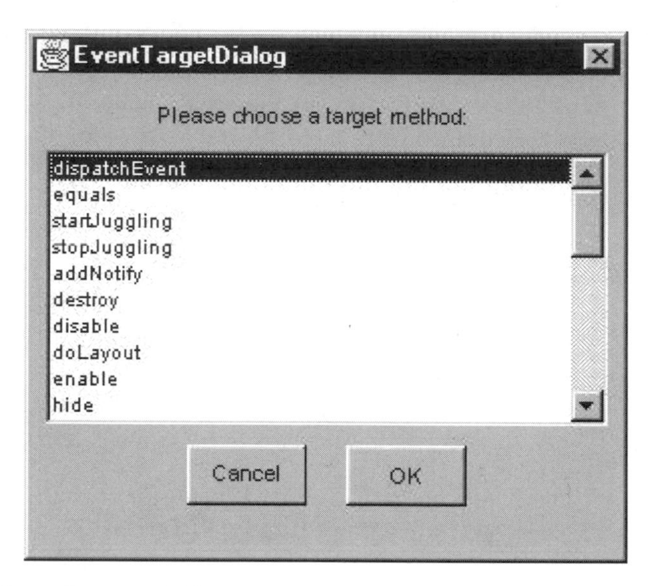

Figure 33 The `EventTargetDialog`.

Clicking on the Start and Stop buttons will now start and stop the `Juggler`. Here is a general description of what happened.

- The Start and Stop buttons are *event sources*. Event sources *fire events* at *event targets*. In this example the Juggler Bean is the event target.
- You choose the type of event that the event source will fire when you choose the Start button and choose an event method (via the Edit > Event menu item).
- You select the event target Bean when you connect the rubber band line to another Bean.
- The `EventTargetDialog` lists methods that can accept that type of event or that take no parameters. When you choose a method in the `EventTargetDialog`, you are specifying the method that will receive the fired event and act on it.

Use the File > Save menu item to save this example to a file of your choice.

Generating Event Adapter Classes

The BeanBox generates an adapter class that interposes between the event source and the target. The adapter class implements the appropriate event listener interface (and thus is the actual listener), catches the event fired by the button, and then calls the selected target Bean method. Here is the BeanBox-generated adapter class that interposes between the Start button and the Juggler Bean:

```
// Automatically generated event hookup file.

package tmp.sunw.beanbox;
import sunw.demo.juggler.Juggler;
import java.awt.event.ActionListener;
import java.awt.event.ActionEvent;

public class ___Hookup_1474c0159e implements
         java.awt.event.ActionListener, java.io.Serializable {

    public void setTarget(sunw.demo.juggler.Juggler t) {
        target = t;
    }

    public void
    actionPerformed(java.awt.event.ActionEvent arg0) {
        target.startJuggling(arg0);
    }

    private sunw.demo.juggler.Juggler target;
}
```

The adapter implements the `ActionListener` interface that you chose in the BeanBox's Edit > Events menu. `ActionListener` declares one method, `actionPerformed()`, which is implemented by the adapter to call the target Bean method (`startJuggling`) that you selected. The adapter's `setTarget` method is called by the BeanBox to set the actual target Bean, in this case `Juggler`.

The EventMonitor Demo Bean

The `EventMonitor` Bean prints out source Bean event reports, as they occur, in a scrolling list box. To see how this works, take the following steps.

1. Drop `OurButton` and `EventMonitor` instances into the BeanBox. You might want to resize the `EventMonitor` (and the BeanBox) to accommodate viewing the event reports.
2. Select the `OurButton` instance and choose any event method in the Edit > Events menu.
3. Connect the rubber band line to the `EventMonitor` and choose its `initiateEventSourcMonitoring` in the `EventTargetDialog`.

4. Select the `OurButton` Bean. You will begin seeing event reports in the `EventMonitor`.

When the first event is delivered, `EventMonitor` analyzes the source Bean to discover all of the events it fires, creates and registers an event listener for each event type, and then reports whenever any event is fired. This is useful for debugging. Try connecting other demo Beans to `EventMonitor` to observer their events.

http://java.sun.com/docs/books/tutorial/javabeans/beaninfo/index.html

23 The BeanInfo Interface

HOW does a builder tool examine a Bean and expose its features (properties, events, and methods) in a Properties sheet? A builder tool does so by using the `java.beans.Introspector` class. The `Introspector` class uses the JDK *core reflection* API to discover a Bean's methods and then applies the JavaBeans design patterns to discover the Bean's features. This discovery process is termed *introspection.*

Alternatively you can *explicitly* expose a Bean's features in a separate, associated class that implements the `BeanInfo` interface. By associating a `BeanInfo` class with your Bean, you can

- Expose only those features you want to expose
- Rely on `BeanInfo` to expose some Bean features while relying on low-level reflection to expose others
- Associate an icon with the target Bean
- Specify a customizer class
- Segregate features into normal and expert categories
- Provide a more descriptive display name or additional information about a Bean feature

BeanInfo defines methods that return descriptors for each property, method, or event that you want exposed. The prototypes for these methods are

```
PropertyDescriptor[] getPropertyDescriptors();
MethodDescriptor[]   getMethodDescriptors();
EventSetDescriptor[] getEventSetDescriptors();
```

Each of these methods returns an array of *descriptors* for each feature. The first section in this lesson identifies the BDK descriptor classes. The second section, Creating a BeanInfo Class (page 274), outlines the steps you need to take.

Feature Descriptors

BeanInfo classes contain *descriptors* that precisely describe the target Bean's features. The BDK implements the following descriptor classes.

- `FeatureDescriptor`, the base class for the other descriptor classes, declares the aspects common to all descriptor types.
- `BeanDescriptor` defines the target Bean's class type and name and customizer class, if it exists.
- `PropertyDescriptor` describes the target Bean's properties.
- `IndexedPropertyDescriptor`, a subclass of `PropertyDescriptor`, describes the target Bean's indexed properties.
- `EventSetDescriptor` describes the events the target Bean fires.
- `MethodDescriptor` describes the target Bean's methods.
- `ParameterDescriptor` describes method parameters.

The `BeanInfo` interface declares methods that return arrays of these descriptors.

Creating a BeanInfo Class

This section uses the `ExplicitButtonBeanInfo` demo class to illustrate creating a `BeanInfo` class. Here are the general steps to make a `BeanInfo` class.

1. Name your `BeanInfo` class. You must append the string `BeanInfo` to the target class name. If the target class name is `ExplicitButton`, its associated Bean information class must be named `ExplicitButtonBeanInfo`.
2. Subclass `SimpleBeanInfo`. This is a convenience class that implements `BeanInfo` methods to return `null` or an equivalent no-op value.

   ```
   public class ExplicitButtonBeanInfo
                extends SimpleBeanInfo {
   ```

   If you use `SimpleBeanInfo` you don't have to implement all of the `BeanInfo` methods; you only have to override those methods you need.

3. Override the appropriate methods to return the properties, methods, or events that you want exposed. `ExplicitButtonBeanInfo` overrides the `getPropertyDescriptors` method to return four properties, as follows:

```
public PropertyDescriptor[] getPropertyDescriptors() {
    try {
         PropertyDescriptor background =
           new PropertyDescriptor("background", beanClass);
         PropertyDescriptor foreground =
           new PropertyDescriptor("foreground", beanClass);
         PropertyDescriptor font =
           new PropertyDescriptor("font", beanClass);
         PropertyDescriptor label =
           new PropertyDescriptor("label", beanClass);

         background.setBound(true);
         foreground.setBound(true);
         font.setBound(true);
         label.setBound(true);

         PropertyDescriptor rv[] = {background, foreground,
                                    font, label};
             return rv;
         } catch (IntrospectionException e) {
             throw new Error(e.toString());
         }
     }
```

Note two important facts here.

- If you leave a descriptor out, that property, event, or method will *not* be exposed. In other words, you can selectively expose properties, events, or methods by leaving out those you don't want exposed.
- If a feature's getter (for example, `getMethodDescriptor`) method returns `null`, low-level reflection is then used for that feature. This means, for example, that you can explicitly specify properties and let low-level reflection discover the methods. If you don't override the `SimpleBeanInfo` default method, which returns `null`, low-level reflection will be used for that feature.

4. Optionally associate an icon with the target Bean.

```
public java.awt.Image getIcon(int iconKind) {
    if (iconKind == BeanInfo.ICON_MONO_16x16 ||
        iconKind == BeanInfo.ICON_COLOR_16x16) {
        java.awt.Image img =
                 loadImage("ExplicitButtonIcon16.gif");
        return img;
```

```
        }if (iconKind == BeanInfo.ICON_MONO_32x32 ||
              iconKind == BeanInfo.ICON_COLOR_32x32 ) {
            java.awt.Image img =
                    loadImage("ExplicitButtonIcon32.gif");
            return img;
        }
    return null;
    }
```

The BeanBox displays this icon next to the Bean name in the ToolBox. You can expect builder tools to do the same.

5. Specify the target Bean class; if the Bean has a customizer, specify it also.

```
public BeanDescriptor getBeanDescriptor() {
   return new BeanDescriptor(beanClass, customizerClass);
}
...
private final static Class beanClass =
   ExplicitButton.class;

private final static Class customizerClass =
   OurButtonCustomizer.class;
```

Keep the `BeanInfo` class in the same directory as its target class. The BeanBox first searches for a target Bean's `BeanInfo` class in the target Bean's package path. If no `BeanInfo` is found, the Bean information package search path (maintained by the `Introspector`) is searched. The default Bean information search path is `sun.beans.infos`. If no `BeanInfo` class is found, low-level reflection is used to discover a Bean's features.

Using BeanInfo to Control Feature Exposure

If you rely on low-level reflection to discover your Bean's features, all of those properties, methods, and events that conform to the appropriate design patterns will be exposed in a builder tool. This includes any features in all base classes. If the BeanBox finds an associated `BeanInfo` class, that information is used instead, and no more base classes are examined using reflection. In other words, `BeanInfo` information overrides low-level reflection information and prevents base-class examination.

By using a `BeanInfo` class, you can expose subsets of a particular Bean feature. For example, by not returning a method descriptor for a particular method, that method will not be exposed in a builder tool.

When you use a `BeanInfo` class, the following conditions apply.

- Base-class features will *not* be exposed. You can retrieve base-class features by using the `BeanInfo.getAdditionalBeanInfo` method.
- Properties, events, or methods that have no descriptor will *not* be exposed. For a particular feature, only those items returned in the descriptor array will be exposed. For example, if you return descriptors for all of your Bean methods except `foo`, `foo` will not be exposed.
- Low-level reflection will be used for features with getter methods returning `null`. For example, suppose that your `BeanInfo` class contains this method implementation:

```
public MethodDescriptor[]
getMethodDescriptors() {
    return null;
}
```

  Low-level reflection will be used to discover your Bean's public methods.

Locating BeanInfo Classes

Before examining a Bean, the `Introspector` will attempt to find a `BeanInfo` class associated with the Bean. By default the `Introspector` takes the target Bean's fully qualified package name and appends `BeanInfo` to form a new class name. For example, if the target Bean is `sunw.demo.buttons.ExplicitButton`, the `Introspector` will attempt to locate `sunw.demo.buttons.ExplicitButtonBeanInfo`.

If that fails, each package in the `BeanInfo` search path is searched. The `BeanInfo` search path is maintained by `Introspector.setBeanInfoSearchPath` and `Introspector.getBeanInfoSearchPath`.

http://java.sun.com/docs/books/tutorial/javabeans/customization/index.html

24 Bean Customization

A Bean's appearance and behavior can be customized at design time within Beans-compliant builder tools. Typically there are two ways to customize a Bean:

- By using a *property editor*. Each Bean property has its own property editor. A builder tool usually displays a Bean's property editors in a *Properties sheet*. A property editor is associated with and edits a particular property type.
- By using *customizers*. Customizers give you complete GUI control over Bean customization. Customizers are used when property editors are not practical or applicable. Unlike a property editor, which is associated with a property, a customizer is associated with a Bean.

The sections in this lesson focus on these two ways to customize Beans:

Property Editors

A property editor is a tool for customizing a particular property *type*. Property editors are displayed in or activated from Properties sheets. A Properties sheet determines a property's type, searches for a relevant property editor, and displays the property's current value in a relevant way.

Property editors must implement the `PropertyEditor` interface, which provides methods that specify how a property should be displayed in a Properties sheet.

The following figure of the BeanBox's Properties sheet contains `OurButton` properties.

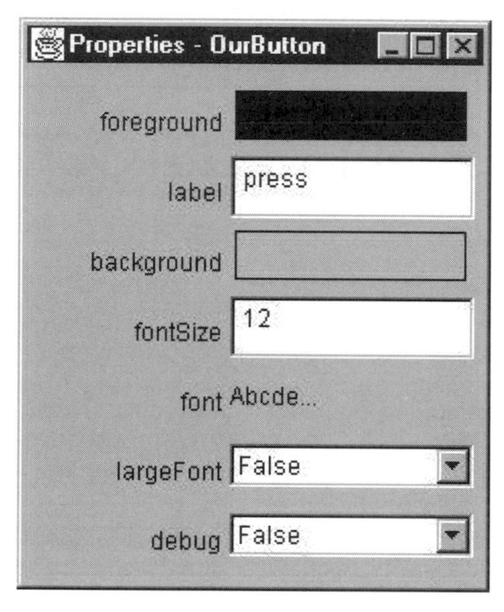

Figure 34 The `OurButton` properties shown in the BeanBox's Properties sheet.

You begin the process of editing these properties by clicking on the property entry in the sheet.

- The `label` and the `fontSize` properties are displayed in an editable text box. Changes can be made in place.
- The `largeFont` and the `debug` properties are selection boxes with discrete choices.
- Clicking on the `foreground`, `background`, and `font` entries brings up separate panels.

How each of these is displayed depends on which `PropertyEditor` methods you implement to return nonnull (or equivalent) values. For example, the `int` property editor implements the `setAsText` method. This indicates to the Properties sheet that the property can be displayed as a `String`; hence an editable text box will be used.

The `Color` and the `Font` property editors use a separate panel and use the Properties sheet merely to display the current property value. The editor is displayed by `sample` within the property sheet. You need to override `isPaintable` to return `true` and to override `paintValue` to paint the current property value in a rectangle in the Properties sheet. Here's how `ColorEditor` implements `paintValue`.

```
public void paintValue(java.awt.Graphics gfx,
                       java.awt.Rectangle box) {
    Color oldColor = gfx.getColor();
    gfx.setColor(Color.black);
    gfx.drawRect(box.x, box.y, box.width-3, box.height-3);
    gfx.setColor(color);
    gfx.fillRect(box.x+1, box.y+1, box.width-4, box.height-4);
    gfx.setColor(oldColor);
}
```

To support the custom property editor, you need to override two more methods. Override `supportsCustomEditor` to return `true`; override `getCustomEditor` to return a custom editor instance. `ColorEditor.getCustomEditor` returns `this`.

The `PropertyEditorSupport` class also maintains a `PropertyChangeListener` list. It also fires property change event notifications to those listeners when a bound property is changed.

Association with Properties

Property editors are discovered and associated with a given property in various ways.

- *Explicit association* via a `BeanInfo` object. The `Molecule` demo Bean uses this technique. Within the `MoleculeBeanInfo` class the `Molecule` Bean's property editor is set with the following line of code:

  ```
  pd.setPropertyEditorClass(MoleculeNameEditor.class);
  ```
- *Explicit registration* via `java.Beans.PropertyEditorManager.registerEditor`. This method takes a pair of arguments: the class type and the editor to be associated with that type.
- *Name search*. If a class has no explicitly associated property editor, the `PropertyEditorManager` searches for that class's property editor by appending `Editor` to either the fully qualified class name or to the simple class name and searching a class search path. In the former case, assuming a property implemented by a class named `java.beans.ComplexNumber`, the property editor manager would search for the `java.beans.ComplexNumberEditor` class. In the latter case, the default class path for the BeanBox is `sun.beans.editors`.

BDK Property Editors

The BDK provides property editors for the primitive data types, such as `int`, `boolean`, and `float`, and the `Color` and `Font` class types. The source code for these property editors is included on the CD-ROM that accompanies this book. These sources make a good starting point for writing your own property editors. Note the following about the BDK property editors.

- All of the "number" properties are represented as `String` objects. The `IntEditor` overrides `PropertyEditorSupport`'s `setAsText` method
- The `boolean` property editor, a menu of discrete choices, overrides the `PropertyEditorSupport`'s `getTags` method to return a `String[]` containing `True` and `False`.

```
public String[] getTags() {
    String result[] = { "True", "False" };
    return result;
}
```

- The `Color` and `Font` property editors implement *custom* property editors. Because these objects require a more sophisticated interface to be easily edited, a separate component pops up to do the property editing. If `supportsCustomEditor` is overridden to return `true`, the Properties sheet is thus signaled that this property's editor is a custom component. The `isPaintable` and the `paintValue` methods are also overridden to provide color and font painting in the editor's Properties sheet sample areas.

Note: If no property editor is found for a property, the BeanBox will not display that property in the Properties sheet.

Customizers

When you use a Bean *customizer*, you get complete control over how to configure or to edit a Bean. A customizer is like an application that specifically targets a Bean's customization. Sometimes properties are insufficient for representing a Bean's configurable attributes. Customizers are used when sophisticated instructions would be needed to change a Bean and when property editors are too primitive to achieve Bean customization.

All customizers must

- Extend `java.awt.Component` or one of its subclasses

- Implement the `java.beans.Customizer` interface: implementing methods to register `PropertyChangeListener` objects and firing property change events at those listeners when a change to the target Bean has occurred
- Implement a default constructor
- Associate the customizer with its target class via `BeanInfo`'s `getBeanDescriptor` method

If a Bean that has an associated customizer is dropped into the BeanBox, you will notice a Customize... item on the Edit menu.

BDK Customizers

The `OurButtonCustomizer` serves as an example that demonstrates the mechanics of building a customizer. The customizer:

- Extends `java.awt.Panel` (a `Component` subclass).
- Implements the `Customizer` interface and uses a `PropertyChangeSupport` object to manage `PropertyChangeListener` registration and notification. See the section Bound Properties (page 254) in the Properties lesson for a `PropertyChangeSupport` description.
- Implements a default constructor.

```
public OurButtonCustomizer() {
    setLayout(null);
}
```

- Is associated with its target class, `ExplicitButton`, by the following `ExplicitButtonBeanInfo` code:

```
public BeanDescriptor getBeanDescriptor() {
    return new BeanDescriptor(beanClass, customizerClass);
}
...
private final static Class customizerClass
                                  = OurButtonCustomizer.class;
```

The `BridgeTester` and the `JDBC Select` demo Beans also have customizers.

http://java.sun.com/docs/books/tutorial/javabeans/persistence/index.html

25 Bean Persistence

A Bean persists by having its properties, fields, and state information saved and restored to and from storage. The mechanism that makes persistence possible is called *serialization*. When a Bean instance is serialized, it is converted into a data stream and is written to storage. Any applet, application, or tool that uses that Bean can then "reconstitute" it by *deserialization*. JavaBeans use the JDK's object serialization API for its serialization needs.

All Beans must persist. To persist, your Beans must support serialization by implementing either the `java.io.Serializable` interface or the `java.io.Externalizable` interface. These interfaces offer you the choice between automatic serialization and "roll your own." As long as one class in a class's inheritance hierarchy implements `Serializable` or `Externalizable`, that class is serializable.

The sections in this lesson discuss various facets of serialization.

This section describes `Serializable`, the default serialization interface, in which everything gets serialized.

This section shows you how to use modifiers to selectively exclude fields you do not want serialized.

This section explains how to write Beans to a specific file format by implementing `Externalizable`, and its two methods to give you complete control over your Bean's serialization.

Automatic Serialization

The `Serializable` interface provides automatic serialization by using the Java object serialization tools. `Serializable` declares no methods; it acts as a marker, telling the object serialization tools that your Bean class is serializable. By marking your class with `Serializable`, you are telling the Java Virtual Machine that you have made sure that your class will work with default serialization. Following are some important points about working with the `Serializable` interface.

- Classes that implement `Serializable` must have a *no-argument constructor.* This constructor will be called when an object is "reconstituted" from a `.ser` file.
- You don't need to implement `Serializable` in your class if it is already implemented in a superclass. You do, however, need to make sure that it works correctly and as you expect with default serialization.
- All fields but `static` and `transient` are serialized. Use the `transient` modifier to specify fields you do not want serialized and to specify classes that are not serializable.

The BeanBox writes serialized Beans to a file with a `.ser` extension.

The `OurButton` demo Bean uses default serialization to make its properties persist. `OurButton` added `Serializable` to its class definition only to make use of default serialization:

```
public class OurButton extends Component
                            implements Serializable,...
```

If you drop an `OurButton` instance into the BeanBox, the properties sheet displays `OurButton`'s properties. Take the following steps to ascertain that serialization is working.

1. Change some `OurButton` properties. For example, change the font size and colors.
2. Serialize the changed `OurButton` instance by choosing the File > Serialize-Component... BeanBox menu item. A file browser will pop up.
3. Put the `.ser` file in a JAR file with a suitable manifest.
4. Clear the BeanBox form by choosing the File > Clear menu item.
5. Reload the serialized instance by choosing the File > LoadJar menu item.

The `OurButton` instance will appear in the BeanBox with your property changes intact. By implementing `Serializable` in your class, simple, primitive properties and fields can be serialized. For more complex class members, different techniques must be used.

Selective Serialization

When you do not want all fields to be serialized, you can use the `transient` keyword to exclude fields from serialization in a `Serializable` object. You use the `transient` modifier to mark the fields.

```
transient int Status;
```

Default serialization will not serialize `transient` and `static` fields.

If your serializable class contains either of the following two methods (the signatures must be exact), the default serialization will not take place.

```
private void writeObject(java.io.ObjectOutputStream out)
    throws IOException;

private void readObject(java.io.ObjectInputStream in)
    throws IOException, ClassNotFoundException;
```

You can control how more complex objects are serialized by writing your own implementations of the `writeObject` and the `readObject` methods. Implement `writeObject` when you need to exercise greater control over what gets serialized, when you need to serialize objects that default serialization cannot handle, or when you need to add data to the serialization stream that is not an object data member. Implement `readObject` to reconstruct the data stream you wrote with `writeObject`.

For example, the `Molecule` demo Bean keeps a version number in a `static` field. Since `static` fields are not serialized by default, `writeObject` and `readObject` are implemented to serialize this field. Here are the `writeObject` and the `readObject` implementations in `Molecule.java`:

```
private void writeObject(java.io.ObjectOutputStream s)
                        throws java.io.IOException {
    s.writeInt(ourVersion);
    s.writeObject(moleculeName);
}
```

```
private void readObject(java.io.ObjectInputStream s)
                    throws java.lang.ClassNotFoundException,
                    java.io.IOException {
    // Compensate for missing constructor.
    reset();
    if (s.readInt() != ourVersion) {
        throw new IOException("Molecule.readObject:
                              version mismatch");
    }
    moleculeName = (String) s.readObject();
}
```

These implementations limit the fields serialized to `ourVersion` and `moleculeName`. Any other data in the class will not be serialized.

It is best to use the `ObjectInputStream`'s `defaultWriteObject` and `defaultReadObject` before doing your own specific stream writing.

```
private void writeObject(java.io.ObjectOutputStream s)
                              throws java.io.IOException {
    //First write out defaults
    s.defaultWriteObject();
    ...
}

private void readObject(java.io.ObjectInputStream s)
                     throws java.lang.ClassNotFoundException,
                     java.io.IOException {
    //First read in defaults
    s.defaultReadObject();
    ...
}
```

Complete Serialization Control

Use the `Externalizable` interface when you need complete control over your Bean's serialization (for example, when writing and reading a specific file format). You need to implement two methods: `readExternal` and `writeExternal`. `Externalizable` classes must also have a no-argument constructor.

When you run the BeanBox, you will see two Beans, `BlueButton` and `OrangeButton`, in the ToolBox. These two Beans are serialized instances of the `ExternalizableButton` class.

ExternalizableButton implements the Externalizable interface. This means that it does all of its own serialization, implementing the readExternal and writeExternal methods defined by Externalizable. The BlueButtonWriter program is used by the buttons makefile to create an ExternalizableButton instance, to change its background property to blue, and to write the Bean to the file BlueButton.ser. Another button, OrangeButton, is created the same way, using OrangeButtonWriter. The button makefile then puts these .ser files in buttons.jar, where the ToolBox can find and reconstitute them.

About the Author

ANDY QUINN is a Sun Microsystems technical writer who specializes in writing for software developers. Andy was one of the original guest authors on *The Java Tutorial* when he posted his first trail on JavaBeans in 1997. Andy graduated from the University of California, Santa Cruz, with a B.S. in Computer Science. He has recently migrated back to the East Coast, where he continues to surf and play the guitar.

Acknowledgments

Special thanks to Bill Nolan and Maureen McPherson.

JDBC Database Access

by Maydene Fisher

JDBC™ was designed to keep simple things simple.[1] This means that the JDBC API makes everyday database tasks, such as simple SELECT statements, very easy. This trail walks you through examples of using JDBC to execute common SQL statements, letting you see for yourself how easy it is to use the basic JDBC API.

This trail is divided into two lessons.

JDBC Basics (page 295) covers the JDBC 1.0 API, which is included in JDK™ 1.1. By the end of the first lesson, you will know how to use the basic JDBC API to create tables, to insert values into them, to query the tables, to retrieve the results of the queries, and to update the tables. In this process you will learn how to use simple statements and prepared statements, and you will see an example of a stored procedure. You will also learn how to perform transactions and how to catch exceptions and warnings. The last part of this lesson shows you how to create an applet.

New Features in the JDBC 2.0 API (page 333) covers the JDBC 2.0 API, which is part of the JDK 1.2 release. This lesson also briefly describes the JDBC extension API, which, like other standard extensions, will be released independently. This lesson teaches you how to move the cursor in a scrollable result set, how to update result sets by using the JDBC 2.0 API, and how to make batch

---

[1] Note that "JDBC" is a trademarked name and not an acronym; nevertheless, it is often associated with *Java Database Connectivity*.

updates. You will also learn about the new SQL3 data types and how to use them in an application written in the Java™ programming language. The final part of this lesson gives you a preview of the JDBC extension API, with features that let you take advantage of JavaBeans™ technology and Enterprise JavaBeans™ technology.

This trail will not cover how to use the metadata API, which is used in more sophisticated programs, such as applications that must dynamically discover and present the table structure of a target database.

Note: The material on the JDBC 1.0 API is based on the first edition of *JDBC Database Access with Java: A Tutorial and Annotated Reference*, written by Graham Hamilton, Rick Cattell, and Maydene Fisher, and published by Addison Wesley Longman, Inc. For more complete information about the JDBC 2.0 API and the JDBC extension API, see the updated Java Series book written by Seth White, Maydene Fisher, Graham Hamilton, Rick Cattell, and Mark Hapner, and published in Spring 1999.

http://java.sun.com/docs/books/tutorial/jdbc/basics/index.html

26 JDBC Basics

IN this lesson you will learn the basics of the JDBC API. We start by giving you setup instructions in Getting Started (page 295), Setting Up a Database (page 296), and Establishing a Connection (page 297). The next several sections explain how to create and update tables and how to use joins, transactions and stored procedures. The final three sections give instructions on how to complete your JDBC application and how to convert it to an applet.

This lesson covers the JDBC 1.0 API, which is included in JDK 1.1, and notes where procedures have changed in JDBC 2.0, which is included in JDK 1.2. For coverage of JDBC 2.0 and more advanced features, see the next lesson, New Features in the JDBC 2.0 API (page 333).

Note: Most JDBC drivers available at the time of this printing are for JDBC 1.0. More drivers will become available for JDBC 2.0 as it gains wider acceptance.

Getting Started

The first thing you need to do is check that you are set up properly. This involves the following steps.

1. Install Java and JDBC on your machine. To install both the Java platform and the JDBC API, simply follow the instructions for downloading the latest release of the JDK. When you download the JDK, you will get JDBC as well. The sample code demonstrating the JDBC 1.0 API was written for JDK1.1 and will run on any version of the Java platform that is compatible

with JDK1.1, including JDK1.2. Note that the sample code illustrating the JDBC 2.0 API requires JDK1.2[1] and will not run on JDK1.1.

2. Install a driver on your machine. Your driver should include instructions for installing it. For JDBC drivers written for a specific database managements system (DBMS), installation consists of copying the driver onto your machine; no special configuration is needed.

   The JDBC–ODBC Bridge driver is not quite as easy to set up. If you download either the Solaris or the Win32 versions of JDK1.1, you will automatically get the JDBC–ODBC Bridge driver, which does not itself require any special configuration. ODBC, however, does. If you do not already have ODBC on your machine, you will need to see your ODBC driver vendor for information on installation and configuration.

3. Install your DBMS, if needed. If you do not already have a DBMS installed, you will need to follow the vendor's instructions for installation. Most users will have a DBMS installed and will be working with an established database.

Setting Up a Database

Creating a database is not at all difficult, but it requires special permissions and is normally done by a database administrator. When you create the tables used as examples in this tutorial, they will be in the default database. We purposely kept the size and number of tables small to keep things manageable. We will assume that the database `COFFEEBREAK` already exists.

Suppose that our sample database is being used by the proprietor of The Coffee Break, a small coffee house where coffee beans are sold by the pound and brewed coffee is sold by the cup. To keep things simple, also suppose that the proprietor needs only two tables, one for types of coffee and one for coffee suppliers.

First, we will show you how to open a connection with your DBMS. Then, since what JDBC does is to send your SQL code to your DBMS, we will demonstrate some SQL code. After that we will show you how easy it is to use JDBC to pass these SQL statements to your DBMS and to process the results that are returned. For your convenience the JDBC code used in this lesson is available on the CD-ROM that accompanies this book.

---

[1] JDK 1.2 is included on the CD-ROM that accompanies this book. You can also download the latest release of JDK 1.2 here: http://java.sun.com/products/jdk/1.2/

This code has been tested on most of the major DBMS products. However, you may encounter some compatibility problems using it with older ODBC drivers with the JDBC–ODBC Bridge.

Establishing a Connection

First, you need to establish a connection with the DBMS you want to use. This involves loading the driver and making the connection.

Loading Drivers

Loading the driver or drivers you want to use is very simple and involves just one line of code. If, for example, you want to use the JDBC–ODBC Bridge driver, the following code will load it:

```
Class.forName("sun.jdbc.odbc.JdbcOdbcDriver");
```

Your driver documentation will give you the class name to use. For instance, if the class name is `jdbc.DriverXYZ`, you would use the following line of code to load the driver:

```
Class.forName("jdbc.DriverXYZ");
```

When you have loaded a driver, it is available for making a connection with a DBMS. You do not need to create an instance of a driver and to register it with the `DriverManager` because calling `Class.forName` will do that for you automatically. If you were to create your own instance, you would be creating an unnecessary duplicate, but it would do no harm.

Making the Connection

The second step in establishing a connection is to have the appropriate driver connect to the DBMS. The following line of code illustrates the general idea:

```
Connection con = DriverManager.getConnection(
                                url, "myLogin", "myPassword");
```

This step is also simple, with the hardest thing being what to supply for *`url`*. If you are using the JDBC–ODBC Bridge driver, the JDBC URL will start with `jdbc:odbc:`. The rest of the URL is generally your data source name or database system. So if you are using ODBC to access an ODBC data source called `Fred`, for example, your JDBC URL could be `jdbc:odbc:Fred`. In place of `myLogin` you put the name you use to log in to the DBMS; in place of `myPassword` you put your password for the DBMS. So if you log in to your DBMS with a login name of `Fernanda` and a password of `J8`, just these two lines of code will establish a connection:

```
String url = "jdbc:odbc:Fred";
Connection con = DriverManager.getConnection(url,
                                        "Fernanda", "J8");
```

If you are using a JDBC driver developed by a third party, the documentation will tell you what subprotocol to use, that is, what to put after `jdbc:` in the JDBC URL. For example, if the driver developer has registered the name *acme* as the subprotocol, the first and second parts of the JDBC URL will be `jdbc:acme:`. The driver documentation will also give you guidelines for the rest of the JDBC URL. This last part of the JDBC URL supplies information for identifying the data source.

If one of the drivers you loaded recognizes the JDBC URL supplied to the method `DriverManager.getConnection`, that driver will establish a connection to the DBMS specified in the JDBC URL. The `DriverManager` class, true to its name, manages all of the details of establishing the connection for you behind the scenes. Unless you are writing a driver, you will probably never use any of the methods in the interface `Driver`, and the only `DriverManager` method you really need to know is `DriverManager.getConnection`.

The connection returned by the method `DriverManager.getConnection` is an open connection you can use to create JDBC statements that pass your SQL statements to the DBMS. In the previous example *con* is an open connection, and we will use it in the examples that follow.

Setting Up Tables

Creating a Table

First, we will create one of the tables in our database. Table 21, "`COFFEES`," on page 299 contains the essential information about the coffees sold at The Coffee Break, including the coffee names, their prices, the number of pounds sold the current week, and the number of pounds sold to date.

Table 21 COFFEES

COF_NAME	SUP_ID	PRICE	SALES	TOTAL
Colombian	101	7.99	0	0
French_Roast	49	8.99	0	0
Espresso	150	9.99	0	0
Colombian_Decaf	101	8.99	0	0
French_Roast_Decaf	49	9.99	0	0

The column storing the coffee name, COF_NAME, holds values with an SQL type of VARCHAR and a maximum length of 32 characters. Since we will use different names for each type of coffee sold, the name will uniquely identify a particular coffee and can therefore serve as the primary key. The second column, SUP_ID, holds a number that identifies the coffee supplier; this number will be of SQL type INTEGER. The third column, PRICE, stores values with an SQL type of FLOAT because it needs to hold values with decimal points. (Note that money values would normally be stored in an SQL type DECIMAL or NUMERIC, but because of differences among DBMSs and to avoid incompatibility with older versions of JDBC, we are using the more standard type FLOAT for this tutorial.) The SALES column stores values of SQL type INTEGER and indicates the number of pounds of coffee sold during the current week. The final column, TOTAL, contains an SQL INTEGER that gives the total number of pounds of coffee sold to date.

Table 22, SUPPLIERS, gives information about each of the suppliers.

Table 22 SUPPLIERS

SUP_ID	SUP_NAME	STREET	CITY	STATE	ZIP
101	Acme, Inc.	99 Market Street	Groundsville	CA	95199
49	Superior Coffee	1 Party Place	Mendocino	CA	95460
150	The High Ground	100 Coffee Lane	Meadows	CA	93966

The tables COFFEES and SUPPLIERS both contain the column SUP_ID, which means that these two tables can be used in SELECT statements to get data based on the information in both tables. The column SUP_ID is the primary key in the table SUPPLIERS, and as such it uniquely identifies each of the coffee suppliers. In the table COFFEES, SUP_ID is called a foreign key. (A foreign key is one that it is imported from another table.) Note that each SUP_ID number appears only once in the SUPPLIERS table; this is required for it to be a primary key. In the

COFFEES table, where SUP_ID is a foreign key, however, duplicate SUP_ID numbers are allowed because one supplier may sell many types of coffee. Later in this lesson, you will see an example of how to use primary and foreign keys in a SELECT statement.

The following SQL statement creates the table COFFEES. The entries within the outer pair of parentheses consist of the name of a column, followed by a space and the SQL type to be stored in that column. A comma separates the entry for one column (consisting of column name and SQL type) from the next one. The type VARCHAR is created with a maximum length, so it takes a parameter indicating that maximum length. The parameter must be in parentheses following the type. The SQL statement shown here, for example, specifies that the name in column COF_NAME may be up to 32 characters long.

```
CREATE TABLE COFFEES
(COF_NAME VARCHAR(32),
 SUP_ID INTEGER,
 PRICE FLOAT,
 SALES INTEGER,
 TOTAL INTEGER)
```

This code does not end with a DBMS statement terminator, which can vary from DBMS to DBMS. For example, Oracle uses a semicolon (;) to indicate the end of a statement, and Sybase uses the word go. The driver you are using will automatically supply the appropriate statement terminator, and you will not need to include it in your JDBC code.

Another thing we should point out about SQL statements is their form. In the CREATE TABLE statement keywords are printed in uppercase letters, and each item is on a separate line. SQL does not require either; these conventions simply make statements easier to read. The standard in SQL is that keywords are not case sensitive. Thus, for example, the following SELECT statement can be written in various equivalent ways.

```
SELECT First_Name, Last_Name
FROM Employees
WHERE Last_Name LIKE "Washington"

select First_Name, Last_Name from Employees where
Last_Name like "Washington"
```

Quoted material, however, is case sensitive: In the name Washington for example, W must be capitalized, and the rest of the letters must be lowercase.

Requirements can vary from one DBMS to another when it comes to identifier names. For example, one DBMS may require that column and table names be given exactly as they were created in the CREATE TABLE statement, whereas another does not. To be safe, we will use all uppercase letters for identifiers, such as COFFEES and SUPPLIERS, because that is how we defined them.

So far we have written the SQL statement that creates the table COFFEES. Now let's put quotation marks around it (making it a string) and assign that string to the variable *createTableCoffees* so that we can use the variable in our JDBC code later. As just shown the DBMS does not care about where lines are divided, but in the Java programming language a String object that extends beyond one line will not compile. Consequently, when you are giving strings, you need to enclose each line in quotation marks and to use a plus sign (+) to concatenate strings.

```
String createTableCoffees = "CREATE TABLE COFFEES " +
    "(COF_NAME VARCHAR(32), SUP_ID INTEGER, PRICE FLOAT, " +
    "SALES INTEGER, TOTAL INTEGER)";
```

The data types we used in our CREATE TABLE statement are the generic SQL types (also called JDBC types) that are defined in the class java.sql.Types. DBMSs generally use these standard types. So when the time comes to try out some JDBC applications, you can just use the application CreateCoffees.java, which uses the CREATE TABLE statement. If your DBMS uses its own local type names, we supply another application for you, which we will explain fully later.

Before running any applications, however, we are going to walk you through the basics of JDBC.

Creating JDBC Statements

A Statement object is what sends your SQL statement to the DBMS. You simply create a Statement object and then execute it, supplying the appropriate execute method with the SQL statement you want to send. Use executeQuery for a SELECT statement. Use executeUpdate for statements that create or modify tables.

It takes an instance of an active connection to create a Statement object. In the following example we use our Connection object *con* to create the Statement object *stmt*:

```
Statement stmt = con.createStatement();
```

At this point *stmt* exists, but it does not have an SQL statement to pass on to the DBMS. We need to supply that to the method we use to execute *stmt*. For example, in the following code fragment we supply `executeUpdate` with the SQL statement from the preceding example:

```
stmt.executeUpdate("CREATE TABLE COFFEES " +
    "(COF_NAME VARCHAR(32), SUP_ID INTEGER, PRICE FLOAT, " +
    "SALES INTEGER, TOTAL INTEGER)");
```

Since we made a string out of the SQL statement and assigned it to the variable *createTableCoffees*, we could have written the code in this alternative form:

```
stmt.executeUpdate(createTableCoffees);
```

Executing Statements

We used the method `executeUpdate` because the SQL statement contained in *createTableCoffees* is a DDL (data definition language) statement. Statements that create, alter, or drop a table are all examples of DDL statements and are executed with the method `executeUpdate`. As you might expect from its name, the method `executeUpdate` is also used to execute SQL statements that update a table. In practice `executeUpdate` is used far more often to update tables than it is to create them because a table is created once but may be updated many times.

The method used most often for executing SQL statements is `executeQuery`. This method is used to execute `SELECT` statements, which comprise the vast majority of SQL statements. You will see how to use this method shortly.

Entering Data into a Table

We have shown how to create the table `COFFEES` by specifying the names of the columns and the data types to be stored in those columns, but this sets up only the structure of the table. The table does not yet contain any data. We will enter our data into the table one row at a time, supplying the information to be stored in each column of that row. Note that the values to be inserted into the columns are listed in the same order that the columns were declared when the table was created, which is the default order.

The following code inserts one row of data, with `Colombian` in the column `COF_NAME`, `101` in `SUP_ID`, `7.99` in `PRICE`, `0` in `SALES`, and `0` in `TOTAL`. (Since The Coffee Break has just opened, the amount sold during the week and the total to date are zero for of all the coffees to start with.) Just as we did in the code that created the table COFFEES, we will create a Statement object and then execute it, using the method executeUpdate.

Since the SQL statement will not quite fit on one line on the page, we have split it into two strings concatenated by a plus sign (+) so that it will compile. Pay special attention to the need for a space between COFFEES and VALUES. This space must be within the quotation marks and may be after COFFEES or before VALUES; without a space the SQL statement will erroneously be read as "INSERT INTO COFFEESVALUES..." and the DBMS will look for the table COFFEESVALUES. Also note that we use single quotation marks around the coffee name because it is nested within double quotation marks. For most DBMSs the general rule is to alternate double quotation marks and single quotation marks to indicate nesting.

```
Statement stmt = con.createStatement();
stmt.executeUpdate("INSERT INTO COFFEES " +
                   "VALUES ('Colombian', 101, 7.99, 0, 0)");
```

The code that follows inserts a second row into the table COFFEES. Note that we can just reuse the Statement object *stmt* rather than having to create a new one for each execution.

```
stmt.executeUpdate("INSERT INTO COFFEES " +
                   "VALUES ('French_Roast', 49, 8.99, 0, 0)");
```

Values for the remaining rows can be inserted as follows:

```
stmt.executeUpdate("INSERT INTO COFFEES " +
             "VALUES ('Espresso', 150, 9.99, 0, 0)");

stmt.executeUpdate("INSERT INTO COFFEES " +
             "VALUES ('Colombian_Decaf', 101, 8.99, 0, 0)");

stmt.executeUpdate("INSERT INTO COFFEES " +
             "VALUES ('French_Roast_Decaf', 49, 9.99, 0, 0)");
```

Getting Data from a Table

Now that the table COFFEES has values in it, we can write a SELECT statement to access those values. The asterisk (*) in the following SQL statement indicates that all columns should be selected. Since there is no WHERE clause to narrow down the rows from which to select, the following SQL statement selects the whole table:

```
SELECT *
FROM COFFEES
```

The result, which is the entire table, will look similar to the following:

```
COF_NAME             SUP_ID          PRICE      SALES       TOTAL
---------------      -----           -----      -----       -----
Colombian             101            7.99         0           0
French_Roast           49            8.99         0           0
Espresso              150            9.99         0           0
Colombian_Decaf       101            8.99         0           0
French_Roast_Decaf     49            9.99         0           0
```

This result is what you would see on your terminal if you entered the SQL query directly to the database system. When we access a database through a Java application, as we will be doing shortly, we will need to retrieve the results so that we can use them. You will see how to do this in the next section.

Here is another example of a `SELECT` statement; this one will get a list of coffees and their respective prices per pound:

```
SELECT COF_NAME, PRICE
FROM COFFEES
```

The results of this query will look something like this:

```
COF_NAME                  PRICE
------------------        -----
Colombian                 7.99
French_Roast              8.99
Espresso                  9.99
Colombian_Decaf           8.99
French_Roast_Decaf        9.99
```

The preceding `SELECT` statement generates the names and the prices of all of the coffees in the table. The following SQL statement limits the coffees selected to those that cost less than $9.00 per pound:

```
SELECT COF_NAME, PRICE
FROM COFFEES
WHERE PRICE < 9.00
```

The results would look similar to this:

```
COF_NAME                 PRICE
---------------          -----
Colombian                7.99
French_Roast             8.99
Colombian Decaf          8.99
```

Retrieving Values from Result Sets

We now show how you send the preceding `SELECT` statements from a program written in the Java programming language and how you get the results we showed. JDBC returns results in a `ResultSet` object, so we need to declare an instance of the class `ResultSet` to hold our results. The following code demonstrates declaring the `ResultSet` object *rs* and assigning to it the results of our earlier query:

```
ResultSet rs = stmt.executeQuery("SELECT COF_NAME, PRICE
                                  FROM COFFEES");
```

Using the Method next

The variable *rs*, which is an instance of `ResultSet`, contains the rows of coffees and prices shown in the preceding result set example. In order to access the names and prices, we will go to each row and retrieve the values according to their types. The method `next` moves a *cursor* to the next row and makes that row (called the *current row*) the one on which we can operate. Since the cursor is initially positioned just above the first row of a `ResultSet` object, the first call to the method `next` moves the cursor to the first row and makes it the current row. Successive invocations of the method `next` move the cursor down one row at a time from top to bottom. As noted in the lesson New Features in the JDBC 2.0 API (page 333), you can move the cursor both forward and backward, to specific positions, and to positions relative to the current row with the JDBC 2.0 API.

Using the *getXXX* Methods

We use the *getXXX* method of the appropriate type to retrieve the value in each column. For example, the first column in each row of *rs* is `COF_NAME`, which stores a value of SQL type `VARCHAR`. The method for retrieving a value of SQL type `VARCHAR` is `getString`. The second column in each row stores a value of SQL type `FLOAT`, and the method for retrieving values of that type is `getFloat`. The following code accesses the values stored in the current row of *rs* and prints a line with the name followed by three spaces and the price. Each time the method next is invoked, the next row becomes the current row, and the loop continues until no more rows are in *rs*.

```
String q uery = "SELECT COF_NAME, PRICE FROM COFFEES";
ResultSet rs = stmt.executeQuery(q uery);
    while (rs.next()) {
    String s = rs.getString("COF_NAME");
    Float n = rs.getFloat("PRICE");
    System.out.println(s + "   " + n);
}
```

The output will look something like this:

```
➥Colombian   7.99
➥French_Roast   8.99
➥Espresso   9.99
➥Colombian_Decaf   8.99
➥French_Roast_Decaf   9.99
```

Note that we use a curved arrow to identify output from JDBC code; it is not part of the output. The arrow is not used for results in a result set, so its use distinguishes between what is contained in a result set and what is printed as the output of an application.

Let's look a little more closely at how the getXXX methods work by examining the two getXXX statements in this code. First, let's examine getString.

```
String s = rs.getString("COF_NAME");
```

The method getString is invoked on the ResultSet object *rs*, so getString will retrieve (*get*) the value stored in the column COF_NAME in the current row of *rs*. The value that getString retrieves has been converted from an SQL VARCHAR to a String in the Java programming language, and it is assigned to the String object *s*. Note that we used the variable *s* in the println expression, that is, println(s + "   " + n). The situation is similar with the method getFloat, except that it retrieves the value stored in the column PRICE, which is an SQL FLOAT, and converts it to a Java float before assigning it to the variable *n*.

JDBC offers two ways to identify the column from which a *getXXX* method gets a value. One way is to give the column name, as was done in the preceding example. The second way is to give the column *index* (number of the column), with 1 signifying the first column, 2 the second, and so on, as follows:

```
String s = rs.getString(1);
float n = rs.getFloat(2);
```

The first line of code gets the value in the first column of the current row of *rs* (column COF_NAME), converts it to a Java String object, and assigns it to *s*. The second line of code gets the value stored in the second column of the current row of *rs*, converts it to a Java float, and assigns it to *n*. Note that the column number refers to the column number in the result set, not in the original table.

In summary, JDBC allows you to use either the column name or the column number as the argument to a *getXXX* method. Using the column number is slightly more efficient, and sometimes the column number is required. In general, though, supplying the column name is essentially equivalent to supplying the column number.

JDBC allows a lot of latitude as to which *getXXX* methods you can use to retrieve the different SQL types. For example, the method getInt can be used to retrieve any of the numeric or character types. The data it retrieves will be converted to an int; that is, if the SQL type is VARCHAR, JDBC will attempt to parse an integer out of the VARCHAR. The method getInt is recommended for retrieving only SQL INTEGER types, however, and it cannot be used for the SQL types BINARY, VARBINARY, LONGVARBINARY, DATE, TIME, or TIMESTAMP.

Table 24, "Methods Used with SQL3 Types," on page 353 shows which methods can legally be used to retrieve SQL types and, more important, which methods are recommended for retrieving the various SQL types. Note that this table uses the term "JDBC type" in place of "SQL type." Both terms refer to the generic SQL types defined in java.sql.Types, and they are interchangeable.

Using the Method getString

Although the method getString is recommended for retrieving the SQL types CHAR and VARCHAR, it can be used to retrieve any of the basic SQL types. (You cannot, however, retrieve the new SQL3 data types with it. We will discuss SQL3 types later in this tutorial.) Getting all of the values with getString can be very useful, but it also has its limitations. For instance, if it is used to retrieve a numeric type, getString will convert the numeric value to a Java String object, and the value will have to be converted back to a numeric type before it can be operated on as a number. If the value will be treated as a string anyway, there is no drawback. Further, if you want an application to retrieve values of any standard SQL type other than SQL3 types, use the getString method.

Table 23 Use of `ResultSet.getXXX` Methods to Retrieve JDBC Types

	TINYINT	SMALLINT	INTEGER	BIGINT	REAL	FLOAT	DOUBLE	DECIMAL	NUMERIC	BIT	CHAR	VARCHAR	LONGVARCHAR	BINARY	VARBINARY	LONGVARBINARY	DATE	TIME	TIMESTAMP
`getByte`	**X**	x	x	x	x	x	x	x	x	x	x	x	x						
`getShort`	x	**X**	x	x	x	x	x	x	x	x	x	x	x						
`getInt`	x	x	**X**	x	x	x	x	x	x	x	x	x	x						
`getLong`	x	x	x	**X**	x	x	x	x	x	x	x	x	x						
`getFloat`	x	x	x	x	**X**	x	x	x	x	x	x	x	x						
`getDouble`	x	x	x	x	x	**X**	**X**	x	x	x	x	x	x						
`getBigDecimal`	x	x	x	x	x	x	x	**X**	**X**	x	x	x	x						
`getBoolean`	x	x	x	x	x	x	x	x	x	**X**	x	x	x						
`getString`	x	x	x	x	x	x	x	x	x	x	**X**	**X**	x	x	x	x	x	x	x
`getBytes`														**X**	**X**	x			
`getDate`											x	x	x				**X**		x
`getTime`											x	x	x					**X**	x
`getTimestamp`											x	x	x				x	x	**X**
`getAsciiStream`											x	x	**X**	x	x	x			
`getUnicodeStream`											x	x	**X**	x	x	x			
`getBinaryStream`														x	x	**X**			
`getObject`	x	x	x	x	x	x	x	x	x	x	x	x	x	x	x	x	x	x	x

In the above table, an "x" indicates that the *`getXXX`* method may legally be used to retrieve the given JDBC type. An "**X**" indicates that the *`getXXX`* method is *recommended* for retrieving the given JDBC type.

Updating Tables

Suppose that after a successful first week, the proprietor of The Coffee Break wants to update the `SALES` column in the table `COFFEES` by entering the number of pounds sold for each type of coffee. The SQL statement to update one row might look like this:

```
String updateString = "UPDATE COFFEES " +
                      "SET SALES = 75 " +
                      "WHERE COF_NAME LIKE 'Colombian'";
```

This JDBC code uses the `Statement` object *`stmt`* to execute the SQL statement contained in *`updateString`*:

```
stmt.executeUpdate(updateString);
```

The table `COFFEES` will now look like this:

COF_NAME	SUP_ID	PRICE	SALES	TOTAL
Colombian	101	7.99	75	0
French_Roast	49	8.99	0	0
Espresso	150	9.99	0	0
Colombian_Decaf	101	8.99	0	0
French_Roast_Decaf	49	9.99	0	0

Note that we have not yet updated the column `TOTAL`, so it still has the value `0`.

Now let's select the row we updated, retrieve the values in the columns `COF_NAME` and `SALES`, and print out those values.

```
String query = "SELECT COF_NAME, SALES FROM COFFEES " +
               "WHERE COF_NAME LIKE 'Colombian'";
ResultSet rs = stmt.executeQuery(query);
while (rs.next()) {
    String s = rs.getString("COF_NAME");
    int n = rs.getInt("SALES");
    System.out.println(n + " pounds of " + s +
                        " sold this week.");
}
```

This will print the following:

```
➥75 pounds of Colombian sold this week.
```

Since the `WHERE` clause limited the selection to only one row, just one row was in the `ResultSet` *`rs`* and one line printed as output. Accordingly it is possible to write the code without a `while` loop as follows:

```
rs.next();
String s = rs.getString(1);
int n = rs.getInt(2);
System.out.println(n + " pounds of " + s + " sold this week.");
```

Even when only one row is in a result set, you need to use the method `next` to access it. A `ResultSet` object is created with a cursor pointing above the first row. The first call to the `next` method positions the cursor on the first (and in this case, only) row of *rs*. In this code `next` is called only once, so if there happened to be another row, it would never be accessed.

Now let's update the `TOTAL` column by adding the weekly amount sold to the existing total, and then let's print out the number of pounds sold to date.

```
String updateString = "UPDATE COFFEES " +
                      "SET TOTAL = TOTAL + 75 " +
                      "WHERE COF_NAME LIKE 'Colombian'";
stmt.executeUpdate(updateString);

String query = "SELECT COF_NAME, TOTAL FROM COFFEES " +
               "WHERE COF_NAME LIKE 'Colombian'";
ResultSet rs = stmt.executeQuery(query);
while (rs.next()) {
    String s = rs.getString(1);
    int n = rs.getInt(2);
    System.out.println(n + " pounds of " + s + " sold to date.");
}
```

Note that in this example we used the column index instead of the column name, supplying the index `1` to `getString` (the first column of the result set is `COF_NAME`), and the index `2` to `getInt` (the second column of the result set is `TOTAL`). It is important to distinguish between a column's index in the database table and its index in the result set table. For example, `TOTAL` is the fifth column in the table `COFFEES` but the second column in the result set generated by the query in the preceding example.

Milestone: The Basics of JDBC

You have just reached a milestone. With what we have done so far, you have learned the basics of JDBC. You have seen how to create a table, to insert values into it, to query the table, to retrieve results, and to update the table. These are the nuts and bolts of using a database, and you can now use them in a program written in the Java programming language, using the JDBC 1.0 API. We have used only very simple queries in our examples so far, but as long as the driver and the DBMS support them, you can send very complicated SQL queries, using only the basic JDBC API we have covered so far.

The rest of this lesson looks at how to use features that are a little more advanced: prepared statements, stored procedures, and transactions. It also illustrates warnings and exceptions and gives an example of how to convert a JDBC application into an applet. The final part of this lesson is sample code that you can run yourself.

Using Prepared Statements

Sometimes it is more convenient or more efficient to use a `PreparedStatement` object for sending SQL statements to the database. This special type of statement is derived from the more general class, `Statement`, that you already know.

When to Use a PreparedStatement Object

If you want to execute a `Statement` object many times, you can reduce execution time by using a `PreparedStatement` object instead. The main feature of a `PreparedStatement` object is that, unlike a `Statement` object, it is given an SQL statement when it is created. The advantage is that in most cases this SQL statement will be sent to the DBMS right away, where it will be compiled. As a result, the `PreparedStatement` object contains not just an SQL statement but also an SQL statement that has been precompiled. This means that when the `PreparedStatement` is executed, the DBMS can just run the `PreparedStatement`'s SQL statement without having to compile it first.

Although `PreparedStatement` objects can be used for SQL statements with no parameters, you will probably use them most often for SQL statements that take parameters. The advantage of using SQL statements that take parameters is that you can use the same statement and supply it with different values each time you execute it. You will see an example of this in the following sections.

Creating a PreparedStatement Object

As with `Statement` objects, you create `PreparedStatement` objects with a `Connection` method. We can use our open connection *con* from previous examples to write the following code to create a `PreparedStatement` object that takes two input parameters:

```
PreparedStatement updateSales = con.prepareStatement(
        "UPDATE COFFEES SET SALES = ? WHERE COF_NAME LIKE ?");
```

The variable *updateSales* now contains the SQL statement `"UPDATE COFFEES SET SALES = ? WHERE COF_NAME LIKE ?"` This statement has also, in most cases, been sent to the DBMS and been precompiled.

Supplying Values for PreparedStatement Parameters

You will need to supply values to be used in place of the question mark placeholders, if any, before you can execute a PreparedStatement object. You do this by calling one of the *setXXX* methods defined in the class PreparedStatement. If the value you want to substitute for a question mark is a Java int, you call the method setInt. If the value you want to substitute for a question mark is a Java String, you call the method setString, and so on. In general each type in the Java programming language has a *setXXX* method.

With the PreparedStatement object *updateSales* from the previous example, the following line of code sets the first question mark placeholder to a Java int with a value of 75:

```
updateSales.setInt(1, 75);
```

As you might surmise from the example, the first argument given to a *setXXX* method indicates which question mark placeholder is to be set, and the second argument indicates the value to which it is to be set. The next example sets the second placeholder parameter to the string Colombian:

```
updateSales.setString(2, "Colombian");
```

After these values have been set for its two input parameters, the SQL statement in *updateSales* will be equivalent to the SQL statement in the String object *updateString* that we used in the previous update example. Therefore the following two code fragments accomplish the same thing:

Code Fragment 1:

```
String updateString = "UPDATE COFFEES SET SALES = 75 " +
                      "WHERE COF_NAME LIKE 'Colombian'";
stmt.executeUpdate(updateString);
```

Code Fragment 2:

```
PreparedStatement updateSales = con.prepareStatement(
        "UPDATE COFFEES SET SALES = ? WHERE COF_NAME LIKE ? ");
updateSales.setInt(1, 75);
updateSales.setString(2, "Colombian");
updateSales.executeUpdate():
```

We used the method executeUpdate to execute both the Statement *stmt* and the PreparedStatement *updateSales*. Notice, however, that no argument is supplied to executeUpdate when it is used to execute *updateSales*. This is true because *updateSales* already contains the SQL statement to be executed.

You might wonder why you would choose to use a PreparedStatement object with parameters instead of just a simple statement, since the simple statement involves fewer steps. If you were going to update the SALES column only once or twice, you would not need to use an SQL statement with input parameters. If you will be updating often, on the other hand, it might be much easier to use a PreparedStatement object, especially when you can use a for loop or a while loop to set a parameter to a succession of values. You will see an example of this later in this section.

Once a parameter has been set with a value, it will retain that value until it is reset to another value or the method clearParameters is called. The following code fragment uses the PreparedStatement object *updateSales* to illustrate reusing a prepared statement after resetting the value of one of its parameters and leaving the other one the same:

```
// changes SALES column of French Roast row to 100
updateSales.setInt(1, 100);
updateSales.setString(2, "French_Roast");
updateSales.executeUpdate();

// changes SALES column of Espresso row to 100 (the first
// parameter stayed 100, and the second parameter was reset
// to "Espresso")
updateSales.setString(2, "Espresso");
updateSales.executeUpdate();
```

Using a Loop to Set Values

You can often make coding easier by using a for loop or a while loop to set values for input parameters. The code fragment that follows demonstrates using a for loop to set values for parameters in the PreparedStatement object *updateSales*. The array *salesForWeek* holds the weekly sales amounts. These sales amounts correspond to the coffee names listed in the array *coffees*. Thus the first amount in *salesForWeek* (175) applies to the first coffee name in *coffees* (Colombian), the second amount in *salesForWeek* (150) applies to the second coffee name in *coffees* (French_Roast), and so on. This code fragment demonstrates updating the SALES column for all the coffees in the table COFFEES.

```
PreparedStatement updateSales;
String updateString = "update COFFEES " +
                "set SALES = ? where COF_NAME like ?";
updateSales = con.prepareStatement(updateString);int []
salesForWeek = {175, 150, 60, 155, 90};
String [] coffees = {"Colombian", "French_Roast", "Espresso",
                    "Colombian_Decaf", "French_Roast_Decaf"};

int len = coffees.length;
for (int i = 0; i < len; i++) {
    updateSales.setInt(1, salesForWeek[i]);
    updateSales.setString(2, coffees[i]);
    updateSales.executeUpdate();
}
```

To update the sales amounts for the next week, the proprietor can use this same code as a template, entering the new sales amounts in the proper order in the array *salesForWeek*. The coffee names in the array *coffees* remain constant, so they do not need to be changed. (In a real application the values would probably be input from the user rather than from an initialized Java array.)

Return Values for the Method executeUpdate

Whereas `executeQuery` returns a `ResultSet` object containing the results of the query sent to the DBMS, the return value for `executeUpdate` is an `int` that indicates how many rows of a table were updated. For instance, the following code shows the return value of `executeUpdate` being assigned to the variable *n*:

```
updateSales.setInt(1, 50);
updateSales.setString(2, "Espresso");
int n = updateSales.executeUpdate();
// n = 1 because one row had a change in it
```

The table `COFFEES` was updated by having the value `50` replace the value in the column `SALES` in the row for `Espresso`. That update affected one row in the table, so *n* is equal to `1`.

When the method `executeUpdate` is used to execute a DDL statement, such as in creating a table, it returns the `int 0`. Consequently, in the following code fragment, which executes the DDL statement used to create the table `COFFEES`, *n* will be assigned a value of `0`:

```
int n = executeUpdate(createTableCoffees); // n = 0
```

Note that when the return value for `executeUpdate` is `0`, it can mean that the statement executed was either an update statement that affected zero rows or a DDL statement.

Using Joins

Sometimes you need to use two or more tables to get the data you want. For example, suppose that the proprietor of The Coffee Break wants a list of the coffees bought from Acme, Inc. This involves information in the `COFFEES` table as well as the yet-to-be-created `SUPPLIERS` table. This case calls for a *join* to be used. A join is a database operation that relates two or more tables by means of values that they share in common. In our example, the tables `COFFEES` and `SUPPLIERS` both have the column `SUP_ID`, which can be used to join them.

Before going any further, we need to create the table `SUPPLIERS` and to populate it with values. The following code creates the table `SUPPLIERS`:

```
String createSUPPLIERS = "create table SUPPLIERS " +
                "(SUP_ID INTEGER, SUP_NAME VARCHAR(40), " +
                "STREET VARCHAR(40), CITY VARCHAR(20), " +
                "STATE CHAR(2), ZIP CHAR(5))";
stmt.executeUpdate(createSUPPLIERS);
```

The following code inserts rows for three suppliers into `SUPPLIERS`:

```
stmt.executeUpdate("insert into SUPPLIERS values (101, " +
    "'Acme, Inc.', '99 Market Street', 'Groundsville', " +
    "'CA', '95199'");
stmt.executeUpdate("Insert into SUPPLIERS values (49," +
    " 'Superior Coffee', '1 Party Place', 'Mendocino', 'CA', " +
    "'95460'");
stmt.executeUpdate("Insert into SUPPLIERS values (150, " +
    "'The High Ground', '100 Coffee Lane', 'Meadows', 'CA', " +
    "'93966'");
```

The following code selects the whole table and lets us see what the table `SUPPLIERS` looks like:

```
ResultSet rs = stmt.executeQuery("select * from SUPPLIERS");
```

The result set will look similar to this:

```
SUP_ID  SUP_NAME        STREET           CITY           STATE  ZIP
------  --------------  ---------------  -------------  -----  -----
101     Acme, Inc.      99 Market Street Groundsville   CA     95199
49      Superior Coffee 1 Party Place    Mendocino      CA     95460
150     The High Ground 100 Coffee Lane  Meadows        CA     93966
```

Now that we have the tables COFFEES and SUPPLIERS, we can proceed. The owner wants to get a list of the coffees bought from a particular supplier. The names of the suppliers are in the table SUPPLIERS, and the names of the coffees are in the table COFFEES. Both tables have the column SUP_ID, so it can be used in a join. It follows that you need a way to distinguish which SUP_ID column you are referring to. This is done by preceding the column name with the table name, as in COFFEES.SUP_ID to indicate that you mean the column SUP_ID in the table COFFEES. The following code, in which *stmt* is a Statement object, will select the coffees bought from Acme, Inc.:

```
String query = "SELECT COFFEES.COF_NAME " +
               "FROM COFFEES, SUPPLIERS " +
               "WHERE SUPPLIERS.SUP_NAME LIKE 'Acme, Inc.' " +
               "and SUPPLIERS.SUP_ID = COFFEES.SUP_ID";

ResultSet rs = stmt.executeQuery(query);
System.out.println("Coffees bought from Acme, Inc.: ");
while (rs.next()) {
    String coffeeName = getString("COF_NAME");
    System.out.println("     " + coffeeName);
}
```

This will produce the following output:

```
➡Coffees bought from Acme, Inc.:
➡     Colombian
➡     Colombian_Decaf
```

Using Transactions

Sometimes you do not want one statement to take effect unless another one also succeeds. For example, when updating the amount of coffee sold each week, the proprietor of The Coffee Break will also want to update the total amount sold to date. However, updating one without also updating the other will yield inconsistent data. The way to be sure that either both actions occur or that neither action occurs is to use a *transaction*. A transaction is a set of one or more statements that are executed together as a unit: Either all of the statements are executed, or none of the statements is executed.

Disabling Auto-commit Mode

When a connection is created, it is in auto-commit mode. This means that each individual SQL statement is treated as a transaction and will be automatically committed right after it is executed. To be more precise, the default is for an SQL statement to be committed when it is *completed*, not when it is *executed*. A statement is completed when all of its result sets and update counts have been retrieved. In almost all cases, however, a statement is completed, and therefore committed, right after it is executed.

The way to allow two or more statements to be grouped into a transaction is to disable auto-commit mode. This is demonstrated in the following line of code, where *con* is an active connection:

```
con.setAutoCommit(false);
```

Committing a Transaction

Once auto-commit mode is disabled, no SQL statements will be committed until you call the method `commit` explicitly. All statements executed after the previous call to the method `commit` will be included in the current transaction and will be committed together as a unit. The following code, in which *con* is an active connection, illustrates a transaction:

```
con.setAutoCommit(false);
PreparedStatement updateSales = con.prepareStatement(
        "UPDATE COFFEES SET SALES = ? WHERE COF_NAME LIKE ?");
updateSales.setInt(1, 50);
updateSales.setString(2, "Colombian");
updateSales.executeUpdate();
PreparedStatement updateTotal =
      con.prepareStatement("UPDATE COFFEES SET TOTAL = " +
                           "TOTAL + ? WHERE COF_NAME LIKE ?");
updateTotal.setInt(1, 50);
updateTotal.setString(2, "Colombian");
updateTotal.executeUpdate();
con.commit();
con.setAutoCommit(true);
```

In this example, auto-commit mode is disabled for the connection *con*, which means that the two prepared statements *updateSales* and *updateTotal* will be committed together when the method `commit` is called. Whenever the `commit` method is called (either automatically when auto-commit mode is enabled or explicitly when it is disabled), all changes resulting from statements in the transaction will be made permanent. Thus the `SALES` and the `TOTAL` columns for Colombian coffee have been changed to `50` (if `TOTAL` had been `0` previously) and will retain this value until they are changed with another update statement. `TransactionPairs.java` (page 827) in the Code Appendix illustrates a similar kind of transaction but uses a `for` loop to supply values to the *setXXX* methods for *updateSales* and *updateTotal*.

The final line of the previous example enables auto-commit mode, which means that each statement will once again be committed automatically when it is completed. You will then be back to the default state, where you do not have to call the method `commit` yourself. It is advisable to disable auto-commit mode only while you want to be in transaction mode. This way, you avoid holding database locks for multiple statements, which increases the likelihood of conflicts with other users.

Using Transactions to Preserve Data Integrity

In addition to grouping statements together for execution as a unit, transactions can help to preserve the integrity of the data in a table. For instance, suppose that an employee was supposed to enter new coffee prices in the table `COFFEES` but delayed doing it for a few days. In the meantime prices rose, and today the owner is in the process of entering the higher prices. The employee finally gets around to entering the now outdated prices at the same time that the owner is trying to update the table. After inserting the outdated prices, the employee realizes that they are no longer valid and calls the `Connection` method `rollback` to undo their effects. (The method `rollback` aborts a transaction and restores values to what they were before the attempted update.) At the same time, however, the owner is executing a `SELECT` statement and printing out the new prices. In this situation, the owner may print a price that was later rolled back to its previous value, making the printed price incorrect.

This kind of situation can be avoided by using transactions. If a DBMS supports transactions, and almost all of them do, it will provide some level of protection against conflicts that can arise when two users access data at the same time.

To avoid conflicts during a transaction, a DBMS will use *locks*, mechanisms for blocking access by others to the data that is being accessed by the transaction.

(Note that in auto-commit mode, with each statement a transaction, locks are held for only one statement.) Once a lock is set, it will remain in force until the transaction is committed or rolled back. For example, a DBMS could lock a row of a table until updates to it have been committed. The effect of this lock would be to prevent a user from getting a *dirty read*, that is, reading a value before it is made permanent. (Accessing an updated value that has not been committed is considered a dirty read because it is possible for that value to be rolled back to its previous value. If you read a value that is later rolled back, you will have read an invalid value.)

How locks are set is determined by what is called a *transaction isolation level*, which can range from not supporting transactions at all to supporting transactions that enforce very strict access rules. One example of a transaction isolation level is `TRANSACTION_READ_COMMITTED`, which will not allow a value to be accessed until after it has been committed. In other words, if the transaction isolation level is set to `TRANSACTION_READ_COMMITTED`, the DBMS will not allow dirty reads to occur. The interface `Connection` includes five values that represent the transaction isolation levels you can use in JDBC.

Normally you do not need to do anything about the transaction isolation level; you can just use the default one for your DBMS. JDBC allows you to find out what transaction isolation level your DBMS is set to (using the `Connection` method `getTransactionIsolation`) and also allows you to set it to another level (using the `Connection` method `setTransactionIsolation`). Keep in mind, however, that even though JDBC allows you to set a transaction isolation level, doing so will have no effect unless the driver and the DBMS you are using support it.

When to Call the Method rollback

As mentioned earlier, calling the method `rollback` aborts a transaction and returns to their previous values any values that were modified. If you are trying to execute one or more statements in a transaction and get an `SQLException`, you should call the method `rollback` to abort the transaction and start the transaction all over again. That is the only way to be sure of what has been committed and what has not been committed. Catching an `SQLException` tells you that something is wrong, but it does not tell you what was or was not committed. Since you cannot count on the fact that nothing was committed, calling the method `rollback` is the only way to be sure.

`TransactionPairs.java` (page 827) in the Code Appendix demonstrates a transaction and includes a `catch` block that invokes the method `rollback`. In this particular situation it is not really necessary to call `rollback`; we do it mainly to illustrate how it is done. If the application continued and used the results of the transaction, however, it would be necessary to include a call to `rollback` in the `catch` block in order to protect against using possibly incorrect data.

Stored Procedures

A stored procedure is a group of SQL statements that form a logical unit and that perform a particular task. Stored procedures are used to encapsulate a set of operations or queries to execute on a database server. For example, operations on an employee database (hire, fire, promote, lookup) could be coded as stored procedures executed by application code. Stored procedures can be compiled and executed with various parameters and results, and they may have any combination of input, output, and input/output parameters.

Stored procedures are supported by most DBMSs but vary considerably in their syntax and capabilities. Therefore, we will show you a simple example of what a stored procedure looks like and how it is invoked from JDBC, but this sample is not intended to be run.

SQL Statements for Creating a Stored Procedure

Here we will look at a very simple stored procedure that has no parameters. Even though most stored procedures do something more complex than this example, it illustrates some basic points about them. As previously stated, the syntax for defining a stored procedure is different for each DBMS. For example, some use `begin ... end` or other keywords to indicate the beginning and ending of the procedure definition. In some DBMSs the following SQL statement creates a stored procedure:

```
create procedure SHOW_SUPPLIERS
as
select SUPPLIERS.SUP_NAME, COFFEES.COF_NAME
from SUPPLIERS, COFFEES
where SUPPLIERS.SUP_ID = COFFEES.SUP_ID
order by SUP_NAME
```

The following code puts the SQL statement into a string and assigns it to the variable *createProcedure*, which we will use later:

```
String createProcedure = "create procedure SHOW_SUPPLIERS " +
            "as " +
            "select SUPPLIERS.SUP_NAME, COFFEES.COF_NAME " +
            "from SUPPLIERS, COFFEES " +
            "where SUPPLIERS.SUP_ID = COFFEES.SUP_ID " +
            "order by SUP_NAME";
```

The following code fragment uses the `Connection` object *con* to create a `Statement` object, which is used to send the SQL statement creating the stored procedure to the database:

```
Statement stmt = con.createStatement();
stmt.executeUpdate(createProcedure);
```

The procedure `SHOW_SUPPLIERS` will be compiled and stored in the database as a database object that can be called, similar to the way you would call a method.

Calling a Stored Procedure from JDBC

JDBC allows you to call a database stored procedure from an application written in the Java programming language. The first step is to create a `CallableStatement` object. As with `Statement` and `PreparedStatement` objects, this is done with an open `Connection` object. A `CallableStatement` object contains a *call* to a stored procedure; it does not contain the stored procedure itself. The first line of code that follows creates a call to the stored procedure `SHOW_SUPPLIERS`, using the connection *con*. The part enclosed in braces is the escape syntax for stored procedures. When the driver encounters `{call SHOW_SUPPLIERS}`, it will translate this escape syntax into the native SQL used by the database to call the stored procedure named `SHOW_SUPPLIERS`.

```
CallableStatement cs =
                con.prepareCall("{call SHOW_SUPPLIERS}");
ResultSet rs = cs.executeQuery();
```

The `ResultSet` *rs* will be similar to the following:

```
SUP_NAME            COF_NAME
----------------    -----------------------
Acme, Inc.          Colombian
Acme, Inc.          Colombian_Decaf
Superior Coffee     French_Roast
Superior Coffee     French_Roast_Decaf
The High Ground     Espresso
```

Note that the method used to execute `cs` is `executeQuery` because `cs` calls a stored procedure that contains one query and thus produces one result set. If the procedure had contained one update or one DDL statement, the method `executeUpdate` would have been the one to use. Sometimes, however, a stored procedure contains more than one SQL statement, in which case it will produce more than one result set, more than one update count, or some combination of result sets and update counts. In the case of multiple results, the method `execute` should be used to execute the `CallableStatement`.

The class `CallableStatement` is a subclass of `PreparedStatement`, so a `CallableStatement` object can take input parameters just as a `PreparedStatement` object can. In addition, a `CallableStatement` object can take output parameters or parameters that are for both input and output. `INOUT` parameters and the method `execute` are used rarely.[1]

Creating Complete JDBC Applications

Up to this point you have seen only code fragments. Later in this section you will see sample programs that are complete applications you can run.

The first sample code creates the table `COFFEES`; the second one inserts values into the table and prints the results of a query. The third application creates the table `SUPPLIERS`, and the fourth populates it with values. After you have run this code, you can try a query that is a join between the tables `COFFEES` and `SUPPLIERS`, as in the fifth code example. The sixth code sample is an application that demonstrates a transaction and also shows how to set placeholder parameters in a `PreparedStatement` object using a `for` loop.

Because they are complete applications, they include some elements of the Java programming language we have not shown before in the code fragments. We will explain these elements briefly here.

Putting Code in a Class Definition

In the Java programming language any code you want to execute must be inside a class definition. You type the class definition in a file and give the file the name of the class, appending `.java` to it. For example, if you have a class named

---

[1] For more information, refer to the forthcoming book that includes the new JDBC 2.0 API and JDBC standard extension API, written by Seth White, Maydene Fisher, Graham Hamilton, Rick Cattell, and Mark Hapner, and published by Addison Wesley Longman, Inc. This Java Series book will be published in Spring 1999.

MySQLStatement, its definition should be in a file named MySQLStatement.java.

Importing Classes to Make Them Visible

The first thing to do is to import the packages or classes you will be using in the new class. The classes in our examples all use the java.sql package (the JDBC API), which is made available when the following line of code precedes the class definition:

```
import java.sql.*;
```

The asterisk (*) indicates that all of the classes in the package java.sql are to be imported. Importing a class makes it visible and means that you do not have to write out the fully qualified name when you use a method or field from that class. If you do not include import java.sql.*; in your code, you will have to write java.sql. plus the class name in front of all of the JDBC fields or methods you use every time you use them. Note that you can import individual classes selectively rather than as a whole package. Java does not require that you import classes or packages, but doing so makes writing code a lot more convenient.

Any lines importing classes appear at the top of all the code samples, as they must if they are going to make the imported classes visible to the class being defined. The actual class definition follows any lines that import classes.

Using the main Method

If a class is to be executed, it must contain a static public main method. This method comes right after the line declaring the class and invokes the other methods in the class. The keyword static indicates that this method operates on a class level rather than on individual instances of a class. The keyword public means that members of any class can access this method. Since we are not just defining classes to be used by other classes but instead want to run them, the applications in this lesson all include a main method.

Using try and catch Blocks

Something else that all of the sample applications include is try and catch blocks, which are the Java programming language's mechanism for handling exceptions. Java requires that when a method throws an exception, a mechanism handle it. Generally a catch block will catch the exception and specify what happens (which you may choose to be nothing). In the sample code we use two `try` blocks and two `catch` blocks. The first `try` block contains the method `Class.forName`, from the `java.lang` package. This method throws a `ClassNotFoundException`, so the `catch` block immediately following it deals with that exception. The second `try` block contains JDBC methods, which all throw `SQLExceptions`, so one `catch` block at the end of the application can handle all of the rest of the exceptions that might be thrown because they will all be `SQLException` objects.

Retrieving Exceptions

JDBC lets you see the warnings and exceptions generated by your DBMS and by the Java compiler. To see exceptions, you can have a `catch` block print them out. For example, the following two `catch` blocks from the sample code print out a message explaining the exception:

```
try {
    // Code that could generate an exception goes here.
    // If an exception is generated, the catch block below
    // will print out information about it.
} catch(SQLException ex) {
    System.err.println("SQLException: " + ex.getMessage());
}

try {
    Class.forName("myDriverClassName");
} catch(java.lang.ClassNotFoundException e) {
    System.err.print("ClassNotFoundException: ");
    System.err.println(e.getMessage());
}
```

If you were to run `CreateCOFFEES.java` twice, you would get an error message similar to this:

```
SQLException: There is already an object named 'COFFEES' in the
database.
Severity 16, State 1, Line 1
```

This example illustrates printing out the message component of an `SQLException` object, which is sufficient for most situations.

There are three components, however, and you can print them all out to be complete. The following code fragment shows a `catch` block that is complete in two ways. First, it prints out all three parts of an `SQLException` object: the message (a string that describes the error), the SQL state (a string identifying the error according to the X/Open SQLState conventions), and the driver vendor's error code number. The `SQLException` object *ex* is caught, and its three components are accessed with the methods `getMessage`, `getSQLState`, and `getErrorCode`.

The second way the following `catch` block is complete is that it gets all of the exceptions that might have been thrown. A second exception, if any, will be chained to *ex*, so `ex.getNextException` is called to see whether there is another exception. If there is, the `while` loop continues and prints out the next exception's message, SQLState, and vendor error code. This continues until there are no more exceptions.

```
try {
    // Code that could generate an exception goes here.
    // If an exception is generated, the catch block below
    // will print out information about it.
} catch(SQLException ex) {
    System.out.println("\n--- SQLException caught ---\n");
    while (ex != null) {
        System.out.println("Message:   " + ex.getMessage ());
        System.out.println("SQLState:  " + ex.getSQLState ());
        System.out.println("ErrorCode: " + ex.getErrorCode ());
        ex = ex.getNextException();
        System.out.println("");
    }
}
```

If you were to substitute the preceding `catch` block into `CreateCoffees.java` (page 820) in the Code Appendix and run it after the table `COFFEES` had already been created, you would get the following printout:

```
➥
➥ --- SQLException caught ---
➥
➥Message:  There is already an object named 'COFFEES' in the
➥database.
➥Severity 16, State 1, Line 1
➥SQLState: 42501
➥ErrorCode:   2714
➥
```

SQLState, a code defined in X/Open and ANSI–92, identifies the exception. Two examples of SQLState code numbers and their meanings follow:

```
08001 – No suitable driver
HY011 – Operation invalid at this time
```

The vendor error code is specific to each driver, so you need to check your driver documentation for a list of error codes and their meanings.

Retrieving Warnings

`SQLWarning` objects, a subclass of `SQLException`, deal with database access warnings. Warnings do not stop the execution of an application, as exceptions do; they simply alert the user that something did not happen as planned. For example, a warning might let you know that a privilege you attempted to revoke was not revoked. Or a warning might tell you that an error occurred during a requested disconnection.

A warning can be reported on a `Connection` object, a `Statement` object (including `PreparedStatement` and `CallableStatement` objects), or a `ResultSet` object. Each of these classes has a `getWarnings` method, which you must invoke in order to see the first warning reported on the calling object. If `getWarnings` returns a warning, you can call the `SQLWarning` method `getNextWarning` on it to get any additional warnings. Executing a statement automatically clears the warnings from a previous statement, so they do not build up. This means, however, that if you want to retrieve warnings reported on a statement, you must do so before you execute another statement.

The following code fragment illustrates how to get complete information about any warnings reported on the `Statement` object *stmt* and also on the `ResultSet` object *rs*:

```
Statement stmt = con.createStatement();
ResultSet rs =
            stmt.executeQuery("select COF_NAME from COFFEES");
while (rs.next()) {
    String coffeeName = rs.getString("COF_NAME");
    System.out.println("Coffees available at the Coffee Break: ");
    System.out.println("    " + coffeeName);
    SQLWarning warning = stmt.getWarnings();
    if (warning != null) {
        System.out.println("\n---Warning---\n");
        while (warning != null) {
            System.out.println("Message: " +
                                   warning.getMessage());
            System.out.println("SQLState: " +
                                   warning.getSQLState());
            System.out.print("Vendor error code: ");
            System.out.println(warning.getErrorCode());
```

```
                System.out.println("");
                warning = warning.getNextWarning();
            }
        }

        SQLWarning warn = rs.getWarnings();
        if (warn != null) {
            System.out.println("\n---Warning---\n");
            while (warn != null) {
                System.out.println("Message: " +
                                    warn.getMessage());
                System.out.println("SQLState: " +
                                    warn.getSQLState());
                System.out.print("Vendor error code: ");
                System.out.println(warn.getErrorCode());
                System.out.println("");
                warn = warn.getNextWarning();
            }
        }
    }
```

Warnings are rather uncommon. Of those that are reported, by far the most common is a `DataTruncation` warning, a subclass of `SQLWarning`. All `DataTruncation` objects have an SQLState of `01004`, indicating a problem with reading or writing data. `DataTruncation` methods let you find out in which column or parameter data was truncated, whether the truncation was on a read or a write operation, how many bytes should have been transferred, and how many bytes were transferred.

Running the Sample Applications

You are now ready to try out some sample code. The directory `book.html` contains complete, runnable applications that illustrate concepts presented in this lesson and the next one.[1]

Before you can run one of these applications, you will need to edit the file by substituting the appropriate information for the following variables:

- `url`—the JDBC URL; the first two parts are supplied by your driver; the third specifies your data source

---

1 The sample code is available on the CD-ROM that accompanies this book. You can also download this sample code from the JDBC Web site at: http://java.sun.com/products/jdbc/book.html

- `myLogin`—your login name or user name
- `myPassword`—your password for the DBMS
- `myDriver.ClassName`—the class name supplied with your driver

The first application is the class `CreateCoffees`, which is in a file named `CreateCoffees.java`. (The full source code, `CreateCoffees.java` (page 820), is in the Code Appendix.) Following are instructions for running `CreateCoffees.java` on the major platforms.

UNIX:

```
javac CreateCoffees.java
java CreateCoffees
```

Win32:

```
javac CreateCoffees.java
java CreateCoffees
```

The first line in the instructions compiles the code in the file `CreateCoffees.java`. The compilation, if successful, will produce a file named `CreateCoffees.class`, which contains the bytecodes translated from the file `CreateCoffees.java`. These bytecodes will be interpreted by the Java Virtual Machine, which is what makes it possible for Java code to run on any machine with a Java Virtual Machine installed on it.

The second line of code is what makes the code run. Note that you use the name of the class, `CreateCoffees`, *not* the name of the file, `CreateCoffees.class`.

Creating an Applet from an Application

Suppose that the owner of The Coffee Break wants to display the current coffee prices in an applet on the shop's Web page. If the applet gets the price directly from the database, the most current price will always be displayed.

In order to do this, the owner needs to create two files of code, one with applet code and one with HTML code. The applet code contains the JDBC code that would appear in a regular application, as well as additional code for running the applet and displaying the results of the database query. In our example the applet code is in the file `OutputApplet.java`. To display our applet in an HTML page, the file `OutputApplet.html` tells the browser what to display and where to display it.

The rest of this section tells you about various applet code elements that are not present in standalone application code. Some of these elements involve advanced aspects of the Java programming language. We will give you some rationale and some basic explanation, but explaining them fully is beyond the scope of this tutorial. For purposes of this sample applet, you need to grasp only the general idea, so don't worry if you don't understand everything. You can use the applet code as a template, substituting your own queries for the one in the applet.

Writing Applet Code

Applets will import classes not used by standalone applications. Our applet imports two classes that are special to applets: the class `Applet`, which is part of the `java.applet` package, and the class `Graphics`, which is part of the `java.awt` package. This applet also imports the general-purpose class `java.util.Vector` so that we have access to an array-like container whose size can be modified. This code uses `Vector` objects to store query results so that they can be displayed later.

All applets extend the `Applet` class; that is, they are subclasses of `Applet`. Therefore every applet definition must contain the words `extends Applet`, as shown here:

```
public class MyAppletName extends Applet {
    ...
}
```

In our applet example this line also includes the words `implements Runnable`, so it looks like this:

```
public class OutputApplet extends Applet implements Runnable {
    ...
}
```

`Runnable` is an interface that makes it possible to run more than one *thread* at a time. A thread is a sequential flow of control, and a program may be multi-threaded, that is, have many threads doing different things concurrently. The class `OutputApplet` implements the interface `Runnable` by defining the method `run`, the only method in `Runnable`. In our example the `run` method contains the JDBC code for opening a connection, executing a query, and getting the results from the result set. Since database connections can be slow, sometimes taking several seconds, it is generally a good idea to structure an applet so that it can handle the database work in a separate thread.

Similar to a standalone application, which must have a `main` method, an applet must implement at least one `init`, `start`, or `paint` method. Our applet defines a `start` method and a `paint` method. Every time `start` is invoked, it creates a new thread (named *`worker`*) to reevaluate the database query. Every time `paint` is invoked, it displays either the query results or a string describing the current status of the applet.

As stated previously, the `run` method defined in `OutputApplet` contains the JDBC code. When the thread *`worker`* invokes the method `start`, the `run` method is called automatically and executes the JDBC code in the thread *`worker`*. The code in `run` is very similar to the code in our other sample code, with three exceptions. First, it uses the class `Vector` to store the results of the query. Second, it does not print out the results but rather adds them to the `Vector` *`results`* for display later. Third, it likewise does not print out exceptions and instead records error messages for later display.

Applets have various ways of drawing, or displaying, their content. This applet, a very simple one that has only text, uses the method `drawString` (part of the `Graphics` class) to display its text. The method `drawString` takes three arguments: the string to be displayed; the `x` coordinate, indicating the horizontal starting point for displaying the string; and the `y` coordinate, indicating the vertical starting point for displaying the string (which is below the text).

The method `paint` is what displays something on the screen, and in `OutputApplet.java` it is defined to contain calls to the method `drawString`. The main thing `drawString` displays is the contents of the `Vector` *`results`* (the stored query results). When there are no query results to display, `drawString` will display the current contents of the `String` *`message`*. This string will be `Initializing` to begin with. It gets set to `Connecting to database` when the method `start` is called, and the method `setError` sets it to an error message when an exception is caught. Thus if the database connection takes much time, the person viewing this applet will see the message `Connecting to database` because that will be the contents of *`message`* at that time. (The method `paint` is called by AWT when it wants the applet to display its current state on the screen.)

In the class `OutputApplet`, the last two methods defined, `setError` and `setResults`, are private, which means that they can be used only by `OutputApplet`. Both of these methods invoke the method `repaint`, which clears the screen and calls `paint`. So if `setResults` calls `repaint`, the query results will be displayed; if `setError` calls `repaint`, an error message will be displayed.

A final point to be made is that all of the methods defined in `OutputApplet` except `run` are `synchronized`. The keyword `synchronized` indicates that while a method is accessing an object, other `synchronized` methods are blocked from accessing that object. The method `run` is not declared `synchronized`, so the applet can still paint itself on the screen while the database connection is in progress. If the database access methods were `synchronized`, they would prevent the applet from being repainted while they are executing, and that could result in delays with no accompanying status message.

To summarize, in an applet it is good programming practice to do some things you would not need to do in a standalone application.

1. Put your JDBC code in a separate thread.
2. Display status messages on the screen during any delays, such as when a database connection is taking a long time.
3. Display error messages on the screen instead of printing them to `System.out` or to `System.err`.

Running an Applet

Before running our sample applet, you need to compile the file `OutputApplet.java`. This creates the file `OutputApplet.class`, which is referenced by the file `OutputApplet.html`.

The easiest way to run an applet is to use the `appletviewer`, which is included as part of the JDK. Simply follow the instructions for your platform to compile and run `OutputApplet.java`.

UNIX:

```
javac OutputApplet.java
appletviewer OutputApplet.html
```

Win32:

```
javac OutputApplet.java
appletviewer OutputApplet.html
```

Applets loaded over the network are subject to various security restrictions. Although this may seem bothersome, it is absolutely necessary for network security, and security is one of the major advantages of using the Java programming language. An applet cannot make network connections except to the host it came from, unless the browser allows it. Whether one is able to treat locally installed applets as "trusted" also depends on the security restrictions imposed by the browser. An applet cannot ordinarily read or write files on the host that is executing it, and it cannot load libraries or define native methods. Applets can usually make network connections to the host they came from, so they can work very well on intranets.

The JDBC–ODBC Bridge driver is a somewhat special case. It can be used quite successfully for intranet access, but it requires that ODBC, the bridge, the bridge native library, and JDBC be installed on every client. With this configuration intranet access works from Java applications and from trusted applets. However, since the bridge requires special client configuration, it is not practical to run applets on the Internet with the JDBC–ODBC Bridge driver. Note that this is a limitation of the JDBC–ODBC Bridge, not of JDBC. With a pure Java JDBC driver, you do not need any special configuration to run applets on the Internet.

New Features in the JDBC 2.0 API

THE `java.sql` package that is included in the JDK 1.2 release (known as the JDBC 2.0 API) includes several new features not included in the `java.sql` package that is part of the JDK 1.1 release (referred to as the JDBC 1.0 API). The code samples in the previous lessons of this tutorial are written using the JDBC 1.0 API.

If you want to run code that uses any of the JDBC 2.0 features, you will need to do the following:

1. Download JDK 1.2, following the download instructions.
2. Install a JDBC driver that implements the JDBC 2.0 features used in the code.
3. Access a DBMS that implements the JDBC 2.0 features used in the code.

To date, no drivers that implement the new features are available, but several are under development. As a consequence it has not been possible to test the code demonstrating JDBC 2.0 features. You can safely learn from the examples, but they are not guaranteed to run.

The JDBC 2.0 API enables you to do the following:

- Scroll forward and backward in a result set or move to a specific row.
- Make updates to database tables, using methods in the Java programming language instead of using SQL commands.
- Send multiple SQL statements to the database as a unit, or batch.

- Use the new SQL3 data types as column values.

The sections in this lesson describe these features in more detail.

Moving the Cursor in Scrollable Result Sets

One of the new features in the JDBC 2.0 API is the ability to move a result set's cursor backward as well as forward. Other methods let you move the cursor to a particular row and check the position of the cursor. Scrollable result sets make it possible to create a GUI (graphical user interface) tool for browsing result sets, which will probably be one of the main uses for this feature. Another use is moving to a row in order to update it.

Before you can take advantage of these features, however, you need to create a scrollable `ResultSet` object. The following line of code illustrates one way to create a scrollable `ResultSet` object:

```
Statement stmt =
        con.createStatement(ResultSet.TYPE_SCROLL_SENSITIVE,
                                     ResultSet.CONCUR_READ_ONLY);
    ResultSet srs = stmt.executeQuery("SELECT COF_NAME,
                                          PRICE FROM COFFEES");
```

This code is similar to what you have used earlier, except that it adds two arguments to the method `createStatement`. The first argument is one of three constants added to the `ResultSet` API to indicate the type of a `ResultSet` object:

```
TYPE_FORWARD_ONLY
TYPE_SCROLL_INSENSITIVE
TYPE_SCROLL_SENSITIVE
```

The second argument is one of two `ResultSet` constants for specifying whether a result set is read-only or updatable:

```
CONCUR_READ_ONLY
CONCUR_UPDATABLE
```

The point to remember here is that if you specify a type, you must also specify whether it is read-only or updatable. Also, you must specify the type first, and because both parameters are of type int, the compiler will not complain if you switch the order.

You specify the constant TYPE_FORWARD_ONLY to create a nonscrollable result set, that is, one in which the cursor moves only forward. If you do not specify any constants for the type and updatability of a ResultSet object, you will automatically get one that is TYPE_FORWARD_ONLY and CONCUR_READ_ONLY (as is the case when you are using only the JDBC 1.0 API).

You will get a scrollable ResultSet object if you specify one of the following two ResultSet constants:

```
TYPE_SCROLL_INSENSITIVE
TYPE_SCROLL_SENSITIVE
```

The difference between the two has to do with whether a result set reflects changes that are made to it while it is open and whether certain methods can be called to detect these changes. A result set that is TYPE_SCROLL_INSENSITIVE generally does not reflect changes made while it is still open; one that is TYPE_SCROLL_SENSITIVE does.

All three types of result sets will make changes visible if they are closed and then reopened. At this stage you do not need to worry about the finer points of a ResultSet object's capabilities, and we will go into a little more detail later. You might keep in mind, though, the fact that no matter what type of result set you specify, you are always limited by what your DBMS and driver provide.

Once you have a scrollable ResultSet object, *srs* in the previous example, you can use it to move the cursor around in the result set. Remember that when you created a new ResultSet object earlier in this tutorial, it had a cursor positioned before the first row. Even when a result set is scrollable, the cursor is initially positioned before the first row. In the JDBC 1.0 API the only way to move the cursor was to call the method next. This is still the appropriate method to call when you want to access each row once, going from the first row to the last row, but now you have many other ways to move the cursor.

The counterpart to the method next, which moves the cursor forward one row (toward the end of the result set), is the new method previous, which moves the cursor backward (one row toward the beginning of the result set). Both methods return false when the cursor goes beyond the result set (to the position after the last row or before the first row), which makes it possible to use them in a while loop. You have already used the method next in a while loop, but to refresh your memory, here is an example in which the cursor moves to the first row and then to the next row each time it goes through the `while` loop. The loop ends when the cursor has gone after the last row, causing the method `next` to return `false`. The following code fragment prints out the values in each row of *srs*, with five spaces between the name and the price:

```
Statement stmt = con.createStatement(
                                ResultSet.TYPE_SCROLL_SENSITIVE,
                                ResultSet.CONCUR_READ_ONLY);
ResultSet srs = stmt.executeQuery("SELECT COF_NAME,
                                    PRICE FROM COFFEES");
while (srs.next()) {
    String name = srs.getString("COF_NAME");
    float price = srs.getFloat("PRICE");
    System.out.println(name + "     " + price);
}
```

The printout will look something like this:

```
➥Colombian     7.99
➥French_Roast     8.99
➥Espresso     9.99
➥Colombian_Decaf     8.99
➥French_Roast_Decaf     9.99
```

As in the following code fragment, you can process all of the rows if *srs* is going backward, but to do this the cursor must start out being after the last row. You can move the cursor explicitly to the position after the last row with the method `afterLast`. Then the method `previous` moves the cursor from the position after the last row to the last row and then to the previous row with each iteration through the `while` loop. The loop ends when the cursor reaches the position before the first row, where the method `previous` returns `false`.

```
Statement stmt = con.createStatement(
                           ResultSet.TYPE_SCROLL_INSENSITIVE,
                           ResultSet.CONCUR_READ_ONLY);
ResultSet srs = stmt.executeQuery("SELECT COF_NAME,
                                     PRICE FROM COFFEES");
srs.afterLast();
while (srs.previous()) {
    String name = srs.getString("COF_NAME");
    float price = srs.getFloat("PRICE");
    System.out.println(name + "     " + price);
}
```

The printout will look similar to this:

```
➥French_Roast_Decaf     9.99
➥Colombian_Decaf     8.99
➥Espresso     9.99
➥French_Roast     8.99
➥Colombian     7.99
```

As you can see, the printout for each will have the same values, but the rows are in the opposite order.

You can move the cursor to a particular row in a `ResultSet` object. The methods `first`, `last`, `beforeFirst`, and `afterLast` move the cursor to the row indicated in their names. The method `absolute` will move the cursor to the row number indicated in the argument passed to it. If the number is positive, the cursor moves the given number from the beginning, so calling `absolute(1)` puts the cursor on the first row. If the number is negative, the cursor moves the given number from the end, so calling `absolute(-1)` puts the cursor on the last row. The following line of code moves the cursor to the fourth row of *srs*:

```
srs.absolute(4);
```

If *srs* has 500 rows, the following line of code will move the cursor to row 497:

```
srs.absolute(-4);
```

Three methods move the cursor to a position relative to its current position. As you have seen, the method `next` moves the cursor forward one row, and the method `previous` moves the cursor backward one row. The method `relative`, lets you specify how many rows to move from the current row and also the direction in which to move. A positive number moves the cursor forward the given number of rows; a negative number moves the cursor backward the given number of rows. For example, in the following code fragment the cursor moves to the fourth row, then to the first row, and finally to the third row:

```
srs.absolute(4); // cursor is on the fourth row
...
srs.relative(-3); // cursor is on the first row
...
srs.relative(2); // cursor is on the third row
```

The method `getRow` lets you check the number of the row where the cursor is positioned. For example, you can use `getRow` to verify the current position of the cursor in the previous example, as follows:

```
srs.absolute(4);
int rowNum = srs.getRow(); // rowNum should be 4
srs.relative(-3);
int rowNum = srs.getRow(); // rowNum should be 1
srs.relative(2);
int rowNum = srs.getRow(); // rowNum should be 3
```

Four additional methods let you verify whether the cursor is at a particular position. The position is stated in their names: `isFirst`, `isLast`, `isBeforeFirst`, `isAfterLast`. These methods all return a `boolean` and can therefore be used in a conditional statement. For example, the following code fragment tests to see whether the cursor is after the last row before invoking the method `previous` in a `while` loop. If the method `isAfterLast` returns `false`, the cursor is not after the last row, so the method `afterLast` is invoked. This guarantees that the cursor will be after the last row and that using the method `previous` in the `while` loop will cover every row in *srs*.

```
if (srs.isAfterLast() == false) {
    srs.afterLast();
}

while (srs.previous()) {
    String name = srs.getString("COF_NAME");
    float price = srs.getFloat("PRICE");
    System.out.println(name + "     " + price);
}
```

In the next section you will see how to use the two remaining `ResultSet` methods for moving the cursor, `moveToInsertRow` and `moveToCurrentRow`. You will also see examples illustrating why you might want to move the cursor to certain positions.

Making Updates to Updatable Result Sets

Another new feature in the JDBC 2.0 API is the ability to update rows in a result set by using methods in the Java programming language rather than having to send an SQL command. But before you can take advantage of this capability, you need to create a `ResultSet` object that is updatable. In order to do this, you must supply the `ResultSet` constant `CONCUR_UPDATABLE` to the `createStatement` method, as you have seen in previous examples. The `Statement` object it creates will produce an updatable `ResultSet` object each time it executes a query. The following code fragment illustrates creating the updatable `ResultSet` object *uprs*. Note that the code also makes *uprs* scrollable. An updatable ResultSet object does not necessarily have to be scrollable, but when you are making changes to a result set, you generally want to be able to move around in it. With a scrollable result set you can move to rows you want to change, and if the type is TYPE_SCROLL_SENSITIVE, you can get the new value in a row after you have changed it.

```
Connection con =
  DriverManager.getConnection("jdbc:mySubProtocol:mySubName");
Statement stmt =
  con.createStatement(ResultSet.TYPE_SCROLL_SENSITIVE,
                      ResultSet.CONCUR_UPDATABLE);
ResultSet uprs = stmt.executeQuery("SELECT COF_NAME,
                      PRICE FROM COFFEES");
```

The ResultSet object *uprs* might look something like this:

```
COF_NAME               PRICE
------------------     -----
Colombian              7.99
French_Roast           8.99
Espresso               9.99
Colombian_Decaf        8.99
French_Roast_Decaf     9.99
```

We can now use the new JDBC 2.0 methods in the ResultSet interface to insert a new row into *uprs*, delete an existing row from *uprs*, or modify a column value in *uprs*.

Updating a Result Set Programmatically

An update is the modification of a column value in the current row. Let's suppose that we want to raise the price of French Roast Decaf coffee to $10.99. If we used the JDBC 1.0 API, the update would look something like this:

```
stmt.executeUpdate("UPDATE COFFEES SET PRICE = 10.99" +
                   "WHERE COF_NAME = FRENCH_ROAST_DECAF");
```

The following code fragment shows another way to accomplish the update, this time using the JDBC 2.0 API:

```
uprs.last();
uprs.updateFloat("PRICE", 10.99);
```

Update operations in the JDBC 2.0 API affect column values in the row where the cursor is positioned. Thus in the first line the ResultSet *uprs* calls the method last to move its cursor to the last row (the row where the column COF_NAME has the value FRENCH_ROAST_DECAF). Once the cursor is on the last row, all of the update methods you call will operate on that row until you move the cursor to another row. The second line changes the value in the PRICE column to 10.99 by calling the method updateFloat. This method is used because the column value we want to update is a float in the Java programming language.

The ResultSet.*updateXXX* methods take two parameters: the column to update and the new value to put in that column. As with the ResultSet.*getXXX* methods, the parameter designating the column may be either the column name or the column number. A different *updateXXX* method is used for updating each data type (updateString, updateBigDecimal, updateInt, and so on), just as different *getXXX* methods retrieve different data types.

At this point the price in *uprs* for French Roast Decaf will be 10.99, but the price in the table COFFEES in the database will still be 9.99. To make the update take effect in the database and not just in the result set, we must call the ResultSet method updateRow. Here is what the code should look like to update both *uprs* and COFFEES:

```
uprs.last();
uprs.updateFloat("PRICE", 10.99);
uprs.updateRow();
```

If you had moved the cursor to a different row before calling updateRow, the update would have been lost. If, on the other hand, you realized that the price should really have been $10.79 instead of $10.99, you could have cancelled the update to $10.99 by calling the method cancelRowUpdates. You have to invoke cancelRowUpdates before invoking the method updateRow; once updateRow is called, calling the method cancelRowUpdates does nothing. Note that cancelRowUpdates cancels all of the updates in a row, so if a row has many invocations of the *updateXXX* methods, you cannot cancel just one of them. The following code fragment first cancels updating the price to $10.99 and then updates it to $10.79:

```
uprs.last();
uprs.updateFloat("PRICE", 10.99);
uprs.cancelRowUpdates();
uprs.updateFloat("PRICE", 10.79);
uprs.updateRow();
```

In this example only one column value was updated, but you can call an appropriate *updateXXX* method for any or all of the column values in a single row. The concept to remember is that updates and related operations apply to the row where the cursor is positioned. Even with many calls to *updateXXX* methods, it takes only one call to the method `updateRow` to update the database with all of the changes made in the current row.

If you want to update the price for `COLOMBIAN_DECAF` as well, you have to move the cursor to the row containing that coffee. Because the row for that coffee immediately precedes the row for `FRENCH_ROAST_DECAF`, you can call the method `previous` to position the cursor on the row for `COLOMBIAN_DECAF`. The following code fragment changes the price in that row to $9.79 in both the result set and the underlying table in the database:

```
uprs.previous();
uprs.updateFloat("PRICE", 9.79);
uprs.updateRow();
```

All cursor movements refer to rows in a `ResultSet` object, not to rows in the underlying database. If a query selects five rows from a database table, the result set will have five rows, with the first row being row 1, the second row being row 2, and so on. Row 1 can also be identified as the first, and, in a result set with five rows, row 5 is the last.

The ordering of the rows in the result set has nothing to do with the order of the rows in the base table. In fact, the order of the rows in a database table is indeterminate. The DBMS keeps track of which rows were selected, and it makes updates to the proper rows, but they may be located anywhere in the table. When a row is inserted, for example, there is no way to know where in the table it has been inserted.

Inserting and Deleting Rows Programmatically

In the previous section you saw how to modify a column value by using methods in the JDBC 2.0 API rather than having to use SQL commands. With the JDBC 2.0 API you can also insert a new row into a table or delete an existing row programmatically.

Let's suppose that our coffee house proprietor is getting a new variety from The High Ground coffee suppliers and wants to add the new coffee to the database. Using the JDBC 1.0 API, the proprietor would write code that passes an SQL insert statement to the DBMS. The following code fragment, in which *stmt* is a `Statement` object, shows this approach:

```
stmt.executeUpdate("INSERT INTO COFFEES " +
                   "VALUES ('Kona', 150, 10.99, 0, 0)");
```

You can do the same thing without using any SQL commands, by using `ResultSet` methods in the JDBC 2.0 API. After you have a `ResultSet` object with results from the table `COFFEES`, you can, in one step, build the new row and then insert it into both the result set and the table `COFFEES`. You build a new row in what is called the *insert row*, a special row associated with every `ResultSet` object. This row is not part of the result set; you can think of it as a separate buffer in which to compose a new row.

Your first step will be to move the cursor to the insert row, which you do by invoking the method `moveToInsertRow`. The next step is to set a value for each column in the row. You do this by calling the appropriate *`updateXXX`* method for each value. Note that these are the same *`updateXXX`* methods you used in the previous section for changing a column value. Finally, call the method `insertRow` to insert into the result set the row you have just populated with values. This one method simultaneously inserts the row into both the `ResultSet` object and the database table from which the result set was selected.

The following code fragment creates the scrollable and updatable `ResultSet` object *`uprs`*, which contains all of the rows and columns in the table `COFFEES`:

```
Connection con =
  DriverManager.getConnection("jdbc:mySubprotocol:mySubName");
Statement stmt =
  con.createStatement(ResultSet.TYPE_SCROLL_SENSITIVE,
                      ResultSet.CONCUR_UPDATABLE);
ResultSet uprs = stmt.executeQuery("SELECT * FROM COFFEES");
```

The next code fragment uses the `ResultSet` object *`uprs`* to insert the row for Kona coffee, shown in the SQL code example. The code moves the cursor to the insert row, sets the five column values, and inserts the new row into *`uprs`* and `COFFEES`:

```
uprs.moveToInsertRow();
uprs.updateString("COF_NAME", "Kona");
uprs.updateInt("SUP_ID", 150);
uprs.updateFloat("PRICE", 10.99);
uprs.updateInt("SALES", 0);
uprs.updateInt("TOTAL", 0);
uprs.insertRow();
```

Because you can use either the column name or the column number to indicate the column to be set, your code for setting the column values could also have looked like this:

```
uprs.updateString(1, "Kona");
uprs.updateInt(2, 150);
uprs.updateFloat(3, 10.99);
uprs.updateInt(4, 0);
uprs.updateInt(5, 0);
```

You might be wondering why the *updateXXX* methods seem to behave differently here from the way they behaved in the update examples. In those examples the value set with an *updateXXX* method immediately replaced the column value in the result set. That was true because the cursor was on a row in the result set. When the cursor is on the insert row, the value set with an *updateXXX* method is likewise immediately set, but it is set in the insert row rather than in the result set. In both updates and insertions calling an *updateXXX* method does not affect the underlying database table. The method `updateRow` must be called to have updates occur in the database. For insertions the method `insertRow` inserts the new row into the result set and the database at the same time.

You might also wonder what happens if you insert a row but do not supply a value for every column in the row. If you fail to supply a value for a column that was defined to accept SQL `NULL` values, the value assigned to that column is `NULL`. If a column does not accept null values, however, you will get an `SQLException` when you do not call an *updateXXX* method to set a value for it. This is also true if a table column is missing in your `ResultSet` object. In the previous example, the query was `SELECT * FROM COFFEES`, which produced a result set with all the columns of all the rows. When you want to insert one or more rows, your query does not have to select all rows, but it is safer to select all columns. Especially if your table has hundreds or thousands of rows, you might want to use a `WHERE` clause to limit the number of rows returned by your `SELECT` statement.

After you have called the method `insertRow`, you can start building another row to be inserted, or you can move the cursor back to a result set row. You can, for instance, invoke any of the methods that put the cursor on a specific row, such as `first`, `last`, `beforeFirst`, `afterLast`, and `absolute`. You can also use the methods `previous`, `relative`, and `moveToCurrentRow`. Note that you can invoke `moveToCurrentRow` only when the cursor is on the insert row.

When you call the method `moveToInsertRow`, the result set records which row the cursor is sitting on, which is by definition the current row. As a consequence, the method moveToCurrentRow can move the cursor from the insert row back to the row that was previously the current row. This also explains why you can use the methods previous and relative, which require movement relative to the current row.

Code Sample for Inserting a Row

The following code sample is a complete program that should run if you have a JDBC 2.0 Compliant driver that implements scrollable result sets. To date there are no such drivers, so this code, although it compiles, has not been tested on a driver and a DBMS.

Here are some things you might notice about the code:

- The ResultSet object *uprs* is updatable, scrollable, and sensitive to changes made by itself and others. Even though this object is TYPE_SCROLL_SENSITIVE, it is possible that the *getXXX* methods called after the insertions will not retrieve values for the newly inserted rows. Certain methods in the DatabaseMetaData interface will tell you what is visible and what is detected in the various types of result sets for your driver and DBMS.[1] In this code sample we wanted to demonstrate cursor movement in the same ResultSet object, so after moving to the insert row and inserting two rows, the code moves the cursor back to the result set, going to the position before the first row. This puts the cursor in position to iterate through the entire result set, using the method next in a while loop. To be absolutely sure that the *getXXX* methods include the inserted row values no matter what driver and DBMS are used, you can close the result set and create another one, reusing the same Statement object *stmt* and again using the query SELECT * FROM COFFEES.
- After all of the values for a row have been set with *updateXXX* methods, the code inserts the row into the result set and the database using the method insertRow. Then, still staying on the insert row, the code sets the values for another row.

```
import java.sql.*;

public class InsertRows {
```

[1] For more information, refer to the forthcoming book that includes the JDBC 2.0 API and JDBC standard extension API, written by Seth White, Maydene Fisher, Graham Hamilton, Rick Cattell, and Mark Hapner. This Java Series book will be published by Addison Wesley Longman, Inc. in Spring 1999.

```
public static void main(String args[]) {
    String url = "jdbc:mySubprotocol:myDataSource";
    Connection con;
    Statement stmt;
try {
    Class.forName("myDriver.ClassName");
} catch(java.lang.ClassNotFoundException e) {
    System.err.print("ClassNotFoundException: ");
    System.err.println(e.getMessage());
}

try {
    con = DriverManager.getConnection(url,
                        "myLogin", "myPassword");
    stmt =
      con.createStatement(ResultSet.TYPE_SCROLL_SENSITIVE,
                        ResultSet.CONCUR_UPDATABLE);
    ResultSet uprs =
       stmt.executeQuery("SELECT * FROM COFFEES");
    uprs.moveToInsertRow();
    uprs.updateString("COF_NAME", "Kona");
    uprs.updateInt("SUP_ID", 150);
    uprs.updateFloat("PRICE", 10.99f);
    uprs.updateInt("SALES", 0);
    uprs.updateInt("TOTAL", 0);
    uprs.insertRow();
    uprs.updateString("COF_NAME", "Kona_Decaf");
    uprs.updateInt("SUP_ID", 150);
    uprs.updateFloat("PRICE", 11.99f);
    uprs.updateInt("SALES", 0);
    uprs.updateInt("TOTAL", 0);
    uprs.insertRow();
    uprs.beforeFirst();

    System.out.println("Table COFFEES after insertion:");
    while (uprs.next()) {
        String name = uprs.getString("COF_NAME");
        int id = uprs.getInt("SUP_ID");
        float price = uprs.getFloat("PRICE");
        int sales = uprs.getInt("SALES");
        int total = uprs.getInt("TOTAL");
        System.out.print(name + "   " + id + "   " + price);
        System.out.println("   " + sales + "   " + total);
    }

    uprs.close();
    stmt.close();
    con.close();
```

```
        } catch(SQLException ex) {
            System.err.println("SQLException: " + ex.getMessage());
        }
    }
```

Deleting a Row

So far you have seen how to update a column value and how to insert a new row. The third and simplest way to modify a `ResultSet` object is to delete a row. All you do is move the cursor to the row you want to delete and then call the method `deleteRow`. For example, if you want to delete the fourth row in the `ResultSet` *`uprs`*, your code will look like this:

```
uprs.absolute(4);
uprs.deleteRow();
```

The fourth row has been removed from *`uprs`* and also from the database.

The only issue about deletions is what the `ResultSet` object does when it deletes a row. With some JDBC drivers a deleted row is removed and is no longer visible in a result set. Some JDBC drivers use a blank row as a placeholder (a "hole") where the deleted row used to be. If a blank row replaces the deleted row, you can use the method `absolute` with the original row positions to move the cursor because the row numbers in the result set are not changed by the deletion.

In any case, you should remember that JDBC drivers handle deletions differently. For example, if you write an application meant to run with various databases, you should not write code that depends on having a hole in a result set.

Seeing Changes in Result Sets

If data in a `ResultSet` object is modified, the change will always be visible if you close it and then reopen it. In other words, if you execute the same query again, you will produce a new result set, based on the data currently in a table. This result set will naturally reflect changes anyone made earlier.

The question is whether you can see changes you or anyone else made while the `ResultSet` object is still open. (Generally you will be most interested in the changes made by others.) The answer depends on the DBMS, the driver, and the type of `ResultSet` object you have.

With a `ResultSet` object that is `TYPE_SCROLL_SENSITIVE`, you can always see updates anyone makes to column values. You can usually see inserts and deletes, but the only way to be sure is to use `DatabaseMetaData` methods that return this information.[1]

You can to some extent regulate what changes are visible by raising or by lowering the transaction isolation level for your connection with the database. For example, the following line of code, where *con* is an active `Connection` object, sets the connection's isolation level to `TRANSACTION_READ_COMMITTED`:

```
con.setTransactionIsolation(TRANSACTION_READ_COMMITTED);
```

With this isolation level your `ResultSet` object will not show any changes before they are committed, but it can show changes that may have other consistency problems. To allow fewer data inconsistencies, you could raise the transaction isolation level to `TRANSACTION_REPEATABLE_READ`. The problem is that the higher the isolation level, the poorer the performance. And, as is always true of databases and drivers, you are limited to what they actually provide. Many programmers just use their database's default transaction isolation level.

In a `ResultSet` object that is `TYPE_SCROLL_INSENSITIVE`, you generally cannot see changes made to it while it is still open. Some programmers use only this type of `ResultSet` object because they want a consistent view of data and do not want to see changes made by others.

You can use the method `refreshRow` to get the latest values for a row straight from the database. This method can be very expensive, especially if the DBMS returns multiple rows each time you call `refreshRow`. Nevertheless, its use can be valuable if it is critical to have the latest data. Even when a result set is sensitive and changes are visible, an application may not always see the very latest changes that have been made to a row if the driver retrieves several rows at a time and caches them. Thus, using the method `refreshRow` is the only way to be sure that you are seeing the most up-to-date data.

The following code sample illustrates how an application might use the method `refreshRow` when it is absolutely critical to see the most current values. Note that the result set should be sensitive; if you use the method `refreshRow` with a `ResultSet` object that is `TYPE_SCROLL_INSENSITIVE`, `refreshRow` does nothing. (The urgency for getting the latest data is a bit improbable for the table `COFFEES`, but a commodities trader's fortunes could depend on knowing the latest prices in a wildly fluctuating coffee market. Or, for example, you would proba-

---

[1] Refer to the forthcoming Java Series book that includes the new JDBC 2.0 API and JDBC standard extension API (Addison Wesley Longman, 1999) for information on getting metadata and for more details regarding the visibility of changes.

bly want the airline reservation clerk to check that the seat you are reserving is still available.)

```
Statement stmt = con.createStatement(
            ResultSet.TYPE_SCROLL_SENSITIVE,
            ResultSet.CONCUR_UPDATABLE);
ResultSet uprs = stmt.executeQuery(SELECT COF_NAME,
                                      PRICE FROM COFFEES);
uprs.absolute(4);
Float price1 = uprs.getFloat("PRICE");
// do something...
uprs.absolute(4);
uprs.refreshRow();
Float price2 = uprs.getFloat("PRICE");
if (price2 > price1) {
    // do something...
}
```

Making Batch Updates

A batch update is a set of multiple update statements submitted to the database for processing as a batch. Sending multiple update statements to the database together as a unit can, in some situations, be much more efficient than sending each update statement separately. This ability to send updates as a unit, referred to as the batch update facility, is one of the features provided with the JDBC 2.0 API.

Using Statement Objects for Batch Updates

In the JDBC 1.0 API `Statement` objects submit updates to the database individually with the method `executeUpdate`. Multiple `executeUpdate` statements can be sent in the same transaction, but even though they are committed or rolled back as a unit, they are still processed individually. The interfaces derived from `Statement`, `PreparedStatement` and `CallableStatement`, have the same capabilities, using their own versions of `executeUpdate`.

With the JDBC 2.0 API `Statement`, `PreparedStatement`, and `CallableStatement` objects have the ability to maintain a list of commands that can be submitted together as a batch. They are created with an associated list, which is initially empty. You can add SQL commands to this list with the method `addBatch`, and you can empty the list with the method `clearBatch`. You send all of the commands in the list to the database with the method `executeBatch`. Now let's see how these methods work.

Let's suppose that our coffee house proprietor wants to start carrying flavored coffees and has determined that the best source is Superior Coffee, a current supplier. Four new coffees will be added to the table COFFEES. Because only four new rows are being inserted, a batch update may not improve performance significantly, but this is a good opportunity to demonstrate batch updates. Remember that the table COFFEES has five columns: column COF_NAME of type VARCHAR(32), column SUP_ID of type INTEGER, column PRICE of type FLOAT, column SALES of type INTEGER, and column TOTAL of type INTEGER. Each row to be inserted will have values for the five columns in order. The code for inserting the new rows as a batch might look similar to this:

```
con.setAutoCommit(false);

Statement stmt = con.createStatement();
stmt.addBatch("INSERT INTO COFFEES" +
            "VALUES('Amaretto', 49, 9.99, 0, 0)");
stmt.addBatch("INSERT INTO COFFEES" +
            "VALUES('Hazelnut', 49, 9.99, 0, 0)");
stmt.addBatch("INSERT INTO COFFEES" +
            "VALUES('Amaretto_decaf', 49, 10.99, 0, 0)");
stmt.addBatch("INSERT INTO COFFEES" +
            "VALUES('Hazelnut_decaf', 49, 10.99, 0, 0)");

int [] updateCounts = stmt.executeBatch();
```

Now let's examine the code line by line.

```
con.setAutoCommit(false);
```

This next line disables auto-commit mode for the Connection object *con* so that the transaction will not be automatically committed or rolled back when the method executeBatch is called. (If you do not recall what a transaction is, review the sections Disabling Auto-commit Mode (page 317) and Committing a Transaction (page 317).) To allow for correct error handling, you should always disable auto-commit mode before beginning a batch update.

This next line of code creates the Statement object *stmt*. As is true of all newly-created Statement objects, *stmt* has a list of commands associated with it, and that list is empty.

```
Statement stmt = con.createStatement();
```

Each of the following lines of code adds a command to the list of commands associated with *stmt*.

```
stmt.addBatch("INSERT INTO COFFEES" +
              "VALUES('Amaretto', 49, 9.99, 0, 0)");
stmt.addBatch("INSERT INTO COFFEES" +
              "VALUES('Hazelnut', 49, 9.99, 0, 0)");

stmt.addBatch("INSERT INTO COFFEES" +
              "VALUES('Amaretto_decaf', 49, 10.99, 0, 0)");
stmt.addBatch("INSERT INTO COFFEES" +
              "VALUES('Hazelnut_decaf', 49, 10.99, 0, 0)");
```

These commands are all `INSERT INTO` statements, each one adding a row consisting of five column values. The values for the columns `COF_NAME` and `PRICE` are self-explanatory. The second value in each row is 49, the identification number for the supplier, Superior Coffee. The last two values, the entries for the columns `SALES` and `TOTAL`, all start out being zero because there have been no sales yet. (`SALES` is the number of pounds of this row's coffee sold in the current week; `TOTAL` is the total of all the cumulative sales of this coffee.)

In the following line, *stmt* sends the four SQL commands that were added to its list of commands off to the database to be executed as a batch.

```
int [] updateCounts = stmt.executeBatch();
```

Note that *stmt* uses the method `executeBatch` to send the batch of insertions, not the method `executeUpdate`, which sends only one command and returns a single update count. The DBMS will execute the commands in the order in which they were added to the list of commands, so it will first add the row of values for Amaretto, then add the row for Hazelnut, then Amaretto decaf, and finally Hazelnut decaf. If all four commands execute successfully, the DBMS will return an update count for each command in the order in which it was executed. The update counts, which indicate how many rows were affected by each command, are stored in the array of `int`, *updateCounts*.

At this point *updateCounts* should contain four elements of type `int`. In this case each `int` will be `1` because an insertion affects one row. The list of commands associated with *stmt* will now be empty because the four commands added previously were sent to the database when *stmt* called the method `executeBatch`. You can at any time empty this list of commands with the method `clearBatch`.

Batch Update Exceptions

Two exceptions can be thrown during a batch update operation: `SQLException` and `BatchUpdateException`.

All methods in the JDBC API will throw an SQLException object when there is a database access problem. In addition, the method executeBatch will throw an SQLException if you have used the method addBatch to add a command that returns a result set to the batch of commands being executed. Typically a query (a SELECT statement) will return a result set, but some methods, such as some of the DatabaseMetaData methods, can also return a result set.

Just using the method addBatch to add a command that produces a result set does not cause an exception to be thrown. There is no problem while the command is just sitting in a Statement object's command list. But there will be a problem when the method executeBatch submits the batch to the DBMS to be executed. When each command is executed, it must return an update count that can be added to the array of update counts returned by the executeBatch method. Trying to put a result set in an array of update counts will cause an error and cause executeBatch to throw an SQLException. In other words, only commands that return an update count (commands such as INSERT INTO, UPDATE, DELETE, CREATE TABLE, DROP TABLE, ALTER TABLE, and so on) can be executed as a batch with the executeBatch method.

If no SQLException was thrown, you know that there were no access problems and that all of the commands produce update counts. If one of the commands cannot be executed for another reason, the method executeBatch will throw a BatchUpdateException. In addition to the information that all exceptions have, this exception contains an array of the update counts for the commands that executed successfully before the exception was thrown. Because the update counts are in the same order as the commands that produced them, you can tell how many commands were successful and which commands they are.

BatchUpdateException is derived from SQLException. This means that you can use all of the methods available to an SQLException object with it. The following code fragment prints the SQLException information and the update counts contained in a BatchUpdateException object. Because getUpdateCounts returns an array of int, it uses a for loop to print each of the update counts.

```
try {
    // make some updates
} catch(BatchUpdateException b) {
    System.err.println("SQLException: " + b.getMessage());
    System.err.println("SQLState:  " + b.getSQLState());
    System.err.println("Message:  " + b.getMessage());
    System.err.println("Vendor:  " + b.getErrorCode());
    System.err.print("Update counts:  ");
    int [] updateCounts = b.getUpdateCounts();
```

```
        for (int i = 0; i < updateCounts.length; i++) {
            System.err.print(updateCounts[i] + "   ");
        }
    }
```

For the complete program, refer to `BatchUpdate.java` (page 832) in the Code Appendix. The following code puts together the code fragments from previous sections to make a complete program. You might notice the two `catch` blocks at the end of the application. If there is a `BatchUpdateException` object, the first `catch` block will catch it. The second one will catch an `SQLException` object that is not a `BatchUpdateException` object.

Using SQL3 Data Types

The new SQL3 data types are being adopted in the next version of the ANSI/ISO SQL standard. The JDBC 2.0 API provides interfaces that represent the mapping of these SQL3 data types into the Java programming language. With these new interfaces you can work with SQL3 data types in the same way that you do other data types.

The new SQL3 data types give a relational database more flexibility in what can be used as a type for a table column. For example, a column may now be used to store the new type `BLOB` (binary large object), which can store very large amounts of data as raw bytes. A column may also be of type `CLOB` (character large object), which is capable of storing very large amounts of data in character format. The new type `ARRAY` makes it possible to use an array as a column value. Even the new SQL user-defined types (UDTs), structured types and distinct types, can now be stored as column values.

The following list gives the JDBC 2.0 interfaces that map the SQL3 types. We will discuss them in more detail later.

- A `Blob` instance maps an SQL `BLOB` instance.
- A `Clob` instance maps an SQL `CLOB` instance.
- An `Array` instance maps an SQL `ARRAY` instance.
- A `Struct` instance maps an SQL structured type instance.
- A `Ref` instance maps an SQL `REF` instance.

You retrieve, store, and update SQL3 data types in the same way that you do other data types. You use either `ResultSet.`*`getXXX`* or `CallableStatement.`*`getXXX`* methods to retrieve them, `PreparedStatement.`*`setXXX`* methods to store them, and *`updateXXX`* methods to update them. Probably 90 percent of the operations performed on SQL3 types use the *getXXX*, *setXXX*, and *updateXXX* methods. Table 24 shows which methods to use.

Table 24 Methods Used with SQL3 Types

SQL3 Type	getXXX Method	setXXX Method	updateXXX Method
BLOB	getBlob	setBlob	updateObject
CLOB	getClob	setClob	updateObject
ARRAY	getArray	setArray	updateObject
Structured type	getObject	setObject	updateObject
REF *(structured type)*	getRef	setRef	updateObject

For example, the following code fragment retrieves an SQL ARRAY value; the column SCORES in the table STUDENTS contains values of type ARRAY. The variable *stmt* is a Statement object.

```
ResultSet rs = stmt.executeQuery("SELECT SCORES FROM STUDENTS
                                  WHERE ID = 2238");
rs.next();
Array scores = rs.getArray("SCORES");
```

The variable *scores* is a logical pointer to the SQL ARRAY object stored in the table STUDENTS in the row for student 2238.

If you want to store a value in the database, you use the appropriate *setXXX* method. For example, the following code fragment, in which *rs* is a ResultSet object, stores a Clob object:

```
Clob notes = rs.getClob("NOTES");
PreparedStatement pstmt = con.prepareStatement("UPDATE MARKETS
                    SET COMMENTS = ? WHERE SALES < 1000000",
                    ResultSet.TYPE_SCROLL_INSENSITIVE,
                    ResultSet.CONCUR_UPDATABLE);
pstmt.setClob(1, notes);
```

This code sets *notes* as the first parameter in the update statement being sent to the database. The CLOB value designated by *notes* will be stored in the table MARKETS in column COMMENTS in every row where the value in the column SALES is less than one million.

Blob, Clob, and Array Objects

An important feature about Blob, Clob, and Array objects is that you can manipulate them without having to bring all of the data from the database server to your client machine. An instance of any of these types is a logical pointer to the database object that the instance represents. Because an SQL BLOB, CLOB, or ARRAY object may be large, this feature can improve performance dramatically.

You can use SQL commands and the JDBC 1.0 and 2.0 API with Blob, Clob, and Array objects just as if you were operating on the object in the database. If you want to work with any of them as an object in the Java programming language, however, you need to bring all of their data over to the client, which we refer to as *materializing* the object. For example, if you want to use an SQL ARRAY object in an application as if it were an array in the Java programming language, you need to materialize the ARRAY object on the client and then convert it to an array in the Java programming language. Then you can use array methods in the Java programming language to operate on the elements of the array. The interfaces Blob, Clob, and Array all have methods for materializing the objects they represent.[1]

Struct and Distinct Types

SQL structured types and distinct types are the two data types that a user can define in SQL. They are often referred to as UDTs (user-defined types), and you create them with an SQL CREATE TYPE statement.

An SQL structured type is similar to structured types in the Java programming language in that it has members, called *attributes*, that may be of any data type. In fact, an attribute may itself be another structured type. Here is an example of a simple definition creating a new SQL data type:

```
CREATE TYPE PLANE_POINT
(
    X FLOAT,
    Y FLOAT
)
```

Unlike Blob, Clob, and Array objects, a Struct object contains values for each of the attributes in the SQL structured type and is not just a logical pointer to the object in the database. For example, suppose that a PLANE_POINT object is stored in column POINTS of table PRICES.

---

1 Refer to the forthcoming Java Series book that includes the new JDBC 2.0 API and JDBC standard extension API (Addison Wesley Longman, 1999) for more details or examples.

```
ResultSet rs = stmt.executeQuery("SELECT POINTS FROM PRICES
                                  WHERE PRICE > 3000.00");
while (rs.next()) {
    Struct point = (Struct)rs.getObject("POINTS");
    // do something with point
}
```

If the `PLANE_POINT` object retrieved has an *X* value of 3 and a *Y* value of -5, the `Struct` object *`point`* will contain the values 3 and -5.

You might have noticed that `Struct` is the only type not to have a *`getXXX`* and a *`setXXX`* method with its name as XXX. You must use `getObject` and `setObject` with `Struct` instances. This means that when you retrieve a value by using the method `getObject`, you will get an `Object` in the Java programming language that you must explicitly cast to a `Struct`, as was done in the previous code example.

The second SQL type that a user can define in an SQL `CREATE TYPE` statement is a distinct type. An SQL distinct type is similar to a `typedef` in C or C++ in that it is a new type based on an existing type. Here is an example of creating a distinct type:

```
CREATE TYPE MONEY AS NUMERIC(10, 2)
```

This definition creates the new type called `MONEY`, which is a number of type `NUMERIC` that is always base 10 with two digits after the decimal point. `MONEY` is now a data type in the schema in which it was defined, and you can store instances of `MONEY` in a table that has a column of type `MONEY`.

An SQL distinct type is mapped to the type in the Java programming language to which its underlying type would be mapped. For example, `NUMERIC` maps to `java.math.BigDecimal`, so the type `MONEY` maps to `java.math.BigDecimal`. To retrieve a `MONEY` object, you use `ResultSet.getBigDecimal` or `CallableStatement.getBigDecimal`; to store a `MONEY` object, you use `PreparedStatement.setBigDecimal`.

SQL3 Advanced Features

Some aspects of working with SQL3 types can get quite complex. We mention some of the more advanced features here to introduce them.[1]

---

[1] Refer to the forthcoming Java Series book that includes the new JDBC 2.0 API and JDBC standard extension API (Addison Wesley Longman, 1999) for more details.

The interface `Struct` is the standard mapping for an SQL structured type. If you want to make working with an SQL structured type easier, you can map it to a class in the Java programming language. The structured type becomes a class, and its attributes become fields. You do not have to use a custom mapping, but it can often be more convenient.

Sometimes you may want to work with a logical pointer to an SQL structured type rather than with all of the values contained in the structured type. This might be true, for instance, if the structured type has many attributes or if the attributes are themselves large. To reference a structured type, you can declare an SQL `REF` type that represents a particular structured type. An SQL `REF` object is mapped to a `Ref` object in the Java programming language, and you can operate on it as if you were operating on the structured type object that it represents.

Standard Extension Features

The package `javax.sql` is a standard extension to the Java programming language. To date, the specification is not yet final, but we can outline the basic functionality that it will provide. The following are features in the JDBC 2.0 standard extension:

Rowsets
A rowset encapsulates a set of rows from a result set and may maintain an open database connection or be disconnected from the data source. A rowset, a JavaBeans™ component, can be created at design time and used in conjunction with other JavaBeans components in a visual JavaBeans builder tool to construct an application.

JNDI™ for Naming Databases
The Java Naming and Directory Interface™ (JNDI) makes it possible to connect to a database by using a logical name instead of having to hardcode a particular database and driver.

Connection Pooling
A connection pool is a cache of open connections that can be used and reused, thus reducing the overhead of creating and destroying database connections.

Distributed Transaction Support
Support for distributed transactions allows a JDBC driver to support the standard two-phase commit protocol used by the Java Transaction API (JTA). This feature facilitates using JDBC functionality in Enterprise JavaBeans components.

About the Author

MAYDENE FISHER has extensive experience as a technical writer specializing in the documentation of object-oriented programming languages. Fisher began her technical writing career on Wall Street, where she documented complex computer models, written in C++, for simulating fixed income derivatives. Before joining the JDBC team at Sun's Java Software division, she wrote documentation for ScriptX, an object-oriented multimedia scripting language, at Kaleida Labs and at Apple Computer.

Acknowledgments

Seth White and Mark Hapner deserve untold thanks for their diligence and perseverance in checking the manuscript for correctness.

Remote Method Invocation

by Ann Wollrath and Jim Waldo

THE Java™ Remote Method Invocation (RMI) system allows an object running in one Java Virtual Machine (VM) to invoke methods on an object running in another Java VM. RMI provides for remote communication between programs written in the Java programming language.

Note: If you are connecting to an existing IDL program, you should use Java IDL rather than RMI. For more information, see Java IDL (page 397).

This trail provides a brief overview of the RMI system and then walks through a complete client/server example that uses RMI's unique capabilities to load and to execute user-defined tasks at runtime. The server in the example implements a generic compute engine, which the client uses to compute the value of π.

This trail contains four lessons.

An Overview of RMI Applications (page 361) describes the RMI system and lists its advantages. Additionally, this lesson provides a description of a typical RMI application, composed of a server and a client, and introduces important terms.

Writing an RMI Server (page 367) walks through the code for the compute engine server. This example will teach you how to design and to implement an RMI server.

Creating a Client Program (page 379) takes a look at one possible compute engine client and uses it to illustrate the important features of an RMI client.

Compiling and Running the Example (page 385) shows you how to compile and to run both the compute engine server and its client.

http://java.sun.com/docs/books/tutorial/rmi/overview/index.html

28 An Overview of RMI Applications

RMI applications are often comprised of two separate programs: a server and a client. A typical server application creates some remote objects, makes references to them accessible, and waits for clients to invoke methods on these remote objects. A typical client application gets a remote reference to one or more remote objects in the server and then invokes methods on them. RMI provides the mechanism by which the server and the client communicate and pass information back and forth. Such an application is sometimes referred to as a *distributed object application*.

Distributed object applications need to

- **Locate remote objects**: Applications can use one of two mechanisms to obtain references to remote objects. An application can register its remote objects with RMI's simple naming facility, the `rmiregistry`, or the application can pass and return remote object references as part of its normal operation.
- **Communicate with remote objects**: Details of communication between remote objects are handled by RMI; to the programmer, remote communication looks like a standard Java method invocation.
- **Load class bytecodes for objects that are passed around**: Because RMI allows a caller to pass objects to remote objects, RMI provides the necessary mechanisms for loading an object's code, as well as for transmitting its data.

The following illustration depicts an RMI distributed application that uses the registry to obtain a reference to a remote object. The server calls the registry to associate (or bind) a name with a remote object. The client looks up the remote object by its name in the server's registry and then invokes a method on it. The illustration also shows that the RMI system uses an existing Web server to load class bytecodes, from server to client and from client to server, for objects when needed.

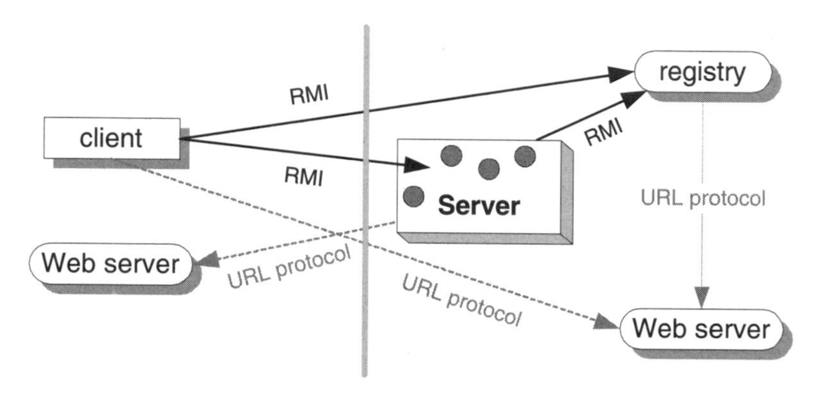

Figure 35 RMI system uses a Web server to load class bytecodes, from server to client and from client to server.

This lesson contains the following sections:

Advantages of Dynamic Code Loading

One of the central and unique features of RMI is its ability to download the *bytecodes* (or simply *code*) of an object's class if the class is not defined in the receiver's virtual machine. The types and the behavior of an object, previously available only in a single virtual machine, can be transmitted to another, possibly remote, virtual machine. RMI passes objects by their true type, so the behavior of those objects is not changed when they are sent to another virtual machine. This allows new types to be introduced into a remote virtual machine, thus extending the behavior of an application dynamically. The compute engine example in this chapter uses RMI's capability to introduce new behavior to a distributed program.

Remote Interfaces, Objects, and Methods

Like any other application, a distributed application built using Java RMI is made up of interfaces and classes. The interfaces define methods, and the classes implement the methods defined in the interfaces and, perhaps, define additional methods as well. In a distributed application some of the implementations are assumed to reside in different virtual machines. Objects that have methods that can be called across virtual machines are *remote objects*.

An object becomes remote by implementing a *remote interface*, which has the following characteristics.

- A remote interface extends the interface `java.rmi.Remote`.
- Each method of the interface declares `java.rmi.RemoteException` in its `throws` clause, in addition to any application-specific exceptions.

RMI treats a remote object differently from a nonremote object when the object is passed from one virtual machine to another. Rather than making a copy of the implementation object in the receiving virtual machine, RMI passes a remote *stub* for a remote object. The stub acts as the local representative, or proxy, for the remote object and basically *is*, to the caller, the remote reference. The caller invokes a method on the local stub, which is responsible for carrying out the method call on the remote object.

A stub for a remote object implements the same set of remote interfaces that the remote object implements. This allows a stub to be cast to any of the interfaces that the remote object implements. However, this also means that *only* those methods defined in a remote interface are available to be called in the receiving virtual machine.

Creating Distributed Applications Using RMI

When you use RMI to develop a distributed application, you follow these general steps.

1. Design and implement the components of your distributed application.
2. Compile sources and generate stubs.
3. Make classes network accessible.
4. Start the application.

Design and Implement the Application Components

First, decide on your application architecture and determine which components are local objects and which ones should be remotely accessible. This step includes:

- **Defining the remote interfaces**: A remote interface specifies the methods that can be invoked remotely by a client. Clients program to remote interfaces, not to the implementation classes of those interfaces. Part of the design of such interfaces is the determination of any local objects that will be used as parameters and return values for these methods; if any of these interfaces or classes do not yet exist, you need to define them as well.
- **Implementing the remote objects**: Remote objects must implement one or more remote interfaces. The remote object class may include implementations of other interfaces (either local or remote) and other methods (which are available only locally). If any local classes are to be used as parameters or return values to any of these methods, they must be implemented as well.
- **Implementing the clients**: Clients that use remote objects can be implemented at any time after the remote interfaces are defined, including after the remote objects have been deployed.

Compile Sources and Generate Stubs

This is a two-step process. In the first step you use the `javac` compiler to compile the source files, which contain the implementation of the remote interfaces and implementations, the server classes, and the client classes. In the second step you use the `rmic` compiler to create stubs for the remote objects. RMI uses a remote object's stub class as a proxy in clients so that clients can communicate with a particular remote object.

Make Classes Network Accessible

In this step you make everything—the class files associated with the remote interfaces, stubs, and other classes that need to be downloaded to clients—accessible via a Web server.

Start the Application

Starting the application includes running the RMI remote object registry, the server, and the client.

The rest of this lesson walks through the steps to create a compute engine.

Building a Generic Compute Engine

This trail focuses on a simple yet powerful distributed application called a compute engine. The compute engine, a remote object in the server, takes tasks from clients, runs them, and returns any results. The tasks are run on the machine where the server is running. This sort of distributed application could allow a number of client machines to make use of a particularly powerful machine or one that has specialized hardware.

The novel aspect of the compute engine is that the tasks it runs do not need to be defined when the compute engine is written. New kinds of tasks can be created at any time and then given to the compute engine to be run. All that is required of a task is that its class implement a particular interface. Such a task can be submitted to the compute engine and run, even if the class that defines that task was written long after the compute engine was written and started. The code needed to accomplish the task can be downloaded by the RMI system to the compute engine, and then the engine runs the task, using the resources on the machine on which the compute engine is running.

The ability to perform arbitrary tasks is enabled by the dynamic nature of the Java platform, which is extended to the network by RMI. RMI dynamically loads the task code into the compute engine's Java virtual machine and runs the task without prior knowledge of the class that implements the task. An application like this, which has the ability to download code dynamically, is often called a behavior-based application. Such applications usually require full agent-enabled infrastructures. With RMI such applications are part of the basic mechanisms for distributed computing on the Java platform.

29 Writing an RMI Server

THE compute engine server accepts tasks from clients, runs the tasks, and returns any results. The server is comprised of an interface and a class. The interface provides the definition for the methods that can be called from the client. Essentially the interface defines the client's view of the remote object. The class provides the implementation.

This section shows you the `Compute` interface, which provides the connection between the client and the server. You will also learn about the RMI API, which supports this communication.

This section explores the class that implements the `Compute` interface, thereby implementing a remote object. This class also provides the rest of the code that makes up the server program: a `main` method that creates an instance of the remote object, registers it with the naming facility, and sets up a security manager.

Designing a Remote Interface

At the heart of the compute engine is a protocol that allows jobs to be submitted to the compute engine, the compute engine to run those jobs, and the results of the job to be returned to the client. This protocol is expressed in interfaces supported by the compute engine and by the objects that are submitted to the compute engine, as shown in the following figure.

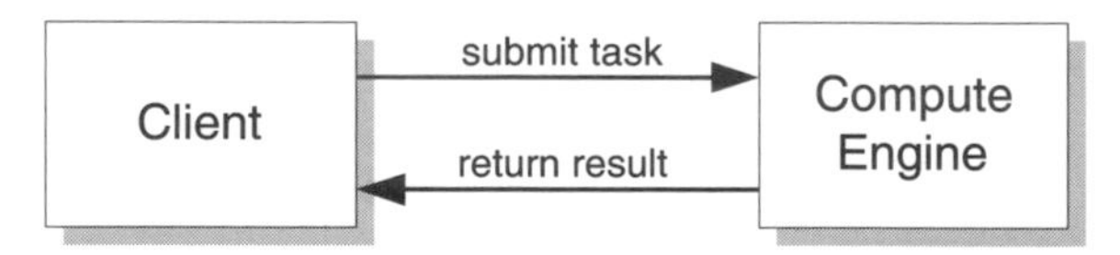

Figure 36 Compute engine protocol in action.

Each of the interfaces contains a single method. The compute engine's interface, `Compute`, allows jobs to be submitted to the engine; the client interface, `Task`, defines how the compute engine executes a submitted task.

The `compute.Compute` interface defines the remotely accessible part—the compute engine itself. Here is the remote interface with its single method:

```
package compute;

import java.rmi.Remote;
import java.rmi.RemoteException;

public interface Compute extends Remote {
    Object executeTask(Task t) throws RemoteException;
}
```

By extending the interface `java.rmi.Remote`, this interface marks itself as one whose methods can be called from any virtual machine. Any object that implements this interface becomes a remote object.

As a member of a remote interface, the `executeTask` method is a remote method. Therefore the method must be defined as being capable of throwing a `java.rmi.RemoteException`. This exception is thrown by the RMI system during a remote method call to indicate that either a communication failure or a protocol error has occurred. A `RemoteException` is a checked exception, so any code making a call to a remote method needs to handle this exception by either catching it or declaring it in its `throws` clause.

The second interface needed for the compute engine defines the type `Task`. This type is used as the argument to the `executeTask` method in the `Compute` interface. The `compute.Task` interface defines the interface between the compute engine and the work that it needs to do, providing the way to start the work.

```
package compute;

import java.io.Serializable;

public interface Task extends Serializable {
    Object execute();
}
```

The `Task` interface defines a single method, `execute`, which returns an `Object`, has no parameters, and throws no exceptions. Since the interface does not extend `Remote`, the method in this interface doesn't need to list `java.rmi.RemoteException` in its `throws` clause.

The return value for the `Compute`'s `executeTask` and `Task`'s `execute` methods is declared to be of type `Object`. This means that any task that wants to return a value of one of the primitive types, such as an `int` or a `float`, needs to create an instance of the equivalent wrapper class for that type, such as an `Integer` or a `Float`, and return that object instead.

Note that the `Task` interface extends the `java.io.Serializable` interface. RMI uses the object serialization mechanism to transport objects by value between Java virtual machines. Implementing `Serializable` marks the class as being capable of conversion into a self-describing byte stream that can be used to reconstruct an exact copy of the serialized object when the object is read back from the stream.

Different kinds of tasks can be run by a `Compute` object as long as they are implementations of the `Task` type. The classes that implement this interface can contain any data needed for the computation of the task and any other methods needed for the computation.

Here is how RMI makes this simple compute engine possible. Since RMI can assume that the `Task` objects are written in the Java programming language, implementations of the `Task` object that were previously unknown to the compute engine are downloaded by RMI into the compute engine's virtual machine as needed. This allows clients of the compute engine to define new kinds of tasks to be run on the server machine without needing the code to be explicitly installed on that machine. In addition, because the `executeTask` method returns a `java.lang.Object`, any type of object can be passed as a return value in the remote call.

The compute engine, implemented by the `ComputeEngine` class, implements the `Compute` interface, allowing different tasks to be submitted to it by calls to its `executeTask` method. These tasks are run using the task's implementation of the `execute` method. The compute engine reports results to the caller through its return value: an `Object`.

Implementing a Remote Interface

Let's turn now to the task of implementing a class for the compute engine. In general the implementation class of a remote interface should at least

- Declare the remote interfaces being implemented
- Define the constructor for the remote object
- Provide an implementation for each remote method in the remote interfaces

The server needs to create and to install the remote objects. This setup procedure can be encapsulated in a `main` method in the remote object implementation class itself, or it can be included in another class entirely. The setup procedure should

- Create and install a security manager
- Create one or more instances of a remote object
- Register at least one of the remote objects with the RMI remote object registry (or another naming service such as one that uses JNDI), for bootstrapping purposes

The complete implementation of the compute engine follows. The `engine.ComputeEngine` class implements the remote interface `Compute` and also includes the `main` method for setting up the compute engine.

```
package engine;

import java.rmi.*;
import java.rmi.server.*;
import compute.*;

public class ComputeEngine extends UnicastRemoteObject
                           implements Compute
{
    public ComputeEngine() throws RemoteException {
        super();
    }

    public Object executeTask(Task t) {
        return t.execute();
    }

    public static void main(String[] args) {
        if (System.getSecurityManager() == null) {
          System.setSecurityManager(new RMISecurityManager());
        }
        String name = "//host/Compute";
        try {
            Compute engine = new ComputeEngine();
            Naming.rebind(name, engine);
            System.out.println("ComputeEngine bound");
        } catch (Exception e) {
```

```
                System.err.println("ComputeEngine exception: " +
                                   e.getMessage());
                e.printStackTrace();
            }
        }
    }
```

Now let's take a closer look at each of the components of the compute engine implementation.

Declare the Remote Interfaces Being Implemented

The implementation class for the compute engine is declared as

```
    public class ComputeEngine extends UnicastRemoteObject
                               implements Compute
```

This declaration states that the class implements the `Compute` remote interface (and therefore defines a remote object) and extends the class `java.rmi.server.UnicastRemoteObject`.

`UnicastRemoteObject` is a convenience class, defined in the RMI public API, that can be used as a superclass for remote object implementations. The superclass `UnicastRemoteObject` supplies implementations for a number of `java.lang.Object` methods (`equals`, `hashCode`, `toString`) so that they are defined appropriately for remote objects. `UnicastRemoteObject` also includes constructors and static methods used to *export* a remote object, that is, make the remote object available to receive incoming calls from clients.

A remote object implementation does not have to extend `UnicastRemoteObject`, but any implementation that does not must supply appropriate implementations of the `java.lang.Object` methods. Furthermore, a remote object implementation must make an explicit call to one of `UnicastRemoteObject`'s `exportObject` methods to make the RMI runtime aware of the remote object so that the object can accept incoming calls. By extending `UnicastRemoteObject`, the `ComputeEngine` class can be used to create a simple remote object that supports unicast (point-to-point) remote communication and that uses RMI's default sockets-based transport for communication.

If you choose to extend a remote object from any class other than `UnicastRemoteObject` or, alternatively, extend from the new JDK 1.2 class `java.rmi.activation.Activatable` (used to construct remote objects that can execute on demand), you need to export the remote object by calling either the `UnicastRemoteObject.exportObject` or `Activatable.exportObject` method explicitly from your class's constructor (or another initialization method, as appropriate).

The compute engine example defines a remote object class that implements only a single remote interface and no other interfaces. The `ComputeEngine` class also contains some methods that can be called only locally. The first of these is a constructor for `ComputeEngine` objects; the second is a `main` method that is used to create a `ComputeEngine` and make it available to clients.

Define the Constructor

The `ComputeEngine` class has a single constructor that takes no arguments. The code for the constructor is

```
public ComputeEngine() throws RemoteException {
    super();
}
```

This constructor simply calls the superclass constructor, which is the no-argument constructor of the `UnicastRemoteObject` class. Although the superclass constructor gets called even if omitted from the `ComputeEngine` constructor, we include it for clarity.

During construction, a `UnicastRemoteObject` is *exported*, meaning that it is available to accept incoming requests by listening for incoming calls from clients on an anonymous port.

Note: In JDK 1.2 you may indicate the specific port that a remote object uses to accept requests.

The no-argument constructor for the superclass, `UnicastRemoteObject`, declares the exception `RemoteException` in its `throws` clause, so the `ComputeEngine` constructor must also declare that it can throw `RemoteException`. A `RemoteException` can occur during construction if the attempt to export the object fails—due to, for example, communication resources being unavailable or the appropriate stub class not being found.

Provide Implementations for Each Remote Method

The class for a remote object provides implementations for each of the remote methods specified in the remote interfaces. The `Compute` interface contains a single remote method, `executeTask`, which is implemented as follows:

```
public Object executeTask(Task t) {
    return t.execute();
}
```

This method implements the protocol between the `ComputeEngine` and its clients. Clients provide the `ComputeEngine` with a `Task` object, which has an implementation of the task's `execute` method. The `ComputeEngine` executes the `Task` and returns the result of the task's `execute` method directly to the caller.

The `executeTask` method does not need to know anything more about the result of the `execute` method than that it is at least an `Object`. The caller presumably knows more about the precise type of the `Object` returned and can cast the result to the appropriate type.

Passing Objects in RMI

Arguments to or return values from remote methods can be of almost any type, including local objects, remote objects, and primitive types. More precisely, any entity of any type can be passed to or from a remote method as long as the entity is an instance of a type that is a primitive data type, a remote object, or a *serializable* object, which means that it implements the interface `java.io.Serializable`.

A few object types do not meet any of these criteria and thus cannot be passed to or returned from a remote method. Most of these objects, such as a file descriptor, encapsulate information that makes sense only within a single address space. Many of the core classes, including those in the packages `java.lang` and `java.util`, implement the `Serializable` interface.

The rules governing how arguments and return values are passed are as follows.

- Remote objects are essentially passed by reference. A *remote object reference* is a stub, which is a client-side proxy that implements the complete set of remote interfaces that the remote object implements.
- Local objects are passed by copy, using object serialization. By default all fields are copied, except those that are marked `static` or `transient`. Default serialization behavior can be overridden on a class-by-class basis.

Passing an object by reference (as is done with remote objects) means that any changes made to the state of the object by remote method calls are reflected in the original remote object. When passing a remote object, only those interfaces that are remote interfaces are available to the receiver; any methods defined in the implementation class or defined in nonremote interfaces implemented by the class are not available to that receiver.

For example, if you were to pass a reference to an instance of the `ComputeEngine` class, the receiver would have access only to the compute engine's `executeTask` method. That receiver would not see either the `ComputeEngine` constructor or its `main` method or any of the methods in `java.lang.Object`.

In remote method calls objects—parameters, return values, and exceptions—that are not remote objects are passed by value. This means that a copy of the object is created in the receiving virtual machine. Any changes to this object's state at the receiver are reflected only in the receiver's copy, not in the original instance.

Implement the Server's main Method

The most involved method of the `ComputeEngine` implementation is the `main` method. The `main` method is used to start the `ComputeEngine` and therefore needs to do the necessary initialization and housekeeping to prepare the server for accepting calls from clients. This method is not a remote method, which means that it cannot be called from a different virtual machine. Since the `main` method is declared `static`, the method is not associated with an object at all but rather with the class `ComputeEngine`.

Create and Install a Security Manager

The first thing that the `main` method does is to create and to install a security manager, which protects access to system resources from untrusted downloaded code running within the virtual machine. The security manager determines whether downloaded code has access to the local file system or can perform any other privileged operations.

All programs using RMI must install a security manager, or RMI will not download classes (other than from the local class path) for objects received as parameters, return values, or exceptions in remote method calls. This restriction ensures that the operations performed by downloaded code go through a set of security checks.

The `ComputeEngine` uses a security manager supplied as part of the RMI system, the `RMISecurityManager`. This security manager enforces a similar security policy as the typical security manager for applets; that is to say, it is very conservative as to what access it allows. An RMI application could define and use another `SecurityManager` class that gave more liberal access to system resources or, in JDK 1.2, use a policy file that grants more permissions.

Here's the code that creates and installs the security manager:

```
if (System.getSecurityManager() == null) {
    System.setSecurityManager(new RMISecurityManager());
}
```

Make the Remote Object Available to Clients

Next, the `main` method creates an instance of the `ComputeEngine`. This is done with the statement

```
Compute engine = new ComputeEngine();
```

As mentioned, this constructor calls the `UnicastRemoteObject` superclass constructor, which in turn exports the newly created object to the RMI runtime. Once the export step is complete, the `ComputeEngine` remote object is ready to accept incoming calls from clients on an anonymous port, one chosen by RMI or the underlying operating system. Note that the type of the variable `engine` is `Compute`, not `ComputeEngine`. This declaration emphasizes that the interface available to clients is the `Compute` interface and its methods, not the `ComputeEngine` class and its methods.

Before a caller can invoke a method on a remote object, that caller must first obtain a reference to the remote object. This can be done in the same way that any other object reference is obtained in a program, such as getting it as part of the return value of a method or as part of a data structure that contains such a reference.

The system provides a particular remote object, the RMI registry, for finding references to remote objects. The RMI registry is a simple remote object name service that allows remote clients to get a reference to a remote object by name. The registry is typically used only to locate the first remote object an RMI client needs to use. That first remote object then provides support for finding other objects.

The `java.rmi.Naming` interface is used as a front-end API for binding, or registering, and looking up remote objects in the registry. Once a remote object is registered with the RMI registry on the local host, callers on any host can look up the remote object by name, obtain its reference, and then invoke remote methods on the object. The registry may be shared by all servers running on a host, or an individual server process may create and use its own registry, if desired.

The `ComputeEngine` class creates a name for the object with the statement

```
String name = "//host/Compute";
```

This name includes the host name, `host`, on which the registry (and remote object) is being run and a name, `Compute`, that identifies the remote object in the registry. The code then needs to add the name to the RMI registry running on the server. This is done later (within the `try` block) with the statement

```
Naming.rebind(name, engine);
```

Calling the `rebind` method makes a remote call to the RMI registry on the local host. This call can result in a `RemoteException` being generated, so the exception needs to be handled. The `ComputeEngine` class handles the exception within the `try/catch` block. If the exception is not handled in this way, `RemoteException` would have to be added to the `throws` clause (currently nonexistent) of the `main` method.

Note the following about the arguments to the call to `Naming.rebind`.

- The first parameter is a URL-formatted `java.lang.String` representing the location and the name of the remote object. You will need to change the value of `host` to be the name, or IP address, of your server machine. If the host is omitted from the URL, the host defaults to the local host. Also, you don't need to specify a protocol in the URL. For example, supplying `Compute` as the name in the `Naming.rebind` call is allowed. Optionally a port number may be supplied in the URL; for example, the name `//host:1234/objectname` is legal. If the port is omitted, it defaults to 1099. You must specify the port number only if a server creates a registry on a port other than the default 1099. The default port is useful in that it provides a well-known place to look for the remote objects that offer services on a particular host.
- The RMI runtime substitutes a reference to the stub for the remote object reference specified by the argument. Remote implementation objects, such as instances of `ComputeEngine`, never leave the VM where they are created, so when a client performs a lookup in a server's remote object registry, a reference to the stub is returned. As discussed earlier, remote objects in such cases are passed by reference rather than by value.
- Note that for security reasons, an application can `bind`, `unbind`, or `rebind` remote object references only with a registry running on the same host. This restriction prevents a remote client from removing or overwriting any of the entries in a server's registry. A `lookup`, however, can be requested from any host, local or remote.

Once the server has registered with the local RMI registry, it prints out a message indicating that it's ready to start handling calls and then the `main` method exits. It is not necessary to have a thread wait to keep the server alive. As long as there is a reference to the `ComputeEngine` object in another virtual machine, local or remote, the `ComputeEngine` object will not be shut down, or garbage collected. Because the program binds a reference to the `ComputeEngine` in the registry, it is reachable from a remote client, the registry itself! The RMI system takes care of keeping the `ComputeEngine`'s process up. The `ComputeEngine` is available to accept calls and won't be reclaimed until its binding is removed from the registry, *and* no remote clients hold a remote reference to the `ComputeEngine` object.

The final piece of code in the `ComputeEngine.main` method deals with handling any exception that might arise. The only exception that could be thrown in the code is a `RemoteException`, thrown either by the constructor of the `ComputeEngine` class or by the call to the RMI registry to bind the object to the name `Compute`. In either case the program can't do much more than exit after printing an error message. In some distributed applications it is possible to recover from the failure to make a remote call. For example, the application could choose another server and continue operation.

Creating a Client Program

THE compute engine is a pretty simple program: it runs tasks that are handed to it. The clients for the compute engine are more complex. A client needs to call the compute engine, but it also has to define the task to be performed by the compute engine.

Two separate classes make up the client in our example. The first class, `ComputePi`, looks up and calls a `Compute` object. The second class, `Pi`, implements the `Task` interface and defines the work to be done by the compute engine. The job of the `Pi` class is to compute the value of π to some number of decimal places.

As you recall, the nonremote `Task` interface is defined as follows:

```
package compute;
public interface Task extends java.io.Serializable {
    Object execute();
}
```

The `Task` interface extends `java.io.Serializable` so that an object that implements the interface can be serialized by the RMI runtime and sent to a remote virtual machine as part of a remote method invocation. We could have chosen to have our implementation classes implement both the `Task` interface and the `Serializable` interface and gotten the same effect. However, the whole purpose of the `Task` interface is to allow implementations of that interface to be passed to a `Compute` object, so having a class that implements the `Task` interface that does not also implement the `Serializable` interface doesn't make sense. Therefore we associate the two interfaces explicitly in the type system, ensuring that all `Task` objects are serializable.

The code that calls a `Compute` object's methods must obtain a reference to that object, create a `Task` object, and then request that the task be executed. The definition of the task `Pi` is shown later. A `Pi` object is constructed with a single argument, the desired precision of the result. The result of the task execution is a `java.math.BigDecimal` representing π calculated to the specified precision.

The client class `client.ComputePi` is as follows.

```
package client;

import java.rmi.*;
import java.math.*;
import compute.*;

public class ComputePi {
    public static void main(String args[]) {
        if (System.getSecurityManager() == null) {
          System.setSecurityManager(new RMISecurityManager());
        }
        try {
            String name = "//" + args[0] + "/Compute";
            Compute comp = (Compute) Naming.lookup(name);
            Pi task = new Pi(Integer.parseInt(args[1]));
         BigDecimal pi = (BigDecimal) (comp.executeTask(task));
            System.out.println(pi);
        } catch (Exception e) {
            System.err.println("ComputePi exception: " +
                               e.getMessage());
            e.printStackTrace();
        }
    }
}
```

Like the `ComputeEngine` server, the client begins by installing a security manager. This is necessary because RMI could be downloading code to the client. In this example the `ComputeEngine`'s stub is downloaded to the client. Any time code is downloaded by RMI, a security manager must be present. As with the server, the client uses the security manager provided by the RMI system for this purpose.

After installing a security manager, the client constructs a name used to look up a `Compute` remote object. The value of the first command line argument, `args[0]`, is the name of the remote host on which the `Compute` object runs. The client uses the `Naming.lookup` method to look up the remote object by name in the remote host's registry. When doing the name lookup, the code creates a URL that specifies the host where the compute server is running. The name passed in the `Naming.lookup` call has the same URL syntax as the name passed in the `Naming.rebind` call, which was discussed earlier.

Next, the client creates a new `Pi` object, passing to the `Pi` constructor the second command line argument, `args[1]`, which indicates the number of decimal places to use in the calculation. Finally, the client invokes the `executeTask` method of the `Compute` remote object. The object passed into the `executeTask` call returns an object of type `java.math.BigDecimal`, so the program casts the result to that type and stores the return value in the variable `result`. Then, the program prints out the result. The following figure depicts the flow of messages among the `ComputePi` client, the `rmiregistry`, and the `ComputeEngine`.

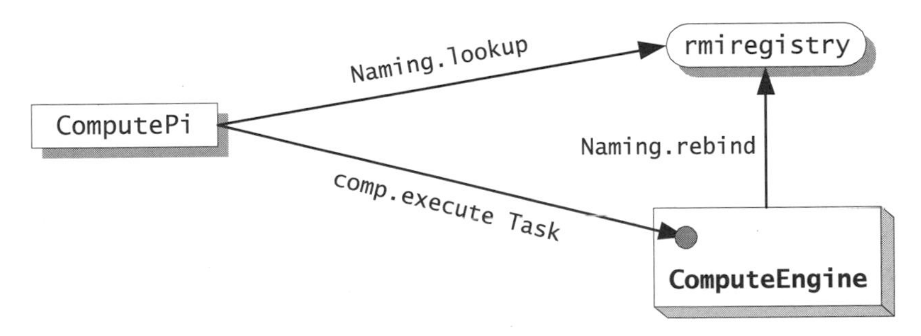

Figure 37 Flow of messages among the `ComputePi` client, the `rmiregistry`, and the `ComputeEngine`.

Finally, let's look at the reason for all of this in the first place: the `Pi` class. This class implements the `Task` interface and computes the value of π to a specified number of decimal places. For this example the actual algorithm is unimportant except, of course, for the accuracy of the computation. All that is important is that the computation is numerically rather expensive and thus the sort of thing that you would want to have occur on a more capable server.

Here is the code for the class `client.Pi`, which implements `Task`.

```
package client;
import compute.*;
import java.math.*;

public class Pi implements Task {

    /** constants used in pi computation */
```

```
private static final BigDecimal ZERO =
    BigDecimal.valueOf(0);
private static final BigDecimal  ONE =
    BigDecimal.valueOf(1);
private static final BigDecimal FOUR =
    BigDecimal.valueOf(4);

/** rounding mode to use during pi computation */
private static final int roundingMode =
    BigDecimal.ROUND_HALF_EVEN;

/** digits of precision after the decimal point */
private int digits;

/**
 * Construct a task to calculate pi to the specified
 * precision.
 */
public Pi(int digits) {
    this.digits = digits;
}

/**
 * Calculate pi.
 */
public Object execute() {
    return computePi(digits);
}

/**
 * Compute the value of pi to the specified number of
 * digits after the decimal point.  The value is
 * computed using Machin's formula:
 *
 *          pi/4 = 4*arctan(1/5) - arctan(1/239)
 *
 * and a power series expansion of arctan(x) to
 * sufficient precision.
 */
public static BigDecimal computePi(int digits) {
    int scale = digits + 5;
    BigDecimal arctan1_5 = arctan(5, scale);
    BigDecimal arctan1_239 = arctan(239, scale);
    BigDecimal pi = arctan1_5.multiply(FOUR).subtract(
                              arctan1_239).multiply(FOUR);
     return pi.setScale(digits,
                      BigDecimal.ROUND_HALF_UP);
}
```

```
    /**
     * Compute the value, in radians, of the arctangent of
     * the inverse of the supplied integer to the speficied
     * number of digits after the decimal point.  The value
     * is computed using the power series expansion for the
     * arc tangent:
     *
     * arctan(x) = x - (x^3)/3 + (x^5)/5 - (x^7)/7 +
     *     (x^9)/9 ...
     */
    public static BigDecimal arctan(int inverseX,
                                    int scale)
    {
        BigDecimal result, numer, term;
        BigDecimal invX = BigDecimal.valueOf(inverseX);
        BigDecimal invX2 =
            BigDecimal.valueOf(inverseX * inverseX);

        numer = ONE.divide(invX, scale, roundingMode);

        result = numer;
        int i = 1;
        do {
            numer =
                numer.divide(invX2, scale, roundingMode);
            int denom = 2 * i + 1;
            term =
                numer.divide(BigDecimal.valueOf(denom),
                             scale, roundingMode);
            if ((i % 2) != 0) {
                result = result.subtract(term);
            } else {
                result = result.add(term);
            }
            i++;
        } while (term.compareTo(ZERO) != 0);
        return result;
    }
}
```

The most interesting feature of this example is that the `Compute` object never needs `Pi`'s class definition until a `Pi` object is passed in as an argument to the `executeTask` method. At that point the code for the class is loaded by RMI into the `Compute` object's virtual machine, the `execute` method is called, and the task's code is executed. The resulting `Object`, which in the case of the `Pi` task is a `java.math.BigDecimal` object, is handed back to the calling client, where it is used to print out the result of the calculation.

The fact that the supplied `Task` object computes the value of `Pi` is irrelevant to the `ComputeEngine` object. You could also implement a task that, for example, generated a random prime number by using a probabilistic algorithm. That would also be numerically intensive and therefore a candidate for being shipped over to the `ComputeEngine`, but it would involve very different code. This code could also be downloaded when the `Task` object was passed to a `Compute` object. In just the way that the algorithm for computing `Pi` is brought in when needed, the code that generates the random prime would be brought in when needed. The `Compute` object knows only that each object it receives implements the `execute` method; it does not know, and does not need to know, what the implementation does.

31 Compiling and Running the Example

NOW that you've seen the code that makes up the client and the server for the compute engine example, let's compile and run that code.

Compiling the Programs

In a real-world scenario in which a service like the compute engine is deployed, a developer would likely create a JAR (Java ARchive) file that contains the `Compute` and `Task` interfaces for server classes to implement and client program to use. Next, a developer, perhaps the same developer of the interface JAR file, would write an implementation of the `Compute` interface and deploy that service on a machine available to clients. Developers of client programs can use the `Compute` and the `Task` interfaces, contained in the JAR file, and independently develop a task and client program that uses a `Compute` service.

In this section you learn how to set up the JAR file, server classes, and client classes. You will see that the client's `Pi` class will be downloaded to the server at runtime. Also, the ComputeEngine's remote stub will be downloaded from the server to the client at runtime.

The example separates the interfaces, remote object implementation, and client code into three packages:

- compute (Compute and Task interfaces)
- engine (ComputeEngine implementation class and its stub)
- client (ComputePi client code and Pi task implementation)

Let's first build the interface JAR file to provide to server and client developers.

Build a JAR File of Interface Classes

First, you need to compile the interface source files in the compute package and then build a JAR file that contains their class files. Let's suppose a user, waldo, has written these particular interfaces and has placed the source files in c:\home\waldo\src\compute (on UNIX: /home/waldo/src/compute). Given these paths, you can use the following commands to compile the interfaces and create the JAR file.

Win32:

```
cd c:\home\waldo\src
javac compute\Compute.java
javac compute\Task.java
jar cvf compute.jar compute\*.class
```

UNIX:

```
cd /home/waldo/src
javac compute/Compute.java
javac compute/Task.java
jar cvf compute.jar compute/*.class
```

The jar command displays the following output (due to the -v option):

```
added manifest
adding: compute/Compute.class (in=281) (out=196)
    (deflated 30%)
adding: compute/Task.class (in=200) (out=164)
    (deflated 18%)
```

Now you can distribute the compute.jar file to developers of server and client applications so that they can make use of the interfaces.

When you build either server- or client-side classes with the javac and rmic compilers, you generally need to specify where the resulting class files should reside so that they are network accessible. In this example this location is, for UNIX, /home/user/public_html/classes, because some web servers allow accessing a user's public_html directory via an HTTP URL constructed as http://host/~user/. If your web server does not support this convention, you could use a file URL instead. The file URLs take the form file:/home/user/public_html/classes/ on UNIX or, on the Win32 platform, file:/c:/home/user/public_html/classes/. You may also select another type of URL, as appropriate.

The network accessibility of the class files allows the RMI runtime to download code when needed. Rather than defining its own protocol for code downloading, RMI uses URL protocols supported by the Java platform (for example, HTTP) to download code. Note that a full, heavyweight web server is not needed to accomplish this downloading of class files. In fact, a simple HTTP server that provides all of the functionality needed to make classes available for downloading in RMI via HTTP can be found at

```
ftp://java.sun.com/pub/jdk1.1/rmi/class-server.zip
```

Build the Server Classes

The engine package contains only one server-side implementation class, ComputeEngine, the remote object implementation of the Compute interface. Since ComputeEngine is an implementation of a remote interface, you need to generate a stub for the remote object so that clients can contact the remote object.

Let's say that ann, the developer of the ComputeEngine class, has placed ComputeEngine.java in the c:\home\ann\src\engine directory and is deploying the class files for clients to use in a subdirectory of her public_html directory, c:\home\ann\public_html\classes (on UNIX that would be /home/ann/public_html/classes, accessible via some web servers as http://host/~ann/classes/).

Now let's assume that the compute.jar file is located in the directory c:\home\ann\public_html\classes. To compile the ComputeEngine class, your class path must include the compute.jar file and the source directory itself.

Note: Normally we recommend that you set the class path on the command line, using the -classpath option. However, for several compounding reasons this example uses the CLASSPATH environment variable, because both javac and rmic require a class path and the -classpath option is treated differently in JDK 1.1 and

JDK 1.2.[1] We recommend that you do not set CLASSPATH in a login or startup file and that you remember to unset it when you're finished working with this example.

Here's how to set the CLASSPATH environment variable

Win32:

```
set CLASSPATH=c:\home\ann\src;
    c:\home\ann\public_html\classes\compute.jar
```

UNIX:

```
setenv CLASSPATH /home/ann/src:
    /home/ann/public_html/classes/compute.jar
```

Now you compile the `ComputeEngine.java` source file, generate a stub for the `ComputeEngine` class, and make that stub network accessible. To create stub (and optionally skeleton files), run the `rmic` compiler on the fully qualified class names of the remote object implementations that must be found in the class path. The `rmic` command takes one or more class names as input and produces as output class files of the form `ClassName_Stub.class` and `ClassName_Skel.class`. A skeleton file will not be generated if you run `rmic` with the `-v1.2` option. This option should be used only if all of your clients will be running JDK 1.2 or compatible versions.

Win32:

```
cd c:\home\ann\src
javac engine\ComputeEngine.java
rmic -d . engine.ComputeEngine
mkdir c:\home\ann\public_html\classes\engine
cp engine\ComputeEngine_*.class
    c:\home\ann\public_html\classes\engine
```

UNIX:

```
cd /home/ann/src
javac engine/ComputeEngine.java
rmic -d . engine.ComputeEngine
mkdir /home/ann/public_html/classes/engine
cp engine/ComputeEngine_*.class
    /home/ann/public_html/classes/engine
```

The `-d` option tells the `rmic` compiler to place the generated class files, `ComputeEngine_Stub.class` and `ComputeEngine_Skel.class`, in the directory `c:\home\ann\src\engine`. You also need to make the stubs and the skeletons network accessible, so you must copy the stub and the skeleton class to the area: `public_html\classes`.

---

[1] For more detailed information on CLASSPATH, refer to http://java.sun.com/products/jdk/1.2/docs/install.html.

Since the ComputeEngine's stub implements the Compute interface, which refers to the Task interface, you need to make these two interface class files network accessible along with the stub. So the final step is to unpack the compute.jar file in the directory c:\home\ann\public_html\classes to make the Compute and the Task interfaces available for downloading.

Win32:

```
cd c:\home\ann\public_html\classes
jar xvf compute.jar
```

UNIX:

```
cd /home/ann/public_html/classes
jar xvf compute.jar
```

The jar command displays the following output:

```
created: META-INF/
extracted: META-INF/MANIFEST.MF
extracted: compute/Compute.class
extracted: compute/Task.class
```

Now the compute engine is ready to deploy. You could do that now or wait until after you have built the client. While we are on a building spree, let's build the client-side program next.

Build the Client Classes

Let's assume that user jones has created the client code in the directory c:\home\jones\src\client and will deploy the Pi class, so that it can be downloaded to the compute engine, in the network-accessible directory c:\home\jones\public_html\classes, also available via some web servers as http://host/~jones/classes/. The two client-side classes are contained in the files Pi.java and ComputePi.java in the client subdirectory.

In order to build the client code, you need the compute.jar file that contains the Compute and the Task interfaces that the client uses. Let's say that the compute.jar file is located in c:\home\jones\public_html\classes. The client classes can be built as follows:

Win32:

```
set
CLASSPATH=c:\home\jones\src;
    c:\home\jones\public_html\classes\compute.jar
cd c:\home\jones\src
javac client\ComputePi.java
javac -d c:\home\jones\public_html\classes client\Pi.java
```

UNIX:

```
setenv CLASSPATH /home/jones/src:
    /home/jones/public_html/classes/compute.jar
cd /home/jones/src
javac client/ComputePi.java
javac -d /home/jones/public_html/classes client/Pi.java
```

Only the `Pi` class needs to be placed in the directory `public_html\classes\client`. (The `client` directory is created by `javac` if it does not exist.) The reason is that only the `Pi` class needs to be available for downloading to the compute engine's virtual machine. Now you can run the server and then the client.

Running the Programs

A Note about Security

The JDK 1.2 security model is more sophisticated than the model used for JDK 1.1. JDK 1.2 contains enhancements for finer-grained security and requires code to be granted specific permissions to be allowed to perform certain operations.

In JDK 1.1 code in the class path is trusted and can perform any operation; downloaded code is governed by the rules of the installed security manager. If you run this example in JDK 1.2, you need to specify a policy file when you run your server and client. Here is a general policy file that allows downloaded code, from any code base, to do two things:

- Connect to or accept connections on unprivileged ports (ports greater than 1024) on any host
- Connect to port 80 (the port for HTTP)

Here is the code for the general policy file:

```
grant {
    permission java.net.SocketPermission "*:1024-65535",
        "connect,accept";
    permission java.net.SocketPermission "*:80", "connect";
};
```

If you make your code available for downloading via HTTP URLs, you should use the preceding policy file when you run this example. However, if you use file URLs instead, you can use the following policy file. Note that in Windows-style file names, the backslash character needs to be represented by two backslash characters in the policy file.

```
grant {
    permission java.net.SocketPermission "*:1024-65535",
        "connect,accept";
    permission java.io.FilePermission
        "c:\\home\\ann\\public_html\\classes\\-", "read";
    permission java.io.FilePermission
        "c:\\home\\jones\\public_html\\classes\\-", "read";
};
```

This example assumes that the policy file is called `java.policy` and that it contains the appropriate permissions. If you run this example on JDK 1.1, you will not need to use a policy file, since the `RMISecurityManager` provides all of the protection you need.

Start the Server

Before starting the compute engine, you need to start RMI's registry, using the `rmiregistry` command. As discussed earlier, the RMI registry is a simple server-side bootstrap naming facility that allows remote clients to get a reference to a remote object. Note that before you start the `rmiregistry`, you must make sure that the shell or window in which you will run `rmiregistry` either has no `CLASSPATH` environment variable set or has a `CLASSPATH` environment variable that does not include the path to any classes, including the stubs for your remote object implementation classes, that you want downloaded to clients of your remote objects.

If you *do* start the `rmiregistry` and it *can* find your stub classes in `CLASSPATH`, it will not remember that the loaded stub class can be loaded from your server's code base, specified by the `java.rmi.server.codebase` property when you started up your server application. Therefore, the `rmiregistry` will not convey to clients the true code base associated with the stub class and, consequently, your clients will not be able to locate and to load the stub class or other server-side classes.

To start the registry on the server, execute the `rmiregistry` command. This command produces no output and is typically run in the background. For this example, we will start the registry on the host `zaphod`.

Win32 (use `javaw` if `start` is not available):

```
unset CLASSPATH
start rmiregistry
```

UNIX:

```
unsetenv CLASSPATH
rmiregistry &
```

By default, the registry runs on port 1099. To start the registry on a different port, specify the port number on the command line. Do not forget to unset your CLASSPATH.

Win32:
```
start rmiregistry 2001
```
UNIX:
```
rmiregistry 2001 &
```

Once the registry is started, you can start the server. First, you need to make sure that both the `compute.jar` file and the remote object implementation class (since that is what you are starting) are in your class path.

Win32:
```
set CLASSPATH=c:\home\ann\src;
    c:\home\ann\public_html\classes\compute.jar
```
UNIX:
```
setenv CLASSPATH /home/ann/src:
    /home/ann/public_html/classes/compute.jar
```

When you start the compute engine, you need to specify, using the `java.rmi.server.codebase` property, where the server's classes will be made available. In this example the server-side classes to be made available for downloading are the `ComputeEngine`'s stub and the `Compute` and the `Task` interfaces, available in `ann`'s `public_html\classes` directory. Here, we start the compute engine server on the host `zaphod`, the same host where we started the registry.

Win32:
```
java -Djava.rmi.server.codebase=
file:c:\home\ann\public_html\classes/
     -Djava.rmi.server.hostname=zaphod.east.sun.com
     -Djava.security.policy=java.policy
      engine.ComputeEngine
```
UNIX:
```
java -Djava.rmi.server.codebase=http://zaphod/~ann/classes/
     -Djava.rmi.server.hostname=zaphod.east.sun.com
     -Djava.security.policy=java.policy
      engine.ComputeEngine
```

The preceding `java` command defines several properties.

- The `java.rmi.server.codebase` property specifies the location, a code base URL, of classes originating *from* this server so that class information for objects sent to other virtual machines will include the location of the class so that a receiver can load it. If the code base specifies a directory (as opposed to a JAR file), you must include the trailing slash in the code base URL.

- The `java.rmi.server.hostname` property indicates the fully qualified host name of your server. In some networked environments a fully qualified host name is not obtainable by using the Java APIs. RMI makes a best-effort attempt to obtain the fully qualified host name. If one cannot be determined, it will fall back and use the IP address. To ensure that RMI will use a host name that is usable from potential clients, you may want to set the `java.rmi.server.hostname` property as a safety measure.
- The `java.security.policy` property is used to specify the policy file that contains the permissions you intend to grant specific code bases.

The `ComputeEngine`'s stub class is dynamically loaded into a client's virtual machine only when the class is not already available locally *and* the `java.rmi.server.codebase` property has been set properly, to the network-accessible location of the stub class, when the *server* is started. Once such a stub is loaded, it will not need to be reloaded for additional references to `ComputeEngine`'s objects.

Start the Client

Once the registry and the engine are running, you can start the client, specifying

- The location where the client serves up its classes (the `Pi` class), using the `java.rmi.server.codebase` property
- As command line arguments the host name of the server—so that the client knows where to locate the `Compute` remote object—and the number of decimal places to use in the π calculation
- The `java.security.policy` property, used to specify the policy file that contains the permissions you intend to grant specific code bases

First, set the `CLASSPATH` to see `jones`'s client and the JAR file containing the interfaces. Then start the client on another host (one named `ford`, for example) as follows:

Win32:

```
set CLASSPATH c:\home\jones\src;
     c:\home\jones\public_html\classes\compute.jar
java -Djava.rmi.server.codebase=file:
     c:\home\jones\public_html\classes/
     -Djava.security.policy=java.policy
     client.ComputePi zaphod.east.sun.com 20
```

UNIX:

```
setenv CLASSPATH /home/jones/src:
     /home/jones/public_html/classes/compute.jar
java -Djava.rmi.server.codebase=http://ford/~jones/classes/
     -Djava.security.policy=java.policy
      client.ComputePi zaphod.east.sun.com 20
```

Note that the class path is set on the command line so that the interpreter can find `jones`'s client and the JAR file containing the interfaces.

After starting the client, you should see the following output on your display:

```
3.14159265358979323846
```

The following figure illustrates where the `rmiregistry`, the `ComputeEngine` server, and the `ComputePi` client obtain classes during program execution.

When the `ComputeEngine` server binds its remote object reference in the registry, the registry downloads the `ComputeEngine_Stub`, as well as the `Compute` and the `Task` interfaces on which the stub class depends. These classes are downloaded from the `ComputeEngine`'s web server or file system, as the case may be.

The `ComputePi` client loads the `ComputeEngine_Stub`, also from the `ComputeEngine`'s web server, as a result of the `Naming.lookup` call. Since the `ComputePi` client has both the `Compute` and the `Task` interfaces available in its class path, those classes are loaded from the class path, not the remote location.

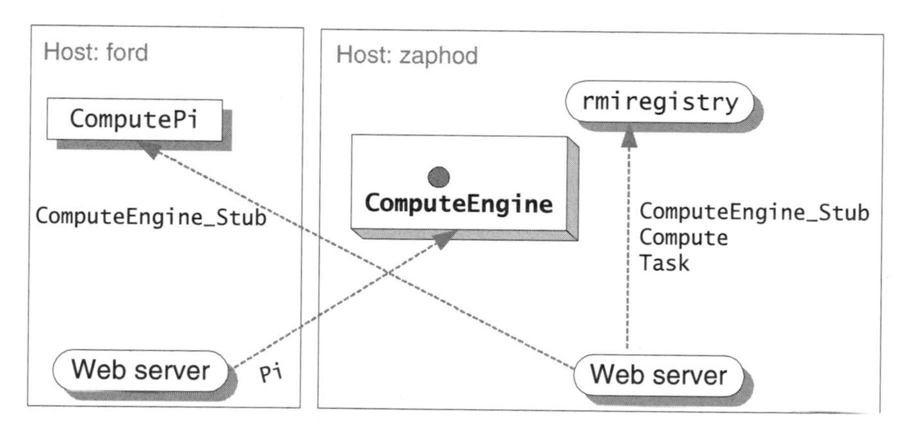

Figure 38 The `rmiregistry`, `ComputeEngine` server, and `ComputePi` client obtaining classes during program execution.

Finally, the `Pi` class is loaded into the `ComputeEngine`'s virtual machine when the `Pi` object is passed in the `executeTask` remote call to the `ComputeEngine` object. The `Pi` class is loaded from the client's web server.

About the Authors

ANN WOLLRATH is a Senior Staff Engineer with Sun Microsystems where she is the architect and project lead of the Java Remote Method Invocation system. Previously during her tenure at Sun Microsystems Laboratories and at the MITRE Corporation, she researched reliable, large-scale distributed systems and parallel computation. Ann received an M.S. in computer science from the University of Massachusetts, Lowell, and a B.S. in computer science from Merrimack College.

JIM WALDO is a Senior Staff Engineer with Sun Microsystems, where he leads a team developing a distributed programming infrastructure for Java. Before joining Sun's Java Software division, he was a Principal Investigator in Sun Labs, doing research into the areas of object-oriented programming and systems, distributed computing, and user environments. Jim is also on the faculty of Harvard University, where he teaches distributed computing in the department of computer science. He received his Ph.D. in philosophy from the University of Massachusetts (Amherst). He also holds M.A. degrees in both linguistics and philosophy.

Acknowledgments

We'd like to thank Peter Jones for his contribution of the code to calculate π and both Peter Jones and Jennifer McGinn for their detailed reviews and comments on this chapter.

Java IDL

by Jim Inscore

THIS trail introduces Java™ IDL, the CORBA-compliant distributed object technology included in JDK™ 1.2. Java IDL enables applications and applets written in the Java programming language to communicate with objects written in any language that supports CORBA, anywhere on the Web.

> If both the client and the server are written in the Java programming language, consider using Java RMI. Refer to the trail Remote Method Invocation (page 359) .

This trail is divided into two lessons.

Introducing Java IDL (page 399) explains the basic concepts and standards behind Java IDL and defines the key terms used in the CORBA technology.

The Hello Client/Server Example (page 403) steps through a very simple but complete client and server that use Java IDL.

For definitions of common IDL terms, refer to the Java IDL Glossary (page 908) in the Appendix.

Introducing Java IDL

IN this lesson, you'll learn what Java IDL is and how it is useful. We'll also introduce several terms and concepts that you need to understand before proceeding with the other sections in the lesson. If you know CORBA and have used IDL, you may want to skip to the next lesson, The Hello Client/Server Example (page 403), and start programming with Java IDL.

This lesson contains the following sections:

What Is Java IDL?

Java IDL is a technology for distributed objects—that is, objects interacting on different platforms across a network. Java IDL is similar to RMI (remote method invocation), which supports distributed objects written entirely in the Java programming language. However, Java IDL enables objects to interact regardless of whether they're written in the Java programming language or another language, such as C, C++, COBOL, or others.

This is possible because Java IDL is based on the Common Object Request Broker Architecture (CORBA), an industry-standard distributed object model. A key feature of CORBA is IDL, a language-neutral interface definition language (IDL). Each language that supports CORBA has its own IDL mapping; as its name implies, Java IDL supports the mapping for the Java programming language. CORBA and the IDL mappings are the work of an industry consortium known as the OMG, or Object Management Group. Sun is a founding member of the OMG, and the Java IDL team has played an active role in defining the mapping of IDL to the Java programming language.

To support interaction between objects in separate programs, Java IDL provides an object request broker, or ORB. The ORB is a class library that enables low-level communication between Java IDL applications and other CORBA-compliant applications.

This trail walks you through designing and developing a simple pair of interacting Java IDL applications. It starts by showing you the general architecture of CORBA, then follows with an overview of the steps to building CORBA applications in Java IDL. Finally, it takes you through each step to produce a running server and client that interact by using CORBA.

The CORBA Architecture

Any relationship between distributed objects has two sides: the *client* and the *server*. The server provides a remote interface, and the client calls a remote interface. These relationships are common to most distributed object standards, including RMI and CORBA. Note that in this context the terms client and server define object-level rather than application-level interaction: Any application could be a server for some objects and a client of others. In fact, a single object could be the client of an interface provided by a remote object and at the same time implement an interface to be called remotely by other objects.

The following figure shows how a one-method distributed object is shared between a CORBA client and server to implement the classic "Hello World" program.

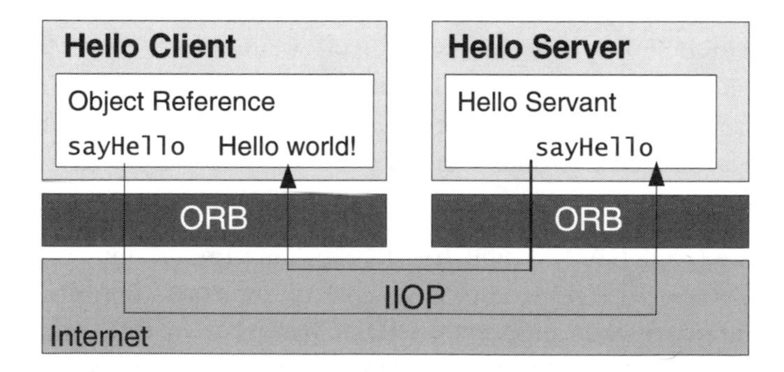

Figure 39 A one-method distributed object shared between a CORBA client and server.

On the client side the application includes a reference for the remote object. The object reference has a stub method, which is a stand-in for the method being called remotely. The stub is wired into the ORB, so that calling it invokes the ORB's connection capabilities, which forwards the invocation to the server.

On the server side the ORB uses skeleton code to translate the remote invocation into a method call on the local object. The skeleton translates the call and any parameters to their implementation-specific format and calls the method being invoked. When the method returns, the skeleton code transforms results or errors and sends them back to the client via the ORBs.

Between the ORBs, communication proceeds by means of a shared protocol, IIOP—the Internet Inter-ORB Protocol. IIOP, which is based on the standard Transmission Control Protocol/Internet Protocol (TCP/IP), defines how CORBA-compliant ORBs pass information back and forth. Like CORBA and IDL, the IIOP standard is defined by OMG, the Object Management Group.

In addition to these simple distributed object capabilities, CORBA-compliant ORBs can provide a number of optional services defined by the OMG. These include services for looking up objects by name, maintaining persistent objects, supporting transaction processing, enabling messaging, and many other abilities useful in today's distributed, multitiered computing environments. Several third-party vendors provide ORBs written in the Java programming language that support some or all of these additional capabilities. The ORB provided with Java IDL supports one optional service, the ability to locate objects by name.

The Java IDL Development Process

Now that you've seen the relationships between client and server in CORBA, you're ready to step through the process of designing and developing a distributed object application with Java IDL. You define the interface for the remote object by using the OMG's interface definition language. You use IDL instead of the Java programming language because the `idltojava` compiler automatically maps from IDL, generating all Java programming language stub and skeleton source files, along with the infrastructure code for connecting to the ORB. Also, by using IDL, you make it possible for developers to implement clients and servers in any other CORBA-compliant language.

Note that if you're implementing a client for an existing CORBA service or a server for an existing client, you would get the IDL interfaces from the implementer—such as a service provider or a vendor. You would then run the `idltojava` compiler over those interfaces and follow the steps described in this lesson for creating the client or server.

The development process consists of four steps.

1. Compile the remote interface. You run the `idltojava` compiler over your interface definition file to generate a version of the interface defined in the Java programming language, as well as the class code files for the stubs and skeletons that enable your applications to hook into the ORB.
2. Implement the server. Once you run the `idltojava` compiler, you can use the skeletons it generates to put together your server application. In addition to implementing the methods of the remote interface, your server code includes a mechanism to start the ORB and to wait for invocation from a remote client.
3. Implement the client. Similarly you use the stubs generated by the `idltojava` compiler as the basis of your client application. The client code builds on the stubs to start its ORB, to look up the server by using the name service provided with Java IDL, to obtain a reference for the remote object, and to call its method.
4. Start the applications. Once you implement a server and a client, you can start the name service, then start the server, then run the client.

You'll see the details of each of these steps in the next lesson, The Hello Client/Server Example (page 403), a simple client/server model based on the classic "Hello World" application.

http://java.sun.com/docs/books/tutorial/idl/hello/index.html

33 The Hello Client/Server Example

THIS lesson teaches you the basic tasks in building a CORBA distributed application using Java IDL. You will build the classic "Hello World" program as a distributed application, with both applet and application clients. The "Hello World" program has a single operation that rcturns a string to be displayed. CORBA terminology and the underlying functionality of the application are discussed in the section The CORBA Architecture (page 400) in the previous lesson. The application diagram is repeated here, along with a review of the steps in the process of communication between the client and the server.

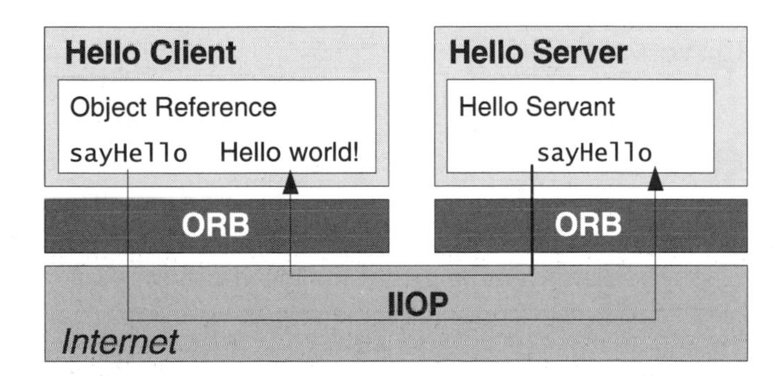

Figure 40 Communication between the client and the server.

1. The client (applet or application) invokes the `sayHello` operation of the Hello Server.

2. The ORB transfers that invocation to the servant object registered for that IDL interface.
3. The servant's `sayHello` method runs, returning a `String`.
4. The ORB transfers that `String` back to the client.
5. The client displays the `String`.

Despite its simple design, the "Hello World" program lets you learn and experiment with all of the tasks required to develop almost any CORBA program that uses static invocation. This lesson contains the following sections:

Getting Started

Before you start working with Java IDL, you need two things: JDK 1.2 and the `idltojava` compiler. The JDK provides the API and ORB needed to enable CORBA-based distributed object interaction. The `idltojava` compiler uses the mapping defined by the OMG to convert IDL interface definitions to corresponding interfaces, classes, and methods in the Java programming language, which you can then use to implement your client and server code. You can get the `idltojava` compiler from the CD-ROM that accompanies this book or from the Java Developer's Connection.[1]

Writing the IDL Interface

This section dissects a simple IDL interface for the "Hello World" application. The IDL interface defines the contract between the client and server parts of your application, specifying what operations and attributes are available. OMG IDL is programming language independent. You must map from IDL to the Java programming language before writing any of the implementation code. (Running `idltojava` on the IDL file does this for you automatically.) The IDL for the "Hello World" application is contained in a file `Hello.idl` (page 841) in the Appendix.

---

[1] http://java.sun.com/jdc/

Writing Hello.idl

OMG IDL is a purely declarative language designed for specifying programming language–independent operational interfaces for distributed applications. OMG specifies a mapping from IDL to several languages, including C, C++, Small-Talk, COBOL, Ada, and the Java programming language. When mapped, each statement in OMG IDL is translated to a corresponding statement in the programming language of choice. You can use the tool `idltojava` to map an IDL interface to the Java programming language and to implement the client class. When you map the same IDL to C++ and implement the server in that language, the client written in the Java programming language and the server written in C++ interoperate through the ORB as though they were written in the same language.

Following is the complete IDL for the "Hello World" application. This IDL, contained in a file named `Hello.idl`, is quite simple.

```
module HelloApp {
    interface Hello
    {
        string sayHello();
    };
};
```

This code declares the CORBA IDL module, the interface through which the client and the server interact, and the operation implemented by the server.

Declare the CORBA IDL Module

A CORBA module is a name space that acts as a container for related interfaces and declarations. It corresponds closely to a package in the Java programming language. Each module statement in an IDL file is mapped to a Java programming language package statement. The following code shows the module statement from `Hello.idl` in bold font.

```
module HelloApp {
    interface Hello
    {
        string sayHello();
    };
};
```

When you run `idltojava` on `Hello.idl`, the module statement generates a package statement in the Java programming language.

Declare the Interface

Like interfaces in the Java programming language, CORBA interfaces declare the API contract that an object has with other objects. Each interface statement in the IDL is converted to an interface statement when mapped to the Java programming language. The following code shows the interface statement from Hello.idl in bold font.

```
module HelloApp {
    interface Hello
    {
        string sayHello();
    };
};
```

When you compile the IDL, this statement generates an interface statement in this code. Both the client and the server classes implement the Hello interface but in different ways.

Declare the Operations

CORBA operations are the behaviors that servers promise to perform on behalf of clients that invoke them. Each operation statement in the IDL generates a corresponding method statement in the generated interface. The "Hello World" application has a single operation, whose declaration is shown here in bold font.

```
module HelloApp {
    interface Hello
    {
        string sayHello();
    };
};
```

Mapping Hello.idl to the Java Programming Language

The tool idltojava reads OMG IDL files and creates the required Java programming language source code files. The idltojava defaults are set up so that if you need both client and server files (as you do for the "Hello World" application), you simply enter the tool name and the name of your IDL file, as follows.

```
idltojava Hello.idl
```

The idltojava compiler creates a directory called HelloApp and five files in that directory. One of the files is named Hello.java, which looks like this:

```
/* Hello.java as generated by idltojava */
package HelloApp;
public interface Hello
    extends org.omg.CORBA.Object {
    String sayHello();
}
```

With an interface this simple, it is easy to see how the IDL statements map to the generated statements in the Java programming language. The following table shows the mapping.

Table 25 Mapping of IDL to the Java Programming Language

IDL	Java Programming Language
module HelloApp	package HelloApp;
interface Hello	public interface Hello
string sayHello();	String sayHello();

The single surprising item is the `extends` statement. All CORBA objects are derived from `org.omg.CORBA.Object` to ensure required CORBA functionality. The required code is generated by `idltojava`; you do not need to do any mapping yourself.

Understanding the idltojava Compiler Output

Based on the options chosen on the command line, the `idltojava` compiler generates a number of files. Because these files provide standard functionality, you can ignore them until it is time to deploy and to run your application. The five files generated by the `idltojava` compiler are

- `_HelloImplBase.java`: This abstract class is the server skeleton, providing basic CORBA functionality for the server. This class implements the `Hello.java` interface. The server class `HelloServant` extends `_HelloImplBase`.
- `_HelloStub.java`: This class is the client stub, providing CORBA functionality for the client. This class implements the `Hello.java` interface.
- `Hello.java`: This interface contains the version of our IDL interface and the single method `sayHello`. The `Hello.java` interface extends `org.omg.CORBA.Object`, providing standard CORBA object functionality as well.

- HelloHelper.java: This class provides auxiliary functionality, notably the narrow method required to cast CORBA object references to their proper types.
- HelloHolder.java: This final class holds a public instance member of type Hello. This class provides operations for out and inout arguments, which CORBA has, although they do not map easily to the semantics of the Java programming language.

When you write the IDL interface, you do all of the programming required to generate all of these files for your distributed application. The only additional work required is the implementation of client and server classes. The lessons that follow describe the HelloClient.java client class and the HelloServer.java class. Additionally, notes are provided for creating an applet client, HelloApplet.java.

Troubleshooting

Error Message: "idltojava" not found

If you try to run idltojava on the file Hello.idl and the system cannot find idltojava, it is most likely not in your executable path. Make certain that the location of idltojava is in your path, and try again.

Error Message: preprocessor failed

By default, idltojava uses a C/C++ preprocessor. You can change the default by setting two environment variables, CPP and CPPARGS. If you do not want to use a preprocessor, you can turn it off by adding -fno-cpp to the idltojava command line.

Developing a Client Application

This section introduces the basics of writing a CORBA client application. Here's the complete implementation of the client for the "Hello World" application, which is coded in a file named HelloClient.java (page 841) in the Appendix.

```
import HelloApp.*;          // The package containing our stubs.

// HelloClient will use the naming service.
import org.omg.CosNaming.*;

import org.omg.CORBA.*;     // All CORBA apps need these classes.

public class HelloClient {
    public static void main(String args[]) {
```

```
        try {
            // Create and initialize the ORB
            ORB orb = ORB.init(args, null);
            // Get the root naming context
            org.omg.CORBA.Object objRef =
              orb.resolve_initial_references("NameService");
            NamingContext ncRef =
              NamingContextHelper.narrow(objRef);

            // Resolve the object reference in naming
            NameComponent nc = new NameComponent("Hello", "");
            NameComponent path[] = {nc};
            Hello helloRef =
              HelloHelper.narrow(ncRef.resolve(path));

            // Call the Hello server object and print results
            String Hello = helloRef.sayHello();
            System.out.println(Hello);
        } catch(Exception e) {
            System.out.println("ERROR : " + e);
            e.printStackTrace(System.out);
        }
    }
}
```

Applet Note: Although this section focuses on writing a CORBA client application, many of the steps are identical to those required for writing applets. The major difference is that the applet code appears in the `init` method rather than in `main`. For information on how to set up the applet's HTML page, see the section Setting Up the HTML File (Applets Only) (page 413). You can find the complete code for the applet version, `HelloApplet.java` (page 842), in the Appendix.

Performing Basic Setup

The basic shell of a CORBA client is the same as for many Java applications: You import required packages, declare the application class, define a `main` method, and remember to handle any exceptions.

Importing Required Packages

The following statements, which appear at the beginning of the client code, import the packages required for the client class.

```
// The package containing our stubs.
import HelloApp.*;
```

```
// HelloClient will use the naming service.
import org.omg.CosNaming.*;

// All CORBA applications need the following classes.
import org.omg.CORBA.*;
```

Applet Note: If you are writing an applet, you must also import `java.awt.Graphics` and `org.omg.CosNaming.NamingContextPackage.*`. The latter package contains special exceptions thrown by the name service.

Declaring the Client Class

`HelloClient.java` declares the client for the "Hello World" application like this:

```
public class HelloClient {
    ...
}
```

Applet Note: In the applet version of the client, `HelloApplet.java`, you declare the applet class like this:

```
public class HelloApplet extends java.applet.Applet {
    ...
}
```

Defining a main Method

Every Java application needs a `main` method. The `HelloClient` class declares the `main` method for the client as follows:

```
public static void main(String args[]) {
    ...
}
```

Handling CORBA System Exceptions

Because all CORBA programs can throw CORBA system exceptions at runtime, the code in the `main` method appears within a `try/catch` block. CORBA programs throw system exceptions whenever trouble occurs during any of the processes involved in invoking the server from the client.

```
try {
    ...
```

```
} catch(Exception e) {
    System.out.println("ERROR : " + e);
    e.printStackTrace(System.out);
}
```

The client's exception handler simply prints the name of the exception and its stack trace to standard output so you can see what has gone wrong. Now, let's look at the code that does the real work in the client—the code governed by the `try` statement.

Creating an ORB Object

A CORBA client needs a local ORB object to perform all of its marshaling and IIOP work. Every client instantiates an `org.omg.CORBA.ORB` object and initializes it by passing to the object certain information about itself. The following line of code from `HelloClient.java`'s `try/catch` block declares and initializes an ORB variable.

```
ORB orb = ORB.init(args, null);
```

The call to the ORB's `init` method passes in your application's command line arguments, allowing you to set certain properties at runtime.

Applet Note: To create an ORB from an applet, you call a different version of the `init` method, which takes the applet itself (`this`) as the first argument. The applet provides information about parameters set in the applet tag to the ORB.

```
ORB orb = ORB.init(this, null)
```

Finding the Hello Server

Once the application has an ORB, it can ask the ORB to locate the service it needs, in this case the Hello server. A CORBA client can get an initial object reference in a number of ways; our client application will use the COS naming service specified by OMG and provided with Java IDL. See the section Using Stringified Object References (page 420) for information on how to get an initial object reference when no naming service is available.

Obtaining the Initial Naming Context

The first step in using the naming service is to get the initial naming context. In the `try/catch` block, below the ORB initialization, the client calls `orb.resolve_initial_references` to get an object reference to the name server.

```
org.omg.CORBA.Object objRef =
                    orb.resolve_initial_references("NameService");
```

The string NameService is defined for all CORBA ORBs. When you pass in that string, the ORB returns the initial naming context, an object reference to the name service.

Narrowing the Object Reference

As with all CORBA object references, objRef is a generic CORBA object. To use it as a NamingContext object, you must narrow it to its proper type by calling the narrow method, as shown.

```
NamingContext ncRef = NamingContextHelper.narrow(objRef);
```

Here you see the use of an idltojava-generated helper class, NamingContextHelper, similar in function to HelloHelper. The ncRef object is now an org.omg.CosNaming.NamingContext, and you can use it to access the naming service and to find other services.

Finding a Service in Naming

Names can have different structures, depending on the implementation of the naming service. Consequently CORBA name servers handle complex names by way of NameComponent objects. Each NameComponent holds a single part, or element, of the name. An array of NameComponent objects can hold a fully specified path to an object on any computer file or disk system.

To find the Hello server, you first need a NameComponent to hold an identifying string for the Hello server.

```
NameComponent nc = new NameComponent("Hello", "");
```

This statement sets the id field of nc, the new NameComponent, to Hello and the kind field to an empty string.

The NamingContext.resolve method requires an array. Because the path to the Hello object has just one element, the client code creates a single-element array out of nc.

```
NameComponent path[] = {nc};
```

Finally, the code calls the naming service's resolve method, with path as an argument, to get an object reference to the Hello server and narrows it to a Hello object:

```
Hello helloRef = HelloHelper.narrow(ncRef.resolve(path));
```

Here you see the `HelloHelper` helper class at work. The `resolve` method returns a generic CORBA object as you saw earlier when locating the name service itself. Therefore you immediately narrow it to a `Hello` object, which is the object reference you need to perform the rest of your work.

Invoking the sayHello Operation

CORBA invocations look like a method call on a local object. The complications of marshaling parameters to the wire, routing them to the server-side ORB, unmarshaling, and placing the upcall to the server method are completely transparent to the client programmer. Because so much is done for you by generated code, invocation is really the easiest part of CORBA programming. Here's the code from `HelloClient.java` that invokes the `sayHello` method and displays the results:

```
String Hello = helloRef.sayHello();
System.out.println(Hello);
```

Setting Up the HTML File (Applets Only)

`Tutorial.html` (page 843) in the Appendix is provided to display your finished applet, but you need to customize a few attributes and parameters within it.

1. Inside the `APPLET` tag enter the name of your project directory as the value for the `CODEBASE` attribute.
2. In the first `PARAM` tag enter the name of the machine where the CORBA name server runs (most likely your local machine name) as the value for `ORBInitialHost`.
3. Make sure that the second `PARAM` tag is set to the value of `ORBInitialPort` that you are using to run the name server (it's preset to 1050 to work with the default used in the examples in this trail). In any case it should be a value above 1028.

Developing the "Hello World" Server

This section introduces the basics of writing a CORBA transient server. The following listing shows the complete version of `HelloServer.java` (page 844) in the Appendix.

```
// The package containing our stubs.
import HelloApp.*;

// HelloServer will use the naming service.
import org.omg.CosNaming.*;

// Package containing special exceptions thrown by name service.
import org.omg.CosNaming.NamingContextPackage.*;

// All CORBA applications need these classes.
import org.omg.CORBA.*;

public class HelloServer
{
    public static void main(String args[])
    {
        try {
            // Create and initialize the ORB
            ORB orb = ORB.init(args, null);
            // Create the servant and register it with the ORB
            HelloServant helloRef = new HelloServant();
            orb.connect(helloRef);

            // Get the root naming context
            org.omg.CORBA.Object objRef =
               orb.resolve_initial_references("NameService");
            NamingContext ncRef =
               NamingContextHelper.narrow(objRef);

            // Bind the object reference in naming
            NameComponent nc = new NameComponent("Hello", "");
            NameComponent path[] = {nc};
            ncRef.rebind(path, helloRef);

            // Wait for invocations from clients
            java.lang.Object sync = new java.lang.Object();
            synchronized(sync){
                sync.wait();
            }
        } catch(Exception e) {
            System.err.println("ERROR: " + e);
            e.printStackTrace(System.out);
        }
    }
}

class HelloServant extends _HelloImplBase
{
```

```
        public String sayHello()
        {
            return "\nHello world!!\n";
        }
    }
```

Performing Basic Setup

The structure of a CORBA server program is the same as for most Java applications: You import required library packages, declare the server class, define a `main` method, and remember to handle any exceptions.

Importing Required Packages

The following lines of code import the packages required for the server class.

```
// The package containing our stubs.
import HelloApp.*;

// HelloServer will use the naming service.
import org.omg.CosNaming.*;

// Package containing special exceptions thrown by name service.
import org.omg.CosNaming.NamingContextPackage.*;

// All CORBA applications need these classes.
import org.omg.CORBA.*;
```

Declaring the Server Class

Below is the declaration for the server class:

```
public class HelloServer {
    ...
}
```

Defining the main Method

And here's the `main` method for the server, which is the standard one for Java applications:

```
public static void main(String args[]) {
    ...
}
```

Handling CORBA System Exceptions

Because all CORBA programs can throw CORBA system exceptions at runtime, the server's `main` method needs a `try/catch` block. CORBA programs throw runtime exceptions whenever trouble occurs during any of the processes (marshaling, unmarshaling, upcall) involved in invocation. The exception handler simply prints the exception and its stack trace to standard output so you can see what has gone wrong.

The following is the `try/catch` block for the server's `main` method.

```
try {
    ...
} catch(Exception e) {
    System.err.println("ERROR: " + e);
    e.printStackTrace(System.out);
}
```

Creating an ORB Object

Just like a client, a CORBA server also needs a local ORB object. Every server instantiates an ORB and registers its servant objects so that the ORB can find the server when it receives an invocation for it.

The following statement appears within `HelloServer.java`'s `try/catch` block and declares and initializes an ORB variable.

```
ORB orb = ORB.init(args, null);
```

The call to the ORB's `init` method passes in the server's command line arguments, allowing you to set certain properties at runtime.

Managing the Servant Object

A server is a process that instantiates one or more servant objects. The servant implements the interface generated by `idltojava` and performs the work of the operations on that interface. Our `HelloServer` needs a `HelloServant`.

Instantiating the Servant Object

Inside the `try/catch` block, just below the call to `init`, the following statement instantiates the servant object:

```
HelloServant helloRef = new HelloServant();
```

You will see the definition for the servant class in the following section. Next, the program connects the servant to the ORB, so that the ORB can recognize invocations on it and pass them along to the correct servant.

```
orb.connect(helloRef);
```

Defining the Servant Class

The definition for the servant class appears in the `HelloServer.java` file, outside the `HelloServer` class. Here's the complete definition for `HelloServant`.

```
class HelloServant extends _HelloImplBase {
    public String sayHello() {
        return "\nHello World!!\n";
    }
}
```

The servant is a subclass of `_HelloImplBase` so that it inherits the general CORBA functionality generated for it by the `idltojava` compiler.

Working with COS Naming

The `HelloServer` works with the naming service to make the servant object's operations available to clients. The server needs an object reference to the name service so that it can register itself and ensure that invocations on the `Hello` interface are routed to its servant object.

Obtaining the Initial Naming Context

The program calls `orb.resolve_initial_references` after the servant is instantiated to get an object reference to the name server.

```
org.omg.CORBA.Object objRef =
orb.resolve_initial_references("NameService");
```

The string `NameService` is defined for all CORBA ORBs. When you pass in that string, the ORB returns a naming context object that is an object reference for the name service.

Narrowing the Object Reference

As with all CORBA object references, `objRef` is a generic CORBA object. To use it as a `NamingContext` object, you must narrow it to its proper type, by calling the `narrow` method.

```
NamingContext ncRef = NamingContextHelper.narrow(objRef);
```

Here you see the use of an idltojava-generated helper class, similar in function to HelloHelper. The ncRef object is now an org.omg.CosNaming.NamingContext, and you can use it to access the naming service and to register the server. You will do that in the next step.

Registering the Servant with the Name Server

Just below the call to narrow, the code creates a new NameComponent member.

```
NameComponent nc = new NameComponent("Hello", "");
```

This statement sets the id field of nc, the new NameComponent, to Hello and the kind component to the empty string. Because the path to the Hello has a single element, create the single-element array that NamingContext.resolve requires for its work.

```
NameComponent path[] = {nc};
```

Finally, the server binds the servant object to the Hello ID:

```
ncRef.rebind(path, helloRef);
```

Now, when the client calls resolve("Hello") on the initial naming context, the naming service returns an object reference to the Hello servant.

Waiting for Invocation

The set up for the server is complete. Now, the server just needs to wait around for a client to request its service.

```
java.lang.Object sync = new java.lang.Object();
synchronized(sync) {
    sync.wait();
}
```

This form of Object.wait requires HelloServer to remain alive (though quiescent) until an invocation comes from the ORB. Because of its placement in main, after an invocation completes and sayHello returns, the server will wait again.

Compiling and Running the "Hello World" Application

This section shows you how to compile and run the server and the client programs that together make up the "Hello World" application.

Compiling the Files Generated by the idltojava Compiler:

Both the server and the client need the files generated by the `idltojava` compiler. Run the Java progamming language compiler on all of the source files generated by `idltojava`, which are in the `HelloApp` directory:

```
javac HelloApp/*.java
```

The compiler puts the corresponding class files in the `HelloApp` directory.

Compiling the Client

Run the Java programming language compiler on `HelloClient.java`:

```
javac HelloClient.java
```

As usual, the compiler puts `HelloClient.class` in the current directory.

Compiling the Server

Run the compiler for the Java programming language on `HelloServer.java`:

```
javac HelloServer.java
```

The compiler creates two class files, `HelloServer.class` and `HelloServant.class`, in the current directory.

Running the Client/Server Application

Start the Java IDL name server:

```
tnameserv -ORBInitialPort 1050
```

Start the Hello server:

```
java HelloServer -ORBInitialPort 1050
```

Run the Hello client:

```
java HelloClient -ORBInitialPort 1050
```

The client displays the string from the server.

```
Hello world!!
```

Remember to stop both the NameServer and the HelloServer processes after the client application returns successfully.

Troubleshooting

Specifying ORB Initial Port

The default ORB initial port is port 900. If you prefer, you can omit the port specifications if you start the name server on port 900. Using Solaris software, you must become root to start a process on a port under 1024. Remember to exit from root access before continuing with the tutorial if you choose to use this port for your name server.

Class Definition Not Found Error

If the compiler for the Java programming language (javac) throws a NoClassDefFoundError, try using -cp (class path) command line option when compiling the source files.

```
javac -cp . *.java HelloApp/*.java
```

Using Stringified Object References

To invoke an operation on a CORBA object, a client application needs a reference to the object. You can get such references in a number of ways, such as calling ORB.resolve_initial_references or using another CORBA object, such as the name service. In previous sections you used both of these methods to get an initial object reference.

Often, however, no naming service is available in the distributed environment. In that situation CORBA clients use a stringified object reference to find their first object.

In this section, you will learn how to create a stringified object reference as a part of the server startup and how the client gets that reference and destringifies it for use as a real object reference.

Making a Stringified Object Reference

For a stringified object reference to be available to the client, the server must create the reference and store it somewhere that the client can access. Your reference will be written to disk in the form of a text file. Here's the modified version of the server, `HelloStringifiedServer.java`.

```
// Stringified object reference version of the server
import java.io.*;
import org.omg.CORBA.*;
import HelloApp.*;

class HelloServant extends _HelloImplBase
{
    public String sayHello()
    {
        return "\nHello world !!\n";
    }
}

public class HelloStringifiedServer {
    public static void main(String args[])
    {
        try {
            // create and initialize the ORB
            ORB orb = ORB.init(args, null);

            // create servant and register it with the ORB
            HelloServant helloRef = new HelloServant();
            orb.connect(helloRef);

            // stringify the helloRef and dump it in a file
            String str = orb.object_to_string(helloRef);
            String filename = System.getProperty("user.home") +
              System.getProperty("file.separator")+"HelloIOR";
            FileOutputStream fos =
              new FileOutputStream(filename);
            PrintStream ps = new PrintStream(fos);
            ps.print(str);
            ps.close();

            // wait for invocations from clients
            java.lang.Object sync = new java.lang.Object();
            synchronized (sync) {
                sync.wait();
            }
        } catch (Exception e) {
            System.err.println("ERROR: " + e);
            e.printStackTrace(System.out);
        }
    }
}
```

The following list describes the changes made to `HelloServer.java` to create `HelloStringifiedServer.java`.

1. Because the new server will write a file to disk, another import statement is required.

   ```
   import java.io.*; // needed for output to the file system.
   ```

2. The new server won't use the naming service, so you don't need the `CosNaming` packages. The following import statements can be deleted.

   ```
   import org.omg.CosNaming.*;
   import org.omg.CosNaming.NamingContextPackage.*;
   ```

3. The new server doesn't need the code that gets the initial naming context and resolves the reference to a `Hello` object. So the following lines of code are deleted.

   ```
   // Get the root naming context
   org.omg.CORBA.Object objRef =
   orb.resolve_initial_references("NameService");
   NamingContext ncRef = NamingContextHelper.narrow(objRef);

   // Bind the object reference in naming
   NameComponent nc = new NameComponent("Hello", "");
   NameComponent path[] = {nc};
   ncRef.rebind(path, helloRef);
   ```

4. The new server needs to call the ORB's `object_to_string` method and pass it the reference to the servant object. This returns the object reference in a string form that can be saved in a file on disk.

   ```
   String ior = orb.object_to_string(helloRef);
   ```

5. Next, the server builds the path to the file that will be stored, using system properties to determine the path structure and syntax.

   ```
   String filename = System.getProperty("user.home") +
            System.getProperty("file.separator")+"HelloIOR";
   ```

6. Finally, the server uses standard File IO objects to write the stringified `ior` to disk.

   ```
   FileOutputStream fos = new FileOutputStream(filename);
   PrintStream ps = new PrintStream(fos);
   ps.print(ior);
   ps.close();
   ```

When `HelloServer` runs, instead of calling the ORB and registering the servant object with naming, it creates the text file `HelloIOR` containing a stringified reference to the servant. The file is stored in your home directory.

Getting a Stringified Object Reference

To find the server, the client reads the HelloIOR file created by the server and gets the stringified object reference from the file. Here's the new version of the client, HelloStringifiedClient.java.

```
// Stringified object reference version of the client
import java.io.*;
import org.omg.CORBA.*;
import HelloApp.*;

public class HelloStringifiedClient
{
    public static void main(String args[])
    {
        try {
            // create and initialize the ORB
            ORB orb = ORB.init(args, null);

            // Get the stringified object reference and
            // destringify it.
            String filename = System.getProperty("user.home") +
                        System.getProperty("file.separator") +
                        "HelloIOR";
            FileInputStream fis =
                        new FileInputStream(filename);
            DataInputStream dis = new DataInputStream(fis) ;
            String ior = dis.readLine() ;
            org.omg.CORBA.Object obj =
                        orb.string_to_object(ior) ;
            Hello helloRef = HelloHelper.narrow(obj);

            // call the Hello server object and print results
            String Hello = helloRef.sayHello();
            System.out.println(Hello);
        } catch (Exception e) {
            System.out.println("ERROR : " + e) ;
            e.printStackTrace(System.out);
        }
    }
}
```

The following describes the changes made to HelloClient.java to create HelloStringifiedClient.java.

1. Because the new client will read a file from the disk, the new client needs the following import statement.

```
import java.io.*; // needed for input from the file system.
```

2. The new client won't use the naming service, so it doesn't need the `CosNaming` package. This import statement can be deleted.

```
import org.omg.CosNaming.*; // not needed for stringified
version
```

3. The new client doesn't need the code that gets the initial naming context and registers the servant with the naming service. So, the following statements can be deleted.

```
// Get the root naming context
org.omg.CORBA.Object objRef =
            orb.resolve_initial_references("NameService");
NamingContext ncRef = NamingContextHelper.narrow(objRef);

// Resolve the object reference in naming
NameComponent nc = new NameComponent("Hello", "");
NameComponent path[] = {nc};
Hello helloRef = HelloHelper.narrow(ncRef.resolve(path));
```

4. The new client uses standard File IO operations to read the file that has the object reference. Note that both the client and the server programs must know the name of the file and where it is stored.

```
String filename = System.getProperty("user.home") +
             System.getProperty("file.separator") +
             "HelloIOR";
FileInputStream fis = new FileInputStream(filename);
DataInputStream dis = new DataInputStream(fis);
String ior = dis.readLine();
```

The `HelloClient` application now has a `String` object containing the stringified object reference.

Destringifying the Object Reference

To destringify the object reference in `ior`, call the standard ORB method.

```
org.omg.CORBA.Object obj = orb.string_to_object(ior);
```

Finally, narrow the CORBA object to its proper type, so that the client can invoke on it.

```
Hello helloRef = HelloHelper.narrow(obj);
```

The rest of the client code stays the same.

Compiling and Running a Stringified Hello World

To compile Hello World, run the compiler on the source code for both the client and the server, and on the source files generated by the `idltojava` compiler.

```
javac HelloStringifiedClient.java HelloStringifiedServer.java
HelloApp/*.java
```

Start the Hello server.

```
java HelloStringifiedServer -ORBInitialPort 1050 &
```

Run the Hello application client.

```
java HelloStringifiedClient -ORBInitialPort 1050
```

The client displays the string from the server.

```
Hello world!!
```

Remember to stop the `HelloStringifiedServer` process after the client application returns successfully.

For More Information

In this trail you've seen how to use Java IDL, the CORBA-compliant remote object technology, to develop a simple client/server application, as well as two ways to locate remote CORBA objects. The Java IDL Glossary (page 908) in the Appendix gives definitions for new terms you may have encountered throughout the tutorial. You can read more background information and details in the Java IDL documentation included in the JDK 1.2 on the CD-ROM that accompanies this book and online.[1]

Additional information on the OMG and CORBA standard is available from the OMG Web site.[2] In particular, take a look at *CORBA for Beginners* section on the OMG site.[3]

---

1 http://java.sun.com/products/jdk/idl/index.html
2 http://www.omg.org/
3 http://www.omg.org/news/begin.htm

About the Author

JIM INSCORE has worked as a technical writer for the past 18 years, documenting API for NeXT, Kaleida, Macromedia, Oracle, Objectivity, and a number of other companies. He is currently publications manager for enterprise, server, and multimedia technologies in Java Software.

In his spare time, Jim hangs out with his family and works on remodeling his house.

Acknowledgments

Thanks to Victoria Camgros for creating the original Java IDL tutorial and to Maydene Fisher for all her work on the whole Java IDL documentation set, including this tutorial. I'd also like to thank Brian Preston and Jennifer Ball for reviewing the material and making sure it all works as advertised.

Servlets

by Cynthia Bloch

THIS trail teaches you about servlets, the bodies of code that run inside servers and that extend servers' functionality. For example, servlets offer an efficient platform-independent replacement for CGI (Common Gateway Interface) scripts. Servers that can host servlets are Java-enabled servers that respond to client requests.

Overview of Servlets (page 431) tells you what servlets are and how you can use them. The lesson also introduces the sample servlets used in this trail.

Interacting with Clients (page 437) shows you how to write servlets that interact with clients. The servlets in this lesson respond to `HTTP GET`, `HEAD`, and `POST` requests. The lesson also discusses issues concerning threads and shows you how to avoid certain problems by creating a servlet that responds to one client at a time.

The Life Cycle of a Servlet (page 445) discusses the significant events in the life of a servlet and shows you how to customize servlet initialization and shutdown.

Saving Client State (page 453) shows you how to use session tracking and how to use cookies.

The servletrunner Utility (page 465) describes how to set up and to run a utility called `servletrunner` to test your servlets. The `servletrunner` is a small, multithreaded process that handles requests for servlets. The `servletrunner` utility comes with the Servlet Development Kit, and is part of the servlet extension to the Java Development Kit.

Running Servlets (page 469) shows you how to call servlets in a variety of ways: from a browser, within an HTML page, and from another servlet.

Note: The servlet API is a standard extension to the Java Development Kit. The lessons in this trail use the Java Servlet Development Kit 2.0, which is available on the CD-ROM that accompanies this book. Or you can download the SDK online from `http://java.sun.com/products/java-server/servlets`.

http://java.sun.com/docs/books/tutorial/servlets/overview/index.html

34 Overview of Servlets

SERVLETS are modules that extend request/response-oriented servers, such as Java-enabled Web servers. For example, a servlet might be responsible for taking data in an HTML order-entry form and applying the business logic used to update a company's order database.

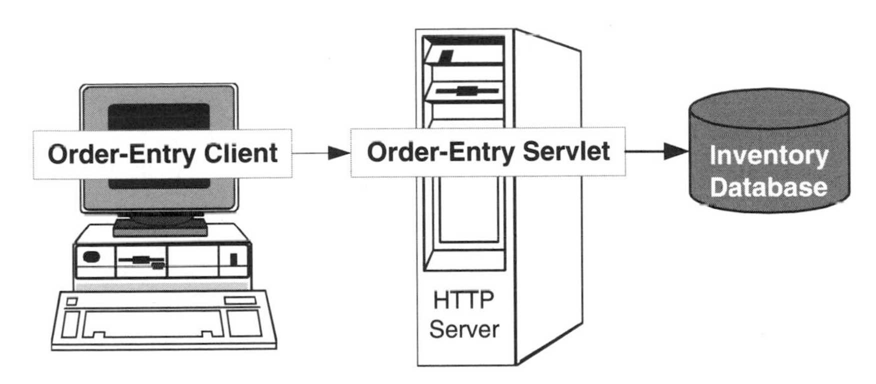

Figure 41 Overview of a servlet's role in a client/server database transaction.

Servlets are to servers what applets are to browsers. Unlike applets, however, servlets have no graphical user interface.

Servlets can be embedded in many different servers because the servlet API, used to write servlets, assumes nothing about the server's environment or protocol. Servlets have become most widely used within HTTP servers; many Web servers support the servlet API.[1]

[1] A list of third-party products that run servlets is maintained online here: http://jserv.javasoft.com/products/java-server/servlets/environments.html

Use Servlets instead of CGI Scripts

Servlets are an effective replacement for CGI scripts, providing a way to generate dynamic documents that is both easier to write and faster to run. Servlets also address the problem of doing server-side programming with platform-specific APIs: Servlets are developed with the Java servlet API, a standard Java extension.

So use servlets to handle HTTP client requests. For example, have a servlet process data posted over HTTPs using an HTML form, including purchase order or credit card data. A servlet like this could be part of an order-entry and processing system, working with product and inventory databases and, perhaps, an online payment system.

Other Uses for Servlets

Here are two more of the many other uses for servlets:

- Allow collaboration between people. A servlet can handle multiple requests concurrently and can synchronize requests. This allows servlets to support such systems as online conferencing.
- Forward requests. Servlets can forward requests to other servers and servlets. Thus servlets can be used to balance the load among several servers that mirror the same content and to partition a single logical service over several servers, according to task type or organizational boundaries.

Architecture of the Servlet Package

The `javax.servlet` package provides interfaces and classes for writing servlets.

The Servlet Interface

The central abstraction in the servlet API is the `Servlet` interface. All servlets implement this interface, either directly or, more commonly, by extending a class that implements it, such as `HttpServlet`.

The `Servlet` interface declares, but does not implement, methods that manage the servlet and its communications with clients. Servlet writers provide some or all of these methods when developing a servlet.

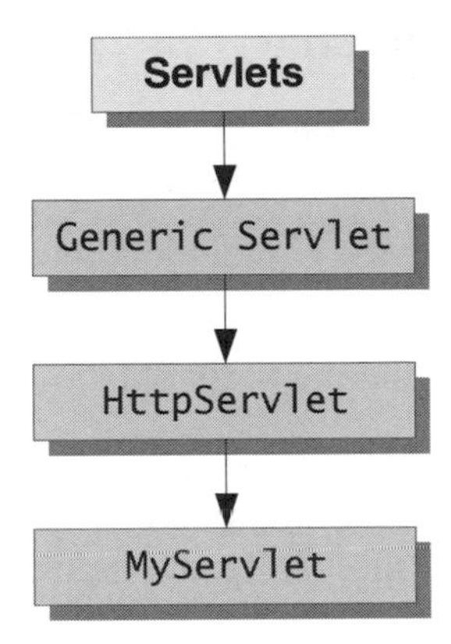

Figure 42 The inheritance of the `Servlet` interface.

Client Interaction

When a servlet accepts a call from a client, it receives two objects:

- A `ServletRequest`, which encapsulates the communication from the client to the server
- A `ServletResponse`, which encapsulates the communication from the servlet back to the client

Both `ServletRequest` and `ServletResponse` are interfaces defined by the `javax.servlet` package.

The ServletRequest Interface

The `ServletRequest` interface allows the servlet access to:

- Such information as the names of the parameters passed in by the client, the protocol (scheme) being used by the client, and the names of the remote host that made the request and the server that received it
- The input stream, `ServletInputStream`, which servlets use to get data from clients that use application protocols such as the HTTP `POST` and `PUT` methods

Interfaces that extend the `ServletRequest` interface allow the servlet to retrieve more protocol-specific data. For example, the `HttpServletRequest` interface contains methods for accessing HTTP-specific header information.

The ServletResponse Interface

The `ServletResponse` interface gives the servlet methods for replying to the client. This interface

- Allows the servlet to set the content length and MIME type of the reply
- Provides an output stream, `ServletOutputStream`, and a `Writer` through which the servlet can send the reply data

Interfaces that extend the `ServletResponse` interface give the servlet more protocol-specific capabilities. For example, the `HttpServletResponse` interface contains methods that allow the servlet to manipulate HTTP-specific header information.

Additional Capabilities of HTTP Servlets

The preceding classes and interfaces make up a basic servlet. HTTP servlets have some additional objects that provide session-tracking capabilities. The servlet writer uses these APIs to maintain, between the servlet and the client, state that persists across multiple connections over some time period. HTTP servlets also have objects that provide cookies. The servlet writer uses the cookie API to save data with the client and to retrieve this data. Cookies are discussed in the section Using Cookies (page 458).

A Simple Servlet

The following class completely defines a servlet. The classes mentioned in the section Architecture of the Servlet Package (page 432) are shown in the example in bold.

```
public class SimpleServlet extends HttpServlet {
    /**
     * Handle the HTTP GET method by building a simple web page.
     */

    public void doGet (HttpServletRequest request,
                       HttpServletResponse response)
                       throws ServletException, IOException {
        PrintWriter out;
        String title = "Simple Servlet Output";

        // set content type and response header fields first
        response.setContentType("text/html");
```

```
        // then write the data of the response
        out = response.getWriter();

        out.println("<HTML><HEAD><TITLE>");
        out.println(title);
        out.println("</TITLE></HEAD><BODY>");
        out.println("<H1>" + title + "</H1>");
        out.println("<P>This is output from SimpleServlet.");
        out.println("</BODY></HTML>");
        out.close();
    }
}
```

That's it!

The preceding code shows the following:

- `SimpleServlet` extends the `HttpServlet` class, which implements the `Servlet` interface.
- `SimpleServlet` overrides the `doGet` method in the `HttpServlet` class. The `doGet` method is called when a client makes a `GET` request (the default HTTP request method), which results in the simple HTML page being returned to the client.
- Within the `doGet` method:
  - The user's request is represented by an `HttpServletRequest` object.
  - The response to the user is represented by an `HttpServletResponse` object.
  - Because text data is returned to the client, the reply is sent by using the `Writer` object obtained from the `HttpServletResponse` object.

The Sample Servlets

The remaining lessons in this trail show you how to write HTTP servlets. Some knowledge of the HTTP protocol is assumed. To learn more about the HTTP protocol, you can refer to the HTTP 1.1 Request for Comments (RFC).[1]

The lessons use an example called *Duke's Bookstore*, a simple online bookstore that allows a customer to perform various functions. Each function is provided by a servlet, as shown in the following table.

---

1 http://info.internet.isi.edu:80/in-notes/rfc/files/rfc2068.txt

Table 26 Servlets Used in the *Duke's Bookstore* Example

Function	Servlet
Browse the books offered for sale	`CatalogServlet`
Buy a book by placing it in a "shopping cart"	`CatalogServlet`
Get more information on a specific book	`BookDetailServlet`
Manage the bookstore database	`BookDBServlet`
See the books that have been selected for purchase	`ShowCartServlet`
Remove one or more books from the shopping cart	`ShowCartServlet`
Buy the books in the shopping cart	`CashierServlet`
Receive a thank-you for the purchase	`ReceiptServlet`

The lessons use the servlets to illustrate various tasks. Several source files comprise the *Duke's Bookstore* example. For your convenience these source files are included on the CD-ROM that accompanies this book.

To run the example, you will need to start a Web server or `servletrunner`, a small, multithreaded process that handles requests for servlets; see the lesson The servletrunner Utility (page 465). To call the servlet from a browser, see the section Calling Servlets from Browsers (page 470), in the lesson Running Servlets (page 469).

http://java.sun.com/docs/books/tutorial/servlets/client-interaction/index.html 35

Interacting with Clients

AN HTTP servlet handles client requests through its `service` method, which supports standard HTTP client requests by dispatching each request to a method designed to handle that request. For example, the `service` method calls the `doGet` method shown earlier, in the section A Simple Servlet (page 434).

This lesson contains the following sections.

This section discusses using the objects that represent the client's request (an `HttpServletRequest` object) and the servlet's response (an `HttpServletResponse` object). These objects are provided to the `service` method and to the methods that `service` calls to handle HTTP requests.

The methods to which the `service` method delegates HTTP requests include

- `doGet`: for handling `GET`, conditional `GET`, and `HEAD` requests
- `doPost`: for handling `POST` requests
- `doPut`: for handling `PUT` requests
- `doDelete`: for handling `DELETE` requests

By default these methods return a `BAD_REQUEST (400)` error. Your servlet should override the method or methods designed to handle the HTTP interactions that it supports. This section shows you how to implement methods that handle the most common HTTP requests: `GET` and `POST`.

The `HttpServlet`'s `service` method also calls the `doOptions` method when the servlet receives an `OPTIONS` request and the `doTrace` methlod when the servlet receives a `TRACE` request. The default implementation of `doOptions` automatically determines which HTTP options are supported and returns that information. The default implementation of `doTrace` causes a response with a message containing all of the headers sent in the trace request. These methods are not typically overridden.

Threading Issues (page 442)

HTTP servlets are typically capable of serving multiple clients concurrently. If any methods in your servlet access a shared resource, you must do one of the following:

- Synchronize access to that resource
- Create a servlet that handles only one client request at a time

This section shows you how to implement the second option.[1]

Providing Servlet Descriptions (page 442)

In addition to handling HTTP client requests, servlets are also called on to supply descriptions of themselves. This section shows you how to provide a description by overriding the method, `getServletInfo`, that supplies the servlet description.

Requests and Responses

In the `HttpServlet` class methods that handle client requests take two arguments:

- An `HttpServletRequest` object, which encapsulates the data *from* the client
- An `HttpServletResponse` object, which encapsulates the response *to* the client

HttpServletRequest Objects

An `HttpServletRequest` object provides access to HTTP header data, such as any cookies found in the request and the HTTP method with which the request was made. The `HttpServletRequest` object also allows you to obtain the arguments that the client sent as part of the request.

The following methods access client data.

[1] The first option, thread synchronization, is covered in *The Java Tutorial, Second Edition,* and in the online tutorial here: http://java.sun.com/docs/books/tutorial/essential/threads/index.html.

- The `getParameter` method returns the value of a named parameter. If your parameter could have more than one value, use `getParameterValues` instead. The `getParameterValues` method returns an array of values for the named parameter. (The method `getParameterNames` provides the names of the parameters.)
- For HTTP `GET` requests the `getQueryString` method returns a `String` of raw data from the client. You must parse this data yourself to obtain the parameters and the values.
- For HTTP `POST`, `PUT`, and `DELETE` requests:
  - If you expect text data, the `getReader` method returns a `BufferedReader` for you to use to read the raw data.
  - If you expect binary data, the `getInputStream` method returns a `ServletInputStream` for use in reading the raw data.

Note: Use either a `getParameter[Values]` method or one of the methods that allows you to parse the data yourself. The two styles cannot be used together in a single request.

HttpServletResponse Objects

An `HttpServletResponse` object provides two ways of returning data to the user:

- The `getWriter` method, which returns a `Writer`
- The `getOutputStream` method, which returns a `ServletOutputStream`

Use the `getWriter` method to return text data to the user; use the `getOutputStream` method for binary data.

Closing the `Writer` or `ServletOutputStream` after you send the response informs the server that the response is complete.

HTTP Header Data

You must set HTTP header data *before* you access the `Writer` or `OutputStream`. The `HttpServletResponse` class provides methods to access the header data. For example, the `setContentType` method sets the content type. (This header is often the only one set manually.)

Handling GET and POST Requests

To handle HTTP requests in a servlet, extend the HttpServlet class and override the servlet methods that handle the HTTP requests that your servlet supports. This section illustrates the handling of GET and POST requests. The methods that handle these requests are doGet and doPost.

Handling GET requests

Handling GET requests involves overriding the doGet method. The following example shows the BookDetailServlet doing this. The methods discussed in the previous section, Requests and Responses (page 438), are shown in bold.

```
public class BookDetailServlet extends HttpServlet {

    public void doGet (HttpServletRequest request,
                       HttpServletResponse response)
                       throws ServletException, IOException {
        ...
        // set content-type header before accessing the Writer
        response.setContentType("text/html");
        PrintWriter out = response.getWriter();

        // then write the response
        out.println("<html>" +
            "<head><title>Book Description</title></head>" +
            ...);

        //Get the identifier of the book to display
        String bookId = request.getParameter("bookId");
        if (bookId != null) {
            // and the information about the book and print it
            ...
        }
        out.println("</body></html>");
        out.close();
    }
    ...
}
```

The servlet extends the HttpServlet class and overrides the doGet method.

Within the doGet method the getParameter method gets the servlet's expected argument.

To respond to the client in the example, the doGet method uses a Writer from the HttpServletResponse object to return text data to the client. Before accessing the Writer, the example sets the content-type header. At the end of the doGet method, after the response has been sent, the Writer is closed.

Handling POST Requests

Handling POST requests involves overriding the doPost method. The following example shows the ReceiptServlet doing this. Again, the methods discussed in the previous section, Requests and Responses (page 438), are shown in bold.

```
public class ReceiptServlet extends HttpServlet {

    public void doPost(HttpServletRequest request,
                       HttpServletResponse response)
                       throws ServletException, IOException {
        ...

        // set content type header before accessing the Writer
        response.setContentType("text/html");
        PrintWriter out = response.getWriter();

        // then write the response
        out.println("<html>" +
                    "<head><title> Receipt </title>" +
                    ...);

        out.println("<h3>Thank you for purchasing your books “ +
                    “from us "+
                    request.getParameter("cardname") +
                    ...);
        out.close();
    }
    ...
}
```

The servlet extends the HttpServlet class and overrides the doPostmethod.

Within the doPost method the getParameter method gets the servlet's expected argument.

To respond to the client in the example, the doPost method uses a Writer from the HttpServletResponse object to return text data to the client. Before accessing the writer, the example sets the content-type header. At the end of the doPost method, after the response has been sent, the Writer is closed.

Threading Issues

HTTP servlets are typically capable of serving multiple clients concurrently. However, if the servlet methods that support multiple clients access the same resource, you must make special accommodations. You can handle the concurrency by creating a servlet that handles only one client request at a time. (You could also synchronize access to the resource.)

To have your servlet handle only one client at a time, have your servlet implement the `SingleThreadModel` interface in addition to extending the `HttpServlet` class. Implementing the `SingleThreadModel` interface does not involve writing any extra methods. You simply declare that the servlet implements the interface, and the server makes sure that your servlet runs only one `service` method at a time.

For example, the `ReceiptServlet` accepts a user's name and credit card number and thanks the user for ordering. If this servlet updated an inventory database, for example, the database connection might be a shared resource. The servlet could either synchronize access to that resource or implement the `SingleThreadModel` interface. If the servlet implemented the interface, the only change in the code from the section Handling GET and POST Requests (page 440) is the one line shown in bold.

```
public class ReceiptServlet extends HttpServlet
                                  implements SingleThreadModel {

    public void doPost(HttpServletRequest request,
                       HttpServletResponse response)
                       throws ServletException, IOException {
        ...
    }
    ...
}
```

Providing Servlet Descriptions

Some applications, such as the Java Web Server Administration Tool,[1] get descriptive information from the servlet and display it. The servlet description is a string that can describe the purpose of the servlet, its author, its version number, or whatever the servlet author deems important.

[1] http://jserv.java.sun.com/products/webserver/features/index.html

The method that returns this information is `getServletInfo`, which returns `null` by default. You are not required to override this method, but applications are unable to supply a description of your servlet unless you do.

The following example shows the description of the `BookStoreServlet`.

```
public class BookStoreServlet extends HttpServlet {
    ...
    public String getServletInfo() {
        return "The BookStore servlet returns the " +
                "main web page for Duke's Bookstore.";
    }
}
```

http://java.sun.com/docs/books/tutorial/servlets/lifecycle/index.html

36 The Life Cycle of a Servlet

SERVLETS have the following life cycle.

1. A server loads and initializes the servlet.
2. The servlet handles zero or more client requests.
3. The server removes the servlet. (Note that some servers do this step only when they shut down.)

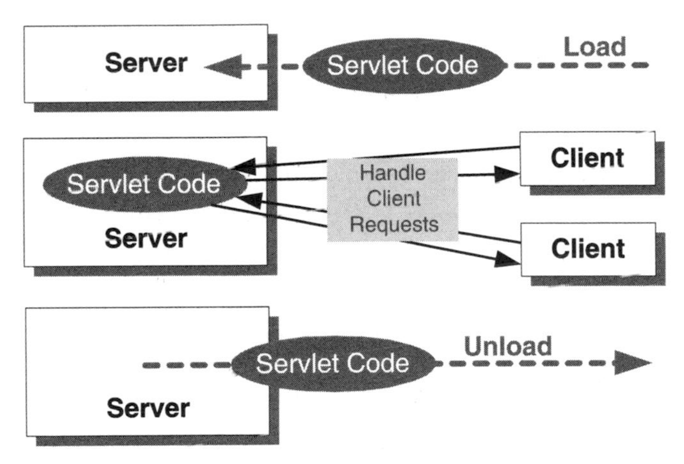

Figure 43 A servlet's life cycle.

The sections in this lesson discuss each aspect of the life cycle.

Initializing a Servlet (page 446)

When a server loads a servlet, the server runs the servlet's `init` method. Initialization completes before client requests are handled and before the servlet is destroyed.

Even though most servlets are run in multithreaded servers, servlets have no concurrency issues during servlet initialization. The server calls the `init` method once, when the server loads the servlet, and will not call the `init` method again unless the server is reloading the servlet. The server cannot reload a servlet until after the server has destroyed the servlet by calling the `destroy` method.

Destroying a Servlet (page 448)

Servlets run until the server destroys them, for example, at the request of a system administrator. When a server destroys a servlet, the server runs the servlet's `destroy` method. The method is run once; the server will not run the `destroy` method again until after the server reloads and reinitializes the servlet.

Handling Service Threads at Servlet Termination (page 448)

When the `destroy` method runs, another thread might be running a service request. This section shows you how to provide a clean shutdown when long-running threads could still be running service requests.

Initializing a Servlet

The `init` method of the `HttpServlet` class initializes the servlet and logs the initialization. To customize initialization for your servlet, follow these rules to override the `init` method.

- If an initialization error occurs that renders the servlet incapable of handling client requests, throw an UnavailableException. The inability to establish a required network connection is an example of this type of error.
- Do not call the `System.exit` method.
- Save the `ServletConfig` parameter so the `getServletConfig` method can return the value. The simplest way to do this is to have the new `init` method call `super.init`. If you store the object yourself, override the `getServletConfig` method to return the object from its new location.

Here is a sample `init` method:

```
public class BookDBServlet ... {
    private BookstoreDB books;
    public void init(ServletConfig config)
                                        throws ServletException {
```

```
        // Store ServletConfig object and log initialization
        super.init(config);
        // Load the database to prepare for requests
        books = new BookstoreDB();
    }
    ...
}
```

The `init` method is quite simple: It calls the `super.init` method to manage the `ServletConfig` object and to log the initialization and then the `init` method sets a private field.

If the `BookDBServlet` used a database instead of simulating one with an object, the `init` method would be more complex. Here is pseudocode for what the `init` method might look like.

```
public class BookDBServlet ... {

    public void init(ServletConfig config)
                                throws ServletException {

        // Store ServletConfig object and log initialization
        super.init(config);
        // Open a database connection to prepare for requests
        try {
            databaseUrl = getInitParameter("databaseUrl");
            ... // get user and password parameters the same way
            connection =
                DriverManager.getConnection(databaseUrl,
                                            user, password);
        } catch(Exception e) {
            throw new UnavailableException (this,
                "Could not open a connection to the database");
        }
    }
    ...
}
```

Initialization Parameters

The second version of the `init` method calls the `getInitParameter` method. This method takes the parameter name as an argument and returns a `String` representation of the parameter's value.

The specification of initialization parameters is server specific. For example, the parameters are specified with a property when a servlet is run with the `servletrunner`. The lesson The servletrunner Utility (page 465) contains a general explanation of properties and how to create them. If for some reason you need to get the parameter names, use the `getParameterNames` method.

Destroying a Servlet

The `destroy` method provided by the `HttpServlet` class destroys the servlet and logs the destruction. To destroy any resources specific to your servlet, override the `destroy` method. The `destroy` method should undo any initialization work and synchronize persistent state with the current in-memory state.

The following example shows the `destroy` method that accompanies the `init` method in the previous section.

```
public class BookDBServlet extends GenericServlet {

    private BookstoreDB books;

    ... // the init method

    public void destroy() {
        // Allow the database to be garbage collected
        books = null;
    }
}
```

A server calls the `destroy` method after all service calls have been completed or after a server-specific number of seconds have passed, whichever comes first. If your servlet handles any long-running operations, `service` methods may still be running when the server calls the `destroy` method. You are responsible for making sure that those threads complete. The next section shows you how.

The `destroy` method shown previously expects all client interactions to be completed when the `destroy` method is called, because the servlet has no long-running operations.

Handling Service Threads at Servlet Termination

All of a servlet's `service` methods should be complete when a servlet is removed. The server tries to ensure this completion by calling the `destroy` method only after all service requests have returned or after a server-specific grace period, whichever comes first.

If your servlet has potentially long-running service requests, use the techniques in this section to

- Keep track of how many threads are currently running the `service` method
- Provide a clean shutdown by having the `destroy` method notify long-running threads of the shutdown and wait for them to complete
- Have the long-running methods poll periodically to check for shutdown and, if necessary, stop working, clean up and return

Tracking Service Requests

To track service requests, include in your servlet class a field that counts the number of service methods that are running. The field should have access methods to increment, decrement, and return its value.

```
public ShutdownExample extends HttpServlet {
    private int serviceCounter = 0;
    ...
    //Access methods for serviceCounter
    protected synchronized void enteringServiceMethod() {
        serviceCounter++;
    }
    protected synchronized void leavingServiceMethod() {
        serviceCounter--;
    }
    protected synchronized int numServices() {
        return serviceCounter;
    }
}
```

The `service` method should increment the service counter each time the method is entered and should decrement the counter each time the method returns. This is one of the few times that your `HttpServlet` subclass should override the `service` method. The new method should call `super.service` to preserve all of the original `HttpServlet.service` method's functionality.

```
protected void service(HttpServletRequest req,
                       HttpServletResponse resp)
                       throws ServletException, IOException {
    enteringServiceMethod();
    try {
        super.service(req, resp);
    } finally {
        leavingServiceMethod();
    }
}
```

Providing a Clean Shutdown

To ensure a clean shutdown, your destroy method should not kill any shared resources until all of the service requests have completed. One step of doing this is to check the service counter. Another step is to notify the long-running methods that it is time to shut down. For this notification another field is required. The field should have the usual access methods.

```
public ShutdownExample extends HttpServlet {
    private boolean shuttingDown;
    ...
    //Access methods for shuttingDown
    protected setShuttingDown(boolean flag) {
        shuttingDown = flag;
    }
    protected boolean isShuttingDown() {
        return shuttingDown;
    }
}
```

An example of the destroy method using these fields to provide a clean shutdown follows.

```
public void destroy() {

    /* Check to see whether there are still service methods
     * running, and if there are, tell them to stop. */
    if (numServices() > 0) {
        setShuttingDown(true);
    }

    /* Wait for the service methods to stop. */
    while(numServices() > 0) {
        try {
            Thread.sleep(interval);
        } catch (InterruptedException e) {
        }
    }
}
```

Creating Polite Long-Running Methods

The final step to provide a clean shutdown is to make any long-running methods behave politely. Methods that might run for a long time should check the value of the field that notifies them of shutdowns and should interrupt their work, if neceesary.

```
public void doPost(...) {
    ...
    for(i = 0; ((i < lotsOfStuffToDo) &&
                !isShuttingDown()); i++) {
        try {
            partOfLongRunningOperation(i);
        } catch (InterruptedException e) {
        }
    }
}
```

http://java.sun.com/docs/books/tutorial/servlets/client-state/index.html

37 Saving Client State

THE servlet API provides two ways to track client state: session tracking and cookies.

: This section discusses session tracking, a mechanism that servlets use to maintain state about a series of requests from the same user (that is, the same browser) across a period of time.

: This section discusses cookies, a mechanism that servlets use to have clients hold a small amount of their own state information. Servlets can use the information in a cookie as the user enters a site (as a low-security user sign-on, for example), as the user navigates around a site (as a repository of user preferences, for example), or both.

Session Tracking

Servlets use session tracking to maintain state about a series of requests from the same user across a period of time. Sessions are shared among the servlets a client accesses. This sharing scheme is convenient for applications made up of multiple servlets. For example, *Duke's Bookstore* uses session tracking to keep track of the books a user orders. All of the servlets in the example have access to the user's session.

Follow these steps to use session tracking.

1. Obtain a session (an `HttpSession` object) for a user.
2. Store or get data from the `HttpSession` object.
3. Invalidate the session (optional).

Obtaining a Session

The getSession method of the HttpServletRequest object returns a user's session. When you call the method with its create argument as true, the implementation creates a session, if necessary.

To properly maintain the session, you must call getSession before any output is written to the response. (If you respond by using a Writer, you must call getSession before accessing the Writer, not just before sending any response data.)

As we've noted, the *Duke's Bookstore* example uses session tracking to keep track of the books in the user's shopping cart. Here is an example of the CatalogServlet obtaining a session for a user.

```
public class CatalogServlet extends HttpServlet {

    public void doGet (HttpServletRequest request,
                       HttpServletResponse response)
                       throws ServletException, IOException {
        // Get the user's session and shopping cart
        HttpSession session = request.getSession(true);
        ...
        out = response.getWriter();
        ...
    }
}
```

Storing and Getting Data from a Session

The HttpSession interface provides methods that store and return

- Standard session properties, such as a session identifier.
- Application data, stored as a name-value pair, where the name is a String and the value is an object in the Java programming language. Because multiple servlets have access to a user's session, you should adopt a naming convention for organizing the names associated with application data. This naming scheme avoids servlets accidentally overwriting one another's values in a session. One such convention is servletname.name, where servletname is the servlet's full name, including its package. For example, com.acme.WidgetSerlet.state is a cookie with the *servletname* com.acme.WidgetServlet and the *name* state.

Here is an example of the CatalogServlet getting a user's session identifier and getting and setting the application data associated with the user's session.

```
public class CatalogServlet extends HttpServlet {
    public void doGet (HttpServletRequest request,
                       HttpServletResponse response)
                       throws ServletException, IOException {
        // Get the user's session and shopping cart
        HttpSession session = request.getSession(true);
        ShoppingCart cart =
            (ShoppingCart)session.getValue(session.getId());

        // If the user has no cart, create a new one
        if (cart == null) {
            cart = new ShoppingCart();
            session.putValue(session.getId(), cart);
        }
        ...
    }
}
```

Because an object can be associated with a session, the *Duke's Bookstore* example uses an object to keep track of the books a user has ordered. The object is type `ShoppingCart`, and each book that a user orders is stored in the shopping cart as a `ShoppingCartItem` object. Look at the following code snippet from the `doGet` method of the `CatalogServlet`.

```
public void doGet (HttpServletRequest request,
                   HttpServletResponse response)
                   throws ServletException, IOException {
    HttpSession session = request.getSession(true);
    ShoppingCart cart =
        (ShoppingCart)session.getValue(session.getId());
    ...
    // Check for pending adds to the shopping cart
    String bookId = request.getParameter("Buy");

    //If the user wants to add a book, add it and print result
    String bookToAdd = request.getParameter("Buy");
    if (bookToAdd != null) {
        BookDetails book = database.getBookDetails(bookToAdd);

        cart.add(bookToAdd, book);
        out.println("<p><h3>" + ...);
    }
}
```

Finally, note that a session can be designated as *new*. A new session causes the `isNew` method of the `HttpSession` class to return `true`, indicating that, for example, the client does not yet know about the session. A new session has no associated data.

You must deal with situations involving new sessions. If the user in the *Duke's Bookstore* example has no shopping cart (the only data associated with a session), the servlet creates a new one. Alternatively if you need information from the user to start a session (such as a user name), you might want to redirect the user to a Web page where you collect the necessary information.

Invalidating the Session

A user's session can be invalidated manually or, depending on where the servlet is running, automatically. (For example, the Java Web Server™ automatically invalidates a session when no page requests have been made in a specified period of time, 30 minutes by default.) To invalidate a session means to remove the `HttpSession` object and its values from the system.

To manually invalidate a session, use the session's `invalidate` method. Some applications have a natural point at which to invalidate the session. The *Duke's Bookstore* example invalidates a user's session after the user has bought the books. This happens in the `ReceiptServlet`.

```
public class ReceiptServlet extends HttpServlet {

    public void doPost(HttpServletRequest request,
                       HttpServletResponse response)
                       throws ServletException, IOException {
        ...
        scart =
              (ShoppingCart)session.getValue(session.getId());
        ...
        // Clear out shopping cart by invalidating the session
        session.invalidate();

        // set content type header before accessing the Writer
        response.setContentType("text/html");
        out = response.getWriter();
        ...
    }
}
```

Handling All Browsers

Session tracking uses cookies by default to associate a session identifier with a user. To support users whose browsers do not support cookies or purposely reject cookies, you must use URL rewriting instead.

Note: Although some Web servers support URL rewriting, the `servletrunner` utility does not. For session tracking to work when a servlet is running within `servletrunner`, the user agent must support cookies.

When you use URL rewriting, you call methods that, when necessary, include the session ID in a link. You must call these methods for every link in the servlet response.

The method `HttpServletResponse.encodeUrl` associates a session ID with a URL. If you redirect the user to another page, use the `HttpServletResponse.encodeRedirectUrl` method to associate the session ID with the redirected URL.

The `encodeUrl` and the `encodeRedirectUrl` methods decide whether the URL needs to be rewritten and return the URL either changed or unchanged. The rules for URLs and redirected URLS differ, but in general if the server detects that the browser supports cookies, the URL is not rewritten.

The *Duke's Bookstore* example uses URL rewriting for all of the links that it returns to its users. For example, the `CatalogServlet` returns the catalog with two links for each book. One link offers details about the book, and the other allows you to add the book to your shopping cart. Both URLs are rewritten.

```
public class CatalogServlet extends HttpServlet {

    public void doGet (HttpServletRequest request,
                       HttpServletResponse response)
                       throws ServletException, IOException {
        // Get user's session and shopping cart, Writer, etc.
        ...
        // then write the data of the response
        out.println("<html>" + ...);
        ...
        // Get the catalog and send it, nicely formatted
        BookDetails[] books =
                      database.getBooksSortedByTitle();
        ...
        for(int i=0; i < numBooks; i++) {
            ...
            //Print out info on each book in its own two rows
            out.println("<tr>" + ...
                        "<a href=\"" +
                          response.encodeUrl(
                              "/servlet/bookdetails?bookId=" +
                               bookId) +
```

```
                                   "\"><strong>" + books[i].getTitle() +
                                   "  </strong></a></td>" + ...
                                   "<a href=\"" +
                                   response.encodeUrl(
                                       "/servlet/catalog?Buy=" +
                                       bookId) +
                                   "\">  Add to Cart_ </a></td></tr>" +
            }
        }
    }
```

If the user clicks on a link with a rewritten URL, the servlet recognizes and extracts the session ID. Then the `getSession` method uses the session ID to get the user's `HttpSession` object.

On the other hand, if the user's browser does not support cookies and the user clicks on an unrewritten URL, the user's session is lost. The servlet contacted through that link creates a new session, but it does not have the data associated with the previous session. Once a servlet loses the session data, the data is lost for all servlets that share the session. You should consistently use URL rewriting if your servlet will support clients that do not support or accept cookies.

Using Cookies

Cookies are a way for a server (or a servlet, as part of a server) to send information to a client to store and for the server to later retrieve its data from that client. Servlets send cookies to clients by adding fields to HTTP response headers. Clients automatically return cookies by adding fields to HTTP request headers.

Each HTTP request and response header is named and has a single value. For example, a cookie could be a header named `BookToBuy` with a value `304qty1`, indicating to the calling application that the user wants to buy one copy of the book with stock number 304. (Cookies and their values are application specific.)

Multiple cookies can have the same name. For example, a servlet could send two cookies with headers named `BookToBuy`; one could have the value shown previously, `304qty1`, and the other could have a value `301qty3`. These cookies would indicate that the user wants to buy one copy of the book with stock number 304 and three copies of the book with stock number 301.

In addition to a name and a value, a cookie may also contain optional attributes, such as comments. Current Web browsers do not always treat the optional attributes correctly, so you should not rely on them.

A server can provide one or more cookies to a client. Client software, such as a Web browser, is expected to support 20 cookies per host, of at least 4KB each.

When you send a cookie to a client, standard HTTP 1.0 caches will not cache the page. Currently the `javax.servlet.http.Cookie` does not support HTTP 1.1 cache control models.

A client storing cookies for a server returns them to that server and only that server. A server can contain multiple servlets: The *Duke's Bookstore* example is made up of multiple servlets running within a single server. Because cookies are returned to a *server*, servlets running within a server share cookies. The examples in this section illustrate this by showing the `CatalogServlet` and `ShowCart` servlet working with the same cookies.

Note: This section shows code that is not a part of the *Duke's Bookstore* example. *Duke's Bookstore* could use code like that shown in this section if it used cookies instead of session tracking to keep track of the client's book order. Because cookies are not a part of *Duke's Bookstore*, think of the examples in this section as pseudocode.

Do the following to send a cookie.

1. Instantiate a `Cookie` object.
2. Set any attributes.
3. Send the cookie.

Do the following to get information from a cookie.

1. Retrieve all of the cookies from the user's request.
2. Find the cookie or cookies with the name that you are interested in, using standard programming techniques.
3. Get the values of the cookies that you found.

Each of these steps is covered in the following sections.

Creating a Cookie

The constructor for the `javax.servlet.http.Cookie` class creates a cookie with an initial name and a value. You can change the value of the cookie later with its `setValue` method.

The name of the cookie must be an HTTP 1.1 *token*. Tokens are strings that contain none of the special characters listed in the specification RFC 2068.[1] Alpha-

---

1 http://info.internet.isi.edu:80/in-notes/rfc/files/rfc2068.txt

numeric strings qualify as tokens. In addition, names that start with the dollar-sign character ($) are reserved by RFC 2109.[1]

The value of the cookie can be any string, although null values are not guaranteed to work the same way on all browsers. In addition, if you are sending a cookie that complies with Netscape's original cookie specification, do not use white space or any of these characters:

```
[ ] ( ) = , " / ? @ : ;
```

If your servlet returns a response to the user with a `Writer`, create the cookie before accessing the `Writer`. (Cookies are sent to the client as a header, and headers must be written before accessing the `Writer`.)

If the `CatalogServlet` used cookies to keep track of a client's book order, the servlet could create cookies like this.

```
public void doGet (HttpServletRequest request,
                   HttpServletResponse response)
                   throws ServletException, IOException {
    BookDBServlet database = (BookDBServlet)
            getServletConfig().getServletContext().getServlet(
                                                        "bookdb");

    // Check for pending adds to the shopping cart
    String bookId = request.getParameter("Buy");

    //If user wants to add a book, remember it by adding a cookie
    if (bookId != null) {
        Cookie getBook = new Cookie("Buy", bookId);
        ...
    }

    // set content-type header before accessing the Writer
    response.setContentType("text/html");

    // now get the writer and write the data of the response
    PrintWriter out = response.getWriter();
    out.println("<html>" +
                "<head><title> Book Catalog </title></head>" +
                ...);
    ...
}
```

[1] http://info.internet.isi.edu:80/in-notes/rfc/files/rfc2109.txt

Setting Cookie Attributes

The Cookie class provides a number of methods for setting a cookie's values and attributes. Using these methods is straightforward; they are explained in the javadoc for the Cookie[1] class.

The following example sets the comment field of the cookie for CatalogServlet. The comment field describes the purpose of the cookie.

```
public void doGet (HttpServletRequest request,
                   HttpServletResponse response)
                   throws ServletException, IOException {
    ...
    //If user wants to add a book, remember it by adding a cookie
    if (values != null) {
        bookId = values[0];
        Cookie getBook = new Cookie("Buy", bookId);
        getBook.setComment("User wants to buy this book " +
                           "from the bookstore.");
    }
    ...
}
```

You can also set the maximum age of the cookie. This attribute is useful, for example, for deleting a cookie. Once again, if *Duke's Bookstore* used cookies to keep track of a user's order, the example would use this attribute to delete a book from the user's order. The user removes a book from the shopping cart in the ShowCartServlet; its code would look something like this:

```
public void doGet (HttpServletRequest request,
                   HttpServletResponse response)
                   throws ServletException, IOException {
    ...
    // Handle any pending deletes from the shopping cart
    String bookId = request.getParameter("Remove");
    ...
    if (bookId != null) {
        // Find the cookie that pertains to the book to remove
        ...
            // Delete cookie by setting its maximum age to zero
            thisCookie.setMaxAge(0);
        ...
    }
```

[1] You can find the Cookie class javadoc in the Servlets directory on the CD-ROM that accompanies this book.

```
        // also set content-type header before accessing the Writer
        response.setContentType("text/html");
        PrintWriter out = response.getWriter();

        //Print out the response
        out.println("<html> <head>" +
                    "<title>Your Shopping Cart</title>" + ...);
    }
```

Sending the Cookie

Cookies are sent as headers of the response from the server to the client and are added with the `addCookie` method of the `HttpServletResponse` class. If you are using a `Writer` to return text data to the client, you must call the `addCookie` method *before* calling the `HttpServletResponse`'s `getWriter` method.

Continuing the example of the `CatalogServlet`, the following code sends the cookie.

```
    public void doGet (HttpServletRequest request,
                       HttpServletResponse response)
                       throws ServletException, IOException {
        ...
        //If user wants to add a book, remember it by adding a cookie
        if (values != null) {
            bookId = values[0];
            Cookie getBook = new Cookie("Buy", bookId);
            getBook.setComment("User has indicated a desire to " +
                               "buy this book from the bookstore.");
            response.addCookie(getBook);
        }
        ...
    }
```

Retrieving Cookies

Clients return cookies as fields added to HTTP request headers. To retrieve any cookie, you must retrieve all of the cookies, using the `getCookies` method of the `HttpServletRequest` class.

The `getCookies` method returns an array of `Cookie` objects, which you can search to find the cookie or cookies you want. (Remember that multiple cookies can have the same name.) To get the name of a cookie, use its `getName` method.

To continue the `ShowCartServlet` example:

```
public void doGet (HttpServletRequest request,
                   HttpServletResponse response)
                   throws ServletException, IOException {
    ...
    // Handle any pending deletes from the shopping cart
    String bookId = request.getParameter("Remove");
    ...
    if (bookId != null) {

        // Find the cookie that pertains to the book to remove
        Cookie[] cookies = request.getCookies();
        ...

            // Delete book's cookie by setting its maximum age
            // to zero
            thisCookie.setMaxAge(0);
    }

    // also set content-type header before accessing the Writer
    response.setContentType("text/html");
    PrintWriter out = response.getWriter();

    //Print out the response
    out.println("<html> <head>" +
        "<title>Your Shopping Cart</title>" + ...);
}
```

Getting the Value of a Cookie

To find the value of a cookie, use its `getValue` method. To continue the `ShowCartServlet` example:

```
public void doGet (HttpServletRequest request,
                   HttpServletResponse response)
                   throws ServletException, IOException {
    ...
    // Handle any pending deletes from the shopping cart
    String bookId = request.getParameter("Remove");
    ...
    if (bookId != null) {
        // Find the cookie that pertains to that book
        Cookie[] cookies = request.getCookies();
        for(i=0; i < cookies.length; i++) {
            Cookie thisCookie = cookie[i];
            if (thisCookie.getName().equals("Buy") &&
                thisCookie.getValue().equals(bookId)) {
                // Delete the cookie by setting its maximum age
```

```
                // to zero
                thisCookie.setMaxAge(0);
            }
        }
    }

    // also set content-type header before accessing the Writer
    response.setContentType("text/html");
    PrintWriter out = response.getWriter();

    //Print out the response
    out.println("<html> <head>" +
                "<title>Your Shopping Cart</title>" + ...);
}
```

http://java.sun.com/docs/books/tutorial/servlets/servletrunner/index.html 38

The servletrunner Utility

ONCE you have written your servlet, you can test it in the `servletrunner` utility, a small, multithreaded process that handles requests for servlets. Because `servletrunner` is multithreaded, it can be used to run multiple servlets simultaneously or to test one servlet that calls other servlets to satisfy client requests.

Unlike some Web servers, `servletrunner` does not automatically reload updated servlets. However, you can stop and restart `servletrunner` with very little overhead to run a new version of a servlet.

This lesson contains the following sections.

You might have to specify certain pieces of data to run a servlet. For example, if a servlet requires initialization parameters, you must set up this data before starting `servletrunner`. This section tells you how.

After the property file is set up, you can run the `servletrunner` utility.

Setting Servlet Properties

Properties are key-value pairs used for the configuration, creation, and initialization of a servlet. For example, `servlet.catalog.code=CatalogServlet` is a property whose key is `servlet.catalog.code` and whose value is `CatalogServlet`.

The `servletrunner` utility has two properties for servlets:

- `servlet.name.code`
- `servlet.name.initargs`

The code Property

The value of the `servlet.name.code` property is the servlet's full class name, including its package.

```
servlet.bookdb.code=database.BookDBServlet
```

The `servlet.name.code` property names your servlet by associating a *name* (in the example, bookdb) with a class (in the example, `database.BookDBServlet`).

The initargs Property

The value of the `servlet.name.initArgs` property holds the servlet's initialization parameters. The syntax of a single parameter is `parameterName=parameterValue`. The entire property (or entire key-value pair) must be a single logical line. For readability you can use the backslash syntax to allow the property to span multiple lines in the file. For example, if the database servlet read its data from a file, the servlet's initial argument might look like this:

```
servlet.bookdb.initArgs=\
    dbfile=servlets/DatabaseData
```

Multiple initialization parameters are specified as a comma-delimited list. For example, if the database servlet is connected to a real database, its initial arguments might look like this:

```
servlet.bookdb.initArgs=\
    user=duke,\
    password=dukes_password,\
    url=fill_in_the_database_url
```

The Property File

Properties are stored in a text file with a default name of `servlet.properties`. (You can specify another name when you start `servletrunner`.) The file holds the properties for all of the servlets that `servletrunner` will run. Here is the `servlet.properties` file for the *Duke's Bookstore* example.

```
# This file contains properties for Duke's Bookstore servlets.

# Duke's Book Store -- main page
servlet.bookstore.code=BookStoreServlet
```

```
# The servlet that manages the database of books
servlet.bookdb.code=database.BookDBServlet

# View all the books in the bookstore
servlet.catalog.code=CatalogServlet

# Show information about a specific book
servlet.bookdetails.code=BookDetailServlet

# See the books that you've chosen to buy
servlet.showcart.code=ShowCartServlet

# Collects information for buying the chosen books
servlet.cashier.code=CashierServlet

# Provide a receipt to the user who's bought books
servlet.receipt.code=ReceiptServlet
```

Starting servletrunner

The `servletrunner` is in the `jsdk/bin` directory. You can run the utility more easily if this directory is on your search path.

Win32:

```
C> set PATH=C:%PATH%(on Win32)
```

UNIX:

```
% setenv PATH /usr/local/jsdk/bin:
```

Invoking `servletrunner` with the `-help` flag shows a usage message without running it.

```
% servletrunner -help
Usage: servletrunner [options]
Options:
    -p port      the port number to listen on
    -b backlog   the listen backlog
    -m max       maximum number of connection handlers
    -t timeout   connection timeout in milliseconds
    -d dir       servlet directory
    -r root      document root directory
    -s filename  servlet property file name
    -v           verbose output
%
```

To see the default values of these options, call `servletrunner` with the -v option. This call starts the utility. If you are not ready to run it yet or don't want to run with the default value, stop it once you have obtained the information. For example, on UNIX you use the `kill` command to stop `servletrunner`.

```
% servletrunner -v
Server settings:
    port = 8080
    backlog = 50
    max handlers = 100
    timeout = 5000
    servlet dir = ./examples
    document dir = ./examples
    servlet propfile = ./examples/servlet.properties
```

Note: In the default values printed here, `servlet dir`, `document dir`, and the directory for the `servlet propfile` contain a period (`.`). The period designates the current working directory, typically the directory from which the executable was started. In this case, however, the period refers to the directory in which the servlet development kit is *installed*.

If you start `servletrunner` from a directory other than the installation directory, `servletrunner` first changes its current working directory (and, therefore, what you consider as the value of the period).

Once `servletrunner` is executing, you can use it to test your servlets, as described in the next lesson, Running Servlets (page 469).

39 Running Servlets

THIS lesson shows you a number of ways to invoke servlets. You can

- Type a servlet URL into a browser window
- Call a servlet from within an HTML page
- Call a servlet from another servlet

A servlet can be called directly by typing its URL into a browser's location window. This procedure is the one you use to access the main page of the *Duke's Bookstore* example. The section Calling Servlets from Browsers (page 470) shows you the general form of a servlet URL.

Servlet URLs can be used in HTML tags, where a URL for a CGI-bin script or a file URL might be found. The section Calling Servlets from an HTML Page (page 470) shows servlet URLs being used as the destination of an anchor, as the action in a form, and as the location to be used when a META tag directs that a page be refreshed. This section assumes knowledge of HTML. For more information on HTML, refer to the HTML Reference Specification.[1]

Servlets can call other servlets. If the two servlets are run in different servers, one can make an HTTP request of the other. If the two servlets are being run by the same network service, one servlet can call another servlet's public methods directly. The last section, Calling Servlets from Servlets (page 473), assumes that

- Your machine, `localhost`, is running `servletrunner` or a servlet-enabled Web server, such as the Java Web server, at port 8080.

[1] http://w3c.org/TR/index.html

- The servlet example, *Duke's Bookstore*, is located in the top level of that process's directory for servlets. For `servletrunner` this means that the class files are in the servlet directory specified by the `-d` option.

If these two conditions are true, you should be able to run the servlet example by typing in the URLs given in the example.

Calling Servlets from Browsers

The URL for a servlet has the following general form, where *servlet-name* corresponds to the name you have given your servlet:

```
http://machine-name:port/servlet/servlet-name
```

For example, the servlet that delivers the main page of *Duke's Bookstore* has the property `servlet.bookstore.code=BookStoreServlet`. To see the main page of the example, type the following URL into your browser:

```
http://localhost:8080/servlet/bookstore
```

Servlet URLs can contain queries, such as for HTTP `GET` requests. For example, the servlet that delivers details about a particuar book takes the stock number of the book as a query. The servlet's name is `bookdetails`; the URL for the servlet to `GET` and to display all of the information about the bookstore's featured book is

```
http://localhost:8080/servlet/bookdetails?bookId=203
```

Calling Servlets from an HTML Page

To invoke a servlet from within an HTML page, just use the servlet URL in the appropriate HTML tag. Tags that take URLs include those that begin anchors and forms, as well as metatags.

This section uses the *Duke's Bookstore* `ShowCart`, `Cashier`, and `Receipt` servlets. Luckily this is the order that the servlets are displayed when you look at your cart and buy your books.

For the most direct access to the ShowCart servlet, click the *Show Cart* link from the *Duke's Bookstore* main page. If you have `servletrunner` or a Web server set up to run the example, go to the main page of the bookstore as shown in the section Calling Servlets from Browsers (page 470). Just for fun, you might want to add a book to your cart before accessing the `ShowCart` servlet.

Sample Servlet URLs in HTML Tags

The page returned by the ShowCartServlet has a number of anchors, each of which has a servlet as a destination. The following shows the code for one of those anchors.

```
public class ShowCartServlet extends HttpServlet {

    public void doGet (HttpServletRequest request,
                       HttpServletResponse response)
                       throws ServletException, IOException {
        ...
        out.println(... +
                    "<a href=\"" +
                    response.encodeUrl("/servlet/cashier") +
                    "\">Check Out</a>_____ " +
                    ...);
        ...
    }
    ...
}
```

This code results in an HTML page that has the following anchor:

```
<a href="http://localhost:8080/servlet/cashier>Check Out</a>
```

If the showcart servlet's page is displayed in your browser, you can see the anchor if you view the source of the page. Then click on the link. The cashier servlet will return the page that contains the next example.

The page displayed by the cashier servlet presents a form that requests the user's name and credit card number. The code that prints out the form tag looks like this:

```
public class CashierServlet extends HttpServlet {

    public void doGet (HttpServletRequest request,
                       HttpServletResponse response)
                       throws ServletException, IOException {
        ...
        out.println(... +
                    "<form action=\"" +
                    response.encodeUrl("/servlet/receipt") +
                    "\" method=\"post\">" +
                    ...
                    "<td><input type=\"text\" +
```

```
                    name=\"cardname\"" +
                  "value=\"Gwen Canigetit\" size=\"19\"></td>" +
                  ...
                  "<td><input type=\"submit\"" +
                  "value=\"Submit Information\"></td>" +
                  ...
                  "</form>" +
                  ...);
            out.close();
        }
        ...
    }
```

This code results in an HTML page that has the following tag to begin the form:

```
<form action="http://localhost:8080/servlet/receipt"
method="post">
```

If the cashier servlet's page is displayed in your browser, you can see the tag that begins the form if you view the source of the page. Then submit the form. The receipt servlet will return the page that contains the next example. The receipt servlet's page resets itself, though, so if you want to view the page's HTML source, do it fast.

The page returned by the receipt servlet has a metatag that uses a servlet URL as part of the value of the `http-equiv` attribute. Specifically the tag directs the page to reset to the main page of *Duke's Bookstore* after thanking the user for the order. The following shows the code for this tag:

```
public class ReceiptServlet extends HttpServlet {

    public void doPost(HttpServletRequest request,
                       HttpServletResponse response)
                       throws ServletException, IOException {
        ...
        out.println("<html>" +
            "<head><title> Receipt </title>" +
            "<meta http-equiv=\"refresh\" content=\"4; url=" +
            "http://" + request.getHeader("Host") +
            "/servlet/bookstore;\">" +
            "</head>" +
        ...
    }
    ...

}
```

This code results in an HTML page that has the following tag:

```
<meta http-equiv="refresh"
   content="4; url=http://localhost:8080/servlet/bookstore;">
```

Calling Servlets from Servlets

To have your servlet call another servlet, you can have a servlet either

- Make an HTTP request of another servlet[1]
- Call another servlet's public methods directly, if the two servlets run within the same server

This section addresses the second option. To call another servlet's public methods directly, you must

- Know the name of the servlet that you want to call
- Gain access to that servlet's `Servlet` object
- Call the servlet's public methods

To gain access to the `Servlet` object, use the `ServletContext` object's `getServlet` method. Get the `ServletContext` object from the `ServletConfig` object stored in the `Servlet` object. An example should make this clear. When the `BookDetail` servlet calls the `BookDB` servlet, the `BookDetail` servlet obtains the `BookDB` servlet's `Servlet` object, like this:

```
public class BookDetailServlet extends HttpServlet {

    public void doGet (HttpServletRequest request,
                       HttpServletResponse response)
                       throws ServletException, IOException {
        ...
        BookDBServlet database = (BookDBServlet)
            getServletConfig().getServletContext().getServlet(
                                                     "bookdb");
        ...
    }
}
```

[1] Opening a connection to a URL is discussed in the *Working with URLs* lesson of *The Java Tutorial, Second Edition*. The HTML version of this lesson is available on the CD-ROM that accompanies this book and is also available online at: http://java.sun.com/docs/books/tutorial/networking/urls/index.html.

Once you have the servlet object, you can call any of that servlet's public methods. For example, the BookDetail servlet calls the BookDBservlet's getBookDetails method

```
public class BookDetailServlet extends HttpServlet {

    public void doGet (HttpServletRequest request,
                       HttpServletResponse response)
                       throws ServletException, IOException {
        ...
        BookDBServlet database = (BookDBServlet)
        getServletConfig().getServletContext().getServlet(
                                                    "bookdb");
        BookDetails bd = database.getBookDetails(bookId);
        ...
    }
}
```

You must exercise caution when you call another servlet's methods. If the servlet that you want to call implements the SingleThreadModel interface, your call could violate the called servlet's single-threaded nature. (The server has no way to intervene and make sure that your call happens when the servlet is not interacting with another client.) In this case your servlet should make an HTTP request of the other servlet instead of calling the other servlet's methods directly.

About the Author

CYNTHIA BLOCH writes technical documentation at Sun Microsystems' Java Software division. She has a Masters in Information Science from the University of Pittsburgh. Since graduate school she has worked as a senior software engineer at Carnegie Group Incorporated in Pittsburgh, Pennsylvania, and as a senior technical trainer at Transarc Corporation in Pittsburgh, Pennsylvania.

Acknowledgments

I would like to thank Rob Clark for answering my questions and reviewing drafts, Carola Fellenz for creating the picture of Duke serving books, and the whole Java Server team for having the idea for *Duke's Bookstore* and providing the code to port.

Security

by Mary Dageforde

IN this trail you'll learn how the built-in Java™ security features protect you from malevolent programs. You'll see how to use tools to control access to resources, to generate and to check digital signatures, and to create and to manage keys needed for signature generation and checking. You'll also see how to incorporate cryptography services, such as digital signature generation and checking, into your programs.

The security features provided by the Java Development Kit (JDK™) 1.2 are intended for a variety of audiences:

- Users running programs: Built-in security functionality protects you from malevolent programs (including viruses), maintains the privacy of your files and information about you, and authenticates the identity of each code provider. For the first time, you can subject *applications* to security controls (just as is done for applets), when desired.
- Developers: You can use API methods to incorporate security functionality into your programs, including cryptography services and security checks. The API framework enables you to define and integrate your own permissions (controlling access to specific resources), cryptography service implementations, security manager implementations, and policy implementations. In addition, classes are provided for management of your public/private key pairs and public key certificates from people you trust.
- Systems administrators, developers, and users: JDK 1.2 tools manage your keystore (database of keys and certificates); generate digital signatures for JAR files, and verify the authenticity of such signatures and the integrity of the signed contents; and create and modify the policy files that define your installation's security policy.

Note: Nearly all of the security features documented in this trail were added to the JDK for its 1.2 release. Thus the code examples in the following lessons will work only on Java platforms that are compatible with JDK 1.2. Individual browsers may have some different behavior, unless you use the Java Plug-in to download the latest Java Runtime Environment (JRE™) compatible with JDK 1.2.

Security Features Overview (page 483) briefly describes the security features available in JDK 1.2.

Quick Tour of Controlling Applets (page 491) provides an overview of some of the new features. This lesson shows how resource accesses, such as reading or writing a file, are not permitted for applets unless explicitly allowed by a permission in a policy file.

Quick Tour of Controlling Applications (page 503) builds on the previous lesson, showing that when applications are run under a security manager, resource accesses may be controlled in exactly the same way as for applets.

Secure Code and File Exchanges (page 515) describes digital signatures, certificates, and keystores and discusses why they are needed. This section also provides overview information applicable to the next three lessons regarding the steps commonly needed for using the tools or the API to generate signatures, export/import certificates, and so on.

Signing Code and Granting It Permissions (page 525) illustrates the use of all the security-related tools. It shows the steps that a developer would take to sign and to distribute code for others to run. The lesson also shows how someone who will run the code (or a system administrator) could add an entry in a policy file to grant the code permission for the resource accesses it needs.

Exchanging Files (page 541) shows use of the tools by one person to sign an important document, such as a contract, and to export the public key certificate used to sign the contract. Then the lesson shows how another person, who receives the contract, the signature, and the public key certificate, can import the certificate and verify the signature.

Generating and Verifying Signatures (page 549) walks you step by step through an example of writing a Java program using the JDK Security API to generate keys, to generate a digital signature for data using the private key, and to export the public key and the signature to files. Then the example shows writing a second program, which may be expected to run on a different person's computer, that imports the public key and verifies the authenticity of the signature. Finally, the example discusses potential weaknesses of the approach used by the basic programs and demonstrates possible alternative approaches and methods of supplying and importing keys, including in certificates.

For More Information

The Security Glossary (page 914) in the Appendix provides definitions and usage descriptions of important terms used throughout this trail.

The online version of this trail[1] contains an additional lesson, "Implementing Your Own Permission," as well as summaries of the security tools, the JDK Security API, and the security-related files.

JDK 1.2 security release documentation[2] can be found with the rest of the release documentation. Here you'll find more detailed information about the security features, including architecture specifications, usage guides, API documentation, and tool documentation.

Encryption and decryption are supplied as part of the Java Cryptography Extension. For more information, see the documentation for that release.[3] Information on use of the Java Plug-in[4] to download the latest Java Runtime Environment compatible with JDK 1.2 is also available.

---

[1] This trail is included on the CD-ROM that accompanies this book and is available online here: http://java.sun.com/docs/books/tutorial/security1.2/index.html
[2] http://java.sun.com/products/jdk/1.2/docs/guide/security/index.html
[3] http://java.sun.com/products/jdk/1.2/jce/index.html
[4] http://java.sun.com/products/plugin/index.html

http://java.sun.com/docs/tutorial/security1.2/overview/index.html

40 Security Features Overview

JDK 1.2 contains substantial security features enhancements: policy-based, easily configurable, fine-grained access control; new cryptographic services and certificate and key management classes and interfaces; and three new tools. These topics are discussed in the following sections:

Security Architecture Extensions

Access control has evolved to be far more fine-grained than in previous versions of the Java platform.

The original security model provided by the Java platform, known as the "sandbox" model, existed in order to provide a very restricted environment in which to run untrusted code obtained from the open network. In the sandbox model, shown in the following diagram, local code is trusted to have full access to vital system resources, such as the file system, but downloaded remote code (an applet) is not trusted and can access only the limited resources provided inside the sandbox. A security manager is responsible in this and subsequent platforms for determining which resource accesses are allowed.

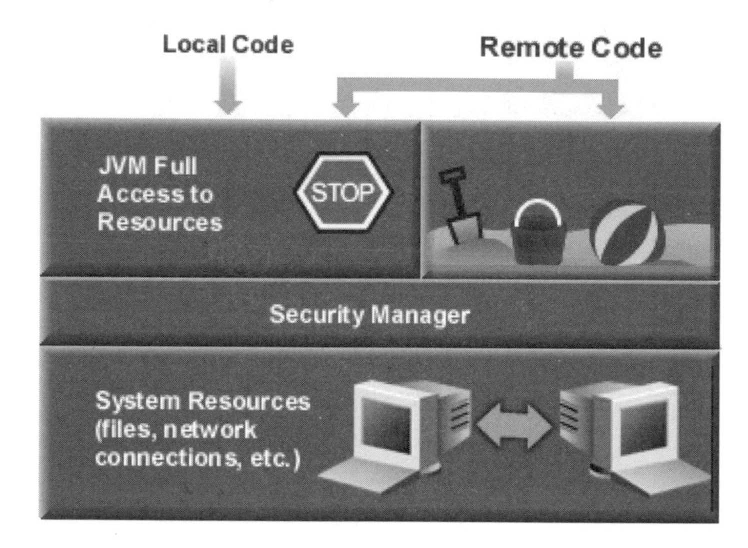

Figure 44 JDK 1.0 sandbox security model.

JDK 1.1 introduced the concept of a "signed applet," as illustrated in the next figure. A digitally signed applet is treated like local code, with full access to resources, if the public key used to verify the signature is trusted. Unsigned applets are still run in the sandbox. Signed applets are delivered, with their respective signatures, in signed JAR (Java ARchive) files.

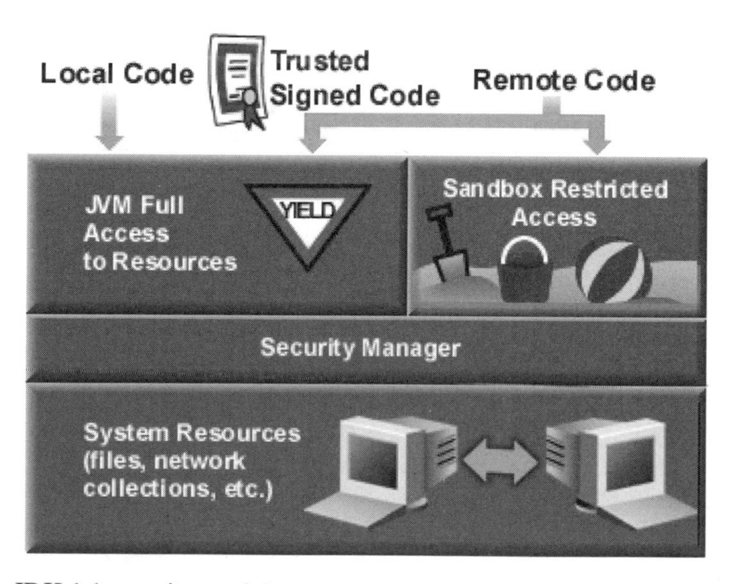

Figure 45 JDK 1.1 security model.

JDK 1.2 introduces a number of improvements over JDK 1.1. First, all code, regardless of whether it is local or remote, can now be subject to a security *policy*. The security policy defines the set of *permissions* available for code from various signers or locations and can be configured by a user or a system administrator. Each permission specifies a permitted access to a particular resource, such as read and write access to a specified file or directory or connect access to a given host and port.

The runtime system organizes code into individual *domains*, each of which encloses a set of classes whose instances are granted the same set of permissions. A domain can be configured to be equivalent to the sandbox, so applets can still be run in a restricted environment if the user or the administrator so chooses. Applications run unrestricted, as before, by default but can optionally be subject to a security policy.

The new security architecture in JDK 1.2 is illustrated in the following figure. The arrow on the left end refers to a domain whose code is granted full access to resources; the arrow on the right refers to the opposite extreme: a domain restricted exactly as the original sandbox. The domains in between have more accesses allowed than the sandbox but less than full access.

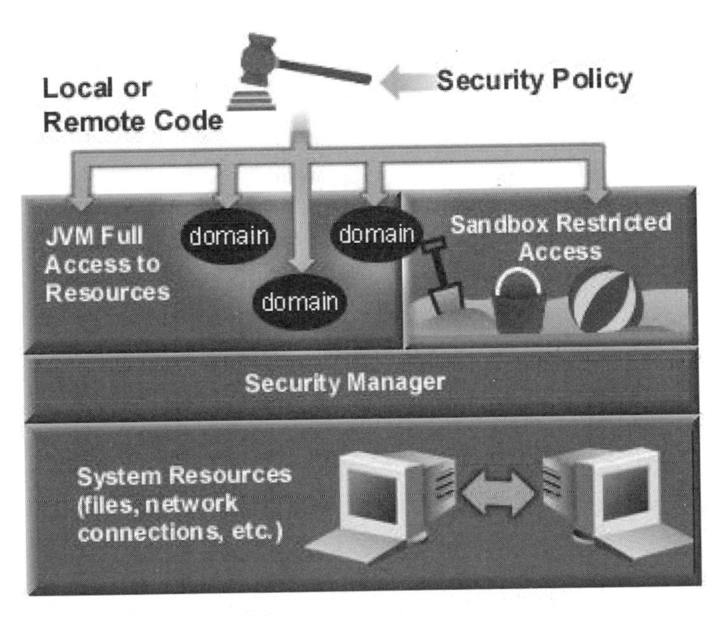

Figure 46 JDK 1.2 security model.

Cryptography Architecture Extensions

This section is of interest mostly to developers already familiar with cryptography concepts. If you're not such a person, you may want to skip ahead to the section Security-Related Tools (page 489). Some of the cryptography terminology is defined in the Security Glossary (page 914) in the Appendix.[1]

The first release of the JDK Security API in JDK 1.1 introduced the Java Cryptography Architecture (JCA), which refers to a framework for accessing and developing cryptographic functionality for the Java platform. The JCA includes a provider architecture that allows for multiple and interoperable cryptography implementations. The term cryptographic service provider (CSP), or simply provider, refers to a package (or a set of packages) that supplies a concrete implementation of a subset of the cryptography aspects of the JDK Security API.

In JDK 1.1 a provider could, for example, contain an implementation of one or more digital signature algorithms, message digest algorithms, and key-generation algorithms. JDK 1.2 adds five more types of services:

- Keystore creation and management
- Algorithm parameter management
- Algorithm parameter generation
- Key factory support to convert between various key representations
- Certificate factory support to generate certificates and certificate revocation lists (CRLs) from their encodings

JDK 1.2 also enables a provider to supply a random-number generation (RNG) algorithm.

Sun Microsystems' version of the JRE comes standard with a default provider, named SUN. The SUN provider package includes implementations of a number of DSA (Digital Signature Algorithm) services, implementations of the MD5 (RFC 1321) and SHA-1 (NIST FIPS 180–1) message digest algorithms, a certificate factory for X.509 certificates and certificate revocation lists, a pseudo-random-number generation algorithm, and a keystore implementation.

The *Java Cryptography Extension (JCE)* extends the JDK to include APIs for encryption, key exchange, and message authentication code (MAC). Together the JCE and the cryptography aspects of the JDK provide a complete, platform-independent cryptography API. The JCE is released separately as an extension to

---

[1] For more information on cryptography, we recommend the book *Applied Cryptography* by Bruce Schneier, published by John Wiley & Sons, Inc., New York, NY, 1996.

the JDK, in accordance with U.S. export control regulations, and is not covered in this trail.

The following figure illustrates the various JCA modules. The SPI (service provider interface) layer, representing methods that must be implemented by cryptographic service providers, is described in the following section.

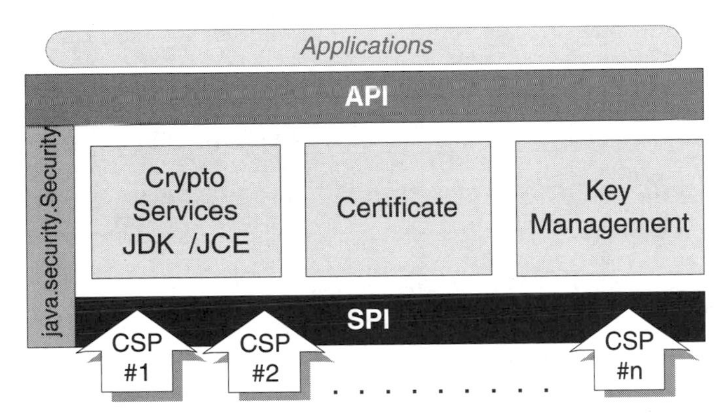

Figure 47 JCA modules.

Cryptographic Services

A number of new "engine" classes have been added in JDK 1.2 to the `Signature`, `MessageDigest`, and `KeyPairGenerator` classes available in JDK 1.1. An engine class defines an abstract cryptographic service (without a concrete implementation). An engine class defines API methods that allow applications to access the specific type of cryptographic service it provides, such as a digital signature algorithm. The actual implementations, from one or more providers, are those for specific algorithms.

The application interfaces supplied by an engine class are implemented in terms of a *service provider interface (SPI)*. That is, each engine class has a corresponding abstract SPI class that defines the service provider interface methods that cryptographic service providers must implement.

For example, an API client may request and use an instance of the `Signature` engine class to access the functionality of a digital signature algorithm to digitally sign a file. The implementation supplied in a `SignatureSpi` subclass would be that for a specific kind of signature algorithm, such as SHA-1 with DSA or MD5 with RSA.

Each instance of an engine class encapsulates an instance of the corresponding SPI class as implemented by a cryptographic service provider. Each API method of an engine class invokes the corresponding SPI method of the encapsulated SPI object.

Certificate Interfaces and Classes

JDK 1.2 introduces certificate interfaces and classes for parsing and managing certificates and provides an X.509 v3 implementation of the certificate interfaces. A certificate is basically a digitally signed statement from one entity, saying that the public key of another entity has some particular value.

Some of the certificate-related classes (all in the `java.security.cert` package) are as follows.

- **`Certificate`:** This class is an abstraction for certificates that have various formats but important common uses. For example, various types of certificates, such as X.509 and PGP, share general certificate functionality, such as encoding and verifying, and some types of information, such as a public key. X.509, PGP, and SDSI certificates can all be implemented by subclassing the `Certificate` class, even though they contain different sets of information and store and retrieve the information in different ways.
- **`CertificateFactory`:** This class defines the functionality of a certificate factory, which is used to generate certificate and certificate revocation list (CRL) objects from their encodings.
- **`X509Certificate`:** This abstract class for X.509 certificates provides a standard way to access all the attributes of an X.509 certificate.

Key Management Classes and Interfaces

JDK 1.1 introduced abstract `Key` interfaces. JDK 1.2 adds

- A `KeyStore` class (an engine class) that supplies well-defined interfaces to access and to modify the information in a keystore, which is a repository of keys and certificates. Multiple different concrete implementations are possible, where each implementation is that for a particular type of keystore. A keystore type defines the storage and data format of the keystore information.
- A default `KeyStore` implementation, which implements the keystore as a file, using a proprietary keystore type (format) named JKS. The keystore implementation protects each private key with its individual password and

also protects the integrity of the entire keystore with a (possibly different) password.

- Key specification interfaces, which are used for "transparent" representations of the key material that constitutes a key. The key material for a key may, for example, consist of the key itself and the algorithm parameters used to calculate the key value. A transparent representation of keys means that you can access each key material value individually.
- A tool for managing keys and certificates.

Security-Related Tools

JDK 1.2 introduces three new tools:

- The `keytool` tool is used to create pairs of public and private keys, to import and display certificate chains, to export certificates, and to generate X.509 v1 self-signed certificates and certificate requests that can be sent to a certification authority.
- The `jarsigner` tool signs JAR files and verifies the authenticity of the signature(s) of signed JAR files.
- The Policy Tool creates and modifies the policy configuration files that define your installation's security policy.

http://java.sun.com/docs/books/tutorial/security1.2/tour1/index.html

41

Quick Tour of Controlling Applets

THIS lesson gives a brief introduction to some of the new security features. It shows how resource accesses, such as reading or writing a file, are not permitted for applets unless explicitly allowed by a permission in a policy file.

The sections for this lesson are

Observe Applet Restrictions

One way the Java platform provides protection from attack from a virus, for example, is through the use of a *security manager.* Currently JDK system code invokes security manager methods to perform resource access control checks.

Most browsers install a security manager, so applets typically run under the scrutiny of a security manager. Each such applet is not allowed to access resources unless it is explicitly granted permission to do so by the security policy in effect. In Java platforms that are compatible with JDK 1.2, the permission must be granted by an entry in a policy file.

In our example an applet named `WriteFile` tries to create and to write to a file named `writetest` in the current directory. The applet shouldn't be able to create the file unless it has explicit permission in a policy file. You can find the complete source code for `WriteFile.java` (page 865) in the Appendix.

Type this command in your command window:

```
appletviewer http://java.sun.com/docs/books/tutorial/
security1.2/tour1/example-1dot2/WriteFile.html
```

Type this command on a single line, without spaces in the URL.

You should see a message about a security exception, as shown in Figure 48. This is the expected behavior; the system caught the applet trying to access a resource it doesn't have permission to access.

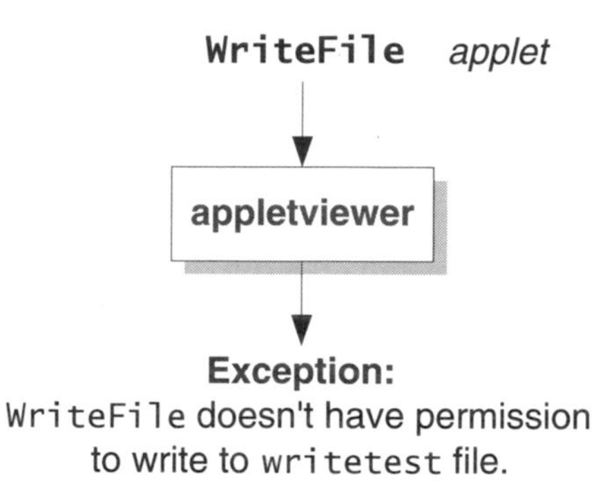

Figure 48 `WriteFile` applet execution.

Set Up a Policy File

A policy file is an ASCII text file and can be composed via a text editor or the graphical Policy Tool utility demonstrated in this section. The Policy Tool saves you typing and eliminates the need for you to know the required syntax of policy files, thus reducing errors.

You will use the Policy Tool to create a policy file, named `mypolicy`, in which you will add a *policy entry* that grants code from the directory where `WriteFile.class` is stored permission to write the `writetest` file. The steps are as follows:

1. Start Policy Tool.
2. Grant the required permission.
3. Save the policy file.

Note for UNIX Users: The steps illustrate creating the policy file for a Win32 system. The steps are exactly the same if you are working on a UNIX system. Where the text says to store the policy file in the `C:\Test` directory, you can store it in another directory. The examples in the section See the Policy File Effects (page 498) and in the lesson Quick Tour of Controlling Applications (page 503) assume that you stored it in the `~/test` directory.

Start Policy Tool

To start Policy Tool, simply type the following at the command line:

```
policytool
```

This brings up the Policy Tool window.

Whenever Policy Tool is started, it tries to fill in this window with policy information from what is sometimes referred to as the "user policy file." The user policy file is by default a file named `.java.policy` in your home directory. If Policy Tool cannot find the user policy file, it reports the situation and displays a blank Policy Tool window (that is, a window with headings and buttons but no data), as shown in Figure 49.

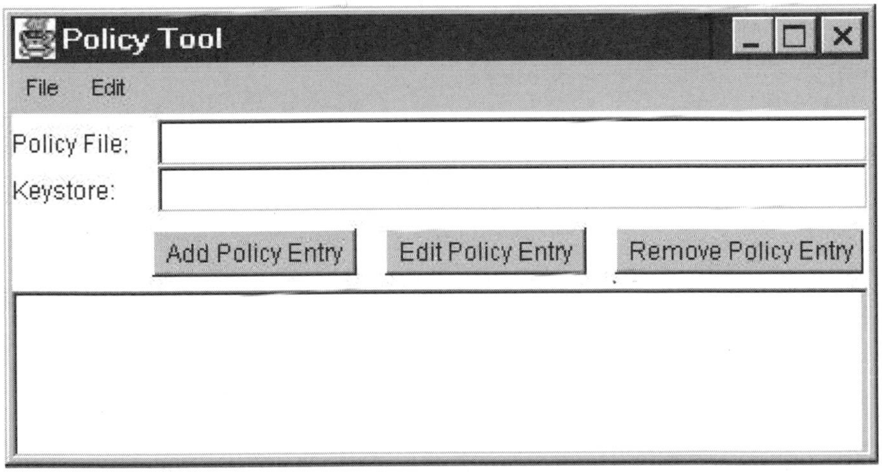

Figure 49 The Policy Tool.

You can then proceed to either open whatever policy file you want to work on or create a new policy file.

The first time you run the Policy Tool, you will see the blank Policy Tool window, since a user policy file does not yet exist. You can immediately proceed to create a new policy file, as described in the next step.

Grant the Required Permission

To grant the `WriteFile` applet permission to create and to write to the `writetest` file, you must create a policy entry granting this permission. To do so, choose the Add Policy Entry button in the main Policy Tool window. This brings up the Policy Entry dialog box, as shown in Figure 50.

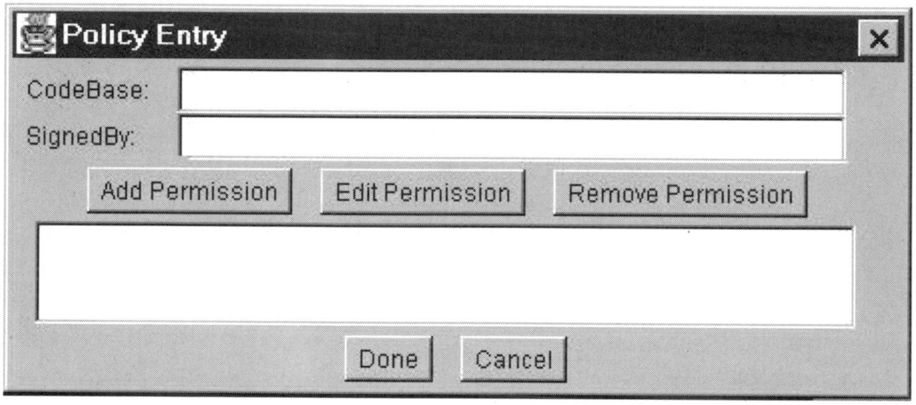

Figure 50 The Policy Entry dialog box.

A policy entry specifies one or more permissions for code from a particular *code source*—code from a particular location (URL), code signed by a particular entity, or both.

The CodeBase and the SignedBy text boxes are used to specify which code you want to grant the permission(s) you will be adding.

- A CodeBase value indicates the code source location; you grant the permission(s) to code from that location. An empty CodeBase entry signifies any code—it doesn't matter where the code originates.
- A SignedBy value indicates the alias for a certificate stored in a keystore. The public key within that certificate is used to verify the digital signature on the code; you grant the permission(s) to code signed by the private key corresponding to the public key in the keystore entry specified by the alias. The SignedBy entry is optional; omitting it signifies any signer, no matter whether the code is signed or by whom.

If you have both a CodeBase and a SignedBy entry, the permission(s) will be granted only to code that is both from the specified location *and* signed by the named alias.

To grant `WriteFile` the permission it needs, you can grant the permission to all code from the location (URL) where `WriteFile.class` is stored. Type the following URL into the CodeBase text box of the Policy Entry dialog box:

```
http://java.sun.com/docs/books/tutorial/security1.2/tour1/
example-1dot2/
```

Note: This is a URL and thus must always have slashes, not backslashes.

Leave the SignedBy text box blank, since the code is not required to be signed.

Note: If you wanted to grant the permission to any code (`.class` file) not just from the directory specified previously but from the `security1.2` directory *and its subdirectories,* you'd type this URL into the CodeBase box: `http://java.sun.com/docs/books/tutorial/security1.2/-` (note the hyphen at the end).

You've specified where the code comes from (the CodeBase) and that the code does not have to be signed (since there's no SignedBy value). Now you are ready to grant permissions to that code. Choose the Add Permission button to bring up the Permissions dialog box as shown in Figure 51.

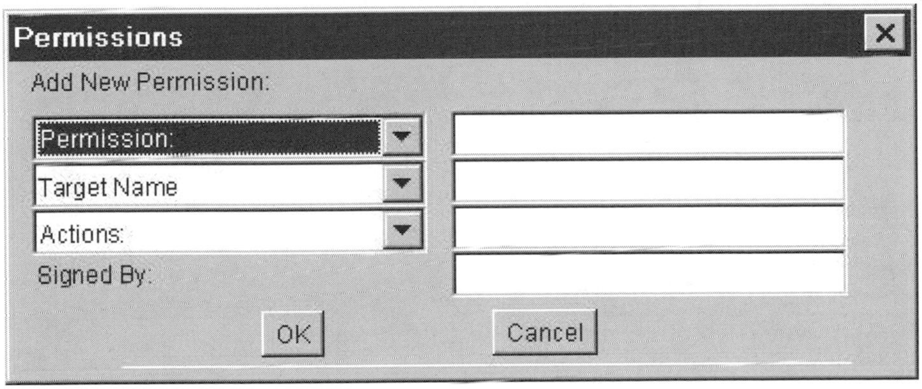

Figure 51 The Permissions dialog box.

Do the following to grant code from the specified CodeBase permission to write (and thus also to create) the file named `writetest`.

- Choose File Permission from the Permission drop-down list. The complete permission type name (`java.io.FilePermission`) now appears in the text box to the right of the drop-down list.
- Type the following in the text box to the right of the list labeled Target Name to specify the file named `writetest`:

  ```
  writetest
  ```

- Specify write access by choosing the write option from the Actions drop-down list.

Now the Permissions dialog box looks like Figure 52.

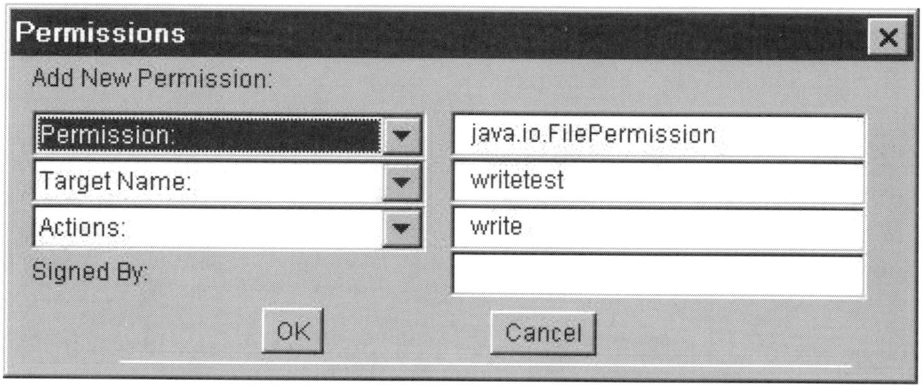

Figure 52 Filled-in Permissions dialog box.

Choose the OK button. The new permission appears in a line in the Policy Entry dialog. So the policy entry window now looks like Figure 53.

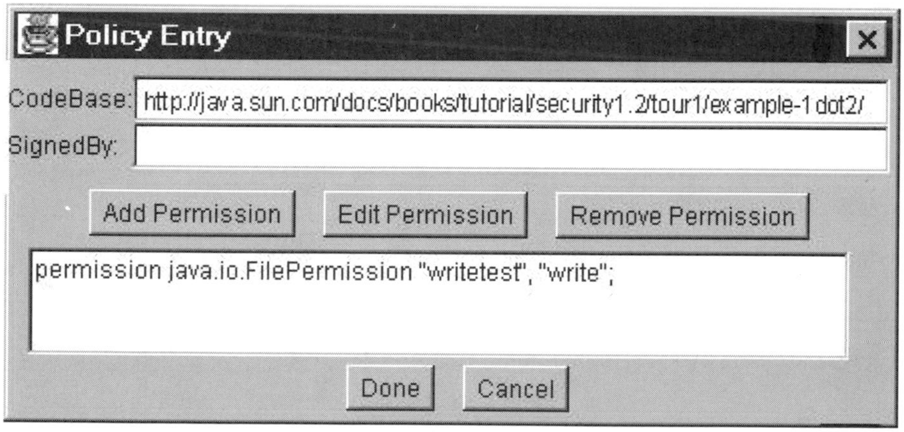

Figure 53 Filled-in Policy Entry dialog box.

You are now done specifying this policy entry, so choose the Done button in the Policy Entry dialog. The Policy Tool window now contains a line representing the policy entry, showing the CodeBase value, as shown in Figure 54.

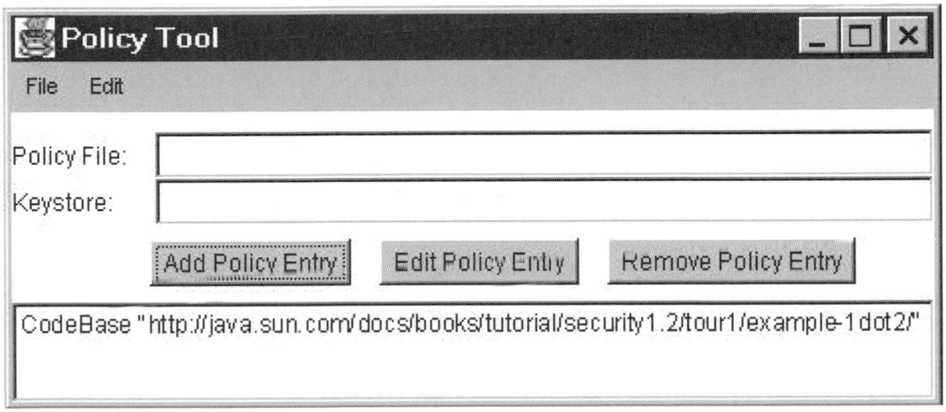

Figure 54 Policy Tool window showing new policy entry.

Save the Policy File

To save the new policy file you've been creating, choose the Save As command from the File menu. This brings up the Save As dialog box.

The examples in this lesson and in the lesson Quick Tour of Controlling Applications (page 503) assume that you stored the policy file in the `Test` directory on the `C:` drive. Navigate the directory structure to get to that directory. Then type the file name `mypolicy` and choose the Save button. The policy file is now saved, and its name and path are shown in the text box labeled Policy File.

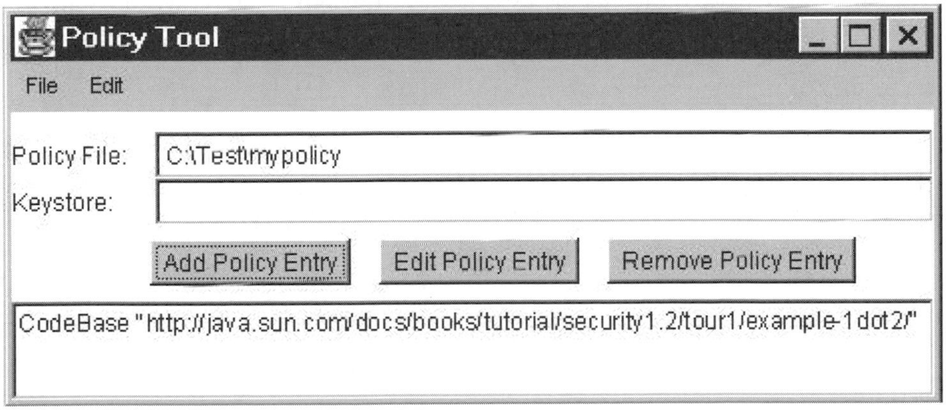

Figure 55 Policy Tool window after policy file is saved.

Exit Policy Tool by choosing the Exit command from the File menu.

See the Policy File Effects

Now that you have created the `mypolicy` policy file, you should be able to successfully execute the `WriteFile` applet to create and to write the file `writetest`, as shown in Figure 56.

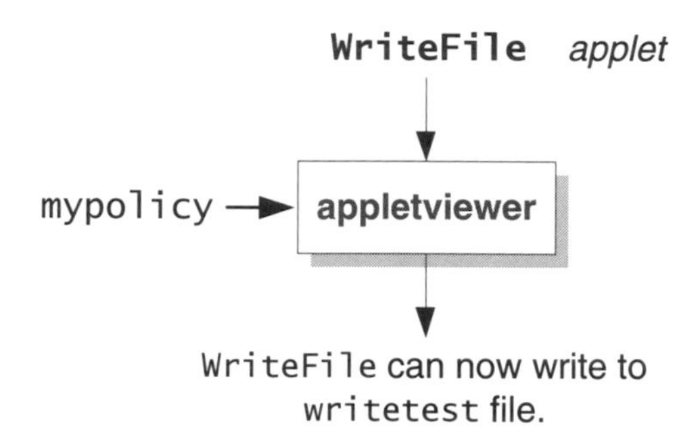

Figure 56 Successful `WriteFile` applet execution.

Whenever you run an applet, or an application with a security manager, the policy files that are loaded and used by default are the ones specified in the *security properties file*, which is located at one of the following:

UNIX:
`java.home/lib/security/java.security`
Win32:
`java.home\lib\security\java.security`

Note that `java.home` indicates the directory into which the JDK was installed.

The policy file locations are specified as the values of properties whose names are of the form

```
policy.url.n
```

Here `n` indicates a number. You specify each such property value in a line of the following form:

```
policy.url.n=URL
```

Here URL is a URL specification. For example, the default policy files, sometimes referred to as the system and user policy files, respectively, are defined in the security properties file as

```
policy.url.1=file:${java.home}/lib/security/java.policy
policy.url.2=file:${user.home}/.java.policy
```

Note: Use of the notation `${propName}` in the security properties file is a way of specifying the value of a property. Thus `${java.home}` will be replaced at runtime by the actual value of the "`java.home`" property, which indicates the directory into which the JDK was stored, and `${user.home}` will be replaced by the value of the `user.home` property, for example, `C:\Windows`.

In the previous step you did not modify one of these policy files. You created a policy file named `mypolicy`. There are two possible ways you can have the `mypolicy` file be considered as part of the overall policy, in addition to the policy files specified in the security properties file. You can either specify the additional policy file in a property passed to the runtime system, described in Approach 1 (page 499), or add a line in the security properties file specifying the additional policy file, discussed in Approach 2 (page 512). To download the program as shown on a UNIX system, you must have DNS configured. Consult your system administrator.

Approach 1

You can use an `appletviewer` command-line argument, `-J-Djava.security.policy`, to specify a policy file that should be used in addition to the ones specified in the security properties file. To run the `WriteFile` applet with the `mypolicy` policy file included, type the following in the directory in which `mypolicy` is stored:

```
appletviewer -J-Djava.security.policy=mypolicy
http://java.sun.com/docs/books/tutorial/security1.2/tour1/
example-1dot2/WriteFile.html
```

This must be typed as a single line, with a space between `mypolicy` and the URL, and no spaces in the URL. Multiple lines are used in the example just for legibility purposes. If this command line is longer than the maximum number of characters you are allowed to type on a single line, do the following. Create a text file containing the full command, and name the file with a `.bat` extension, for example, `wf.bat`. In your command window simply type the name of the `.bat` file instead of the command. This results in execution of the full command.

If the applet still reports an error, something is wrong in the policy file. Use the Policy Tool to open the `mypolicy` file (using File > Open) and check the policy entries you just created in the section Set Up a Policy File (page 492). Change any typos or other errors.

To view or to edit an existing policy entry, select the line for that entry in the main Policy Tool window, then choose the Edit Policy Entry button. Alternatively you can simply double-click the line for that entry.

This brings up the same type of Policy Entry dialog box as appears when you are adding a new policy entry after choosing the Add Policy Entry button, except in this case the dialog box is filled in with the existing policy entry information. To change the information, simply retype it (for the CodeBase and SignedBy values) or add, remove, or modify permissions.

Approach 2

You can specify a number of URLs in `policy.url.n` properties in the security properties file, and all the designated policy files will get loaded. So one way to have our `mypolicy` file's policy entry considered by the `appletviewer` is to add an entry specifying that policy file in the security properties file.

Important: If you are running your own copy of the JDK, you can easily edit your security properties file. If you are running a version shared with others, you may only be able to modify the system-wide security properties file if you have write access to it or if you ask your system administrator to modify the file when appropriate. However, it's probably not appropriate for you to make modifications to a system-wide policy file for this tutorial test. We suggest that you just read the following to see how it's done or that you install your own private version of the JDK to use for the tutorial lessons.

To modify the security properties file, open it in an editor suitable for editing an ASCII text file. Then add the following line after the line starting with `policy.url.2`:

UNIX:

```
policy.url.3=file:${user.home}/test/mypolicy
```

or a line explicitly specifying your home directory, as in:

```
policy.url.3=file:/home/susanj/test/mypolicy
```

Win32:

```
policy.url.3=file:/C:/Test/mypolicy
```

Now you should be able to successfully run the following:

```
appletviewer http://java.sun.com/docs/books/tutorial/
security1.2/tour1/example-1dot2/WriteFile.html
```

Type this command on one line, without spaces in the URL.

As with approach 1, if you still get a security exception, something is wrong in the policy file. Use the Policy Tool to check the policy entry you just created in the previous step, in the section Set Up a Policy File (page 492). Fix any typos or other errors.

Important Note: The `mypolicy` policy file is also used in the lesson Quick Tour of Controlling Applications (page 503). If you will not be completing that lesson, you may want to delete or comment out the line you just added in the security properties file. You probably do not want the `mypolicy` file included when you are not running the lessons in this trail.

http://java.sun.com/docs/books/tutorial/security1.2/tour2/index.html

42

Quick Tour of Controlling Applications

THIS lesson gives another quick tour of how to control access to resources, this time for applications. The lesson shows how resource accesses for applications may be controlled exactly the same as for applets, when the applications are run under a security manager.

This lesson contains the following sections:

Observe Application Freedom

A security manager is *not* automatically installed when an *application* is running. The next section shows how to apply the same security policy to an application found on the local file system as to downloaded applets. But first, let's demonstrate that a security manager is by default not installed for an application, and thus the application has full access to resources, as was always the case in JDK 1.1.

Create a file named `GetProps.java` on your computer. You can find the `GetProps.java` (page 866) source code in the Appendix and on the CD-ROM that accompanies this book.

The examples in this lesson assume that you put `GetProps.java` in the `C:\Test` directory if you're using a Win32 system or in the `~/test` directory on UNIX. As you can see if you examine the source file, this program tries to get (read) the values of various properties, whose names are "`os.name`," "`java.version`," "`user.home`," and "`java.home`." Now compile and run `GetProps.java`. You should see output like the following:

```
C:\TEST>java GetProps
    About to get os.name property value
      The name of your operating system is: Windows 95
    About to get java.version property value
      The version of the JVM you are running is: 1.2
    About to get user.home property value
      Your user home directory is: C:\Windows
    About to get user.name property value
      Your user name is: susanj
    About to get java.home property value
      Your JDK installation directory is: C:\JDK1.2
```

As you can see, the application was allowed to access all the property values, as shown in Figure 57.

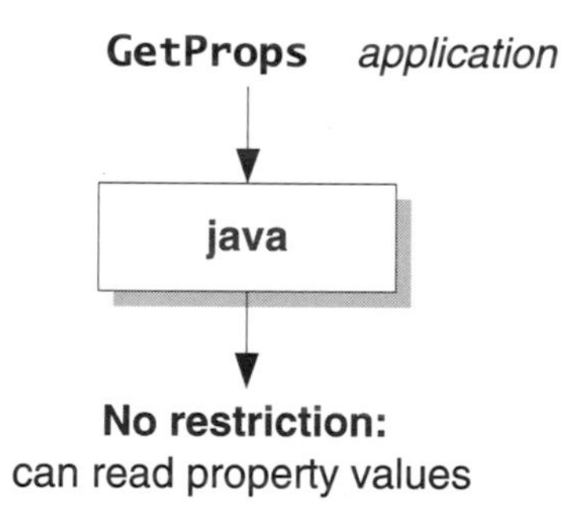

Figure 57 Unrestricted `GetProps` application execution.

See How to Restrict Applications

As you saw in the previous section, a security manager is *not* automatically installed when an *application* is running. To apply the same security policy to an application found on the local file system as to downloaded applcts, you can invoke the interpreter with the new `-Djava.security.manager` command line argument. To execute the `GetProps` application with the default security manager, type the following:

```
java -Djava.security.manager GetProps
```

Here's the output from the program:

```
C:\TEST>java -Djava.security.manager GetProps
   About to get os.name property value
     The name of your operating system is: Windows 95
   About to get java.version property value
     The version of the JVM you are running is: JDK 1.2
   About to get user.home property value
   Caught exception java.security.AccessControlException:
    access denied (java.util.PropertyPermission user.home read)
```

The process is shown in Figure 58.

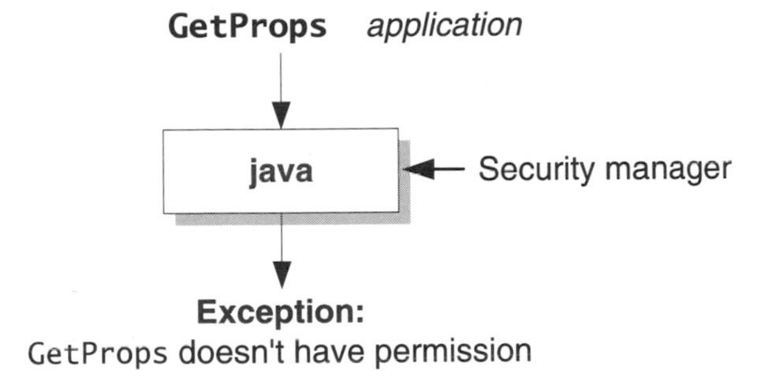

Figure 58 Running GetProps with a security manager.

Security-Sensitive Properties

The system policy file, loaded by default, grants all code permission to access some commonly useful properties, such as "os.name" and "java.version." These properties are not security-sensitive, so granting such permissions does not pose a problem.

The other properties GetProps tries to access, "user.home" and "java.home," are *not* among the properties for which the system policy file grants read permission. Thus as soon as GetProps attempts to access the first of these properties ("user.home"), the security manager prevents the access and reports an AccessControlException. This exception indicates that the policy currently in effect, which consists of entries in one or more policy files, doesn't allow permission to read the "user.home" property.

The System Policy File

The system policy file is by default located at:

UNIX:
```
java.home/lib/security/java.policy
```
Win32:
```
java.home\lib\security\java.policy
```

Note that *java.home* represents the value of the "`java.home`" property, which is a system property specifying the directory into which the JDK was installed. Thus if the JDK was installed in the directory named `C:\jdk1.2` on Win32 and `/jdk1.2` on UNIX, the system policy file is located at

UNIX:
```
/jdk1.2/lib/security/java.policy
```
Win32:
```
C:\jdk1.2\lib\security\java.policy
```

You can see the complete system policy file, java.policy (page 867), in the Appendix.

Set Up the Policy File

You will now use the Policy Tool to open the policy file named `mypolicy` created in the lesson Quick Tour of Controlling Applets (page 491). You will add a new policy entry granting permission for code from the directory where `GetProps.class` is stored to read the "`user.home`" and the "`java.home`" property values, as shown in Figure 59.

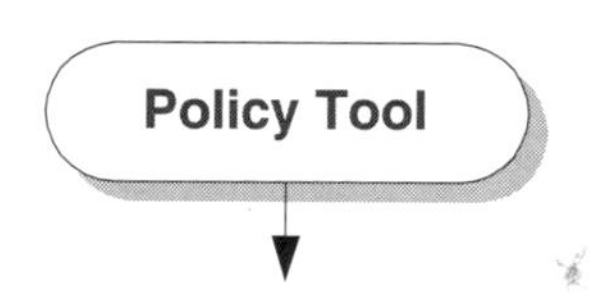

Figure 59 Result of using Policy Tool.

The steps are as follows. First, the policy file is opened. Then the required permissions are granted. Finally, the policy file is saved.

Note for UNIX Users: The instructions illustrate creating the policy file for a Win32 system. The steps are exactly the same if you arc working on a UNIX system, but with the following differences.

- You retrieve the `mypolicy` file from the `test` directory in your home directory.
- For the CodeBase URL in the step for granting the required permissions, you can substitute `file:${user.home}/test/` for `file:/C:/Test/`. Alternatively you could directly specify your home directory rather than referring to the `user.home` property, as in `file:/home/susanj/test/`.

Open the Policy File

Start the Policy Tool by typing the following at the command line:

```
policytool
```

This brings up the Policy Tool window. To open the `mypolicy` policy file, use the Open command in the File menu. This will present you with an Open dialog, which you can use to navigate the directory structure until you get to the directory containing the policy file (that is, the `C:\Test directory).`

Choose the `mypolicy` file in that directory and then the Open button (Figure 60). This will fill in the Policy Tool window with information from the `mypolicy` policy file, including the policy file name and the CodeBase part of the policy entry created in the lesson Quick Tour of Controlling Applets (page 491).

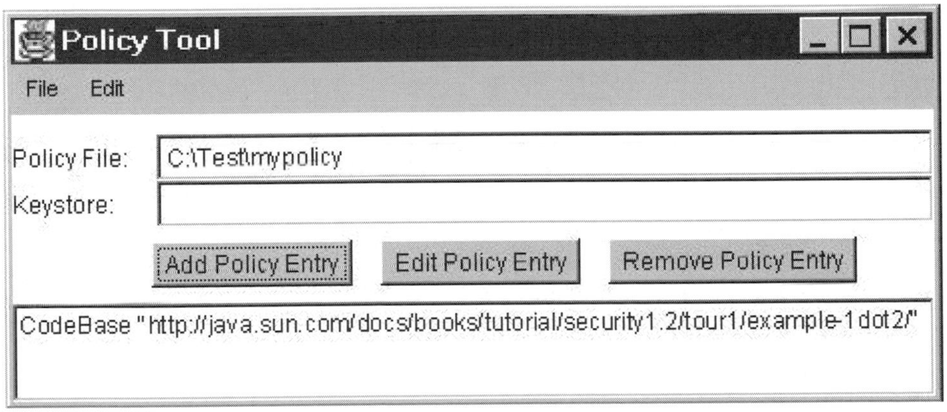

Figure 60 The opened `mypolicy` policy file.

Grant the Required Permissions

To grant the `GetProps` application permission to read the "`user.home`" and the "`java.home`" property values, you must create a policy entry granting those permissions. Choose the Add Policy Entry button in the main Policy Tool window. This brings up the Policy Entry dialog box as shown in Figure 61.

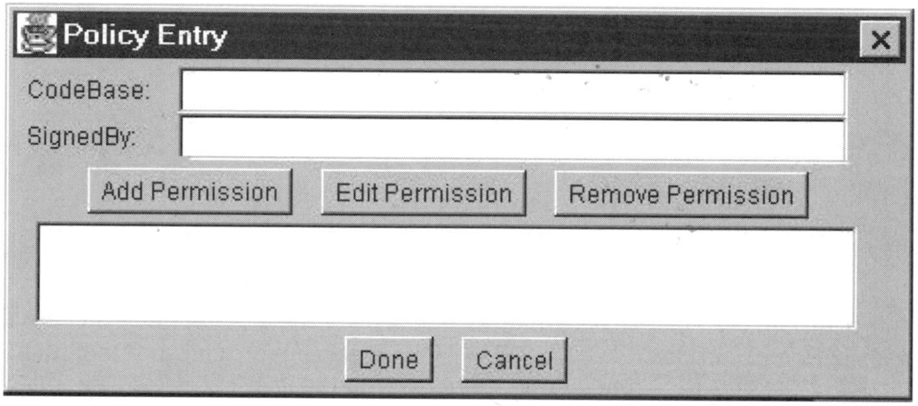

Figure 61 The Policy Entry dialog box.

Type this file URL, `file:/C:/Test/`, into the CodeBase text box to indicate that you are going to be granting a permission to code from the specified directory, which is the directory in which `GetProps.class` is stored. Leave the "Signed By" text box blank, since the code is not required to be signed.

To add permission to read the "`user.home`" property value, choose the Add Permission button. This brings up the Permissions dialog box as shown in Figure 62.

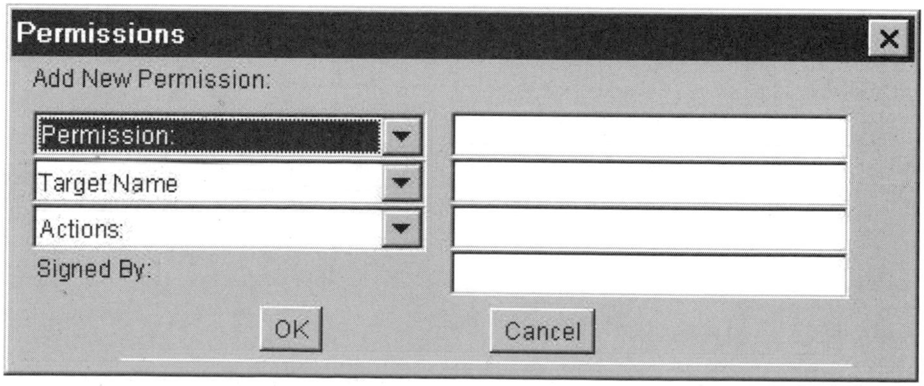

Figure 62 The Permissions dialog box.

Do the following.

1. Choose Property Permission from the Permission drop-down list. The complete permission type name (`java.util.PropertyPermission`) now appears in the text box to the right of the drop-down list.
2. Type the following in the text box to the right of the list labeled Target Name to specify the "`user.home`" property:

   ```
   user.home
   ```
3. Specify permission to read this property by choosing the read option from the Actions drop-down list.

Now the Permissions dialog box looks like Figure 63.

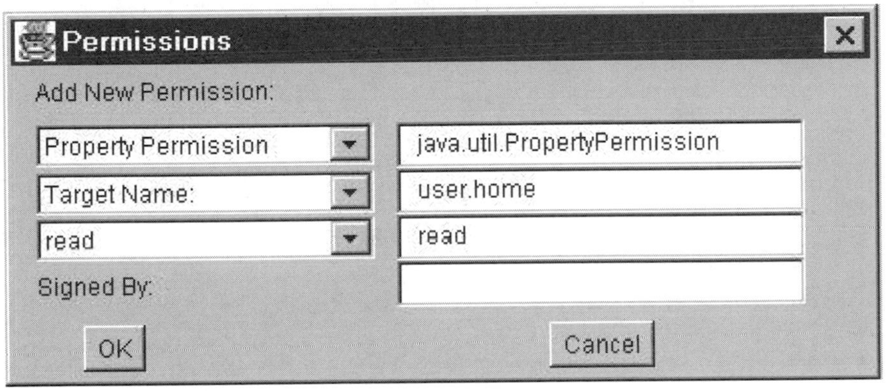

Permissions

Add New Permission:

Property Permission	java.util.PropertyPermission
Target Name:	user.home
read	read
Signed By:	

OK | Cancel

Figure 63 Policy Entry dialog box with first property permission.

Choose the OK button. The new permission appears in a line in the policy entry window, as shown in Figure 64.

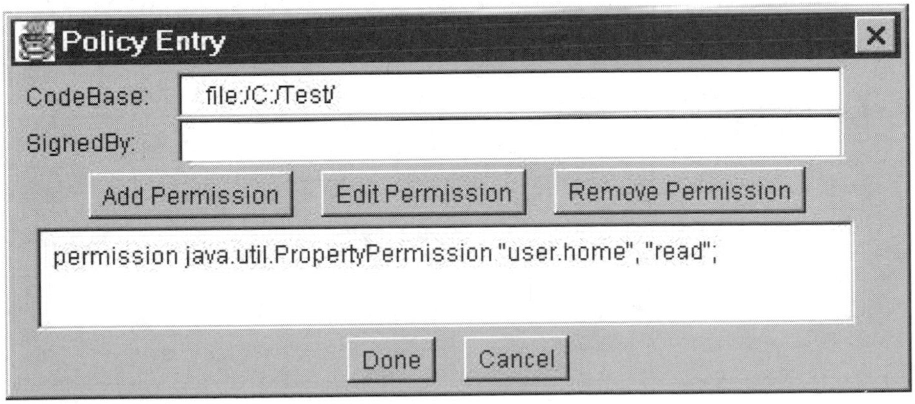

Policy Entry

CodeBase: file:/C:/Test/

SignedBy:

Add Permission | Edit Permission | Remove Permission

permission java.util.PropertyPermission "user.home", "read";

Done | Cancel

Figure 64 Policy Entry dialog box with first permission.

To add permission to read the "`java.home`" property value, choose the Add Permission button again. In the Permissions dialog box, do the following:

1. Choose Property Permission from the Permission drop-down list.
2. Type the following in the text box to the right of the list labeled Target Name to specify the "`java.home`" property:

   ```
   java.home
   ```

3. Specify permission to read this property by choosing the read option from the Actions drop-down list.

Now the Permissions dialog box looks like Figure 65.

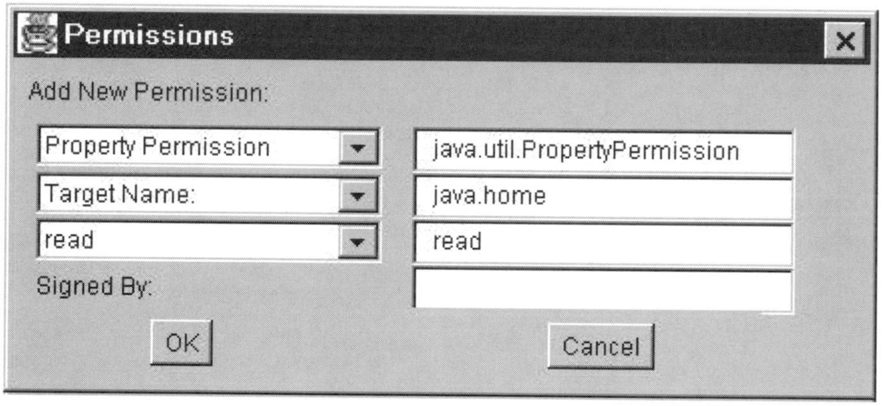

Figure 65 Permissions dialog box with second property permission.

Choose the OK button. The new permission and the previously added permission appear in lines in the Policy Entry window, as shown in Figure 66.

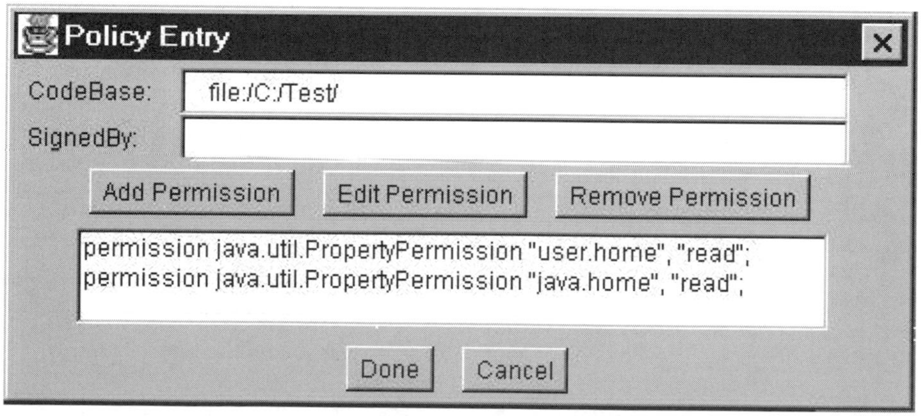

Figure 66 Policy Entry dialog box with both permissions.

You are now done specifying this policy entry, so choose the Done button in the Policy Entry dialog. The Policy Tool window now includes a line representing the new policy entry, showing the CodeBase value.

Save the Policy File

To save the policy file, simply choose the Save command in the File menu.

Then exit Policy Tool by choosing the Exit command from the File menu.

See the Policy File Effects

Now that you have added the required policy entry to the `mypolicy` policy file, you should be able to successfully read the specified properties when you execute the `GetProps` application with a security manager, as shown in Figure 67.

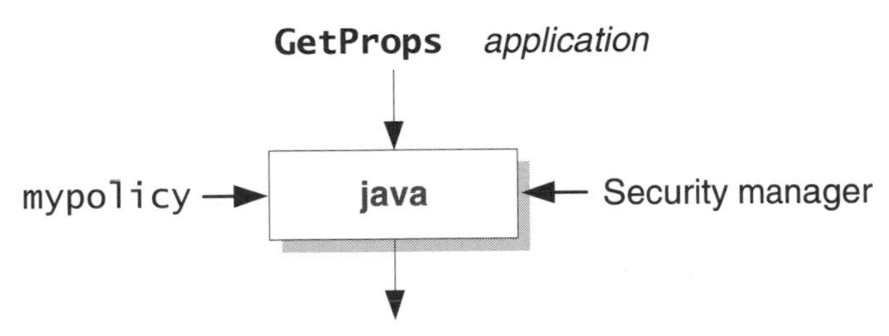

Figure 67 Successful `GetProps` execution with a security manager.

As noted at the end of the lesson Quick Tour of Controlling Applets (page 491), whenever you run an applet, or an application with a security manager, the policy files that are loaded and used by default are the ones specified in the *security properties file*, which is located at

UNIX:
    java.home`/lib/security/java.security`
Win32:
    java.home`\lib\security\java.security`

Note that *`java.home`* indicates the directory into which the JDK was installed.

There are two possible ways you can have the `mypolicy` file be considered as part of the overall policy, in addition to the policy files specified in the security properties file. You can either specify the additional policy file in a property passed to the runtime system (approach 1) or you can add a line in the security properties file specifying the additional policy file (approach 2).

Approach 1

You can use a `-Djava.security.policy` interpreter command line argument to specify a policy file that should be used in addition to the ones specified in the security properties file. Make sure that you are in the directory containing `GetProps.class` and `mypolicy`. Then you can run the `GetProps` application and pass the `mypolicy` policy file to the interpreter by typing

```
java -Djava.security.manager -Djava.security.policy=mypolicy
     GetProps
```

Recall that `-Djava.security.manager` is required in order to run an application with a security manager, as shown in the section See How to Restrict Applications (page 504). The program should report the values of the "`user.home`" and the "`java.home`" properties.

If the application still reports an error, something is wrong in the policy file. Use the Policy Tool to check the policy entry you just created in the section Set Up the Policy File (page 506). Then fix any typos or other errors.

Approach 2

You can specify a number of URLs in `policy.url.n` properties in the security properties file, and all the designated policy files will get loaded. So one way to have your `mypolicy` file's policy entries considered by the `java` interpreter is to add an entry specifying that policy file in the security properties file.

You created such an entry in the last part of the lesson Quick Tour of Controlling Applets (page 491). If your security properties file still has that entry, you're ready to run the application. Otherwise you need to add the entry. To do so, open the security properties file in an editor suitable for editing an ASCII text file. Then add the following line after the line containing `policy.url.2`. If you're on a Win32 system, add

```
policy.url.3=file:/C:/Test/mypolicy
```

If you're on a UNIX system, add

```
policy.url.3=file:${user.home}/test/mypolicy
```

Alternatively you can explicitly specify your home directory, as in

```
policy.url.3=file:/home/susanj/test/mypolicy
```

Run the Application

Now you should be able to successfully run the following

```
java -Djava.security.manager GetProps
```

As with approach 1, if you still get a security exception, something is wrong in the policy file. Use the Policy Tool to check the policy entry you just created in the section Set Up the Policy File (page 506). Then fix any typos or other errors.

Important: Before continuing, you may want to delete the line you just added in the security properties file (or comment it out), since you probably do not want the `mypolicy` file included when you are not running the tutorial lessons.

43 Secure Code and File Exchanges

THIS lesson contains overview information to help you understand why digital signatures, certificates, and keystores are needed. The lesson also compares use of the tools versus the JDK Security API with respect to generating signatures. Such tool usage is demonstrated in the next two lessons, Signing Code and Granting It Permissions (page 525) and Exchanging Files (page 541). API usage is demonstrated in the lesson Generating and Verifying Signatures (page 549).

This lesson contains the following sections.

Code and Document Security

If you electronically send someone an important document (or documents), or an applet or application to run, the recipient needs a way of verifying that the document or code came from you and was not modified in transit (for example, by a malicious user intercepting it). Digital signatures, certificates, and keystores all help ensure the security of the files you send.

Digital Signatures

The basic idea in the use of digital signatures is as follows.

1. You sign the document or code using one of your *private keys*, which you can generate by using `keytool` or security API methods. That is, you generate a digital signature for the document or code, using the `jarsigner` tool or API methods.
2. You send to the other person, the "receiver," the document or code and the signature.
3. You also supply the receiver with the *public key* corresponding to the private key used to generate the signature, if the receiver doesn't already have it.
4. The receiver uses the public key to verify the authenticity of the signature and the integrity of the document/code.

A receiver needs to ensure that the public key *itself* is authentic before reliably using it to check the signature's authenticity. Therefore it is more typical to supply a *certificate* containing the public key rather than just the public key itself.

For more information about the terminology and concepts of signing and verification, and further explanation of the benefits, see Understanding Signing and Verification (page 590) in the JAR File Format trail.

Certificates

A certificate contains the following:

- A public key.
- The "distinguished-name" information of the entity (person, company, or so on) whose certificate it is. This entity is referred to as the certificate *subject* or *owner*. The distinguished-name information includes the following attributes (or a subset): the entity's name, organizational unit, organization, city or locality, state or province, and country code.
- A digital signature. A certificate is signed by one entity, the *issuer*, to vouch for the fact that the enclosed public key is the actual public key of another entity, the owner.
- The distinguished-name information for the signer (issuer).

One way for a recipient to check whether a certificate is valid is by verifying its digital signature, using its issuer's (signer's) public key. That key may itself be stored in another certificate whose signature can be verified by using the public key of that other certificate's issuer, and that key may *also* be stored in yet *another* certificate, and so on. You can stop checking when you reach a public key that you already trust and use it to verify the signature on the corresponding certificate.

If the recipient cannot establish such a trust chain—for example, because the required issuer certificates are not available—the certificate *fingerprint(s)* can be calculated, as may be done by the commands `keytool -import` or `keytool -printcert`. Each fingerprint is a relatively short number that uniquely and reliably identifies the certificate. (Technically the fingerprint is a hash value of the certificate information, using a message digest function.) The recipient can call up the certificate owner and compare the fingerprints of the received certificate with those of the certificate that was sent. If the fingerprints are the same, the certificates are the same.

Thus you can ensure that a certificate was not modified in transit. One other potential uncertainty when working with certificates is the identity of the sender. Sometimes a certificate is *self-signed*, that is, signed using the private key corresponding to the public key in the certificate; the issuer is the same as the subject. This is okay if the receiver already knows and trusts the sender.

Otherwise the sender needs to obtain a certificate from a trusted third party, referred to as a certification authority (CA). To do so, you send a self-signed certificate signing request (CSR) to the CA. The CA verifies the signature on the CSR and your identity, perhaps by checking your driver's license or other information. The CA then vouches for your being the owner of the public key by issuing a certificate and signing it with its own (the CA's) private key. Anybody who trusts the issuing CA's public key can now verify the signature on the certificate. In many cases the issuing CA itself may have a certificate from a CA higher up in the CA hierarchy, leading to *certificate chains*.

Certificates of entities you trust are typically imported into your keystore as *trusted certificates*. The public key in each such certificate may then be used to verify signatures generated using the corresponding private key. Such verifications can be done by the `jarsigner` tool (if the document/code and signature appear in a JAR file), API methods, or the runtime system, when a resource access is attempted and a policy file specifies that the resource access is allowed for the code attempting the access if its signature is authentic. The code's class file(s) and signature must be in a JAR file.

If you are sending signed code or documents to others, you need to supply them with the certificate containing the public key corresponding to the private key used to sign the code/document. The `keytool -export` command or API methods can export your certificate from your keystore to a file, which can then be sent to anyone needing it. A person who receives the certificate can import it into the keystore as a trusted certificate, using, for example, API methods or the `keytool -import` command.

If you use the `jarsigner` tool to generate a signature for a JAR file, the tool retrieves your certificate and its supporting certificate chain from your keystore. The tool then stores them, along with the signature, in the JAR file.

Keystores

Private keys and their associated public key certificates are stored in password-protected databases called *keystores*. A keystore can contain two types of entries: the trusted certificate entries and key/certificate entries, each containing a private key and the corresponding public key certificate. Each entry in a keystore is identified by an *alias*.

A keystore owner can have multiple keys in the keystore, accessed via different aliases. An alias is typically named after a particular role in which the keystore owner uses the associated key. An alias may also identify the purpose of the key. For example, the alias `signPersonalEmail` might be used to identify a keystore entry whose private key is used for signing personal e-mail, and the alias `signJarFiles` might be used to identify an entry whose private key is used for signing JAR files.

The `keytool` tool can be used to

- Create private keys and their associated public key certificates
- Issue certificate requests, which you send to the appropriate certification authority
- Import certificate replies, obtained from the certification authority you contacted
- Import public key certificates belonging to other parties as trusted certificates
- Manage your keystore

API methods can also be used to access and to modify a keystore.

Tool and API Notes

Note the following regarding use of the tools and the API related to digital signatures.

- You can use the JDK Security API, tools, or a combination to generate keys and signatures and to import certificates. You can use these API or tool features to securely exchange documents with others.
- To use the *tools* for document exchange, the document(s) must be placed in a JAR (Java ARchive) file, which may be created by the `jar` tool. A JAR file is a good way of encapsulating multiple files in one spot. When a file is "signed," the resulting digital signature bytes need to be stored somewhere. When a JAR file is signed, the signature can go in the JAR file itself. This is what happens when you use the `jarsigner` tool to sign a JAR file.
- If you are creating applet code that you will sign, it needs to be placed in a JAR file. The same is true if you are creating application code that may be similarly restricted by running it with a security manager. The reason you need the JAR file is that when a policy file specifies that code signed by a particular entity is permitted one or more operations, such as specific file reads or writes, the code is expected to come from a signed JAR file. (The term "signed code" is an abbreviated way of saying "code in a class file that appears in a JAR file that was signed.")
- In order for the runtime system to check a code signature, the person/organization that will run the code first needs to import into their keystore a certificate authenticating the public key corresponding to the private key used to sign the code.
- In order for the `jarsigner` tool to verify the authenticity of a JAR file signature, the person/organization that received the JAR file first needs to import into their keystore a certificate authenticating the public key corresponding to the private key used to sign the code.
- At this time there are no APIs for certificate creation.

Use of the Security API to Sign Documents

The lesson Generating and Verifying Signatures (page 549) demonstrates the use of the JDK Security API with respect to signing documents. The lesson shows what one program, executed by the person who has the original document, would do to generate keys, generate a digital signature for the document using the private key, and export the public key and the signature to files. Then it shows an example of another program, executed by the receiver of the document, signature, and public key. It shows how the program could import the public key and verify the authenticity of the signature. The lesson also discusses and demonstrates possible alternative approaches and methods of supplying and importing keys, including in certificates.

Use of the Tools to Sign Code or Documents

The lesson Signing Code and Granting It Permissions (page 525) shows use of the tools by a code developer to put code into a JAR file, sign it, and export the public key. Then it shows use of the tools by someone who will run the code or a system administrator to import the signer's public key certificate and add an entry into a policy file granting the code permission for the resource accesses it needs.

The lesson Exchanging Files (page 541) shows use of the tools by one person to sign an important document, such as a contract, and export the public key certificate for the public key corresponding to the private key used to sign the contract. Then it shows how another person receiving the contract, the signature, and the public key certificate would use `keytool` to import the certificate and the `jarsigner` tool to verify the signature.

These two lessons have much in common. In both cases the first two steps for the code or document sender are to

1. Create a JAR file containing the document or class file, using the `jar` tool.
2. Generate keys (if they don't already exist), using the `keytool -genkey` command.

The next two steps are optional.

3. Use the `keytool -certreq` command; then send the resulting certificate signing request to a certification authority (CA), such as VeriSign.
4. Use the `keytool -import` command to import the CA's response.

The next two steps are required.

5. Sign the JAR file, using the `jarsigner` tool and the private key generated in step 2.
6. Export the public key certificate, using the `keytool -export` command. Then supply the signed JAR file and the certificate to the receiver.

In both cases the receiver of the signed JAR file and the certificate should import the certificate as a trusted certificate, using the `keytool -import` command. The `keytool` will try to construct a trust chain from the certificate to be imported to an already trusted certificate in the keystore. If that fails, the `keytool` will display the certificate fingerprint and prompt you to verify it.

If what was sent was code, the receiver also needs to modify a policy file to permit the required resource accesses to code signed by the private key corresponding to the public key in the imported certificate. The Policy Tool can be used to do this.

If what was sent was one or more documents, the receiver needs to verify the authenticity of the JAR file signature, using the `jarsigner` tool.

This section discusses the two optional steps 3 and 4. The other steps are covered in the next two lessons, Signing Code and Granting It Permissions (page 525) and Exchanging Files (page 541).

Generating a Certificate Signing Request (CSR) for a Public Key Certificate

When `keytool` is used to generate public/private key pairs, it creates a keystore entry containing a private key and a self-signed certificate for the public key. (That is, the certificate is signed using the corresponding private key.) This may be adequate if the people receiving your signed files already know and trust your identity.

However, a certificate is more likely to be trusted by others if it is signed by a certification authority (CA). To get a certificate signed by a CA, you first generate a certificate signing request (CSR), via a command such as the following:

```
keytool -certreq -alias alias -file csrFile
```

Here *`alias`* is used to access the keystore entry containing the private key and the public key certificate, and *`csrFile`* specifies the name to be used for the CSR created by this command.

You then submit this file to a CA, such as VeriSign, Inc. The CA will authenticate you, the requestor ("subject"), usually off line, and then will sign and return a certificate authenticating your public key. That is, the CA vouches that you are the owner of the public key by signing the certificate. (In some cases, the CA will return a chain of certificates, each one authenticating the public key of the signer of the previous certificate in the chain.)

Importing the Response from the CA

If you submitted a certificate signing request (CSR) to a certification authority (CA), you need to replace the original self-signed certificate in your keystore with a certificate chain by importing the certificate (or chain of certificates) returned to you by the CA. But first you need a "trusted certificate" entry in your keystore (or in the `cacerts` keystore file) that authenticates the *CA*'s public key. With such an entry the CA's signature can be verified. That is, the CA's signature on the certificate, or on the final certificate in the chain the CA sends to you in response to your CSR, can be verified.

Importing a Certificate from a CA as a "Trusted Certificate"

Before you import the certificate reply from a CA, you need one or more "trusted certificates" in your keystore or in the `cacerts` file.

- If the certificate reply is a certificate chain, you just need the top certificate of the chain—the "root" CA certificate authenticating that CA's public key.
- If the certificate reply is a single certificate, you need a certificate for the issuing CA (the one that signed it). If that certificate is not self-signed, you need a certificate for its signer, and so on, up to a self-signed "root" CA certificate.

The `cacerts` file represents a system-wide keystore with CA certificates. This file resides in the JDK security properties directory, *`java.home`*`/lib/security`, where *`java.home`* is the JDK installation directory.

The `cacerts` file currently ships with five VeriSign root CA certificates. If you sent your CSR to VeriSign, you won't need to import a VeriSign certificate as a trusted certificate in your keystore; you can go on to the next section to see how to import the certificate reply from the CA.

A certificate from a CA is usually either self-signed or signed by another CA, in which case you also need a certificate authenticating that CA's public key. Suppose that company ABC, Inc., is a CA and that you obtain a file named `ABCCA.cer`, purportedly a self-signed certificate from ABC, authenticating that CA's public key.

Be very careful to ensure that the certificate is valid prior to importing it as a "trusted" certificate! View it first (using the `keytool -printcert` command or the `keytool -import` command without the `-noprompt` option), and make sure that the displayed certificate fingerprint(s) match the expected ones. You can call the person who sent the certificate and compare the fingerprint(s) that you see with the ones that they show or that a secure public key repository shows. Only if the fingerprints are equal is it guaranteed that the certificate has not been replaced in transit with somebody else's (for example, an attacker's) certificate. If such an attack took place and you did not check the certificate before you imported it, you would end up trusting anything the attacker has signed.

If you trust that the certificate is valid, you can add it to your keystore via a command such as the following:

```
keytool -import -alias alias -file ABCCA.cer -keystore
        storefile
```

This command creates a "trusted certificate" entry in the keystore whose name is that specified in *storefile*. The entry contains the data from the file ABCCA.cer, and it is assigned the specified alias.

Importing the Certificate Reply from the CA

Once you've imported the required trusted certificate(s), as described in the previous section, or they are already in your keystore or in the cacerts file, you can import the certificate reply and thereby replace your self-signed certificate with a certificate chain. This chain will be either the one returned by the CA in response to your request (if the CA reply is a chain) or one constructed (if the CA reply is a single certificate) by using the certificate reply and trusted certificates that are already available in the keystore or in the cacerts keystore file.

As an example, suppose that you sent your certificate signing request to VeriSign. You can then import the reply via the following, which assumes that the returned certificate is in the file specified by *certReplyFile*:

```
keytool -import -trustcacerts -keystore storefile -alias alias
        -file certReplyFile
```

Type this command on one line.

The certificate reply is validated by using trusted certificates from the keystore and optionally by using the certificates configured in the cacerts keystore file (if the -trustcacerts option is specified). Each certificate in the chain is verified, using the certificate at the next level higher in the chain. You need to trust only the top-level "root" CA certificate in the chain. If you do not already trust the top-level certificate, keytool will display the fingerprint of that certificate and ask whether you want to trust it.

The new certificate chain of the specified (by *alias*) entry replaces the old certificate (or chain) associated with this entry. The old chain can be replaced only if a valid *keypass*, the password used to protect the private key of the entry, is supplied. If no password is provided and if the private key password is different from the keystore password, the user is prompted for it.

For more detailed information about generating CSRs and importing certificate replies, see the keytool documentation.[1]

---

[1] Win32: http://java.sun.com/products/jdk/1.2/docs/tooldocs/win32/keytool.html
UNIX: http://java.sun.com/products/jdk/1.2/docs/tooldocs/solaris/keytool.html

http://java.sun.com/docs/books/tutorial/security1.2/toolsign/index.html

44

Signing Code and Granting It Permissions

THIS lesson illustrates the use of the security-related tools (`keytool`, `jarsigner`, and Policy Tool). It also shows use of the `jar` tool to place files in JAR (Java ARchive) files for subsequent signing by the `jarsigner` tool.

In this lesson you first execute steps to create an application, put it in a JAR file, sign the JAR file, and export the public key certificate corresponding to the private key used to sign the JAR file. For convenience, you pretend to be Susan Jones and you supply information about her when you generate the keys.

Then you act as the recipient of the signed JAR file and the certificate. For convenience, you pretend to be Ray. You see how the signed application cannot normally read a file when it is run under a security manager. Then you use `keytool` to import the certificate into Ray's keystore in an entry aliased by `susan`, and the Policy Tool to create an entry in Ray's policy file to permit code signed by `susan` to read the specified file. Finally, you see how the application running under a security manager can now read the file, since it has been granted permission.

For further information about digital signatures, certificates, keystores, and the tools, see the lesson Secure Code and File Exchanges (page 515).

Important Note: You need to do everything in this lesson while working in the directory in which you store the sample application, but you should store the data file needed by the application in a different directory. All of the examples assume that you are working in the `C:\Test` directory and that the data file is in the `C:\TestData` directory. If you are working on a UNIX system, substitute your own directory names.

The two sections in this lesson outline the steps.

- Steps for the Code Signer (page 526)
- Steps for the Code Receiver (page 530)

Steps for the Code Signer

The steps you take as the code signer are:

1. Download and try the sample application.
2. Create a JAR file.
3. Generate keys, if they don't already exist.

Optional Step: Generate a certificate signing request (CSR) for the public key certificate and import the response from the certification authority. For simplicity (and since you are only pretending to be Susan Jones), this step is omitted. See the section Generating a Certificate Signing Request (CSR) for a Public Key Certificate (page 521) for more information.

---

4. Sign the JAR file, using the `jarsigner` tool and the private key.
5. Export the public key certificate, using the `keytool -export` command. Then supply the signed JAR file and the certificate to the receiver Ray.

These steps are shown in Figure 68.

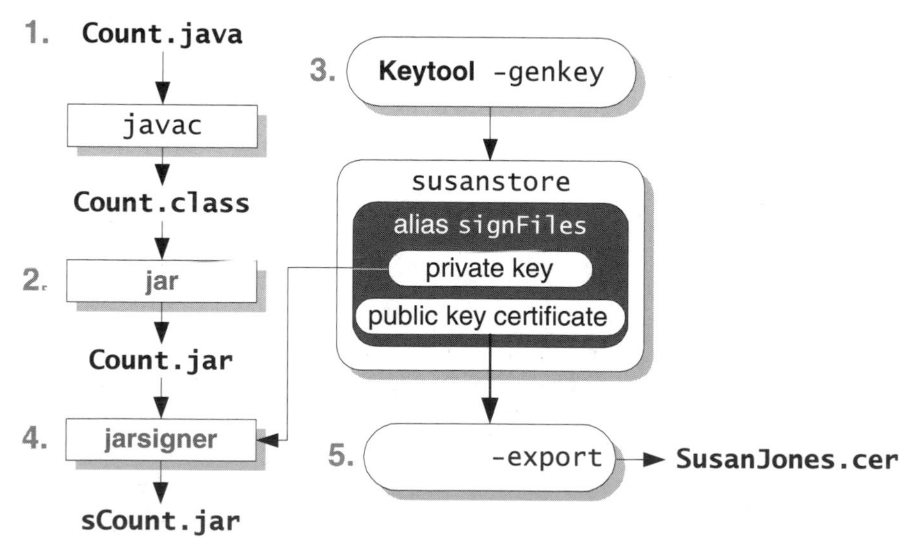

Figure 68 Code signer steps.

Try the Sample Application

The application used by this lesson is supplied for you. Create a file named `Count.java` on your computer. You can find the `Count.java` (page 869) source code in the Appendix and on the CD-ROM that accompanies this book. The examples in this lesson assume that you place the source file in the `C:\Test` directory.

Now compile and then run the `Count` application to see what it does. You need to specify (as an argument) the path name of a file to be read. You can use the sample file named `data`, which is on the CD-ROM that accompanies this book,[1] or any other file you like.

Important: For this lesson put the data file in a directory other than the directory containing the `Count` application.The examples assume that you put the data file in the `C:\TestData` directory. Later in this lesson you will see how an application running under a security manager cannot read a file unless it has explicit permission to do so. However, an application can *always* read a file from the same directory (or a subdirectory); it does not need explicit permission.

A sample run is the following; the bold indicates what you should type.

```
C:\Test>java Count C:\TestData\data
Counted 65 chars.
```

Create a JAR File Containing the Class File

Next, create a JAR file containing the `Count.class` file. Type the following in your command window:

```
jar cvf Count.jar Count.class
```

This command creates a JAR file, `Count.jar`, and places the `Count.class` file inside it.

Generate Keys

If a code signer does not yet have a suitable private key for signing the code, the key must first be generated, along with a corresponding public key that can be used by the code receiver's runtime system to verify the signature. Since this les-

---

[1] The `data` file is also available online here: http://java.sun.com/docs/books/tutorial/security1.2/toolsign/example-1dot2/data.

son assumes that you don't yet have such keys, you are going to create a keystore named `susanstore` and create an entry with a newly generated public/private key pair (with the public key in a certificate).

Now pretend that you are Susan Jones and that you work in company ABC's purchasing department.

Type the following command in your command window to create a keystore named `susanstore` and to generate keys for Susan Jones:

```
keytool -genkey -alias signFiles -keypass kpi135
        -keystore susanstore -storepass ab987c
```

(This must be typed as a single line.)

Subparts of the keytool Command

Let's look at what each of the `keytool` subparts mean.

- The command for generating keys is *`-genkey`*.
- The *`-alias signFiles`* subpart indicates the alias to be used in the future to refer to the keystore entry containing the keys that will be generated.
- The *`-keypass kpi135`* subpart specifies a password for the private key about to be generated. This password will always need to be used in order to access the keystore entry containing that key. The entry doesn't have to have its own password; if you don't include a *`-keypass`* option, you will be prompted for the key password and given the option of letting it be the same as the keystore password.
- The *`-keystore susanstore`* subpart indicates the name (and optionally path) of the keystore you are creating or already using.
- The *`-storepass ab987c`* subpart indicates the keystore password. If you don't include a `-storepass` option, you will be prompted for the keystore password.

For security reasons you actually should not supply your key or keystore passwords on the command line, because they can be intercepted more easily that way. Instead you should leave off the `-keypass` and the `-storepass` options and type your passwords when you are prompted for them.

Distinguished-Name Information

If you use the preceding command, you will be prompted for your distinguished-name information. Following are the prompts; the bold indicates what you should type.

```
What is your first and last name?
  [Unknown]:  Susan Jones
What is the name of your organizational unit?
  [Unknown]:  Purchasing
What is the name of your organization?
  [Unknown]:  ABC
What is the name of your City or Locality?
  [Unknown]:  Cupertino
What is the name of your State or Province?
  [Unknown]:  CA
What is the two-letter country code for this unit?
  [Unknown]:  US
Is <CN=Susan Jones, OU=Purchasing, O=ABC, L=Cupertino, ST=CA,
C=US> correct?
  [no]:  y
```

Command Results

The `keytool` command creates the keystore named `susanstore` (if it doesn't already exist) in the same directory in which the command is executed and assigns it the password `ab987c`. The command generates a public/private key pair for the entity whose distinguished name has a common name of Susan Jones and the organizational unit of Purchasing.

The command creates a self-signed certificate that includes the public key and the distinguished-name information. (The distinguished name you supply will be used as the "subject" field in the certificate.) This certificate will be valid for 90 days, the default validity period if you don't specify a `-validity` option. The certificate is associated with the private key in a keystore entry referred to by the alias `signFiles`. The private key is assigned the password `kpi135`.

The command could be shorter if option defaults are accepted or you wish to be prompted for various values. Whenever you execute a `keytool` command, defaults are used for unspecified options that have default values, and you are prompted for any required values. For the `genkey` command, options with default values include *`alias`* (whose default is `mykey`), *`validity`* (90 days), and *`keystore`* (the file named `.keystore` in your home directory). Required values include *`dname`*, *`storepass`*, and *`keypass`*.

Sign the JAR File

Now you are ready to sign the JAR file. Type the following in your command window to sign the JAR file `Count.jar` using the private key in the keystore entry aliased by `signFiles`, and to name the resulting signed JAR file `sCount.jar`:

```
jarsigner -keystore susanstore -signedjar sCount.jar Count.jar
         signFiles
```

You will be prompted for the store password (ab987c) and the private key password (kpi135).

Note: The jarsigner tool extracts the certificate from the keystore entry whose alias is signFiles and attaches it to the generated signature of the signed JAR file.

Export the Public Key Certificate

You now have a signed JAR file sCount.jar. The runtime system of the code receiver (Ray) will need to authenticate the signature when the Count application in the signed JAR file tries to read a file and a policy file grants that permission to this signed code.

In order for the runtime system to authenticate the signature, Ray's keystore needs to have the public key corresponding to the private key used to generate the signature. You supply this by sending Ray a copy of the certificate authenticating the public key. Copy that certificate from the keystore susanstore to a file named SusanJones.cer via the following:

```
keytool -export -keystore susanstore -alias signFiles -file
        SusanJones.cer
```

You will be prompted for the store password (ab987c).

Steps for the Code Receiver

Now act as Ray, who receives the signed JAR file and the certificate file from Susan. You will perform the following steps, as shown in Figure 69.

1. Observe the restricted application.
2. Import the certificate as a trusted certificate, using the keytool -import command, and give it the alias susan.
3. Set up a policy file to grant the required permission to permit classes signed by susan to read the specified file.
4. See the policy file effects, that is, see how the application can now read the file.

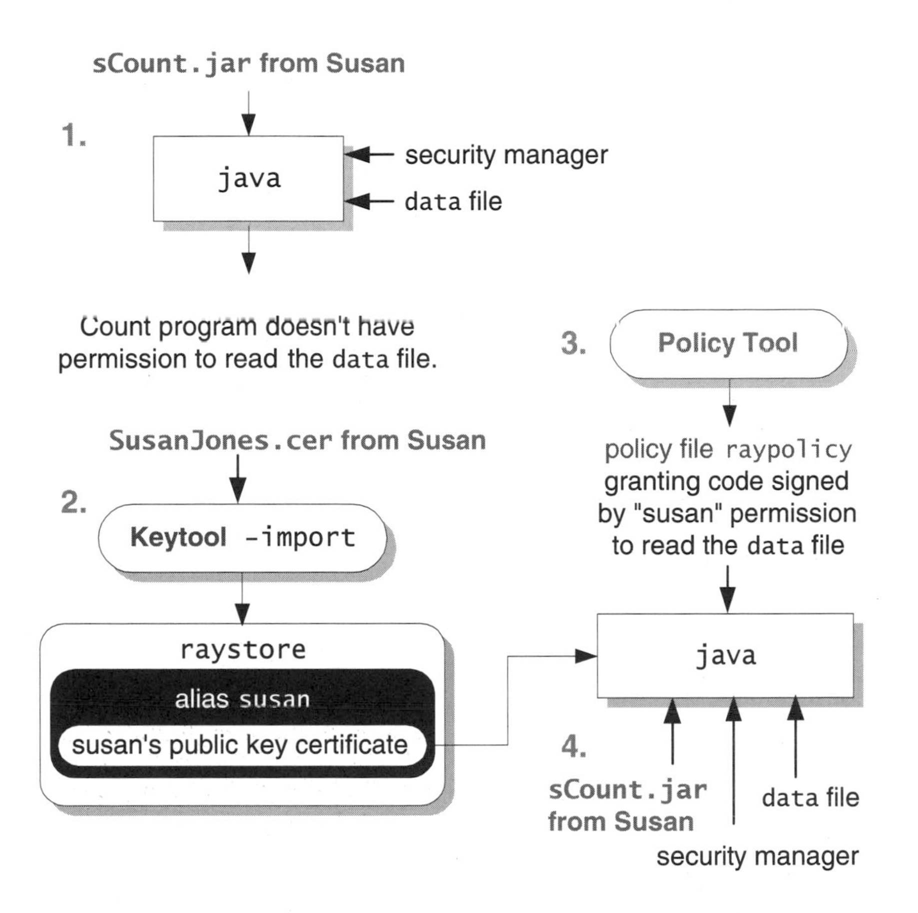

Figure 69 Code receiver steps.

Observe the Restricted Application

The last part of the lesson Quick Tour of Controlling Applications (page 503) shows how an application can be run under a security manager by invoking the interpreter with the new `-Djava.security.manager` command line argument. But what if the application to be invoked resides inside a JAR file?

One of the interpreter options is the `-cp` (for class path) option, whereby you specify a search path for application classes and resources. Thus, for example, to execute the `Count` application inside the `sCount.jar` JAR file, specifying the file `C:\TestData\data` as its argument, you could type the following while in the directory containing `sCount.jar`:

```
java -cp sCount.jar Count C:\TestData\data
```

To execute the application with a security manager, simply add `-Djava.security.manager`, as in

```
java -Djava.security.manager -cp sCount.jar Count
     C:\TestData\data
```

When you run this command, you should get an exception.

```
Exception in thread "main"
java.security.AccessControlException: access denied
   (java.io.FilePermission C:\TestData\data read)
   at java.security.AccessControlContext.checkPermission
                                          (Compiled Code)
   at java.security.AccessController.checkPermission
                                          (Compiled Code)
   at java.lang.SecurityManager.checkPermission(Compiled Code)
   at java.lang.SecurityManager.checkRead(Compiled Code)
   at java.io.FileInputStream.(Compiled Code)
   at Count.main(Compiled Code)
```

This `AccessControlException` is reporting that the application does not have permission to read the file `C:\TestData\data`. This exception is raised because an application running under a security manager cannot read a file or access other resources unless it has explicit permission to do so.

Import the Certificate as a Trusted Certificate

Before you can grant the signed code permission to read a specified file, you need to import Susan's certificate as a trusted certificate in your keystore. Suppose that you have received from Susan the signed JAR file `sCount.jar`, which contains the `Count.class` file, and the file `SusanJones.cer`, which contains the public key certificate for the public key corresponding to the private key used to sign the JAR file.

Even though you created these files and they haven't been transported anywhere, you can simulate being someone other than the creator and sender, Susan. Pretend you are now Ray. Acting as Ray, you will create a keystore named `raystore` and will use it to import the certificate into an entry with an alias of `susan`.

A keystore is created whenever you use a `keytool` command specifying a keystore that doesn't yet exist. Thus you can create the `raystore` and import the certificate by doing the following in your command window.

1. Go to the directory containing the public key certificate file `SusanJones.cer`. (You should actually already be there, since this lesson assumes that you stay in a single directory throughout.)
2. Type the following command:

```
keytool -import -alias susan -file SusanJones.cer -keystore
        raystore
```

Since the keystore doesn't yet exist, it will be created, and you will be prompted for a keystore password; type whatever password you want.

The `keytool` command will print out the certificate information and ask you to verify it, for example, by comparing the displayed certificate fingerprints with those obtained from another (trusted) source of information. (Each fingerprint is a relatively short number that uniquely and reliably identifies the certificate.) For example, in the real world you might call up Susan and ask her what the fingerprints should be. She can get the fingerprints of the `SusanJones.cer` file she created by executing the command

```
keytool -printcert -file SusanJones.cer
```

If the fingerprints she sees are the same as the ones reported to you by `keytool`, the certificate has not been modified in transit. In that case you let `keytool` proceed with placing a trusted-certificate entry in the keystore. The entry contains the public key certificate data from the file `SusanJones.cer` and is assigned the alias `susan`.

Set Up a Policy File to Grant the Required Permission

Next, you will use the Policy Tool to create a policy file named `raypolicy` and in it grant a permission to code from a signed JAR file. The JAR file must have been signed using the private key corresponding to the public key imported into Ray's keystore (`raystore`) in the previous step. The certificate containing the public key is aliased by `susan` in the keystore. We will grant such code permission to read any file in the `C:\TestData\` directory.

The steps are:

1. Start Policy Tool.
2. Specify the keystore.
3. Add a policy entry with a `SignedBy` alias.
4. See the policy file effects.

Start Policy Tool

To start Policy Tool, simply type the following at the command line:

```
policytool
```

This brings up the Policy Tool window. Whenever Policy Tool is started, it tries to fill in this window with policy information from what is sometimes referred to as the "user policy file," which by default is a file named `.java.policy` in your home directory. If Policy Tool cannot find the user policy file, it reports the situation and displays a blank Policy Tool window (that is, a window with headings and buttons but no data in it, as shown in Figure 70).

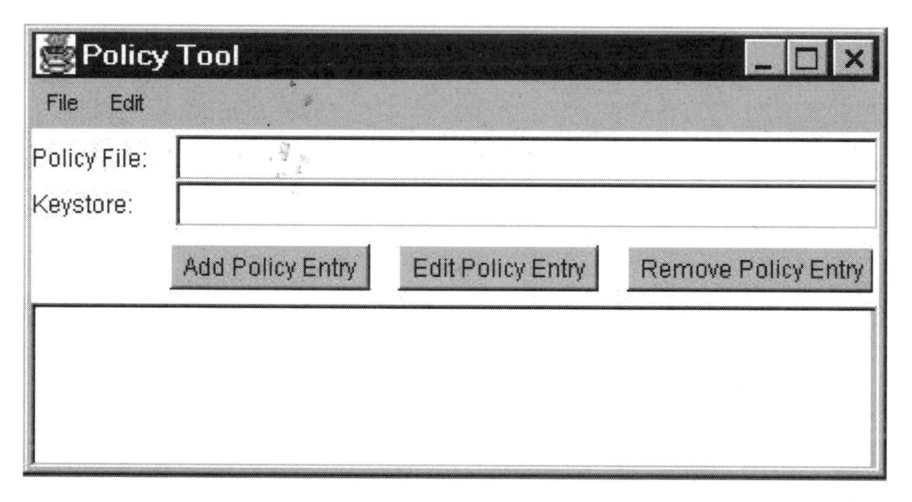

Figure 70 The Policy Tool.

You will create and work on a policy file other than the user policy file, since the lessons of this trail don't expect modifications to be made to your official user policy file. Assuming that you see the blank Policy Tool window (if not, select New in the File menu), you can immediately proceed to create a new policy file.

Specify the Keystore

For this lesson you will grant all code in JAR files signed by the alias `susan` read access to all files in the `C:\TestData\` directory. You need to

1. Specify the keystore containing the certificate information aliased by `susan`.
2. Create the policy entry granting the permission.

The keystore is the one named `raystore` created in the section Import the Certificate as a Trusted Certificate (page 532). To specify the keystore, choose the Change Keystore command in the Edit menu of the main Policy Tool window. This brings up a dialog box in which you can specify the keystore URL and the keystore type.

To specify the keystore named `raystore` in the `Test` directory on the `C:` drive, type the following `file` URL into the text box labeled New KeyStore URL:

```
file:/C:/Test/raystore
```

You can leave the text box labeled New KeyStore Type blank if the keystore type is the default one, as specified in the security properties file.[1] Your keystore will be the default type, so leave the text box blank. The result is shown in Figure 71.

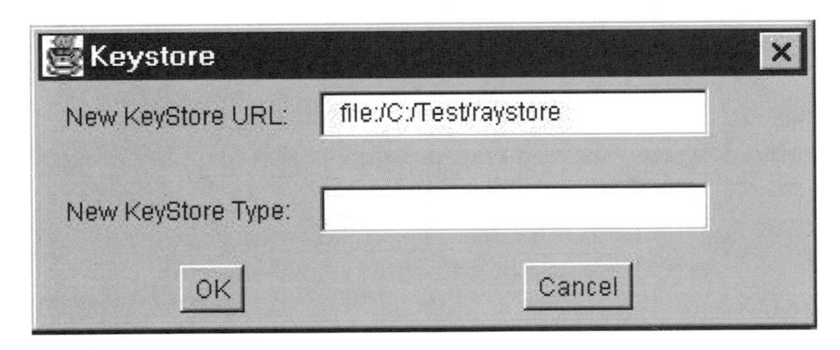

Figure 71 Keystore specification.

Note: The New KeyStore URL value is a URL and thus should always use slashes (never backslashes) as the directory separator.

When you are done specifying the keystore URL, choose OK. The text box labeled Keystore: is now filled in with the URL. Next, you need to specify the new policy entry.

Add a Policy Entry with a SignedBy Alias

To grant code signed by `susan` permission to read any files in the `C:\TestData` directory, you need to create a policy entry granting this permission. Note that "Code signed by `susan`" is an abbreviated way of saying: "Code in a class file

---

1 http://java.sun.com/docs/books/tutorial/security1.2/summary/files.html

contained in a JAR file, where the JAR file was signed using the private key corresponding to the public key that appears in a keystore certificate in an entry aliased by `susan`."

Choose the Add Policy Entry button in the main Policy Tool window. This brings up the Policy Entry dialog box. Using this dialog box, type the following alias into the SignedBy text box: `susan`.

Leave the CodeBase text box blank, to grant *all* code signed by `susan` the permission, no matter where it comes from.

Note: If you wanted to restrict the permission to just code signed by `susan` that comes from the `C:\Test\` directory, you would type the following URL into the CodeBase text box: `file:/C:/Test/*`

To add the permission, choose the Add Permission button. This brings up the Permissions dialog box. Do the following.

1. Choose File Permission from the Permission drop-down list. The complete permission type name (`java.io.FilePermission`) now appears in the text box to the right of the drop-down list.
2. Type the following in the text box to the right of the list labeled Target Name: to specify all files in the `C:\TestData\` directory:

   ```
   C:\TestData\*
   ```

3. Specify read access by choosing the read option from the Actions drop-down list.

Now the Permissions dialog box looks like the following.

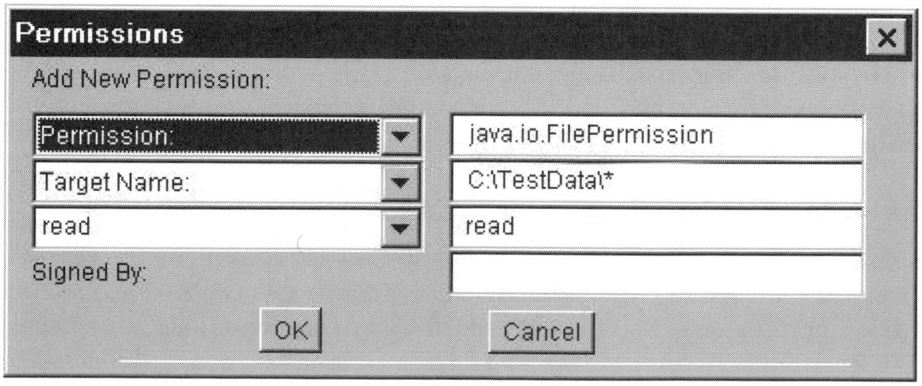

Figure 72 Permissions dialog box with file permission.

Choose the OK button. The new permission appears in a line in the Policy Entry dialog, as shown in Figure 73.

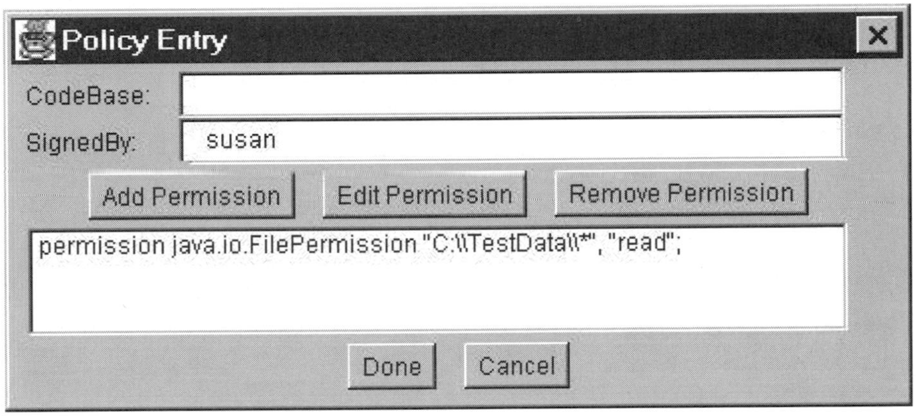

Figure 73 Policy Entry dialog box with file permission.

Note: Each backslash in the file path you typed has been replaced with two backslashes, for your convenience. Strings in a policy file are processed by a tokenizer that allows \ to be used as an escape character (for example, \n to indicate a new line), so the policy file requires two backslashes to indicate a single backslash. If you use single backslashes as your directory separators, Policy Tool automatically converts them to double backslashes for you.

You are now done specifying this policy entry, so choose the Done button in the Policy Entry dialog. The Policy Tool window now contains a line representing the policy entry, showing the SignedBy value, as shown in Figure 74.

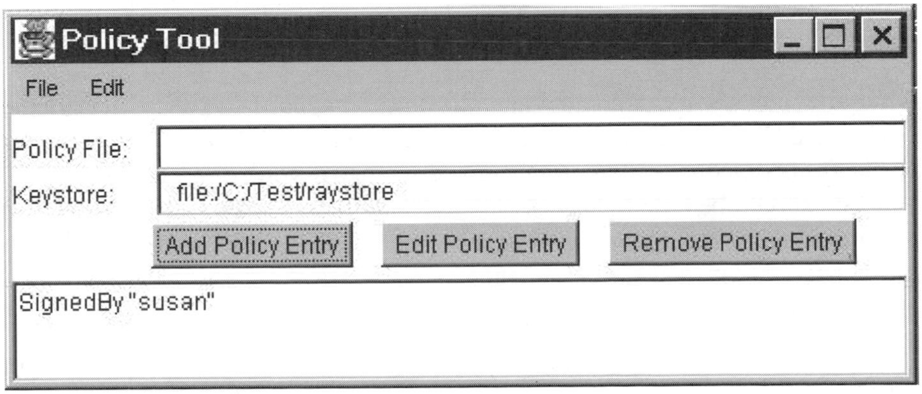

Figure 74 Policy Tool window showing new policy entry.

Save the Policy File

To save the new policy file you've been creating, choose the Save As command from the File menu. This brings up the Save As dialog box.

Navigate the directory structure to get to the directory in which to save the policy file: the `Test` directory on the `C:` drive. Type the file name

```
raypolicy
```

Then choose the Save button. The policy file is now saved, and its name and path are shown in the text box labeled Policy File, as shown in Figure 75.

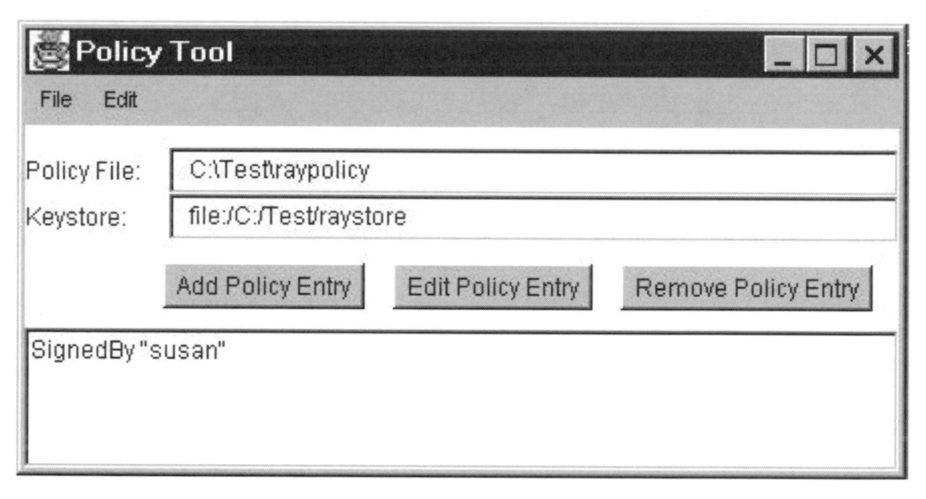

Figure 75 Policy Tool window after policy file is saved.

Then exit Policy Tool by selecting the Exit command from the File menu.

See the Policy File Effects

In the previous steps you created an entry in the `raypolicy` policy file granting code signed by `susan` permission to read files from the `C:\TestData\` directory (or the `testdata` directory in your home directory if you're working on UNIX). Now you should be able to successfully execute the `Count` program to read and to count the characters in a file from the specified directory, even when you run the application with a security manager.

As described at the end of the lesson Quick Tour of Controlling Applications (page 503), there are two possible ways you can have the `raypolicy` file be considered as part of the overall policy, in addition to the policy files specified in the security properties file. The first approach is to specify the additional policy file in a property passed to the runtime system. The second approach is to add a line in the security properties file specifying the additional policy file.

Approach 1

You can use a `-Djava.security.policy` command line argument to specify a policy file that should be used in addition to the ones specified in the security properties file. To run the `Count` application and have the `raypolicy` policy file included, type the following while in the directory containing the `sCount.jar` and `raypolicy` files:

```
java -Djava.security.manager -Djava.security.policy=raypolicy
     -cp sCount.jar Count C:\TestData\data
```

The program should report the number of characters in the specified file.

If it still reports an error, something is wrong in the policy file. Use the Policy Tool to check the permission you just created in the previous step, and change any typos or other errors.

Approach 2

You can specify a number of URLs—including ones of the form `http://`—in `policy.url.n` properties in the security properties file, and all of the designated policy files will get loaded. So one way to have your `raypolicy` file's policy entries considered by the interpreter is to add an entry indicating that file in the security properties file.

Important: If you are running your own copy of the JDK, you can easily edit your security properties file. If you are running a version shared with others, you may only be able to modify the system-wide security properties file if you have write access to it or if you ask your system administrator to modify the file when appropriate. However, it's probably not appropriate for you to make modifications to a system-wide policy file for this tutorial test; we suggest that you just read the following to see how it's done or that you install your own private version of the JDK to use for the tutorial lessons.

The security properties file is located at

UNIX:
`java.home/lib/security/java.security`

Win32:
`java.home\lib\security\java.security`

The *java.home* portion indicates the directory into which the JDK was installed.

To modify the security properties file, open it in an editor suitable for editing an ASCII text file. Then add the following line after the line starting with `policy.url.2`:

UNIX:

```
policy.url.3=file:${user.home}/test/raypolicy
```

or a line explicitly specifying your home directory, as in:

```
policy.url.3=file:/home/susanj/test/raypolicy
```

Win32:

```
policy.url.3=file:/C:/Test/raypolicy
```

Next, in your command window, go to the directory containing the `sCount.jar` file, that is, the `C:\Test` or `~/test` directory. Type the following:

```
java -Djava.security.manager -cp sCount.jar Count
     C:\TestData\data
```

As with approach 1, if the program still reports an error, something is wrong with the policy file. Use the Policy Tool to check the permission you just created in the previous step, and change any typos or other errors.

Important: Before continuing, you may want to delete the line you just added in the security properties file (or comment it out), since you probably do not want the `raypolicy` file included when you are not running the tutorial lessons.

---

http://java.sun.com/docs/books/tutorial/security1.2/toolfilex/index.html

45 Exchanging Files

IF you want to electronically send an important document, such as a contract, to someone else, it is a good idea to digitally "sign" the document, so that the recipient has a way of checking that the document indeed came from you and was not altered in transit. This lesson illustrates the use of security-related tools for the exchange of an important document, in this case a contract. You first pretend that you are the contract sender, Stan Smith. This lesson shows the steps Stan would use to put the contract in a JAR file, sign it, and export the public key certificate for the public key corresponding to the private key used to sign the JAR file. Then you pretend that you are Ruth, who has received the signed JAR file and the certificate. You'll use `keytool` to import the certificate into Ruth's keystore in an entry aliased by `stan`, and the `jarsigner` tool to verify the signature.

The sections in this lesson are:

For further information about digital signatures, certificates, keystores, and the tools, see the lesson Secure Code and File Exchanges (page 515).

Note: Commands in this lesson are presumed to be executed in the same directory.

Steps for the Contract Sender

The steps outlined here for the contract sender are *basically the same* as those listed for a code signer in the lesson Signing Code and Granting It Permissions (page 525). Here, however, you are pretending to be Stan Smith rather than Susan Jones and are storing a data file rather than a class file in the JAR file to be signed.

The steps you take as the contract sender are as follows.

1. Create a JAR file containing the contract, using the `jar` tool.
2. Generate keys if they don't already exist, using the `keytool -genkey` command.

Optional Step: Generate a certificate signing request (CSR) for the public key certificate, and import the response from the certification authority. For simplicity and since you are only pretending to be Stan Smith, this step is omitted. See the section Generating a Certificate Signing Request (CSR) for a Public Key Certificate (page 521) for more information.

---

3. Sign the JAR file, using the `jarsigner` tool and the private key generated in step 2.
4. Export the public key certificate, using the `keytool -export` command. Then supply the signed JAR file and the certificate to the receiver, Ruth.

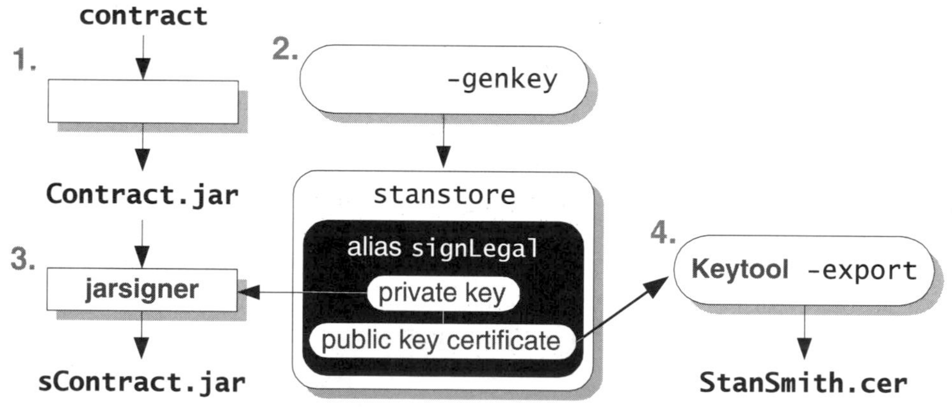

Figure 76 Contract sender steps.

Create a JAR File Containing the Contract

The first thing you need is a contract file. You can use the very basic sample file named `contract`, which is on the CD-ROM that accompanies this book,[1] or any

---

[1] The `contract` file is also available online here: http://java.sun.com/docs/books/tutorial/security1.2/toolfilex/example-1dot2/contract

other file you like. Just be sure to name the file `contract` so it will work with the commands specified in this lesson.

Once you've got a contract file, you can place it in a JAR file. In your command window type the following:

```
jar cvf Contract.jar contract
```

This command creates a JAR file named `Contract.jar` and places the `contract` file inside it.

Generate Keys

Before signing the `Contract.jar` JAR file containing the `contract` file, you need to generate keys, if you don't already have suitable keys available. The private key is needed to sign the JAR file, and the corresponding public key is needed by the contract receiver to verify the signature.

This lesson assumes that you don't yet have such keys. You are going to create a keystore named `stanstore` and create an entry with a newly generated public/private key pair (with the public key in a certificate).

Now pretend that you are Stan Smith and that you work in the legal department of XYZ corporation. Type the following in your command window to create a keystore named `stanstore` and to generate keys for Stan Smith:

```
keytool -genkey -alias signLegal -keystore stanstore
```

You will be prompted for the keystore password, your distinguished-name information, and the key password. Following are the prompts; the bold indicates what you should type.

```
Enter keystore password:  balloon53
What is your first and last name?
  [Unknown]:  Stan Smith
What is the name of your organizational unit?
  [Unknown]:  Legal
What is the name of your organization?
  [Unknown]:  XYZ
What is the name of your City or Locality?
  [Unknown]:  New York
What is the name of your State or Province?
  [Unknown]:  NY
What is the two-letter country code for this unit?
  [Unknown]:  US
```

```
Is <CN=Stan Smith, OU=Legal, O=XYZ, L=New York,
      ST=NY, C=US> correct?
  [no]:  y

Enter key password for <signLegal>
        (RETURN if same as keystore password):  cat876
```

The preceding `keytool` command creates the keystore named `stanstore` in the same directory in which the command is executed (assuming that the specified keystore doesn't already exist) and assigns it the password `balloon53`. The command generates a public/private key pair for the entity whose distinguished name has a common name of Stan Smith and an organizational unit of Legal.

The self-signed certificate created includes the public key and the distinguished name information. (A self-signed certificate is one signed by the private key corresponding to the public key in the certificate.) This certificate will be valid for 90 days, the default validity period if you don't specify a *-validity* option. The certificate is associated with the private key in a keystore entry referred to by the alias `signLegal`. The private key is assigned the password `cat876`.

Sign the JAR File

Now you are ready to sign the JAR file. Type the following in your command window to sign the JAR file `Contract.jar`, using the private key in the keystore entry aliased by `signLegal`, and to name the resulting signed JAR file `sContract.jar`:

```
jarsigner -keystore stanstore -signedjar sContract.jar
          Contract.jar signLegal
```

(Type all of this code on one line.)

You will be prompted for the store password (`balloon53`) and the private key password (`cat876`).

The `jarsigner` tool extracts the certificate from the keystore entry whose alias is `signLegal` and attaches it to the generated signature of the signed JAR file.

Export the Public Key Certificate

You now have a signed JAR file `sContract.jar`. Clients wanting to use the file will want to authenticate the signature. In order to do so, they need the public key corresponding to the private key used to generate the signature. You supply this by sending them a copy of the certificate containing the public key. Copy that certificate from the keystore `stanstore` to a file named `StanSmith.cer` via the following:

```
keytool -export -keystore stanstore -alias signLegal -file
        StanSmith.cer
```

You will be prompted for the store password (`balloon53`).

Given that certificate and the signed JAR file, a client can use the `jarsigner` tool to authenticate your signature, as you will see next.

Steps for the Contract Receiver

Now acting as Ruth, who receives the signed JAR file and the certificate file from Stan, perform the following steps, as shown in Figure 77.

1. Import the certificate as a trusted certificate, using the `keytool -import` command.
2. Verify the JAR file signature, using the `jarsigner` tool.

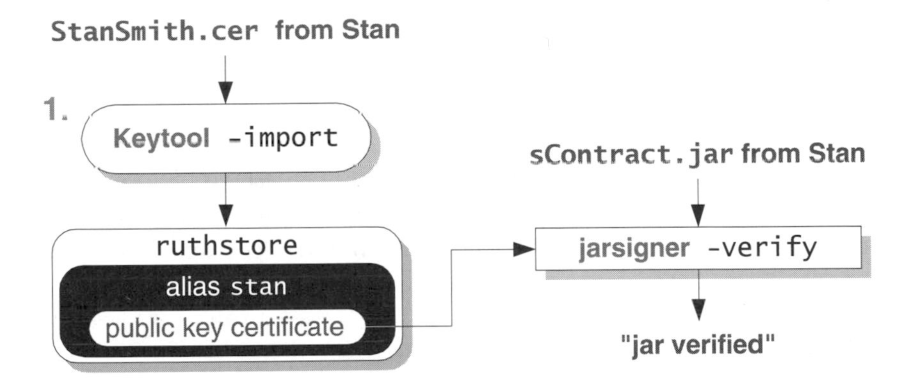

Figure 77 Contract receiver steps.

Import the Certificate as a Trusted Certificate

Suppose that you are Ruth and have received from Stan Smith

- The signed JAR file `sContract.jar` containing a contract

- The file `StanSmith.cer` containing the public key certificate for the public key corresponding to the private key used to sign the JAR file

Before you can use the `jarsigner` tool to check the authenticity of the JAR file's signature, you need to import into your keystore the certificate from Stan.

Even though you (acting as Stan) created these files and they haven't been transported anywhere, you can simulate being someone other than the creator and sender, Stan. Acting as Ruth, type the following to create a keystore named `ruthstore` and import the certificate into an entry with an alias of `stan`.

```
keytool -import -alias stan -file StanSmith.cer -keystore
        ruthstore
```

Since the keystore doesn't yet exist, it will be created. You will be prompted for a keystore password; type whatever password you want.

The `keytool` will print out the certificate information and ask you to verify it, for example, by comparing the displayed certificate fingerprints with those obtained from another (trusted) source of information. (Each fingerprint is a relatively short number that uniquely and reliably identifies the certificate.) For example, in the real world you might call up Stan and ask him what the fingerprints should be. He can get the fingerprints of the `StanSmith.cer` file he created by executing the command

```
keytool -printcert -file StanSmith.cer
```

If the fingerprints he sees are the same as the ones reported to you by `keytool`, the certificate has not been modified in transit. In that case you let `keytool` proceed with placing a "trusted certificate" entry in the keystore. The entry contains the public key certificate data from the file `StanSmith.cer` and is assigned the alias `stan`.

Verify the JAR File Signature

Now that you, acting as Ruth, have imported Stan's public key certificate into the `ruthstore` keystore as a "trusted certificate," you can use the `jarsigner` tool to verify the authenticity of the JAR file signature. When you verify a signed JAR file, you verify that the signature is valid and that the JAR file has not been tampered with. You can do this for the `sContract.jar` file via the following command:

```
jarsigner -verify -verbose -keystore ruthstore sContract.jar
```

You should see something like the following:

```
          183 Fri Jul 31 10:49:54 PDT 1998 META-INF/SIGNLEGAL.SF
         1542 Fri Jul 31 10:49:54 PDT 1998 META-INF/SIGNLEGAL.DSA
          0 Fri Jul 31 10:49:18 PDT 1998 META-INF/
smk       1147 Wed Jul 29 16:06:12 PDT 1998 contract

  s = signature was verified
  m = entry is listed in manifest
  k = at least one certificate was found in keystore
  i = at least one certificate was found in identity scope

jar verified.
```

Be sure to run the command with the `-verbose` option to get enough information to ensure that the contract file is among the files in the JAR file that were signed and its signature was verified (that's what the `s` signifies) and that the public key used to verify the signature is in the specified keystore and thus trusted by you (that's what the `k` signifies).

46 Generating and Verifying Signatures

THIS lesson walks you through the steps necessary to use the JDK Security API to generate a digital signature for data and to verify that a signature is authentic. This lesson is meant for developers who wish to incorporate security functionality into their programs, including cryptography services.

This lesson demonstrates the use of the JDK Security API with respect to signing documents. The lesson shows what one program, executed by the person who has the original document, would do to generate keys, generate a digital signature for the document using the private key, and export the public key and the signature to files. Then it shows an example of another program, executed by the receiver of the document, signature, and public key. It shows how the program could import the public key and verify the authenticity of the signature. The lesson also discusses and demonstrates possible alternative approaches and methods of supplying and importing keys, including in certificates.

For more details on the concepts and terminology (digital signatures, certificates, and keystores), see the lesson Secure Code and File Exchanges (page 515).

In this lesson you create two basic applications, one for the digital signature generation and the other for the verification. This is followed by a discussion and demonstration of potential enhancements. The lesson contains three sections.

Generating a Digital Signature (page 550)
: This section shows using the API to generate keys and a digital signature for data using the private key and to export the public key and the signature to files. The application gets the data file name from the command line.

Generating a Digital Signature

The `GenSig` program you are about to create will use the JDK Security API to generate keys and a digital signature for data using the private key and to export the public key and the signature to files. The application gets the data file name from the command line.

The following steps create the `GenSig` sample program.

1. Prepare the initial program structure. Create a text file named `GenSig.java`. Type in the initial program structure (import statements, class name, `main` method, and so on).
2. Generate public and private keys. Generate a key pair (public key and private key). The private key is needed for signing the data. The public key will be used by the `VerSig` program for verifying the signature.
3. Sign the data. Get a Signature object and initialize it for signing. Supply it with the data to be signed, and generate the signature.
4. Save the signature and the public key in files. Save the signature bytes in one file and the public key bytes in another.
5. Compile and run the program.

Prepare Initial Program Structure

Here's the basic structure of the `GenSig` program. This code is in a file called `GenSig.java`.

```
import java.io.*;
import java.security.*;

class GenSig {

    public static void main(String[] args) {

        /* Generate a DSA signature */
        if (args.length != 1) {
            System.out.println("Usage: GenSig " +
                               "nameOfFileToSign");
        }

        else try {
            // the rest of the code goes here
        } catch (Exception e) {
            System.err.println("Caught exception " +
                               e.toString());
        }
    }
}
```

The methods for signing data are in the `java.security` package, so the program imports everything from that package. The program also imports the `java.io` package, which contains the methods needed to input the file data to be signed. A single argument is expected, specifying the data file to be signed. The code written in subsequent steps will go between the `try` and the `catch` blocks.

Generate Public and Private Keys

To create a digital signature, you need a private key. (Its corresponding public key will be needed in order to verify the authenticity of the signature.)

In some cases the *key pair* (private key and corresponding public key) are already available in files. In that case the program can import and use the private key for signing, as shown in the section Weaknesses and Alternatives (page 559). In other cases the program needs to generate the key pair. A key pair is generated by using the `KeyPairGenerator` class.

In this example you will generate a public/private key pair for the Digital Signature Algorithm (DSA). You will generate keys with a 1024-bit length. Generating a key pair requires several steps.

Create a Key-Pair Generator

The first step is to get a key-pair generator object for generating keys for the DSA signature algorithm. As with all engine classes, the way to get a `KeyPair-`

Generator object for a particular type of algorithm is to call the getInstance static factory method on the KeyPairGenerator class. This method has two forms, both of which have a String algorithm first argument; one form also has a String provider second argument.

A caller may thus optionally specify the name of a provider, which will guarantee that the implementation of the algorithm requested is from the named provider. The sample code of this lesson always specifies the default SUN provider built into the JDK.

Put the following statement after the else try { line in the file created in the previous step.

```
KeyPairGenerator keyGen =
          KeyPairGenerator.getInstance("DSA", "SUN");
```

Initialize the Key-Pair Generator

The next step is to initialize the key-pair generator. All key-pair generators share the concepts of a keysize and a source of randomness. The KeyPairGenerator class has an initialize method that takes these two types of arguments.

- The keysize for a DSA key generator is the key length (in bits), which you will set to 1024.
- The source of randomness must be an instance of the SecureRandom class. This example requests one that uses the SHA1PRNG pseudo-random-number generation algorithm, as provided by the built-in SUN provider. The example then passes this SecureRandom instance to the key-pair generator initialization method.

  ```
  SecureRandom random = SecureRandom.getInstance("SHA1PRNG",
                                                 "SUN");
  keyGen.initialize(1024, random);
  ```

  The SecureRandom implementation attempts to completely randomize the internal state of the generator itself unless the caller follows the call to the getInstance method with a call to the setSeed method. So if you had a specific seed value that you wanted used, you would call the following prior to the initialize call:

  ```
  random.setSeed(seed);
  ```

Generate the Pair of Keys

The final step is to generate the key pair and to store the keys in PrivateKey and PublicKey objects.

```
KeyPair pair = keyGen.generateKeyPair();
PrivateKey priv = pair.getPrivate();
PublicKey pub = pair.getPublic();
```

Sign the Data

Now that you have created a public key and a private key, you are ready to sign the data. In this example you will sign the data contained in a file. `GenSig` gets the file name from the command line. A digital signature is created (or verified) using an instance of the `Signature` class. Signing data, generating a digital signature for that data, is done with the following steps.

Get a Signature Object

The following gets a `Signature` object for generating or verifying signatures using the DSA algorithm, the same algorithm for which the program generated keys in the previous step.

```
Signature dsa = Signature.getInstance("SHA1withDSA", "SUN");
```

Note: When specifying the signature algorithm name, you must include the name of the message digest algorithm used by the signature algorithm. SHA1withDSA is a way of specifying the DSA signature algorithm, using the SHA-1 message digest algorithm.

Initialize the Signature Object

Before a `Signature` object can be used for signing or verifying, it must be initialized. The initialization method for signing requires a private key. Use the private key placed into the `PrivateKey` object named `priv` in the previous step.

```
dsa.initSign(priv);
```

Supply the Signature Object the Data to Be Signed

This program will use the data from the file whose name is specified as the first (and only) command line argument. The program will read in the data a buffer at a time and will supply it to the `Signature` object by calling the `update` method.

```
FileInputStream fis = new FileInputStream(args[0]);
BufferedInputStream bufin = new BufferedInputStream(fis);
byte[] buffer = new byte[1024];
int len;
```

```
while (bufin.available() != 0) {
    len = bufin.read(buffer);
    dsa.update(buffer, 0, len);
};

bufin.close();
```

Generate the Signature

Once all of the data has been supplied to the `Signature` object, you can generate the digital signature of that data.

```
byte[] realSig = dsa.sign();
```

Save the Signature and the Public Key in Files

Now that you have generated a signature for some data, you need to save the signature bytes in one file and the public key bytes in another so you can send (via modem, floppy, mail, and so on) someone else the data for which the signature was generated, the signature, and the public key. The receiver can verify that the data came from you and was not modified in transit by running the `VerSig` program you will generate in the section Verifying a Digital Signature (page 555). That program uses the public key to verify that the signature received is the true signature for the data received.

Recall that the signature was placed in a byte array named `realSig`. You can save the signature bytes in a file named `sig` via the following.

```
/* save the signature in a file */
FileOutputStream sigfos = new FileOutputStream("sig");
sigfos.write(realSig);
sigfos.close();
```

Recall from the section Generate Public and Private Keys (page 551) that the public key was placed in a `PublicKey` object named `pub`. You can get the encoded key bytes by calling the `getEncoded` method and then store them in a file. You can name the file whatever you want. If, for example, your name is Susan, you might name it something like `suepk` (for “Sue’s public key”), as in the following:

```
/* save the public key in a file */
byte[] key = pub.getEncoded();
FileOutputStream keyfos = new FileOutputStream("suepk");
keyfos.write(key);
keyfos.close();
```

Compile and Run the Program

You can refer to the complete source code for GenSig.java (page 869) in the Appendix (also available on this book's CD-ROM). Compile and run it. Remember, you need to specify the name of a file to be signed, as in

```
java GenSig data
```

You can use the sample file named data, which is on the CD-ROM that accompanies this book,[1] or any other file you like. The file will not be modified. It will be read so that a signature can be generated for it. After executing the program, you should see the saved suepk (public key) and sig (signature) files.

Verifying a Digital Signature

If you have data for which a digital signature was generated, you can verify the authenticity of the signature. To do so, you need the data, the signature, and the public key corresponding to the private key used to sign the data.

In this example you write a VerSig program (see VerSig.java (page 871) in the Appendix) to verify the signature generated by the GenSig program. This demonstrates the steps required to verify the authenticity of an alleged signature.

VerSig imports a public key and a signature that is alleged to be the signature of a specified data file and then verifies the authenticity of the signature. The public key, signature, and data file names are specified on the command line.

The steps to create the VerSig sample program to import the files and to verify the signature are the following.

1. Prepare the initial program structure. Create a text file named VerSig.java. Type in the initial program structure (import statements, class name, main method, and so on).
2. Input and convert the encoded public key bytes. Import the encoded public key bytes from the file specified as the first command line argument, and convert them to a PublicKey.
3. Input the signature bytes. Input the signature bytes from the file specified as the second command line argument.

---

[1] The data file is also available online here: http://java.sun.com/docs/books/tutorial/security1.2/apisign/example-1dot2/data.

4. Verify the signature. Get a `Signature` object and initialize it with the public key for verifying the signature. Supply it with the data whose signature is to be verified (from the file specified as the third command line argument), and verify the signature.
5. Compile and run the program.

Prepare Initial Program Structure

Here's the basic structure of the `VerSig` program created in the following parts of this lesson. Place this program structure in a file called `VerSig.java`.

```
import java.io.*;

import java.security.*;
import java.security.spec.*;

class VerSig {
    public static void main(String[] args) {
        /* Verify a DSA signature */
        if (args.length != 3) {
            System.out.println("Usage: VerSig publickeyfile" +
                               " signaturefile datafile");
        } else try {
            // the rest of the code goes here
        } catch (Exception e) {
            System.err.println("Caught exception " +
                                e.toString());
        }
    }
}
```

You should note the following.

- The methods for verifying data are in the `java.security` package, so the program imports everything from that package. The program also imports the `java.io` package for methods needed to input the file data to be signed, as well as the `java.security.spec` package, which contains the `X509EncodedKeySpec` class.
- Three arguments are expected, specifying the public key, the signature, and the data files.
- The code written in subsequent steps of this lesson will go between the `try` and the `catch` blocks.

Input and Convert the Encoded Public Key Bytes

Next, VerSig needs to import the encoded public key bytes from the file specified as the first command line argument and to convert them to a PublicKey. A PublicKey is needed because that is what the Signature initVerify method requires in order to initialize the Signature object for verification.

First, read in the encoded public key bytes.

```
FileInputStream keyfis = new FileInputStream(args[0]);
byte[] encKey = new byte[keyfis.available()];
keyfis.read(encKey);
keyfis.close();
```

Now the byte array encKey contains the encoded public key bytes.

You can use a KeyFactory class in order to instantiate a DSA public key from its encoding. The KeyFactory class provides conversions between opaque keys (of type Key) and key specifications, which are transparent representations of the underlying key material. With an opaque key you can obtain the algorithm name, format name, and encoded key bytes, but not the key material, which, for example, may consist of the key itself and the algorithm parameters used to calculate the key. (Note that PublicKey, because it extends Key, is itself a Key.)

So, first you need a key specification. You can obtain one via the following, assuming that the key was encoded according to the X.509 standard, which is the case, for example, if the key was generated with the built-in DSA key pair generator supplied by the SUN provider:

```
X509EncodedKeySpec pubKeySpec = new X509EncodedKeySpec(encKey);
```

Now you need a KeyFactory object to do the conversion. That object must be one that works with DSA keys.

```
KeyFactory keyFactory = KeyFactory.getInstance("DSA", "SUN");
```

Finally, you can use the KeyFactory object to generate a PublicKey from the key specification.

```
PublicKey pubKey = keyFactory.generatePublic(pubKeySpec);
```

Input the Signature Bytes

Next, input the signature bytes from the file specified as the second command line argument.

```
FileInputStream sigfis = new FileInputStream(args[1]);
byte[] sigToVerify = new byte[sigfis.available()];
sigfis.read(sigToVerify);
sigfis.close();
```

Now the byte array `sigToVerify` contains the signature bytes.

Verify the Signature

You've added code to the `VerSig` program to

- Input the encoded key bytes and convert them to a `PublicKey`, `pubKey`
- Input the signature bytes into a byte array named `sigToVerify`

You can now proceed to do the verification.

Initialize the Signature Object for Verification

As with signature generation, a signature is verified by using an instance of the `Signature` class. You need to create a `Signature` object that uses the same signature algorithm as was used to generate the signature. The algorithm used by the `GenSig` program was the SHA1withDSA algorithm from the SUN provider.

```
Signature sig = Signature.getInstance("SHA1withDSA", "SUN");
```

Next, you need to initialize the `Signature` object. The initialization method for verification requires the public key.

```
sig.initVerify(pubKey);
```

Supply the Signature Object with the Data to Be Verified

You now need to supply the `Signature` object with the data for which a signature was generated. This data is in the file whose name was specified as the third command line argument. As you did when signing, read in the data one buffer at a time, and supply it to the `Signature` object by calling the `update` method.

```
FileInputStream datafis = new FileInputStream(args[2]);
BufferedInputStream bufin = new BufferedInputStream(datafis);
byte[] buffer = new byte[1024];
int len;
while (bufin.available() != 0) {
    len = bufin.read(buffer);
    sig.update(buffer, 0, len);
};
bufin.close();
```

Verify the Signature

Once you have supplied all of the data to the `Signature` object, you can verify the digital signature of that data and report the result. Recall that the alleged signature was read into a byte array called `sigToVerify`.

```
boolean verifies = sig.verify(sigToVerify);
System.out.println("signature verifies: " + verifies);
```

The `verifies` value will be `true` if the alleged signature (`sigToVerify`) is the actual signature of the specified data file generated by the private key corresponding to the public key `pubKey`.

Compile and Run the Program

Refer to the complete source code for <u>`VerSig.java`</u> (page 871) in the Appendix, with some comments added.

Compile and run the program. Remember, you need to specify three arguments on the command line:

- The name of the file containing the encoded public key bytes
- The name of the file containing the signature bytes
- The name of the data file (the one for which the signature was generated)

Since you will be testing the output of the `GenSig` program, the file names you should use are `suepk`, `sig`, and `data`.

Here's a sample run; the bold indicates what you type.

```
% java VerSig suepk sig data
signature verifies: true
```

Weaknesses and Alternatives

The `GenSig` and `VerSig` programs in this lesson illustrate the use of the JDK Security API to generate a digital signature for data and to verify that a signature is authentic. However, the actual scenario depicted by those programs, in which a sender uses the JDK Security API to generate a new public/private key pair, the sender stores the encoded public key bytes in a file, and the receiver reads in the key bytes, is not necessarily realistic and has a potential major flaw.

In many cases the keys do not need to be generated; they already exist, either as encoded keys in files or as entries in a keystore. The potential major flaw is that nothing guarantees the authenticity of the public key the receiver receives, and the `VerSig` program correctly verifies the authenticity of a signature only if the public key it is supplied is *itself* authentic!

These are not issues in some cases, as when a single program is doing both signing and verification. For example, in *The Java Tutorial*'s online trail Putting It All Together,[1] the `NotaryPublic` class constructor creates a key pair. Subsequently whenever a `Player` joins a game, the `Game` class generates the cards for the `Player` to play with. Before sending the cards back to the `Player`, the `Game` digitally signs the cards, using the private key. Later, when a `Player` claims to have a winning card, the `Game` verifies the signature by using the public key, to make sure that the card was actually created by this `Game` for the current game.

Working with Encoded Key Bytes

Sometimes encoded key bytes already exist in files for the key pair to be used for signing and verification. If that's the case the `GenSig` program can import the encoded private key bytes and convert them to a `PrivateKey` needed for signing, via the following, assuming that the name of the file containing the private key bytes is in the `privkeyfile String` and that the bytes represent a DSA key that has been encoded by using the PKCS #8 standard.

```
FileInputStream keyfis = new FileInputStream(privkeyfile);
byte[] encKey = new byte[keyfis.available()];
keyfis.read(encKey);
keyfis.close();
PKCS8EncodedKeySpec privKeySpec =
                              new PKCS8EncodedKeySpec(encKey);
KeyFactory keyFactory = KeyFactory.getInstance("DSA");
PrivateKey privKey = keyFactory.generatePrivate(privKeySpec);
```

`GenSig` no longer needs to save the public key bytes in a file, as they're already in one.

In this case the sender sends the receiver the already existing file containing the encoded public key bytes—unless the receiver already has this—and the data file and the signature file exported by `GenSig`. The `VerSig` program remains unchanged, as it already expects encoded public key bytes in a file.

But what about the potential problem of a malicious user intercepting the files and replacing them all in such a way that their switch cannot be detected? In

[1] This trail is available on the CD-ROM that accompanies this book and online here: http://java.sun.com/docs/books/tutorial/together/index.html

some cases this is not an issue because people have already exchanged public keys face to face or via a trusted third party that does the face-to-face exchange. After that multiple subsequent file and signature exchanges may be done remotely (that is, between two people in different locations), and the public keys may be used to verify their authenticity. If a malicious user tries to change the data or signature, this is detected by `VerSig`.

If a face-to-face key exchange is not possible, you can try other methods of increasing the likelihood of proper receipt. For example, you could send your public key via the most secure method possible prior to subsequent exchanges of data and signature files, perhaps using less secure mediums.

In general, sending the data and the signature separately from your public key greatly reduces the likelihood of an attack. Unless all three files are changed, and in a certain manner discussed in the next paragraph, `VerSig` will detect any tampering.

If all three files—data document, public key, and signature—were intercepted by a malicious user, that person could replace the document with something else, sign it with a private key, and forward on to you the replaced document, the new signature, and the public key corresponding to the private key used to generate the new signature. Then `VerSig` would report a successful verification, and you'd think that the document came from the original sender. Thus you should take steps to ensure that at least the public key is received intact (`VerSig` detects any tampering of the other files), or you can use certificates to facilitate authentication of the public key, as described in the next section.

Working with Certificates

It is more common in cryptography to exchange *certificates* containing public keys rather than the keys themselves. One benefit is that a certificate is signed by one entity (the *issuer*) to verify that the enclosed public key is the actual public key of another entity (the *subject*, or *owner*). Typically a trusted third-party *certification authority* (CA) verifies the identity of the subject and then vouches for its being the owner of the public key by signing the certificate. Another benefit of using certificates is that you can check to ensure the validity of a certificate you received by verifying its digital signature, using its issuer's (signer's) public key, which itself may be stored in a certificate whose signature can be verified by using the public key of that certificate issuer; that public key itself may be stored in a certificate, and so on, until you reach a public key that you already trust.

If you cannot establish a trust chain—perhaps because the required issuer certificates are not available to you—the certificate *fingerprint(s)* can be calculated.

Each fingerprint is a relatively short number that uniquely and reliably identifies the certificate. (Technically it's a hash value of the certificate information, using a message digest, also known as a one-way hash function.) You can call up the certificate owner and compare the fingerprints of the certificate you received with the ones sent. If they're the same, the certificates are the same.

It would be more secure for `GenSig` to create a certificate containing the public key and for `VerSig` to then import the certificate and extract the public key. However, currently the JDK has no public certificate APIs that would allow you to create a certificate from a public key, so the `GenSig` program cannot create a certificate from the public key it generated. (There *are* public APIs for extracting a public key from a certificate, though.)

If you want, you can use the various security tools, not APIs, to sign your important document(s) and work with certificates from a keystore, as was done in the lesson Exchanging Files (page 541).

Alternatively you can use the API to modify your programs to work with an already existing private key and corresponding public key (in a certificate) from your keystore. To start, modify the `GenSig` program to extract a private key from a keystore rather than generate new keys. First, let's assume the following.

- The keystore name is in the `String ksName`.
- The keystore type is JKS, the proprietary type created by Sun Microsystems.
- The keystore password is in the char array `spass`.
- The alias to the keystore entry containing the private key and the public key certificate is in the `String alias`.
- The private key password is in the char array `kpass`.

Then you can extract the private key from the keystore via the following.

```
KeyStore ks = KeyStore.getInstance("JKS");
FileInputStream ksfis = new FileInputStream(ksName);
BufferedInputStream ksbufin = new BufferedInputStream(ksfis);
ks.load(ksbufin, spass);
PrivateKey priv = (PrivateKey) ks.getKey(alias, kpass);
```

You can extract the public key certificate from the keystore and save its encoded bytes to a file named `suecert`, via the following.

```
java.security.cert.Certificate cert = ks.getCertificate(alias);
byte[] encodedCert = cert.getEncoded();
```

```
/* save the certificate in a file named "suecert" */
FileOutputStream certfos = new FileOutputStream("suecert");
certfos.write(encodedCert);
certfos.close();
```

Then you send the data file, the signature, and the certificate to the receiver. The receiver verifies the authenticity of the certificate by first getting the certificate's fingerprints, via the `keytool -printcert` command as shown in the following; the bold indicates what you should type.

```
keytool -printcert -file suecert
Owner: CN=Susan Jones, OU=Purchasing, O=ABC, L=SF,ST=CA, C=US
Issuer: CN=Susan Jones, OU=Purchasing, O=ABC, L=SF, ST=CA, C=US
Serial number: 35aaed17
Valid from: Mon Jul 13 22:31:03 PDT 1998 until: Sun Oct 11
22:31:03 PDT 1998

Certificate fingerprints:
   MD5:_ 1E:B8:04:59:86:7A:78:6B:40:AC:64:89:2C:0F:DD:13
   SHA1:
1C:79:BD:26:A1:34:C0:0A:30:63:11:6A:F2:B9:67:DF:E5:8D:7B:5E
```

Then the receiver verifies the fingerprints, perhaps by calling the sender up and comparing them with those of the sender's certificate or by looking them up in a public repository. The receiver's verification program (a modified `VerSig`) can then import the certificate and extract the public key from it via the following, assuming that the certificate file name (for example, `suecert`) is in the `String` `certName`.

```
FileInputStream certfis = new FileInputStream(certName);
CertificateFactory cf=CertificateFactory.getInstance("X.509");
java.security.cert.Certificate cert =
                          cf.generateCertificate(certfis);
PublicKey pub = cert.getPublicKey();
```

Ensuring Data Confidentiality

Suppose that you want to keep the contents of the data confidential so people accidentally or maliciously trying to view it in transit (or on your own machine or disk) cannot do so. To keep the data confidential, you should encrypt it and store and send only the encryption result (referred to as *ciphertext*). The receiver can decrypt the ciphertext to obtain a copy of the original data. APIs for data encryption and decryption, together with some default algorithm implementations, are released separately in the Java Cryptography Extension (JCE), an add-on package to the JDK, in accordance with U.S. export control regulations.

About the Author

MARY DAGEFORDE writes software documentation for various Silicon Valley computer companies, including Sun Microsystems. She has a Master's in Computer Science from Stanford University. She spent ten years working primarily on the design and implementation of the English-like customer programming language for the pioneering Xerox Star GUI environment and its successors. For the past eight years she has concentrated on documenting APIs, languages, tools, and systems.

Acknowledgments

I would like to thank Charlie Lai, Jan Luehe, and Roland Schemers for their lesson ideas, wonderfully thorough technical reviews, and excellent suggestions. Roland and Jan also designed the images in the "Security Features Overview" lesson. These images include enhancements made by Duarte Designs, Inc. I would also like to thank Li Gong for some of the technical information (especially regarding the evolution of the security architecture) and Marianne Mueller for a sample program. My final thanks go to my husband, Tom Wills, for his much-appreciated encouragement and understanding, as well as his willingness to provide hardware, software, or emotional support whenever it was needed!

JAR File Format

by Alan Sommerer

THE Java™ Archive (JAR) file format enables you to bundle multiple files into a single archive file. Typically a JAR file contains the class files and auxiliary resources associated with applets and applications.

Note: The JAR file format was introduced in the Java Development Kit (JDK™) 1.1, and the 1.2 version includes several enhancements to JAR file functionality. Unless otherwise noted, features covered in this trail pertain to both 1.1 and 1.2. If a feature description or example pertains to only one version, you'll be alerted with an annotation.

The JAR file format provides many benefits.

- **Security**: You can digitally sign the contents of a JAR file. Users who recognize your signature can then optionally grant your software security privileges it wouldn't otherwise have.
- **Decreased download time**: If your applet is bundled in a JAR file, the applet's class files and associated resources can be downloaded to a browser in a single HTTP transaction, without the need for opening a new connection for each file.
- **Compression**: The JAR format allows you to compress your files for efficient storage.
- **Packaging for extensions** (JDK 1.2): The extensions framework provides a means by which you can add functionality to the Java core platform, and the JAR file format defines the packaging for extensions. Java 3D and JavaMail™ are examples of extensions developed by Sun Microsystems. By using the JAR file format, you can turn your software into extensions as well.

- **Package sealing** (JDK 1.2): Packages stored in JAR files can be optionally sealed so that the package can enforce version consistency. Sealing a package within a JAR file means that all classes defined in that package must be found in the same JAR file.
- **Package versioning** *(*JDK 1.2*)*: A JAR file can hold data about the files it contains, such as vendor and version information.
- **Portability**: The mechanism for handling JAR files is a standard part of the Java platform's core API.

This trail contains the following three lessons:

Using JAR Files: The Basics (page 569) shows you how to perform basic JAR file operations and how to run software that is bundled in JAR files. This lesson also introduces you to the concept of the JAR file's manifest, which plays an important role in more advanced JAR functionality.

Signing and Verifying JAR Files (page 589) shows you how to use the JDK tools to digitally sign JAR files and to verify the signatures of signed JAR files.

Using JAR-Related APIs Introduced in 1.2 (page 599) introduces you to some of the new JAR-handling features in the Java 1.2 platform.

The JAR file format is an important part of the Java platform's extension mechanism. You can learn more about that aspect of JAR files in the trail Java Extension Mechanism (page 607).

47

Using JAR Files: The Basics

JAR files are packaged with the ZIP file format, so you can use them for "ZIP-like" tasks, such as lossless data compression, archiving, decompression, and archive unpacking. These are among the most common uses of JAR files, and you can realize many JAR file benefits by using only these basic features.

Even if you want to take advantage of advanced functionality provided by the JAR file format, such as electronic signing, you'll first need to become familiar with the fundamental operations. To perform basic tasks with JAR files, you use the Java Archive tool provided as part of the Java Development Kit. Because you invoke the Java Archive tool by using the `jar` command, we'll call it the Jar tool.

The sections in this lesson show you how to perform the most common JAR-file operations, with examples for each of the basic features.

The following table summarizes common JAR file operations as a synopsis and preview of some of the topics covered in this lesson.

Table 27 JAR File Operations

Operation	Command
Create a JAR file.	`jar cf` *jar-file input-file(s)*
View the contents of a JAR file.	`jar tf` *jar-file*
Extract the contents of a JAR file.	`jar xf` *jar-file*
Extract specific files from a JAR file.	`jar xf` *jar-file archived-file(s)*
Run an application packaged as a JAR file (version 1.1).	`jre -cp` *app.jar MainClass*
Run an application packaged as a JAR file (version 1.2—requires `Main-Class` manifest header).	`java -jar` *app.jar*
Invoke an applet packaged as a JAR file.	<applet code=*AppletClassName*.class archive="*JarFileName.jar*" width=*width* height=*height*> </applet>

The documentation for the Java Development Kit includes the following reference pages for the Jar tool:

- Jar tool reference for Win32 platform[1]
- Jar tool reference for Solaris platform[2]

Creating a JAR File

The basic format of the command for creating a JAR file is

```
jar cf jar-file input-file(s)
```

Let's look at the options and arguments used in this command.

- The `c` option indicates that you want to *create* a JAR file.
- The `f` option indicates that you want the output to go to a *file* rather than to `stdout`.
- The name that you want the resulting JAR file to have is `jar-file`. You can use any file name for a JAR file. By convention JAR file names are given a `.jar` extension, although this is not required.

---

[1] http://java.sun.com/products/jdk/1.2/docs/tooldocs/win32/jar.html
[2] http://java.sun.com/products/jdk/1.2/docs/tooldocs/solaris/jar.html

- The `input-file(s)` argument is a space-delimited list of one or more files that you want to be placed in your JAR file. The `input-file(s)` argument can contain the wildcard (`*`) symbol. If any of the input files are directories, they are added to the JAR archive recursively.

The `c` and `f` options can appear in either order, but there must not be any space between them.

This command will generate a compressed JAR file and will place it in the current directory. The command will also generate a default manifest file for the JAR archive. See the section Understanding the Manifest (page 585) for more information on the manifest file.

The following table lists additional options to the `cf` options of the basic command.

Table 28 More Options for Creating a JAR File

Option	Description
`v`	Produces *verbose* output on `stderr` (in 1.1) or `stdout` (in 1.2) while the JAR file is being built. The verbose output tells you the name of each file as it's added to the JAR file.
`0`	Zero indicates that you don't want the JAR file to be compressed.
`M`	Indicates that the default manifest file should not be produced.
`m`	Used to include manifest information from an existing manifest file. The format for using this option is `jar cmf existing-manifest jar-file input-file(s)` See the section Modifying a Manifest File (page 577) for more information about this option.
`-C`	Used to change directories during execution of the command (1.2 only).

In 1.1 the JAR file format supports only ASCII file names. Names encoded in UTF-8 are supported in 1.2.

An Example

Let's look at an example. The JDK demos include a simple TicTacToe applet. This demo contains a byte code class file, audio files, and images, all housed in a directory called `TicTacToe` with the following structure:

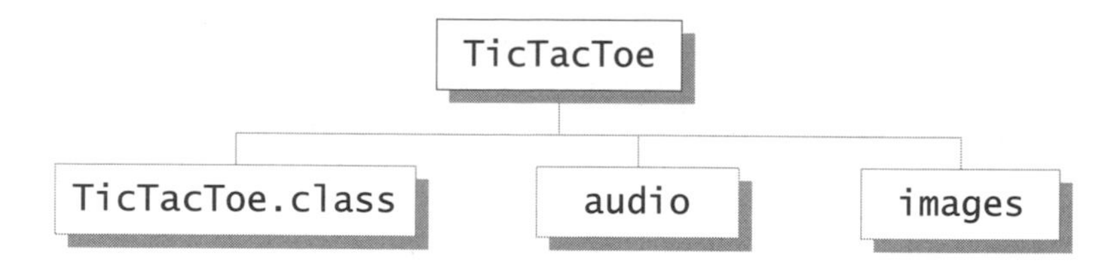

Figure 78 Directory structure of the TicTacToe applet.

The `audio` and `images` subdirectories contain sound files and GIF images that the applet uses.

To package this demo into a single JAR file named `TicTacToe.jar`, run this command from inside the `TicTacToe` directory:

```
jar cvf TicTacToe.jar TicTacToe.class audio images
```

The `audio` and `images` arguments represent directories, so the Jar tool will recursively place them and their contents in the JAR file. The generated JAR file `TicTacToe.jar` will be placed in the current directory. Because the command used the `v` option for verbose output, something similar to this output would appear when you run the command:

```
adding: TicTacToe.class (in=3825) (out=2222) (deflated 41%)
adding: audio/ (in=0) (out=0) (stored 0%)
adding: audio/beep.au (in=4032) (out=3572) (deflated 11%)
adding: audio/ding.au (in=2566) (out=2055) (deflated 19%)
adding: audio/return.au (in=6558) (out=4401) (deflated 32%)
adding: audio/yahoo1.au (in=7834) (out=6985) (deflated 10%)
adding: audio/yahoo2.au (in=7463) (out=4607) (deflated 38%)
adding: images/ (in=0) (out=0) (stored 0%)
adding: images/cross.gif (in=157) (out=160) (deflated -1%)
adding: images/not.gif (in=158) (out=161) (deflated -1%)
```

You can see from this output that the JAR file `TicTacToe.jar` is compressed. The Jar tool compresses files by default. You can turn off the compression feature by using the `0` (zero) option, so that the command would look like

```
jar cvf0 TicTacToe.jar TicTacToe.class audio images
```

You might want to avoid compression, for example, to increase the speed with which a JAR file could be loaded by a browser. Uncompressed JAR files can generally be loaded more quickly than compressed files because the need to decompress the files during loading is eliminated. However, there's a trade-off in that download time over a network may be longer for larger, uncompressed files.

The Jar tool will accept arguments that use the wildcard (*) symbol. As long as no unwanted files were in the TicTacToe directory, you could have used this alternative command to construct the JAR file:

```
jar cvf TicTacToe.jar *
```

Although the verbose output doesn't indicate it, the Jar tool automatically adds a manifest file to the JAR archive with path name META-INF/MANIFEST.MF. See the section Understanding the Manifest (page 585) for more information on the manifest file.

In the preceding example, the files in the archive retained their relative pathnames and directory structure. The Jar tool in the Java Development Kit 1.2 provides the -C option, which you can use to create a JAR file in which the relative paths of the archived files are not preserved. This option is modeled after GZIP's -C option.

As an example, suppose that you wanted to put audio files and GIF images used by the TicTacToe demo into a JAR file and that you wanted all of the files to be on the top level, with no directory hierarchy. You could accomplish that by issuing this command from the parent directory of the images and audio directories:

```
jar cf ImageAudio.jar -C images * -C audio *
```

The -C images part of this command directs the Jar tool to go to the images directory, and the * following -C images directs the Jar tool to archive all of the contents of that directory. The -C audio * part of the command then does the same with the audio directory. The resulting JAR file would have this table of contents:

```
META-INF/MANIFEST.MF
cross.gif
not.gif
beep.au
ding.au
return.au
yahoo1.au
yahoo2.au
```

By contrast, suppose that you used a command that didn't use the -C option:

```
jar cf ImageAudio.jar images audio
```

The resulting JAR file would have this table of contents:

```
META-INF/MANIFEST.MF
images/cross.gif
images/not.gif
audio/beep.au
audio/ding.au
audio/return.au
audio/yahoo1.au
audio/yahoo2.au
```

Viewing the Contents of a JAR File

The basic format of the command for viewing the contents of a JAR file is

```
jar tf jar-file
```

Let's look at the options and argument used in this command.

- The `t` option indicates that you want to view the *table* of contents of the JAR file.
- The `f` option indicates that the JAR file whose contents are to be viewed is specified on the command line. Without the `f` option, the Jar tool would expect a file name on `stdin`.
- The `jar-file` argument is the file name (or path and file name) of the JAR file whose contents you want to view.

The `t` and `f` options can appear in either order, but there must not be any space between them.

This command will display the JAR file's table of contents to `stdout`.

You can optionally add the verbose option, `v`, to produce additional information about file sizes and last-modified dates in the output.

An Example

Let's use the Jar tool to list the contents of the `TicTacToe.jar` file we created in the previous section.

```
jar tf TicTacToe.jar
```

This command displays the contents of the JAR file to `stdout`:

```
META-INF/MANIFEST.MF
TicTacToe.class
audio/
audio/beep.au
audio/ding.au
audio/return.au
audio/yahoo1.auaudio/yahoo2.au
images/
images/cross.gif
images/not.gif
```

The JAR file contains the `TicTacToe` class file and the audio and images directory, as expected. The output also shows that the JAR file contains a manifest file, `META-INF/MANIFEST.MF`, which the JAR tool automatically placed in the archive.

All path names are displayed with forward slashes, regardless of the platform or operating system you're using. Paths in JAR files are always relative; you'll never see a path beginning with `C:`, for example.

The JAR tool will display additional information if you use the `v` option:

```
jar tvf TicTacToe.jar
```

For example, the verbose output for the `TicTacToe` JAR file would look similar to this:

```
 256 Mon Apr 20 10:50:28 PDT 1998 META-INF/MANIFEST.MF
3885 Mon Apr 20 10:49:50 PDT 1998 TicTacToe.class
   0 Wed Apr 15 16:39:32 PDT 1998 audio/
4032 Wed Apr 15 16:39:32 PDT 1998 audio/beep.au
2566 Wed Apr 15 16:39:32 PDT 1998 audio/ding.au
6558 Wed Apr 15 16:39:32 PDT 1998 audio/return.au
7834 Wed Apr 15 16:39:32 PDT 1998 audio/yahoo1.au
7463 Wed Apr 15 16:39:32 PDT 1998 audio/yahoo2.au
   0 Wed Apr 15 16:39:44 PDT 1998 images/
 157 Wed Apr 15 16:39:44 PDT 1998 images/cross.gif
 158 Wed Apr 15 16:39:44 PDT 1998 images/n
```

Extracting the Contents of a JAR File

The basic command to use for extracting the contents of a JAR file is

```
jar xf jar-file [archived-file(s)]
```

Let's look at the options and arguments in this command.

- The `x` option indicates that you want to *extract* files from the JAR archive.
- The `f` option indicates that the JAR *file* from which files are to be extracted is specified on the command line rather than through `stdin`.
- The `jar-file` argument is the file name (or path and file name) of the JAR file from which to extract files.
- The optional argument `archived-file(s)` consists of a space-delimited list of the files to be extracted from the archive. If this argument is not present, the Jar tool will extract all of the files in the archive.

As usual, the order in which the `x` and `f` options appear in the command doesn't matter, but there must not be a space between them.

When extracting files, the Jar tool makes copies of the desired files and writes them to the current directory, reproducing the directory structure that the files have in the archive. The original JAR file remains unchanged.

Caution: When the Jar tool extracts files, it will overwrite any existing files having the same path name as the extracted files.

An Example

Let's extract some files from the `TicTacToe` JAR file we've been using in previous sections. Recall that the contents of `TicTacToe.jar` are

```
META-INF/MANIFEST.MF
TicTacToe.class
audio/
audio/beep.au
audio/ding.au
audio/return.auaudio/yahoo1.au
audio/yahoo2.au
images/
images/cross.gif
images/not.gif
```

Suppose that you want to extract the `TicTacToe` class file and the `cross.gif` image file. To do so, you can use the following command:

```
jar xf TicTacToe.jar TicTacToe.class images/cross.gif
```

This command does two things.

- It places a copy of `TicTacToe.class` in the current directory.
- It creates the directory `images`, if it doesn't already exist, and places a copy of `cross.gif` within it.

The original `TicTacToe` JAR file remains unchanged.

As many files as desired can be extracted from the JAR file in the same way. When the command doesn't specify which files to extract, the Jar tool extracts all files in the archive. For example, you can extract all of the files in the `TicTacToe` archive by using this command:

```
jar xf TicTacToe.jar
```

Modifying a Manifest File

You can modify the contents of a JAR file in a couple of ways. One method, available in both versions 1.1 and 1.2 of the Jar tool, uses the `m` command line option to add custom information to the manifest during creation of a JAR file. The `m` option is described in this section.

Version 1.2 of the Jar tool also provides the `u` option, which you can used to update the contents of an existing JAR file, including its manifest. The `u` option is covered in the next section, Updating a JAR File (page 580).

The Jar tool automatically puts a default manifest with path name `META-INF/MANIFEST.MF` into any JAR file you create. You can enable special JAR file functionality, such as package sealing, by modifying the default manifest. Typically this involves adding to the manifest special-purpose *headers* that allow the JAR file to perform a particular desired function. For examples of some special-purpose headers, and for more information about manifest files in general, see the section Understanding the Manifest (page 585).

The Jar tool's `m` option allows you to add information to the default manifest during creation of a JAR file. You must first prepare a text file containing the information you wish to add to the default manifest. You can then use the Jar tool's `m` option to add the information in your file to the default manifest.

The basic command has the format

```
jar cmf manifest-addition jar-file input-file(s)
```

Let's look at the options and arguments used in this command:

- The `c` option indicates that you want to *create* a JAR file.
- The `m` option indicates that you want to merge information from an existing *manifest* file into the manifest file of the JAR file you're creating.
- The `f` option indicates that you want the output to go to a *file* (the JAR file you're creating) rather than to `stdout`.
- The name (or path and name) `manifest-addition` is the existing text file whose contents you want included in the JAR file's manifest.
- The name `jar-file` is what you want the resulting JAR file to have.
- The `input-file(s)` argument is a space-delimited list of one or more files that you want to be placed in your JAR file.

The `c`, `m`, and `f` options can appear in any order, but there must not be any white space between them.

An Example

In the Java 1.2 platform, packages within JAR files can be optionally sealed, which means that all classes defined in that package must be archived in the same JAR file. You might want to seal a package, for example, to ensure version consistency among the classes in your software.

A package can be sealed by adding the `Sealed` header beneath the header naming the package that's to be sealed, as follows:

```
Name: myCompany/myPackage/
Sealed: true
```

The default manifest created by the Jar tool does not contain any `Sealed` headers, of course, because packages are not sealed by default. To seal a package, you therefore have to add the `Sealed` header yourself. To insert the `Sealed` header in a JAR file's manifest, you first need to write a text file containing the appropriate headers. The file you write doesn't have to be a complete manifest file; it can contain only the text that you want to merge into the default manifest, along with any `Name` headers that might be necessary to tell the Jar tool where to place your text within the manifest. Each header in your file must end with a line feed in order for the text to be merged properly into the manifest.

Let's suppose, for example, that your JAR file is to contain four packages:

```
myCompany/firstPackage/
myCompany/secondPackage/
myCompany/thirdPackage/
myCompany/fourthPackage/
```

To seal `firstPackage` and `thirdPackage`, you would write a text file with contents that look like this:

```
Name: myCompany/firstPackage/
Sealed: true

Name: myCompany/thirdPackage/
Sealed: true
```

Note that the package names end with a `/`. This file contains the information that needs to be added to the default manifest to seal the desired packages. Each `Sealed` header is immediately preceded by a `Name` header that indicates which package is to be sealed.

Let's suppose that:

- You named your text file `sealInfo`
- The JAR file you want to create will have the name `myJar.jar`
- The current directory is the parent directory of `myCompany`

You would create the JAR file with this command:

```
jar cmf sealInfo myJar.jar myCompany
```

The precise look of the resulting manifest file in `myJar.jar` would depend on whether you were using the Java Development Kit 1.1 or 1.2. In either case the `Sealed` header would be included for `firstPackage` and `thirdPackage`. If you were using the Jar tool 1.2, the manifest would look like this:

```
Manifest-Version: 1.0
Name: myCompany/firstPackage/
Sealed: true

Name: myCompany/thirdPackage/
Sealed: true
```

Only the first line, `Manifest-Version: 1.0`, is part of the default manifest. The other lines are in the manifest because you added them by using the `m` option when the Jar file was created.

Updating a JAR File

The Jar tool in the Java Development Kit 1.2 provides the `u` option, which you can use to update the contents of an existing JAR file by modifying its manifest or by adding files. The basic command for adding files has this format:

```
jar uf jar-file input-file(s)
```

In this command

- The `u` option indicates that you want to *update* an existing JAR file.
- The `f` option indicates that the JAR file to update is specified on the command line. If the `f` option is not present, the Jar tool will expect a JAR file name on `stdin`.
- The existing JAR file that's to be updated is `jar-file`.
- A space-deliminated list of one or more files that you want to add to the Jar file is denoted by `input-file`(s).

In the archive any files already having the same path name as a file being added will be overwritten.

As when creating a new JAR file, you can optionally use the `-C` option to indicate a change of directory.

You can combine the `u` option with the `m` option to update an existing JAR file's manifest:

```
jar umf manifest jar-file
```

In this command

- The `m` option indicates that you want to update the JAR file's *manifest*.
- The manifest whose contents you want to merge into the manifest of the existing JAR file is `manifest`.

Examples

Recall that `TicTacToe.jar` has these contents:

```
META-INF/MANIFEST.MF
TicTacToe.class
audio/
audio/beep.au
```

```
audio/ding.au
audio/return.au
audio/yahoo1.au
audio/yahoo2.au
images/
images/cross.gif
images/not.gif
```

Suppose that you want to add the file `images/new.gif` to the JAR file. You could accomplish that by issuing the following command from the parent directory of the `images` directory:

```
jar uf TicTacToe.jar images/new.gif
```

The revised JAR file would have this table of contents:

```
META-INF/MANIFEST.MF
TicTacToe.class
audio/
audio/beep.au
audio/ding.au
audio/return.au
audio/yahoo1.au
audio/yahoo2.au
images/
images/cross.gif
images/not.gif
images/new.gif
```

You can use the `-C` option to "change directories" during execution of the command. For example:

```
jar uf TicTacToe.jar -C images new.gif
```

This command would change to the `images` directory before adding `new.gif` to the JAR file. The `images` directory would not be included in the path name of `new.gif` when it's added to the archive, resulting in a table of contents that looks like this:

```
META-INF/MANIFEST.MF
TicTacToe.class
audio/
audio/beep.au
audio/ding.au
audio/return.au
audio/yahoo1.au
```

```
audio/yahoo2.au
images/
images/cross.gif
images/not.gif
new.gif
```

As a final example, suppose that you want to modify the default manifest of `TicTacToe.jar` by adding some version and vendor information. (Version and vendor information is contained in special headers that you can add to a JAR file's manifest. See the section Understanding the Manifest (page 585) for information about special headers.) You would first prepare a text file containing the headers that you wish to add to the default manifest. Your text file might consist of the following information, for example:

```
Name: TicTacToe.class
Implementation-Title: "TicTacToe demo"
Implementation-Version: "build57"
Implementation-Vendor: "Sun Microsystems, Inc."
```

If the file containing this information were called `versionInfo`, you would add the information to the manifest in `TicTacToe.jar` by using this command:

```
jar umf versionInfo TicTacToe.jar
```

After running this command, the manifest for `TicTacToe.jar` would contain the information from your `versionInfo` file.

Running JAR-Packaged Software

Now that you've learned how to create JAR files, how do you run the code that you've packaged? Consider these three scenarios.

- Your JAR file contains an applet that is to be run inside a browser.
- Your JAR file contains an application that is to be invoked from the command line.
- Your JAR file contains code that you want to use as an extension.

This section will cover the first two situations. A separate trail, Java Extension Mechanism (page 607), covers the use of JAR files as extensions.

Applets Packaged in JAR Files

To invoke any applet from an HTML file for running inside a browser, you need to use the APPLET tag.[1] If the applet is bundled as a JAR file, the only thing you need to do differently is to use the *ARCHIVE* parameter to specify the relative path to the JAR file.

As an example, let's use (again!) the TicTacToe demo applet that ships with the Java Development Kit. The APPLET tag in the HTML file that calls the demo looks like this:

```
<Applet code=TicTacToe.class
        width=120 height=120>
</Applet>
```

If the TicTacToe demo were packaged in a JAR file named TicTacToe.jar, you could modify the APPLET tag with the simple addition of an ARCHIVE parameter, as follows:

```
<Applet code=TicTacToe.class
        Archive="TicTacToe.jar"
        Width=120 height=120>
</Applet>
```

The ARCHIVE parameter specifies the relative path to the JAR file that contains TicTacToe.class. This example assumes that the JAR file and the HTML file are in the same directory. If they're not, you would need to include the JAR file's relative path in the ARCHIVE parameter's value. For example, if the JAR file were one directory below the HTML file in a directory called applets, the APPLET tag would look like this:

```
<Applet code=TicTacToe.class
        Archive="applets/TicTacToe.jar"
        Width=120 height=120>
</Applet>
```

Applications Packaged in JAR Files — *1.1 platform*

You can run applications that are bundled as JAR files by using the JDK 1.1 jre tool.

---

[1] See the *Writing Applets* lesson in *The Java Tutorial, Second Edition*. The HTML version of this lesson is available on the CD-ROM that accompanies this book and is also available online at: http://java.sun.com/docs/books/tutorial/applet/index.html.

```
jre -cp app.jar MainClass
```

In the JDK 1.1 software the `-cp` option prepends the `app.jar` file to the system class path. `MainClass` identifies the class that is the application's entry point within the JAR file. (Recall that one of the classes in an application must have a method with the signature `public static void main(String[] args)`, which serves as entry, or starting, point for the application.)

JAR Files as Applications — *1.2 platform only*

In the JDK 1.2 software, you can run JAR-packaged applications with the Java interpreter. The basic command is

```
java -jar jar-file
```

The `-jar` flag tells the interpreter that the application is packaged in the JAR file format.

Note: The `-jar` option is not available for interpreters prior to JDK 1.2.

Before this command will work, however, the runtime environment needs to know which class within the JAR file is the application's entry point. To indicate that class, you must add a `Main-Class` header to the JAR file's manifest. The header takes the form

```
Main-Class: classname
```

The header's value, `classname`, is the name of the class that's the application's entry point.

To create a JAR file having a manifest with the appropriate `Main-Class` header, you can use the Jar tool's `m` flag as described in the section Modifying a Manifest File (page 577). You would first prepare a single-line text file with the `Main-Class` header and value. For example, if your application were the single-class `HelloWorld` application, the entry point would of course be the `HelloWorld` class, and your text file would have this line:

```
Main-Class: HelloWorld
```

Assuming that your text file was in a file called `mainClass`, you could merge it into a JAR file's manifest with a command such as this:

```
jar cmf mainClass app.jar HelloWorld.class
```

With your JAR file prepared in this way, you can run the `HelloWorld` application from the command line, as follows:

```
java -jar app.jar
```

Understanding the Manifest

JAR files can support a wide range of functionality, including electronic signing, version control, package sealing, extensions, and others. What gives JAR files their versatility? The answer is embodied in the JAR file's *manifest*.

The manifest is a special file that can contain information about the files packaged in a JAR file. By tailoring this "meta" information that the manifest contains, you enable the JAR file to be used for a variety of purposes.

Before looking at some of the ways manifests can be modified to enable special JAR file functionality, let's take a look at the baseline default manifest.

The Default Manifest

When you create a JAR file, it automatically receives a default manifest file. An archive can contain only one manifest file, and it always has the path name

```
META-INF/MANIFEST.MF
```

When a JAR file is created with the Java Development Kit 1.2, the default manifest file is very simple. Here are its full contents:

```
Manifest-Version: 1.0
```

This line shows that a manifest's entries take the form of "header: value" pairs. The name of a header is separated from its value by a colon. The default manifest shows that it conforms to version 1.0 of the manifest specification.

The manifest can also contain information about the other files that are packaged in the archive. Exactly what file information is recorded in the manifest will depend on what use you intend for the JAR file. The default manifest file makes no assumptions about what information it should record about other files, so its single line contains data only about itself.

The format of the default manifest file changed between JDK 1.1 and 1.2. If you create a JAR file for the `java.math` package, for example, the JDK 1.1 default manifest file would look something like this:

```
Manifest-Version: 1.0

Name: java/math/BigDecimal.class
SHA1-Digest: TD1GZt8G11dXY2p4olSZPc5Rj64=
MD5-Digest: z6z8xPj2AW/Q9AkRSPF0cg==

Name: java/math/BigInteger.class
SHA1-Digest: oBmrvIkBnSxdNZzPh5iLyF0S+bE=
MD5-Digest: wFymhDKjNreNZ4AzDWWg1Q==
```

Like the JDK 1.2 manifest file, the JDK 1.1 manifest has an entry for `Manifest-Version`. The version number is the same, indicating that the manifest specification didn't change between JDK 1.1 and 1.2.

Unlike the JDK 1.2 manifest file, the JDK 1.1 manifest has entries for each file contained in the archive, including the files' path names and digest values. See the Digests and the Signature File (page 591) section in the next lesson. The path names are given as values of the `Name` header. Any headers that immediately follow a `Name` header, without any intervening blank lines, pertain to the file specified by the `Name` header. In the preceding manifest, for example, the first `Name` header is followed by the lines

```
SHA1-Digest: TD1GZt8G11dXY2p4olSZPc5Rj64=
MD5-Digest: z6z8xPj2AW/Q9AkRSPF0cg==
```

Because these lines follow the `Name` header without any intervening blank lines, you know that the digest values they specify are for the file `java/math/BigDecimal.class`.

Digest values are relevant only with respect to signing JAR files. In fact, that's why the digest information isn't in the JDK 1.2 default manifest; it isn't always needed. To learn more about digests and signing, see the next lesson, Signing and Verifying JAR Files (page 589).

Special-Purpose Manifest Headers

Depending on what role you want your JAR file to play, you may need to modify the default manifest. If you're interested only in the ZIP-like features of JAR files, such as compression and archiving, you don't have to worry about the manifest file, as it doesn't really play a role in those situations.

Beyond simple archiving and compression, most uses of JAR files require special information to be in the manifest file. Following are brief descriptions of the headers required for some special-purpose JAR file functions:

- Applications bundled as JAR files
- Download extensions
- Package sealing
- Package versioning

Applications Bundled as JAR Files — *version 1.2 only*

If you have an application bundled in a JAR file, you need some way to indicate which class within the JAR file is your application's entry point. (Recall that the entry point is the class having a method with signature `public static void main(String[] args)`.) You provide this information with the `Main-Class`- header, which has the general form

```
Main-Class: classname
```

The value `classname` identifies your application's entry point.

Download Extensions — *version 1.2 only*

Download extensions are JAR files that are referenced by the manifest files of other JAR files. See the trail Java Extension Mechanism (page 607) for information about extensions.

In a typical situation an applet will be bundled in a JAR file whose manifest references a JAR file (or several JAR files) that will serve as an extension for the purposes of that applet. Extensions may reference each other in the same way.

Download extensions are specified in the `Class-Path` header field in the manifest file of an applet, application, or another extension. A `Class-Path` header might look like this, for example:

```
Class-Path: servlet.jar infobus.jar acme/beans.jar
```

With this header the classes in the files `servlet.jar`, `infobus.jar`, and `acme/beans.jar` will serve as extensions for purposes of the applet or application. The URLs in the `Class-Path` header are given relative to the URL of the JAR file of the applet or application.

Package Sealing — *version 1.2 only*

A package within a JAR file can be optionally sealed, which means that all classes defined in that package must be archived in the same JAR file. You might want to seal a package, for example, to ensure version consistency among the classes in your software or as a security measure.

To seal a package, you need to add a `Name` header for the package, followed by a `Sealed` header:

```
Name: myCompany/myPackage/
Sealed: true
```

The `Name` header's value is the package's relative path name. Note that it ends with a / to distinguish it from a file name. Any headers following a `Name` header, without any intervening blank lines, apply to the file or package specified in the `Name` header. Since the `Sealed` header in the preceding example occurs after the `Name:_myCompany/myPackage` header with no blank lines between, the `Sealed` header will be interpreted as applying only to the package `myCompany/myPackage`.

Package Versioning — *version 1.2 only*

The Package Versioning specification[1] defines several manifest headers to hold versioning information. One set of such headers can be assigned to each package. The versioning headers should appear directly beneath the `Name` header for the package. The following example shows all of the versioning headers:

```
Name: java/util/
Specification-Title: "Java Utility Classes"
Specification-Version: "1.2"
Specification-Vendor: "Sun Microsystems, Inc.".
Implementation-Title: "java.util"
Implementation-Version: "build57"
Implementation-Vendor: "Sun Microsystems, Inc."
```

Additional Information

A specification of the manifest format is part of the online JDK documentation.[2]

---

1 http://java.sun.com/products/jdk/1.2/docs/guide/versioning/spec/VersioningSpecification.html#PackageVersioning

2 http://java.sun.com/products/jdk/1.2/docs/guide/jar/manifest.html

http://java.sun.com/docs/books/tutorial/jar/sign/index.html

48 Signing and Verifying JAR Files

YOU can optionally sign a JAR file with your electronic "signature." Users who verify your signature can grant your JAR-bundled software security privileges that it wouldn't ordinarily have. Conversely, you can verify the signatures of signed JAR files that you want to use.

This lesson shows you how to use the tools provided in the Java Development Kit to sign and to verify JAR files.

Understanding Signing and Verification (page 590)
This section will bring you up to speed on concepts of signing and verification, defining the relevant terms, describing some of the benefits provided by signing, and outlining the signing mechanism used by the Java platform as it relates to JAR files.

Signing JAR Files (page 593)
This section teaches you how to use the JDK tools to digitally sign your JAR files.

Verifying Signed JAR Files (page 597)
In this section you learn how to use the JDK tool set to verify signed JAR files.

Understanding Signing and Verification

The Java platform enables you to digitally sign JAR files. You digitally sign a file for the same reason you might sign a paper document with pen and ink—to let readers know that you wrote the document or at least that it has your approval.

When you sign a letter, for example, everyone who recognizes your signature can confirm that you wrote the letter. Similarly anyone who "recognizes" your digital signature knows that the file came from you. The process of "recognizing" electronic signatures is called *verification*.

The ability to sign and to verify files is an important part of the Java platform's security architecture. In the 1.2 platform, security is controlled by the security *policy* in force at runtime. You can configure the policy to grant security privileges to applets and to applications. For example, you could grant permission to an applet to perform normally forbidden operations, such as reading and writing local files or running local executable programs. If you have downloaded some code that's signed by a trusted entity, you can use that fact as a criterion in deciding which security permissions to assign to the code.

Once you (or your browser) have verified that an applet is from a trusted source, you can have the platform relax security restrictions to let the applet perform operations that would ordinarily be forbidden. On the 1.1 Java platform, a trusted applet has the same freedom to perform operations as a local application. On the 1.2 platform, a trusted applet would have freedoms as specified by the *policy file* in force.

The Java platform enables signing and verification by using special numbers, called public and private *keys*. Public keys and private keys come in pairs and play complementary roles.

The private key is the electronic "pen" with which you can sign a file. As its name implies, your private key is known only to you, so no one else can "forge" your signature. A file signed with your private key can be verified only by the corresponding public key.

Public and private keys alone, however, aren't enough to truly verify a signature. Even if you've verified that a signed file contains a matching key pair, you still need a way to confirm that the public key comes from the signer it purports to come from.

One more element, therefore, is required to make signing and verification work. That additional element is the *certificate* that the signer includes in a signed JAR file. A certificate, a digitally signed statement from a recognized *certification authority*, indicates who owns a particular public key. A certification authority is an entity (typically a firm specializing in digital security) that is trusted throughout the industry to sign and to issue certificates for keys and their owners. In the case of signed JAR files the certificate indicates who owns the public key contained in the JAR file. When you sign a JAR file, your public key is placed inside the archive, along with an associated certificate so that it's easily available for use by anyone wanting to verify your signature.

To summarize digital signing: First, the signer signs the JAR file, using a private key. Then the corresponding public key is placed in the JAR file, together with its certificate, so that it's available for use by anyone who wants to verify the signature.

Digests and the Signature File

When you sign a JAR file using the tools in the JDK 1.2 software, each file in the archive is given a digest entry in the archive's manifest. The following example shows what such an entry might look like.

```
Name: test/classes/ClassOne.class
SHA1-Digest: TD1GZt8G11dXY2p4olSZPc5Rj64=
```

The digest values are hashes, or encoded representations of the contents of the files as they were at the time of signing. A file's digest will change if and only if the file itself changes. In the 1.1 platform, digest-value entries are added to the manifest when you *create* the JAR file rather than when you sign it.

When a JAR file is signed, a *signature* file is automatically generated and placed in the JAR file's `META-INF` directory, the same directory that contains the archive's manifest. Signature files have file names with an `.SF` extension. The following example shows the contents of a signature file.

```
Signature-Version: 1.0
SHA1-Digest-Manifest: h1yS+K9T7DyHtZrtI+LxvgqaMYM=
Created-By: SignatureFile JDK 1.2

Name: test/classes/ClassOne.class
SHA1-Digest: fcav7ShIG6i86xPepmitOVo4vWY=

Name: test/classes/ClassTwo.class
SHA1-Digest: xrQem9snnPhLySDiZyclMlsFdtM=

Name: test/images/ImageOne.gif
```

```
SHA1-Digest: kdHbE7kL9ZHLgK7akHttYV4XIa0=

Name: test/images/ImageTwo.gif
SHA1-Digest: mF0D5zpk68R4oaxEqoS9Q7nhm60=
```

As you can see, the signature file contains digest entries for the archive's files that look similar to the digest-value entries in the manifest. See the section Understanding the Manifest (page 585) in the previous lesson for more information on the manifest. However, whereas the digest values in the manifest are computed from the files, the digest values in the signature file are computed from the corresponding entries in the manifest. Signature files produced with the 1.2 platform also contain a digest value for the entire manifest (see the `SHA1-Digest-Manifest` header in the preceding example).

When a signed JAR file is being verified, the digests of each of its files are re-computed and compared with the digests recorded in the manifest to ensure that the contents of the JAR file haven't changed since it was signed. As an additional check, digest values for the manifest file are recomputed and compared against the values recorded in the signature file.

You can read additional information about signature files on the Manifest Format page of the JDK documentation.[1]

The Signature Block File

In addition to the signature file, a *signature block* file is automatically placed in the `META-INF` directory when a JAR file is signed. Unlike the manifest file or the signature file, signature block files are not human-readable.

The signature block file contains two elements essential for verification:

- The JAR file's digital signature that was generated with the signer's private key
- The certificate containing the signer's public key, to be used by anyone wanting to verify the signed JAR file

Signature block file names typically have a `.DSA` extension, indicating that they were created by the default digital signature algorithm. Other file name extensions are possible if keys associated with another standard algorithm are used for signing.

---

[1] http://java.sun.com/products/jdk/1.2/docs/guide/jar/manifest.html

Related Documentation

For additional information about keys, certificates, and certification authorities, see The JDK 1.2 Key and Certificate Management Tool[1] and X.509 Certificates.[2] For more information about the Java platform's security architecture, see the trail Security (page 477). Also see The Java Cryptography Architecture API Specification and Reference[3] and JDK 1.2 Security Documentation.[4]

Signing JAR Files

The Java Development Kit contains the tools that you need to sign JAR files. Depending on which version of the Java Development Kit you're using, you will use either the JAR Signing and Verification Tool or the Java Security Tool.

The JDK 1.2 JAR Signing and Verification Tool

The JAR Signing and Verification tool is invoked by using the `jarsigner` command, so we'll refer to it as "Jarsigner" for short. To sign a JAR file, you must first have a private key. Private keys and their associated public-key certificates are stored in password-protected databases called *keystores*. A keystore can hold the keys of many potential signers. Each key in the keystore can be identified by an *alias,* typically the name of the signer who owns the key. The key belonging to Rita Jones might have the alias "rita," for example.

The basic form of the command for signing a JAR file is

```
jarsigner jar-file alias
```

In this command

- The path name of the JAR file to be signed is `jar-file`.
- The alias identifying the private key to be used to sign the JAR file, and the key's associated certificate is `alias`.

The Jarsigner tool will prompt you for the passwords for the keystore and the alias.

---

1 http://java.sun.com/products/jdk/1.2/docs/tooldocs/solaris/keytool.html
2 http://java.sun.com/products/jdk/1.2/docs/guide/security/cert3.html
3 http://java.sun.com/products/jdk/1.1/docs/guide/security/CryptoSpec.html
4 http://java.sun.com/products/jdk/1.2/docs/guide/security/index.html

The basic form of the command assumes that the keystore to be used is in a file named `.keystore` in your home directory. This command will create signature and signature block files with names `x.SF` and `x.DSA`, respectively, where `x` comprises the first eight letters of the alias, all converted to uppercase. This basic command will *overwrite* the original JAR file with the signed JAR file.

In practice you may want to use this command in conjunction with one or more of these options, which must precede the `jar-file` pathname.

Table 29 Additional Options for Use with the Jarsigner Tool

Option	Description
`-keystore` *url*	Specifies a keystore to be used if you don't want to use the `.keystore` default database.
`-storepass` *password*	Allows you to enter the keystore's password on the command line rather than be prompted for it.
`-keypass` *password*	Allows you to enter your alias's password on the command line rather than be prompted for it.
`-sigfile` *file*	Specifies the base name for the `.SF` and `.DSA` files if you don't want the base name to be taken from your alias; `file` must be composed only of uppercase letters (A–Z), numerals (0–9), hyphens, and underscores.
`-signedjar` *file*	Specifies the name of the signed JAR file to be generated if you don't want the original unsigned file to be overwritten with the signed file.

Example

Let's look at a couple of examples of signing a JAR file with the Jarsigner tool. In these examples we will assume that

- Your alias is `johndoe`
- The keystore you want to use is in the file `mykeys` in the current working directory
- The keystore's password is `abc123`
- The password for your alias is `mypass`

Under these assumptions you could use the following command to sign a JAR file named `app.jar`:

```
jarsigner -keystore mykeys -storepass abc123
          -keypass mypass app.jar johndoe
```

Because this command doesn't make use of the `-sigfile` option, the `.SF` and `.DSA` files it creates would be named `JOHNDOE.SF` and `JOHNDOE.DSA`. Because the command doesn't use the `-signedjar` option, the resulting signed file will overwrite the original version of `app.jar`.

Let's look at what would happen if you used a different combination of options:

```
jarsigner -keystore mykeys -sigfile SIG
          -signedjar SignedApp.jar app.jar johndoe
```

This time you would be prompted to enter the passwords for both the keystore and your alias, because the passwords aren't specified on the command line. The signature and signature block files would be named `SIG.SF` and `SIG.DSA`, respectively, and the signed JAR file `SignedApp.jar` would be placed in the current directory. The original unsigned JAR file would remain unchanged.

Jarsigner Reference Page

Complete reference pages for the JAR Signing and Verification tool are online:

- Jarsigner reference page with Win32 examples[1]
- Jarsigner reference page with Solaris examples[2]

The Java Development Kit provides the Key and Certificate Management tool (Keytool) for managing keystores:

- Keytool reference page for Win32[3]
- Keytool reference page for Solaris[4]

The JDK 1.1 Java Security Tool

If you're working with JDK 1.1, you'll use the Java Security tool to sign JAR files. You invoke this tool with the `javakey` command, so we'll call it Javakey for short.

---

1 http://java.sun.com/products/jdk/1.2/docs/tooldocs/win32/jarsigner.html
2 http://java.sun.com/products/jdk/1.2/docs/tooldocs/solaris/jarsigner.html
3 http://java.sun.com/products/jdk/1.2/docs/tooldocs/win32/keytool.html
4 http://java.sun.com/products/jdk/1.2/docs/tooldocs/solaris/keytool.html

The Javakey tool manages a database containing public/private key pairs and related certificates. In order to sign a JAR file with the Javakey tool, you need to have a public/private key pair in Javakey's database. The Javakey tool will look for the database at the location specified by the `identity.database` property in the security properties file, `java.security`, located in the `jre/lib/security` directory of the JDK software. The database typically holds key pairs for many different potential signers, each key pair being associated with the user name of a signer.

In addition to key pairs, Javakey's database contains certificates for the public keys. When a certificate is added to the database, Javakey assigns it a unique number for identification purposes.

To sign a file, you must provide Javakey with several pieces of information:

- User name of the key pair to use
- Number of the certificate to use
- Name that the signature and signature block files are to have
- Name that the signed JAR file is to have

You provide this information to Javakey by using a *directive file*, a property file that Javakey reads when signing a JAR file. Here's a sample directive file:

```
# The signer property specifies the username corresponding to
# the key pair that Javakey is to use to sign the JAR file.
# In this example, Javakey will sign the file using the key pair
# belonging to user "rita".

signer=rita

# The cert property tells Javakey which certificate to use. Each
# certificate in Javakey's database is identified by a number.
# To see a list of all the certificates and associated numbers
# in the database, use the command 'javakey -ld'.

cert=1

# The signature.file property specifies the name that the
# signature file and signature block file are to have.  In this
# example, the files will be named SIGFILE.SF and SIGFILE.DSA,
# respectively.

signature.file=sigfile
```

```
# The out.file property specifies the name that Javakey should
# give to the signed JAR file it produces.  This property is
# optional. If it's not present, Javakey will give the signed
# file the name of the original JAR file, but with a .sig
# filename extension.

out.file=rita.jar
```

Once your directive file is ready, you sign a JAR file by using a command of the form

```
javakey -gs directive-file jar-file
```

In this command

- The `-gs` option tells Javakey to sign a JAR file.
- The path name `directive-file` indicates the directive file that Javakey should use.
- The path name `jar-file` refers to the JAR file you want to sign.

Javakey will place the signed JAR file in the current directory.

Javakey can perform many other functions related to managing the key/certificate database. See the online JDK documentation for more information about Javakey:

- Javakey reference page for Win32[1]
- Javakey reference page for Solaris[2]

Verifying Signed JAR Files

Typically, verification of signed JAR files will be the responsibility of your Java runtime environment. Assuming that your browser uses a 1.1 or later runtime environment, it will verify signed applets that it downloads. In version 1.2 of the Java platform, signed applications invoked with the `-jar` option of the interpreter will be verified by the runtime environment.

However, you can verify signed JAR files yourself by using the JDK 1.2 Jarsigner tool. You might want to do this, for example, to test a signed JAR file that

---

1 http://java.sun.com/products/jdk/1.1/docs/tooldocs/win32/javakey.html
2 http://java.sun.com/products/jdk/1.1/docs/tooldocs/solaris/javakey.html

you've prepared. The Jarsigner tool can verify files that were signed with either Jarsigner or the JDK 1.1 Javakey tool.

Note: JDK 1.1 does not provide a utility for verifying signed JAR files.

The basic command to use for verifying a signed JAR file is

```
jarsigner -verify jar-file
```

This command will verify the JAR file's signature and ensure that the files in the archive haven't changed since it was signed. You'll see the following message if the verification is successful:

```
jar verified.
```

If you try to verify an unsigned JAR file, the following message results:

```
jar is unsigned. (signatures missing or not parsable)
```

If the verification fails, an appropriate message is displayed. For example, if the contents of a JAR file have changed since the JAR file was signed, a message similar to the following will result if you try to verify the file:

```
jarsigner: java.lang.SecurityException: invalid SHA1
signature file digest for test/classes/Manifest.class
```

49 Using JAR-Related APIs Introduced in 1.2

VERSION 1.2 of the Java platform contains several new classes that greatly expand the number of ways that you can use JAR files. Some of these new APIs are the

- `java.util.jar` package
- `java.net.JarURLConnection` class
- `java.net.URLClassLoader` class

To give you an idea of the possibilities these new APIs open up, this lesson guides you through the inner workings of a sample application, `JarRunner`.

`JarRunner` enables you to run an application that's bundled in a JAR file by specifying the JAR file's URL on the command line. For example, if an application called `TargetApp` were bundled in a JAR file at `http://www.xxx.yyy/TargetApp.jar`, you could run the application by using this command:

```
java JarRunner http://www.xxx.yyy/TargetApp.jar
```

In order for `JarRunner` to work, it must be able to perform the following tasks, all of which are accomplished by using the new APIs:

- Access the remote JAR file and establish a communications link with it
- Inspect the JAR file's manifest to see which of the classes in the archive is the main class
- Load the classes in the JAR file

The JarRunner application consists of two classes, JarRunner and JarClassLoader. JarRunner delegates most of the JAR-handling tasks to the JarClassLoader class. JarClassLoader extends the new java.net.URLClassLoader class of the 1.2 platform. You can browse the source code for the JarRunner and JarClassLoader classes before proceeding with the lesson:

- JarRunner.java (page 875)
- JarClassLoader.java (page 873)

This lesson has two sections.

The JarClassLoader Class (page 600)
This section shows you how JarClassLoader uses some of the new APIs to perform tasks required for the JarRunner application to work.

The JarRunner Class (page 603)
This section summarizes the JarRunner class that comprises the JarRunner application.

The JarClassLoader Class

The JarClassLoader class extends jar.net.URLClassLoader, a new class in the Java 1.2 platform. As its name implies, URLClassLoader is designed to be used for loading classes and resources that are accessed by searching a set of URLs. The URLs can refer either to directories or to JAR files.

In addition to subclassing URLClassLoader, JarClassLoader makes use of features in two other new JAR-related APIs: the java.util.jar package and the java.net.JarURLConnection class. In this section we'll look in detail at the constructor and two methods of JarClassLoader.

The JarClassLoader Constructor

The constructor takes an instance of java.net.URL as an argument. The URL passed to this constructor will be used elsewhere in JarClassLoader to find the JAR file from which classes are to be loaded.

```
public JarClassLoader(URL url) {
    super(new URL[] { url });
    this.url = url;
}
```

The URL object is passed to the constructor of the superclass, URLClassLoader, which takes as an argument a URL[] array rather than a single URL instance.

The getMainClassName Method

Once a JarClassLoader object is constructed with the URL of a JAR-bundled application, it's going to need a way to determine which class in the JAR file is the application's entry point. That's the job of the getMainClassName method.

```
public String getMainClassName() throws IOException {
    URL u = new URL("jar", "", url + "!/");
    JarURLConnection uc = (JarURLConnection)u.openConnection();
    Attributes attr = uc.getMainAttributes();

    return attr !=
      (null ? attr.getValue(Attributes.Name.MAIN_CLASS) : null);
}
```

You may recall from section JAR Files as Applications — *1.2 platform only* (page 20) in the previous lesson that a JAR-bundled application's entry point is specified by the Main-Class header of the JAR file's manifest. To understand how getMainClassName accesses the Main-Class header value, let's look at the method in detail, paying special attention to the new JAR-handling features it uses.

The JarURLConnection class and JAR URLs

The getMainClassName method uses the JAR URL format specified by the java.net.JarURLConnection class. The syntax for the URL of a JAR file is as in this example:

```
jar:http://www.xxx.yyy/jarfile.jar!/
```

The terminating !/ separator indicates that the URL refers to an entire JAR file. Anything following the separator refers to specific JAR-file contents, as in this example:

```
jar:http://www.xxx.yyy/jarfile.jar!/mypackage/myclass.class
```

The first line in the getMainClassName method is

```
URL u = new URL("jar", "", url + "!/");
```

This statement constructs a new URL object representing a JAR URL, appending the !/ separator to the URL that was used in creating the JarClassLoader instance.

The java.net.JarURLConnection Class

This new class in the 1.2 platform represents a communications link between an application and a JAR file. This class has methods for accessing the JAR file's manifest. The second line of getMainClassName is

```
JarURLConnection uc = (JarURLConnection)u.openConnection();
```

In this statement a URL instance created in the first line opens a URLConnection. The URLConnection instance is then cast to JarURLConnection so it can take advantage of the JAR-handling features of JarURLConnection.

Fetching Manifest Attributes: java.util.jar.Attributes

With a JarURLConnection open to a JAR file, you can access the header information in the JAR file's manifest by using the getMainAttributes method of JarURLConnection. This method returns an instance of a new class in the 1.2 platform, java.util.jar.Attributes, which maps header names in JAR-file manifests with their associated string values. The third line in getMainClassName creates an Attributes object, as follows:

```
Attributes attr = uc.getMainAttributes();
```

To get the value of the manifest's Main-Class header, the fourth line of getMainClassName invokes the Attributes.getValue method.

```
return attr !=
    null ? attr.getValue(Attributes.Name.MAIN_CLASS) : null;
```

The method's argument, Attributes.Name.MAIN_CLASS, specifies that it's the value of the Main-Class header that you want. (The Attributes.Name class also provides static fields, such as MANIFEST_VERSION, CLASS_PATH, and SEALED for specifying other standard manifest headers.)

The invokeClass Method

You've seen how JarURLClassLoader can identify the main class in a JAR-bundled application. The last method to consider, JarURLClassLoader.invokeClass, enables that main class to be invoked to launch the JAR-bundled application, as follows:

```
public void invokeClass(String name, String[] args)
    throws ClassNotFoundException,
           NoSuchMethodException,
           InvocationTargetException
{
    Class c = loadClass(name);
    Method m =
        c.getMethod("main", new Class[] { args.getClass() });
    m.setAccessible(true);
    int mods = m.getModifiers();
    if (m.getReturnType() != void.class ||
                         !Modifier.isStatic(mods) ||
                         !Modifier.isPublic(mods)) {
        throw new NoSuchMethodException("main");
    }
    try {
        m.invoke(null, new Object[] { args });
    } catch (IllegalAccessException e) {
        // This should not happen,
        // as we have disabled access checks
    }
}
```

The `invokeClass` method takes two arguments: the name of the application's entry point class and an array of string arguments to pass to the entry point class's `main` method. First, the main class is loaded:

```
Class c = loadClass(name);
```

The `loadClass` method is inherited from `java.lang.ClassLoader`.

Once the `main` class is loaded, the reflection API of the `java.lang.reflect` package is used to pass the arguments to the class and to launch it. You can refer to the trail Reflection (page 681) for a review of reflection.

The JarRunner Class

The `JarRunner` application is launched with a command of the form

```
java JarRunner url [arguments]
```

The previous section showed how `JarClassLoader` is able to identify and to load the main class of a JAR-bundled application from a given URL. To complete the `JarRunner` application, therefore, we need to be able to take a URL and any arguments from the command line and to pass them to an instance of `JarClassLoader`. These tasks belong to the `JarRunner` class, the entry point of the `JarRunner` application.

It begins by creating a `java.net.URL` object from the URL specified on the command line.

```
public static void main(String[] args) {
    if (args.length < 1) {
        usage();
    }
    URL url = null;
    try {
        url = new URL(args[0]);
    } catch (MalformedURLException e) {
        fatal("Invalid URL: " + args[0]);
    }
    ...
```

If `args.length < 1`, no URL was specified on the command line, so a usage message is printed. If the first command line argument is a good URL, a new `URL` object is created to represent it.

Next, `JarRunner` creates a new instance of `JarClassLoader`, passing to the constructor the URL that was specified on the command line.

```
JarClassLoader cl = new JarClassLoader(url);
```

As we saw in the previous section, it's through `JarClassLoader` that JarRunner taps into the new JAR-handling APIs of the 1.2 platform.

The URL passed to the `JarClassLoader` constructor is that of the JAR-bundled application that you want to run. `JarRunner` next calls the class loader's `getMainClassName` method to identify the entry point class for the application.

```
String name = null;
try {
    name = cl.getMainClassName();
} catch (IOException e) {
    System.err.println("I/O error while loading JAR file:");
    e.printStackTrace();
    System.exit(1);
}
```

```
if (name == null) {
    fatal("Specified jar file does not contain a 'Main-Class'" +
          " manifest attribute");
}
```

The key statement is highlighted in bold. The other statements are for error handling.

Once `JarRunner` has identified the application's entry point class, only two steps remain: passing any arguments to the application and launching the application. `JarRunner` performs these steps with this code:

```
// Get arguments for the application
String[] newArgs = new String[args.length - 1];
System.arraycopy(args, 1, newArgs, 0, newArgs.length);

// Invoke application's main class
try {
    cl.invokeClass(name, newArgs);
} catch (ClassNotFoundException e) {
    fatal("Class not found: " + name);
} catch (NoSuchMethodException e) {
    fatal("Class does not define a 'main' method: " + name);
} catch (InvocationTargetException e) {
    e.getTargetException().printStackTrace();
    System.exit(1);
}
```

Recall that the first command line argument was the URL of the JAR-bundled application. Any arguments to be passed to that application are therefore in element `1` and beyond in the `args` array. `JarRunner` takes those elements and creates a new array, called `newArgs`, to pass to the application (bold highlighting). `JarRunner` then passes the entry-point's class name and the new argument list to the `invokeClass` method of `JarClassLoader`. As we saw in the previous section, `invokeClass` will load the application's entry point class, pass it any arguments, and launch the application.

About the Author

ALAN SOMMERER was a physicist on the staff of the International Institute of Theoretical and Applied Physics at Iowa State University before moving to the Silicon Valley. After moving to California, he joined Warthman Associates in Palo Alto, where he did technical writing and applet programming for a variety of high-tech firms. Alan now writes documentation about the Java Development Kit for Sun Microsystems.

Acknowledgments

David Connelly, Roland Schemers, Hemma Prafullchandra, Benedict Gomes, Anand Palaniswamy, and Mary Dageforde all reviewed this lesson and/or provided code samples.

Java Extension Mechanism

by Alan Sommerer

THE extension mechanism is a new feature in the Java™ 1.2 platform. The extension mechanism provides a standard, scalable way to make custom APIs available to all applications running on the Java platform.

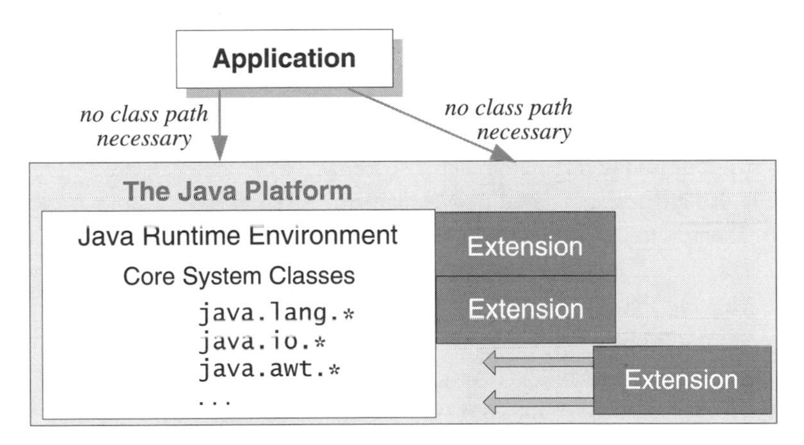

Figure 79 Extensions act as "add-on" modules to the Java platform. Their classes and public APIs are automatically available to any applications running on the platform.

Extensions are groups of packages and classes that augment the Java platform through the extension mechanism. As shown in the figure, the extension mechanism enables the runtime environment to find and to load extension classes without their having to be named on the class path. In that respect extension classes are similar to the Java platform's core classes. That's also where extensions get their name; they extend the platform's core API. The extension mechanism also provides a means for extension classes to be downloaded from remote locations for use by applets.[1]

Extensions are bundled as Java Archive (JAR) files, and this trail assumes that you are familiar with the JAR file format, as covered in the trail JAR File Format (page 565).

This trail has the following two lessons:

Creating and Using Extensions (page 609) shows you what you need to do to add an extension to your Java platform and how applets can benefit from the extension mechanism by downloading remote extension classes.

Making Extensions Secure (page 617) shows you how to control the security privileges and permissions that are granted to extensions on your platform. You'll see how to use the Java platform's security architecture if you're writing extensions classes of your own.

[1] You can find further information about extensions in The Java Extensions Framework section of the JDK 1.2 documentation on the CD-ROM that accompanies this book and online at: http://java.sun.com/products/jdk/1.2/docs/guide/extensions/index.html

http://java.sun.com/docs/books/tutorial/ext/basics/index.html

50 Creating and Using Extensions

ANY set of packages or classes can easily be made to play the role of an extension. The first step in turning a set of classes into an extension is to bundle them in a JAR file. Once that's done, you can turn the software into an extension. You can do so in two ways, as follows.

- Place the JAR file in a special location in the directory structure of the Java runtime environment, in which case it's called an *installed* extension.
- Reference the JAR file in a specified way from the manifest of the another JAR file, in which case it's called a *download* extension.

The three sections in this lesson show you how the extension mechanism works, using a simple "toy" extension as an example.

In this section, you'll create a simple installed extension and see how the runtime environment treats extension software as a part of the platform.

This section shows you how modify a JAR file's manifest so that the JAR-bundled software can make use of download extensions.

This short detour summarizes the 1.2 platform's new delegation model for loading classes and shows how it relates to loading classes in extensions.

The next lesson, Making Extensions Secure (page 617), uses the same extension to show how the Java platform controls the security permissions that are granted to extensions.

Installed Extensions

Installed extensions are JAR files in the lib/ext directory of the Java runtime environment (JRE) software. As its name implies, the JRE is the runtime portion of the Java Development Kit and contains the platform's core API but not development tools, such as compilers and debuggers. The JRE is available either by itself or as part of the Java Development Kit.

In the 1.2 platform the JRE is a strict subset of the JDK software. The following figure shows the JDK 1.2 software directory tree.

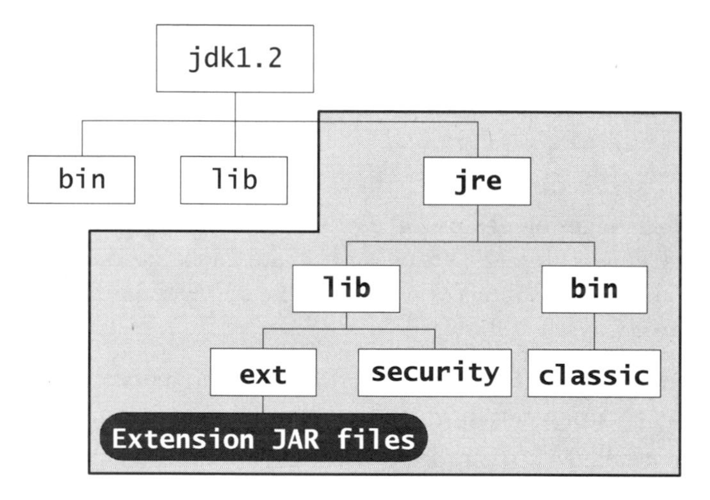

Figure 80 The JDK 1.2 software directory structure. The JRE consists of those directories within the highlighted box. Any JAR file in the JRE's lib/ext directory is automatically treated by the runtime environment as an extension.

A Simple Example

Let's create a simple installed extension. Our extension consists of one class, RectangleArea, that computes the areas of rectangles.

```
public final class RectangleArea {
    public static int area(java.awt.Rectangle r) {
        return r.width * r.height;
    }
}
```

This class has a single method, area, that takes an instance of java.awt.Rectangle and returns the rectangle's area.

Suppose that you want to test RectangleArea with an application called AreaApp.

```
import java.awt.*;

public class AreaApp {
   public static void main(String[] args) {
        int width = 10;
        int height = 5;
        Rectangle r = new Rectangle(width, height);
        System.out.println("The rectangle's area is "
                             + RectangleArea.area(r));
   }
}
```

This application instantiates a 10 x 5 rectangle and then prints out its area, using the RectangleArea.area method.

Running AreaApp without the Extension Mechanism

Let's first review how you would run the AreaApp application without using the extension mechanism. We'll assume that the RectangleArea class is bundled in a JAR file named area.jar.

The RectangleArea class is not part of the Java platform, of course, so you would need to place the area.jar file on the class path in order to run AreaApp without getting a runtime exception. If area.jar were in the directory /home/user, for example, you could use this command:

```
java -classpath .:/home/user/area.jar AreaApp
```

The class path specified in this command contains both the current directory, containing AreaApp.class, and the path to the JAR file containing the RectangleArea package. You would get the desired output by running this command:

```
The rectangle's area is 50
```

Running AreaApp by Using the Extension Mechanism

Now let's look at how you would run AreaApp by using the RectangleArea class as an extension. To make the RectangleArea class into an extension, you place the file area.jar into the lib/ext directory of the JRE. That automatically gives the RectangleArea the status of being an installed extension.

With area.jar installed as an extension, you can run AreaApp without needing to specify the class path.

```
java AreaApp
```

Because you're using area.jar as an installed extension, the runtime environment will be able to find and to load the RectangleArea class, even though you haven't specified it on the class path. Similarly, any applet or application being run by any user on your system would be able to find and to use the RectangleArea class.

Download Extensions

Download extensions are classes, including those in JAR files, that are specified in the Class-Path headers in the manifests of other JAR files. Assume, for example, that a.jar and b.jar are two JAR files in the same directory and that the manifest of a.jar contains this header:

```
Class-Path: b.jar
```

Then the classes in b.jar serve as extension classes for purposes of the classes in a.jar. The classes in a.jar can invoke classes in b.jar without those in b.jar having to be named on the class path; a.jar may or may not itself be an extension. If b.jar weren't in the same directory as a.jar, the value of the Class-Path header should be set to the relative path name of b.jar.

There's nothing special about the classes that are playing the role of a download extension. They are treated as extensions solely because they're referenced by the manifest of another JAR file. To get a better understanding of how download extensions work, let's create one and put it to use.

An Example

Suppose that you want to create an applet that makes use of the RectangleArea class of the previous section.

```
public final class RectangleArea {
    public static int area(java.awt.Rectangle r) {
        return r.width * r.height;
    }
}
```

In the previous section you made the RectangleArea class into an installed extension by placing the JAR file containing it into the lib/ext directory of the JRE. By making it an installed extension, you enabled any application to use the RectangleArea class as if it were part of the Java platform.

If you want to be able to use the RectangleArea class from an applet, the situation is a little different. Suppose, for example, that you have an applet, AreaApplet, that makes use of class RectangleArea.

```
import java.applet.Applet;
import java.awt.*;

public class AreaApplet extends Applet {
    Rectangle r;

    public void init() {
        int width = 10;
        int height = 5;
        r = new Rectangle(width, height);
    }

    public void paint(Graphics g) {
        g.drawString("The rectangle's area is "
                         + RectangleArea.area(r), 10, 10);
    }
}
```

This applet instantiates a 10 x 5 rectangle and then displays its area by using the RectangleArea.area method.

However, you can't assume that everyone who downloads and uses your applet is going to have the RectangleArea class available on the system, as an installed extension or otherwise. One way around that problem is to make the RectangleArea class available from the server side, and you can do that by using it as a download extension.

To see how that's done, let's assume that you've bundled AreaApplet in a JAR file called AreaApplet.jar and that the class RectangleArea is bundled in RectangleArea.jar. In order for RectangleArea.jar to be treated as a download extension, RectangleArea.jar must be listed in the Class-Path header in the manifest of AreaApplet.jar. That manifest might look like this, for example:

```
Manifest-Version: 1.0
Class-Path: RectangleArea.jar
```

The value of the `Class-Path` header in this manifest is `RectangleArea.jar` with no path specified, indicating that `RectangleArea.jar` is located in the same directory as the applet's JAR file.

More about the Class-Path Header

If an applet or application uses more than one extension, you can list multiple URLs in a manifest. For example, the following is a valid header:

```
Class-Path: area.jar servlet.jar images/
```

In the `Class-Path` header any URLs listed that don't end with a slash (/) are assumed to be JAR files. URLs ending in / indicate directories. In the preceding example, `images/` might be a directory containing resources needed by the applet or the application.

You can also specify multiple extension URLs by using more than one `Class-Path` header in the manifest.

```
Class-Path: area.jar
Class-Path: servlet.jar
```

Download extensions can be "daisy chained," meaning that the manifest of one download extension can have a `Class-Path` header that refers to a second extension, which can refer to a third extension, and so on.

Understanding Extension Class Loading

The extension framework makes use of the new class-loading mechanism in the Java 1.2 platform. When the runtime environment needs to load a new class, it looks for the class in the following locations, in order:

1. **Bootstrap classes**: the runtime classes in `rt.jar` and internationalization classes in `i18n.jar`.
2. **Installed extensions**: classes in JAR files in the `lib/ext` directory of the JRE.
3. **The class path**: classes, including classes in JAR files, on paths specified by the system property `java.class.path`. If a JAR file on the class path has a manifest with a `Class-Path` attribute, JAR files specified by the `Class-Path` attribute will be searched also. By default, the `java.class.path`'s property's value is `.`, the current directory. You can

change the value by setting the `CLASSPATH` environment variable or by using the `-classpath` or `-cp` command-line options. These command-line options override the setting of the `CLASSPATH` environment variable. Note that in the Java 1.2 software, `java.class.path` no longer includes the bootstrap classes in `rt.jar` and `i18n.jar`.

The precedence list tells you, for example, that the class path is searched only if a class to be loaded hasn't been found among the classes in `rt.jar`, `i18n.jar`, or the installed extensions.

Unless your software instantiates its own class loaders for special purposes, you don't really need to know much more than to keep this precedence list in mind. In particular you should be aware of any class name conflicts that might be present. For example, if you list a class on the class path, you'll get unexpected results if the runtime environment instead loads another class of the same name that it found in an installed extension.

The 1.2 Class-Loading Mechanism

The Java 1.2 platform uses a new delegation model for loading classes. The basic idea is that every class loader has a "parent" class loader. When loading a class, a class loader first "delegates" the search for the class to its parent class loader before attempting to find the class itself.

Here are some highlights of the class-loading API:

- Constructors in `java.lang.ClassLoader` and its subclasses allow you to specify a parent when you instantiate a new class loader. If you don't explicitly specify a parent, the virtual machine's system class loader will be assigned as the default parent.
- The `loadClass` method in `ClassLoader` performs these tasks, in order, when called to load a class:
    1. If a class has already been loaded, it returns it.
    2. Otherwise it delegates the search for the new class to the parent class loader.
    3. If the parent class loader doesn't find the class, `loadClass` calls the method `findClass` to find and to load the class.
- The `findClass` method of `ClassLoader` searches for the class in the current class loader if the class wasn't found by the parent class loader. You will probably want to override this method when you instantiate a class loader subclass in your application.

- The class `java.net.URLClassLoader` has been added to the core API. This class serves as the basic class loader for extensions and other JAR files, overriding the `findClass` method of `java.lang.ClassLoader` to search one or more specified URLs for classes and resources.

To see a sample application that uses some of the new API as it relates to JAR files, see the trail JAR File Format (page 565).

Changes to the java Command

The 1.2 platform's class-loading mechanism is reflected in some changes to the `java` command.

- The 1.2 JRE now includes the same Java interpreter, invoked with the `java` command, as is in the JDK 1.2 software. This tool replaces the old `jre` tool in JRE 1.1.
- In the 1.2 `java` tool the `-classpath` option is a shorthand way to set the `java.class.path` property. Formerly the `-classpath` option was used to override the search path for system classes.
- The `-cp` option, formerly part of the `jre` utility, has been added as an option to the `java` command. The `-cp` and `-classpath` options are equivalent.
- The `-jar` option has been added for running applications that are packaged in JAR files. For a description and examples of this new option, see the trail JAR File Format (page 565).

http://java.sun.com/docs/books/tutorial/ext/security/index.html

51 Making Extensions Secure

NOW that you've seen how to use extensions, you may be wondering what security privileges extensions have. If you're developing an extension that does file I/O, for example, you'll need to know how your extension is granted the appropriate permissions for reading and writing files. Conversely if you're thinking about using an extension developed by someone else, you'll want to understand clearly what security privileges the extension has and how to change those privileges should you desire to do so.

This lesson shows you how the Java platform's security architecture treats extensions. You'll see how to tell what privileges are granted to extension software, and you'll learn how to modify extension privileges by following some simple steps. In addition, you'll learn how to seal packages within your extensions to restrict access to specified parts of your code.

This lesson has the following two sections:

Setting Privileges for Extensions (page 618)
: This section contains some examples that show you what conditions must be met for extensions to be granted permissions to perform security-sensitive operations. Security-sensitive operations are those which involve accessing system resources such as the file system.

Sealing Packages in Extensions (page 622)
: This section shows you how to modify an extension's manifest to seal extension packages. You can optionally seal packages in extension JAR files as an

additional security measure. If a package is sealed, all classes defined in that package must originate from a single JAR file.

You'll find links and references to relevant security documentation at appropriate places throughout this lesson. For complete information on security, you can refer to the following:

- The trail Security (page 477)
- The security section of the JDK documentation[1]

Setting Privileges for Extensions

If a security manager is in force, the following conditions must be met to enable extension software, any software, including to perform security-sensitive operations.

- The security-sensitive code in the extension must be wrapped in a `PrivilegedAction` object.
- The security policy implemented by the security manager must grant the appropriate permission to the extension. By default, installed extensions are granted all security permissions as if they were part of the core platform API. The permissions granted by the security policy apply only to code wrapped in the `PrivilegedAction` instance.

Let's look at each of these conditions in a little more detail, with some examples.

Using the PrivilegedAction Class

Suppose that you want to modify the `RectangleArea` class in the extension example of the previous lesson to write rectangle areas to a file rather than to `stdout`. Writing to a file, however, is a security-sensitive operation, so if your software is going to be running under a security manager, you'll need to mark your code as being privileged. There are two steps you need to take to do so.

1. You need to place code that performs security-sensitive operations within the `run` method of an object of type `java.security.PrivilegedAction`.
2. You must use that `PrivilegedAction` object as the argument in a call to the `doPrivileged` method of `java.security.AccessController`.

If we apply those guidelines to the `RectangleArea` class, our class definition would look something like this:

---

[1] http://java.sun.com/products/jdk/1.2/docs/guide/security/index.html

```
import java.io.*;
import java.security.*;

public final class RectangleArea {
    public static void writeArea(final java.awt.Rectangle r) {
        AccessController.doPrivileged(new PrivilegedAction() {
            public Object run() {
                try {
                    int area = r.width * r.height;
                    FileWriter fw =
                            new FileWriter("/tmp/AreaOutput");
                    fw.write("Rectangle's area is " + area);
                    fw.flush();
                    fw.close();
                } catch(IOException ioe) {
                    System.err.println(ioe);
                }
                return null;
            }
        });
    }
}
```

The single method in this class, `writeArea`, computes the area of a rectangle and writes the area to a file called `AreaOutput` in the `/tmp` directory.

The security-sensitive statements dealing with the output file are placed within the `run` method of a new instance of `PrivilegedAction`. (Note that `run` requires that an `Object` instance be returned. The returned object can be `null`.) The new `PrivilegedAction` instance is then passed as an argument in a call to `AccessController.doPrivileged`.

For more information about using `doPrivileged`, see New API for Privileged Blocks in the JDK documentation.[1]

Wrapping security-sensitive code in a `PrivilegedAction` object in this manner is the first requirement for enabling an extension to perform security-sensitive operations. The second requirement is: getting the security manager to grant the privileged code the appropriate permissions.

Specifying Permissions with the Security Policy

The security policy in force at runtime is specified by a *policy file*. The default policy is set by the file `lib/security/java.policy` in the JRE software.

---

[1] The API documentation is available on the CD-ROM that accompanies this book and online at: http://java.sun.com/products/jdk/1.2/docs/guide/security/doprivileged.html

The policy file assigns security privileges to software by using *grant* entries. The policy file can contain any number of grant entries. The default policy file has this grant entry for installed extensions:

```
grant codeBase "file:${java.home}/lib/ext/" {
    permission java.security.AllPermission;
};
```

This entry specifies that files at the location `file:${java.home}/lib/ext/` are to be granted the permission called `java.security.AllPermission`. (Note that in the Java 1.2 platform `java.home` refers to the `jre` directory.) It's not too hard to guess that `java.security.AllPermission` grants installed extensions all the security privileges that it's possible to grant.

By default, then, installed extensions have no security restrictions. Extension software can perform security-sensitive operations as if there were no security manager installed, provided that security-sensitive code is contained in an instance of `PrivilegedAction` passed as an argument in a `doPrivileged` call.

To limit the privileges granted to extensions, you need to modify the policy file. To deny all privileges to all extensions, you could simply remove the default grant entry.

Not all permissions are as comprehensive as the `java.security.AllPermission` granted by default. After deleting the default grant entry, you can enter a new grant entry for one or more of the following limited permissions:

- `java.awt.AWTPermission`
- `java.io.FilePermission`
- `java.net.NetPermission`
- `java.util.PropertyPermission`
- `java.lang.reflect.ReflectPermission`
- `java.lang.RuntimePermission`
- `java.security.SecurityPermission`
- `java.io.SerializablePermission`
- `java.net.SocketPermission`

The Policy Permissions[1] file in the JDK documentation provides details about each of these permissions. Let's look at just one, `java.io.FilePermission`, as an example.

---

[1] The API documentation is available on the CD-ROM that accompanies this book and online at: http://java.sun.com/products/jdk/1.2/docs/guide/security/permissions.html

The only permission that the RectangleArea.writeArea method really needs is the permission to write to a file. Assuming that the RectangleArea class is bundled in the file area.jar, you could grant write privileges by adding this entry to the policy file:

```
grant codeBase "file:${java.home}/lib/ext/area.jar" {
    permission java.io.FilePermission "/tmp/*", "write";
};
```

The codeBase "file:${java.home}/lib/ext/area.jar" part of this entry guarantees that any permissions specified by this entry will apply only to your JAR file. The java.io.FilePermission permits access to files. The first string argument, "/tmp/*", indicates that area.jar is being granted permission to access all files in the /tmp directory. The second argument indicates that the file access being granted is only for writing. (Other choices for the second argument are "read", "delete", and "execute".)

Signing Extensions

You can use the policy file to place additional restrictions on the permissions granted to extensions by requiring them to be signed by a trusted entity. For a review of signing and verifying JAR files, see the trail JAR File Format (page 565).

To allow signature verification of extensions or other software in conjunction with granting permissions, the policy file must contain a *keystore entry*. The keystore entry specifies which keystore is to be used in the verification. Keystore entries have the form

```
keystore "keystore_url";
```

The URL *keystore_url* is either an absolute or relative. If it's relative, the URL is relative to the location of the policy file.

To indicate that an extension must be signed in order to be granted security privileges, you use the signedBy field. For example, the following entry indicates that the extension area.jar is to be granted write privileges only if it is signed by the users identified in the keystore by the aliases Robert and Rita:

```
grant signedBy "Robert,Rita", codeBase
               "file:${java.home}/lib/ext/area.jar" {
    permission java.io.FilePermission "*", "write";
};
```

If the `codeBase` field is omitted, the permissions are granted to *any* software, including installed or download extensions, that are signed by `Robert` or `Rita`.

```
grant signedBy "Robert,Rita" {
    permission java.io.FilePermission "*", "write";
};
```

For further details about the policy file format, see Signing Code and Granting It Permissions (page 525) in the Security trail.

Sealing Packages in Extensions

You can optionally *seal* packages in extension JAR files as an additional security measure. If a package is sealed, all classes defined in that package must originate from a single JAR file.

Without sealing, a "hostile" program could create a class and define it to be a member of one of your extension packages. The hostile software would then have free access to package-protected members of your extension package.

Sealing packages in extensions is no different than sealing any JAR-packaged classes. To seal your extension packages, you must add the `Sealed` header to the manifest of the JAR file containing your extension. You can seal individual packages by associating a `Sealed`header with the packages' `Name` headers. A `Sealed` header not associated with an individual package in the archive signals that all packages are sealed. Such a "global" `Sealed` header is overridden by any `Sealed` headers associated with individual packages. The value associated with the `Sealed` header is either `true` or `false`.

Examples

Let's look at a few sample manifest files. For these examples suppose that the JAR file contains these packages:

```
com/myCompany/package_1/
com/myCompany/package_2/
com/myCompany/package_3/
com/myCompany/package_4/
```

Suppose that you want to seal all four packages. You could do so by simply adding an archive-level `Sealed` header to the manifest, like this:

```
Manifest-Version: 1.0
Sealed: true
```

All packages in any JAR file having this manifest will be sealed.

If you wanted to seal only `com.myCompany.package_3`, you could do so with this manifest:

```
Manifest-Version: 1.0

Name: com/myCompany/package_3/
Sealed: true
```

In this example the only `Sealed` header is that associated with the `Name` header of package `com.myCompany.package_3`, so only that package is sealed. (The `Sealed` header is associated with the `Name` header because there are no blank lines between them.)

For a final example, suppose that you wanted to seal all packages *except for* `com.myCompany.package_2`. You could accomplish that with a manifest like this:

```
Manifest-Version: 1.0
Sealed: true

Name: com/myCompany/package_2/
Sealed: false
```

In this example the archive-level `Sealed: true` header indicates that all of the packages in the JAR file are to be sealed. However, the manifest also has a `Sealed: false` header associated with package `com.myCompany.package_2`, and that header overrides the archive-level sealing for that package. Therefore this manifest will cause all packages to be sealed except for `com.myCompany.package_2`.

About the Author

ALAN SOMMERER was a physicist on the staff of the International Institute of Theoretical and Applied Physics at Iowa State University before moving to the Silicon Valley. After moving to California, he joined Warthman Associates in Palo Alto, where he did technical writing and applet programming for a variety of high-tech firms. Alan now writes documentation about the Java Development Kit™ for Sun Microsystems.

Acknowledgments

David Connelly, Roland Schemers, Hemma Prafullchandra, Benedict Gomes, Anand Palaniswamy, Rosanna Lee, Jan Luehe and Mary Dageforde all reviewed this chapter and/or provided code samples.

http://java.sun.com/docs/books/tutorial/native1.1/index.html

Java Native Interface

by Beth Stearns

LESSONS in this trail show you how to integrate native code with programs written in the Java™ programming language. You will learn how to write *native methods*. Native methods are implemented in another programming language, such as C.

The Java™ Native Interface (JNI) is for programmers who want to run code from native language libraries or take advantage of components written in other programming languages outside the Java platform. Therefore, only experienced programmers should attempt to write native methods or to use the invocation API.

Overview of the JNI (page 629) introduces JNI concepts.

Writing a Java Program with Native Methods (page 633) explains how to compile and to run a Java program with a native method. This lesson walks you step by step through a simple example (the "Hello World!" of native methods) to illustrate how to write, compile, and run a program written in the Java programming language that includes native methods.

Integrating Java and Native Programs (page 643) shows you how to map Java types to native types. This lesson includes information about passing arguments of various data types into a native method and returning values of various data types from a native method. The lesson also shows how to implement a native method within a program written in the Java programming language.

Interacting with Java from the Native Side (page 649) describes many useful functions that your native language code can use to access Java objects and their members, create Java objects, throw exceptions, and more.

Invoking the Java Virtual Machine (page 671) explains how to invoke the Java Virtual Machine from your native application.

Summary of the JNI (page 675) lists the JNI methods and mapping tables to synthesize what you've learned.

Note: MacOS programmers should refer to MacOS Runtime for Java (MRJ). See `http://devworld.apple.com/java/`.

Security Consideration: The ability to load dynamic libraries is subject to approval by the current security manager. When working with native methods, you must load dynamic libraries. Some applets may not be able to use native methods because the browser or viewer they are running in restricts the ability to load dynamic libraries. For more information see the trail Security (page 477).

http://java.sun.com/docs/books/tutorial/native1.1/overview/index.html

52 Overview of the JNI

THE Java Native Interface (JNI) is the native programming interface for Java that is part of the JDK™. By writing programs using the JNI, you can run the same native library binary code on different virtual machine implementations on the same platform.

The material in this chapter covers the JNI for JDK 1.1. The JDK 1.2 contains additional JNI enhancements. See the API documentation included on the CD-ROM that accompanies this book and online here: `http://java.sun.com/products/jdk/1.2/docs/guide/jni/index.html`.

The JNI allows Java code that runs within a Java Virtual Machine (VM) to operate with applications and libraries written in other languages, such as C, C++, and assembly. In addition, the *invocation API* allows you to embed the Java Virtual Machine into your native applications.

Programmers use the JNI to write native methods when an application cannot be written entirely in the Java programming language. For example, you may need to use native methods and the JNI in the following situations:

- The standard Java class library may not support the platform-dependent features your application needs.
- You may already have a library or an application written in another programming language and wish to make it accessible to Java applications.
- You may want to implement a small portion of time-critical code in a lower-level programming language, such as assembly, and then have your Java application call these functions.

Programming through the JNI lets you use native methods to do many operations. Native methods may be written to leverage legacy applications, or they may be written explicitly to solve a problem that is best handled outside of the Java programming environment.

The JNI lets your native method use Java objects in the same way that Java code uses them. A native method can create Java objects, including arrays and strings, and then inspect and use these objects to perform its tasks. A native method can also inspect and use objects created by Java application code. A native method can even update Java objects that it created or that were passed to it, and these updated objects are available to the Java application. Thus both sides of an application—native language and Java—can create, update, and access Java objects and then share them.

Native methods can also easily call Java methods. Often you will already have developed a library of Java methods. Your native method does not need to "re-invent the wheel" to implement functionality already incorporated in existing Java methods. The native method, using the JNI, can call the existing Java method, pass it the required parameters, and get the results back when the method completes.

The JNI enables you to use the features of the Java programming language from your native method. In particular, you can catch and throw exceptions from the native method and have them handled in the Java application. Native methods can also get information about Java classes. By calling special JNI functions, native methods can load Java classes and obtain class information. Finally, native methods can use the JNI to perform runtime type checking.

For example, the following figure shows how a legacy C program can use the JNI to link with Java libraries, call Java methods, use Java classes, and so on.

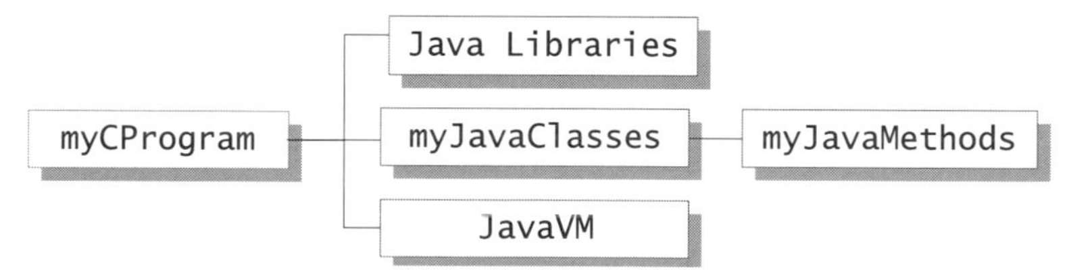

Figure 81 How legacy programs use the JNI.

The next figure illustrates calling native language functions from a Java application. This diagram shows the many possibilities for using the JNI from a Java program, including calling C routines, using C++ classes, calling assembler routines, and so on.

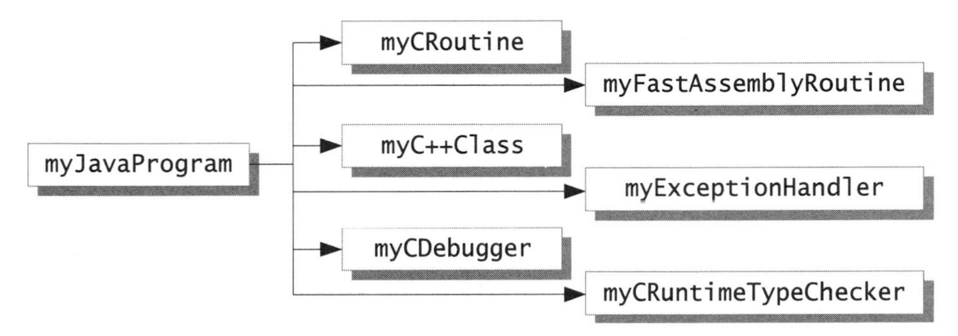

Figure 82 How Java applications use the JNI.

It is easy to see that the JNI serves as the glue between Java and native applications. The following diagram shows how the JNI ties the C side of an application to the Java side.

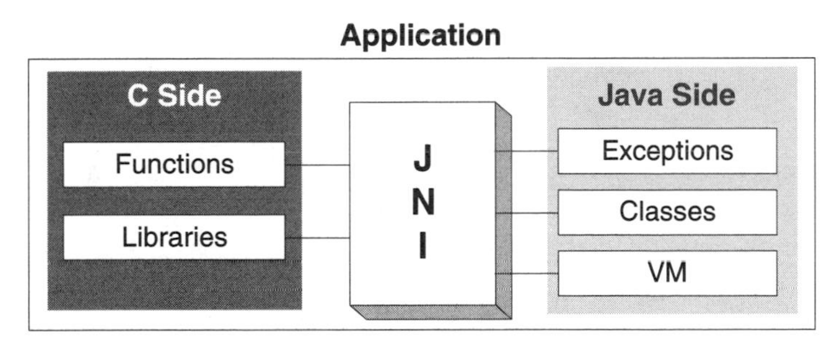

Figure 83 JNI with Java and native applications.

http://java.sun.com/docs/books/tutorial/native1.1/stepbystep/index.html

53 Writing a Java Program with Native Methods

THIS lesson walks you through the steps necessary to integrate native code with programs written in Java. In this lesson you implement the canonical "Hello World!" program. This program has one Java class, `HelloWorld`. `HelloWorld.java` declares a native method that displays "Hello World!" and also implements the `main` method for the overall program. The implementation for the native method is provided in C.

Note: This lesson assumes that you are starting with neither existing C functions nor Java classes. Although in the real world you probably have existing C functions that you wish to integrate with Java programs, you will still need to modify the types for these C functions to work with the JNI. To be sure that you use the correct types, it is best to begin by writing and compiling the Java code, as described here.

Writing native methods for Java programs is a multistep process. Each section in this lesson describes one of those steps.

Step 1: Write the Java Code (page 635)
: Your first step is to write the Java program. Create a Java class that declares the native method; this class contains the declaration for the native method and also includes a `main` method, which calls the native method.

Step 2: Compile the Java Code (page 637)
: Compile the Java class, which declares the native method and the `main` method.

Step 3: Create the .h File (page 637)
: Generate a header file for the native method, using `javah` with the native interface flag `-jni`. Once you've generated the header file, you have the formal signature for your native method.

Step 4: Write the Native Method Implementation (page 639)
: Write the implementation of the native method in the programming language of your choice, such as C or C++.

Step 5: Create a Shared Library (page 640)
: Compile the header and the implementation files into a shared library file.

Step 6: Run the Program (page 641)

The following figure illustrates these steps for the "Hello World" program.

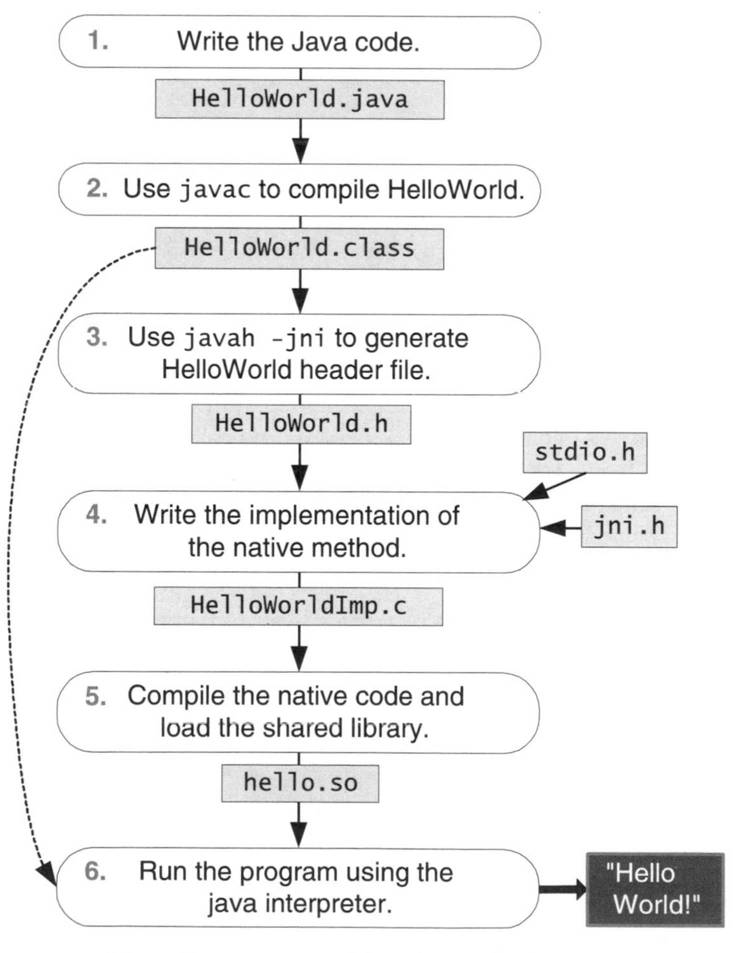

Figure 84 Steps to writing a Java program with native methods.

First, you create a Java class named HelloWorld that declares a native method. This class also includes a main method that creates a HelloWorld object and that calls the native method.

Next, you use javac to compile the Java code that you wrote in step 1. Then you use javah to create a JNI-style header file (a .h file) from the HelloWorld class. The header file provides a function signature for the implementation of the native method displayHelloWorld. (Note that, to be consistent with the rest of the tutorial, this lesson uses the term "signature" rather than the more correct term "prototype.")

In step 4 you write the implementation for the native method in a native language (such as ANSI C) source file. The implementation will be a regular C function that's integrated with your Java class.

In step 5 you use the C compiler to compile the .h file and the .c file that you created in steps 3 and 4 into a shared library. In Win32 terminology a shared library is called a dynamic link library (DLL).

Finally, you use java, the Java interpreter, to run the program.

The next sections describe each of these six steps in detail.

Step 1: Write the Java Code

The following Java code segment defines a class named HelloWorld, which declares one native method, implements a main method, and has a static code segment.

```
class HelloWorld {
    public native void displayHelloWorld();
    static {
        System.loadLibrary("hello");
    }

    public static void main(String[] args) {
        new HelloWorld().displayHelloWorld();
    }
}
```

Declare a Native Method

You must declare all methods, whether Java methods or native methods, within a class on the Java side. When you write a method implementation in a language other than Java, you must include the keyword `native` as part of the method's definition within the Java class. The `native` keyword signals to the Java compiler that the function is a native language function. It is easy to tell that the implementation for the `HelloWorld` class's `displayHelloWorld` method is written in another programming language, because the `native` keyword appears as part of its method definition:

```
public native void displayHelloWorld();
```

This native method declaration in your Java class provides only the method signature for `displayHelloWorld`. It provides no implementation for the method. You must provide the implementation for `displayHelloWorld` in a separate native language source file.

The method declaration for `displayHelloWorld` also indicates that the method is a public instance method, accepts no arguments, and returns no value. For more information about arguments to and return values from native methods, see the lesson Interacting with Java from the Native Side (page 649).

Load the Library

Compile the native language code that implements `displayHelloWorld` into a shared library. You will do this in the section Step 5: Create a Shared Library (page 640). The runtime system later loads the shared library into the Java class that requires it. Loading the library into the Java class maps the implementation of the native method to its declaration.

The `HelloWorld` class uses the `System.loadLibrary` method, which loads the shared library that will be created when you compile the implementation code. Place this method within a static initializer. The argument to `System.loadLibrary` is the name of the shared library. This can be any name that you choose. The system uses a standard, platform-specific approach to convert the library name to a native library name. For example, the Solaris system converts the library name `hello` to `libhello.so`, whereas a Win32 system converts the same name to `hello.dll`.

The following static initializer from the `HelloWorld` class loads the appropriate library, named `hello`. The runtime system executes a class's static initializer when it loads the class.

```
static {
    System.loadLibrary("hello");
}
```

Write the Main Method

The `HelloWorld` class, because it is an application, also includes a `main` method to instantiate the class and to call the native method. The `main` method instantiates `HelloWorld` and calls the `displayHelloWorld` native method.

```
public static void main(String[] args) {
    new HelloWorld().displayHelloWorld();
}
```

You can see from the code sample that you call a native method in the same manner as you call a regular method. Just append the name of the method to the end of the object name, separated with a period (`.`). A matched set of parentheses `()`, follows the method name and encloses any arguments to pass into the method. The `displayHelloWorld` method doesn't take any arguments.

Step 2: Compile the Java Code

Use the Java compiler to compile the class that you created in the previous section, Step 1: Write the Java Code (page 635). Here's the command to use:

```
javac HelloWorld.java
```

Step 3: Create the .h File

In this step you use the `javah` utility program to generate a header file (a `.h` file) from the `HelloWorld` class. The header file provides a `C` function signature for the implementation of the native method `displayHelloWorld` defined in that class.

Run `javah -jni` now on the `HelloWorld` class that you created in the previous steps.

The name of the header file is the Java class name with a `.h` appended to the end. For example, the previous command will generate a file named `HelloWorld.h`.

By default, `javah` places the new `.h` file in the same directory as the `.class` file. Use the `-d` option to instruct `javah` to put the header files in a different directory.

The Function Definition

Look at the header file `HelloWorld.h`.

```
/* DO NOT EDIT THIS FILE - it is machine generated */
#include <jni.h>
/* Header for class HelloWorld */

#ifndef _Included_HelloWorld
#define _Included_HelloWorld
#ifdef __cplusplus
extern "C" {
#endif
/*
 * Class:     HelloWorld
 * Method:    displayHelloWorld
 * Signature: ()V
 */
JNIEXPORT void JNICALL Java_HelloWorld_displayHelloWorld
  (JNIEnv *, jobject);

#ifdef __cplusplus
}
```

The `Java_HelloWorld_displayHelloWorld` function provides the implementation for the `HelloWorld` class's native method `displayHelloWorld`, which you will write in the next section, Step 4: Write the Native Method Implementation (page 639). You use the same function signature when you write the implementation for the native method. If `HelloWorld` contained any other native methods, their function signatures would appear here as well.

The name of thc nativc language function that implements the native method consists of the prefix `Java_`, the package name, the class name, and the name of the native method. Between each name component is an underscore (_) separator. Graphically this looks as follows:

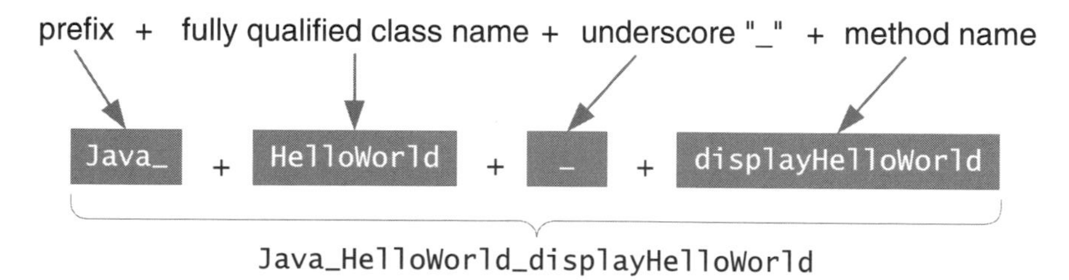

Figure 85 Constructing the `HelloWorld` native method name.

The native method `displayHelloWorld` within the `HelloWorld` class becomes `Java_HelloWorld_displayHelloWorld`. No package name appears in our example because `HelloWorld` is in the default package, which has no name.

Notice that the implementation of the native function, as it appears in the header file, accepts two parameters, even though in its definition on the Java side it accepts no parameters. The JNI requires every native method to have these two parameters.

The first parameter for every native method is a `JNIEnv` interface pointer. It is through this pointer that your native code accesses parameters and objects passed to it from the Java application. The second parameter is `jobject`, which references the current object. In a sense you can think of the `jobject` parameter as the `this` variable in Java. For a native instance method, such as the `displayHelloWorld` method in our example, the `jobject` argument is a reference to the current instance of the object. For native class methods this argument would be a reference to the method's Java class. Our example ignores both parameters. The next lesson, Integrating Java and Native Programs (page 643), explains how to access data by using the JNI interface pointer `env` parameter. The next lesson also provides more information about `jobject`.

Step 4: Write the Native Method Implementation

Now you can finally write the implementation for the native method in a language other than Java.

Note: Back to that "real world": C and C++ programmers may already have existing implementations of native methods. For those "real" methods, you must ensure that the native method signature matches the signature generated on the Java side. You should read this step so that you know how to match the native method signature to the Java one.

The function that you write must have the same function signature as the one generated by `javah` in the `HelloWorld.h` file in the section Step 3: Create the .h File (page 637). Recall that the function signature generated for the `HelloWorld` class's `displayHelloWorld` native method looks like this:

```
JNIEXPORT void JNICALL Java_HelloWorld_displayHelloWorld
     (JNIEnv *, jobject);
```

Here's the C language implementation for the native method `Java_HelloWorld_displayHelloWorld`. This implementation can be found in full in the Appendix in the file named `HelloWorldImp.c` (page 878).

```
#include <jni.h>
#include "HelloWorld.h"
#include <stdio.h>
JNIEXPORT void JNICALL_
Java_HelloWorld_displayHelloWorld(JNIEnv *env, jobject obj){
    printf("Hello world!);
    return;
}
```

The implementation for `Java_HelloWorld_displayHelloWorld` is straightforward. The function uses the `printf` function to display the string "`Hello World!`" and then returns.

The `HelloWorldImp.c` file includes three header files:

- `jni.h`: This header file provides information that the native language code requires to interact with the Java runtime system. When writing native methods, you must always include this file in your native language source files.
- `HelloWorld.h`: The `.h` file that you generated in the section Step 3: Create the .h File (page 637).
- `stdio.h`: The previous code snippet includes `stdio.h` because it uses the `printf` function. The `printf` function is part of the `stdio.h` library.

Step 5: Create a Shared Library

Remember that in the section Step 1: Write the Java Code (page 635) you used the following method call to load a shared library named `hello` into your program at runtime:

```
System.loadLibrary("hello");
```

Now you are ready to create this shared library.

In the previous section, Step 4: Write the Native Method Implementation (page 639), you created a C file in which you wrote the implementation for the `displayHelloWorld` native method. You saved the native method in the file `HelloWorldImp.c`. Now you must compile `HelloWorldImp.c` into a shared library, which you name `hello` to match the library name used in the `System.loadLibrary` method.

Compile the native language code that you created in the previous two steps into a shared library. On Solaris you'll create a shared library; on Win32 you'll create a dynamic link library (DLL). Remember to specify the path or paths to all necessary header files. See Creating and Loading Shared Libraries (page 919) in the Reference Appendix for information on forming a shared library name.

On Solaris the following command builds a shared library, `libhello.so`:

```
cc -G -I/usr/local/java/include \
      -I/usr/local/java/include/solaris \
      HelloWorldImp.c -o libhello.so
```

On Win32 the following command builds a dynamic link library, `hello.dll`, using Microsoft Visual C++ 4.0:

```
cl -Ic:\java\include -Ic:\java\include\win32
   -LD HelloWorldImp.c -Fehello.dll
```

Of course, you need to specify the `include` path that corresponds to the setup on your own machine.

For more information on the system-dependent mechanisms for loading a shared library, see Creating and Loading Shared Libraries (page 919) in the Reference Appendix.

Step 6: Run the Program

Now run the Java application (the `HelloWorld` class) with the Java interpreter, as follows:

```
java HelloWorld
```

You should see the following output:

```
Hello World!
```

If you see an exception like the following, you don't have your library path set up correctly.

```
java.lang.UnsatisfiedLinkError: no hello in shared library path
        at java.lang.Runtime.loadLibrary(Runtime.java)
        at java.lang.System.loadLibrary(System.java)
        at
        at java.lang.Thread.init(Thread.java)
```

The library path is a list of directories that the Java runtime system searches when loading libraries. Set your library path now, and make sure that the name of the directory where the `hello` library lives is in it. Refer to Set Your Library Path (page 921) in the Reference Appendix for details.

http://java.sun.com/docs/books/tutorial/native1.1/integrating/index.html

54 Integrating Java and Native Programs

THE Java Native Interface (JNI) defines a standard naming and calling convention so that the Java Virtual Machine (VM) can locate and invoke your native methods. This lesson shows you how to follow the JNI naming and calling conventions in order to use JNI functions from a native method. This lesson also teaches you how to declare types so that they can be correctly recognized by both the Java program and the native method.

This lesson consists of two sections.

On the Java side you declare a native method with the `native` keyword and an empty method body. On the native side you provide an implementation for the native method. You must be careful when writing native methods to "match" the native function implementation with the method signature in the Java header file. The `javah` tool, which is explained in the section Step 3: Create the .h File (page 637) in the previous lesson, helps you to generate native function prototypes that match the Java-side native method declaration.

The JNI defines a mapping of Java types and native language (C/C++) types. This section introduces the native types corresponding to both primitive Java types, such as `int` and `double`, and Java objects, including strings and arrays.

Declaring Native Methods

This section illustrates how to declare a native method in Java and how to generate the corresponding C/C++ function prototype.

The Java Side

Our first example, Prompt.java (page 879) found in full in the Appendix, contains a native method that accepts and prints a Java string. The program calls the native method, which waits for user input and then returns the line the user typed in.

The Prompt class contains a main method, which is used to invoke the program, and a native method, getLine, which is declared as follows:

```
private native String getLine(String prompt);
```

Notice that the declarations for native methods are almost identical to the declarations for regular, nonnative Java methods. However, you declare native methods differently, as follows:

- First, native methods must have the native keyword. The native keyword informs the Java compiler that the implementation for this method is provided in another language.
- Second, the native method declaration is terminated with a semicolon (the statement terminator symbol) because the Java class file does not include implementations for native methods.

The Native Language Side

You must declare and implement native methods in a native language, such as C or C++. Before you do this, however, it is helpful to generate the header file that contains the function prototype for the native method implementation.

Compile the Prompt.java file and then generate the .h file. First, compile the Prompt.java file as follows:

```
javac Prompt.java
```

Once you have successfully compiled Prompt.java and have created the Prompt.class file, you can generate a JNI-style header file by specifying a -jni option to javah.

```
javah -jni Prompt
```

Examine the full source code for Prompt.h (page 879) in the Appendix. Note the function prototype for the native method getLine that you declared in Prompt.java.

```
JNIEXPORT jstring JNICALL Java_Prompt_getLine
    (JNIEnv *, jobject, jstring);
```

The native method function definition in the implementation code must match the generated function signature in the header file. Always include JNIEXPORT and JNICALL in your native method function signatures. JNIEXPORT and JNICALL ensure that the source code compiles on platforms, such as Win32, that require special keywords for functions exported from dynamic link libraries.

Native method names are concatenated from the following components:

- The prefix Java_
- The fully qualified class name
- An underscore (_) separator
- The method name

Graphically, this looks as follows:

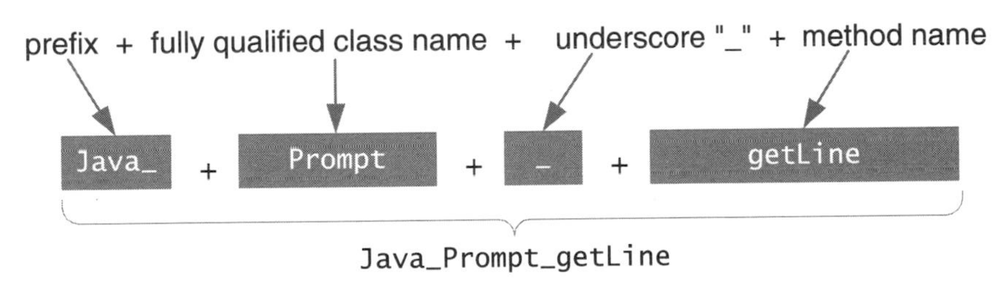

Figure 86 Forming native method names.

Thus the native code implementation for the Prompt.getLine method becomes Java_Prompt_getLine. (Remember that no package name component appears, because the Prompt class is in the default package.)

Overloaded native method names, in addition to the preceding components, have an extra two underscores (__) appended to the method name, followed by the argument signature. To illustrate, we created a second version of the Java program, Prompt2.java (page 880), and overloaded the getLine method by adding a second argument of type int. The two getLine method names in the Prompt2.h (page 880) header file look as follows:

```
Java_Prompt2_getLine__Ljava_lang_String_2
Java_Prompt2_getLine__Ljava_lang_String_2I
```

Recall from the section Step 3: Create the .h File (page 637) in the previous lesson that each native method has two parameters in addition to those that you declared on the Java side. The first parameter, `JNIEnv *`, is the JNI interface pointer, which is organized as a function table, with every JNI function at a known table entry point. Your native method invokes specific JNI functions to access Java objects through the `JNIEnv *` pointer. The `jobject` parameter is a reference to the object itself (it is like the `this` pointer in Java).

Finally, notice that the JNI has a set of type names, such as `jobject` and `jstring`, and that each type corresponds to Java types. This is covered in the next section.

Mapping between Java and Native Types

In this section you will learn how to reference Java types in your native method. You need to do this when you want to

- Access arguments passed in to a native method from a Java application
- Create Java objects in your native method
- Have your native method return results to the caller

Java Primitive Types

Your native method can directly access Java *primitive* types, such as Booleans, integers, floats, and so on, that are passed from programs written in Java. For example, the Java type `boolean` maps to the native language type `jboolean` (represented as unsigned 8 bits), whereas the Java type `float` maps to the native language type `jfloat` (represented by 32 bits). The following table describes the mapping of Java primitive types to native types.

Table 30 Primitive Types and Native Equivalents

Java Type	Native Type	Size in Bits
`boolean`	`jboolean`	8, unsigned
`byte`	`jbyte`	8
`char`	`jchar`	16, unsigned
`short`	`jshort`	16

Table 30 Primitive Types and Native Equivalents

Java Type	Native Type	Size in Bits
`int`	`jint`	32
`long`	`jlong`	64
`float`	`jfloat`	32
`double`	`jdouble`	64
`void`	`void`	N/A

Java Object Types

Java objects are passed by reference. All references to Java objects have the type `jobject`. For convenience and to avoid programming errors, the JNI implements a set of types that are conceptually all subclassed from (or are "subtypes" of) `jobject`, as follows:

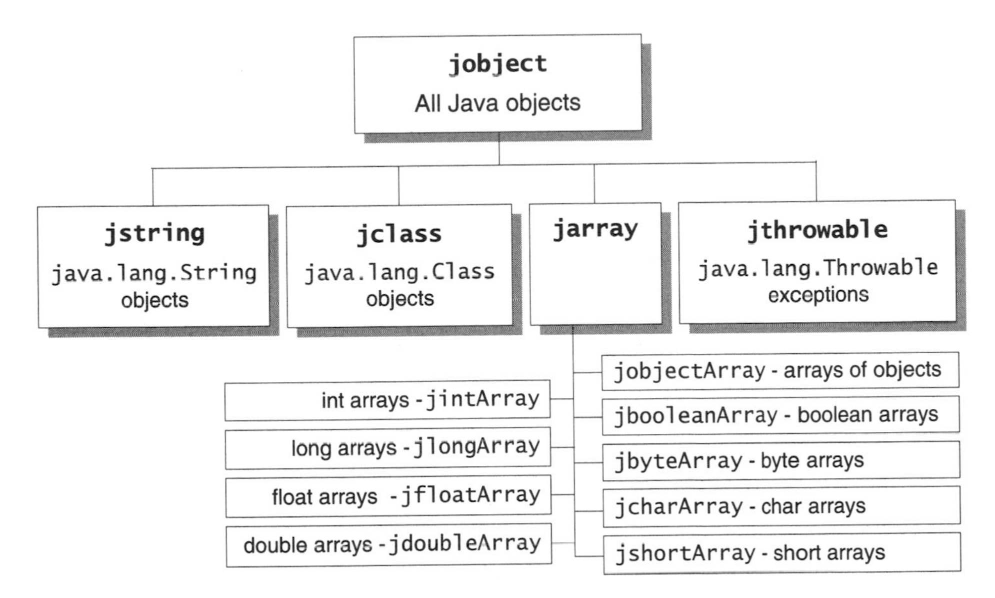

Figure 87 JNI `jobject` subtypes.

In our `Prompt.java` example the native method `getLine` takes a Java string as an argument and returns a Java string.

```
private native String getLine(String prompt);
```

The corresponding native implementation has type `jstring` for both the argument and the return value:

```
JNIEXPORT jstring JNICALL Java_Prompt_getLine
     (JNIEnv *, jobject, jstring);
```

Graphically, this looks as follows:

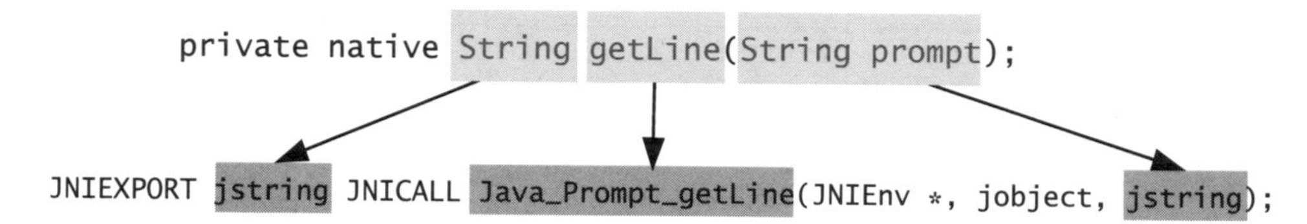

Figure 88 Mapping Java and native method types.

As mentioned, `jstring` corresponds to the Java type `String`. Notice that the second argument to `Java_Prompt_getLine`, which is the reference to the object itself, has type `jobject`.

http://java.sun.com/docs/books/tutorial/native1.1/interacting/index.html

55 Interacting with Java from the Native Side

THE JNI offers a set of standard interface functions. You can use these interface functions to call JNI functions from your native method code to access and manipulate Java objects, release Java objects, create new objects, call Java methods, and so on.

This lesson shows you how to use JNI functions from a native method. Each example consists of a Java program that calls various native methods implemented in the C programming language. The native methods, in turn, may call JNI functions to access the Java objects.

This lesson contains the following sections.

Strings are a particularly useful kind of object. The JNI provides a set of string-manipulation functions to ease the task of handling Java strings in native code. The programmer can use these functions to translate between Java strings and native strings in Unicode and UTF-8 formats.

Arrays are another kind of frequently used Java object. You can use JNI array-manipulation functions to create arrays and to access array elements.

The JNI-supported set of "callback" operations allow you to invoke a Java method from the native code. You locate the method by using its name and signature. You can also invoke both class and instance methods. Use the `javap` tool to generate JNI-style method signatures from class files.

Java Strings

In passing a string to a native method, a Java application passes the string as a `jstring` type. This `jstring` type is different from the regular C string type (`char *`). If your code tries to print a `jstring` directly, the likely result will be a VM crash. For example, the following code segment incorrectly tries to print a `jstring` and may result in a VM crash:

```
/* DO NOT USE jstring THIS WAY !!! */
JNIEXPORT jstring JNICALL
Java_Prompt_getLine(JNIEnv *env, jobject obj, jstring prompt){
    printf("%s", prompt);
    ...
```

Your native method code must use JNI functions to convert Java strings to native strings. The JNI supports the conversion to and from native Unicode and UTF-8 strings. In particular, UTF-8 strings use the highest bit-to-signal multibyte characters; they are therefore upward compatible with 7-bit ASCII. In Java UTF-8 strings are always zero-terminated.

Accessing Java Strings

Your native method needs to call `GetStringUTFChars` to correctly print the string passed to it from a Java application. `GetStringUTFChars` converts the built-in Unicode representation of a Java string into a UTF-8 string. Once you are certain that the string contains only 7-bit ASCII characters, you can directly pass the string to regular C language functions, such as `printf`, as is shown in `Prompt.c`:

```
JNIEXPORT jstring JNICALL
Java_Prompt_getLine(JNIEnv *env, jobject obj, jstring prompt){
    char buf[128];
    const char *str = (*env)->GetStringUTFChars(env, prompt, 0);
    printf("%s", str);
    (*env)->ReleaseStringUTFChars(env, prompt, str);
    ...
```

Note: When finished using the UTF-8 string, your native code must call `ReleaseStringUTFChars`, which informs the VM that the native method is finished with the string. The VM can then free the memory taken by the UTF-8 string. Failing to call `ReleaseStringUTFChars` results in a memory leak, which will ultimately lead to system memory exhaustion.

The native method can also construct a new string, using the JNI function `NewStringUTF`. The following lines of code from `Java_Prompt_getLine` show this:

```
    ...
    scanf("%s", buf);
    return (*env)->NewStringUTF(env, buf);
}
```

Using the JNIEnv Interface Pointer

Native methods must access and manipulate Java objects, such as strings, through the `env` interface pointer. In C this requires using the `env` pointer to reference the JNI function. Notice how the native method uses the `env` interface pointer to reference the two functions, `GetStringUTFChars` and `ReleaseStringUTFChars`, that it calls. The native method uses `env` as an interface pointer, passed as the first parameter to these functions.

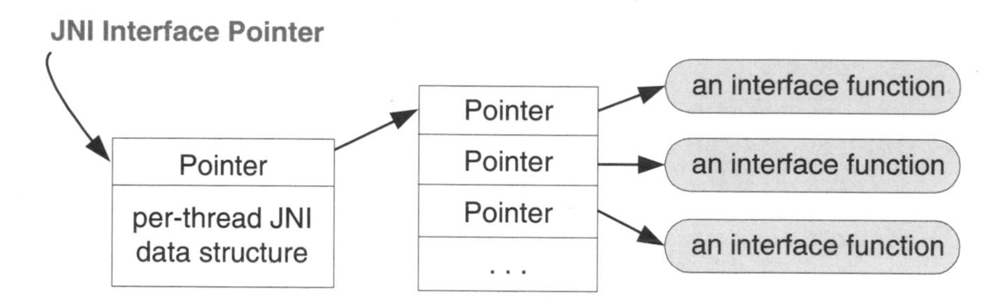

Figure 89 The JNI interface pointer.

Other JNI Functions for Accessing Java Strings

The JNI also provides functions to obtain the Unicode representation of Java strings. This is useful, for example, on operating systems that support Unicode as the native format. There are also utility functions to obtain both the UTF-8 and Unicode length of Java strings.

- `GetStringChars` takes the Java string and returns a pointer to an array of Unicode characters comprising the string.
- `ReleaseStringChars` releases the pointer to the array of Unicode characters.
- `NewString` constructs a new `java.lang.String` object from an array of Unicode characters.
- `GetStringLength` returns the length of a string comprised of an array of Unicode characters.
- `GetStringUTFLength` returns the length of a string if it is represented in the UTF-8 format.

Accessing Java Arrays

The JNI uses the `jarray` type to represent references to Java arrays. As with `jstring`, you cannot directly access `jarray` types in your native method C code. Instead you use JNI-provided functions that allow you to obtain pointers to elements of integer arrays.

Our second example, `IntArray.java`, contains a native method that totals the contents of an integer array passed to it from a Java application. You cannot implement the native method by directly addressing the array elements. The following code snippet incorrectly tries to access the array elements directly:

```
/*_ This program is illegal! */
JNIEXPORT jint JNICALL
Java_IntArray_sumArray(JNIEnv *env, jobject obj, jintArray arr)
{

    int i, sum = 0;
    for (i=0; i<10; i++) {
        sum += arr[i];
    }
    ...
```

The C program IntArray.c (page 881) in the Appendix shows the correct way to implement the preceding function Java_IntArray_sumArray. In this example you use one JNI function to get the length of the array and another JNI function to obtain a pointer to the individual elements of the array. Then you can retrieve the elements. Finally, you use a third JNI function to release the array memory.

Accessing Arrays of Primitive Elements

First, obtain the length of the array by calling the JNI function GetArrayLength. Note that, unlike C language arrays, Java arrays carry length information.

```
JNIEXPORT jint JNICALL
Java_IntArray_sumArray(JNIEnv *env, jobject obj,
                          jintArray arr){
    int i, sum = 0;
    jsize len = (*env)->GetArrayLength(env, arr);
    ...
```

Next, obtain a pointer to the elements of the array. Our example contains an integer array, so we use the JNI function GetIntArrayElements to obtain this pointer. Once you obtain the pointer, you can use normal C language operations on the resulting integer array.

```
{
    ...
    jint *body = (*env)->GetIntArrayElements(env, arr, 0);
    for (i=0; i<len; i++) {
        sum += body[i];
    }
    ...
```

The JNI provides a set of functions to obtain array element pointers; use the function that corresponds to the primitive type of the array. Had our example contained a float array arr, for example, we would have used the JNI function GetFloatArrayElements to obtain a pointer to its elements, as follows:

```
    ...
    int i;
    float sum = 0;
    ...
    jfloat *body = (*env)->GetFloatArrayElements(env, arr, 0);
    for (i=0; i<len; i++) {
        sum += body[i];
    }
    ...
```

In general, the garbage collector may move Java arrays. However, the Java Virtual Machine guarantees that the result of `GetIntArrayElements` points to a nonmovable array of integers. The JNI will either "pin" down the array or make a copy of the array into nonmovable memory. Therefore, the native code must call `ReleaseIntArrayElements` when it has finished using the array, as follows:

```
    ...
    (*env)->ReleaseIntArrayElements(env, arr, body, 0);
    return sum;
}
```

`ReleaseIntArrayElements` enables the JNI to copy back and to free the memory referenced by the `body` parameter if it is a copy of the original Java array. The "copy back" action enables the calling program to obtain the new values of array elements that the native method may have modified. `ReleaseIntArrayElements` will "unpin" the Java array if it has been pinned in memory.

Similar to the `Get<type>ArrayElements` functions, the JNI provides a set of `Release<type>ArrayElements` functions. Do not forget to call the appropriate `Release<type>ArrayElements` function, such as `ReleaseIntArrayElements`. If you forget to make this call, the array stays pinned for an extended period of time, or the Java Virtual Machine is unable to reclaim the memory used to store the nonmovable copy of the array.

The JNI provides a set of functions to access arrays of every primitive type, including `boolean`, `byte`, `char`, `short`, `int`, `long`, `float`, and `double`. Each function in the following table accesses elements in the specified type of array.

Table 31 JNI Functions for Accessing Arrays

Function	Array Type
GetBooleanArrayElements	boolean
GetByteArrayElements	byte
GetCharArrayElements	char

Table 31 JNI Functions for Accessing Arrays

Function	Array Type
`GetShortArrayElements`	`short`
`GetIntArrayElements`	`int`
`GetLongArrayElements`	`long`
`GetFloatArrayElements`	`float`
`GetDoubleArrayElements`	`double`

The JNI also provides a set of functions to release arrays of different primitive types. The following table summarizes these functions.

Table 32 JNI Functions for Releasing Arrays

Function	Array Type
`ReleaseBooleanArrayElements`	`boolean`
`ReleaseByteArrayElements`	`byte`
`ReleaseCharArrayElements`	`char`
`ReleaseShortArrayElements`	`short`
`ReleaseIntArrayElements`	`int`
`ReleaseLongArrayElements`	`long`
`ReleaseFloatArrayElements`	`float`
`ReleaseDoubleArrayElements`	`double`

Accessing a Small Number of Elements

Note that the `Get<type>ArrayElements` function might potentially copy the entire array. You may want to limit the number of elements that are copied, especially if your array is large. If you are interested only in a small number of elements in a (potentially) large array, you should instead use the `Get/Set<type>ArrayRegion` functions. These functions allow you to acccss, via copying, a small set of elements in an array.

Accessing Arrays of Objects

The JNI provides a separate set of functions to access elements of object arrays. You can use these functions to get and to set individual object array elements. However, you cannot get all of the object array elements at once.

- GetObjectArrayElement returns the object element at a given index.
- SetObjectArrayElement updates the object element at a given index.

Calling Java Methods

This section illustrates how to call Java methods from native language methods. Our sample program, Callbacks.java (page 882) invokes a native method, which then makes a call back to a Java method. To make things a little more interesting, the Java method again (recursively) calls the native method. This process continues until the recursion is five levels deep, at which time the Java method returns without making any more calls to the native method. To help you see this, the Java method and the native method print a sequence of tracing data.

Calling a Java Method from Native Code

To see how native code calls a Java method, let us focus on the implementation of Callbacks_nativeMethod, which is implemented in Callbacks.c. This native method contains a call back to the Java method Callbacks.callback.

```
JNIEXPORT void JNICALL
Java_Callbacks_nativeMethod(JNIEnv *env, jobject obj,
                            jint depth) {
    jclass cls = (*env)->GetObjectClass(env, obj);
    jmethodID mid = (*env)->GetMethodID(env, cls,
                                        "callback", "(I)V");
    if (mid == 0) {
        return;
    }
    printf("In C, depth = %d, about to enter Java, depth);
    (*env)->CallVoidMethod(env, obj, mid, depth);
    printf("In C, depth = %d, back from Java, depth);
}
```

You can call an instance method by following three steps.

1. Your native method calls the JNI function GetObjectClass, which returns the Java class object that is the type of the Java object.
2. Your native method then calls the JNI function GetMethodID, which performs a lookup for the Java method in a given class. The lookup is based on both the name of the method and the method signature. If the method does not exist, GetMethodID returns 0. An immediate return from the native method at that point causes a NoSuchMethodError to be thrown in the Java application code.

3. Your native method calls the JNI function `CallVoidMethod`, which invokes an instance method that has `void` return type. You pass the object, method ID, and the actual arguments to `CallVoidMethod`.

Forming the Method Name and Method Signature

The JNI performs a symbolic lookup, based on the method's name and type signature. This ensures that the same native method will work even after new methods have been added to the corresponding Java class.

The method name is the Java method name in UTF-8 form. Specify the constructor of a class by enclosing the word `init` within angle brackets: `<init>`.

Note that the JNI uses the method signature to denote the return type of a Java method. The signature `(I)V`, for example, denotes a Java method that takes one argument of type `int` and has a return type `void`. The general form of a method signature argument is

```
"(argument-types)return-type"
```

The following table summarizes the encoding for the Java type signatures.

Table 33 Java VM Type Signatures

Signature	Java Type
`Z`	`boolean`
`B`	`byte`
`C`	`char`
`S`	`short`
`I`	`int`
`J`	`long`
`F`	`float`
`D`	`double`
`L` *`fully-qualified-class`*`;`	fully-qualified-class
`[` *`type`*	*type*`[]`
`(` *`arg-types`* `)` *`ret-type`*	method type

For example, the `Prompt.getLine` method has the signature

```
(Ljava/lang/String;)Ljava/lang/String;
```

Prompt.getLine takes one parameter, a Java String object, and the method type is also String.

The Callbacks.main method has the signature

```
([Ljava/lang/String;)V
```

The signature indicates that the Callbacks.main method takes one parameter, a Java String object, and that the method type is void.

Array types are indicated by a leading square bracket ([) followed by the type of the array elements.

Using javap to Generate Method Signatures

The Java class file disassembler tool, javap, helps you to eliminate the mistakes that can occur when deriving method signatures by hand. You can use the javap tool to print out member variables and method signatures for specified classes. Run the javap tool with the options -s and -p and give it the name of a Java class, as follows:

```
javap -s -p Prompt
```

This gives you the following output:

```
Compiled from Prompt.java
class Prompt extends java.lang.Object
    /* ACC_SUPER bit set */
{
    private native getLine (Ljava/lang/String;)
                           Ljava/lang/String;
    public static main ([Ljava/lang/String;)V
    <init> ()V
    static <clinit> ()V
}
```

The -s flag informs javap to output signatures rather than normal Java types. The -p flag instructs javap to include private members.

Calling Java Methods by Using Method IDs

When you invoke a method in the JNI, you pass the method ID to the actual method invocation function. Obtaining a method ID is a relatively expensive operation. Because you obtain the method ID separately from the method invocation, you need perform this operation only once. Thus it is possible to first obtain the method ID one time and to then use the method ID many times at later points to invoke the same method.

It is important to keep in mind that *a method ID is valid for only as long as the class from which it is derived is not unloaded.* Once the class is unloaded, the method ID becomes invalid. Therefore, if you want to cache the method ID, be sure to keep a live reference to the Java class from which the method ID is derived. As long as the reference to the Java class (the jclass value) exists, the native code keeps a live reference to the class. The section Local and Global References (page 665) explains how to keep a live reference even after the native method returns and the jclass value goes out of scope.

Passing Arguments to Java Methods

The JNI provides several ways to pass arguments to a Java method. Most often you pass the arguments following the method ID. There are also two variations of method invocation functions that take arguments in an alternative format. For example, the CallVoidMethodV function receives all of its arguments in one va_list type argument. A va_list type is a special C type that allows a C function to accept a variable number of arguments. The CallVoidMethodA function expects the arguments in an array of jvalue union types. The array of jvalue union types are as follows:

```
typedef union jvalue {
    jboolean z;
    jbyte    b;
    jchar    c;
    jshort   s;
    jint     i;
    jlong    j;
    jfloat   f;
    jdouble  d;
    jobject  l;
} jvalue;
```

In addition to the CallVoidMethod function, the JNI supports instance method invocation functions with other return types, such as CallBooleanMethod, CallIntMethod, and so on. The return type of the method invocation function must match with the type of the Java method you wish to invoke.

Calling Class Methods

You can call a Java class method from your native code in a similar manner to calling an instance method. Call a class method by following these steps.

1. Obtain the method ID by using the JNI function GetStaticMethodID rather than the function GetMethodID.
2. Pass the class, method ID, and arguments to the family of class method invocation functions: CallStaticVoidMethod, CallStaticBoolean-Method, and so on.

If you compare instance method invocation functions to class method invocation functions, you will notice that the former receive the *object*, rather than the class, as the second argument following the JNIEnv argument. For example, suppose that we add an incDepth class method into Callback.java.

```
static int incDepth(int depth) {return depth + 1};
```

We can call this class method incDepth from Java_Callback_nativeMethod using the following JNI functions:

```
JNIEXPORT void JNICALL
Java_Callbacks_nativeMethod(JNIEnv *env, jobject obj,
                            jint depth){
    jclass cls = (*env)->GetObjectClass(env, obj);
    jmethodID mid = (*env)->GetStaticMethodID
                        (env, cls, "incDepth", "(I)I");
    if (mid == 0) {
        return;
    }
    depth = (*env)->CallStaticIntMethod(env, cls, mid, depth);
    ...
```

Calling Instance Methods of a Superclass

You can call superclass-defined instance methods that have been overridden in the class to which the object belongs. The JNI provides a set of CallNonvirtual<type>Method functions for this purpose. To call instance methods from the superclass that defined them, you do the following.

- Obtain the method ID from the superclass, using GetMethodID rather than GetStaticMethodID.
- Pass the object, superclass, method ID, and arguments to the family of non-virtual invocation functions: CallNonvirtualVoidMethod, CallNonvirtualBooleanMethod, and so on.

It is rare that you will need to invoke the instance methods of a superclass. This facility is similar to calling a superclass method, such as f, in Java, using the following construct:

```
super.f();
```

Accessing Java Member Variables

The JNI provides functions that native methods use to get and to set Java member variables. You can get and set both instance and class member variables. As with accessing methods, you use one set of JNI functions to access instance member variables and another set of JNI functions to access class member variables.

Our sample program, FieldAccess.java (page 883) in the Appendix, contains a class with one class integer member variable, si, and an instance string member variable, s. The sample program calls the native method accessFields, which prints out the value of these two member variables and then sets the member variables to new values. To verify that the member variables have indeed changed, we print out their values again in the Java application after returning from the native method.

Procedure for Accessing a Java Member Variable

To get and to set Java member variables from a native language method, you must do the following:

- Obtain the identifier for that member variable from its class, name, and type signature. For example, in FieldAccess.c (page 884) in the Appendix, we get the identifier for the class integer member variable si like this:

```
fid = (*env)->GetStaticFieldID(env, cls, "si", "I");
```

  We get the identifier for the instance string member variable s as follows:

```
fid = (*env)->GetFieldID(env, cls, "s", "Ljava/lang/String;");
```

- Use one of several JNI functions to either get or set the member variable specified by the member variable identifier. To get the value of a class member variable, pass the class to one of the appropriate class member variable access functions. To get the value of an instance member variable, pass the object to the appropriate instance member variable access function. For example, in FieldAccess.c we use GetStaticIntField to get the value of the class integer member variable si, as follows:

```
si = (*env)->GetStaticIntField(env, cls, fid);
```

We use the function GetObjectField to get the value of the instance string member variable s:

```
jstr = (*env)->GetObjectField(env, obj, fid);
```

Just as we did when calling a Java method, we factor out the cost of member variable lookup using a two-step process. First, we obtain the member variable ID; then we use the member variable ID to access the member variable. The member variable ID uniquely identifies a member variable in a given class. Similar to method IDs, a member variable ID remains valid until the class from which it is derived is unloaded.

Member Variable Signatures

Specify member variable signatures following the same encoding scheme as method signatures. The general form of a member variable signature is

```
"member variable type"
```

The member variable signature is the encoded symbol for the type of the member variable, enclosed in quotation marks. The member variable symbols are the same as the argument symbols in the method signature. That is, you represent an integer member variable with “I”, a float member variable with “F”, a double member variable with “D”, a Boolean member variable with “Z”, and so on.

The signature for a Java object, such as a String, begins with the letter L, followed by the fully qualified class for the object, and terminated by a semicolon (;). Thus you form the member variable signature for a String variable, such as c.s in FieldAccess.java, as follows:

```
"Ljava/lang/String;"
```

To indicate an array, use a leading bracket ([), followed by the type of the array. For example, you designate an integer array as follows:

```
"[I"
```

Refer to Table 33, “Java VM Type Signatures,” on page 657, which summarizes the encoding for the Java type signatures and their matching Java types.

You can use the Java class disassembler tool javap with option “-s” to generate the member variable signatures from class files. For example, run

```
javap -s -p FieldAccess
```

This gives you output containing the following two member variable signatures:

```
...
static si I
s Ljava/lang/String;
...
```

Catching and Throwing Exceptions

When an exception is thrown in Java, the Java Virtual Machine automatically looks for the nearest enclosing exception handler and unwinds the stack, if necessary. This style of exception handling frees the programmer from caring about and handling unusual error cases at every operation in the program. Instead the Java Virtual Machine propagates the error conditions automatically to a location (the `catch` clause in Java) that can handle the same class of error conditions in a centralized way.

Although other languages, such as C++, support a similar notion of exception handling, there is no uniform and general way to throw and to catch exceptions in native languages. The JNI therefore requires you to check for possible exceptions after calling JNI functions. The JNI also provides functions that allow your native methods to throw Java exceptions. These exceptions can then be handled either by other parts of your native code or by the Java Virtual Machine. After the native code catches and handles an exception, it can either clear the pending exception so that the computation can continue or throw another exception for an outer exception handler.

Many JNI functions may cause an exception to be thrown. For example, the `GetFieldID` function, described in the section Accessing Java Member Variables (page 661), throws a `NoSuchFieldError` if the specified field does not exist. To simplify error checking, most JNI functions use a combination of error codes and Java exceptions to report error conditions. For example, you may check whether the `jfieldID` returned from `GetFieldID` is `0` instead of calling the JNI function `ExceptionOccurred`. When the result of `GetFieldID` is not `0`, you are guaranteed that there is no pending exception.

The remainder of this section illustrates how to catch and to throw exceptions in native code. The code example is in `CatchThrow.java` (page 885) in the Appendix.

The `CatchThrow.main` method calls the native method. The native method, defined in `CatchThrow.c` (page 885) in the Appendix, first invokes the Java method `CatchThrow.callback`, as follows:

```
...
jclass cls = (*env)->GetObjectClass(env, obj);
jmethodID mid = (*env)->GetMethodID
                      (env, cls, "callback", "()V");
jthrowable exc;
if (mid == 0) {
    return;
}
(*env)->CallVoidMethod(env, obj, mid);
...
```

Since `CallVoidMethod` throws a `NullPointerException`, the native code can detect this exception after `CallVoidMethod` returns by calling the method `ExceptionOccurred`:

```
...
exc = (*env)->ExceptionOccurred(env);
if (exc) {
    ...
```

You can see that it is a simple matter to catch and handle an exception. In our example we do not do much about the exception in `CatchThrow.c` except to use the method `ExceptionDescribe` to output a debugging message. The native method then throws an `IllegalArgumentException`, which the Java code invoking the native method will see.

```
...
(*env)->ExceptionDescribe(env);
(*env)->ExceptionClear(env);
newExcCls = (*env)->FindClass
            (env, "java/lang/IllegalArgumentException");
if (newExcCls == 0) { /* Unable to find the new
                         exception class, give up. */
    return;
}
(*env)->ThrowNew(env, newExcCls, "thrown from C code");
...
```

The `ThrowNew` function constructs an exception object from the given exception class and message string and posts the exception in the current thread.

Note: It is *extremely* important to check, handle, and clear the pending exception before calling subsequent JNI functions. Calling arbitrary JNI functions with a pending exception may lead to unexpected results. You can safely call only a small number of JNI functions when there is a pending exception. These functions are `ExceptionOccurred`, `ExceptionDescribe`, and `ExceptionClear`.

Local and Global References

So far we have used such data types as `jobject`, `jclass`, and `jstring` to denote references to Java objects. However, the JNI creates references for all object arguments passed to native methods, as well as for all objects returned from JNI functions.

References serve to keep the Java objects from being garbage collected. By default the JNI creates *local references*, which ensure that the Java Virtual Machine can eventually free the Java objects. Local references become invalid when program execution returns from the native method in which the local reference is created. Therefore a native method must not store away a local reference and expect to reuse it in subsequent invocations.

For example, the following program, which is a variation of the native method in `FieldAccess.c` (page 884) in the Appendix, mistakenly caches the Java class for the member variable ID so that it does not have to repeatedly search for the member variable ID based on the member variable name and signature at each invocation:

```
/* This code is illegal */
static jclass cls = 0;
static jfieldID fld;
JNIEXPORT void JNICALL
Java_FieldAccess_accessFields(JNIEnv *env, jobject obj)
{
    ...
    if (cls == 0) {
        cls = (*env)->GetObjectClass(env, obj);
        if (cls == 0) {
            ... /* error */
        }
        fid = (*env)->GetStaticFieldID(env, cls, "si", "I");
    }
    /* access the member variable using cls and fid */
    ...
}
```

This program is illegal because the local reference returned from `GetObjectClass` is valid only until the native method returns. When the Java application calls the native method `Java_FieldAccess_accessFields` a second time, the native method tries to use an invalid local reference. This leads to either the wrong results or a VM crash.

You can overcome this problem by creating a *global reference*, which remains valid until it is explicitly freed. The following code rewrites the previous program and correctly uses a global reference to cache the class for the member variable ID:

```
/* This code is correct. */
static jclass cls = 0;
static jfieldID fld;

JNIEXPORT void JNICALL
Java_FieldAccess_accessFields(JNIEnv *env, jobject obj)
{
    ...
    if (cls == 0) {
         jclass cls1 = (*env)->GetObjectClass(env, obj);
         if (cls1 == 0) {
              ... /* error */
         }
         cls = (*env)->NewGlobalRef(env, cls1);
         if (cls == 0) {
              ... /* error */
         }
         fid = (*env)->GetStaticFieldID
                        (env, cls, "si", "I");
    }
    /* access the member variable using cls and fid */
    ...
}
```

A global reference keeps the Java Virtual Machine from unloading the Java class and therefore also ensures that the member variable ID remains valid, as discussed in the section Accessing Java Member Variables (page 661). However, the native code must call `DeleteGlobalRef` when it no longer needs access to the global reference. Otherwise the Java Virtual Machine will never unload the corresponding Java object, the Java class referenced by `cls`.

In most cases the native programmer should rely on the Java Virtual Machine to free all local references after the native method returns. In certain situations, however, the native code may need to call the `DeleteLocalRef` function to explicitly delete a local reference.

- You may know that you are holding the only reference to a large Java object and you do not want to wait until the current native method returns before the garbage collector can reclaim the object. For example, in the following program segment the garbage collector may be able to free the Java object referred to by `lref` when it is running inside `lengthyComputation`:

```
...
lref = ...            /* a large Java object */
...                   /* last use of lref */
(*env)->DeleteLocalRef(env, lref);
lengthyComputation(); /* may take some time */
return;               /* all local refs will now be freed */
```

- You may need to create a large number of local references in a single native method invocation. This may result in an overflow of the internal JNI local reference table. It is a good idea to delete those local references that will not be needed. For example, in the following program segment the native code iterates through a potentially large array `arr` consisting of Java strings. After each iteration, the program can free the local reference to the string element.

```
...
for(i = 0; i < len; i++) {
    jstring jstr = (*env)->GetObjectArrayElement
                          (env, arr, i);
    ...                               /* processes jstr */
    (*env)->DeleteLocalRef(env, jstr); /* no longer needs
                                        jstr */
}
...
```

Threads and Native Methods

The Java platform is a multithreaded system. Therefore, native methods must be thread-safe programs. Unless you have knowledge to the contrary, such as knowing that the native method is synchronized, you must assume that there can be multiple threads of control executing a native method at any given time. Native methods therefore must not modify sensitive global variables in unprotected ways. That is, the native methods must share and coordinate their access to variables in certain critical sections of code.

Before reading further, you should be familiar with the concepts of threads of control and multithreaded programming. Threads of Control[1] covers programming with threads. In particular, Multithreaded Programs[2] covers issues, including synchronization, related to writing programs that contain multiple threads.

---

[1] Refer to *The Java Tutorial, Second Edition*, or to the HTML version on this book's CD-ROM or at: http://java.sun.com/docs/books/tutorial/essential/threads/index.html.

[2] Refer to *The Java Tutorial, Second Edition*, or to the HTML version on this book's CD-ROM or at: http://java.sun.com/docs/books/tutorial/essential/threads/multithreaded.html.

Threads and JNI

- The JNI interface pointer (`JNIEnv *`) is valid only in the current thread. You must not pass the interface pointer from one thread to another or cache an interface pointer and use it in multiple threads. The Java Virtual Machine will pass you the *same* interface pointer in consecutive invocations of a native method from the same thread. However, different threads pass *different* interface pointers to native methods.
- You must not pass local references from one thread to another. In particular, a local reference may become invalid before the other thread has had a chance to use it. You should always convert local references to global references when different threads may be using the same reference to a Java object.
- Check the use of global variables carefully. Multiple threads might be accessing these global variables at the same time. Make sure to put in appropriate locks to ensure safety.

Thread Synchronization in Native Methods

The JNI provides two synchronization functions that allow you to implement *synchronized blocks*. In Java you implement synchronized blocks by using the `synchronized` statement.

```
synchronized (obj) {
    ...                     /* synchronized block */
    ...
}
```

The Java Virtual Machine guarantees that a thread must acquire the monitor associated with a Java object `obj` before it can execute the statements in the block. At any given time, therefore, at most one thread can be running inside the synchronized block.

Native code can perform equivalent synchronization on objects by using the JNI functions `MonitorEnter` and `MonitorExit`.

```
...
(*env)->MonitorEnter(env, obj);
...                                 /* synchronized block */
(*env)->MonitorExit(env, obj);
...
```

A thread must enter the monitor associated with obj before it can continue its execution. A thread is allowed to enter a monitor multiple times. The monitor contains a counter signaling how many times it has been entered by a given thread. MonitorEnter increments the counter when the thread enters a monitor it has already entered. MonitorExit decrements the counter. Other threads can enter the monitor when the counter reaches 0.

Wait and Notify

The functions Object.wait, Object.notify, and Object.notifyAll provide another useful thread-synchronization mechanism. Although the JNI does not directly support these functions, a native method can always follow the JNI method call mechanism to invoke them, as detailed in the section Calling Java Methods (page 656).

JNI Programming in C++

The JNI provides a slightly cleaner interface for C++ programmers. The jni.h file contains a set of inline C++ functions. This allows the native method programmer to simply write

```
jclass cls = env->FindClass("java/lang/String");
```

instead of

```
jclass cls = (*env)->FindClass(env, "java/lang/String");
```

The extra level of indirection on env and the env argument to FindClass is hidden from the programmer. The C++ compiler simply expands the C++ member function calls to their C counterparts; therefore the resulting code is exactly the same.

The jni.h file also defines a set of dummy C++ classes to enforce the subtyping relationships among variations of jobject types, as follows:

```
class _jobject {};
class _jclass : public _jobject {};
class _jthrowable : public _jobject {};
class _jstring : public _jobject {};
... /* more on jarray */

typedef _jobject *jobject;
```

```
typedef _jclass *jclass;
typedef _jthrowable *jthrowable;
typedef _jstring *jstring;
... /* more on jarray */
```

The C++ compiler is therefore better able than the C compiler to detect when incorrect types are passed to methods. For example, it is incorrect to pass a `jobject` to `GetMethodID`, because `GetMethodID` expects a `jclass`. You can see this by examining the `GetMethodID` signature.

```
jmethodID GetMethodID(jclass clazz, const char *name,
                      const char *sig);
```

The C compiler treats `jclass` the same as `jobject` because it makes this determination, using the following `typedef` statement:

```
typedef jobject jclass;
```

Therefore a C compiler is not able to detect that you have mistakenly passed the method a `jobject` instead of a `jclass`.

The added type safety in C++ comes with a small inconvenience. Recall from the section Accessing Java Member Variables (page 661) that in C you can fetch a Java string from an array of strings and directly assign the result to a `jstring`, as follows:

```
jstring jstr = (*env)->GetObjectArrayElement(env, arr, i);
```

In C++, however, you need to insert an explicit conversion of the Java string to `jstring`.

```
jstring jstr = (jstring)env->GetObjectArrayElement(arr, i);
```

You must make this explicit conversion because `jstring` is a subtype of `jobject`, which is the return type of `GetObjectArrayElement`.

56 Invoking the Java Virtual Machine

THIS lesson teaches you how to embed the Java Virtual Machine into a native application. Embedding the VM into your native application gives it the full power of the VM. For example, you might want to do this if your application is a Web browser that supports the execution of Java applets.

The JDK 1.2 ships the Java Virtual Machine as a shared library (or dynamic link library on Win32). You can embed the Java Virtual Machine into your native application by linking the native application with the shared library.

The JNI supports an invocation API that allows you to load, initialize, and invoke the Java Virtual Machine. Indeed the normal way of starting the Java interpreter, `java`, is no more than a simple C program that parses the command line arguments and invokes the Java Virtual Machine through the invocation API.

To illustrate, we will write a C program that invokes the Java Virtual Machine and calls the `Prog.main` method defined in `Prog.java`.

```
public class Prog {
    public static void main(String[] args) {
        System.out.println("Hello World" + args[0]);
    }
}
```

The C code in `invoke.c` (page 886) in the Appendix begins with a call to `JNI_GetDefaultJavaVMInitArgs` to obtain the default initialization settings, such as heap size, stack size, and so on. The C code then calls `JNI_Create-`

`JavaVM` to load and to initialize the Virtual Machine. `JNI_CreateJavaVM` fills in two return values:

- The created Java Virtual Machine `jvm`. You can use this value to destroy the Virtual Machine at a later time, for example.
- The value `env` is a JNI interface pointer that the current thread can use to access Java features, such as calling a Java method.

Note that after `JNI_CreateJavaVM` successfully returns, the current native thread has bootstrapped itself into the Java Virtual Machine and is therefore running just like a native method. The only difference is that there is no concept of returning to the Java Virtual Machine. Therefore any local references that you subsequently create will not be freed until you call `DestroyJavaVM`. See the section Local and Global References (page 665) for more information on local references.

Once you have created the Java Virtual Machine, you can issue regular JNI calls to invoke, for example, `Prog.main`. `DestroyJavaVM` attempts to unload the Java Virtual Machine. Note that the JDK 1.2 Java Virtual Machine cannot be unloaded; therefore `DestroyJavaVM` always returns an error code.

You need to compile and to link `invoke.c` with the Java libraries shipped with JDK 1.2. On Solaris you can use the following command to do this:

```
cc -I<where jni.h is> -L<where libjava.so is> -ljava invoke.c
```

On Win32 with Microsoft Visual C++ 4.0 the command line is:

```
cl -I<where jni.h is> -MT invoke.c -link <where javai.lib is>lib
```

Those working in the MacOS environment should refer to the JManager API, which is part of the online MacOS Runtime for Java (MRJ) documentation.[1] You use the JManager API to embed Java applications into your application.

Run the resulting executable from the command line. You may get the following error message:

```
Unable to initialize threads: cannot find class
        java/lang/Thread

Can't create Java VM
```

---

[1] http://devworld.apple.com/java/index.html

This error message indicates that you have set the wrong value for the `vm_args.classpath` variable.

You might get an error indicating that it cannot find either `libjava.so` (on Solaris) or `javai.dll` (on Win32). If so, add `libjava.so` into your `LD_LIBRARY_PATH` on Solaris, or add `javai.dll` into your executable path on Win32.

The program may report an error that it cannot find the class `Prog`. If so, make sure that the directory containing `Prog.class` is in the `vm_args.classpath` variable as well.

Attaching Native Threads

The invocation API also allows you to *attach* native threads to a running Java Virtual Machine and to have the threads bootstrap themselves into Java threads. This requires that the Java Virtual Machine internally use native threads. In JDK 1.2 this feature works only on Win32. The Solaris version of the Java Virtual Machine uses user-level thread support and is therefore incapable of attaching native threads. In the future the JDK on Solaris will support native threads.

Our sample program, `attach.c` (page 888), therefore, will work only on Win32. This program is a variation of `invoke.c`. Instead of calling `Prog.main` in the `main` thread, the native code spawns five threads and then waits for them to finish before it destroys the Java Virtual Machine. Each thread attaches itself to the Java Virtual Machine, invokes the `Prog.main` method, and finally detaches itself from the Virtual Machine before it terminates. Note that the third argument to `AttachCurrentThread` is reserved and should be set to `NULL`.

When you call `DetachCurrentThread`, you free all local references belonging to the current thread.

Limitations of the JDK1.2 Invocation API

As mentioned, the invocation API implementation in JDK 1.2 has a number of limitations.

- The user-level Java thread implementation on Solaris requires the Java Virtual Machine to redirect certain Solaris system calls. The set of redirected system calls currently includes `read`, `readv`, `write`, `writev`, `getmsg`, `putmsg`, `poll`, `open`, `close`, `pipe`, `fcntl`, `dup`, `create`, `accept`, `recv`, `send`, and so on. This may cause undesirable effects on a hosting native application that also depends on these system calls.

- You cannot attach a native thread to the user thread-based Java Virtual Machine on Solaris. `AttachCurrentThread` simply fails on Solaris (unless your code calls it from the `main` thread that created the Virtual Machine).
- You cannot unload the Java Virtual Machine without terminating the process. The `DestroyJavaVM` call simply returns an error code.

Note: Currently the JDK supports attaching only native threads on Win32. The support for Solaris native threads will be available in a future release.

---

57 Summary of the JNI

YOU have learned a great deal about the JNI. To help you remember everything you have learned, this lesson summarizes the JNI functions and mapping types.

Mapping between JNI and Native Types

The following two tables summarize how Java types map to native types and the rules for encoding Java types in JNI signatures.

Table 34 Primitive Types and Native Equivalents

Java Type	Native Type	Size in bits
`boolean`	`jboolean`	8, unsigned
`byte`	`jbyte`	8
`char`	`jchar`	16, unsigned
`short`	`jshort`	16
`int`	`jint`	32
`long`	`jlong`	64
`float`	`jfloat`	32
`double`	`jdouble`	64
`void`	`void`	n/a

Table 35 Encoding for Java Type Signatures

Signature	**Java Type**
`Z`	`boolean`
`B`	`byte`
`C`	`char`
`S`	`short`
`I`	`int`
`J`	`long`
`F`	`float`
`D`	`double`
`L` *`fully-qualified-class`*`;`	fully-qualified-class
`[` *`type`*	*type*`[]`
`(` *`arg-types`* `)` *`ret-type`*	method type

JNI has the following string-handling functions:

- `GetStringChars`
- `GetStringLength`
- `GetStringUTFChars`
- `GetStringUTFLength`
- `NewString`
- `NewStringUTF`
- `ReleaseStringChars`
- `ReleaseStringUTFChars`

JNI has the following array-handling functions:

- `GetArrayLength`
- Get<*type*>ArrayElements
- `GetBooleanArrayElements`
- `GetByteArrayElements`
- `GetCharArrayElements`
- `GetDoubleArrayElements`
- `GetFloatArrayElements`
- `GetIntArrayElements`

- GetLongArrayElements
- GetShortArrayElements
- Release<*type*>ArrayElements
- Get<*type*>ArrayRegion
- Set<*type*>ArrayRegion
- GetObjectArrayElement
- SetObjectArrayElement

JNI method-handling functions are as follows:

- GetObjectClass
- GetMethodID
- GetStaticMethodID
- Call<*returntype*>Method
- CallBooleanMethod
- CallByteMethod
- CallCharMethod
- CallDoubleMethod
- CallFloatMethod
- CallIntMethod
- CallLongMethod
- CallObjectMethod
- CallShortMethod
- CallVoidMethod
- CallStatic<*returntype*>Method
- CallNonvirtual<*returntype*>Method
- Call<*returntype*>MethodV
- Call<*returntype*>MethodA

JNI member variable-handling functions are as follows:

- GetFieldID
- GetStaticFieldID
- Get<*type*>Field
- GetBooleanField
- GetByteField

- `GetCharField`
- `GetDoubleField`
- `GetFloatField`
- `GetIntField`
- `GetLongField`
- `GetObjectField`
- `GetShortField`
- `Set`<*type*>`Field`
- `GetStatic`<*type*>`Field`
- `SetStatic`<*type*>`Field`

JNI exception-handling functions are

- `ExceptionClear`
- `ExceptionDescribe`
- `ExceptionOccurred`

JNI local and global reference-handling functions are

- `NewGlobalRef`
- `DeleteGlobalRef`
- `DeleteLocalRef`

JNI thread-synchronization functions are

- `MonitorEnter`
- `MonitorExit`

About the Author

BETH STEARNS is the president of Computer Ease Publishing, a computer consulting firm she founded in 1982. Her client list includes Sun Microsystems Inc., Silicon Graphics Inc., Oracle Corporation, and Xerox Corporation. Her "Understanding EDT," a guide to Digital Equipment Corporation's text editor, has sold throughout the world. She received her B.S. degree from Cornell University and a master's degree from Adelphi University.

Beth is an avid cyclist, hiker, gourmet cook, and Francophile, and she plans to retire with her two cats and husband to the southwest of France.

Acknowledgments

I'd like to thank my husband John for his thoughtful and insightful comments, not to mention encouragement and support, and my two boys Woody and Charlie, for enthusiastically digging through the JNI pages and ripping out unnecessary material.

I would like to acknowledge Sheng Liang, architect of the JNI specification, for his early collaboration on this chapter and subsequent review, and Dan Sears for his review of this chapter.

Reflection

by Dale Green

THE reflection API represents, or reflects, the classes, interfaces, and objects in the current Java™ Virtual Machine. You'll want to use the reflection API if you are writing development tools such as debuggers, class browsers, and GUI builders. With the reflection API you can:

- Determine the class of an object
- Get information about a class's modifiers, fields, methods, constructors, and superclasses
- Find out what constants and method declarations belong to an interface
- Create an instance of a class whose name is not known until runtime
- Get and set the value of an object's field, even if the field name is unknown to your program until runtime
- Invoke a method on an object, even if the method is not known until runtime
- Create a new array, whose size and component type are not known until runtime, and then modify the array's components

First, a note of caution. Don't use the reflection API when other tools more natural to the Java programming language would suffice. For example, if you are in the habit of using function pointers in another language, you might be tempted to use the `Method` objects of the reflection API in the same way. Resist the temptation! Your program will be easier to debug and maintain if you don't use `Method` objects. Instead you should define an interface and then implement it in the classes that perform the needed action.

Other trails use the term "member variable" instead of "field." The two terms are synonymous. Because the `Field` class is part of the reflection API, this trail uses the term "field."

This trail uses a task-oriented approach to the reflection API. Each lesson includes a set of related tasks, and every task is explained, step by step, with a sample program. The lessons are as follows:

Examining Classes (page 685) explains how to determine the class of an object and how to get information about classes and interfaces.

Manipulating Objects (page 697) shows you how to instantiate classes, get or set field values, and invoke methods. With the reflection API you can perform these tasks even if the names of the classes, fields, and methods are unknown until runtime.

Working with Arrays (page 707) describes the APIs used to create and to modify arrays whose names are not known until runtime.

Summary of Classes (page 713) lists the classes that comprise the reflection API and provides links to the appropriate API documentation.

Note: Many of the APIs documented in this trail were added to the Java Development Kit (JDK) for its 1.1 release. Therefore the code examples in this trail will work only on Java platforms that are compatible with release 1.1 of the JDK software.

http://java.sun.com/docs/books/tutorial/reflect/class/index.html

58 Examining Classes

IF you are writing a class browser, you need a way to get information about classes at runtime. For example, you might want to display the names of the class fields, methods, and constructors. Or you might want to show which interfaces are implemented by a class. To get this information, you need to get the `Class`[1] object that reflects the class.

For each class, the Java Runtime Environment (JRE) maintains an immutable `Class` object that contains information about the class. A `Class` object represents, or reflects, the class. With the reflection API you can invoke methods on a `Class` object that return `Constructor`,[2] `Method`,[3] and `Field`[4] objects. You can use these objects to get information about the corresponding constructors, methods, and fields defined in the class.

Class objects also represent interfaces. You invoke `Class` methods to find out about an interface's modifiers, methods, and public constants. Not all of the `Class` methods are appropriate when a `Class` object reflects an interface. For example, it doesn't make sense to invoke `getConstructors` when the `Class` object represents an interface. The section Examining Interfaces (page 690) explains which `Class` methods you may use to get information about interfaces.

---

1 The API documentation is available on the CD-ROM that accompanies this book and online here: http://java.sun.com/products/jdk/1.1/docs/api/java.lang.Class.html

2 The API documentation is available on the CD-ROM that accompanies this book and online here: http://java.sun.com/products/jdk/1.1/docs/api/java.lang.reflect.Constructor.html

3 The API documentation is available on the CD-ROM that accompanies this book and online here: http://java.sun.com/products/jdk/1.1/docs/api/java.lang.reflect.Method.html

4 The API documentation is available on the CD-ROM that accompanies this book and online here: http://java.sun.com/products/jdk/1.1/docs/api/java.lang.reflect.Field.html

This lesson contains the following sections:

Retrieving Class Objects

You can retrieve a `Class` object in several ways:

- If an instance of the class is available, you can invoke `Object.getClass`. The `getClass` method is useful when you want to examine an object but don't know its class. The following line of code gets the `Class` object for an object named `mystery`:

```
Class c = mystery.getClass();
```

- If you want to retrieve the `Class` object for the superclass that another `Class` object reflects, invoke the `getSuperclass` method. In the following example, `getSuperclass` returns the `Class` object associated with the `TextComponent` class, because `TextComponent` is the superclass of `TextField`:

```
TextField t = new TextField();
Class c = t.getClass();
Class s = c.getSuperclass();
```

- If you know the name of the class at compile time, you can retrieve its `Class` object by appending `.class` to its name. In the next example the `Class` object that represents the `Button` class is retrieved:

```
Class c = java.awt.Button.class;
```

- If the class name is unknown at compile time but is available at runtime, you can use the `forName` method. In the following example if the `String` named `strg` is set to `java.awt.Button`, then `forName` returns the `Class` object associated with the `Button` class:

```
Class c = Class.forName(strg);
```

Getting the Class Name

Every class in the Java programming language has a name. When you declare a class, the name immediately follows the `class` keyword. In the following class declaration the class name is `Point`:

```
public class Point {int x, y;}
```

At runtime you can determine the name of a `Class` object by invoking the `getName` method. The `String` returned by `getName` is the fully qualified name of the class.

The following program gets the class name of an object. First, the program retrieves the corresponding `Class` object; then it invokes the `getName` method on that `Class` object.

```
import java.lang.reflect.*;
import java.awt.*;

class SampleName {
   public static void main(String[] args) {
        Button b = new Button();
        printName(b);
   }

   static void printName(Object o) {
        Class c = o.getClass();
        String s = c.getName();
        System.out.println(s);
   }
}
```

The sample program prints the following line:

```
java.awt.Button
```

Discovering Class Modifiers

A class declaration may include the following modifiers: `public`, `abstract`, or `final`. The class modifiers precede the `class` keyword in the class definition. In the following example the class modifiers are `public` and `final`:

```
public final Coordinate {int x, int y, int z}
```

To identify the modifiers of a class at runtime you perform these steps:

1. Invoke `getModifiers` on a `Class` object to retrieve a set of modifiers.
2. Check the modifiers by calling `isPublic`, `isAbstract`, and `isFinal`.

The following program identifies the modifiers of the `String` class.

```
import java.lang.reflect.*;
import java.awt.*;

class SampleModifier {
    public static void main(String[] args) {
        String s = new String();
        printModifiers(s);
    }

    public static void printModifiers(Object o) {
        Class c = o.getClass();
        int m = c.getModifiers();
        if (Modifier.isPublic(m))
            System.out.println("public");
        if (Modifier.isAbstract(m))
            System.out.println("abstract");
        if (Modifier.isFinal(m))
            System.out.println("final");
    }
}
```

The output of the sample program reveals that the modifiers of the `String` class are `public` and `final`:

```
public
final
```

Finding Superclasses

Because the Java programming language supports inheritance, an application such as a class browser must be able to identify superclasses. To determine the superclass of a class, you invoke the `getSuperclass` method. This method returns a `Class` object representing the superclass, or returns `null` if the class has no superclass. To identify all ancestors of a class, call `getSuperclass` iteratively until it returns `null`.

The program that follows finds the names of the `Button` class's ancestors by calling `getSuperclass` iteratively.

```
import java.lang.reflect.*;
import java.awt.*;

class SampleSuper {
```

```
    public static void main(String[] args) {
        Button b = new Button();
        printSuperclasses(b);
    }

    static void printSuperclasses(Object o) {
        Class subclass = o.getClass();
        Class superclass = subclass.getSuperclass();
        while (superclass != null) {
            String className = superclass.getName();
            System.out.println(className);
            subclass = superclass;
            superclass = subclass.getSuperclass();
        }
    }
}
```

The output of the sample program verifies that the parent of `Button` is `Component` and that the parent of `Component` is `Object`:

```
java.awt.Component
java.lang.Object
```

Identifying the Interfaces Implemented by a Class

The type of an object is determined by not only its class and superclass but also its interfaces. In a class declaration, the interfaces are listed after the `implements` keyword. For example, the `RandomAccessFile` class implements the `DataOutput` and `DataInput` interfaces:

```
public class RandomAccessFile implements DataOutput, DataInput
```

You invoke the `getInterfaces` method to determine which interfaces a class implements. The `getInterfaces` method returns an array of `Class` objects. The reflection API represents interfaces with `Class` objects. Each `Class` object in the array returned by `getInterfaces` represents one of the interfaces implemented by the class. You can invoke the `getName` method on the `Class` objects in the array returned by `getInterfaces` to retrieve the interface names. To find out how to get additional information about interfaces, see the section Examining Interfaces (page 690).

The program that follows prints the interfaces implemented by the `RandomAccessFile` class.

```
import java.lang.reflect.*;
import java.io.*;

class SampleInterface {
    public static void main(String[] args) {
        try {
            RandomAccessFile r =
                new RandomAccessFile("myfile", "r");
            printInterfaceNames(r);
        } catch (IOException e) {
            System.out.println(e);
        }
    }

    static void printInterfaceNames(Object o) {
        Class c = o.getClass();
        Class[] theInterfaces = c.getInterfaces();
        for (int i = 0; i < theInterfaces.length; i++) {
            String interfaceName = theInterfaces[i].getName();
            System.out.println(interfaceName);
        }
    }
}
```

Note that the interface names printed by the sample program are fully qualified:

```
java.io.DataOutput
java.io.DataInput
```

Examining Interfaces

`Class` objects represent interfaces as well as classes. If you aren't sure whether a `Class` object represents an interface or a class, call the `isInterface` method.

You invoke `Class` methods to get information about an interface. To find the public constants of an interface, invoke the `getFields` method on the `Class` object that represents the interface. The section Identifying Class Fields (page 691) has an example containing `getFields`. You can use `getMethods` to get information about an interface's methods. See the section Obtaining Method Information (page 694). To find out about an interface's modifiers, invoke the `getModifiers` method. See the section Discovering Class Constructors (page 693) for an example.

By calling `isInterface`, the following program reveals that `Observer` is an interface and that `Observable` is a class:

```
import java.lang.reflect.*;
import java.util.*;

class SampleCheckInterface {

   public static void main(String[] args) {
       Class observer = Observer.class;
       Class observable = Observable.class;
       verifyInterface(observer);
       verifyInterface(observable);
   }

   static void verifyInterface(Class c) {
       String name = c.getName();
       if (c.isInterface()) {
           System.out.println(name + " is an interface.");
       } else {
           System.out.println(name + " is a class.");
       }
   }
}
```

The output of the preceding program is:

```
java.util.Observer is an interface.
java.util.Observable is a class.
```

Identifying Class Fields

If you are writing an application such as a class browser, you might want to find out what fields belong to a particular class. You can identify a class's public fields by invoking the `getFields` method on a `Class` object. The `getFields` method returns an array of `Field` objects containing one object per accessible public field.

A public field is accessible if it is a member of any of the following:

- This class
- A superclass of this class
- An interface implemented by this class
- An interface extended from an interface implemented by this class

The methods provided by the Field[1] class allow you to retrieve the field's name, type, and set of modifiers. You can even get and set the value of a field, as described in the sections Getting Field Values (page 701) and Setting Field Values (page 703).

The following program prints the names and types of fields belonging to the GridBagConstraints class. Note that the program first retrieves the Field objects for the class by calling getFields, and then invokes the getName and getType methods on each of these Field objects.

```
import java.lang.reflect.*;
import java.awt.*;

class SampleField {
    public static void main(String[] args) {
        GridBagConstraints g = new GridBagConstraints();
        printFieldNames(g);
    }

    static void printFieldNames(Object o) {
        Class c = o.getClass();
        Field[] publicFields = c.getFields();
        for (int i = 0; i < publicFields.length; i++) {
            String fieldName = publicFields[i].getName();
            Class typeClass = publicFields[i].getType();
            String fieldType = typeClass.getName();
            System.out.println("Name: " + fieldName +
                                 ", Type: " + fieldType);
        }
    }
}
```

A truncated listing of the output generated by the preceding program follows:

```
Name: RELATIVE, Type: int
Name: REMAINDER, Type: int
Name: NONE, Type: int
Name: BOTH, Type: int
Name: HORIZONTAL, Type: int
Name: VERTICAL, Type: int
.
.
.
```

---

[1] The API documentation for java.lang.reflect.Field is available on this book's CD-ROM and here: http://java.sun.com/products/jdk/1.1/docs/api/java.lang.reflect.Field.html

Discovering Class Constructors

To create an instance of a class, you invoke a special method called a constructor. Like methods, constructors can be overloaded and are distinguished from one another by their signatures.

You can get information about a class's public constructors by invoking the `getConstructors` method, which returns an array of `Constructor` objects. You can use the methods provided by the `Constructor` class to determine the constructor's name, set of modifiers, parameter types, and set of throwable exceptions. You can also create a new instance of the `Constructor` object's class with the `Constructor.newInstance` method. You'll learn how to invoke `Constructor.newInstance` in the section Manipulating Objects (page 697).

The sample program that follows prints out the parameter types for each constructor in the `Rectangle` class. The program performs the following steps:

1. It retrieves an array of `Constructor` objects from the `Class` object by calling `getConstructors`.
2. For every element in the `Constructor` array, it creates an array of `Class` objects by invoking `getParameterTypes`. The `Class` objects in the array represent the parameters of the constructor.
3. The program calls `getName` to fetch the class name for every parameter in the `Class` array created in the preceding step.

The sample program is not as complicated as it sounds. Here's the source code:

```
import java.lang.reflect.*;
import java.awt.*;

class SampleConstructor {

   public static void main(String[] args) {
      Rectangle r = new Rectangle();
      showConstructors(r);
   }

   static void showConstructors(Object o) {
      Class c = o.getClass();
      Constructor[] theConstructors = c.getConstructors();
      for (int i = 0; i < theConstructors.length; i++) {
         System.out.print("( ");
         Class[] parameterTypes =
            theConstructors[i].getParameterTypes();
         for (int k = 0; k < parameterTypes.length; k++) {
```

```
                String parameterString =
                  parameterTypes[k].getName();
                System.out.print(parameterString + " ");
                }
            System.out.println(")");
            }
        }
    }
```

In the first line of output generated by the sample program, no parameter types appear, because that particular `Constructor` object represents a no-argument constructor. In subsequent lines the parameters listed are either `int` types or fully qualified object names. The output of the sample program is:

```
( )
( int int )
( int int int int )
( java.awt.Dimension )
( java.awt.Point )
( java.awt.Point java.awt.Dimension )
( java.awt.Rectangle )
```

Obtaining Method Information

To find out what public methods belong to a class, invoke the method named `getMethods`. The array returned by `getMethods` contains `Method` objects. You can use a `Method` object to uncover a method's name, return type, parameter types, set of modifiers, and set of throwable exceptions. All of this information would be useful if you were writing a class browser or a debugger. With `Method.invoke` you can even call the method itself. To see how to do this, see the section Invoking Methods (page 704).

The following sample program prints the name, return type, and parameter types of every public method in the `Polygon` class. The program performs the following tasks:

1. It retrieves an array of `Method` objects from the `Class` object by calling `getMethods`.
2. For every element in the `Method` array, the program:
    - retrieves the method name by calling `getName`
    - gets the return type by invoking `getReturnType`
    - creates an array of `Class` objects by invoking `getParameterTypes`

3. The array of `Class` objects created in the preceding step represents the parameters of the method. To retrieve the class name for every one of these parameters, the program invokes `getName` against each `Class` object in the array.

Not many lines of source code are required to accomplish these tasks:

```
import java.lang.reflect.*;
import java.awt.*;

class SampleMethod {

    public static void main(String[] args) {
        Polygon p = new Polygon();
        showMethods(p);
    }

    static void showMethods(Object o) {
        Class c = o.getClass();
        Method[] theMethods = c.getMethods();
        for (int i = 0; i < theMethods.length; i++) {
            String methodString = theMethods[i].getName();
            System.out.println("Name: " + methodString);
            String returnString =
                theMethods[i].getReturnType().getName();
            System.out.println("   Return Type: " +
                                returnString);
            Class[] parameterTypes =
                theMethods[i].getParameterTypes();
            System.out.print("   Parameter Types:");
            for (int k = 0; k < parameterTypes.length; k ++) {
                String parameterString =
                    parameterTypes[k].getName();
                System.out.print(" " + parameterString);
            }
        System.out.println();
        }
    }
}
```

An abbreviated version of the output generated by the sample program follows:

```
Name: equals
   Return Type: boolean
   Parameter Types: java.lang.Object
Name: getClass
   Return Type: java.lang.Class
```

```
   Parameter Types:Name: hashCode
   Return Type: int
   Parameter Types:
.
.
.
Name: intersects
   Return Type: boolean
   Parameter Types: double double double double
Name: intersects
   Return Type: boolean
   Parameter Types: java.awt.geom.Rectangle2D
Name: translate
   Return Type: void
   Parameter Types: int int
```

Manipulating Objects

SOFTWARE development tools, such as GUI builders and debuggers, need to manipulate objects at runtime. For example, a GUI builder may allow the end user to select a `Button` from a menu of components, create the `Button` object, and then click the `Button` while running the application within the GUI builder. If you're in the business of creating software development tools, you'll want to take advantage of the reflection API features described in this lesson.

This lesson has the following sections:

Creating Objects

The simplest way to create an object in the Java programming language is to use the `new` operator:

```
Rectangle r = new Rectangle();
```

This technique is adequate for nearly all applications, because usually you know the class of the object at compile time. However, if you are writing development tools, you may not know the class of an object until runtime. For example, a GUI builder might allow the user to drag and drop a variety of GUI components onto the page being designed. In this situation you may be tempted to create the GUI components as follows:

```
String className;

// . . . load className from the user interface

Object o = new (className); // WRONG!
```

The preceding statement is invalid because the `new` operator does not accept arguments. Fortunately, with the reflection API you can create an object whose class is unknown until runtime. The method you invoke to create an object dynamically depends on whether the constructor you want to use has arguments. The next sections discuss these topics:

- Using No-Argument Constructors (page 698)
- Using Constructors that Have Arguments (page 699)

Using No-Argument Constructors

If you need to create an object with the no-argument constructor, you can invoke the `newInstance` method on a `Class`[1] object. The `newInstance` method throws a `NoSuchMethodException` if the class does not have a no-argument constructor. For more information on working with `Constructor`[2] objects, see the section Discovering Class Constructors (page 693).

The following sample program creates an instance of the `Rectangle` class, using the no-argument constructor by calling the `newInstance` method:

```
import java.lang.reflect.*;
import java.awt.*;

class SampleNoArg {

   public static void main(String[] args) {
       Rectangle r = (Rectangle)createObject
                   ("java.awt.Rectangle");
       System.out.println(r.toString());
   }
```

---

[1] The API documentation is available on the CD-ROM that accompanies this book and online here: http://java.sun.com/products/jdk/1.1/docs/api/java.lang.Class.html

[2] The API documentation is available on the CD-ROM that accompanies this book and online here: http://java.sun.com/products/jdk/1.1/docs/api/java.lang.reflect.Constructor.html

```
    static Object createObject(String className) {
        Object object = null;
        try {
            Class classDefinition = Class.forName(className);
            object = classDefinition.newInstance();
        } catch (InstantiationException e) {
            System.out.println(e);
        } catch (IllegalAccessException e) {
            System.out.println(e);
        } catch (ClassNotFoundException e) {
            System.out.println(e);
        }
        return object;
    }
}
```

The output of the preceding program is:

```
java.awt.Rectangle[x=0,y=0,width=0,height=0]
```

Using Constructors that Have Arguments

To create an object with a constructor that has arguments, you invoke the `newInstance` method on a `Constructor`[1] object, not a `Class` object. This technique involves several steps:

1. Create a `Class` object for the object you want to create.
2. Create a `Constructor` object by invoking `getConstructor` on the `Class` object. The `getConstructor` method has one parameter: an array of `Class` objects that correspond to the constructor's parameters.
3. Create the object by invoking `newInstance` on the `Constructor` object. The `newInstance` method has one parameter: an `Object` array whose elements are the argument values being passed to the constructor.

The sample program that follows creates a `Rectangle` with the constructor that accepts two integers as parameters. Invoking `newInstance` on this constructor is analogous to this statement:

```
Rectangle rectangle = new Rectangle(12, 34);
```

This constructor's arguments are primitive types, but the argument values passed to `newInstance` must be objects. Therefore each of the primitive `int` types is wrapped in an `Integer` object.

---

[1] The API documentation is available on the CD-ROM that accompanies this book and online here: http://java.sun.com/products/jdk/1.1/docs/api/java.lang.reflect.Constructor.html

The sample program hardcodes the argument passed to the `getConstructor` method. In a real-life application, such as a debugger, you would probably let the user select the constructor. To verify the user's selection, you could use the methods described in the section Discovering Class Constructors (page 693).

The source code for the sample program follows:

```
import java.lang.reflect.*;
import java.awt.*;

class SampleInstance {

   public static void main(String[] args) {

        Rectangle rectangle;
        Class rectangleDefinition;
        Class[] intArgsClass = new Class[]
                               {int.class, int.class};
        Integer height = new Integer(12);
        Integer width = new Integer(34);
        Object[] intArgs = new Object[] {height, width};
        Constructor intArgsConstructor;

        try {
            rectangleDefinition =
                Class.forName("java.awt.Rectangle");
            intArgsConstructor =
                rectangleDefinition.getConstructor
                (intArgsClass);
            rectangle = (Rectangle)
                createObject(intArgsConstructor, intArgs);
        } catch (ClassNotFoundException e) {
            System.out.println(e);
        } catch (NoSuchMethodException e) {
            System.out.println(e);
        }
   }

   public static Object createObject(Constructor constructor,
                                     Object[] arguments) {

        System.out.println ("Constructor: " +
                            constructor.toString());
        Object object = null;
```

```
        try {
            object = constructor.newInstance(arguments);
            System.out.println ("Object: " +
                                object.toString());
            return object;
        } catch (InstantiationException e) {
            System.out.println(e);
        } catch (IllegalAccessException e) {
            System.out.println(e);
        } catch (IllegalArgumentException e) {
            System.out.println(e);
        } catch (InvocationTargetException e) {
            System.out.println(e);
        }

        return object;
    }
}
```

The sample program prints a description of the constructor and the object that it creates:

```
Constructor: public java.awt.Rectangle(int,int)
Object: java.awt.Rectangle[x=0,y=0,width=12,height=34]
```

Getting Field Values

If you are writing a development tool such as a debugger, you must be able to obtain field values. This is a three-step process:

1. Create a `Class` object. The section Retrieving Class Objects (page 686) shows you how to do this.
2. Create a `Field` object by invoking `getField` on the `Class` object. For more information, see the section Identifying Class Fields (page 691).
3. Invoke one of the `get` methods on the `Field` object.

The `Field`[1] class has specialized methods for getting the values of primitive types. For example, the `getInt` method returns the contents as an `int` value, `getFloat` returns a `float`, and so forth. If the field stores an object instead of a primitive, use the `get` method to retrieve the object.

---

1 The API documentation is available on the CD-ROM that accompanies this book and online here: http://java.sun.com/products/jdk/1.1/docs/api/java.lang.reflect.Field.html

The following sample program demonstrates the three steps listed previously. This program gets the value of the `height` field from a `Rectangle` object. Because `height` is a primitive type (`int`), the object returned by the `get` method is a wrapper object (`Integer`).

In the sample program the name of the `height` field is known at compile time. However, in a development tool such as a GUI builder, the field name might not be known until runtime. To find out what fields belong to a class, you can use the techniques described in the section Identifying Class Fields (page 691).

Here is the source code for the sample program:

```
import java.lang.reflect.*;
import java.awt.*;

class SampleGet {

    public static void main(String[] args) {
        Rectangle r = new Rectangle(100, 325);
        printHeight(r);
    }

    static void printHeight(Rectangle r) {
        Field heightField;
        Integer heightValue;
        Class c = r.getClass();
        try {
            heightField = c.getField("height");
            heightValue = (Integer) heightField.get(r);
            System.out.println("Height: " +
                                   heightValue.toString());
        } catch (NoSuchFieldException e) {
            System.out.println(e);
        } catch (SecurityException e) {
            System.out.println(e);
        } catch (IllegalAccessException e) {
            System.out.println(e);
        }
    }
}
```

The output of the sample program verifies the value of the height field:

```
Height: 325
```

Setting Field Values

Some debuggers allow users to change field values during a debugging session. If you are writing a tool that has this capability, you must call one of the `Field` class's `set` methods. To modify the value of a field, perform the following steps:

1. Create a `Class` object. For more information, see the section Retrieving Class Objects (page 686).
2. Create a `Field` object by invoking `getField` on the `Class` object. The section Identifying Class Fields (page 691) shows you how.
3. Invoke the appropriate `set` method on the `Field` object.

The `Field` class provides several `set` methods. Specialized methods, such as `setBoolean` and `setInt`, are for modifying primitive types. If the field you want to change is an object, invoke the `set` method. You can call `set` to modify a primitive type, but you must use the appropriate wrapper object for the value parameter.

The sample program that follows modifies the `width` field of a `Rectangle` object by invoking the `set` method. Since the `width` is a primitive type, an `int`, the value passed by `set` is an `Integer`, which is an object wrapper.

```
import java.lang.reflect.*;
import java.awt.*;

class SampleSet {

   public static void main(String[] args) {
       Rectangle r = new Rectangle(100, 20);
       System.out.println("original: " + r.toString());
       modifyWidth(r, new Integer(300));
       System.out.println("modified: " + r.toString());
   }

   static void modifyWidth(Rectangle r, Integer widthParam ) {
       Field widthField;
       Integer widthValue;
       Class c = r.getClass();
       try {
           widthField = c.getField("width");
           widthField.set(r, widthParam);
       } catch (NoSuchFieldException e) {
           System.out.println(e);
       } catch (IllegalAccessException e) {
```

```
                System.out.println(e);
            }
        }
    }
```

The output of the sample program verifies that the width changed from 100 to 300:

```
original: java.awt.Rectangle[x=0,y=0,width=100,height=20]
modified: java.awt.Rectangle[x=0,y=0,width=300,height=20]
```

Invoking Methods

Suppose that you are writing a debugger that allows the user to select and then invoke methods during a debugging session. Since you don't know at compile time which methods the user will invoke, you cannot hardcode the method name in your source code. Instead you must follow these steps:

1. Create a `Class` object that corresponds to the object whose method you want to invoke. See the section Retrieving Class Objects (page 686) for more information.
2. Create a `Method`[1] object by invoking `getMethod` on the `Class` object. The `getMethod` method has two arguments: a `String` containing the method name, and an array of `Class` objects. Each element in the array corresponds to a parameter of the method you want to invoke. For more information on retrieving `Method` objects, see the section Obtaining Method Information (page 694).
3. Invoke the method by calling `invoke`. The `invoke` method has two arguments: an array of argument values to be passed to the invoked method, and an object whose class declares or inherits the method.

The sample program that follows shows you how to invoke a method dynamically. The program retrieves the `Method` object for the `String.concat` method and then uses `invoke` to concatenate two `String` objects.

```
import java.lang.reflect.*;

class SampleInvoke {
```

[1] The API documentation is available on the CD-ROM that accompanies this book and online here: http://java.sun.com/products/jdk/1.1/docs/api/java.lang.reflect.Method.html

```
    public static void main(String[] args) {
        String firstWord = "Hello ";
        String secondWord = "everybody.";
        String bothWords = append(firstWord, secondWord);
        System.out.println(bothWords);
    }

    public static String append(String firstWord,
                                String secondWord) {
        String result = null;
        Class c = String.class;
        Class[] parameterTypes = new Class[] {String.class};
        Method concatMethod;
        Object[] arguments = new Object[] {secondWord};
        try {
            concatMethod = c.getMethod("concat",
                                       parameterTypes);
            result = (String) concatMethod.invoke(firstWord,
                                                  arguments);
        } catch (NoSuchMethodException e) {
            System.out.println(e);
        } catch (IllegalAccessException e) {
            System.out.println(e);
        } catch (InvocationTargetException e) {
            System.out.println(e);
        }
        return result;
    }
}
```

The output of the preceding program is:

```
Hello everybody.
```

http://java.sun.com/docs/books/tutorial/reflect/array/index.html

60 Working with Arrays

THE Array[1] class provides methods that allow you to dynamically create and access arrays. In this lesson you'll learn how to use these methods. The section Identifying Arrays (page 707) shows you how to determine if an object really is an array. If you want to find out the component type of an array, you'll want to check out the programming example in the section Retrieving Component Types (page 709). The section Creating Arrays (page 710) shows you how simple it is to create arrays at runtime. Even if you don't know the name of an array until runtime, you can examine or modify the values of its elements. The section Getting and Setting Element Values (page 711) shows you how.

Identifying Arrays

If you aren't certain that a particular object is an array, you can check it with the `Class.isArray` method. Let's take a look at an example.

The sample program that follows prints the names of the arrays that are encapsulated in an object. The program performs these steps:

1. It retrieves the `Class` object that represents the target object.
2. It gets the `Field` objects for the `Class` object retrieved in step 1.
3. For each `Field` object, the program gets a corresponding `Class` object by invoking the `getType` method.

[1] The API documentation is available on the CD-ROM that accompanies this book and online here: http://java.sun.com/products/jdk/1.1/docs/api/java.lang.reflect.Array.html

4. To verify that the `Class` object retrieved in the preceding step represents an array, the program invokes the `isArray` method.

Here's the source code for the sample program:

```
import java.lang.reflect.*;
import java.awt.*;

class SampleArray {

   public static void main(String[] args) {
        KeyPad target = new KeyPad();
        printArrayNames(target);
   }

   static void printArrayNames(Object target) {
        Class targetClass = target.getClass();
        Field[] publicFields = targetClass.getFields();
        for (int i = 0; i < publicFields.length; i++) {
             String fieldName = publicFields[i].getName();
             Class typeClass = publicFields[i].getType();
             String fieldType = typeClass.getName();
             if (typeClass.isArray()) {
             System.out.println("Name: " + fieldName +
                                 ", Type: " + fieldType);
             }
        }
    }
}

class KeyPad {
    public boolean alive;
    public Button power;
    public Button[] letters;
    public int[] codes;
    public TextField[] rows;
    public boolean[] states;
}
```

The output of the sample program follows. Note that the left bracket indicates that the object is an array. For a detailed description of the type descriptors that `getName` returns, see section 4.3.1 of *The Java Virtual Machine Specification.*

```
Name: letters, Type: [Ljava.awt.Button;
Name: codes, Type: [I
Name: rows, Type: [Ljava.awt.TextField;
Name: states, Type: [Z
```

Retrieving Component Types

The component type is the type of an array's elements. For example, the component type of the `arrowKeys` array in the following line of code is `Button`:

```
Button[] arrowKeys = new Button[4];
```

The component type of a multidimensional array is an array. In the next line of code the component type of the array named `matrix` is `int[]`:

```
int[][] matrix = new int[100][100];
```

By invoking the `getComponentType` method against the `Class` object that represents an array, you can retrieve the component type of the array's elements.

The sample program that follows invokes the `getComponentType` method and prints out the class name of each array's component type.

```
import java.lang.reflect.*;
import java.awt.*;

class SampleComponent {
   public static void main(String[] args) {
        int[] ints = new int[2];
        Button[]  buttons = new Button[6];
        String[][] twoDim = new String[4][5];

        printComponentType(ints);
        printComponentType(buttons);
        printComponentType(twoDim);
   }

   static void printComponentType(Object array) {
        Class arrayClass = array.getClass();
        String arrayName = arrayClass.getName();
        Class componentClass = arrayClass.getComponentType();
        String componentName = componentClass.getName();
        System.out.println("Array: " + arrayName +
                           ", Component: " + componentName);
   }
}
```

The output of the sample program is:

```
Array: [I, Component: int
Array: [Ljava.awt.Button;, Component: java.awt.Button
Array: [[Ljava.lang.String;, Component: [Ljava.lang.String;
```

Creating Arrays

If you are writing a development tool such as an application builder, you may want to allow the end user to create arrays at runtime. Your program can provide this capability by invoking the `Array.newInstance` method.

The following sample program uses the `newInstance` method to create a copy of an array that is twice the size of the original array. The `newInstance` method accepts as arguments the length and the component type of the new array. The source code follows:

```
import java.lang.reflect.*;

class SampleCreateArray {
    public static void main(String[] args) {
        int[] originalArray =  {55, 66};
        int[] biggerArray = (int[])doubleArray(originalArray);
        System.out.println("originalArray:");
        for (int k = 0;k < Array.getLength(originalArray);k++)
            System.out.println(originalArray[k]);
        System.out.println("biggerArray:");
        for (int k = 0; k < Array.getLength(biggerArray); k++)
            System.out.println(biggerArray[k]);
    }

    static Object doubleArray(Object source) {
        int sourceLength = Array.getLength(source);
        Class arrayClass = source.getClass();
        Class componentClass = arrayClass.getComponentType();
        Object result = Array.newInstance(componentClass,
                                          sourceLength * 2);
        System.arraycopy(source, 0, result, 0, sourceLength);
        return result;
    }
}
```

The output of the preceding program is:

```
originalArray:
55
66
biggerArray:
55
66
0
0
```

You can also use the `newInstance` method to create multidimensional arrays. In this case the parameters of the method are the component type and an array of `int` types representing the dimensions of the new array.

The next sample program shows how to use `newInstance` to create multidimensional arrays:

```
import java.lang.reflect.*;

class SampleMultiArray {

    public static void main(String[] args) {

        // The oneDimA and oneDimB objects are one
        // dimensional int arrays with 5 elements.

        int[] dim1 = {5};
        int[] oneDimA =
            (int[]) Array.newInstance(int.class, dim1);
        int[] oneDimB =
            (int[]) Array.newInstance(int.class, 5);

        // The twoDimStr object is a 5 X 10 array of
        // String objects.

        int[] dimStr = {5, 10};
        String[][] twoDimStr =
           (String[][])Array.newInstance(String.class,dimStr);

        // The twoDimA object is an array of 12 int arrays. The
        // tail dimension is not defined. It is equivalent
        // to the array created as follows:
        //    int[][] ints = new int[12][];

        int[] dimA = {12};
        int[][] twoDimA =
           (int[][]) Array.newInstance(int[].class,dimA);
    }
}
```

Getting and Setting Element Values

In most programs to access array elements you merely use an assignment expression as follows:

```
int[10] codes;
codes[3] = 22;
aValue = codes[3];
```

This technique will not work if you don't know the name of the array until runtime.

Fortunately, you can use the `Array` class `set` and `get` methods to access array elements when the name of the array is unknown at compile time. In addition to `get` and `set`, the `Array` class has specialized methods that work with specific primitive types. For example, the value parameter of `setInt` is an `int`, and the object returned by `getBoolean` is a wrapper for a `boolean` type.

The sample program that follows uses the `set` and `get` methods to copy the contents of one array to another.

```
import java.lang.reflect.*;

class SampleGetArray {

   public static void main(String[] args) {
        int[] sourceInts = {12, 78};
        int[] destInts = new int[2];
        copyArray(sourceInts, destInts);
        String[] sourceStrgs =
             {"Hello ", "there ", "everybody"};
        String[] destStrgs = new String[3];
        copyArray(sourceStrgs, destStrgs);
   }

   public static void copyArray(Object source, Object dest) {
        for (int i = 0; i < Array.getLength(source); i++) {
             Array.set(dest, i, Array.get(source, i));
              System.out.println(Array.get(dest, i));
        }
   }
}
```

The output of the sample program is:

```
12
78
Hello
there
everybody
```

http://java.sun.com/docs/books/tutorial/reflect/summary/index.html

61 Summary of Classes

THE following table summarizes the classes that compose the reflection API. The `Class` and `Object` classes are in the `java.lang`[1] package. The other classes are contained in the `java.lang.reflect`[2] package.

Table 36 Reflection API Classes

Class	Description
`Array`	Provides static methods to dynamically create and access arrays.
`Class`	Represents, or reflects, classes and interfaces.
`Constructor`	Provides information about, and access to, a constructor for a class. Allows you to instantiate a class dynamically.
`Field`	Provides information about, and dynamic access to, a field of a class or an interface.
`Method`	Provides information about, and access to, a single method on a class or interface. Allows you to invoke the method dynamically.
`Modifier`	Provides static methods and constants that allow you to get information about the access modifiers of a class and its members.
`Object`	Provides the `getClass` method.

1 The API documentation is available on the CD-ROM that accompanies this book and online here: http://java.sun.com/products/jdk/1.1/docs/api/Package-java.lang.html

2 The API documentation is available on the CD-ROM that accompanies this book and online here: http://java.sun.com/products/jdk/1.1/docs/api/Package-java.lang.reflect.html

About the Author

DALE GREEN is a staff writer with Sun Microsystems, where he documents APIs for the Java programming language. In previous lives he programmed business applications, designed databases, taught technical classes, and documented RDBMS products. In his current incarnation he writes about internationalization and reflection APIs for *The Java Tutorial*.

Acknowledgments

The following people provided thoughtful and detailed reviews: Waleed Hosny and Greg White. I'd also like to thank our many readers on the Internet for their comments and suggestions.

Appendices

APPENDIX A

Code Examples

THIS appendix lists every complete Java example program featured in this tutorial. It also includes a few HTML and data files that you might need to copy.

Each example lists the section(s) in which it is explained, the names of the source files that comprise the example, and the location of each source file on our Web site. Most applets have an additional field that lists the HTML pages on which you can find the applet running.

Collections

LESSON 2: Interfaces

EXAMPLE: The Find Duplicates Application

Where Explained:
Basic Operations (page 32)

FindDups.java

SOURCE CODE: *http://java.sun.com/docs/books/tutorial/collections/interfaces/example-1dot2/FindDups.java*

```
import java.util.*;

public class FindDups {
    public static void main(String args[]) {
        Set s = new HashSet();
        for (int i=0; i<args.length; i++)
            if (!s.add(args[i]))
                System.out.println("Duplicate detected:" +
                                   args[i]);
        System.out.println(s.size()+" distinct words " +
                           "detected: "+s);
    }
}
```

EXAMPLE: The Find Duplicates 2 Application

Where Explained:
Bulk Operations (page 33)

FindDups2.java

SOURCE CODE: *http://java.sun.com/docs/books/tutorial/collections/interfaces/example-1dot2/FindDups2.java*

```
import java.util.*;

public class FindDups2 {
    public static void main(String args[]) {
        Set uniques = new HashSet();
        Set dups = new HashSet();

        for (int i=0; i<args.length; i++)
            if (!uniques.add(args[i]))
                dups.add(args[i]);

        uniques.removeAll(dups); // Destructive set-difference

        System.out.println("Unique words:    " + uniques);
        System.out.println("Duplicate words: " + dups);
    }
}
```

EXAMPLE: The Shuffle Application

Shuffle.java

SOURCE CODE: *http://java.sun.com/docs/books/tutorial/collections/interfaces/example-1dot2/Shuffle.java*

Where Explained:
Positional Access and Search Operations (page 37)

```
import java.util.*;

public class Shuffle {
    public static void main(String args[]) {
        List l = Arrays.asList(args);
        Collections.shuffle(l);
        System.out.println(l);
    }
}
```

EXAMPLE: The Deal Application

Deal.java

SOURCE CODE: *http://java.sun.com/docs/books/tutorial/collections/interfaces/example-1dot2/Deal.java*

Where Explained:
List Interface (page 35)

```
import java.util.*;

class Deal {
    public static void main(String args[]) {
        int numHands = Integer.parseInt(args[0]);
        int cardsPerHand = Integer.parseInt(args[1]);
        // Make a normal 52-card deck
        String[] suit = new String[] {"spades",
                        "hearts", "diamonds", "clubs"};
        String[] rank = new String[]
                         {"ace","2","3","4","5","6","7",
                         "8","9","10","jack","queen","king"};
        List deck = new ArrayList();
        for (int i=0; i<suit.length; i++)
            for (int j=0; j<rank.length; j++)
                deck.add(rank[j] + " of " + suit[i]);

        Collections.shuffle(deck);

        for (int i=0; i<numHands; i++)
            System.out.println(dealHand(deck, cardsPerHand));
    }

    public static List dealHand(List deck, int n) {
        int deckSize = deck.size();
```

```
            List handView = deck.subList(deckSize-n, deckSize);
            List hand = new ArrayList(handView);
            handView.clear();
            return hand;
        }
    }
```

EXAMPLE: Simple Program to Generate Frequency Table

Where Explained:
Map Interface
(page 45)

Freq.java

SOURCE CODE: *http://java.sun.com/docs/books/tutorial/collections/interfaces/example-1dot2/Freq.java*

```
import java.util.*;

public class Freq {
    private static final Integer ONE = new Integer(1);
    public static void main(String args[]) {
        Map m = new TreeMap();

        // Initialize frequency table from command line
        for (int i=0; i<args.length; i++) {
            Integer freq = (Integer) m.get(args[i]);
            m.put(args[i], (freq==null ? ONE :
                               new Integer(freq.intValue() + 1)));
}

        System.out.println(m.size() + " distinct words " +
                                " detected:");
        System.out.println(m);
    }
}
```

EXAMPLE: Permutation Groups Program

Where Explained:
Multimaps
(page 51)

Perm.java

SOURCE CODE: *http://java.sun.com/docs/books/tutorial/collections/interfaces/example-1dot2/Perm.java*

```
import java.util.*;
import java.io.*;

public class Perm {
    public static void main(String[] args) {
        int minGroupSize = Integer.parseInt(args[1]);

        // Read words from file & put into simulated multimap
```

```
        Map m = new HashMap();
        try {
            BufferedReader in =
                  new BufferedReader(new FileReader(args[0]));
            String word;
            while((word = in.readLine()) != null) {
                String alpha = alphabetize(word);
                List l = (List) m.get(alpha);
                if (l==null)
                    m.put(alpha, l=new ArrayList());
                l.add(word);
            }
        } catch(IOException e) {
            System.err.println(e);
            System.exit(1);
        }

        // Print all permutation groups above size threshold
        for (Iterator i=m.values().iterator(); i.hasNext();) {
            List l = (List) i.next();
            if (l.size() >= minGroupSize)
                System.out.println(l.size() + ": " + l);
        }
    }

    private static String alphabetize(String s) {
        int count[] = new int[256];
        int len = s.length();
        for (int i=0; i<len; i++)
            count[s.charAt(i)]++;
        StringBuffer result = new StringBuffer(len);
        for (char c='a'; c<='z'; c++)
            for (int i=0; i<count[c]; i++)
                result.append(c);
        return result.toString();
    }
}
```

EXAMPLE: The Name Application

Where Explained:
Writing Your Own Comparable Types (page 55)

EXAMPLE:

Name.java

SOURCE CODE: *http://java.sun.com/docs/books/tutorial/collections/interfaces/example-1dot2/Name.java*

```
import java.util.*;
```

```
public class Name implements Comparable {
    private String firstName, lastName;

    public Name(String firstName, String lastName) {
        if (firstName==null || lastName==null)
            throw new NullPointerException();
        this.firstName = firstName;
        this.lastName = lastName;
    }

    public String firstName()    {return firstName;}
    public String lastName()     {return lastName;}

    public boolean equals(Object o) {
        if (!(o instanceof Name))
            return false;
        Name n = (Name)o;
        return n.firstName.equals(firstName) &&
               n.lastName.equals(lastName);
    }

    public int hashCode() {
        return 31*firstName.hashCode() + lastName.hashCode();
    }

    public String toString() {return firstName + " " +
                                 lastName;}

    public int compareTo(Object o) {
        Name n = (Name)o;
        int lastCmp = lastName.compareTo(n.lastName);
        return (lastCmp!=0 ? lastCmp :
                firstName.compareTo(n.firstName));
    }
}
```

NameSort.java

SOURCE CODE: *http://java.sun.com/docs/books/tutorial/collections/interfaces/example-1dot2/NameSort.java*

```
import java.util.*;

class NameSort {
    public static void main(String args[]) {
        Name n[] = {
            new Name("John", "Lennon"),
            new Name("Karl", "Marx"),
            new Name("Groucho", "Marx"),
```

```
            new Name("Oscar", "Grouch")
        };
        List l = Arrays.asList(n);
        Collections.sort(l);
        System.out.println(l);
    }
}
```

LESSON 4: Algorithms

EXAMPLE: The Sort Application

Sort.java

SOURCE CODE: *http://java.sun.com/docs/books/tutorial/collections/algorithms/example-1dot2/Sort.java*

Where Explained:
Sorting (page 77)

```
import java.util.*;

public class Sort {
    public static void main(String args[]) {
        List l = Arrays.asList(args);
        Collections.sort(l);
        System.out.println(l);
    }
}
```

EXAMPLE: Permutation Groups Program (Prints in Reverse Order)

Perm2.java

SOURCE CODE: *http://java.sun.com/docs/books/tutorial/collections/algorithms/example-1dot2/Perm2.java*

Where Explained:
Sorting (page 77)

```
import java.util.*;
import java.io.*;

public class Perm2 {
    public static void main(String[] args) {
        int minGroupSize = Integer.parseInt(args[1]);

        // Read words from file & put into simulated multimap
        Map m = new HashMap();
        try {
            BufferedReader in =
                   new BufferedReader(new FileReader(args[0]));
            String word;
```

```
            while((word = in.readLine()) != null) {
                String alpha = alphabetize(word);
                List l = (List) m.get(alpha);
                if (l==null)
                    m.put(alpha, l=new ArrayList());
                l.add(word);
            }
        } catch(IOException e) {
            System.err.println(e);
            System.exit(1);
        }
        // Make a List of all permutation groups above size
        // threshold
        List winners = new ArrayList();
        for (Iterator i = m.values().iterator(); i.hasNext();) {
            List l = (List) i.next();
            if (l.size() >= minGroupSize)
                winners.add(l);
        }



        // Sort permutation groups according to size
        Collections.sort(winners, new Comparator() {
            public int compare(Object o1, Object o2) {
                return ((List)o2).size() - ((List)o1).size();
            }
        });


        // Print permutation groups
        for (Iterator i=winners.iterator(); i.hasNext(); ) {
            List l = (List) i.next();
            System.out.println(l.size() + ": " + l);
        }
    }

    private static String alphabetize(String s) {
        int count[] = new int[256];
        int len = s.length();
        for (int i=0; i<len; i++)
            count[s.charAt(i)]++;
        StringBuffer result = new StringBuffer(len);
        for (char c='a'; c<='z'; c++)
            for (int i=0; i<count[c]; i++)
                result.append(c);
        return result.toString();
    }
}
```

Internationalization

LESSON 5: Introduction

Where Explained:
After Internationalization (page 101)

EXAMPLE: An Internationalized Program

I18NSample.java

SOURCE CODE: *http://java.sun.com/docs/books/tutorial/i18n/intro/after.html*

```
import java.util.*;

public class I18NSample {

   static public void main(String[] args) {

        ResourceBundle messages =
            ResourceBundle.getBundle("MessagesBundle",
                                      Locale.getDefault());
        System.out.println(messages.getString("greetings"));
        System.out.println(messages.getString("inquiry"));
        System.out.println(messages.getString("farewell"));
   }
}
```

LESSON 6: Setting the Locale

EXAMPLE: Identifying Available Locales

Where Explained: *Identifying Available Locales* (page 112)

Available.java

SOURCE CODE: *http://java.sun.com/docs/books/tutorial/i18n/locale/example-1dot1/Available.java*

```
import java.util.*;
import java.text.*;

public class Available {

   static public void main(String[] args) {
        Locale list[] = DateFormat.getAvailableLocales();
        for (int i = 0; i < list.length; i++) {
            System.out.println (list[i].getLanguage() + " " +
                                list[i].getCountry());
        }
   }
}
```

LESSON 7: Isolating Locale-Specific Data

EXAMPLE: Backing a ResourceBundle with Properties Files

Where Explained: *Backing a ResourceBundle with Properties Files* (page 120)

PropertiesDemo.java

SOURCE CODE: *http://java.sun.com/docs/books/tutorial/i18n/resbundle/example-1dot1/PropertiesDemo.java*

```
import java.util.*;

public class PropertiesDemo {

    static void displayValue(
                Locale currentLocale, String key) {
        ResourceBundle labels =
                    ResourceBundle.getBundle(
                    "LabelsBundle", currentLocale);
        String value  = labels.getString(key);
        System.out.println(
            "Locale = " + currentLocale.toString() + ", " +
            "key = " + key + ", " +
            "value = " + value);
    } // displayValue

    static void iterateKeys(Locale currentLocale) {
        ResourceBundle labels =
            ResourceBundle.getBundle("LabelsBundle",
                                     currentLocale);
        Enumeration bundleKeys = labels.getKeys();

        while (bundleKeys.hasMoreElements()) {
            String key = (String)bundleKeys.nextElement();
            String value  = labels.getString(key);
            System.out.println("key = " + key + ", " +
                               "value = " + value);
        }
    } // iterateKeys

    static public void main(String[] args) {
        Locale[] supportedLocales = {
            Locale.FRENCH,
            Locale.GERMAN,
            Locale.ENGLISH
        };
        for (int i = 0; i < supportedLocales.length; i ++) {
            displayValue(supportedLocales[i], "s2");
        }

        System.out.println();

        iterateKeys(supportedLocales[0]);
    } // main
} // class
```

EXAMPLE: Using a ListResourceBundle

Where Explained:
Using a ListResource Bundle
(page 123)

ListDemo.java

SOURCE CODE: *http://java.sun.com/docs/books/tutorial/i18n/resbundle/example-1dot1/ListDemo.java*

```
import java.util.*;

public class ListDemo {

    static void displayValues(Locale currentLocale) {

        ResourceBundle stats = ResourceBundle.getBundle(
                                   "StatsBundle",currentLocale);
        Integer gdp = (Integer)stats.getObject("GDP");
        System.out.println("GDP = " + gdp.toString());
        Integer pop = (Integer)stats.getObject("Population");
        System.out.println("Population = " + pop.toString());
        Double lit = (Double)stats.getObject("Literacy");
        System.out.println("Literacy = " + lit.toString());

    } // displayValues

    static public void main(String[] args) {

        Locale[] supportedLocales = {
            new Locale("en","CA"),
            new Locale("ja","JA"),
            new Locale("fr","FR")
        };

        for (int i = 0; i < supportedLocales.length; i ++) {
            System.out.println("Locale = " +
                                   supportedLocales[i]);
            displayValues(supportedLocales[i]);
            System.out.println();
        }

    } // main

} // class
```

StatsBundle.java

SOURCE CODE: *http://java.sun.com/docs/books/tutorial/i18n/resbundle/example-1dot1/StatsBundle.java*

```
import java.util.*;

public class StatsBundle extends ListResourceBundle {

    public Object[][] getContents() {
        return contents;
    }

    private Object[][] contents = {
        {"GDP", new Integer(0)},
        {"Population", new Integer(0)},
        {"Literacy", new Double(0.00)},
    };
}
```

StatsBundle_en_CA.java

```
import java.util.*;

public class StatsBundle_en_CA extends ListResourceBundle {

    public Object[][] getContents() {
        return contents;
    }

    private Object[][] contents = {
        {"GDP", new Integer(24400)},
        {"Population", new Integer(28802671)},
        {"Literacy", new Double(0.97)},
    };
}
```

StatsBundle_ja_JA.java

```
import java.util.*;

public class StatsBundle_ja_JP extends ListResourceBundle {

    public Object[][] getContents() {
        return contents;
    }
```

```
    private Object[][] contents = {
        {"GDP", new Integer(21300)},
        {"Population", new Integer(125449703)},
        {"Literacy", new Double(0.99)},
    };
}
```

StatsBundle_fr_FR.java

```
import java.util.*;

public class StatsBundle_fr_FR extends ListResourceBundle {

   public Object[][] getContents() {
      return contents;
   }

   private Object[][] contents = {
      {"GDP", new Integer(20200)},
      {"Population", new Integer(58317450)},
      {"Literacy", new Double(0.99)},
   };
}
```

LESSON 8: Formatting

EXAMPLE: Application with Predefined Formats

Where Explained: *Using Predefined Formats* (page 128)

NumberFormatDemo.java

SOURCE CODE: *http://java.sun.com/docs/books/tutorial/i18n/format/example-1dot1/NumberFormatDemo.java*

```
import java.util.*;
import java.text.*;

public class NumberFormatDemo {

    static public void displayNumber(Locale currentLocale) {

        Integer quantity = new Integer(123456);
        Double amount = new Double(345987.246);
        NumberFormat numberFormatter;
        String quantityOut;
        String amountOut;
```

```
    numberFormatter =
        NumberFormat.getNumberInstance(currentLocale);
    quantityOut = numberFormatter.format(quantity);
    amountOut = numberFormatter.format(amount);
    System.out.println(quantityOut + "   " +
                        currentLocale.toString());
    System.out.println(amountOut + "   " +
                        currentLocale.toString());
}

static public void displayCurrency(Locale currentLocale) {
    Double currency = new Double(9876543.21);
    NumberFormat currencyFormatter;
    String currencyOut;

    currencyFormatter =
        NumberFormat.getCurrencyInstance(currentLocale);
    currencyOut = currencyFormatter.format(currency);
    System.out.println(currencyOut + "   " +
                        currentLocale.toString());
}

static public void displayPercent(Locale currentLocale) {
    Double percent = new Double(0.75);
    NumberFormat percentFormatter;
    String percentOut;
    percentFormatter =
        NumberFormat.getPercentInstance(currentLocale);
    percentOut = percentFormatter.format(percent);
    System.out.println(percentOut + "   " +
                        currentLocale.toString());
}

static public void main(String[] args) {

    Locale[] locales = {
        new Locale("fr","FR"),
        new Locale("de","DE"),
        new Locale("en","US")
    };

    for (int i = 0; i < locales.length; i++) {
        System.out.println();
        displayNumber(locales[i]);
        displayCurrency(locales[i]);
```

```
                displayPercent(locales[i]);
            }
        }
    }
```

EXAMPLE: Customizing Formats

Where Explained: *Customizing Formats* (page 130)

DecimalFormatDemo.java

SOURCE CODE: *http://java.sun.com/docs/books/tutorial/i18n/format/example-1dot1/DecimalFormatDemo.java*

```
import java.util.*;
import java.text.*;

public class DecimalFormatDemo {

    static public void customFormat(String pattern,
                                    double value ) {
        DecimalFormat myFormatter =
                    new DecimalFormat(pattern);
        String output = myFormatter.format(value);
        System.out.println(value + "  " + pattern + "  " +
                       output);
    }

    static public void localizedFormat(String pattern,
                                       double value,
                                       Locale loc ) {
        NumberFormat nf = NumberFormat.getNumberInstance(loc);
        DecimalFormat df = (DecimalFormat)nf;
        df.applyPattern(pattern);
        String output = df.format(value);
        System.out.println(pattern + "  " + output + "  " +
                           loc.toString());
    }

    static public void main(String[] args) {

        customFormat("###,###.###", 123456.789);
        customFormat("###.##", 123456.789);
        customFormat("000000.000", 123.78);
        customFormat("$###,###.###", 12345.67);
        customFormat("\u00a5###,###.###", 12345.67);

        Locale currentLocale = new Locale("en", "US");

        DecimalFormatSymbols unusualSymbols =
                  new DecimalFormatSymbols(currentLocale);
```

```
            unusualSymbols.setDecimalSeparator('|');
            unusualSymbols.setGroupingSeparator('^');
            String strange = "#,##0.###";
            DecimalFormat weirdFormatter = new DecimalFormat(
                                        strange, unusualSymbols);
            weirdFormatter.setGroupingSize(4);
            String bizarre = weirdFormatter.format(12345.678);
            System.out.println(bizarre);

            Locale[] locales = {
                new Locale("en", "US"),
                new Locale("de", "DE"),
                new Locale("fr", "FR")
            };

            for (int i = 0; i < locales.length; i++) {
                localizedFormat("###,###.###", 123456.789,
                                locales[i]);
            }
        }
    }
```

EXAMPLE: Using Predefined Formats

DateFormatDemo.java

Where Explained:
Using Predefined Formats (page 133)

SOURCE CODE: *http://java.sun.com/docs/books/tutorial/i18n/format/example-1dot1/DateFormatDemo.java*

```
import java.util.*;
import java.text.*;

public class DateFormatDemo {

    static public void displayDate(Locale currentLocale) {

        Date today;
        String dateOut;
        DateFormat dateFormatter;
        dateFormatter = DateFormat.getDateInstance(
                            DateFormat.DEFAULT, currentLocale);
        today = new Date();
        dateOut = dateFormatter.format(today);

        System.out.println(dateOut + "   " +
                            currentLocale.toString());
    }
```

```
static public void showBothStyles(Locale currentLocale) {

     Date today;
     String result;
     DateFormat formatter;

     int[] styles = {
         DateFormat.DEFAULT,
         DateFormat.SHORT,
         DateFormat.MEDIUM,
         DateFormat.LONG,
         DateFormat.FULL
     };

     System.out.println();
     System.out.println("Locale: " +
                              currentLocale.toString());
     System.out.println();

     today = new Date();

     for (int k = 0; k < styles.length; k++) {
         formatter = DateFormat.getDateTimeInstance(
                      styles[k], styles[k], currentLocale);
         result = formatter.format(today);
         System.out.println(result);
     }
}

static public void showDateStyles(Locale currentLocale) {

     Date today = new Date();
     String result;
     DateFormat formatter;

     int[] styles = {
         DateFormat.DEFAULT,
         DateFormat.SHORT,
         DateFormat.MEDIUM,
         DateFormat.LONG,
         DateFormat.FULL
     };

     System.out.println();
     System.out.println("Locale: " +
                              currentLocale.toString());
     System.out.println();
```

```
        for (int k = 0; k < styles.length; k++) {
            formatter = DateFormat.getDateInstance(
                                         styles[k], currentLocale);
            result = formatter.format(today);
            System.out.println(result);
        }
    }

    static public void showTimeStyles(Locale currentLocale) {

        Date today = new Date();
        String result;
        DateFormat formatter;
        int[] styles = {
            DateFormat.DEFAULT,
            DateFormat.SHORT,
            DateFormat.MEDIUM,
            DateFormat.LONG,
            DateFormat.FULL
        };

        System.out.println();
        System.out.println("Locale: " +
                           currentLocale.toString());
        System.out.println();

        for (int k = 0; k < styles.length; k++) {
            formatter = DateFormat.getTimeInstance(
                             styles[k], currentLocale);
            result = formatter.format(today);
            System.out.println(result);
        }
    }

    static public void main(String[] args) {

        Locale[] locales = {
            new Locale("fr","FR"),
            new Locale("de","DE"),
            new Locale("en","US")
        };

        for (int i = 0; i < locales.length; i++) {
            displayDate(locales[i]);
        }

        showDateStyles(new Locale("en","US"));
        showDateStyles(new Locale("fr","FR"));
```

```
        showTimeStyles(new Locale("en","US"));
        showTimeStyles(new Locale("de","DE"));

        showBothStyles(new Locale("en","US"));
        showBothStyles(new Locale("fr","FR"));

    }
}
```

EXAMPLE: Customizing Formats

Where Explained: *Customizing Formats* (page 135)

SimpleDateFormatDemo.java

SOURCE CODE: *http://java.sun.com/docs/books/tutorial/i18n/format/example-1dot1/SimpleDateFormatDemo.java*

```
import java.util.*;
import java.text.*;

public class SimpleDateFormatDemo {

    static public void displayDate(Locale currentLocale) {
        Date today;
        String result;
        SimpleDateFormat formatter;

        formatter = new SimpleDateFormat("EEE d MMM yy",
                                         currentLocale);
        today = new Date();
        result = formatter.format(today);

        System.out.println("Locale: " +
                           currentLocale.toString());
        System.out.println("Result: " + result);
    }

    static public void displayPattern(String pattern,
                                      Locale currentLocale) {
        Date today;
        SimpleDateFormat formatter;
        String output;

        formatter = new SimpleDateFormat(
                                      pattern, currentLocale);
        today = new Date();
        output = formatter.format(today);

        System.out.println(pattern + "   " + output);
    }
```

```
    static public void main(String[] args) {

        Locale[] locales = {
            new Locale("fr","FR"),
            new Locale("de","DE"),
            new Locale("en","US")
        };

        for (int i = 0; i < locales.length; i++) {
            displayDate(locales[i]);
            System.out.println();
        }

        String[] patterns = {
            "dd.MM.yy",
            "yyyy.MM.dd G 'at' hh:mm:ss z",
            "EEE, MMM d, ''yy",
            "h:mm a",
            "H:mm",
            "H:mm:ss:SSS",
            "K:mm a,z",
            "yyyy.MMMMM.dd GGG hh:mm aaa"
        };

        for (int k = 0; k < patterns.length; k++) {
            displayPattern(patterns[k],
                           new Locale("en","US"));
            System.out.println();
        }
        System.out.println();
    }
}
```

EXAMPLE: Changing Date Format Symbols

DateFormatSymbolsDemo.java

SOURCE CODE: *http://java.sun.com/docs/books/tutorial/i18n/format/example-1dot1/DateFormatSymbolsDemo.java*

Where Explained:
Changing Date Format Symbols (page 137)

```
import java.util.*;
import java.text.*;

public class DateFormatSymbolsDemo {

    static public void changeWeekDays() {
        Date today;
        String result;
        SimpleDateFormat formatter;
```

```
            DateFormatSymbols symbols;
            String[] defaultDays;
            String[] modifiedDays;

            symbols = new DateFormatSymbols(
                              new Locale("en","US"));
            defaultDays = symbols.getShortWeekdays();

            for (int i = 0; i < defaultDays.length; i++) {
                System.out.print(defaultDays[i] + "  ");
            }
            System.out.println();

            String[] capitalDays = {
             "", "SUN", "MON", "TUE", "WED", "THU", "FRI", "SAT"};
            symbols.setShortWeekdays(capitalDays);
            modifiedDays = symbols.getShortWeekdays();

            for (int i = 0; i < modifiedDays.length; i++) {
                System.out.print(modifiedDays[i] + "  ");
            }

            System.out.println();
            System.out.println();

            formatter = new SimpleDateFormat("E", symbols);
            today = new Date();
            result = formatter.format(today);
            System.out.println(result);
        }

        static public void main(String[] args) {
            changeWeekDays();
        }
    }
```

EXAMPLE: Dealing with Compound Messages

Where Explained: *Dealing with Compound Messages* (page 140)

MessageFormatDemo.java

SOURCE CODE: *http://java.sun.com/docs/books/tutorial/i18n/format/example-1dot1/MessageFormatDemo.java*

```
import java.util.*;
import java.text.*;

public class MessageFormatDemo {

    static void displayMessage(Locale currentLocale) {
```

```
        System.out.println("currentLocale = " +
                           currentLocale.toString());
        System.out.println();

        ResourceBundle messages = ResourceBundle.getBundle(
                                  "MessageBundle",
                                  currentLocale);

        Object[] messageArguments = {
            messages.getString("planet"),
            new Integer(7),
            new Date()
        };

        MessageFormat formatter = new MessageFormat("");
        formatter.setLocale(currentLocale);
        formatter.applyPattern(messages.getString(
                                       "template"));
        String output = formatter.format(messageArguments);

        System.out.println(output);
    }

    static public void main(String[] args) {
        displayMessage(new Locale("en", "US"));
        System.out.println();
        displayMessage(new Locale("de", "DE"));
    }
}
```

EXAMPLE: Handling Plurals

ChoiceFormatDemo.java

SOURCE CODE: *http://java.sun.com/docs/books/tutorial/i18n/format/example-1dot1/ChoiceFormatDemo.java*

Where Explained: *Handling Plurals* (page 143)

```
import java.util.*;
import java.text.*;

public class ChoiceFormatDemo {

    static void displayMessages(Locale currentLocale) {

        System.out.println("currentLocale = " +
                           currentLocale.toString());
        System.out.println();
```

```
        ResourceBundle bundle = ResourceBundle.getBundle(
                                "ChoiceBundle",currentLocale);
        MessageFormat messageForm = new MessageFormat("");
        messageForm.setLocale(currentLocale);

        double[] fileLimits = {0,1,2};

        String [] fileStrings = {
            bundle.getString("noFiles"),
            bundle.getString("oneFile"),
            bundle.getString("multipleFiles")
        };

        ChoiceFormat choiceForm = new ChoiceFormat(fileLimits,
                                              fileStrings);

        String pattern = bundle.getString("pattern");
        Format[] formats = {choiceForm, null,
                            NumberFormat.getInstance()};

        messageForm.applyPattern(pattern);
        messageForm.setFormats(formats);

        Object[] messageArguments = {null, "XDisk", null};

        for (int numFiles = 0; numFiles < 4; numFiles++) {
            messageArguments[0] = new Integer(numFiles);
            messageArguments[2] = new Integer(numFiles);
            String result =
                       messageForm.format(messageArguments);
            System.out.println(result);
        }
    }

    static public void main(String[] args) {
        displayMessages(new Locale("en", "US"));
        System.out.println();
        displayMessages(new Locale("fr", "FR"));
    }
}
```

Where Explained: *Performing Locale-Independent Comparisons* (page 152)

LESSON 9: Working with Text

EXAMPLE: Performing Locale-Independent Comparisons

CollatorDemo.java

SOURCE CODE: *http://java.sun.com/docs/books/tutorial/i18n/text/example-1dot1/CollatorDemo.java*

```
import java.util.*;
import java.text.*;

public class CollatorDemo {

    public static void sortStrings(Collator collator,
                                   String[] words) {
        String tmp;
        for (int i = 0; i < words.length; i++) {
            for (int j = i + 1; j < words.length; j++) {
                // Compare elements of array two at a time.
                if (collator.compare(words[i], words[j])> 0) {
                    // Swap words[i] and words[j]
                    tmp = words[i];
                    words[i] = words[j];
                    words[j] = tmp;
                }
            }
        }
    }

    public static void printStrings(String [] words) {
        for (int i = 0; i < words.length; i++) {
            System.out.println(words[i]);
        }
    }

    public static void testCompare() {

        Collator myCollator =
                Collator.getInstance(new Locale("en", "US"));

        System.out.println(myCollator.compare("abc", "def"));
        System.out.println(myCollator.compare("rtf", "rtf"));
        System.out.println(myCollator.compare("xyz", "abc"));
    }

    static public void main(String[] args) {

        testCompare();
        System.out.println();

        Collator fr_FRCollator =
            Collator.getInstance(new Locale("fr","FR"));
```

```
            Collator en_USCollator =
                Collator.getInstance(new Locale("en","US"));

            String eWithCircumflex = new String("\u00EA");
            String eWithAcute = new String("\u00E9");
            String peachfr = "p" + eWithAcute + "ch" + eWithAcute;
            String sinfr = "p" + eWithCircumflex + "che";

            String [] words = {
                peachfr,
                sinfr,
                "peach",
                "sin"
            };

            sortStrings(fr_FRCollator, words);
            printStrings(words);

            System.out.println();

            sortStrings(en_USCollator, words);
            printStrings(words);
        }
    }
```

EXAMPLE: Customizing Collation Rules

Where Explained: *Customizing Collation Rules* (page 154)

RulesDemo.java

SOURCE CODE: *http://java.sun.com/docs/books/tutorial/i18n/text/example-1dot1/RulesDemo.java*

```
import java.util.*;
import java.text.*;

public class RulesDemo {

    public static void sortStrings(Collator collator,
                                   String[] words) {
        String tmp;
        for (int i = 0; i < words.length; i++) {
            for (int j = i + 1; j < words.length; j++) {
                // Compare elements of the words array
                if(collator.compare(words[i], words[j]) > 0) {
                    // Swap words[i] and words[j]
                    tmp = words[i];
                    words[i] = words[j];
                    words[j] = tmp;
```

```
                }
            }
        }
    }

    public static void printStrings(String [] words) {
        for (int i = 0; i < words.length; i++) {
            System.out.println(words[i]);
        }
    }

    static public void main(String[] args) {
        String englishRules =
           ("< a,A < b,B < c,C < d,D < e,E < f,F " +
            "< g,G < h,H < i,I < j,J < k,K < l,L " +
            "< m,M < n,N < o,O < p,P < q,Q < r,R " +
            "< s,S < t,T < u,U < v,V < w,W < x,X " +
            "< y,Y < z,Z");

        String smallnTilde  = new String("\u00F1");
        String capitalNTilde = new String("\u00D1");

        String traditionalSpanishRules =
           ("< a,A < b,B < c,C " +
            "< ch, cH, Ch, CH "  +
            "< d,D < e,E < f,F " +
            "< g,G < h,H < i,I < j,J < k,K < l,L " +
            "< ll, lL, Ll, LL "  +
            "< m,M < n,N " +
            "< " + smallnTilde + "," + capitalNTilde + " " +
            "< o,O < p,P < q,Q < r,R " +
            "< s,S < t,T < u,U < v,V < w,W < x,X " +
            "< y,Y < z,Z");
        String [] words = {
            "luz",
            "curioso",
            "llama",
            "chalina"
        };

        try {
            RuleBasedCollator enCollator =
               new RuleBasedCollator(englishRules);
            RuleBasedCollator spCollator =
               new RuleBasedCollator(traditionalSpanishRules);
            sortStrings(enCollator, words);
            printStrings(words);
```

```
                System.out.println();

                sortStrings(spCollator, words);
                printStrings(words);

            } catch (ParseException pe) {
                System.out.println("Parse exception for rules");
            }
        }
    }
```

EXAMPLE: Improving Collation Performance

Where Explained: *Improving Collation Performance* (page 156)

KeysDemo.java

SOURCE CODE: *http://java.sun.com/docs/books/tutorial/i18n/text/example-1dot1/KeysDemo.java*

```
import java.util.*;
import java.text.*;

public class KeysDemo  {

    public static void sortArray(CollationKey[] keys) {

        CollationKey tmp;
        for (int i = 0; i < keys.length; i++) {
            for (int j = i + 1; j < keys.length; j++) {
                // Compare the keys
                if( keys[i].compareTo( keys[j] ) > 0 ) {
                    // Swap keys[i] and keys[j]
                    tmp = keys[i];
                    keys[i] = keys[j];
                    keys[j] = tmp;
                }
            }
        }
    }

    static void displayWords(CollationKey[] keys) {
        for (int i = 0; i < keys.length; i++) {
            System.out.println(keys[i].getSourceString());
        }
    }

    static public void main(String[] args) {
        Collator enUSCollator =
            Collator.getInstance(new Locale("en","US"));
        String [] words = {
            "peach",
```

```
            "apricot",
            "grape",
            "lemon"
        };

        CollationKey[] keys = new CollationKey[words.length];

        for (int k = 0; k < keys.length; k ++) {
            keys[k] = enUSCollator.getCollationKey(words[k]);
        }

        sortArray(keys);
        displayWords(keys);
    }
}
```

EXAMPLE: About the Break Iterator Class

Where Explained: *About the BreakIterator Class* (page 158)

BreakIteratorDemo.java

SOURCE CODE: *http://java.sun.com/docs/books/tutorial/i18n/text/example-1dot1/BreakIteratorDemo.java*

```
import java.util.*;
import java.text.*;
import java.io.*;

public class BreakIteratorDemo {

    static void extractWords(String target,
                             BreakIterator wordIterator) {

        wordIterator.setText(target);
        int start = wordIterator.first();
        int end = wordIterator.next();

        while (end != BreakIterator.DONE) {
            String word = target.substring(start,end);
            if (Character.isLetterOrDigit(word.charAt(0))) {
                System.out.println(word);
            }

            start = end;
            end = wordIterator.next();
        }
    }

    static void reverseWords(String target,
                             BreakIterator wordIterator) {
```

```
        wordIterator.setText(target);
        int end = wordIterator.last();
        int start = wordIterator.previous();


        while (start != BreakIterator.DONE) {
            String word = target.substring(start,end);
            if (Character.isLetterOrDigit(word.charAt(0)))
                System.out.println(word);
            end = start;
            start = wordIterator.previous();
        }
    }

    static void markBoundaries(String target,
                               BreakIterator iterator) {

        StringBuffer markers = new StringBuffer();
        markers.setLength(target.length() + 1);
        for (int k = 0; k < markers.length(); k++) {
            markers.setCharAt(k,' ');
        }

        iterator.setText(target);
        int boundary = iterator.first();

        while (boundary != BreakIterator.DONE) {
            markers.setCharAt(boundary,'^');
            boundary = iterator.next();
        }
        System.out.println(target);
        System.out.println(markers);
    }

    static void formatLines(String target, int maxLength,
                            Locale currentLocale) {

        BreakIterator boundary =
                BreakIterator.getLineInstance(currentLocale);
        boundary.setText(target);
        int start = boundary.first();
        int end = boundary.next();
        int lineLength = 0;

        while (end != BreakIterator.DONE) {
            String word = target.substring(start,end);
            lineLength = lineLength + word.length();
            if (lineLength >= maxLength) {
```

```
                System.out.println();
                lineLength = word.length();
            }

            System.out.print(word);
            start = end;
            end = boundary.next();
        }
    }

    static void listPositions(String target,
                               BreakIterator iterator) {

        iterator.setText(target);
        int boundary = iterator.first();

        while (boundary != BreakIterator.DONE) {
            System.out.println (boundary);
            boundary = iterator.next();
        }
    }

    static void characterExamples() {

        BreakIterator arCharIterator =
             BreakIterator.getCharacterInstance(new Locale
                                                ("ar","SA"));
        // Arabic word for "house"
        String house = "\u0628" + "\u064e" + "\u064a" +
                       "\u0652" + "\u067a" + "\u064f";
        listPositions (house,arCharIterator);
    }

    static void wordExamples() {

        Locale currentLocale = new Locale ("en","US");
        BreakIterator wordIterator =
             BreakIterator.getWordInstance(currentLocale);
        String someText = "She stopped.  " +
                          "She said, \"Hello there,\" and " +
                          "then went on.";
        markBoundaries(someText, wordIterator);
        System.out.println();
        extractWords(someText, wordIterator);
    }

    static void sentenceExamples() {

        Locale currentLocale = new Locale ("en","US");
```

```
        BreakIterator sentenceIterator =
             BreakIterator.getSentenceInstance(currentLocale);
        String someText = "She stopped.  " +
                          "She said, \"Hello there,\" and " +
                          "then went on.";
        markBoundaries(someText, sentenceIterator);
        String variousText = "He's vanished!  " +
                             "What will we do? It's up to us.";
        markBoundaries(variousText, sentenceIterator);
        String decimalText =
                          "Please add 1.5 liters to the tank.";
        markBoundaries(decimalText, sentenceIterator);
        String  donneText = "\"No man is an island . . . " +
                             "every man . . . \"";
        markBoundaries(donneText, sentenceIterator);
        String dogText =
                       "My friend, Mr. Jones, has a new dog." +
                       "The dog's name is Spot.";
        markBoundaries(dogText, sentenceIterator);
    }

    static void lineExamples() {
        Locale currentLocale = new Locale ("en","US");
        BreakIterator lineIterator =
             BreakIterator.getLineInstance(currentLocale);
        String someText = "She stopped.  " +
                          "She said, \"Hello there,\" and " +
                                "then went on.";
        markBoundaries(someText, lineIterator);
        String hardHyphen =
                       "There are twenty-four hours in a day.";
        markBoundaries(hardHyphen, lineIterator);
        System.out.println();
        String moreText =
                  "She said, \"Hello there,\" and then " +
                  "went on down the street.  When she " +
                  "stopped to look at the fur coats " +
                  "in a shop window, her dog growled. " +
                  " \"Sorry Jake,\" she said. " +
                  " \"I didn't know you would take it " +
                  "personally.\"";
        formatLines(moreText, 30, currentLocale);
        System.out.println();
    }

    static public void main(String[] args) {
        characterExamples();
        System.out.println();
        wordExamples();
        System.out.println();
```

```
        sentenceExamples();
        System.out.println();
        lineExamples();
    }
} // class
```

EXAMPLE: Byte Encodings and Strings

StringConverter.java

SOURCE CODE: *http://java.sun.com/docs/books/tutorial/i18n/text/example-1dot1/StringConverter.java*

Where Explained:
Byte Encodings and Strings (page 167)

```
import java.io.*;
import java.util.*;

public class StringConverter {

    public static void printBytes(byte[] array, String name) {

        for (int k = 0; k < array.length; k++) {
            System.out.println(name + "["+ k + "] = " + "0x" +
                       UnicodeFormatter.byteToHex(array[k]));
        }
    }

    public static void main(String[] args) {

        String original = new String("A" + "\u00ea" +
                                     "\u00f1" + "\u00fc" +
                                     "C");

        System.out.println("original = " + original);
        System.out.println();

        try {
            byte[] utf8Bytes = original.getBytes("UTF8");
            byte[] defaultBytes = original.getBytes();

            String roundTrip = new String(utf8Bytes, "UTF8");
            System.out.println("roundTrip = " + roundTrip);

            System.out.println();
            printBytes(utf8Bytes, "utf8Bytes");
            System.out.println();
            printBytes(defaultBytes, "defaultBytes");

        } catch (UnsupportedEncodingException e) {
            e.printStackTrace();
        }
```

```
    } // main
}
```

UnicodeFormatter.java

SOURCE CODE: *http://java.sun.com/docs/books/tutorial/i18n/text/example-1dot1/UnicodeFormatter.java*

```
import java.io.*;

public class UnicodeFormatter  {

    static public String byteToHex(byte b) {
        // Returns hex String representation of byte b
        char hexDigit[] = {
             '0', '1', '2', '3', '4', '5', '6', '7',
             '8', '9', 'a', 'b', 'c', 'd', 'e', 'f'
        };
        char[] array = { hexDigit[(b >> 4) & 0x0f],
                         hexDigit[b & 0x0f] };
        return new String(array);
    }

    static public String charToHex(char c) {
        // Returns hex String representation of char c
        byte hi = (byte) (c >>> 8);
        byte lo = (byte) (c & 0xff);
        return byteToHex(hi) + byteToHex(lo);
    }

} // class
```

EXAMPLE: Stream Converter Application

Where Explained: *Character and Byte Streams* (page 168)

StreamConverter.java

SOURCE CODE: *http://java.sun.com/docs/books/tutorial/i18n/text/example-1dot1/StreamConverter.java*

```
import java.io.*;
import java.util.*;

public class StreamConverter {

    static void writeOutput(String str) {
```

```
        try {
            FileOutputStream fos =
                              new FileOutputStream("test.txt");
            Writer out = new OutputStreamWriter(fos, "UTF8");
            out.write(str);
            out.close();
        } catch (IOException e) {
            e.printStackTrace();
        }
    }

    static String readInput() {

        StringBuffer buffer = new StringBuffer();
        try {
            FileInputStream fis =
                              new FileInputStream("test.txt");
            InputStreamReader isr =
                           new InputStreamReader(fis, "UTF8");
            Reader in = new BufferedReader(isr);
            int ch;
            while ((ch = in.read()) > -1) {
                buffer.append((char)ch);
            }
            in.close();
            return buffer.toString();
        } catch (IOException e) {
            e.printStackTrace();
            return null;
        }
    }

    public static void main(String[] args) {

        String jaString  =
           new String("\u65e5\u672c\u8a9e\u6587\u5b57\u5217");
        writeOutput(jaString);
        String inputString = readInput();
        String displayString = jaString + " " + inputString;
        new ShowString(displayString, "Conversion Demo");
    }
}
```

ShowString.java

SOURCE CODE: *http://java.sun.com/docs/books/tutorial/i18n/text/example-1dot1/ShowString.java*

```
import java.awt.*;
```

```
class ShowString extends Frame {

    FontMetrics fontM;
    String outString;

    ShowString (String target, String title) {
        setTitle(title);
        outString = target;

        Font font = new Font("Monospaced", Font.PLAIN, 36);
        fontM = getFontMetrics(font);
        setFont(font);

        int size = 0;
        for (int i = 0; i < outString.length(); i++) {
           size += fontM.charWidth(outString.charAt(i));
        }
        size += 24;

        setSize(size, fontM.getHeight() + 60);
        setLocation(getSize().width/2, getSize().height/2);
        show();
    }

    public void paint(Graphics g) {
        Insets insets = getInsets();
        int x = insets.left;
        int y = insets.top;
        g.drawString(outString, x + 6,
                     y + fontM.getAscent() + 14);
    }
}
```

Java 2D

LESSON 12: Overview of the Java 2D API

EXAMPLE: 2D ShapesDemo

ShapesDemo2D.java

SOURCE CODE: *http://java.sun.com/docs/books/tutorial/2d/display/example-1dot2/ShapesDemo2D.java*

Where Explained:
Overview of the Java 2D API (page 177)

```
import java.awt.*;
import java.awt.event.*;
import java.awt.geom.*;
import javax.swing.*;

/*
 * This is like the FontDemo applet in volume 1, except it
 * uses Java 2D APIs to define and render graphics and text.
 */
```

```
public class ShapesDemo2D extends JApplet {
    final static int maxCharHeight = 15;
    final static int minFontSize = 6;

    final static Color bg = Color.white;
    final static Color fg = Color.black;
    final static Color red = Color.red;
    final static Color white = Color.white;

    final static BasicStroke stroke = new BasicStroke(2.0f);
    final static BasicStroke wideStroke =
                 new BasicStroke(8.0f);

    final static float dash1[] = {10.0f};
    final static BasicStroke dashed =
                 new BasicStroke(1.0f, BasicStroke.CAP_BUTT,
                                 BasicStroke.JOIN_MITER,
                                 10.0f, dash1, 0.0f);
    Dimension totalSize;
    FontMetrics fontMetrics;

    public void init() {
        //Initialize drawing colors
        setBackground(bg);
        setForeground(fg);
    }

    FontMetrics pickFont(Graphics2D g2,
                         String longString,
                         int xSpace) {
        boolean fontFits = false;
        Font font = g2.getFont();
        FontMetrics fontMetrics = g2.getFontMetrics();
        int size = font.getSize();
        String name = font.getName();
        int style = font.getStyle();

        while ( !fontFits ) {
            if ( (fontMetrics.getHeight() <= maxCharHeight) &&
                 (fontMetrics.stringWidth(longString)
                                     <= xSpace) ) {
                fontFits = true;
            }else {
                if ( size <= minFontSize ) {
                    fontFits = true;
                }else {
                    g2.setFont(font = new Font(name,
                                               style,
                                               --size));
```

```
                fontMetrics = g2.getFontMetrics();
            }
        }
    }

    return fontMetrics;
}

public void paint(Graphics g) {
    Graphics2D g2 = (Graphics2D) g;
    g2.setRenderingHint(
                    RenderingHints.KEY_ANTIALIASING,
                    RenderingHints.VALUE_ANTIALIAS_ON);
    Dimension d = getSize();
    int gridWidth = d.width / 6;
    int gridHeight = d.height / 2;

    fontMetrics = pickFont(g2, "Filled and Stroked " +
                        "GeneralPath", gridWidth);

    Color fg3D = Color.lightGray;

    g2.setPaint(fg3D);
    g2.draw3DRect(0, 0, d.width - 1, d.height - 1, true);
    g2.draw3DRect(3, 3, d.width - 7, d.height - 7, false);
    g2.setPaint(fg);

    int x = 5;
    int y = 7;
    int rectWidth = gridWidth - 2*x;
    int stringY = gridHeight -
              3 - fontMetrics.getDescent();
    int rectHeight = stringY -
                fontMetrics.getMaxAscent() - y - 2;

    // draw Line2D.Double
    g2.draw(new Line2D.Double(x, y+rectHeight-1,
                         x + rectWidth, y));
    g2.drawString("Line2D", x, stringY);
    x += gridWidth;

    // draw Rectangle2D.Double
    g2.setStroke(stroke);
    g2.draw(new Rectangle2D.Double(x, y, rectWidth,
                              rectHeight));
    g2.drawString("Rectangle2D", x, stringY);
    x += gridWidth;
```

```
// draw  RoundRectangle2D.Double
g2.setStroke(dashed);
g2.draw(new RoundRectangle2D.Double(x, y, rectWidth,
                                    rectHeight, 10,
                                    10));
g2.drawString("RoundRectangle2D", x, stringY);
x += gridWidth;

// draw Arc2D.Double
g2.setStroke(wideStroke);
g2.draw(new Arc2D.Double(x, y, rectWidth, rectHeight,
                         90, 135, Arc2D.OPEN));
g2.drawString("Arc2D", x, stringY);
x += gridWidth;

// draw Ellipse2D.Double
g2.setStroke(stroke);
g2.draw(new Ellipse2D.Double(x, y, rectWidth,
                             rectHeight));
g2.drawString("Ellipse2D", x, stringY);
x += gridWidth;

// draw GeneralPath (polygon)
int x1Points[] = {x, x+rectWidth, x, x+rectWidth};
int y1Points[] = {y, y+rectHeight, y+rectHeight, y};
GeneralPath polygon =
            new GeneralPath(GeneralPath.WIND_EVEN_ODD,
                            x1Points.length);
polygon.moveTo(x1Points[0], y1Points[0]);
for (int index = 1; index<x1Points.length; index++) {
    polygon.lineTo(x1Points[index], y1Points[index]);
};
polygon.closePath();

g2.draw(polygon);
g2.drawString("GeneralPath", x, stringY);

// NEW ROW
x = 5;
y += gridHeight;
stringY += gridHeight;

// draw GeneralPath (polyline)
int x2Points[] = {x, x+rectWidth, x, x+rectWidth};
int y2Points[] = {y, y+rectHeight, y+rectHeight, y};
GeneralPath polyline =
            new GeneralPath(GeneralPath.WIND_EVEN_ODD,
                            x2Points.length);
```

```
polyline.moveTo (x2Points[0], y2Points[0]);
for (int index=1; index < x2Points.length; index++) {
    polyline.lineTo(x2Points[index], y2Points[index]);
};

g2.draw(polyline);
g2.drawString("GeneralPath (open)", x, stringY);
x += gridWidth;

// fill Rectangle2D.Double (red)
g2.setPaint(red);
g2.fill(new Rectangle2D.Double(x, y, rectWidth,
                               rectHeight));
g2.setPaint(fg);
g2.drawString("Filled Rectangle2D", x, stringY);
x += gridWidth;

// fill RoundRectangle2D.Double
GradientPaint redtowhite =
       new GradientPaint(x,y,red,x+rectWidth,y,white);
g2.setPaint(redtowhite);
g2.fill(new RoundRectangle2D.Double(x, y, rectWidth,
                                    rectHeight, 10,
                                    10));
g2.setPaint(fg);
g2.drawString("Filled RoundRectangle2D", x, stringY);
x += gridWidth;

// fill Arc2D
g2.setPaint(red);
g2.fill(new Arc2D.Double(x, y, rectWidth, rectHeight,
                         90, 135, Arc2D.OPEN));
g2.setPaint(fg);
g2.drawString("Filled Arc2D", x, stringY);
x += gridWidth;

// fill Ellipse2D.Double
redtowhite = new GradientPaint(x,y,red,x+rectWidth,
                               y,white);
g2.setPaint(redtowhite);
g2.fill (new Ellipse2D.Double(x, y, rectWidth,
                              rectHeight));
g2.setPaint(fg);
g2.drawString("Filled Ellipse2D", x, stringY);
x += gridWidth;

// fill and stroke GeneralPath
int x3Points[] = {x, x+rectWidth, x, x+rectWidth};
int y3Points[] = {y, y+rectHeight, y+rectHeight, y};
```

```
        GeneralPath filledPolygon =
                    new GeneralPath(GeneralPath.WIND_EVEN_ODD,
                                    x3Points.length);
        filledPolygon.moveTo(x3Points[0], y3Points[0]);
        for (int index=1; index < x3Points.length; index++) {
            filledPolygon.lineTo(x3Points[index],
                                 y3Points[index]);
        };
        filledPolygon.closePath();
        g2.setPaint(red);
        g2.fill(filledPolygon);
        g2.setPaint(fg);
        g2.draw(filledPolygon);
        g2.drawString("Filled and Stroked GeneralPath",
                      x, stringY);
    }

    public static void main(String s[]) {
        JFrame f = new JFrame("ShapesDemo2D");
        f.addWindowListener(new WindowAdapter() {
            public void windowClosing(
                                  WindowEvent e)
                                  {System.exit(0);}
        });
        JApplet applet = new ShapesDemo2D();
        f.getContentPane().add("Center", applet);
        applet.init();
        f.pack();
        f.setSize(new Dimension(550,100));
        f.show();
    }

}
```

ShapesDemo2D.html

```
<!DOCTYPE HTML PUBLIC "-//IETF//DTD HTML//EN">
<html>
  <head>
    <title>Shapes Demo Using Java 2D</title>
  </head>
<body>
This is the Java 2D version of the Shapes Demo applet:
<applet code="ShapesDemo2D.class" width="550" height="100">
</applet>
</body>
</html>
```

LESSON 13: Displaying Graphics with Graphics2D

EXAMPLE: Stroke and Fill Applet

StrokeAndFill.java

SOURCE CODE: *http://java.sun.com/docs/books/tutorial/2d/display/example-1dot2/StrokeAndFill.java*

Where Explained:
Stroking and Filling Graphics Primitives (page 188)

```
import java.lang.Integer;
import java.awt.*;
import java.awt.event.*;
import java.awt.font.*;
import java.awt.geom.*;
import java.awt.image.*;
import java.awt.event.ActionListener;
import java.awt.event.ActionEvent;
import java.awt.event.ItemListener;
import java.awt.event.ItemEvent;
import javax.swing.*;

/*
 * This applet renders a Shape, selected by the user, using
 * the Stroke and Paint attributes and rendering method
 * also selected by the user.
*/

public class StrokeAndFill extends JApplet
                           implements ItemListener {
    JLabel primLabel, lineLabel, paintLabel, strokeLabel;
    ShapePanel display;
    static JComboBox primitive, line, paint, stroke;
    int index = 0;
    public static boolean no2D = false;

    public void init() {
        GridBagLayout layOut = new GridBagLayout();
        getContentPane().setLayout(layOut);
        GridBagConstraints c = new GridBagConstraints();

        c.weightx = 1.0;
        c.fill = GridBagConstraints.BOTH;
        primLabel = new JLabel();
        primLabel.setText("Primitive");
        Font newFont = getFont().deriveFont(1);
        primLabel.setFont(newFont);
```

```
primLabel.setHorizontalAlignment(JLabel.CENTER);
layOut.setConstraints(primLabel, c);
getContentPane().add(primLabel);

lineLabel = new JLabel();
lineLabel.setText("Lines");
lineLabel.setFont(newFont);
lineLabel.setHorizontalAlignment(JLabel.CENTER);
layOut.setConstraints(lineLabel, c);
getContentPane().add(lineLabel);

c.gridwidth = GridBagConstraints.RELATIVE;
paintLabel = new JLabel();
paintLabel.setText("Paints");
paintLabel.setFont(newFont);
paintLabel.setHorizontalAlignment(JLabel.CENTER);
layOut.setConstraints(paintLabel, c);
getContentPane().add(paintLabel);

c.gridwidth = GridBagConstraints.REMAINDER;
strokeLabel = new JLabel();
strokeLabel.setText("Rendering");
strokeLabel.setFont(newFont);
strokeLabel.setHorizontalAlignment(JLabel.CENTER);
layOut.setConstraints(strokeLabel, c);
getContentPane().add(strokeLabel);

GridBagConstraints ls = new GridBagConstraints();
ls.weightx = 1.0;
ls.fill = GridBagConstraints.BOTH;
primitive = new JComboBox( new Object []{
                           "rectangle",
                           "ellipse",
                           "text"});
primitive.addItemListener(this);
newFont = newFont.deriveFont(0, 14.0f);
primitive.setFont(newFont);
layOut.setConstraints(primitive, ls);
getContentPane().add(primitive);

line = new JComboBox( new Object []{
                      "thin",
                      "thick",
                      "dashed"});
line.addItemListener(this);
line.setFont(newFont);
layOut.setConstraints(line, ls);
getContentPane().add(line);
```

```
        ls.gridwidth = GridBagConstraints.RELATIVE;
        paint = new JComboBox( new Object[]{
                                "solid",
                                "gradient",
                                "polka"});
        paint.addItemListener(this);
        paint.setFont(newFont);
        layOut.setConstraints(paint, ls);
        getContentPane().add(paint);

        ls.gridwidth = GridBagConstraints.REMAINDER;
        stroke = new JComboBox( new Object[]{
                                "Stroke",
                                "Fill",
                                "Stroke & Fill"});
        stroke.addItemListener(this);
        stroke.setFont(newFont);
        layOut.setConstraints(stroke, ls);
        getContentPane().add(stroke);

        GridBagConstraints sC = new GridBagConstraints();
        sC.fill = GridBagConstraints.BOTH;
        sC.weightx = 1.0;
        sC.weighty = 1.0;
        sC.gridwidth = GridBagConstraints.REMAINDER;
        display = new ShapePanel();
        layOut.setConstraints(display, sC);
        display.setBackground(Color.white);
        getContentPane().add(display);

        validate();

    }

    public void itemStateChanged(ItemEvent e) {
        display.renderShape();
    }

    public static void main( String[] argv ) {
        if ( argv.length > 0 && argv[0].equals( "-no2d" ) ) {
            StrokeAndFill.no2D = true;
        }

        JFrame frame = new JFrame( "StrokeAndFill" );
        frame.addWindowListener( new WindowAdapter(){
            public void windowClosing( WindowEvent e ){
                System.exit( 0 );
            }
        });
```

```
        JApplet applet = new StrokeAndFill();
        frame.getContentPane().add(BorderLayout.CENTER,applet);

        applet.init();

        frame.setSize( 450, 250 );
        frame.show();
    }
}

class ShapePanel extends JPanel {
    BasicStroke bstroke = new BasicStroke(3.0f);
    int w, h;
    Shape shapes[] = new Shape[3];

    public ShapePanel(){
        setBackground(Color.white);
        shapes[0] = new Rectangle(0, 0, 100, 100);
        shapes[1] = new Ellipse2D.Double(0.0, 0.0,
                                    100.0, 100.0);
        TextLayout textTl = new TextLayout(
                            "Text",
                            new Font("Helvetica", 1, 96),
                            new FontRenderContext(
                                    null, false, false));
        AffineTransform textAt = new AffineTransform();
        textAt.translate(
                0, (float)textTl.getBounds().getHeight());
        shapes[2] = textTl.getOutline(textAt);
    }

    // Invokes the paint method.
    public void renderShape() {
        repaint();
    }

    public void paintComponent (Graphics g) {
        super.paintComponent(g);

if ( !StrokeAndFill.no2D ) {
    Graphics2D g2 = (Graphics2D) g;
    Dimension d = getSize();
    w = d.width;
    h = d.height;
    int width, height;

    // Prints the initial instructions.
```

```
String instruct  = "Pick a primitive, line style, " +
                   "paint, and rendering method.";
TextLayout thisTl = new TextLayout(instruct,
                            new Font("Helvetica", 0, 10),
                            g2.getFontRenderContext());
Rectangle2D bounds = thisTl.getBounds();
width = (int)bounds.getWidth();
thisTl.draw(g2, w/2-width/2, 20);

Stroke oldStroke = g2.getStroke();

// Sets the Stroke.
switch ( StrokeAndFill.line.getSelectedIndex() ) {
    case 0 : g2.setStroke(new BasicStroke(3.0f)); break;
    case 1 : g2.setStroke(new BasicStroke(8.0f)); break;
    case 2 : float dash[] = {10.0f};
             g2.setStroke(new BasicStroke(3.0f,
                                BasicStroke.CAP_BUTT,
                                BasicStroke.JOIN_MITER,
                                10.0f, dash, 0.0f));
    break;
}

Paint oldPaint = g2.getPaint();

// Sets the Paint.
switch ( StrokeAndFill.paint.getSelectedIndex() ) {
    case 0 : g2.setPaint(Color.blue); break;
    case 1 : g2.setPaint(new GradientPaint(0, 0,
                               Color.lightGray, w-250,
                               h, Color.blue, false));
             break;
    case 2 : BufferedImage bi = new BufferedImage(5, 5,
                              BufferedImage.TYPE_INT_RGB);
             Graphics2D big = bi.createGraphics();
             big.setColor(Color.blue);
             big.fillRect(0, 0, 5, 5);
             big.setColor(Color.lightGray);
             big.fillOval(0, 0, 5, 5);
             Rectangle r = new Rectangle(0,0,5,5);
             g2.setPaint(new TexturePaint(bi, r));
             break;
}

// Sets the Shape.
Shape shape =
      shapes[StrokeAndFill.primitive.getSelectedIndex()];
Rectangle r = shape.getBounds();
```

```
        // Sets the selected Shape to the center of the Canvas.
        AffineTransform saveXform = g2.getTransform();
        AffineTransform toCenterAt = new AffineTransform();
        toCenterAt.translate(w/2-(r.width/2), h/2-(r.height/2));
        g2.transform(toCenterAt);

        // Determines whether to fill, stroke, or fill and stroke.
        switch ( StrokeAndFill.stroke.getSelectedIndex() ) {
            case 0 : g2.draw(shape); break;
            case 1 : g2.fill(shape); break;
            case 2 : Graphics2D tempg2 = g2;
                     g2.fill(shape);
                     g2.setColor(Color.darkGray);
                     g2.draw(shape);
                     g2.setPaint(tempg2.getPaint()); break;
        }
        g2.setTransform(saveXform);
        g2.setStroke(oldStroke);
        g2.setPaint(oldPaint);

        } else {
            g.drawRect(0, 0, 100, 100);
        }
    }
```

EXAMPLE: Transform Applet

Where Explained: *Transforming Shapes, Text, and Images* (page 194)

Transform.java

SOURCE CODE: *http://java.sun.com/docs/books/tutorial/2d/display/example-1dot2/Transform.java*

```
import java.lang.Integer;
import java.awt.*;
import java.awt.event.*;
import java.awt.font.*;
import java.awt.geom.*;
import java.awt.image.*;
import java.awt.event.ActionListener;
import java.awt.event.ActionEvent;
import javax.swing.*;

/*
 * This applet renders a shape, selected by the user, with a
 * paint,stroke, and rendering method,
 * also selected by the user.
*/
```

```
public class Transform extends JApplet
                        implements ActionListener {

    JLabel primLabel, lineLabel, paintLabel, transLabel,
           strokeLabel;
    TransPanel display;
    static JComboBox primitive, line, paint, trans, stroke;
    JButton redraw;
    public static boolean no2D = false;

    public void init() {
        GridBagLayout layOut = new GridBagLayout();
        getContentPane().setLayout(layOut);
        GridBagConstraints c = new GridBagConstraints();

        c.weightx = 1.0;
        c.fill = GridBagConstraints.BOTH;
        primLabel = new JLabel();
        primLabel.setText("Primitive");
        Font newFont = getFont().deriveFont(1);
        primLabel.setFont(newFont);
        primLabel.setHorizontalAlignment(JLabel.CENTER);
        layOut.setConstraints(primLabel, c);
        getContentPane().add(primLabel);

        lineLabel = new JLabel();
        lineLabel.setText("Lines");
        lineLabel.setFont(newFont);
        lineLabel.setHorizontalAlignment(JLabel.CENTER);
        layOut.setConstraints(lineLabel, c);
        getContentPane().add(lineLabel);

        paintLabel = new JLabel();
        paintLabel.setText("Paints");
        paintLabel.setFont(newFont);
        paintLabel.setHorizontalAlignment(JLabel.CENTER);
        layOut.setConstraints(paintLabel, c);
        getContentPane().add(paintLabel);

        c.gridwidth = GridBagConstraints.RELATIVE;
        transLabel = new JLabel();
        transLabel.setText("Transforms");
        transLabel.setFont(newFont);
        transLabel.setHorizontalAlignment(JLabel.CENTER);
        layOut.setConstraints(transLabel, c);
        getContentPane().add(transLabel);

        c.gridwidth = GridBagConstraints.REMAINDER;
        strokeLabel = new JLabel();
```

```
strokeLabel.setText("Rendering");
strokeLabel.setFont(newFont);
strokeLabel.setHorizontalAlignment(JLabel.CENTER);
layOut.setConstraints(strokeLabel, c);
getContentPane().add(strokeLabel);

GridBagConstraints ls = new GridBagConstraints();
ls.weightx = 1.0;
ls.fill = GridBagConstraints.BOTH;
primitive = new JComboBox( new Object []{
                            "rectangle",
                            "ellipse",
                            "text"});
primitive.addItemListener(this);
newFont = newFont.deriveFont(0, 14.0f);
primitive.setFont(newFont);
layOut.setConstraints(primitive, ls);
getContentPane().add(primitive);

line = new JComboBox( new Object []{
                       "thin",
                       "thick",
                       "dashed"});
line.addItemListener(this);
line.setFont(newFont);
layOut.setConstraints(line, ls);
getContentPane().add(line);

paint = new JComboBox( new Object[]{
                        "solid",
                        "gradient",
                        "polka"});
paint.addItemListener(this);
paint.setFont(newFont);
layOut.setConstraints(paint, ls);
getContentPane().add(paint);

ls.gridwidth = GridBagConstraints.RELATIVE;

trans = new JComboBox(new Object[]{
    "Identity",
    "rotate",
    "scale",
    "shear"});

trans.addItemListener(this);
trans.setFont(newFont);
layOut.setConstraints(trans, ls);
getContentPane().add(trans);
```

```
        ls.gridwidth = GridBagConstraints.REMAINDER;
        stroke = new JComboBox( new Object[]{
                                "Stroke",
                                "Fill",
                                "Stroke & Fill"});
        stroke.setFont(newFont);
        layOut.setConstraints(stroke, ls);
        getContentPane().add(stroke);

        GridBagConstraints button = new GridBaqConstraints();
        button.gridwidth = GridBagConstraints.REMAINDER;
        redraw = new JButton("Redraw");
        redraw.addActionListener(this);
        redraw.setFont(newFont);
        layOut.setConstraints(redraw, button);
        getContentPane().add(redraw);

        GridBagConstraints tP = new GridBagConstraints();
        tP.fill = GridBagConstraints.BOTH;
        tP.weightx = 1.0;
        tP.weighty = 1.0;
        tP.gridwidth = GridBagConstraints.REMAINDER;
        display = new TransPanel();
        layOut.setConstraints(display, tP);
        display.setBackground(Color.white);
        getContentPane().add(display);
        validate();
    }

    public void actionPerformed(ActionEvent e) {
        display.setTrans(trans.getSelectedIndex());
        display.renderShape();
    }

    public static void main( String[] argv ) {
        if ( argv.length > 0 && argv[0].equals( "-no2d" ) ) {
            Transform.no2D = true;
        }

        JFrame frame = new JFrame( "Transform" );
        frame.addWindowListener( new WindowAdapter() {
            public void windowClosing( WindowEvent e ) {
                System.exit(0);
            }
        });

        JApplet applet = new Transform();
        frame.getContentPane().add(BorderLayout.CENTER,
                                   applet);
        applet.init();
```

```
        frame.setSize( 550, 400 );
        frame.show();
    }
}

class TransPanel extends JPanel {
    AffineTransform at = new AffineTransform();
    int w, h;
    Shape shapes[] = new Shape[3];
    BufferedImage bi;
    boolean firstTime = true;

    public TransPanel(){
        setBackground(Color.white);
        shapes[0] = new Rectangle(0, 0, 100, 100);
        shapes[1] = new Ellipse2D.Double(0.0, 0.0,
                                          100.0, 100.0);
        TextLayout textTl = new TextLayout("Text",
                                 new Font("Helvetica", 1, 96),
                                 new FontRenderContext(null,
                                                 false, false));
        AffineTransform textAt = new AffineTransform();
        textAt.translate(0,
                    (float)textTl.getBounds().getHeight());
        shapes[2] = textTl.getOutline(textAt);
    }

    public void setTrans(int transIndex) {
        // Sets the AffineTransform.
        switch ( transIndex ) {
            case 0 : at.setToIdentity();
                     at.translate(w/2, h/2); break;
            case 1 : at.rotate(Math.toRadians(45)); break;
            case 2 : at.scale(0.5, 0.5); break;
            case 3 : at.shear(0.5, 0.0); break;
        }
    }

    public void renderShape() {
        repaint();
    }

    public void paintComponent(Graphics g) {
        super.paintComponent(g);
        if ( !Transform.no2D ) {
            Graphics2D g2 = (Graphics2D) g;
            Dimension d = getSize();
            w = d.width;
            h = d.height;
```

```
// Prints out the intructions.
String instruct = "Pick a primitive, line style, "
                + "paint, transform,";
TextLayout thisTl = new TextLayout(instruct,
                        new Font("Helvetica",
                                 0, 10),
                        g2.getFontRenderContext());
float width =
      (float)thisTl.getBounds().getWidth();
float height =
       (float)thisTl.getBounds().getHeight();
thisTl.draw(g2, w/2-width/2, 15);

instruct = "and rendering method and click the "+
           Redraw button.";
thisTl = new TextLayout(instruct,
                         new Font("Helvetica",
                                  0, 10),
                        g2.getFontRenderContext());
width = (float)thisTl.getBounds().getWidth();
thisTl.draw(g2, w/2-width/2, height + 17);

// Initialize the transform.
if (firstTime) {
    at.setToIdentity();
    at.translate(w/2, h/2);
    firstTime = false;
}

// Sets the Stroke.
Stroke oldStroke = g2.getStroke();
switch ( Transform.line.getSelectedIndex() ) {
    case 0 : g2.setStroke(new BasicStroke(3.0f));
             break;
    case 1 : g2.setStroke(new BasicStroke(8.0f));
             break;
    case 2 : float dash[] = {10.0f};
            g2.setStroke(new BasicStroke(3.0f,
                          BasicStroke.CAP_BUTT,
                          BasicStroke.JOIN_MITER,
                           10.0f, dash, 0.0f));
      break;
}

// Sets the Paint.
Paint oldPaint = g2.getPaint();
switch ( Transform.paint.getSelectedIndex() ) {
case 0 : g2.setPaint(Color.blue);break;
```

```
                case 1 : g2.setPaint(new GradientPaint(0, 0,
                                        Color.lightGray, w-250, h,
                                        Color.blue, false));
                        break;
                case 2 : BufferedImage buffi =
                                new BufferedImage(15,
                                 15, BufferedImage.TYPE_INT_RGB);
                        Graphics2D buffig =
                                   buffi.createGraphics();
                        buffig.setColor(Color.blue);
                        buffig.fillRect(0, 0, 15, 15);
                        buffig.setColor(Color.lightGray);
                        buffig.translate((15/2)-(5/2),
                                              (15/2)-(5/2));
                        buffig.fillOval(0, 0, 7, 7);
                        Rectangle r = new Rectangle(0,0,25,25);
                        g2.setPaint(new TexturePaint(buffi, r));
                        break;
                }

                // Sets the Shape.
                Shape shape =
                   shapes[Transform.primitive.getSelectedIndex()];
                Rectangle r = shape.getBounds();

                // Sets selected Shape to the center of Canvas.
                AffineTransform saveXform = g2.getTransform();
                AffineTransform toCenterAt = new AffineTransform();
                toCenterAt.concatenate(at);
                toCenterAt.translate(-(r.width/2), -(r.height/2));

                g2.transform(toCenterAt);

                // Sets the rendering method.
                switch ( Transform.stroke.getSelectedIndex() ) {
                case 0 : g2.draw(shape); break;
                case 1 : g2.fill(shape); break;
                case 2 : Graphics2D tempg2 = g2;
                        g2.fill(shape);
                        g2.setColor(Color.darkGray);
                        g2.draw(shape);
                        g2.setPaint(tempg2.getPaint()); break;
                }
                g2.setStroke(oldStroke);
                g2.setPaint(oldPaint);
                g2.setTransform(saveXform);
            }
        }
    }
```

EXAMPLE: ClipImage Applet

ClipImage.java

Where Explained:
Clipping the Drawing Region (page 196)

SOURCE CODE: *http://java.sun.com/docs/books/tutorial/2d/display/example-1dot2/ClipImage.java*

```
import javax.swing.*;
import java.awt.*;
import java.awt.geom.*;
import java.awt.event.WindowEvent;
import java.awt.event.WindowListener;
import java.awt.event.WindowAdapter;
import java.awt.image.BufferedImage;

/**
 * Animated clipping of an image & shapes with alpha.
 */
public class ClipImage extends JApplet implements Runnable {

    private Image img;
    private final double OINC[] = {5.0, 3.0};
    private final double SINC[] = {5.0, 5.0};
    private double x, y;
    private double ix = OINC[0];
    private double iy = OINC[1];
    private double iw = SINC[0];
    private double ih = SINC[1];
    private double ew, eh;   // ellipse width & height
    private GeneralPath p = new GeneralPath();
    private AffineTransform at = new AffineTransform();
    private BasicStroke bs = new BasicStroke(20.0f);
    private Arc2D arc = new Arc2D.Float();
    private Ellipse2D ellipse = new Ellipse2D.Float();
    private RoundRectangle2D roundRect = new

RoundRectangle2D.Float();
    private Rectangle2D rect = new Rectangle2D.Float();
    private Color redBlend = new Color(255, 0, 0, 120);
    private Color greenBlend = new Color(0, 255, 0, 120);
    private Thread thread;
    private BufferedImage offImg;
    private int w, h;
    private boolean newBufferedImage;

    public ClipImage() {
        setBackground(Color.white);
        img = getToolkit().getImage("images/clouds.jpg");
        try {
            MediaTracker tracker = new MediaTracker(this);
```

```
            tracker.addImage(img, 0);
            tracker.waitForID(0);
        }
        catch ( Exception e ) {}
    }

    public void drawDemo(Graphics2D g2) {

        if ( newBufferedImage ) {
            x = Math.random()*w;
            y = Math.random()*h;
            ew = (Math.random()*w)/2;
            eh = (Math.random()*h)/2;
        }
        x += ix;
        y += iy;
        ew += iw;
        eh += ih;
        if ( ew > w/2 ) {
            ew = w/2;
            iw = Math.random() * -w/16 - 1;
        }
        if ( ew < w/8 ) {
            ew = w/8;
            iw = Math.random() * w/16 + 1;
        }
        if ( eh > h/2 ) {
            eh = h/2;
            ih = Math.random() * -h/16 - 1;
        }
        if ( eh < h/8 ) {
            eh = h/8;
            ih = Math.random() * h/16 + 1;
        }
        if ( (x+ew) > w ) {
            x = (w - ew)-1;
            ix = Math.random() * -w/32 - 1;
        }
        if ( x < 0 ) {
            x = 2;
            ix = Math.random() * w/32 + 1;
        }
        if ( (y+eh) > h ) {
            y = (h - eh)-2;
            iy = Math.random() * -h/32 - 1;
        }
        if ( y < 0 ) {
            y = 2;
            iy = Math.random() * h/32 + 1;
        }
```

```
    ellipse.setFrame(x, y, ew, eh);
    g2.setClip(ellipse);

    rect.setRect(x+5, y+5, ew-10, eh-10);
    g2.clip(rect);

    g2.drawImage(img, 0, 0, w, h, this);

    p.reset();
    p.moveTo(- w / 2.0f, - h / 8.0f);
    p.lineTo(+ w / 2.0f, - h / 8.0f);
    p.lineTo(- w / 4.0f, + h / 2.0f);
    p.lineTo(+         0.0f, - h / 2.0f);
    p.lineTo(+ w / 4.0f, + h / 2.0f);
    p.closePath();

    at.setToIdentity();
    at.translate(w*.5f, h*.5f);
    g2.transform(at);
    g2.setStroke(bs);
    g2.setPaint(redBlend);
    g2.draw(p);

    at.setToIdentity();
    g2.setTransform(at);

    g2.setPaint(greenBlend);

    for ( int yy = 0; yy < h; yy += 50 ) {
        for ( int xx = 0, i=0; xx < w; i++, xx += 50 ) {
            switch ( i ) {
                case 0 : arc.setArc(xx, yy, 25, 25, 45,
                                    270, Arc2D.PIE);
                         g2.fill(arc); break;
                case 1 : ellipse.setFrame(xx, yy, 25, 25);
                          g2.fill(ellipse); break;
                case 2 : roundRect.setRoundRect(xx, yy,
                                                25, 25,
                                                 4, 4);
                          g2.fill(roundRect); break;
                case 3 : rect.setRect(xx, yy, 25, 25);
                         g2.fill(rect);
                          i = -1;
            }
        }
    }
}
```

```
public Graphics2D createDemoGraphics2D(Graphics g) {
    Graphics2D g2 = null;

    if ( offImg == null || offImg.getWidth() != w ||
         offImg.getHeight() != h ) {
        offImg = (BufferedImage) createImage(w, h);
        newBufferedImage = true;
    }

    if ( offImg != null ) {
        g2 = offImg.createGraphics();
        g2.setBackground(getBackground());
    }

    // .. set attributes ..
    g2.setRenderingHint(RenderingHints.KEY_ANTIALIASING,
                        RenderingHints.VALUE_ANTIALIAS_ON);
    g2.setRenderingHint(RenderingHints.KEY_RENDERING,
                        RenderingHints.VALUE_RENDER_QUALITY);
    // .. clear canvas ..
    g2.clearRect(0, 0, w, h);

    return g2;
}

public void paint(Graphics g) {
    w = getWidth();
    h = getHeight();

    if ( w <= 0 || h <= 0 )
        return;

    Graphics2D g2 = createDemoGraphics2D(g);
    drawDemo(g2);
    g2.dispose();

    if ( offImg != null && isShowing() ) {
        g.drawImage(offImg, 0, 0, this);
    }

    newBufferedImage = false;
}

public void start() {
    thread = new Thread(this);
    thread.start();
}
```

```
    public synchronized void stop() {
        thread = null;
    }

    public void run() {
        Thread me = Thread.currentThread();

        while ( thread == me && isShowing() ) {
            Graphics g = getGraphics();
            paint(g);
            g.dispose();
            thread.yield();
        }
        thread = null;
    }

    public static void main(String s[]) {
        final ClipImage demo = new ClipImage();
        WindowListener l = new WindowAdapter() {
            public void windowClosing(WindowEvent e)
                                            { System.exit(0); }
            public void windowDeiconified(WindowEvent e)
                                            { demo.start(); }
            public void windowIconified(WindowEvent e)
                                            { demo.stop(); }
        };
        JFrame f = new JFrame("Java 2D Demo - ClipImage");
        f.addWindowListener(l);
        f.getContentPane().add("Center", demo);
        f.setSize(new Dimension(400,300));
        f.show();
        demo.start();
    }
}
```

EXAMPLE: Composite Applet

Where Explained:
Compositing Graphics
(page 197)

Composite.java

SOURCE CODE: *http://java.sun.com/docs/books/tutorial/2d/display/example-1dot2/Composite.java*

```
import java.lang.Integer;
import java.awt.*;
import java.awt.event.*;
import java.awt.font.*;
import java.awt.geom.*;
import java.awt.image.*;
```

```
import java.awt.event.ItemListener;
import java.awt.event.ItemEvent;
import javax.swing.*;

/*
 * This applet renders an ellipse overlapping a rectangle
 * with the compositing rule and
 * alpha value selected by the user.
*/

public class Composite extends JApplet implements ItemListener
{
    CompPanel comp;
    JLabel alphaLabel, rulesLabel;
    JComboBox alphas, rules;
    String alpha = "1.0";
    int rule = 0;

    // Initializes the layout of the components.
    public void init() {
        GridBagLayout layOut = new GridBagLayout();
        getContentPane().setLayout(layOut);

        GridBagConstraints l = new GridBagConstraints();
        l.weightx = 1.0;
        l.fill = GridBagConstraints.BOTH;
        l.gridwidth = GridBagConstraints.RELATIVE;
        alphaLabel = new JLabel();
        alphaLabel.setText("Alphas");
        Font newFont = getFont().deriveFont(1);
        alphaLabel.setFont(newFont);
        alphaLabel.setHorizontalAlignment(JLabel.CENTER);
        layOut.setConstraints(alphaLabel, l);
        getContentPane().add(alphaLabel);
        GridBagConstraints c = new GridBagConstraints();
        getContentPane().setLayout(layOut);

        l.gridwidth = GridBagConstraints.REMAINDER;
        rulesLabel = new JLabel();
        rulesLabel.setText("Rules");
        newFont = getFont().deriveFont(1);
        rulesLabel.setFont(newFont);
        rulesLabel.setHorizontalAlignment(JLabel.CENTER);
        layOut.setConstraints(rulesLabel, l);
        getContentPane().add(rulesLabel);

        GridBagConstraints a = new GridBagConstraints();
        a.gridwidth = GridBagConstraints.RELATIVE;
```

```
        a.weightx = 1.0;
        a.fill = GridBagConstraints.BOTH;
        alphas = new JComboBox();
        layOut.setConstraints(alphas, a);
        alphas.addItem("1.0");
        alphas.addItem("0.75");
        alphas.addItem("0.50");
        alphas.addItem("0.25");
        alphas.addItem("0.0");
        alphas.addItemListener(this);
        getContentPane().add(alphas);

        a.gridwidth = GridBagConstraints.REMAINDER;
        rules = new JComboBox();
        layOut.setConstraints(rules, a);
        rules.addItem("SRC");
        rules.addItem("DST_IN");
        rules.addItem("DST_OUT");
        rules.addItem("DST_OVER");
        rules.addItem("SRC_IN");
        rules.addItem("SRC_OVER");
        rules.addItem("SRC_OUT");
        rules.addItem("CLEAR");
        rules.addItemListener(this);
        getContentPane().add(rules);

        GridBagConstraints fC = new GridBagConstraints();
        fC.fill = GridBagConstraints.BOTH;
        fC.weightx = 1.0;
        fC.weighty = 1.0;
        fC.gridwidth = GridBagConstraints.REMAINDER;
        comp = new CompPanel();
        layOut.setConstraints(comp, fC);
        getContentPane().add(comp);

        validate();
    }

/*
 * Detects a change in either of the Choice components.
 * Resets the variable corresponding to the Choice whose
 * state is changed. Invokes changeRule in CompPanel
 * with the current alpha and composite rules.
*/
    public void itemStateChanged(ItemEvent e) {
        if ( e.getStateChange() != ItemEvent.SELECTED ) {
            return;
        }
```

```
        Object choice = e.getSource();
        if ( choice == alphas ) {
            alpha = (String)alphas.getSelectedItem();
        } else {
            rule = rules.getSelectedIndex();
        }
        comp.changeRule(alpha, rule);
    }

    public static void main(String s[]) {
        JFrame f = new JFrame("Composite");
        f.addWindowListener(new WindowAdapter() {
            public void windowClosing(WindowEvent e)
                                         {System.exit(0);}
        });
        JApplet applet = new Composite();
        f.getContentPane().add("Center", applet);
        applet.init();
        f.pack();
        f.setSize(new Dimension(300,300));
        f.show();
    }
}

class CompPanel extends JPanel {
    AlphaComposite ac =
          AlphaComposite.getInstance(AlphaComposite.SRC);
    float alpha = 1.0f;

    public CompPanel(){}

// Resets the alpha and composite rules with selected items.
    public void changeRule(String a, int rule) {
        alpha = Float.valueOf(a).floatValue();
        ac = AlphaComposite.getInstance(getRule(rule), alpha);
        repaint();
    }

// Gets the requested compositing rule.
    public int getRule(int rule){
        int alphaComp = 0;
        switch ( rule ) {
        case 0: alphaComp = AlphaComposite.SRC; break;
        case 1: alphaComp = AlphaComposite.DST_IN; break;
        case 2: alphaComp = AlphaComposite.DST_OUT; break;
        case 3: alphaComp = AlphaComposite.DST_OVER; break;
        case 4: alphaComp = AlphaComposite.SRC_IN; break;
        case 5: alphaComp = AlphaComposite.SRC_OVER; break;
```

```
            case 6: alphaComp = AlphaComposite.SRC_OUT; break;
            case 7: alphaComp = AlphaComposite.CLEAR; break;
            }
            return alphaComp;
        }

        public void paintComponent(Graphics g) {
            super.paintComponent( g );
            Graphics2D g2 = (Graphics2D) g;

            Dimension d = getSize();
            int w = d.width;
            int h = d.height;

            // Creates the buffered image.
            BufferedImage buffImg = new BufferedImage(w, h,
                                    BufferedImage.TYPE_INT_ARGB);
            Graphics2D gbi = buffImg.createGraphics();

            // Clears the previously drawn image.
            g2.setColor(Color.white);
            g2.fillRect(0, 0, d.width, d.height);

            int rectx = w/4;
            int recty = h/4;

            // Draws rectangle and ellipse into buffered image.
            gbi.setColor(new Color(0.0f, 0.0f, 1.0f, 1.0f));
            gbi.fill(new Rectangle2D.Double(rectx, recty,
                                            150, 100));
            gbi.setColor(new Color(1.0f, 0.0f, 0.0f, 1.0f));
            gbi.setComposite(ac);
            gbi.fill(new Ellipse2D.Double(rectx+rectx/2,
                                          recty+recty/2,
                                          150,100));

            // Draws the buffered image.
            g2.drawImage(buffImg, null, 0, 0);
        }
    }
```

EXAMPLE: Pear Applet

Where Explained:
Constructing Complex Shapes from Geometry Primitives (page 200)

Pear.java

SOURCE CODE: *http://java.sun.com/docs/books/tutorial/2d/display/example-1dot2/Pear.java*

```
import java.awt.*;
import java.awt.event.*;
```

```
import java.awt.font.*;
import java.awt.geom.*;
import javax.swing.*;

/*
 * This applet renders a pear, using Constructive Area
 * Geometry (CSG) methods, add, intersect, and subtract.
*/

public class Pear extends JApplet {

    Ellipse2D.Double circle, oval, leaf, stem;
    Area circ, ov, leaf1, leaf2, st1, st2;

    public void init() {
        circle = new Ellipse2D.Double();
        oval = new Ellipse2D.Double();
        leaf = new Ellipse2D.Double();
        stem = new Ellipse2D.Double();
        circ = new Area(circle);
        ov = new Area(oval);
        leaf1 = new Area(leaf);
        leaf2 = new Area(leaf);
        st1 = new Area(stem);
        st2 = new Area(stem);

        setBackground(Color.white);
    }

    public void paint (Graphics g) {
        Graphics2D g2 = (Graphics2D) g;
        Dimension d = getSize();
        int w = d.width;
        int h = d.height;
        double ew = w/2;
        double eh = h/2;

        g2.setColor(Color.green);

        // Creates the first leaf by filling the intersection
        // of two Area objects created from an ellipse.
        leaf.setFrame(ew-16, eh-29, 15.0, 15.0);
        leaf1 = new Area(leaf);
        leaf.setFrame(ew-14, eh-47, 30.0, 30.0);
        leaf2 = new Area(leaf);
        leaf1.intersect(leaf2);
        g2.fill(leaf1);
```

```
        // Creates the second leaf.
        leaf.setFrame(ew+1, eh-29, 15.0, 15.0);
        leaf1 = new Area(leaf);
        leaf2.intersect(leaf1);
        g2.fill(leaf2);

        g2.setColor(Color.black);

        // Creates the stem by filling the Area resulting
        // from the subtraction of two Area objects created
        // from an ellipse.
        stem.setFrame(ew, eh-42, 40.0, 40.0);
        st1 = new Area(stem);
        stem.setFrame(ew+3, eh-47, 50.0, 50.0);
        st2 = new Area(stem);
        st1.subtract(st2);
        g2.fill(st1);

        g2.setColor(Color.yellow);

        // Creates the pear itself by filling the Area
        // resulting from the union of two Area objects
        // created by two different ellipses.
        circle.setFrame(ew-25, eh, 50.0, 50.0);
        oval.setFrame(ew-19, eh-20, 40.0, 70.0);
        circ = new Area(circle);
        ov = new Area(oval);
        circ.add(ov);
        g2.fill(circ);
    }

    public static void main(String s[]) {
        JFrame f = new JFrame("Pear");
        f.addWindowListener(new WindowAdapter() {
            public void windowClosing(WindowEvent e)
                                      {System.exit(0);}
        });
        JApplet applet = new Pear();
        f.getContentPane().add("Center", applet);
        applet.init();
        f.pack();
        f.setSize(new Dimension(150,200));
        f.show();
    }
}
```

EXAMPLE: ShapeMover Applet

Where Explained: *Supporting User Interaction* (page 202)

ShapeMover.java

SOURCE CODE: *http://java.sun.com/docs/books/tutorial/2d/display/example-1dot2/ShapeMover.java*

```
import java.awt.*;
import java.awt.event.*;
import java.applet.Applet;
import java.awt.image.*;

/*
 * This applet allows the user to move a texture painted
 * rectangle around the applet window. The rectangle flickers
 * and draws slowly because this applet does not use
 * double buffering.
*/

public class ShapeMover extends Applet{
static protected Label label;

   public void init(){

        setLayout(new BorderLayout());
        add(new SMCanvas());

        label = new Label("Drag rectangle around within " +
                              "the area");
        add("South", label);
    }

    public static void main(String s[]) {
         Frame f = new Frame("ShapeMover");
         f.addWindowListener(new WindowAdapter() {
             public void windowClosing(WindowEvent e)
                                             {System.exit(0);}
         });
         Applet applet = new ShapeMover();
         f.add("Center", applet);
         applet.init();
         f.pack();
         f.setSize(new Dimension(550,250));
         f.show();
    }

}
```

```
class SMCanvas extends Canvas
            implements MouseListener,
                       MouseMotionListener {
    Rectangle rect = new Rectangle(0, 0, 100, 50);
    BufferedImage bi;
    Graphics2D big;

    // Holds coordinates of user's last
    // mousePressed event.
    int last_x, last_y;
    boolean firstTime = true;
    TexturePaint fillPolka, strokePolka;
    Rectangle area;

    // True if the user pressed, dragged or released
    // the mouse outside of the rectangle; else, false.
    boolean pressOut = false;

    public SMCanvas() {
        setBackground(Color.white);
        addMouseMotionListener(this);
        addMouseListener(this);

        // Creates the fill texture paint pattern.
        bi = new BufferedImage(5, 5,
                           BufferedImage.TYPE_INT_RGB);
        big = bi.createGraphics();
        big.setColor(Color.pink);
        big.fillRect(0, 0, 7, 7);
        big.setColor(Color.cyan);
        big.fillOval(0, 0, 3, 3);
        Rectangle r = new Rectangle(0,0,5,5);
        fillPolka = new TexturePaint(bi, r);
        big.dispose();

        //Creates the stroke texture paint pattern.
        bi = new BufferedImage(5, 5,
                           BufferedImage.TYPE_INT_RGB);
        big = bi.createGraphics();
        big.setColor(Color.cyan);
        big.fillRect(0, 0, 7, 7);
        big.setColor(Color.pink);
        big.fillOval(0, 0, 3, 3);
        r = new Rectangle(0,0,5,5);
        strokePolka = new TexturePaint(bi, r);
        big.dispose();
    }
```

```
// Handles event of user pressing down mouse button.
public void mousePressed(MouseEvent e) {
    last_x = rect.x - e.getX();
    last_y = rect.y - e.getY();

     // Checks whether or not the cursor is inside the
     // rectangle while the user is pressing the mouse.
    if(rect.contains(e.getX(), e.getY()))
         updateLocation(e);
    else {
         ShapeMover.label.setText("First position the"+
             " cursor on the rectangle and then drag.");
         pressOut = true;
    }
}

// Handles the event of a user dragging mouse while
// holding down the mouse button.
public void mouseDragged(MouseEvent e) {
    if(!pressOut)
         updateLocation(e);
    else {
         ShapeMover.label.setText("First position the"+
             " cursor on the rectangle and then drag.");
    }
}

// Handles event of a user releasing the mouse button.
public void mouseReleased(MouseEvent e) {

// Checks whether or not the cursor is inside of the
// rectangle when the user releases the mouse button.
    if(rect.contains(e.getX(), e.getY()))
                        updateLocation(e);
     else {
         ShapeMover.label.setText("First position " +
                           "the cursor on the  " +
                           "rectangle and then drag.");
         pressOut = false;
     }
}

 // This method required by MouseListener.
 public void mouseMoved(MouseEvent e) {}

 // These methods are required by MouseMotionListener.
 public void mouseClicked(MouseEvent e) {}
 public void mouseExited(MouseEvent e) {}
 public void mouseEntered(MouseEvent e) {}
```

```
// Updates the coordinates representing the location
// of the current rectangle.
public void updateLocation(MouseEvent e) {

    rect.setLocation(last_x + e.getX(),
                     last_y + e.getY());
    /*
     * Updates the label to reflect the location
     * of the current rectangle if checkRect
     * returns true; otherwise, returns error message.
     */
    if (checkRect()) {
        ShapeMover.label.setText("Rectangle " +
                                 "located at " +
                                 rect.getX() + ", " +
                                 rect.getY());
    } else {
        ShapeMover.label.setText("Please don't try " +
                                 "to drag outside the area.");
    }
    repaint();
}

public void paint(Graphics g){
    update(g);
}

public void update(Graphics g){
    Graphics2D g2 = (Graphics2D)g;
    Dimension dim = getSize();
    int w = (int)dim.getWidth();
    int h = (int)dim.getHeight();
    g2.setStroke(new BasicStroke(8.0f));
    if(firstTime){
        area = new Rectangle(dim);
        rect.setLocation(w/2-50, h/2-25);
        firstTime = false;
    }

    // Clears the rectangle that was previously drawn.
    g2.setPaint(Color.white);
    g2.fillRect(0, 0, w, h);

    // Draws and fills the newly positioned rectangle.
    g2.setPaint(strokePolka);
    g2.draw(rect);
    g2.setPaint(fillPolka);
    g2.fill(rect);
}
```

```
            /*
             * Checks if the rectangle is contained within applet
             * window.  If the rectangle is not contained within
             * applet window, it is redrawn so that it is adjacent
             * to the edge of the window and just inside window.
            */

            boolean checkRect() {
                if (area == null) {
                    return false;
                }

                if (area.contains(rect.x, rect.y, 100, 50)) {
                    return true;
                }
                int new_x = rect.x;
                int new_y = rect.y;

                if ((rect.x+100)>area.getWidth()) {
                    new_x = (int)area.getWidth()-99;
                }
                if (rect.x < 0) {
                    new_x = -1;
                }
                if ((rect.y+50)>area.getHeight()) {
                    new_y = (int)area.getHeight()-49;
                }
                if (rect.y < 0) {
                    new_y = -1;
                }
                rect.setLocation(new_x, new_y);
                return false;
            }
        }
    }
```

EXAMPLE: SwingShapeMover Applet

Where Explained: *Supporting User Interaction* (page 202)

SwingShapeMover.java

SOURCE CODE: *http://java.sun.com/docs/books/tutorial/2d/display/example-1dot2/SwingShapeMover.java*

```
import java.awt.*;
import java.awt.event.*;
import java.awt.image.*;
import javax.swing.*;
```

```
/*
 * This applet allows the user to move a texture
 * painted rectangle around the applet window.
 * The rectangle flickers and draws slowly because
 * this applet does not use double buffering.
*/

public class SwingShapeMover extends JApplet {
    static protected JLabel label;
    DPanel d;

    public void init(){
        getContentPane().setLayout(new BorderLayout());

        d = new DPanel();
        d.setBackground(Color.white);
        getContentPane().add(d);

        label = new JLabel("Drag rectangle around within " +
                           "the area");
        getContentPane().add("South", label);
    }

    public static void main(String s[]) {
        JFrame f = new JFrame("SwingShapeMover");
        f.addWindowListener(new WindowAdapter() {
            public void windowClosing(WindowEvent e)
                       {System.exit(0);}
        });
        JApplet applet = new SwingShapeMover();
        f.getContentPane().add("Center", applet);
        applet.init();
        f.pack();
        f.setSize(new Dimension(550,250));
        f.show();
    }
}

class DPanel extends JPanel
             implements MouseListener, MouseMotionListener {
    Rectangle rect = new Rectangle(0, 0, 100, 50);
    BufferedImage bi;
    Graphics2D big;

    // Holds coordinates of user's last mousePressed event.
    int last_x, last_y;
    boolean firstTime = true;
```

```
TexturePaint fillPolka, strokePolka;
Rectangle area;

// True if the user pressed, dragged or released the mouse
// outside the rectangle; false otherwise.
boolean pressOut = false;

public DPanel(){
    setBackground(Color.white);
    addMouseMotionListener(this);
    addMouseListener(this);

    // Creates the fill texture paint pattern.
    bi = new BufferedImage(5, 5, BufferedImage.TYPE_INT_RGB);
    big = bi.createGraphics();
    big.setColor(Color.pink);
    big.fillRect(0, 0, 7, 7);
    big.setColor(Color.cyan);
    big.fillOval(0, 0, 3, 3);
    Rectangle r = new Rectangle(0,0,5,5);
    fillPolka = new TexturePaint(bi, r);
    big.dispose();

    //Creates the stroke texture paint pattern.
    bi = new BufferedImage(5, 5,
                               BufferedImage.TYPE_INT_RGB);
    big = bi.createGraphics();
    big.setColor(Color.cyan);
    big.fillRect(0, 0, 7, 7);
    big.setColor(Color.pink);
    big.fillOval(0, 0, 3, 3);
    r = new Rectangle(0,0,5,5);
    strokePolka = new TexturePaint(bi, r);
    big.dispose();
}

// Handles event of user pressing down the mouse button.
public void mousePressed(MouseEvent e){
    last_x = rect.x - e.getX();
    last_y = rect.y - e.getY();
    // Checks whether or not the cursor is inside the
    // rectangle while the user is pressing the mouse.
    if ( rect.contains(e.getX(), e.getY()) ) {
        updateLocation(e);
    } else {
        SwingShapeMover.label.setText("First position " +
                                   "the cursor on the " +
                                  "rectangle and then drag.");
```

```
            pressOut = true;
        }
    }

    // Handles the event of a user dragging the mouse
    // while holding down the mouse button.
    public void mouseDragged(MouseEvent e){
        if ( !pressOut ) {
            updateLocation(e);
        } else {
            SwingShapeMover.label.setText("First position " +
                                    "the cursor on the " +
                                    "rectangle and then drag.");
        }
    }

    // Handles the event of a user releasing the mouse button.
    public void mouseReleased(MouseEvent e){
        // Checks whether or not the cursor is inside the
        // rectangle when the user releases the mouse button.
        if ( rect.contains(e.getX(), e.getY()) ) {
            updateLocation(e);
        } else {
            SwingShapeMover.label.setText("First position " +
                              "the cursor on the rectangle " +
                              "and then drag.");
            pressOut = false;
        }
    }

    // This method is required by MouseListener.
    public void mouseMoved(MouseEvent e){}

    // These methods are required by MouseMotionListener.
    public void mouseClicked(MouseEvent e){}
    public void mouseExited(MouseEvent e){}
    public void mouseEntered(MouseEvent e){}

    // Updates the coordinates representing the
    // location of the current rectangle.
    public void updateLocation(MouseEvent e){
        rect.setLocation(last_x + e.getX(),
                         last_y + e.getY());
    /*
     * Updates the label to reflect the location of the
     * current rectangle if checkRect returns true;
     * otherwise, returns error message.
     */
```

```
        if (checkRect()) {
            SwingShapeMover.label.setText("Rectangle "+
                                          " located at " +
                                          rect.getX() +  ", "
                                          + rect.getY());
        } else {
             SwingShapeMover.label.setText("Please don't " +
                                 "try to drag outside the area.");
        }
        repaint();
    }

    public void paintComponent(Graphics g){
        super.paintComponent(g);
        Graphics2D g2 = (Graphics2D)g;
        g2.setStroke(new BasicStroke(8.0f));
        Dimension dim = getSize();
        int w = (int)dim.getWidth();
        int h = (int)dim.getHeight();

        if ( firstTime ) {
            area = new Rectangle(dim);
            rect.setLocation(w/2-50, h/2-25);
            firstTime = false;
        }
        // Clears the rectangle that was previously drawn.
        g2.setPaint(Color.white);
        g2.fillRect(0, 0, w, h);

        // Draws and fills the newly positioned rectangle.
        g2.setPaint(fillPolka);
        g2.fill(rect);
        g2.setPaint(strokePolka);
        g2.draw(rect);
    }

    /*
     * Checks if the rectangle is contained within the
     * applet window.  If the rectangle is not contained
     * within the applet window, it is redrawn so that
     * it is adjacent to the window's edge and just inside.
    */
    boolean checkRect(){

    if (area == null) {
        return false;
    }
    if (area.contains(rect.x, rect.y, 100, 50)) {
```

```
            return true;
        }
        int new_x = rect.x;
        int new_y = rect.y;

        if ((rect.x+100)>area.getWidth()) {
            new_x = (int)area.getWidth()-99;
        }
        if (rect.x < 0){
            new_x = -1;
        }
        if ((rect.y+50)>area.getHeight()) {
            new_y = (int)area.getHeight()-49;
        }
        if (rect.y < 0){
            new_y = -1;
        }
        rect.setLocation(new_x, new_y);
        return false;
        }
    }
```

LESSON 14: Manipulating and Displaying Images

EXAMPLE: ImageOps Applet

ImageOps.java

SOURCE CODE: *http://java.sun.com/docs/books/tutorial/2d/images/example-1dot2/ImageOps.java*

Where Explained:
Filtering a BufferedImage (page 206)

```
    import java.awt.*;
    import java.awt.event.*;
    import javax.swing.*;
    import java.awt.image.*;
    import java.awt.geom.AffineTransform;
    import java.awt.font.TextLayout;

    public class ImageOps extends JApplet {

        private BufferedImage bi[];
        public static final float[] SHARPEN3x3_3 = {
            0.f, -1.f,  0.f,
            -1.f,  5.f, -1.f,
            0.f, -1.f,  0.f};
```

```
    public void init() {
        setBackground(Color.white);

        bi = new BufferedImage[4];
        String s[] = { "bld.jpg", "bld.jpg", "boat.gif",
                       "boat.gif"};
        for ( int i = 0; i < bi.length; i++ ) {
            Image img = getToolkit().getImage("images/" +
                                                s[i]);
            try {
                MediaTracker tracker = new MediaTracker(this);
                tracker.addImage(img, 0);
                tracker.waitForID(0);
            }
            catch ( Exception e ) {}
            int iw = img.getWidth(this);
            int ih = img.getHeight(this);
            bi[i] = new BufferedImage(iw, ih,
                        BufferedImage.TYPE_INT_RGB);
            Graphics2D big = bi[i].createGraphics();
            big.drawImage(img,0,0,this);
        }
    }


    public void paint(Graphics g) {
        Graphics2D g2 = (Graphics2D) g;
        g2.setRenderingHint(RenderingHints.KEY_ANTIALIASING,

RenderingHints.VALUE_ANTIALIAS_ON);
        g2.setRenderingHint(RenderingHints.KEY_RENDERING,
                         RenderingHints.VALUE_RENDER_QUALITY);
        int w = getSize().width;
        int h = getSize().height;

        g2.setColor(Color.black);
        float[][] data = {{0.1f, 0.1f, 0.1f, //low-pass filter
                0.1f, 0.2f, 0.1f,
                0.1f, 0.1f, 0.1f},
                SHARPEN3x3_3};

        String theDesc[] = { "Convolve LowPass",
                             "Convolve Sharpen", "LookupOp",
                             "RescaleOp"};
        for ( int i = 0; i < bi.length; i++ ) {
            int iw = bi[i].getWidth(this);
            int ih = bi[i].getHeight(this);
            int x = 0, y = 0;
```

```
            AffineTransform at = new AffineTransform();
            at.scale((w-14)/2.0/iw, (h-34)/2.0/ih);
            BufferedImageOp biop = null;
            BufferedImage bimg =
                    new BufferedImage(
                         iw, ih, BufferedImage.TYPE_INT_RGB);
            switch ( i ) {
            case 0 :
            case 1 : x = i==0?5:w/2+3; y = 15;
                     Kernel kernel = new Kernel(3,3,data[i]);
                     ConvolveOp cop = new ConvolveOp(kernel,
                                      ConvolveOp.EDGE_NO_OP,
                                      null);
                     cop.filter(bi[i],bimg);
                     biop = new AffineTransformOp(at,
                                      AffineTransformOp.
                                      TYPE_NEAREST_NEIGHBOR);
                      break;
            case 2 : x = 5; y = h/2+15;
                     byte chlut[] = new byte[256];
                     for ( int j=0;j<200 ;j++ )
                         chlut[j]=(byte)(256-j);
                     ByteLookupTable blut =
                          new ByteLookupTable(0,chlut);
                     LookupOp lop = new LookupOp(blut,
                                                 null);
                     lop.filter(bi[i],bimg);
                     biop = new AffineTransformOp(at,
                            AffineTransformOp.TYPE_BILINEAR);
                      break;
            case 3 : x = w/2+3; y = h/2+15;
                     RescaleOp rop =
                            new RescaleOp(1.1f,20.0f, null);
                     rop.filter(bi[i],bimg);
                     biop = new AffineTransformOp(at,
                            AffineTransformOp.TYPE_BILINEAR);
            }
            g2.drawImage(bimg,biop,x,y);
            TextLayout tl = new TextLayout(theDesc[i],
                      g2.getFont(),g2.getFontRenderContext());
            tl.draw(g2, (float) x, (float) y-4);
        }
    }

    public static void main(String s[]) {
        JFrame f = new JFrame("ImageOps");
        f.addWindowListener(new WindowAdapter() {
            public void windowClosing(WindowEvent e)
                                     {System.exit(0);}
        });
```

```
            JApplet applet = new ImageOps();
            f.getContentPane().add("Center", applet);
            applet.init();
            f.pack();
            f.setSize(new Dimension(550,550));
            f.show();
        }
    }
```

EXAMPLE: BufferedShapeMover Applet

Where Explained: *Using a BufferedImage for Double Buffering* (page 208)

BufferedShapeMover.java

SOURCE CODE: *http://java.sun.com/docs/books/tutorial/2d/images/example-1dot2/BufferedShapeMover.java*

```
import java.awt.*;
import java.awt.event.*;
import java.applet.Applet;
import java.awt.image.*;

public class BufferedShapeMover extends Applet {

    static protected Label label;
    public void init(){
        //Initialize the layout.
        setLayout(new BorderLayout());
        add(new BSMCanvas());
        label = new Label("Drag rectangle around within " +
                          "the area");
        add("South", label);
    }

    public static void main(String s[]) {
        Frame f = new Frame("BufferedShapeMover");
        f.addWindowListener(new WindowAdapter() {
            public void windowClosing(WindowEvent e)
            {System.exit(0);}
            });
            Applet applet = new BufferedShapeMover();
            f.add("Center", applet);
            applet.init();
            f.pack();
            f.setSize(new Dimension(550,250));
            f.show();
        }
    }
    class BSMCanvas extends Canvas
                implements MouseListener,
                           MouseMotionListener{
    Rectangle rect = new Rectangle(0, 0, 100, 50);
```

```
BufferedImage bi;
Graphics2D big;

// Holds coordinates of user's last mousePressed event.
int last_x, last_y;
boolean firstTime = true;
TexturePaint fillPolka, strokePolka;
Rectangle area;

// True if user pressed, dragged or released the mouse
// outside of the rectangle; false otherwise.
boolean pressOut = false;

public BSMCanvas(){
    setBackground(Color.white);
    addMouseMotionListener(this);
    addMouseListener(this);

    // Creates the fill texture paint pattern.
    bi = new BufferedImage(5, 5,
                               BufferedImage.TYPE_INT_RGB);
    big = bi.createGraphics();
    big.setColor(Color.pink);
    big.fillRect(0, 0, 7, 7);
    big.setColor(Color.cyan);
    big.fillOval(0, 0, 3, 3);
    Rectangle r = new Rectangle(0,0,5,5);
    fillPolka = new TexturePaint(bi, r);
    big.dispose();

    //Creates the stroke texture paint pattern.
    bi = new BufferedImage(5, 5,
                               BufferedImage.TYPE_INT_RGB);
    big = bi.createGraphics();
    big.setColor(Color.cyan);
    big.fillRect(0, 0, 7, 7);
    big.setColor(Color.pink);
    big.fillOval(0, 0, 3, 3);
    r = new Rectangle(0,0,5,5);
    strokePolka = new TexturePaint(bi, r);
    big.dispose();
}

// Handles event of the user pressing down the mouse button.
public void mousePressed(MouseEvent e){
    last_x = rect.x - e.getX();
    last_y = rect.y - e.getY();
    // Checks if the cursor is inside of the rectangle
    // while the user is pressing themouse.
```

```
        if(rect.contains(e.getX(), e.getY())){
            updateLocation(e);
        } else {
            BufferedShapeMover.label.setText("First position"+
                  " the cursor on the rectangle and then drag.");
            pressOut = true;
        }
    }

    // Handles the event of a user dragging the mouse while
    // holding down the mouse button.
    public void mouseDragged(MouseEvent e){
        if(!pressOut){
            updateLocation(e);
        } else {
            BufferedShapeMover.label.setText("First position"+
                " the cursor on the rectangle and then drag.");
        }
    }

    // Handles the event of a user releasing the mouse button.
    public void mouseReleased(MouseEvent e){
        // Checks if the cursor is inside the
        // rectangle when the user releases the mouse button.
        if (rect.contains(e.getX(), e.getY())){
            updateLocation(e);
        } else {
            BufferedShapeMover.label.setText("First " +
                    "position the cursor on the " +
                    "rectangle, then drag.");
            vpressOut = false;
        }
    }

    // This method required by MouseListener.
    public void mouseMoved(MouseEvent e) {}

    // These methods are required by MouseMotionListener.
    public void mouseClicked(MouseEvent e) {}
    public void mouseExited(MouseEvent e) {}
    public void mouseEntered(MouseEvent e) {}
    public void updateLocation(MouseEvent e) {

    rect.setLocation(last_x + e.getX(), last_y + e.getY());

        /*
         * Updates the label to reflect the location of the
```

```
        * current rectangle if checkRect returns true;
        * otherwise, returns error message.
        */
        if (checkRect()) {
            BufferedShapeMover.label.setText("Rectangle " +
                    "located at " + rect.getX() + ", "
                     + rect.getY());
        } else {
            BufferedShapeMover.label.setText("Please don't" +
                        " try to drag outside the area.");
        }
        repaint();
    }

    public void paint(Graphics g){
        update(g);
    }

    public void update(Graphics g) {
        Graphics2D g2 = (Graphics2D)g;
        if(firstTime){
            Dimension dim = getSize();
            int w = dim.width;
            int h = dim.height;
            area = new Rectangle(dim);
            bi = (BufferedImage)createImage(w, h);
            big = bi.createGraphics();
            rect.setLocation(w/2-50, h/2-25);
            big.setStroke(new BasicStroke(8.0f));
            firstTime = false;
        }

        // Clears the rectangle that was previously drawn.
        big.setColor(Color.white);
        big.clearRect(0, 0, area.width, area.height);

        // Draws and fills newly positioned rectangle
        // to the buffer.
        big.setPaint(strokePolka);
        big.draw(rect);
        big.setPaint(fillPolka);
        big.fill(rect);

        // Draws the buffered image to the screen.
```

```
            g2.drawImage(bi, 0, 0, this);
        }


        /*
         * Checks if the rectangle is contained within the applet
         * window. If the rectangle is not contained withing the
         * applet window, it is redrawn so that it is adjacent to
         * the edge of the window and just inside the window.
         */
        boolean checkRect() {
            if (area == null) {
                return false;
            }
            if (area.contains(rect.x, rect.y, 100, 50)) {
                return true;
            }
            int new_x = rect.x;
            int new_y = rect.y;

            if ((rect.x+100)>area.width) {
                new_x = area.width-99;
            }
            if (rect.x < 0) {
                new_x = -1;
            }
            if ((rect.y+50)>area.height) {
                new_y = area.height-49;
            }
            if (rect.y < 0) {
                new_y = -1;
            }
            rect.setLocation(new_x, new_y);
            return false;
        }
    }
```

LESSON 15: Printing

Where Explained: *Printing the Contents of a Component* (page 213)

EXAMPLE: ShapesPrint Applet

ShapesPrint.java

SOURCE CODE: *http://java.sun.com/docs/books/tutorial/2d/printing/example-1dot2/ShapesPrint.java*

```
import java.awt.geom.*;
import java.awt.print.PrinterJob;
```

```
import java.awt.event.*;
import java.awt.*;
import javax.swing.*;
import java.awt.print.*;
public class ShapesPrint extends JPanel
                         implements Printable,
                                    ActionListener {
    final static Color bg = Color.white;
    final static Color fg = Color.black;
    final static Color red = Color.red;
    final static Color white = Color.white;

    final static BasicStroke stroke = new BasicStroke(2.0f);
    final static BasicStroke wideStroke =
                new BasicStroke(8.0f);

    final static float dash1[] = {10.0f};
    final static BasicStroke dashed =
                new BasicStroke(1.0f,
                                BasicStroke.CAP_BUTT,
                                BasicStroke.JOIN_MITER,
                                10.0f, dash1, 0.0f);
    final static JButton button = new JButton("Print");

    public ShapesPrint() {
        setBackground(bg);
        button.addActionListener(this);
    }

    public void actionPerformed(ActionEvent e) {
        if (e.getSource() instanceof JButton) {
            PrinterJob printJob = PrinterJob.getPrinterJob();
            printJob.setPrintable(this);
            if (printJob.printDialog()) {
                try {
                    printJob.print();
                } catch (Exception ex) {
                    ex.printStackTrace();
                }
            }
        }
    }

    public void paintComponent(Graphics g) {
        super.paintComponent(g);
        Graphics2D g2 = (Graphics2D) g;
        drawShapes(g2);
```

```
    }


    public void drawShapes(Graphics2D g2){
        Dimension d = getSize();
        int gridWidth = 400 / 6;
        int gridHeight = 300 / 2;

        int rowspacing = 5;
        int columnspacing = 7;
        int rectWidth = gridWidth - columnspacing;
        int rectHeight = gridHeight - rowspacing;

        Color fg3D = Color.lightGray;

        g2.setPaint(fg3D);
        g2.drawRect(80, 80, 400 - 1, 310);
        g2.setPaint(fg);

        int x = 85;
        int y = 87;


        // draw Line2D.Double
        g2.draw(new Line2D.Double(x, y+rectHeight-1,
                                  x + rectWidth, y));
        x += gridWidth;

        // draw Rectangle2D.Double
        g2.setStroke(stroke);
        g2.draw(new Rectangle2D.Double(x, y, rectWidth,
                                       rectHeight));
        x += gridWidth;
        // draw  RoundRectangle2D.Double
        g2.setStroke(dashed);
        g2.draw(new RoundRectangle2D.Double(x, y, rectWidth,
                                            rectHeight, 10,
                                             10));
        x += gridWidth;

        // draw Arc2D.Double
        g2.setStroke(wideStroke);
        g2.draw(new Arc2D.Double(x, y, rectWidth, rectHeight,
                                 90, 135, Arc2D.OPEN));
        x += gridWidth;

        // draw Ellipse2D.Double
        g2.setStroke(stroke);
```

```
g2.draw(new Ellipse2D.Double(x, y, rectWidth,
                             rectHeight));
x += gridWidth;
// draw GeneralPath (polygon)
int x1Points[] = {x, x+rectWidth, x, x+rectWidth};
int y1Points[] = {y, y+rectHeight, y+rectHeight, y};
GeneralPath polygon =
            new GeneralPath(GeneralPath.WIND_EVEN_ODD,
                            x1Points.length);
polygon.moveTo(x1Points[0], y1Points[0]);
for (int index=1; index < x1Points.length; index++) {
    polygon.lineTo(x1Points[index], y1Points[index]);
};
polygon.closePath();
g2.draw(polygon);

// NEW ROW
x = 85;
y += gridHeight;

// draw GeneralPath (polyline)
int x2Points[] = {x, x+rectWidth, x, x+rectWidth};
int y2Points[] = {y, y+rectHeight, y+rectHeight, y};
GeneralPath polyline =
            new GeneralPath(
                        GeneralPath.WIND_EVEN_ODD,
                        x2Points.length);
polyline.moveTo (x2Points[0], y2Points[0]);

for (int index=1; index < x2Points.length; index++) {
    polyline.lineTo(x2Points[index], y2Points[index]);
};
g2.draw(polyline);
x += gridWidth;

// fill Rectangle2D.Double (red)
g2.setPaint(red);
g2.fill(new Rectangle2D.Double(x, y, rectWidth,
                               rectHeight));
g2.setPaint(fg);
x += gridWidth;

// fill RoundRectangle2D.Double
GradientPaint redtowhite = new GradientPaint(x, y,
                           red, x+rectWidth,
                           y,white);
g2.setPaint(redtowhite);
```

```
        g2.fill(new RoundRectangle2D.Double(x, y, rectWidth,
                                            rectHeight, 10,
                                             10));
        g2.setPaint(fg);
        x += gridWidth;
        // fill Arc2D
        g2.setPaint(red);
        g2.fill(new Arc2D.Double(x, y, rectWidth, rectHeight,
                                 90, 135, Arc2D.OPEN));
        g2.setPaint(fg);
        x += gridWidth;
        // fill Ellipse2D.Double
       redtowhite = new GradientPaint(x, y, red, x+rectWidth,
                                      y,white);
        g2.setPaint(redtowhite);
        g2.fill (new Ellipse2D.Double(x, y, rectWidth,
                                      rectHeight));
        g2.setPaint(fg);
        x += gridWidth;
        // fill and stroke GeneralPath
        int x3Points[] = {x, x+rectWidth, x, x+rectWidth};
        int y3Points[] = {y, y+rectHeight, y+rectHeight, y};
        GeneralPath filledPolygon =
                    newGeneralPath(GeneralPath.WIND_EVEN_ODD,
                                   x3Points.length);
        filledPolygon.moveTo(x3Points[0], y3Points[0]);
        for (int index=1; index < x3Points.length; index++) {
            filledPolygon.lineTo(x3Points[index],
                                 y3Points[index]);
        };
        filledPolygon.closePath();
        g2.setPaint(red);
        g2.fill(filledPolygon);
        g2.setPaint(fg);
        g2.draw(filledPolygon);
    }

    public int print(Graphics g, PageFormat pf, int pi)
                throws PrinterException {
        if (pi >= 1) {
            return Printable.NO_SUCH_PAGE;
        }
        drawShapes((Graphics2D) g);
        return Printable.PAGE_EXISTS;
    }

    public static void main(String s[]) {
        WindowListener l = new WindowAdapter() {
            public void windowClosing(WindowEvent e)
                                  { System.exit(0); }
```

```
            public void windowClosed(WindowEvent e)
                                    { System.exit(0); }
        };
        JFrame f = new JFrame();
        f.addWindowListener(l);
        JPanel panel = new JPanel();
        panel.add(button);
        f.getContentPane().add(BorderLayout.SOUTH, panel);
        f.getContentPane().add(BorderLayout.CENTER,
                               new ShapesPrint());
        f.setSize(580, 500);
        f.show();
    }
}
```

EXAMPLE: SimpleBook Applet

Where Explained:
Printing a Collection of Pages (page 216)

SimpleBook.java

SOURCE CODE: *http://java.sun.com/docs/books/tutorial/2d/printing/example-1dot2/SimpleBook.java*

```
import java.awt.event.*;
import javax.swing.*;
import java.awt.*;
import java.awt.geom.*;
import java.awt.print.*;

public class SimpleBook extends JPanel
                        implements ActionListener{

    final static Color bg = Color.white;
    final static Color fg = Color.black;
    final static Color red = Color.red;
    final static Color white = Color.white;

    final static BasicStroke stroke = new BasicStroke(2.0f);
    final static BasicStroke wideStroke =
                 new BasicStroke(8.0f);

    final static float dash1[] = {10.0f};
    final static BasicStroke dashed = new BasicStroke(
                                    1.0f,
                                    BasicStroke.CAP_BUTT,
                                    BasicStroke.JOIN_MITER,
                                    10.0f, dash1, 0.0f);
    final static JButton button = new JButton("Print");

    public SimpleBook() {
```

```
        setBackground(bg);
        button.addActionListener(this);
    }

    public void actionPerformed(ActionEvent e) {
        // Get a PrinterJob
        PrinterJob job = PrinterJob.getPrinterJob();
        // Create a landscape page format
        PageFormat landscape = job.defaultPage();
        landscape.setOrientation(PageFormat.LANDSCAPE);
        // Set up a book
        Book bk = new Book();
        bk.append(new PaintCover(), job.defaultPage());
        bk.append(new PaintContent(), landscape);
        // Pass the book to the PrinterJob
        job.setPageable(bk);
        // Put up the dialog box
        if (job.printDialog()) {
            // Print the job if user didn't cancel printing
            try { job.print(); }
            catch (Exception exc) { /* Handle Exception */ }
        }
    }

    public void paintComponent(Graphics g) {
        super.paintComponent(g);
        Graphics2D g2 = (Graphics2D) g;
        drawShapes(g2);
    }

    static void drawShapes(Graphics2D g2){
        int gridWidth = 600 / 6;
        int gridHeight = 250 / 2;

        int rowspacing = 5;
        int columnspacing = 7;
        int rectWidth = gridWidth - columnspacing;
        int rectHeight = gridHeight - rowspacing;

        Color fg3D = Color.lightGray;

        g2.setPaint(fg3D);
        g2.drawRect(80, 80, 605 - 1, 265);
        g2.setPaint(fg);

        int x = 85;
        int y = 87;
        // draw Line2D.Double
```

```
g2.draw(new Line2D.Double(x, y+rectHeight-1,
                          x + rectWidth, y));
x += gridWidth;
Graphics2D temp = g2;
// draw Rectangle2D.Double
g2.setStroke(stroke);
g2.draw(new Rectangle2D.Double(x, y, rectWidth,
                               rectHeight));
x += gridWidth;

// draw  RoundRectangle2D.Double
g2.setStroke(dashed);
g2.draw(new RoundRectangle2D.Double(x, y, rectWidth,
                                    rectHeight,
                                    10, 10));
x += gridWidth;

// draw Arc2D.Double
g2.setStroke(wideStroke);
g2.draw(new Arc2D.Double(x, y, rectWidth, rectHeight,
                         90, 135, Arc2D.OPEN));
x += gridWidth;

// draw Ellipse2D.Double
g2.setStroke(stroke);

g2.draw(new Ellipse2D.Double(x, y, rectWidth,
                             rectHeight));
x += gridWidth;

// draw GeneralPath (polygon)
int x1Points[] = {x, x+rectWidth, x, x+rectWidth};
int y1Points[] = {y, y+rectHeight, y+rectHeight, y};
GeneralPath polygon =
            new GeneralPath(GeneralPath.WIND_EVEN_ODD,
                            x1Points.length);
polygon.moveTo(x1Points[0], y1Points[0]);
for (int index=1; index < x1Points.length; index++) {
    polygon.lineTo(x1Points[index], y1Points[index]);
};
polygon.closePath();

g2.draw(polygon);

// NEW ROW
x = 85;
y += gridHeight;
// draw GeneralPath (polyline)
int x2Points[] = {x, x+rectWidth, x, x+rectWidth};
```

```
int y2Points[] = {y, y+rectHeight, y+rectHeight, y};
GeneralPath polyline =
            new GeneralPath(GeneralPath.WIND_EVEN_ODD,
                                    x2Points.length);
polyline.moveTo (x2Points[0], y2Points[0]);
for (int index=1; index < x2Points.length; index++) {
    polyline.lineTo(x2Points[index], y2Points[index]);
};

g2.draw(polyline);
x += gridWidth;
// fill Rectangle2D.Double (red)
g2.setPaint(red);
g2.fill(new Rectangle2D.Double(x, y, rectWidth,
                                   rectHeight));
g2.setPaint(fg);
x += gridWidth;

// fill RoundRectangle2D.Double
GradientPaint redtowhite =
      new GradientPaint(x,y,red,x+rectWidth,y,white);
g2.setPaint(redtowhite);
g2.fill(new RoundRectangle2D.Double(x, y, rectWidth,
                                        rectHeight,
                                         10, 10));
g2.setPaint(fg);
x += gridWidth;

// fill Arc2D
g2.setPaint(red);
g2.fill(new Arc2D.Double(x, y, rectWidth, rectHeight,
                              90, 135, Arc2D.OPEN));
g2.setPaint(fg);
x += gridWidth;

// fill Ellipse2D.Double
redtowhite = new GradientPaint(x, y, red, x+rectWidth,
                                   y, white);
g2.setPaint(redtowhite);
g2.fill (new Ellipse2D.Double(x, y, rectWidth,
                                  rectHeight));
g2.setPaint(fg);
x += gridWidth;
// fill and stroke GeneralPath
int x3Points[] = {x, x+rectWidth, x, x+rectWidth};
int y3Points[] = {y, y+rectHeight, y+rectHeight, y};
GeneralPath filledPolygon =
            new GeneralPath(GeneralPath.WIND_EVEN_ODD,
                                    x3Points.length);
```

```
        filledPolygon.moveTo(x3Points[0], y3Points[0]);
        for (int index=1; index < x3Points.length; index++) {
            filledPolygon.lineTo(x3Points[index],
                                 y3Points[index]);
        };
        filledPolygon.closePath();
        g2.setPaint(red);
        g2.fill(filledPolygon);
        g2.setPaint(fg);
        g2.draw(filledPolygon);
        g2.setStroke(temp.getStroke());
    }

    public static void main(String[] args) {
        WindowListener l = new WindowAdapter() {
            public void windowClosing(WindowEvent e)
                                  { System.exit(0); }
            public void windowClosed(WindowEvent e)
                                { System.exit(0); }
            };
        JFrame f = new JFrame();
        f.addWindowListener(l);
        JPanel panel = new JPanel();
        panel.add(button);
        f.getContentPane().add(BorderLayout.SOUTH, panel);
        f.getContentPane().add(BorderLayout.CENTER,
                               new SimpleBook());
        f.setSize(775, 450);
        f.show();
    }
}

class PaintCover implements Printable {
    Font fnt = new Font("Helvetica-Bold", Font.PLAIN, 48);

    public int print(Graphics g, PageFormat pf, int pageIndex)
        throws PrinterException {
        g.setFont(fnt);
        g.setColor(Color.black);
        g.drawString("Sample Shapes", 100, 200);
        return Printable.PAGE_EXISTS;
    }
}

class PaintContent implements Printable {
    public int print(Graphics g, PageFormat pf, int pageIndex)
              throws PrinterException {
        SimpleBook.drawShapes((Graphics2D) g);
        return Printable.PAGE_EXISTS;
    }
}
```

Sound

LESSON 17: Playing Sounds

EXAMPLE: Sound Applet

SoundApplet.java

SOURCE CODE: *http://java.sun.com/docs/books/tutorial/sound/example-1dot2/SoundApplet.java*

Where Explained:
Playing Sounds from an Applet (page 223)

```
import javax.swing.*;
import java.applet.*;
import java.awt.*;
import java.awt.event.*;

public class SoundApplet extends JApplet
                         implements ActionListener,
                                    ItemListener {
    AppletSoundList soundList;
    String auFile = "spacemusic.au";
    String aiffFile = "flute+hrn+mrmba.aif";
    String midiFile = "trippygaia1.mid";
    String rmfFile = "jungle.rmf";
    String wavFile = "bottle-open.wav";
    String chosenFile;
    AudioClip onceClip, loopClip;

    JComboBox formats;
    JButton playButton, loopButton, stopButton;
    boolean looping = false;

    public void init() {
        String [] fileTypes = {auFile,
                               aiffFile,
```

```
                                midiFile,
                                rmfFile,
                                wavFile};
        formats = new JComboBox(fileTypes);
        formats.setSelectedIndex(0);
        chosenFile = (String)formats.getSelectedItem();
        formats.addItemListener(this);

        playButton = new JButton("Play");
        playButton.addActionListener(this);

        loopButton = new JButton("Loop");
        loopButton.addActionListener(this);

        stopButton = new JButton("Stop");
        stopButton.addActionListener(this);
        stopButton.setEnabled(false);

        JPanel controlPanel = new JPanel();
        controlPanel.add(formats);
        controlPanel.add(playButton);
        controlPanel.add(loopButton);
        controlPanel.add(stopButton);
        getContentPane().add(controlPanel);

        startLoadingSounds();
    }

    public void itemStateChanged(ItemEvent e) {
        chosenFile = (String)formats.getSelectedItem();
        soundList.startLoading(chosenFile);
    }

    void startLoadingSounds() {
        //Start asynchronous sound loading.
        soundList = new AppletSoundList(this, getCodeBase());
        soundList.startLoading(auFile);
        soundList.startLoading(aiffFile);
        soundList.startLoading(midiFile);
        soundList.startLoading(rmfFile);
        soundList.startLoading(wavFile);
   }

    public void stop() {
        onceClip.stop();        //Cut short the one-time sound.
        if (looping) {
            loopClip.stop();    //Stop the sound loop.
        }
    }
```

```
public void start() {
    if (looping) {
        loopClip.loop();    //Restart the sound loop.
    }
}

public void actionPerformed(ActionEvent event) {
    //PLAY BUTTON
    Object source = event.getSource();
    if (source == playButton) {
        //Try to get the AudioClip.
        onceClip = soundList.getClip(chosenFile);
        onceClip.play();     //Play it once.
        stopButton.setEnabled(true);
        showStatus("Playing sound " + chosenFile + ".");
        if (onceClip == null) {
            showStatus("Sound " + chosenFile +
                       " not loaded yet.");
        }
        return;
    }

    //START LOOP BUTTON
    if (source == loopButton) {
        loopClip = soundList.getClip(chosenFile);

        looping = true;
        loopClip.loop();     //Start the sound loop.
        loopButton.setEnabled(false);  //Disable loop
                                        //button.
        stopButton.setEnabled(true);
        showStatus("Playing sound " + chosenFile +
                   " continuously.");
        if (loopClip == null) {
            showStatus("Sound " + chosenFile +
                       " not loaded yet.");
        }
        return;
    }

    //STOP LOOP BUTTON
    if (source == stopButton) {
        if (looping) {
            looping = false;
            loopClip.stop();    //Stop the sound loop.
            //Enable start button.
            loopButton.setEnabled(true);

        }
```

```
                else if (onceClip != null) {
                    onceClip.stop();
                }
                stopButton.setEnabled(false);
                showStatus("Stopped playing " + chosenFile + ".");
                return;
            }
        }
    }
```

AppletSoundList.java

SOURCE CODE: *http://java.sun.com/docs/books/tutorial/sound/example-1dot2/AppletSoundList.java*

```
import javax.swing.*;
import java.applet.*;
import java.net.URL;

//Loads and holds a bunch of audio files whose locations are
//specified relative to a fixed base URL.
public class AppletSoundList extends java.util.Hashtable {
    JApplet applet;
    URL baseURL;

    public AppletSoundList(JApplet applet, URL baseURL) {
        super(5); //Initialize Hashtable with capacity
                  //of 5 entries.
        this.applet = applet;
        this.baseURL = baseURL;
    }

    public void startLoading(String relativeURL) {
        new AppletSoundLoader(applet, this,
                              baseURL, relativeURL);
    }

    public AudioClip getClip(String relativeURL) {
        return (AudioClip)get(relativeURL);
    }

    public void putClip(AudioClip clip, String relativeURL) {
        put(relativeURL, clip);
    }
}
```

AppletSoundLoader.java

SOURCE CODE: *http://java.sun.com/docs/books/tutorial/sound/example-1dot2/AppletSoundLoader.java*

```
import javax.swing.*;
import java.applet.*;
import java.net.URL;

public class AppletSoundLoader extends Thread {
    JApplet applet;
    AppletSoundList soundList;
    URL baseURL;
    String relativeURL;

    public AppletSoundLoader(JApplet applet,
                             AppletSoundList soundList,
                             URL baseURL,
                             String relativeURL) {
        this.applet = applet;
        this.soundList = soundList;
        this.baseURL = baseURL;
        this.relativeURL = relativeURL;
        setPriority(MIN_PRIORITY);
        start();
    }

    public void run() {
        AudioClip audioClip = applet.getAudioClip(
                                        baseURL, relativeURL);
        soundList.putClip(audioClip, relativeURL);
    }
}
```

SoundApplet.html

SOURCE CODE: *http://java.sun.com/docs/books/tutorial/sound/example-1dot2/AppletSoundApplet.html*

```
<HTML>
<HEAD>
<TITLE> SoundApplet<BODY>
<APPLET CODE="SoundApplet.class" WIDTH = 500 HEIGHT = 200>
</APPLET>
</BODY>
</HTML>
```

EXAMPLE: Sound Application

Where Explained: *Playing Sounds from an Application* (page 225)

SoundApplication.java

SOURCE CODE: *http://java.sun.com/docs/books/tutorial/sound/example-1dot2/SoundApplication.java*

```
import java.applet.AudioClip;
import javax.swing.*;
import java.awt.*;
import java.awt.event.*;
import java.net.URL;
import java.net.MalformedURLException;
import java.awt.GridBagLayout;

public class SoundApplication extends JPanel
                              implements ActionListener,
                                         ItemListener {
    SoundList soundList;
    String auFile = "spacemusic.au";
    String aiffFile = "flute+hrn+mrmba.aif";
    String midiFile = "trippygaia1.mid";
    String rmfFile = "jungle.rmf";
    String wavFile = "bottle-open.wav";
    String chosenFile;

    AudioClip onceClip, loopClip;
    URL codeBase;

    JComboBox formats;
    JButton playButton, loopButton, stopButton;
    JLabel status;

    boolean looping = false;

    public SoundApplication() {
        String [] fileTypes = {auFile,
                               aiffFile,
                               midiFile,
                               rmfFile,
                               wavFile};
        formats = new JComboBox(fileTypes);
        formats.setSelectedIndex(0);
        chosenFile = (String)formats.getSelectedItem();
        formats.addItemListener(this);

        playButton = new JButton("Play");
        playButton.addActionListener(this);
```

```
        loopButton = new JButton("Loop");
        loopButton.addActionListener(this);

        stopButton = new JButton("Stop");
        stopButton.addActionListener(this);
        stopButton.setEnabled(false);

        status = new JLabel("Click Play or Loop to " +
                            "play the selected sound file.");

        JPanel controlPanel = new JPanel();
        controlPanel.add(formats);
        controlPanel.add(playButton);
        controlPanel.add(loopButton);
        controlPanel.add(stopButton);

        JPanel statusPanel = new JPanel();
        statusPanel.add(status);

        add(controlPanel);
        add(statusPanel);

        startLoadingSounds();
    }

    public void itemStateChanged(ItemEvent e){
        chosenFile = (String)formats.getSelectedItem();
        soundList.startLoading(chosenFile);
    }

    void startLoadingSounds() {
        //Start asynchronous sound loading.
        try {
            codeBase = new URL("file:" +
                        System.getProperty("user.dir") + "/");
        } catch (MalformedURLException e) {
            System.err.println(e.getMessage());
        }
        soundList = new SoundList(codeBase);
        soundList.startLoading(auFile);
        soundList.startLoading(aiffFile);
        soundList.startLoading(midiFile);
        soundList.startLoading(rmfFile);
        soundList.startLoading(wavFile);
    }

    public void stop() {
        onceClip.stop();      //Cut short the one-time sound.
```

```
        if (looping) {
            loopClip.stop();    //Stop the sound loop.
        }
    }

    public void start() {
        if (looping) {
            loopClip.loop();    //Restart the sound loop.
        }
    }

    public void actionPerformed(ActionEvent event) {
        //PLAY BUTTON
        Object source = event.getSource();
        if (source == playButton) {
            //Try to get the AudioClip.
            onceClip = soundList.getClip(chosenFile);
            stopButton.setEnabled(true);
            onceClip.play();     //Play it once.
            status.setText("Playing sound " +
                           chosenFile + ".");
            if (onceClip == null) {
                status.setText("Sound " + chosenFile +
                               " not loaded yet.");
            }
            return;
        }

        //START LOOP BUTTON
        if (source == loopButton) {
            loopClip = soundList.getClip(chosenFile);

            looping = true;
            loopClip.loop();     //Start the sound loop.
            loopButton.setEnabled(false); //Disable start
                                          //button.
            stopButton.setEnabled(true);
            status.setText("Playing sound " + chosenFile +
                           " continuously.");
            if (loopClip == null) {
                status.setText("Sound " + chosenFile +
                               " not loaded yet.");
            }
            return;
        }

        //STOP LOOP BUTTON
        if (source == stopButton) {
            if (looping) {
```

```
                looping = false;
                loopClip.stop();    //Stop the sound loop.
                //Enable start button.
                loopButton.setEnabled(true);
             } else if (onceClip != null) {
                onceClip.stop();
            }
            stopButton.setEnabled(false);
            status.setText("Stopped playing " + chosenFile +
                           ".");
            return;
        }
    }

    public static void main(String s[]) {
        WindowListener l = new WindowAdapter() {
            public void windowClosing(WindowEvent e)
                                        {System.exit(0);}
        };
        JFrame f = new JFrame("SoundApplication");
        f.addWindowListener(l);
        f.getContentPane().add(new SoundApplication());
        f.setSize(new Dimension(400,100));
        f.show();
    }
}
```

SoundList.java

SOURCE CODE: *http://java.sun.com/docs/books/tutorial/sound/example-1dot2/SoundList.java*

```
import java.applet.AudioClip;
import javax.swing.*;
import java.net.URL;

/**
 * Loads and holds a bunch of audio files whose locations are
 * specified relative to a fixed base URL.
 */
public class SoundList extends java.util.Hashtable {
    JApplet applet;
    URL baseURL;

    public SoundList(URL baseURL) {
        super(5); //Initialize Hashtable with capacity of 5
                  // entries.
        this.baseURL = baseURL;
    }
```

```
    public void startLoading(String relativeURL) {
        new SoundLoader(this, baseURL, relativeURL);
    }

    public AudioClip getClip(String relativeURL) {
        return (AudioClip)get(relativeURL);
    }

    public void putClip(AudioClip clip, String relativeURL) {
        put(relativeURL, clip);
    }
}
```

SoundLoader.java

SOURCE CODE: *http://java.sun.com/docs/books/tutorial/sound/example-1dot2/SoundLoader.java*

```
import java.applet.*;
import javax.swing.*;
import java.net.URL;
import java.net.MalformedURLException;

public class SoundLoader extends Thread {
    SoundList soundList;
    URL completeURL;
    String relativeURL;

    public SoundLoader(SoundList soundList,
                       URL baseURL, String relativeURL) {
        this.soundList = soundList;
        try {
            completeURL = new URL(baseURL, relativeURL);
        } catch (MalformedURLException e){
            System.err.println(e.getMessage());
        }
        this.relativeURL = relativeURL;
        setPriority(MIN_PRIORITY);
        start();
    }

    public void run() {
        AudioClip audioClip =
                 Applet.newAudioClip(completeURL);
        soundList.putClip(audioClip, relativeURL);
    }
}
```

JDBC Database Access

LESSON 26: JDBC Basics

EXAMPLE: Sample Code 1 and 2

Sample Code 1 is `CreateCoffees.java`, and Sample Code 2 is `InsertCoffees.java`. After you have created the table `COFFEES` with Sample Code 1, you can use Sample Code 2 to populate it with values.

Where Explained:
Setting Up Tables (page 298)

You create the table `COFFEES` by simply running the application `CreateCoffees.java`, (the first sample code below), following the steps previously described in Running the Sample Applications (page 327). `CreateCoffees.java` uses standard SQL data types and will work for most DBMSs.

It is possible that your DBMS uses nonstandard names for data types or that it uses its own types that are specific to it. Because of this possibility, we have provided an application, called `SQLTypesCreate.java`, that will discover the local type names for you and then use them to create your table. This application is included in the code samples you can download.

Before running `SQLTypesCreate.java`, you will need to modify it by substituting the appropriate URL, login name, password, and driver class name, as is true with all of the sample code. Then, on Solaris and Win32 platforms, run the application by typing the following two lines at the command line:

```
javac SQLTypesCreate.java
java SQLTypesCreate
```

The application will prompt you for the table name, column names, and column types. You just type the following after the appropriate prompts:

```
COFFEES
COF_NAME
VARCHAR
32
SUP_ID
INTEGER
PRICE
FLOAT
SALES
INTEGER
TOTAL
INTEGER
```

The output from `SQLTypesCreate` is printed after the application. This output shows what you will see on the screen when you run the application, and it also includes the responses you need to type (the responses just listed) in order to create the table we use in later applications.

After you have created the table `COFFEES`, you are ready to run `InsertCoffees.java`, which inserts values into `COFFEES`, sends a `select` statement, retrieves the results of the query, and prints out the results. If you ran `CreateCoffees.java` and got no results after running `InsertCoffees.java`, your DBMS probably did not create the table `COFFEES`. Try creating the table again by running `SQLTypesCreate.java` and then run `InsertCoffees.java` again.

CreateCoffees.java

```
import java.sql.*;

public class CreateCoffees {

public static void main(String args[]) {

    String url = "jdbc:mySubprotocol:myDataSource";
    Connection con;
    String createString;
    createString = "create table COFFEES " +
                   "(COF_NAME VARCHAR(32), " +
                   "SUP_ID INTEGER, " +
                   "PRICE FLOAT, " +
                   "SALES INTEGER, " +
                   "TOTAL INTEGER)";
```

```
        Statement stmt;

        try {
            Class.forName("myDriver.ClassName");

        } catch(java.lang.ClassNotFoundException e) {
            System.err.print("ClassNotFoundException: ");
            System.err.println(e.getMessage());
        }

        try {
            con = DriverManager.getConnection(url, "myLogin",
                                              "myPassword");

            stmt = con.createStatement();
            stmt.executeUpdate(createString);

            stmt.close();
            con.close();

        } catch(SQLException ex) {
            System.err.println("SQLException: " +
    ex.getMessage());
        }
    }
    }
```

InsertCoffees.java

```
    import java.sql.*;

    public class InsertCoffees {

    public static void main(String[] args) {

        String url = "jdbc:mySubprotocol:myDataSource";
        Connection con;
        Statement stmt;
        String query = "select COF_NAME, PRICE from COFFEES";

        try {
            Class.forName("myDriver.ClassName");

        } catch(java.lang.ClassNotFoundException e) {
            System.err.print("ClassNotFoundException: ");
            System.err.println(e.getMessage());
        }
```

```
    try {
        con = DriverManager.getConnection(url, "myLogin",
                                         "myPassword");

        stmt = con.createStatement();

        stmt.executeUpdate("insert into COFFEES " +
            "values('Colombian', 101, 7.99, 0, 0)");

        stmt.executeUpdate("insert into COFFEES " +
            "values('French_Roast', 49, 8.99, 0, 0)");

        stmt.executeUpdate("insert into COFFEES " +
            "values('Espresso', 150, 9.99, 0, 0)");

        stmt.executeUpdate("insert into COFFEES " +
             "values('Colombian_Decaf', 101, 8.99, 0, 0)");

        stmt.executeUpdate("insert into COFFEES " +
            "values('French_Roast_Decaf', 49, 9.99, 0, 0)");

        ResultSet rs = stmt.executeQuery(query);

        System.out.println("Coffee Break Coffees and Prices:");
        while (rs.next()) {
            String s = rs.getString("COF_NAME");
            float f = rs.getFloat("PRICE");
            System.out.println(s + "    " + f);
        }

        stmt.close();
        con.close();

    } catch(SQLException ex) {
        System.err.println("SQLException: " +
ex.getMessage());
    }
}
}
```

The printout for `InsertCoffees.java` looks like this:

```
➡Coffee Break Coffees and Prices:
➡Colombian   7.99
➡French_Roast   8.99
➡Espresso   9.99
➡Colombian_Decaf   8.99
➡French_Roast_Decaf   9.99
```

EXAMPLE: Sample Code 3 and 4

Sample Code 3 is `CreateSuppliers.java`, and Sample Code 4 is `InsertSuppliers.java`. These applications are similar to Sample Code 1 and 2 except that `CreateSuppliers.java` creates the table `SUPPLIERS`, and `InsertSuppliers.java` populates the table `SUPPLIERS`.

Where Explained:
Setting Up Tables (page 298)

If you needed to use the generic application `SQLTypesCreate` to create the table `COFFEES`, you will also need to use it to create the table `SUPPLIERS`. Follow the same directions, using the following responses:

```
SUPPLIERS
SUP_NAME
VARCHAR
40
STREET
VARCHAR
40
CITY
VARCHAR
20
STATE
CHAR
2
ZIP
CHAR
5
```

CreateSuppliers.java

```
import java.sql.*;

public class CreateSuppliers {

public static void main(String[] args) {

    String url = "jdbc:mySubprotocol:myDataSource";
    Connection con;
    String createString;
    createString = "create table SUPPLIERS " +
                   "(SUP_ID INTEGER, " +
                   "SUP_NAME VARCHAR(40), " +
                   "STREET VARCHAR(40), " +
                   "CITY VARCHAR(20), " +
                   "STATE CHAR(2), ZIP CHAR(5))";

    Statement stmt;
    try {
        Class.forName("myDriver.ClassName");
```

```
    } catch(java.lang.ClassNotFoundException e) {
        System.err.print("ClassNotFoundException: ");
        System.err.println(e.getMessage());
    }

    try {
        con = DriverManager.getConnection(url, "myLogin",
                                          "myPassword");
        stmt = con.createStatement();
        stmt.executeUpdate(createString);

        stmt.close();
        con.close();

    } catch(SQLException ex) {
        System.err.println("SQLException: " +
ex.getMessage());
    }
}
}
```

The following code, found in the file `InsertSuppliers.java`, inserts values into the table `SUPPLIERS`, queries for the name and supplier identification number for each of the suppliers, and prints out the results.

```
import java.sql.*;

public class InsertSuppliers {

public static void main(String[] args) {

    String url = "jdbc:mySubprotocol:myDataSource";
    Connection con;
    Statement stmt;
    String query = "select SUP_NAME, SUP_ID from SUPPLIERS";

    try {
        Class.forName("myDriver.ClassName");

    } catch(java.lang.ClassNotFoundException e) {
        System.err.print("ClassNotFoundException: ");
        System.err.println(e.getMessage());
    }

    try {
        con = DriverManager.getConnection(url, "myLogin",
                                          "myPassword");

        stmt = con.createStatement();
```

```
        stmt.executeUpdate("insert into SUPPLIERS " +
            "values(49, 'Superior Coffee', '1 Party Place', " +
            "'Mendocino', 'CA', '95460')");

        stmt.executeUpdate("insert into SUPPLIERS " +
            "values(101, 'Acme, Inc.', '99 Market Street', " +
            "'Groundsville', 'CA', '95199')");

        stmt.executeUpdate("insert into SUPPLIERS " +
            "values(150, 'The High Ground', " +
            "'100 Coffee Lane', 'Meadows', 'CA', '93966')");

        ResultSet rs = stmt.executeQuery(query);

        System.out.println("Suppliers and their ID Numbers:");
        while (rs.next()) {
            String s = rs.getString("SUP_NAME");
            int n = rs.getInt("SUP_ID");
            System.out.println(s + "   " + n);
        }

        stmt.close();
        con.close();

    } catch(SQLException ex) {
        System.err.println("SQLException: " + ex.getMessage());
    }
}
}
```

The printout for `InsertSuppliers.java` follows:

```
➥Suppliers and their ID Numbers:
➥Superior Coffee   49
➥Acme, Inc.   101
➥The High Ground   150
```

EXAMPLE: Sample Code 5

Where Explained: *Using Joins* (page 315)

Sample Code 5 is the file `Join.java`. This application does a simple join between the tables `COFFEES` and `SUPPLIERS`. It should look familiar because it incorporates an example used previously into a runnable program.

Join.java

```
import java.sql.*;

public class Join {
```

```
public static void main(String[] args) {

    String url = "jdbc:mySubprotocol:myDataSource";
    Connection con;
    String query = "select SUPPLIERS.SUP_NAME, " +
                   "COFFEES.COF_NAME from COFFEES, " +
                   "SUPPLIERS where SUPPLIERS.SUP_NAME" +
                    "like 'Acme, Inc.' and " +
                    "SUPPLIERS.SUP_ID = COFFEES.SUP_ID";
    Statement stmt;

    try {
        Class.forName("myDriver.ClassName");

    } catch(java.lang.ClassNotFoundException e) {
        System.err.print("ClassNotFoundException: ");
        System.err.println(e.getMessage());
    }

    try {
        con = DriverManager.getConnection (url, "myLogin",
                                                "myPassword");

        stmt = con.createStatement();

        ResultSet rs = stmt.executeQuery(query);
        System.out.println("Supplier, Coffee:");
        while (rs.next()) {
            String supName = rs.getString(1);
            String cofName = rs.getString(2);
            System.out.println("    " + supName + ", " +
                               cofName);
        }

        stmt.close();
        con.close();

    } catch(SQLException ex) {
        System.err.print("SQLException: ");
        System.err.println(ex.getMessage());
    }
}
}
```

The output of `Join.java` looks like this:

```
➥Supplier, Coffee:
➥    Acme, Inc., Colombian
➥    Acme, Inc., Colombian_Decaf
```

EXAMPLE: Sample Code 6

Where Explained:
Using Transactions (page 316)

Sample Code 6 is the file `TransactionPairs.java`. This application uses two `PreparedStatement` objects, one to update the `SALES` column and one to update the `TOTAL` column. The values for the input parameters are set using a `for` loop that iterates through an array. Refer back to Using a Loop to Set Values (page 313) for a more thorough explanation.

In `TransactionPairs.java` there are five transactions, each occurring in one iteration through the `for` loop. In each iteration, the values for the input parameters are set, the two prepared statements are executed, and the method `commit` is called. Thus, each iteration constitutes a transaction, ensuring that neither *updateTotal* nor *updateSales* will be committed unless the other is committed.

This code invokes the method `con.rollback` in a `catch` block, which is explained in the section When to Call the Method rollback (page 319). Because of that, we initialized the `Connection` object *con* to `null`. Then in the `catch` block, we tested to see if *con* is still `null`. If it is, a connection was never even established, and the exception being caught is a result of that failure. In other words, *con* was not assigned a value in the following statement: `con = DriverManager.getConnection(url, "myLogin", "myPassword")`. Consequently, it is not necessary to call the method `rollback` because nothing was committed. If *con* had not originally been set to `null`, the Java compiler would have complained that *con* might not have been initialized.

TransactionPairs.java

```
import java.sql.*;

public class TransactionPairs {

public static void main(String[] args) {

    String url = "jdbc:mySubprotocol:myDataSource";
    Connection con = null;
    Statement stmt;
    PreparedStatement updateSales;
    PreparedStatement updateTotal;
    String updateString = "update COFFEES " +
                      "set SALES = ? where COF_NAME like ?";
    String updateStatement = "update COFFEES " +
            "set TOTAL = TOTAL + ? where COF_NAME like ?";
   String query = "select COF_NAME, SALES, TOTAL from COFFEES";

    try {
        Class.forName("myDriver.ClassName");
```

```
} catch(java.lang.ClassNotFoundException e) {
    System.err.print("ClassNotFoundException: ");
    System.err.println(e.getMessage());
}

try {
    con = DriverManager.getConnection(url, "myLogin",
                                      "myPassword");
    updateSales = con.prepareStatement(updateString);
    updateTotal = con.prepareStatement(updateStatement);
    int [] salesForWeek = {175, 150, 60, 155, 90};
    String [] coffees = {"Colombian", "French_Roast",
                         "Espresso", "Colombian_Decaf",
                         "French_Roast_Decaf"};
    int len = coffees.length;
    con.setAutoCommit(false);
    for (int i = 0; i < len; i++) {
        updateSales.setInt(1, salesForWeek[i]);
        updateSales.setString(2, coffees[i]);
        updateSales.executeUpdate();

        updateTotal.setInt(1, salesForWeek[i]);
        updateTotal.setString(2, coffees[i]);
        updateTotal.executeUpdate();
        con.commit();
    }

    con.setAutoCommit(true);

    updateSales.close();
    updateTotal.close();

    stmt = con.createStatement();
    ResultSet rs = stmt.executeQuery(query);

    while (rs.next()) {
        String c = rs.getString("COF_NAME");
        int s = rs.getInt("SALES");
        int t = rs.getInt("TOTAL");
        System.out.println(c + "     " +  s + "    " + t);
    }

    stmt.close();
    con.close();

} catch(SQLException ex) {
    System.err.println("SQLException: " + ex.getMessage());
    if (con != null) {
```

```
                try {
                    System.err.print("Transaction is being ");
                    System.err.println("rolled back");
                    con.rollback();
                } catch(SQLException excep) {
                     System.err.print("SQLException: ");
                     System.err.println(excep.getMessage());
                }
            }
        }
    }
```

When the initial values for SALES and TOTAL are 0, the output looks like this:

```
➥Colombian     175     175
➥French_Roast     150     150
➥Espresso     60     60
➥Colombian_Decaf     155     155
➥French_Roast_Decaf     90     90
```

If you were to run TransactionPairs a second time, the printout would be:

```
➥Colombian     175     350
➥French_Roast     150     300
➥Espresso     60     120
➥Colombian_Decaf     155     310
➥French_Roast_Decaf     90     180
```

EXAMPLE: Sample Code 7 and 8

Sample Code 7 is OutputApplet.java, and Sample Code 8 is OutputApplet.html. The sample code in this section is a demonstration JDBC applet. It displays some simple standard output from the table COFFEES.

Where Explained:
Creating an Applet from an Application (page 328)

The contents of OutputApplet.java are printed first, and the contents of the file OutputApplet.html follow.

OutputApplet.java

```
import java.applet.Applet;
import java.awt.Graphics;
import java.util.Vector;
import java.sql.*;

public class OutputApplet extends Applet implements Runnable {
    private Thread worker;
    private Vector queryResults;
```

```
private String message = "Initializing";
public synchronized void start() {
    // Every time "start" is called, we create a worker
    // thread to re-evaluate the database query.
    if (worker == null) {
        message = "Connecting to database";
        worker = new Thread(this);
        worker.start();
    }
}

public void run() {
    String url = "jdbc:mySubprotocol:myDataSource";
    String query = "select COF_NAME, PRICE from COFFEES";

    try {
        Class.forName("myDriver.ClassName");
    } catch(Exception ex) {
        setError("Can't find Database driver class: " + ex);
        return;
    }

    try {
        Vector results = new Vector();
        Connection con = DriverManager.getConnection(url,
                                    "myLogin", "myPassword");
        Statement stmt = con.createStatement();
        ResultSet rs = stmt.executeQuery(query);
        while (rs.next()) {
            String s = rs.getString("COF_NAME");
        float f = rs.getFloat("PRICE");
            String text = s + "     " + f;
            results.addElement(text);
        }

        stmt.close();
        con.close();

        setResults(results);

    } catch(SQLException ex) {
        setError("SQLException: " + ex);
    }
}

public synchronized void paint(Graphics g) {
    // If there are no results available, display the
    // current message.
```

```
        if (queryResults == null) {
            g.drawString(message, 5, 50);
            return;
        }

        // Display the results.
        g.drawString("Prices of coffee per pound:  ", 5, 10);
        int y = 30;
        java.util.Enumeration enum = queryResults.elements();
        while (enum.hasMoreElements()) {
            String text = (String)enum.nextElement();
            g.drawString(text, 5, y);
            y = y + 15;
        }
    }

    private synchronized void setError(String mess) {
        queryResults = null;
        message = mess;
        worker = null;
        // And ask AWT to repaint this applet.
        repaint();
    }

    private synchronized void setResults(Vector results) {
        queryResults = results;
        worker = null;
        // And ask AWT to repaint this applet.
        repaint();
    }
}
```

What follows is the `html` file that places our applet on the HTML page.

```
<HTML>
<HEAD>
      <TITLE> Query Output </TITLE>
</HEAD>
<BODY>
<CENTER>
Output from query select NAME, PRICE from COFFEES
<BR>
<APPLET CODEBASE=. CODE="OutputApplet.class" WIDTH=350
HEIGHT=200>
</CENTER>
</APPLET>
</BODY>
</HTML>
```

LESSON 27: New Features in the JDBC 2.0 API

EXAMPLE: Sample Code for Batch Update

Where Explained: *Making Batch Updates* (page 348)

The following code puts together the code fragments from previous sections to make a complete program. One thing you might notice is that there are two `catch` blocks at the end of the application. If there is a `BatchUpdateException` object, the first `catch` block will catch it. The second one will catch an `SQLException` object that is not a `BatchUpdateException` object.

Note that this code compiles, but as of this writing, there are no JDBC 2.0 drivers with which to test it.

BatchUpdate.java

```
import java.sql.*;

public class BatchUpdate {

    public static void main(String[] args) {

        String url = "jdbc:mySubprotocol:myDataSource";
        Connection con;
        Statement stmt;
        try {
            Class.forName("myDriver.ClassName");

        } catch(java.lang.ClassNotFoundException e) {
            System.err.print("ClassNotFoundException: ");
            System.err.println(e.getMessage());
        }

        try {
            con = DriverManager.getConnection(url,
                                     "myLogin", "myPassword");

            stmt = con.createStatement(
                             ResultSet.TYPE_SCROLL_SENSITIVE,
                             ResultSet.CONCUR_UPDATABLE);

            con.setAutoCommit(false);

            stmt.addBatch("INSERT INTO COFFEES" +
                "VALUES('Amaretto', 49, 9.99, 0, 0)");
            stmt.addBatch("INSERT INTO COFFEES" +
                "VALUES('Hazelnut', 49, 9.99, 0, 0)");
            stmt.addBatch("INSERT INTO COFFEES" +
                "VALUES('Amaretto_decaf', 49, 10.99, 0, 0)");
```

```
            stmt.addBatch("INSERT INTO COFFEES" +
                "VALUES('Hazelnut_decaf', 49, 10.99, 0, 0)");
            int [] updateCounts = stmt.executeBatch();
            ResultSet uprs = stmt.executeQuery("SELECT * " +
                                            "FROM COFFEES");
            System.out.println("Table COFFEES after " +
                                "insertion:");
            while (uprs.next()) {
                String name = uprs.getString("COF_NAME");
                int id = uprs.getInt("SUP_ID");
                float price = uprs.getFloat("PRICE");
                int sales = uprs.getInt("SALES");
                int total = uprs.getInt("TOTAL");
                System.out.print(name + "   " + id + "   " +
                                price);
                System.out.println("   " + sales + "   " +
                                total);
            }

            uprs.close();
            stmt.close();
            con.close();

        } catch(BatchUpdateException b) {
            System.err.println("SQLException: " +
                                b.getMessage());
            System.err.println("SQLState: " +
                                b.getSQLState());
            System.err.println("Message:  " + b.getMessage());
            System.err.println("Vendor:  " +
                                b.getErrorCode());
            System.err.print("Update counts:  ");
            int [] updateCounts = b.getUpdateCounts();
            for (int i = 0; i < updateCounts.length; i++) {
                System.err.print(updateCounts[i] + "   ");
            }

        } catch(SQLException ex) {
            System.err.println("SQLException: " +
                                ex.getMessage());
            System.err.println("SQLState:  " +
                                ex.getSQLState());
            System.err.println("Message:  " +
                                ex.getMessage());
            System.err.println("Vendor: " +
                                ex.getErrorCode());
        }
    }
}
```

RMI

LESSON 29: Writing an RMI Server

EXAMPLE: Compute.java

Where Explained:
Designing a Remote Interface (page 367)

Compute.java

SOURCE CODE: *http://java.sun.com/docs/books/tutorial/rmi/example-1dot2/compute/Compute.java*

```
package compute;

import java.rmi.Remote;
import java.rmi.RemoteException;

public interface Compute extends Remote {
    Object executeTask(Task t) throws RemoteException;
}
```

Task.java

SOURCE CODE: *http://java.sun.com/docs/books/tutorial/rmi/example-1dot2/compute/Task.java*

```
package compute;

import java.io.Serializable;

public interface Task extends Serializable {
    Object execute();
}
```

EXAMPLE: Compute Engine

Where Explained:
Implementing a Remote Interface (page 369)

ComputeEngine.java

SOURCE CODE: *http://java.sun.com/docs/books/tutorial/rmi/example-1dot2/engine/ComputeEngine.java*

```
package engine;

import java.rmi.*;
import java.rmi.server.*;
import compute.*;

public class ComputeEngine extends UnicastRemoteObject
                           implements Compute
{
    public ComputeEngine() throws RemoteException {
        super();
    }

    public Object executeTask(Task t) {
        return t.execute();
    }

    public static void main(String[] args) {


        if (System.getSecurityManager() == null) {
            System.setSecurityManager(
                      new RMISecurityManager());
        }

        String name = "//localhost/Compute";

        try {
            Compute engine = new ComputeEngine();
            Naming.rebind(name, engine);
            System.out.println("ComputeEngine bound");
        } catch (Exception e) {
            System.err.println("ComputeEngine exception: " +
                                   e.getMessage());
            e.printStackTrace();
        }
    }
}
```

LESSON 30: Creating a Client Program

EXAMPLE: Compute Pi

Where Explained: *Creating a Client Program* (page 379)

ComputePi.java

SOURCE CODE: *http://java.sun.com/docs/books/tutorial/rmi/example-1dot2/client/ComputePi.java*

```
package client;

import java.rmi.*;
import java.math.*;
import compute.*;

public class ComputePi {
    public static void main(String[] args) {
        if (System.getSecurityManager() == null) {
            System.setSecurityManager(new
RMISecurityManager());
        }
        try {
            String name = "//" + args[0] + "/Compute";
            Compute comp = (Compute) Naming.lookup(name);
            Pi task = new Pi(Integer.parseInt(args[1]));
            BigDecimal pi = (BigDecimal)
                            (comp.executeTask(task));
            System.out.println(pi);
        } catch (Exception e) {
            System.err.println("ComputePi exception: " +
                               e.getMessage());
            e.printStackTrace();
        }
    }
}
```

Pi.java

SOURCE CODE: *http://java.sun.com/docs/books/tutorial/rmi/example-1dot2/client/Pi.java*

```
package client;

import compute.*;
import java.math.*;

public class Pi implements Task {

    /** constants used in pi computation */
```

```
private static final BigDecimal ZERO =
    BigDecimal.valueOf(0);
private static final BigDecimal ONE =
    BigDecimal.valueOf(1);
private static final BigDecimal FOUR =
    BigDecimal.valueOf(4);

/** rounding mode to use during pi computation */
private static final int roundingMode =
    BigDecimal.ROUND_HALF_EVEN;

/** digits of precision after the decimal point */
private int digits;

/**
 * Construct a task to calculate pi to the specified
 * precision.
 */
public Pi(int digits) {
    this.digits = digits;
}

/**
 * Calculate pi.
 */
public Object execute() {
    return computePi(digits);
}

/**
 * Compute the value of pi to the specified number of
 * digits after the decimal point.  The value is
 * computed using Machin's formula:
 *
 *          pi/4 = 4*arctan(1/5) - arctan(1/239)
 *
 * and a power series expansion of arctan(x) to
 * sufficient precision.
 */
public static BigDecimal computePi(int digits) {
    int scale = digits + 5;
    BigDecimal arctan1_5 = arctan(5, scale);
    BigDecimal arctan1_239 = arctan(239, scale);
    BigDecimal pi = arctan1_5.multiply(FOUR).subtract(
                             arctan1_239).multiply(FOUR);
    return pi.setScale(digits, BigDecimal.ROUND_HALF_UP);
}
/**
 * Compute the value, in radians, of the arctangent of the
```

```
     * inverse of the supplied integer to the speficied number
     * of digits after the decimal. The value is computed
     * using the power series expansion for the arctangent:
     *
     * arctan(x) = x - (x^3)/3 + (x^5)/5 - (x^7)/7 +
     *     (x^9)/9 ...
     */

    public static BigDecimal arctan(int inverseX, int scale)
    {
        BigDecimal result, numer, term;
        BigDecimal invX = BigDecimal.valueOf(inverseX);
        BigDecimal invX2 =
               BigDecimal.valueOf(inverseX * inverseX);

        numer = ONE.divide(invX, scale, roundingMode);

        result = numer;
        int i = 1;
        do {
            numer = numer.divide(invX2, scale, roundingMode);
            int denom = 2 * i + 1;
            term = numer.divide(BigDecimal.valueOf(denom),
                                scale, roundingMode);
            if ((i % 2) != 0) {
                result = result.subtract(term);
            } else {
                result = result.add(term);
            }
            i++;
        } while (term.compareTo(ZERO) != 0);
        return result;
    }
}
```

LESSON 31: Compiling and Running the Example

EXAMPLE: General Policy File

java.policy

SOURCE CODE: *http://java.sun.com/docs/books/tutorial/rmi/example-1dot2/java.policy*

Where Explained:
A Note about Security (page 390)

```
grant {
```

```
        permission java.net.SocketPermission "*:1024-65535",
            "connect,accept";
        permission java.net.SocketPermission "*:80", "connect";
};
```

java.policy 2

SOURCE CODE: *http://java.sun.com/docs/books/tutorial/rmi/example-1dot2/java.policy2*

```
grant {
        permission java.net.SocketPermission "*:1024-65535",
            "connect,accept";
        permission java.io.FilePermission
            "c:\\home\\ann\\public_html\\classes\\-", "read";
        permission java.io.FilePermission
            "c:\\home\\jones\\public_html\\classes\\-", "read";
};
```

IDL

LESSON 33: The Hello Client/Server Example

EXAMPLE: Hello.idl

Hello.idl

SOURCE CODE: *http://java.sun.com/docs/books/tutorial/idl/hello/example-1dot2/Hello.idl*

Where Explained: *Writing Hello.idl* (page 405)

```
module HelloApp {
    interface Hello {
        string sayHello();
    };
};
```

EXAMPLE: HelloClient dl

HelloClient.java

SOURCE CODE: *http://java.sun.com/docs/books/tutorial/idl/hello/example-1dot2/HelloClient.java*

Where Explained: *Developing a Client Application* (page 408)

```
import HelloApp.*;           // Package containing our stubs.
import org.omg.CosNaming.*; // HelloClient will use the naming
                             // service.
import org.omg.CORBA.*;      // All CORBA applications need
                             // these classes.

public class HelloClient {

    public static void main(String[] args) {
```

```
            try {
                // Create and initialize the ORB
                ORB orb = ORB.init(args, null);

                // Get the root naming context
                org.omg.CORBA.Object objRef =
                    orb.resolve_initial_references("NameService");
                NamingContext ncRef =
                                NamingContextHelper.narrow(objRef);

                // Resolve the object reference in naming
                NameComponent nc = new NameComponent("Hello", "");
                NameComponent path[] = {nc};
                Hello helloRef =
                      HelloHelper.narrow(ncRef.resolve(path));

                // Call the Hello server object and print results
                String Hello = helloRef.sayHello();
                System.out.println(Hello);

            } catch(Exception e) {
                System.out.println("ERROR : " + e);
                e.printStackTrace(System.out);
            }
        }
    }
```

Where Explained:
Developing a Client Application (page 408)

EXAMPLE: Applet Version of the HelloClient

HelloApplet.java

SOURCE CODE: *http://java.sun.com/docs/books/tutorial/idl/hello/example-1dot2/HelloApplet.java*

```
// The package containing our stubs.
import HelloApp.*;

// HelloClient will use the naming service.
import org.omg.CosNaming.*;

// The package containing special exceptions thrown
// by the name service.
import org.omg.CosNaming.NamingContextPackage.*;

// All CORBA applications need these classes.
import org.omg.CORBA.*;

// Needed for the applet.
import java.awt.Graphics;
```

```
    public class HelloApplet extends java.applet.Applet {
        String message = "";

        public void init() {

            try{

            // Create and initialize the ORB
            ORB orb = ORB.init(this, null);

            // Get the root naming context
            org.omg.CORBA.Object objRef =
                    orb.resolve_initial_references("NameService");
            NamingContext ncRef =
                  NamingContextHelper.narrow(objRef);

            // Resolve the object reference in naming
            NameComponent nc = new NameComponent("Hello", "");
            NameComponent path[] = {nc};
            Hello helloRef =
                  HelloHelper.narrow(ncRef.resolve(path));

            // Call the Hello server object and print the results
            message = helloRef.sayHello();

            } catch(Exception e) {
                System.out.println("HelloApplet exception: " + e);
                e.printStackTrace(System.out);
            }
        }

        public void paint(Graphics g) {
            g.drawString(message, 25, 50);
        }
    }
}
```

Tutorial.html

SOURCE CODE: *http://java.sun.com/docs/books/tutorial/idl/*

```
    <HTML>
    <!--Copyright 1997, Sun Microsystems, Inc. -->
    <HEAD>
       <TITLE>Java IDL Getting Started: Running HelloApplet</
    TITLE>
    <!-- Changed by: vlc, 7/30/97 -->
       <X-SAS-WINDOW TOP=42 BOTTOM=477 LEFT=4 RIGHT=534>
    </HEAD>
    <BODY BGCOLOR="#FFFFFF">
```

```
<H1 ALIGN=CENTER>Running the Hello World Applet</H1>
<HR>
<P>If all goes well, the applet appears below:
<P>
<APPLET CODE=HelloApplet.class

CODEBASE='enter_the_path_to_your_project_directory_here'
        WIDTH=500
        HEIGHT=300>
<PARAM name="org.omg.CORBA.ORBInitialHost"
value=enter_server_machine_name>
<PARAM name="org.omg.CORBA.ORBInitialPort" value=1050>
</APPLET>
</BODY>
</HTML>
```

EXAMPLE: HelloServer

Where Explained: *Developing the "Hello World" Server* (page 413)

HelloServer.java

SOURCE CODE: *http://java.sun.com/docs/books/tutorial/idl/hello/example-1dot2/HelloServer.java*

```
// The package containing our stubs.
import HelloApp.*;

// HelloServer will use the naming service.
import org.omg.CosNaming.*;

// The package containing special exceptions thrown by the
name service.
import org.omg.CosNaming.NamingContextPackage.*;

// All CORBA applications need these classes.
import org.omg.CORBA.*;

public class HelloServer {
    public static void main(String[] args) {
        try{
            // Create and initialize the ORB
            ORB orb = ORB.init(args, null);

            // Create the servant and register it with the ORB
            HelloServant helloRef = new HelloServant();
            orb.connect(helloRef);
            // Get the root naming context
            org.omg.CORBA.Object objRef =
                orb.resolve_initial_references("NameService");
```

```
            NamingContext ncRef =
                 NamingContextHelper.narrow(objRef);

            // Bind the object reference in naming
            NameComponent nc = new NameComponent("Hello", "");
            NameComponent path[] = {nc};
            ncRef.rebind(path, helloRef);

            // Wait for invocations from clients
            java.lang.Object sync = new java.lang.Object();
            synchronized(sync){
                sync.wait();
            }

        } catch(Exception e) {
            System.err.println("ERROR: " + e);
            e.printStackTrace(System.out);
        }
    }
}

class HelloServant extends _HelloImplBase {
    public String sayHello() {
        return "\nHello world!!\n";
    }
}
```

EXAMPLE: Stringified HelloServer and HelloClient

Where Explained:
Using Stringified Object References (page 420)

HelloStringifiedServer.java

SOURCE CODE: *http://java.sun.com/docs/books/tutorial/idl/hello/example-1dot2/HelloStringifiedServer.java*

```
// HelloStringifiedServer.java, stringified object
// reference version

import java.io.*;
import org.omg.CORBA.*;
import HelloApp.*;

class HelloServant extends _HelloImplBase {

    public String sayHello() {
        return "\nHello world !!\n";
    }
}

public class HelloStringifiedServer {
    public static void main(String[] args) {
```

```
        try{
            // create and initialize the ORB
            ORB orb = ORB.init(args, null);

            // create servant and register it with the ORB
            HelloServant helloRef = new HelloServant();
            orb.connect(helloRef);

            // stringify the helloRef and dump it in a file
            String str = orb.object_to_string(helloRef);
            String filename =
                    System.getProperty("user.home") +
                    System.getProperty("file.separator") +
                    "HelloIOR";
            FileOutputStream fos =
                                 new FileOutputStream(filename);
            PrintStream ps = new PrintStream(fos);
            ps.print(str);
            ps.close();

            // wait for invocations from clients
            java.lang.Object sync = new java.lang.Object();
            synchronized (sync) {
            sync.wait();
        }

        } catch (Exception e) {
            System.err.println("ERROR: " + e);
            e.printStackTrace(System.out);
        }
    }
}
```

HelloStringifiedClient.java

SOURCE CODE: *http://java.sun.com/docs/books/tutorial/idl/hello/example-1dot2/HelloStringifiedClient.java*

```
// HelloStringifiedClient.java, stringified object
// reference version

import java.io.*;
import org.omg.CORBA.*;
import HelloApp.*;

public class HelloStringifiedClient {

    public static void main(String[] args) {
        try {
            // create and initialize the ORB
```

```
            ORB orb = ORB.init(args, null);

            // Get the stringified object reference and
            // destringify it.
            String filename =
                   System.getProperty("user.home") +
                   System.getProperty("file.separator") +
                   "HelloIOR";
            FileInputStream fis =
                            new FileInputStream(filename);
            DataInputStream dis = new DataInputStream(fis);
            String ior = dis.readLine();
            org.omg.CORBA.Object obj =
                                orb.string_to_object(ior);
            Hello helloRef = HelloHelper.narrow(obj);

            // call the Hello server object and print results
            String Hello = helloRef.sayHello();
            System.out.println(Hello);

        } catch (Exception e) {
            System.out.println("ERROR : " + e) ;
            e.printStackTrace(System.out);
        }
    }
}
```

Servlets

LESSON 34: Overview of Servlets

EXAMPLE: A Simple Servlet Client

SimpleServlet.java

Where Explained:
A Simple Servlet (page 434)

SOURCE CODE: *http://java.sun.com/docs/books/tutorial/servlets/overview/simple.html*

```
public class SimpleServlet extends HttpServlet {
    // Handle the HTTP GET method by building
    // a simple web page.
    public void doGet (HttpServletRequest request,
                       HttpServletResponse response)
                       throws ServletException, IOException {
        PrintWriter out;
        String title = "Simple Servlet Output";

        // Set content type and other response header
        // fields first
        response.setContentType("text/html");

        //then write the data of the response

        out.println("<HTML><HEAD><TITLE>");
        out.println(title);
        out.println("</TITLE></HEAD><BODY>");
        out.println("<H1>" + title + "</H1>");
        out.println("<P>This is output from SimpleServlet.");
        out.println("</BODY></HTML>");
        out.close();
    }
}
```

EXAMPLE: Duke's Bookstore

Where Explained: *The Sample Servlets* (page 435)

CatalogServlet.java

SOURCE CODE: *http://java.sun.com/docs/books/tutorial/servlets/example-1dot2/CatalogServlet.java*

```
import java.io.*;
import javax.servlet.*;
import javax.servlet.http.*;

import database.*;
import cart.ShoppingCart;

/**
 * This is a simple example of an HTTP Servlet. It responds to
 * the GET and HEAD methods of the HTTP protocol. This servlet
 * calls other servlets.  This catalog calls other servlets.
 */
public class CatalogServlet extends HttpServlet {

    public void doGet (HttpServletRequest request,
                       HttpServletResponse response)
        throws ServletException, IOException {
        // Get the user's session and shopping cart
        HttpSession session = request.getSession(true);
        ShoppingCart cart =

(ShoppingCart)session.getValue(session.getId());

        // If the user has no cart, create a new one
        if (cart == null) {
            cart = new ShoppingCart();
            session.putValue(session.getId(), cart);
        }

        // set content-type header before accessing the Writer
        response.setContentType("text/html");
        PrintWriter out = response.getWriter();

        // then write the data of the response
        out.println("<html>" +
             "<head><title> Book Catalog </title></head>"+
             "<body  bgcolor=\"#ffffff\">" +
             "<center>" +
             "<hr> <br>  " +
             "<h1>" +
             "<font size=\"+3\" color=\"red\">Duke's <font>" +
       "<font size=\"+3\" color=\"purple\">Bookstore</font>" +
```

```
        "</h1>" +
        "</center>" +
        "<br>   <hr> <br>  ");

    //Data on the books are from the database servlet
    BookDBServlet database =
                (BookDBServlet)getServletConfig().
                 getServletContext().getServlet("bookdb");

    //Additions to the shopping cart
    String bookToAdd = request.getParameter("Buy");
    if (bookToAdd != null) {
        BookDetails book =
                database.getBookDetails(bookToAdd);

        cart.add(bookToAdd, book);
        out.println("<p><h3>" +
                    "<font color=\"#ff0000\">" +
                    "You just added <i>"+ book.getTitle() +
                    "</i> "+
                    "to your shopping cart</font></h3>");
    }

    //Give the option of checking cart or checking out
    //if cart not empty
    if (cart.getNumberOfItems() > 0) {
        out.println("<table><tr>" +
                  "<th align=\"left\"><a href=\"" +
                  response.encodeUrl("/servlet/showcart") +
                  "\"> Check Shopping Cart</a></th>" +
                  "<th> </th>" +
                  "<th align=\"right\"><a href=\"" +
                  response.encodeUrl("/servlet/cashier") +
                  "\"> Buy your Books</a></th>" +
                  "</tr></table");
    }

    //Always prompt the user to buy more--get and
    //show the catalog
    out.println("<br>  " +
            "<h3>Please choose from our selections</h3>"+
            "<center> <table>");

    BookDetails[] books =
                  database.getBooksSortedByTitle();
    int numBooks = database.getNumberOfBooks();
```

```
        for(int i=0; i < numBooks; i++) {
            String bookId = books[i].getBookId();

            //Print out info on each book in its own two rows
            out.println("<tr>" +
                    "<td bgcolor=\"#ffffaa\">" +
                    "<a href=\"" +
                    response.encodeUrl("/servlet/" +
                                       "bookdetails?bookId=" +
                                       bookId) +
                     "\"> <strong>" + books[i].getTitle() +
                     "  </strong></a></td>" +
                     "<td bgcolor=\"#ffffaa\" rowspan=2>" +
                     "$" + books[i].getPrice() +
                     "  </td>" +
                     "<td bgcolor=\"#ffffaa\" rowspan=2>" +
                     "<a href=\"" +
                     response.encodeUrl("/servlet/" +
                                  "catalog?Buy=" + bookId) +
                     "\">   Add to Cart  " +
                                   </a><td></tr>" +
                      "<tr>" +
                      "<td bgcolor=\"#ffffff\">" +
                      "    by <em> " +
                      books[i].getFirstName() +
                      " " + books[i].getSurname() +
                      "</em></td></tr>");
        }

        out.println("</table></center></body></html>");
        out.close();
    }

    public String getServletInfo() {
        return "The Catalog servlet adds books to the " +
               "user's shopping cart and prints the catalog.";

    }
}
```

EXAMPLE: Book Detail Servlet

Where Explained: *Backing a ResourceBundle with Properties Files* (page 120)

BookDetailServlet.java

SOURCE CODE: *http://java.sun.com/docs/books/tutorial/servlets/example-1dot2/BookDetailServlet.java*

```
import java.io.*;
import javax.servlet.*;
import javax.servlet.http.*;
```

```
import database.*;
import cart.ShoppingCart;

/**
 * This is a simple example of an HTTP Servlet. It responds to
 * the GET and HEAD methods of the HTTP protocol. This servlet
 * calls other servlets.
 */
public class BookDetailServlet extends HttpServlet {

    public void doGet (HttpServletRequest request,
                       HttpServletResponse response)
        throws ServletException, IOException
    {
        // Get the user's session and shopping cart
        HttpSession session = request.getSession(true);
        ShoppingCart cart =
            (ShoppingCart)session.getValue(session.getId());

        // If the user has no cart, create a new one
        if (cart == null) {
            cart = new ShoppingCart();
            session.putValue(session.getId(), cart);
        }

        // set content-type header before accessing the Writer
        response.setContentType("text/html");
        PrintWriter out = response.getWriter();

        // then write the response
        out.println("<html>" +
            "<head><title>Book Description</title></head>" +
            "<body  bgcolor=\"#FFFFFF\">" +
            "<center>" +
            "<hr> <br>  " +
            "<h1>" +
            "<font size=\"+3\" color=\"red\">Duke's </font>" +
      "<font size=\"+3\" color=\"purple\">Bookstore</font>" +
            "</h1>" +
            "</center>" +
            "<br>   <hr> <br>  ");

        //Get the identifier of the book to display
        String bookId = request.getParameter("bookId");
        if (bookId != null) {

            // and the information about the book
```

```
            BookDBServlet database = (BookDBServlet)
                                  getServletConfig().
                                  getServletContext().
                                  getServlet("bookdb");
            BookDetails bd = database.getBookDetails(bookId);

            //Print out the information obtained
            out.println("<h2>" + bd.getTitle() + "</h2>" +
                "  By <em>" + bd.getFirstName() + ", " +
                bd.getSurname() + "</em>     " +
                "(" + bd.getYear() + ")<br>   <br>" +
                "<h4>Here's what the critics say: </h4>" +
                "<blockquote>" + bd.getDescription() +
                "</blockquote>" +
                "<h4>Our price: $" +bd.getPrice()+"</h4>" +
                "<center>" +
                "<p><a href=\"" +
                response.encodeUrl("/servlet/" +
                                 "catalog?Buy=" + bookId) +
                "\"> Add this item to your " +
                                 "shopping cart.</a></p>" +
                 "</center>");
        }
        out.println("</body></html>");
        out.close();
    }

    public String getServletInfo() {
        return "The BookDetail servlet returns information " +
               "about any book that is available from the " +
               "bookstore.";
    }
}
```

BookDBServlet.java

SOURCE CODE: *http://java.sun.com/docs/books/tutorial/servlets/example-1dot2/database/BookDBServlet.java*

```
package database;

import java.io.*;
import javax.servlet.*;

/**
 * This is a simple example of a Generic Servlet.  Other
 * servlets call its public methods; it does not accept
 * calls from clients.
 */
```

```
public class BookDBServlet extends GenericServlet {

    private BookstoreDB books;

    public void init(ServletConfig config)
                throws ServletException {
        //Store the ServletConfig object and log the
        //initialization
        super.init(config);

        //Load the database to prepare for requests
        books = new BookstoreDB();
    }

    public void destroy() {
        //Allow the database to be garbage collected
        books = null;
    }

    public void service(ServletRequest req,
                        ServletResponse res)
                throws ServletException, IOException {
        throw new UnavailableException(this,
            "This servlet does not accept client requests.");
    }

    public BookDetails getBookDetails(String bookId) {
        return books.getBookDetails(bookId);
    }

    public BookDetails[] getBooksSortedByTitle() {
        return books.getBooksSortedByTitle();
    }

    public int getNumberOfBooks() {
        return books.getNumberOfBooks();
    }

    public String getServletInfo() {
        return "The BookDB servlet manages the bookstore " +
               "database.  It is called by other servlets, " +
               "not directly by a user.";
    }
}
```

ShowCart.java

SOURCE CODE: *http://java.sun.com/docs/books/tutorial/servlets/example-1dot2/ShowCartServlet.java*

```
import java.io.*;
import java.util.*;
import javax.servlet.*;
import javax.servlet.http.*;
import database.*;
import cart.*;

/**
 * An HTTP servlet that displays the contents of a customer's
 * shopping cart at Duke's Bookstore.  It responds to the GET
 * and HEAD methods of the HTTP protocol.  This servlet calls
 * other servlets.
 */
public class ShowCartServlet extends HttpServlet {

    public void doGet (HttpServletRequest request,
                       HttpServletResponse response)
        throws ServletException, IOException
    {
        // Get the user's session and shopping cart
        HttpSession session = request.getSession(true);
        ShoppingCart cart =
              (ShoppingCart)session.getValue(session.getId());

        // If the user has no cart, create a new one
        if (cart == null) {
            cart = new ShoppingCart();
            session.putValue(session.getId(), cart);
        }

        // set content type header before accessing the Writer
        response.setContentType("text/html");
        PrintWriter out = response.getWriter();

        //Print out the response
        out.println("<html>" +
            "<head><title>Your Shopping Cart</title></head>" +
            "<body  bgcolor=\"#ffffff\">" +
            "<center> <hr> <br>  " +
            "<h1>" +
            "<font size=\"+3\" color=\"red\">Duke's </font>" +
       "<font size=\"+3\" color=\"purple\">Bookstore</font>" +
            "</h1>" +
            "</center>" +
            "<br>   <hr> <br>  ");
```

```
/* Handle any pending deletes from shopping cart and
  indicate the outcome as part of the response */

String bookId =request.getParameter("Remove");
if (bookId != null) {
    cart.remove(bookId);

    BookDBServlet database = (
            BookDBServlet)getServletConfig().
            getServletContext().getServlet("bookdb");
    BookDetails book =
                database.getBookDetails(bookId);
    out.println("<font color=\"#ff00000\ +
                "size=\"+2\">" +
                "You just removed: <strong>" +
                book.getTitle() +
                "</strong> <br>   <br>" +
                "</font>");

} else if (request.getParameter("Clear") != null) {
    cart.clear();

    out.println("<font color=\"#ff0000\"
              size=\"+2\"><strong>" +
              "You just cleared your shopping cart!" +
              "</strong> <br>  <br> </font>");
}

// Print a summary of the shopping cart
int num = cart.getNumberOfItems();
if (num > 0) {
    out.println("<font size=\"+2\">" +
             "You have " + num + (num==1 ? " item" :
                                        " items") +
             " in your shopping cart </h2>" +
             "<font>");

    // Return the Shopping Cart Nice and Pretty
    out.println("<table>" +
             "<tr>" +
             "<th align=left>Quantity</TH>" +
             "<th align=left>Title</TH>" +
             "<th align=left>Price</TH>" +
             "</tr>");

    Enumeration e = cart.getItems();
    while (e.hasMoreElements()) {
```

```
        ShoppingCartItem item =
                  (ShoppingCartItem) e.nextElement();
        BookDetails bookDetails =
                  (BookDetails) item.getItem();

        out.println("<tr>" +
                    "<td align=\"right\" +
                    bgcolor=\"#ffffff\">" +
                    item.getQuantity() +
                    "</td>" +
                    "<td bgcolor=\"#ffffaa\">" +
                    "<strong><a href=\"" +
                    response.encodeUrl("/servlet/" +
                            "bookdetails?bookId=" +
                            bookDetails.getBookId()) +
                    "\">" + bookDetails.getTitle() +
                    "</a></strong>" +
                    "</td>" +
                    "<td bgcolor=\"#ffffaa\" +
                    "align=\"right\">" +
                    Cashier.format(
                            bookDetails.getPrice()) +
                    "</td>" +
                    "<td bgcolor=\"#ffffaa\">" +
                    "<strong>" + "<a href=\"" +
                   response.encodeUrl("/servlet/" +
                             "showcart?Remove=" +
                             bookDetails.getBookId()) +
                    "\">Remove Item</a></strong>" +
                    "</td></tr>");
    }

    // Print the total at the bottom of the table
    Cashier cashier = new Cashier(cart);
    out.println("<tr><td colspan=\"5\" +
                bgcolor=\"#ffffff\">" +
                "<br></td></tr>" +
                "<tr>" +
                "<td colspan=\"2\" align=\"right\"" +
                "bgcolor=\"#ffffff\">" +
                "Subtotal:</td>" +
                "<td bgcolor=\"#ffffaa\" +
                align=\"right\">" +
                cashier.format(cashier.getAmount()) +
                "</td>" +
                "</td><td><br></td></tr>" +
                "<tr>" +
                "<td colspan=\"2\" align=\"right\"" +
```

```
                    "bgcolor=\"#ffffff\">" +
                    "CA Sales Tax:</td>" +
                    "<td bgcolor=\"#ffffaa\" align=\" +
                    right\">" +
                    cashier.format(cashier.getTax()) +
                    "</td>" +
                    "</td><td><br></td></tr>" +
                    "<tr>" +
                    "<td colspan=\"2\" align=\"right\"" +
                    "bgcolor=\"ffffff\">" +
                    "<font color=\"ff0000\">" +
                    "<strong>Grand Total:</strong>" +
                    "</font> </td>" +
                    "<td bgcolor=\"ffffaa\" +
                    align=\"right\">" +
                    cashier.format(cashier.getTotal()) +
                    "</td>" +
                    "</td><td><br></td></tr>" +
                    "</table>");

        // Where to go and what to do next
        out.println("<p>   <p><a href=\"" +
             response.encodeUrl("/servlet/catalog") +
             "\">See the Catalog</a>   " +
             "   " +
             "<a href=\"" +
             response.encodeUrl("/servlet/cashier") +
             "\">Check Out</a>      " +
             "<a href=\"" +
             response.encodeUrl("/servlet" +
             "showcart?Clear=clear") +
             "\">Clear Cart</a>");
    } else {

        // Shopping cart is empty!
        out.println("<font size=\"+2\">" + "There is " +
                 "nothing in your shopping cart.</font>" +
                 "<br>   <br>" +
                 "<center><a href=\""+
                 response.encodeUrl("/servlet/catalog") +
                 "\">Back to the Catalog</a> </center>");
    }

    out.println("</body> </html>");
    out.close();
}
```

```
    public String getServletInfo() {
        return "The ShowCart servlet returns information " +
               "about the books that the user is in the " +
                "process of ordering.";
    }
}
```

CashierServlet.java

SOURCE CODE: *http://java.sun.com/docs/books/tutorial/servlets/example-1dot2/CashierServlet.java*

```
import java.io.*;
import javax.servlet.*;
import javax.servlet.http.*;
import cart.*;

/**
 * An HTTP Servlet that responds to the GET and HEAD methods
 * of the HTTP protocol.  It returns a form to the user that
 * gathers data. The form POSTs to another servlet.
 */
public class CashierServlet extends HttpServlet {

    public void doGet (HttpServletRequest request,
                       HttpServletResponse response)
        throws ServletException, IOException {

        // Get the user's session and shopping cart
        HttpSession session = request.getSession(true);
        ShoppingCart cart =
            (ShoppingCart)session.getValue(session.getId());

        // If the user has no cart, create a new one
        if (cart == null) {
            cart = new ShoppingCart();
            session.putValue(session.getId(), cart);
        }

        // set content-type header before accessing Writer
        response.setContentType("text/html");
        PrintWriter out = response.getWriter();

        // then write the data of the response
        out.println("<html>" +
                "<head><title> Cashier </title></head>" +
                "<body  bgcolor=\"#ffffff\">" +
                "<center>" +
                "<hr> <br>  " +
```

```
    "<h1>" +
    "<font size=\"+3\" color=\"red\">Duke's </font>" +
    "<font size=\"+3\" color=\"purple\">Bookstore</font>" +
    "</h1>" +
    "</center>" +
    "<br>   <hr> <br>  ");

     // Determine the total price of the user's books
     Cashier cashier = new Cashier(cart);
     double total = cashier.getTotal();

     // Print out the total and the form for the user
     out.println("<p>Your total purchase amount is: " +
        "<strong>" + cashier.format(total) + "</strong>" +
        "<p>To purchase the items in your shopping cart," +
        "please provide the following information:" +
        "<form action=\"" +
        response.encodeUrl("/servlet/receipt") +
        "\" method=\"post\">" +
        "<table>" +
        "<tr>" +
        "<td><strong>Name:</strong></td>" +
        "<td><input type=\"text\" name=\"cardname\"" +
        "value=\"Gwen Canigetit\" size=\"19\"></td>" +
        "</tr>" +
        "<tr>" +
        "<td><strong>Credit Card Number:</strong></td>" +
        "<td>" +
        "<input type=\"text\" name=\"cardnum\" " +
        "value=\"xxxx xxxx xxxx xxxx\" size=\"19\"></td>" +
        "</tr>" +
        "<tr>" +
        "<td></td>" +
        "<td><input type=\"submit\"" +
        "value=\"Submit Information\"></td>" +
        "</tr>" +
        "</table>" +
        "</form>" +
        "</body>" +
        "</html>");
     out.close();
  }

  public String getServletInfo() {
     return "The Cashier servlet takes the user's name " +
            "and credit-card number so that the user " +
            "can buy the books.";
  }
}
```

ReceiptServlet.java

SOURCE CODE: *http://java.sun.com/docs/books/tutorial/servlets/example-1dot2/ReceiptServlet.java*

```
import java.io.*;
import javax.servlet.*;
import javax.servlet.http.*;
import cart.ShoppingCart;

/**
 * An HTTP servlet that responds to the POST method of the
 * HTTP protocol.
 * It clears the shopping cart, thanks the user for the order,
 * and resets the page to the BookStore's main page.
 */

public class ReceiptServlet extends HttpServlet {

    public void doPost(HttpServletRequest request,
                       HttpServletResponse response)
        throws ServletException, IOException {

        // Get the user's session and shopping cart
        HttpSession session = request.getSession(true);
        ShoppingCart cart =
            (ShoppingCart)session.getValue(session.getId());

        // If the user has no cart, create a new one
        if (cart == null) {
            cart = new ShoppingCart();
            session.putValue(session.getId(), cart);
        }

        // Payment received -- invalidate the session
        session.invalidate();

        // set content type header before accessing the Writer
        response.setContentType("text/html");
        PrintWriter out = response.getWriter();

        // then write the response
        out.println("<html>" +
                    "<head><title> Receipt </title>" +
                    "<meta http-equiv=\"refresh\" " +
                           content=\"4; + url=" +
                    "http://" + request.getHeader("Host") +
                    "/servlet/bookstore;\">" +
                    "</head>" +
```

```
            "<body  bgcolor=\"#FFFFFF\">" +
            "<center>" +
            "<hr> <br>  " +
            "<h1>" +
            "<font size=\"+3\" color=\"red\">Duke's </font>" +
            "<font size=\"+3\" color=\"purple\">Bookstore</font>" +
            "</h1>" +
            "</center>" +
            "<br>   <hr> <br>  ");

        out.println("<h3>Thank you for purchasing your " +
                    "books from us " +
                    request.getParameter("cardname") +
                    "<p>Please shop with us again soon!</h3>" +
                    "<p><i>This page automatically " +
                    "resets.</i>" +
                    "</body></html>");
        out.close();
    }

    public String getServletInfo() {
        return "The Receipt servlet clears the shopping  " +
               "cart, thanks the user for the order, and " +
               "resets the page to the BookStore's main " +
               "page.";
    }
}
```

Security Architecture

LESSON 41: Quick Tour of Controlling Applets

EXAMPLE: WriteFile

Where Explained:
Quick Tour of Controlling Applets (page 491)

WriteFile.java

```
/**
  * By default, this applet raises a security exception,
  * unless you configure your policy to allow applets from its
  * location to write to the file "writetest."
  */

import java.awt.*;
import java.io.*;
import java.lang.*;
import java.applet.*;

public class WriteFile extends Applet {
    String myFile = "writetest";
    File f = new File(myFile);
    DataOutputStream dos;

    public void init() {

        String osname = System.getProperty("os.name");
    }
```

```
        public void paint(Graphics g) {
            try {
                dos = new DataOutputStream(
                          new BufferedOutputStream(
                          new FileOutputStream(myFile),128));
                dos.writeChars("Cats can hypnotize you when " +
                               "you least expect it\n");
                dos.flush();
                g.drawString("Successfully wrote to the file " +
                             "named " + myFile + " -- go take " +
                             "a look at it!", 10, 10);
            }
            catch (SecurityException e) {
                g.drawString("writeFile: caught security " +
                             "exception: " + e, 10, 10);
            }
            catch (IOException ioe) {
                g.drawString("writeFile: caught i/o" +
                             "exception", 10, 10);
            }
        }
    }
```

LESSON 42: Quick Tour of Controlling Applications

EXAMPLE: Get Properties

Where Explained:
Quick Tour of Controlling Applications (page 503)

GetProps.java

```
    import java.lang.*;
    import java.security.*;

    class GetProps {

        public static void main(String[] args) {

            //Test reading properties w & w/out security manager

            String s;

            try {

                System.out.println("About to get os.name " +
                                   "property value");
```

```
            s = System.getProperty("os.name","not specified");
            System.out.println("  The name of your " +
                               "operating system is: " + s);

            System.out.println("About to get java.version " +
                               "property value");

            s = System.getProperty("java.version",
                                     "not specified");
            System.out.println("  The version of the JVM  " +
                              "you are running is: " + s);

            System.out.println("About to get user.home " +
                               "property value");

            s = System.getProperty("user.home",
                                     "not specified");
            System.out.println("  Your user home directory " +
                               "is: " + s);

            System.out.println("About to get java.home " +
                               "property value");

            s = System.getProperty("java.home",
                                     "not specified");
            System.out.println("  Your JDK installation " +
                               "directory is: " + s);


        } catch (Exception e) {
            System.err.println("Caught exception " +
                               e.toString());
        }

    }

}
```

java.policy

SOURCE CODE: *http://java.sun.com/docs/books/tutorial/security1.2/tour2/example-1dot2/java.policy*

```
// Standard extensions get all permissions by default

grant codeBase "file:${java.home}/lib/ext/" {
        permission java.security.AllPermission;
};
```

```
// default permissions granted to all domains

grant {
        // allows anyone to listen on un-privileged ports
        permission java.net.SocketPermission "localhost:1024-",
                                              "listen";

        // "standard" properies that can be read by anyone
        permission java.util.PropertyPermission
                        "java.version", "read";
        permission java.util.PropertyPermission
                      "java.vendor", "read";
        permission java.util.PropertyPermission
                      "java.vendor.url", "read";
        permission java.util.PropertyPermission
                      "java.class.version", "read";
        permission java.util.PropertyPermission "os.name",
                                                "read";
        permission java.util.PropertyPermission "os.version",
                                                "read";
        permission java.util.PropertyPermission "os.arch",
                                                "read";
        permission java.util.PropertyPermission
                                 "file.separator", "read";
        permission java.util.PropertyPermission
                                 "path.separator", "read";
        permission java.util.PropertyPermission
                                 "line.separator", "read";

        permission java.util.PropertyPermission
                      "java.specification.version", "read";
        permission java.util.PropertyPermission
                      "java.specification.vendor", "read";
        permission java.util.PropertyPermission
                      "java.specification.name", "read";

        permission java.util.PropertyPermission
                  "java.vm.specification.version", "read";
        permission java.util.PropertyPermission
                  "java.vm.specification.vendor", "read";
        permission java.util.PropertyPermission
                      "java.vm.specification.name", "read";
        permission java.util.PropertyPermission
                                 "java.vm.version", "read";
        permission java.util.PropertyPermission
                                 "java.vm.vendor", "read";
        permission java.util.PropertyPermission
                                 "java.vm.name", "read";
};
```

LESSON 44: Signing Code and Granting It Permissions

EXAMPLE: Counting Application

Where Explained:
Signing Code and Granting It Permissions (page 525)

Count.java

```
import java.io.*;

public class Count {
    public static void countChars(InputStream in)
                                       throws IOException
    {
        int count = 0;

        while (in.read() != -1)
            count++;

        System.out.println("Counted " + count + " chars.");
    }

    public static void main(String[] args) throws Exception
    {
        if (args.length >= 1)
            countChars(new FileInputStream(args[0]));
        else
            System.err.println("Usage: Count filename");
    }
}
```

LESSON 46: Generating and Verifying Signatures

EXAMPLE: Generate Signature

Where Explained:
Generating a Digital Signature (page 550)

GenSig.java

```
import java.io.*;
import java.security.*;

class GenSig {

    public static void main(String[] args) {

        /* Generate a DSA signature */
```

```
if (args.length != 1) {
    System.out.println("Usage: GenSig " +
                       "nameOfFileToSign");
    }
else try{

    /* Generate a key pair */

    KeyPairGenerator keyGen =
          KeyPairGenerator.getInstance("DSA", "SUN");
    SecureRandom random =
          SecureRandom.getInstance("SHA1PRNG", "SUN");

    keyGen.initialize(1024, random);

    KeyPair pair = keyGen.generateKeyPair();
    PrivateKey priv = pair.getPrivate();
    PublicKey pub = pair.getPublic();


    /* Create a Signature object and initialize it
     * with the private key
     */

    Signature dsa =
         Signature.getInstance("SHA1withDSA", "SUN");

    dsa.initSign(priv);

    /* Update and sign the data */

    FileInputStream fis =
            new FileInputStream(args[0]);
    BufferedInputStream bufin =
                new BufferedInputStream(fis);
    byte[] buffer = new byte[1024];
    int len;
    while (bufin.available() != 0) {
        len = bufin.read(buffer);
        dsa.update(buffer, 0, len);
        };

    bufin.close();

    /* Now that all the data to be signed has been
     * read in, generate a signature for it
     */

    byte[] realSig = dsa.sign();
```

```
            /* Save the signature in a file */
            FileOutputStream sigfos = new FileOutputStream(
                                                     "sig");
            sigfos.write(realSig);

            sigfos.close();

            /* Save the public key in a file */
            byte[] key = pub.getEncoded();
            FileOutputStream keyfos =
                                new FileOutputStream("suepk");
            keyfos.write(key);

            keyfos.close();

        } catch (Exception e) {
            System.err.println("Caught exception " +
                                     e.toString());
        }
    };
}
```

EXAMPLE: Verify Signature

Where Explained:
Verifying a Digital Signature (page 555)

VerSig.java

```
import java.io.*;
import java.security.*;
import java.security.spec.*;

class VerSig {

    public static void main(String[] args) {

        /* Verify a DSA signature */

        if (args.length != 3) {
            System.out.println("Usage: VerSig publickeyfile" +
                                 " signaturefile datafile");
        }
        else try{

            /* import encoded public key */

            FileInputStream keyfis =
                                new FileInputStream(args[0]);
            byte[] encKey = new byte[keyfis.available()];
            keyfis.read(encKey);

            keyfis.close();
```

```
            X509EncodedKeySpec pubKeySpec =
                                 new X509EncodedKeySpec(encKey);

            KeyFactory keyFactory =
                       KeyFactory.getInstance("DSA", "SUN");
            PublicKey pubKey =
                      keyFactory.generatePublic(pubKeySpec);

            /* input the signature bytes */
            FileInputStream sigfis =
                                new FileInputStream(args[1]);
            byte[] sigToVerify = new byte[sigfis.available()];
            sigfis.read(sigToVerify );

            sigfis.close();

            // create a Signature object and initialize
            // it with the public key
            Signature sig =
                 Signature.getInstance("SHA1withDSA", "SUN");
            sig.initVerify(pubKey);

            /* Update and verify the data */

            FileInputStream datafis =
                                new FileInputStream(args[2]);
            BufferedInputStream bufin =
                             new BufferedInputStream(datafis);

            byte[] buffer = new byte[1024];
            int len;
            while (bufin.available() != 0) {
                len = bufin.read(buffer);
                sig.update(buffer, 0, len);
                };

            bufin.close();
            boolean verifies = sig.verify(sigToVerify);

            System.out.println("signature verifies: " +
                                     verifies);

        } catch (Exception e) {
            System.err.println("Caught exception " +
                                    e.toString());
        };
    }
}
```

JAR

LESSON 49: Using JAR-Related APIs Introduced in 1.2

EXAMPLE: The JarClassLoader Class

JarClassLoader.java

SOURCE CODE: *http://java.sun.com/docs/books/tutorial/jar/api/example-1dot2/JarClassLoader.java*

Where Explained: *The JarClassLoader Class* (page 600)

```
import java.net.URL;
import java.net.URLClassLoader;
import java.net.JarURLConnection;
import java.lang.reflect.Method;
import java.lang.reflect.Modifier;
import java.lang.reflect.InvocationTargetException;
import java.util.jar.Attributes;
import java.io.IOException;

/**
 * Class loader for loading jar files, both local and remote.
 */
class JarClassLoader extends URLClassLoader {
    private URL url;

    /**
     * Creates a new JarClassLoader for the specified url.
     *
     * @param url the url of the jar file
     */
    public JarClassLoader(URL url) {
        super(new URL[] { url });
        this.url = url;
    }

    /**
     * Returns the name of the jar file main class, or null if
     * no "Main-Class" manifest attributes was defined.
     */
```

```
    public String getMainClassName() throws IOException {
        URL u = new URL("jar", "", url + "!/");
        JarURLConnection uc =
                        (JarURLConnection)u.openConnection();
        Attributes attr = uc.getMainAttributes();
        return attr != null ?
                    attr.getValue(Attributes.Name.MAIN_CLASS)
                  : null;
    }

    /**
     * Invokes the application in this jar file given the name
     * of the main class and an array of arguments. The class
     * must define a static method "main" which takes an array
     * of String arguments and is of return type "void".
     *
     * @param name the name of the main class
     * @param args the arguments for the application
     * @exception ClassNotFoundException if the specified
     *    class could not be found
     * @exception NoSuchMethodException if the specified class
     *    does not contain a "main" method
     * @exception InvocationTargetException if the application
     *    raised an exception
     */
    public void invokeClass(String name, String[] args)
        throws ClassNotFoundException,
               NoSuchMethodException,
               InvocationTargetException
    {
        Class c = loadClass(name);
        Method m = c.getMethod("main",
                        new Class[] { args.getClass() });
        m.setAccessible(true);
        int mods = m.getModifiers();
        if (m.getReturnType() != void.class ||
                                !Modifier.isStatic(mods) ||
                                !Modifier.isPublic(mods)) {
            throw new NoSuchMethodException("main");
        }
        try {
            m.invoke(null, new Object[] { args });
        } catch (IllegalAccessException e) {
            // This should not happen, as we have disabled
            // access checks
        }
    }
}
```

EXAMPLE: The JarRunner Class

JarRunner.java

SOURCE CODE: *http://java.sun.com/docs/books/tutorial/jar/api/example-1dot2/JarRunner.java*

Where Explained:
The JarRunner Class (page 603)

```
import java.io.IOException;
import java.net.URL;
import java.net.MalformedURLException;
import java.lang.reflect.InvocationTargetException;

/**
 * Runs a jar application from any url. Usage is 'java
 * JarRunner url [args..]' where url is the url of the jar
 * file and args is optional arguments to be passed to the
 * application's main method.
 */
public class JarRunner {
    public static void main(String[] args) {
        if (args.length < 1) {
            usage();
        }
        URL url = null;
        try {
            url = new URL(args[0]);
        } catch (MalformedURLException e) {
            fatal("Invalid URL: " + args[0]);
        }
        // Create class loader for the application jar file
        JarClassLoader cl = new JarClassLoader(url);
        // Get the application's main class name
        String name = null;
        try {
            name = cl.getMainClassName();
        } catch (IOException e) {
            System.err.println("I/O error while loading " +
                               "JAR file:");
            e.printStackTrace();
            System.exit(1);
        }
        if (name == null) {
            fatal("Specified jar file does not contain " +
                  "a 'Main-Class' manifest attribute");
        }
        // Get arguments for the application
        String[] newArgs = new String[args.length - 1];
        System.arraycopy(args, 1, newArgs, 0, newArgs.length);
```

```
        // Invoke application's main class
        try {
            cl.invokeClass(name, newArgs);
        } catch (ClassNotFoundException e) {
            fatal("Class not found: " + name);
        } catch (NoSuchMethodException e) {
            fatal("Class does not define a 'main' method: " +
                  name);
        } catch (InvocationTargetException e) {
            e.getTargetException().printStackTrace();
            System.exit(1);
        }
    }

    private static void fatal(String s) {
        System.err.println(s);
        System.exit(1);
    }

    private static void usage() {
        fatal("Usage: java JarRunner url [args..]");
    }
}
```

Java Native Interface

LESSON 52: Overview of the JNI

EXAMPLE: HelloWorld Program

HelloWorld.java

SOURCE CODE: *http://java.sun.com/docs/books/tutorial/native1.1/stepbystep/example-1dot1/HelloWorld.java*

Where Explained: *Step 1: Write the Java Code* (page 635)

```
class HelloWorld {
    public native void displayHelloWorld();

    static {
        System.loadLibrary("hello");
    }
```

```
    public static void main(String[] args) {
        new HelloWorld().displayHelloWorld();
    }
}
```

EXAMPLE: HelloWorld Program

Where Explained: *Step 3: Create the .h File* (page 637)

HelloWorld.h

SOURCE CODE: *http://java.sun.com/docs/books/tutorial/native1.1/stepbystep/example-1dot1/HelloWorld.h*

```
/* DO NOT EDIT THIS FILE - it is machine generated */
#include <jni.h>
/* Header for class HelloWorld */

#ifndef _Included_HelloWorld
#define _Included_HelloWorld
#ifdef __cplusplus
extern "C" {
#endif
/*
 * Class:     HelloWorld
 * Method:    displayHelloWorld
 * Signature: ()V
 */
JNIEXPORT void JNICALL Java_HelloWorld_displayHelloWorld
  (JNIEnv *, jobject);

#ifdef __cplusplus
}
#endif
#endif
```

EXAMPLE: HelloWorld Program

Where Explained: *Step 4: Write the Native Method Implementation* (page 639)

HelloWorldImp.c

SOURCE CODE: *http://java.sun.com/docs/books/tutorial/native1.1/stepbystep/example-1dot1/HelloWorldImp.c*

```
#include <jni.h>
#include "HelloWorld.h"
#include <stdio.h>

JNIEXPORT void JNICALL
Java_HelloWorld_displayHelloWorld(JNIEnv *env, jobject obj)
```

```
{
    printf("Hello world!\n");
    return;
}
```

LESSON 53: Writing a Java Program with Native Methods

EXAMPLE: Prompt Program

Prompt.java

SOURCE CODE: *http://java.sun.com/docs/books/tutorial/native1.1/integrating/example-1dot1/Prompt.java*

Where Explained:
Declaring Native Methods (page 644)

```
class Prompt {
    private native String getLine(String prompt);
    public static void main(String[] args) {
        Prompt p = new Prompt();
        String input = p.getLine("Type a line: ");
        System.out.println("User typed: " + input);
    }
    static {
        System.loadLibrary("MyImpOfPrompt");
    }
}
```

Prompt.h

SOURCE CODE: *http://java.sun.com/docs/books/tutorial/native1.1/integrating/example-1dot1/Prompt.h*

```
/* DO NOT EDIT THIS FILE - it is machine generated */
#include <jni.h>
/* Header for class Prompt */

#ifndef _Included_Prompt
#define _Included_Prompt
#ifdef __cplusplus
extern "C" {
#endif
/*
 * Class:     Prompt
 * Method:    getLine
 * Signature: (Ljava/lang/String;)Ljava/lang/String;
 */
```

```
JNIEXPORT jstring JNICALL Java_Prompt_getLine
  (JNIEnv *, jobject, jstring);

#ifdef __cplusplus
}
#endif
#endif
```

Prompt2.java

SOURCE CODE: *http://java.sun.com/docs/books/tutorial/native1.1/integrating/example-1dot1/Prompt2.java*

```
class Prompt2 {
    private native String getLine(String prompt);
    private native String getLine(String prompt, int length);
    public static void main(String[] args) {
        Prompt2 p = new Prompt2();
        String input = p.getLine("Type a line: ");
        System.out.println("User typed: " + input);
    }
    static {
        System.loadLibrary("MyImpOfPrompt2");
    }
}
```

Prompt2.h

SOURCE CODE: *http://java.sun.com/docs/books/tutorial/native1.1/integrating/example-1dot1/Prompt2.h*

```
/* DO NOT EDIT THIS FILE - it is machine generated */
#include <jni.h>
/* Header for class Prompt2 */

#ifndef _Included_Prompt2
#define _Included_Prompt2
#ifdef __cplusplus
extern "C" {
#endif
/*
 * Class:     Prompt2
 * Method:    getLine
 * Signature: (Ljava/lang/String;)Ljava/lang/String;
 */
JNIEXPORT jstring JNICALL
Java_Prompt2_getLine__Ljava_lang_String_2
  (JNIEnv *, jobject, jstring);

/*
```

```
 * Class:     Prompt2
 * Method:    getLine
 * Signature: (Ljava/lang/String;I)Ljava/lang/String;
 */
JNIEXPORT jstring JNICALL
Java_Prompt2_getLine__Ljava_lang_String_2I
  (JNIEnv *, jobject, jstring, jint);

#ifdef __cplusplus
}
#endif
#endif
```

LESSON 54: Integrating Java and Native Programs

EXAMPLE: Prompt Program

Where Explained: *Java Strings* (page 650)

Prompt.c

SOURCE CODE: *http://java.sun.com/docs/books/tutorial/native1.1/implementing/example-1dot1/Prompt.c*

```
#include <stdio.h>
#include <jni.h>
#include "Prompt.h"

JNIEXPORT jstring JNICALL
Java_Prompt_getLine(JNIEnv *env, jobject obj, jstring prompt)
{
  char buf[128];
  const char *str = (*env)->GetStringUTFChars(env, prompt, 0);
  printf("%s", str);
  (*env)->ReleaseStringUTFChars(env, prompt, str);
  scanf("%s", buf);
  return (*env)->NewStringUTF(env, buf);
}
```

EXAMPLE: Interger Array Program

Where Explained: *Accessing Java Arrays* (page 652)

IntArray.c

SOURCE CODE: *http://java.sun.com/docs/books/tutorial/native1.1/implementing/example-1dot1/IntArray.c*

```
#include <jni.h>
#include "IntArray.h"
```

```
JNIEXPORT jint JNICALL
Java_IntArray_sumArray(JNIEnv *env, jobject obj, jintArray
arr)
{
  jsize len = (*env)->GetArrayLength(env, arr);
  int i, sum = 0;
  jint *body = (*env)->GetIntArrayElements(env, arr, 0);
  for (i=0; i<len; i++) {
    sum += body[i];
  }
  (*env)->ReleaseIntArrayElements(env, arr, body, 0);
  return sum;
}
```

EXAMPLE: Callback Program

Where Explained: *Calling Java Methods* (page 656)

Callbacks.java

SOURCE CODE: *http://java.sun.com/docs/books/tutorial/native1.1/implementing/example-1dot1/Callbacks.java*

```
class Callbacks {
    private native void nativeMethod(int depth);
    private void callback(int depth) {
        if (depth < 5) {
            System.out.println("In Java, depth = " + depth +
                               ", about to enter C");
            nativeMethod(depth + 1);
            System.out.println("In Java, depth = " + depth +
                               ", back from C");
        } else
            System.out.println("In Java, depth = " + depth +
                               ", limit exceeded");
    }

    public static void main(String[] args) {
        Callbacks c = new Callbacks();
        c.nativeMethod(0);
    }

    static {
        System.loadLibrary("MyImpOfCallbacks");
    }
}
```

Callbacks.c

SOURCE CODE: *http://java.sun.com/docs/books/tutorial/native1.1/implementing/example-1dot1/Callbacks.java*

```
#include <stdio.h>
#include <jni.h>
#include "Callbacks.h"

JNIEXPORT void JNICALL
Java_Callbacks_nativeMethod(JNIEnv *env, jobject obj,
                                          jint depth)
{
  jclass cls = (*env)->GetObjectClass(env, obj);
  jmethodID mid = (*env)->GetMethodID(env, cls, "callback",
                                        "(I)V");
  if (mid == 0) {
    return;
  }
  printf("In C, depth = %d, about to enter Java\n", depth);
  (*env)->CallVoidMethod(env, obj, mid, depth);
  printf("In C, depth = %d, back from Java\n", depth);
}
```

EXAMPLE: Accessing Java Member Variables

FieldAccess.java

SOURCE CODE: *http://java.sun.com/docs/books/tutorial/native1.1/implementing/example-1dot1/FieldAccess.java*

Where Explained: *Accessing Java Member Variables* (page 661)

```
class FieldAccess {
    static int si;
    String s;

    private native void accessFields();
    public static void main(String[] args) {
        FieldAccess c = new FieldAccess();
        FieldAccess.si = 100;
        c.s = "abc";
        c.accessFields();
        System.out.println("In Java:");
        System.out.println("  FieldAccess.si = " +
                           FieldAccess.si);
        System.out.println("  c.s = \"" + c.s + "\"");
    }
    static {
        System.loadLibrary("MyImpOfFieldAccess");
    }
}
```

FieldAccess.c

http://java.sun.com/docs/books/tutorial/native1.1/implementing/example-1dot1/FieldAccess.c

```
#include <stdio.h>
#include <jni.h>
#include "FieldAccess.h"

JNIEXPORT void JNICALL
Java_FieldAccess_accessFields(JNIEnv *env, jobject obj)
{
  jclass cls = (*env)->GetObjectClass(env, obj);
  jfieldID fid;
  jstring jstr;
  const char *str;
  jint si;

  printf("In C:\n");

  fid = (*env)->GetStaticFieldID(env, cls, "si", "I");
  if (fid == 0) {
    return;
  }
  si = (*env)->GetStaticIntField(env, cls, fid);
  printf("  FieldAccess.si = %d\n", si);
  (*env)->SetStaticIntField(env, cls, fid, 200);

  fid = (*env)->GetFieldID(env, cls, "s",
                           "Ljava/lang/String;");
  if (fid == 0) {
    return;
  }

  jstr = (*env)->GetObjectField(env, obj, fid);
  str = (*env)->GetStringUTFChars(env, jstr, 0);
  printf("  c.s = \"%s\"\n", str);
  (*env)->ReleaseStringUTFChars(env, jstr, str);

  jstr = (*env)->NewStringUTF(env, "123");
  (*env)->SetObjectField(env, obj, fid, jstr);
}
```

EXAMPLE: Catching and Throwing Exceptions

Where Explained: *Catching and Throwing Exceptions* (page 663)

CatchThrow.java

SOURCE CODE: *http://java.sun.com/docs/books/tutorial/native1.1/implementing/example-1dot1/CatchThrow.java*

```
class CatchThrow {
    private native void catchThrow() throws

IllegalArgumentException;
    private void callback() throws NullPointerException {
        throw new NullPointerException("thrown in " +
                                       "CatchThrow.callback");
    }
    public static void main(String[] args) {
        CatchThrow c = new CatchThrow();
        try {
            c.catchThrow();
        } catch (Exception e) {
            System.out.println("In Java:\n    " + e);
        }
    }
    static {
        System.loadLibrary("MyImpOfCatchThrow");
    }
}
```

CatchThrow.c

SOURCE CODE: *http://java.sun.com/docs/books/tutorial/native1.1/implementing/example-1dot1/CatchThrow.c*

```
#include <jni.h>
#include "CatchThrow.h"

JNIEXPORT void JNICALL
Java_CatchThrow_catchThrow(JNIEnv *env, jobject obj)
{
  jclass cls = (*env)->GetObjectClass(env, obj);
  jmethodID mid = (*env)->GetMethodID(env, cls, "callback",
                                      "()V");
  jthrowable exc;
  if (mid == 0) {
    return;
  }
  (*env)->CallVoidMethod(env, obj, mid);
  exc = (*env)->ExceptionOccurred(env);
```

```
    if (exc) {
      /* We don't do much with the exception, except that we
         print a debug message using ExceptionDescribe, clear
         it, and throw a new exception. */
      jclass newExcCls;

      (*env)->ExceptionDescribe(env);
      (*env)->ExceptionClear(env);

      newExcCls = (*env)->FindClass(env,
                           "java/lang/IllegalArgumentException");
      if (newExcCls == 0) {
        /* Unable to find the new exception class, give up. */
        return;
      }
      (*env)->ThrowNew(env, newExcCls, "thrown from C code");
    }
  }
```

LESSON 55: Interacting with Java from the Native Side

EXAMPLE: Invoke Program

Where Explained: *Invoking the Java Virtual Machine* (page 671)

invoke.c

SOURCE CODE: *http://java.sun.com/docs/books/tutorial/native1.1/invoking/example-1dot1/invoke.c*

```
#include <jni.h>

#ifdef _WIN32
#define PATH_SEPARATOR ';'
#else /* UNIX */
#define PATH_SEPARATOR ':'
#endif

#define USER_CLASSPATH "." /* where Prog.class is */

main() {
    JNIEnv *env;
    JavaVM *jvm;
    JDK1_1InitArgs vm_args;
    jint res;
    jclass cls;
    jmethodID mid;
```

```
jstring jstr;
jobjectArray args;
char classpath[1024];


/* IMPORTANT: specify vm_args version # if you use
   JDK1.1.2 and beyond */
vm_args.version = 0x00010001;

JNI_GetDefaultJavaVMInitArgs(&vm_args);

/* Append USER_CLASSPATH to the end of default system
   class path */
sprintf(classpath, "%s%c%s",
       vm_args.classpath, PATH_SEPARATOR, USER_CLASSPATH);
vm_args.classpath = classpath;

/* Create the Java VM */
res = JNI_CreateJavaVM(&jvm,&env,&vm_args);
if (res < 0) {
    fprintf(stderr, "Can't create Java VM\n");
    exit(1);
}

cls = (*env)->FindClass(env, "Prog");
if (cls == 0) {
    fprintf(stderr, "Can't find Prog class\n");
    exit(1);
}

mid = (*env)->GetStaticMethodID(env, cls, "main",
                                "([Ljava/lang/String;)V");
if (mid == 0) {
    fprintf(stderr, "Can't find Prog.main\n");
    exit(1);
}

jstr = (*env)->NewStringUTF(env, " from C!");
if (jstr == 0) {
    fprintf(stderr, "Out of memory\n");
    exit(1);
}
args = (*env)->NewObjectArray(env, 1,
               (*env)->FindClass(env, "java/lang/String"),
                      jstr);
if (args == 0) {
    fprintf(stderr, "Out of memory\n");
    exit(1);
```

```
    }
    (*env)->CallStaticVoidMethod(env, cls, mid, args);

    (*jvm)->DestroyJavaVM(jvm);
}
```

EXAMPLE: Attach Program

Where Explained: *Attaching Native Threads* (page 673)

attach.c

SOURCE CODE: *http://java.sun.com/docs/books/tutorial/native1.1/invoking/example-1dot1/attach.c*

```
/* Note: This program only works on Win32.
*/
#include <windows.h>
#include <jni.h>

JavaVM *jvm;

void thread_fun(void *arg)
{
    jint res;
    jclass cls;
    jmethodID mid;
    jstring jstr;
    jobjectArray args;
    JNIEnv *env;
    char buf[100];
    int threadNum = (int)arg;

    /* Pass NULL as the third argument */
    res = (*jvm)->AttachCurrentThread(jvm, &env, NULL);
    if (res < 0) {
       fprintf(stderr, "Thread %d: attach failed\n",
               threadNum);
       return;
    }

    cls = (*env)->FindClass(env, "Prog");
    if (cls == 0) {
        fprintf(stderr, "Thread %d: Can't find Prog class\n",
                threadNum);
        goto detach;
    }

    mid = (*env)->GetStaticMethodID(env, cls, "main",
                                "([Ljava/lang/String;)V");
```

```
    if (mid == 0) {
        fprintf(stderr, "Thread %d: Can't find Prog.main\n",
                  threadNum);
        goto detach;
    }

    sprintf(buf, " from Thread %d", threadNum);
    jstr = (*env)->NewStringUTF(env, buf);
    if (jstr == 0) {
        fprintf(stderr, "Thread %d: Out of memory\n",
                threadNum);
        goto detach;
    }
    args = (*env)->NewObjectArray(env, 1,
             (*env)->FindClass(env, "java/lang/String"),jstr);
    if (args == 0) {
        fprintf(stderr, "Thread %d: Out of memory\n",
                threadNum);
        goto detach;
    }
    (*env)->CallStaticVoidMethod(env, cls, mid, args);

  detach:
    if ((*env)->ExceptionOccurred(env)) {
        (*env)->ExceptionDescribe(env);
    }
    (*jvm)->DetachCurrentThread(jvm);
}

#ifdef _WIN32
#define PATH_SEPARATOR ';'
#else /* UNIX */
#define PATH_SEPARATOR ':'
#endif

#define USER_CLASSPATH "." /* where Prog.class is */

main() {
    JNIEnv *env;
    JDK1_1InitArgs vm_args;
    int i;
    jint res;
    char classpath[1024];

    /* IMPORTANT: specify vm_args version # if you use
       JDK1.1.2 and beyond */
    vm_args.version = 0x00010001;
```

```
    JNI_GetDefaultJavaVMInitArgs(&vm_args);

    /* Append USER_CLASSPATH to the end of default system
       class path */
    sprintf(classpath, "%s%c%s",
            vm_args.classpath, PATH_SEPARATOR,USER_CLASSPATH);
    vm_args.classpath = classpath;

    /* Create the Java VM */
    res = JNI_CreateJavaVM(&jvm, &env, &vm_args);

    if (res < 0) {
        fprintf(stderr, "Can't create Java VM\n");
        exit(1);
    }

    for (i=0; i<5; i++)
        /* We pass the thread number as the argument to every
           thread */
        _beginthread(thread_fun,0,(void *)i);

    Sleep(5000); /* wait for threads to finish */

    (*jvm)->DestroyJavaVM(jvm);
}
```

Reflection

LESSON 58: Examining Classes

EXAMPLE: Sample Programs to Examine Classes

SampleCheckInterface.java

SOURCE CODE: *http://java.sun.com/docs/books/tutorial/reflect/class/example-1dot1/SampleCheckInterface.java*

Where Explained:
Examining Classes (page 685)

```
import java.lang.reflect.*;
import java.util.*;

class SampleCheckInterface {

   public static void main(String[] args) {
```

```
      Class observer = Observer.class;
      Class observable = Observable.class;
      verifyInterface(observer);
      verifyInterface(observable);
   }

   static void verifyInterface(Class c) {
      String name = c.getName();
      if (c.isInterface()) {
         System.out.println(name + " is an interface.");
      } else {
         System.out.println(name + " is a class.");
      }
   }
}
```

SampleConstructor.java

SOURCE CODE: *http://java.sun.com/docs/books/tutorial/reflect/class/example-1dot1/SampleConstructor.java*

```
import java.lang.reflect.*;
import java.awt.*;

class SampleConstructor {

   public static void main(String[] args) {
      Rectangle r = new Rectangle();
      showConstructors(r);
   }

   static void showConstructors(Object o) {
      Class c = o.getClass();
      Constructor[] theConstructors = c.getConstructors();
      for (int i = 0; i < theConstructors.length; i++) {
         System.out.print("( ");
         Class[] parameterTypes =
                 theConstructors[i].getParameterTypes();
         for (int k = 0; k < parameterTypes.length; k ++) {
            String parameterString =
                               parameterTypes[k].getName();
            System.out.print(parameterString + " ");
            }

         System.out.println(")");
         }
   }
}
```

SampleField.java

SOURCE CODE: *http://java.sun.com/docs/books/tutorial/reflect/class/example-1dot1/SampleField.java*

```
import java.lang.reflect.*;
import java.awt.*;

class SampleField {

    public static void main(String[] args) {
        GridBagConstraints g = new GridBagConstraints();
        printFieldNames(g);
    }

    static void printFieldNames(Object o) {
        Class c = o.getClass();
        Field[] publicFields = c.getFields();
        for (int i = 0; i < publicFields.length; i++) {
            String fieldName = publicFields[i].getName();
            Class typeClass = publicFields[i].getType();
            String fieldType = typeClass.getName();
            System.out.println("Name: " + fieldName +
                               ", Type: " + fieldType);
        }
    }
}
```

SampleInterface.java

SOURCE CODE: *http://java.sun.com/docs/books/tutorial/reflect/class/example-1dot1/SampleInterface.java*

```
import java.lang.reflect.*;
import java.io.*;

class SampleInterface {

   public static void main(String[] args) {
      try {
         RandomAccessFile r =
               new RandomAccessFile("myfile", "r");
         printInterfaceNames(r);
      } catch (IOException e) {
         System.out.println(e);
      }
   }
```

```
    static void printInterfaceNames(Object o) {
        Class c = o.getClass();
        Class[] theInterfaces = c.getInterfaces();
        for (int i = 0; i < theInterfaces.length; i++) {
            String interfaceName = theInterfaces[i].getName();
            System.out.println(interfaceName);
        }
    }
}
```

SampleMethod.java

SOURCE CODE: *http://java.sun.com/docs/books/tutorial/reflect/class/example-1dot1/SampleMethod.java*

```
import java.lang.reflect.*;
import java.awt.*;

class SampleMethod {

    public static void main(String[] args) {
        Polygon p = new Polygon();
        showMethods(p);
    }

    static void showMethods(Object o) {
        Class c = o.getClass();
        Method[] theMethods = c.getMethods();
        for (int i = 0; i < theMethods.length; i++) {
            String methodString = theMethods[i].getName();
            System.out.println("Name: " + methodString);
            String returnString =
                          theMethods[i].getReturnType().getName();
            System.out.println("   Return Type: " +
                                  returnString);
            Class[] parameterTypes =
                           theMethods[i].getParameterTypes();

            System.out.print("   Parameter Types:");

            for (int k = 0; k < parameterTypes.length; k ++) {
                String parameterString =
                        parameterTypes[k].getName();
                System.out.print(" " + parameterString);
                }

            System.out.println();
            }
    }
}
```

SampleModifier.java

SOURCE CODE: *http://java.sun.com/docs/books/tutorial/reflect/class/example-1dot1/SampleModifier.java*

```
import java.lang.reflect.*;
import java.awt.*;

class SampleModifier {

   public static void main(String[] args) {
      String s = new String();
      printModifiers(s);
   }

   public static void printModifiers(Object o) {
      Class c = o.getClass();
      int m = c.getModifiers();
      if (Modifier.isPublic(m))
         System.out.println("public");
      if (Modifier.isAbstract(m))
         System.out.println("abstract");
      if (Modifier.isFinal(m))
         System.out.println("final");
   }
}
```

SampleName.java

SOURCE CODE: *http://java.sun.com/docs/books/tutorial/reflect/class/example-1dot1/SampleName.java*

```
import java.lang.reflect.*;
import java.awt.*;

class SampleName {

   public static void main(String[] args) {
      Button b = new Button();;
      printName(b);
   }

   static void printName(Object o) {
       Class c = o.getClass();
       String s = c.getName();
       System.out.println(s);
   }
}
```

SampleSuper.java

SOURCE CODE: *http://java.sun.com/docs/books/tutorial/reflect/class/example-1dot1/SampleSuper.java*

```
import java.lang.reflect.*;
import java.awt.*;

class SampleSuper {
    public static void main(String[] args) {
        Button b = new Button();
        printSuperclasses(b);
    }

    static void printSuperclasses(Object o) {
        Class subclass = o.getClass();
        Class superclass = subclass.getSuperclass();
        while (superclass != null) {
            String className = superclass.getName();
            System.out.println(className);
            subclass = superclass;
            superclass = subclass.getSuperclass();
        }
    }
}
```

LESSON 59: Manipulating Objects

EXAMPLE: Sample Programs to Manipulate Objects

Where Explained: *Manipulating Objects* (page 697)

SampleSet.java

SOURCE CODE: *http://java.sun.com/docs/books/tutorial/reflect/object/example-1dot1/SampleSet.java*

```
import java.lang.reflect.*;
import java.awt.*;

class SampleSet {

    public static void main(String[] args) {
        Rectangle r = new Rectangle(100, 20);
        System.out.println("original: " + r.toString());
        modifyWidth(r, new Integer(300));
        System.out.println("modified: " + r.toString());
    }
```

```
    static void modifyWidth(Rectangle r, Integer widthParam ){
        Field widthField;
        Integer widthValue;
        Class c = r.getClass();
        try {
            widthField = c.getField("width");
            widthField.set(r, widthParam);
        } catch (NoSuchFieldException e) {
            System.out.println(e);
        } catch (IllegalAccessException e) {
            System.out.println(e);
        }
    }
}
```

SampleGet.java

SOURCE CODE: *http://java.sun.com/docs/books/tutorial/reflect/object/example-1dot1/SampleGet.java*

```
import java.lang.reflect.*;
import java.awt.*;

class SampleGet {

   public static void main(String[] args) {
      Rectangle r = new Rectangle(100, 325);
      printHeight(r);

   }

   static void printHeight(Rectangle r) {
      Field heightField;
      Integer heightValue;
      Class c = r.getClass();
      try {
        heightField = c.getField("height");
        heightValue = (Integer) heightField.get(r);
        System.out.println("Height: " +
                           heightValue.toString());
      } catch (NoSuchFieldException e) {
         System.out.println(e);
      } catch (SecurityException e) {
         System.out.println(e);
      } catch (IllegalAccessException e) {
         System.out.println(e);
      }
   }
}
```

SampleInvoke.java

SOURCE CODE: *http://java.sun.com/docs/books/tutorial/reflect/object/example-1dot1/SampleInvoke.java*

```
import java.lang.reflect.*;

class SampleInvoke {


   public static void main(String[] args) {
      String firstWord = "Hello ";
      String secondWord = "everybody.";
      String bothWords = append(firstWord, secondWord);
      System.out.println(bothWords);
   }

   public static String append(String firstWord,
                               String secondWord) {
      String result = null;
      Class c = String.class;
      Class[] parameterTypes = new Class[] {String.class};
      Method concatMethod;
      Object[] arguments = new Object[] {secondWord};
      try {
        concatMethod = c.getMethod("concat", parameterTypes);
        result = (String) concatMethod.invoke(firstWord,
                                              arguments);
      } catch (NoSuchMethodException e) {
          System.out.println(e);
      } catch (IllegalAccessException e) {
          System.out.println(e);
      } catch (InvocationTargetException e) {
          System.out.println(e);
      }
      return result;
   }
}
```

SampleInstance.java

SOURCE CODE: *http://java.sun.com/docs/books/tutorial/reflect/object/example-1dot1/SampleInstance.java*

```
import java.lang.reflect.*;
import java.awt.*;

class SampleInstance {

   public static void main(String[] args) {
```

```
        Rectangle rectangle;
        Class rectangleDefinition;
        Class[] intArgsClass =
                new Class[] {int.class, int.class};
        Integer height = new Integer(12);
        Integer width = new Integer(34);
        Object[] intArgs = new Object[] {height, width};
        Constructor intArgsConstructor;

        try {
          rectangleDefinition =
                    Class.forName("java.awt.Rectangle");
          intArgsConstructor =
             rectangleDefinition.getConstructor(intArgsClass);
          rectangle = (Rectangle)
                    createObject(intArgsConstructor, intArgs);
        } catch (ClassNotFoundException e) {
            System.out.println(e);
        } catch (NoSuchMethodException e) {
            System.out.println(e);
        }
    }

    public static Object createObject(Constructor constructor,
                                      Object[] arguments) {

        System.out.println ("Constructor: " +
                           constructor.toString());
        Object object = null;

        try {
          object = constructor.newInstance(arguments);
          System.out.println ("Object: " + object.toString());
          return object;
        } catch (InstantiationException e) {
            System.out.println(e);
        } catch (IllegalAccessException e) {
            System.out.println(e);
        } catch (IllegalArgumentException e) {
            System.out.println(e);
        } catch (InvocationTargetException e) {
            System.out.println(e);
        }
        return object;
    }
}
```

SampleNoArg.java

SOURCE CODE: *http://java.sun.com/docs/books/tutorial/reflect/object/example-1dot1/SampleNoArg.java*

```
import java.lang.reflect.*;
import java.awt.*;

class SampleNoArg {

   public static void main(String[] args) {
      Rectangle r = (Rectangle)
                     createObject("java.awt.Rectangle");
      System.out.println(r.toString());
   }

   static Object createObject(String className) {
      Object object = null;
      try {
          Class classDefinition = Class.forName(className);
          object = classDefinition.newInstance();
      } catch (InstantiationException e) {
          System.out.println(e);
      } catch (IllegalAccessException e) {
          System.out.println(e);
      } catch (ClassNotFoundException e) {
          System.out.println(e);
      }
      return object;
   }
}
```

LESSON 60: Working with Arrays

EXAMPLE: Sample Programs that Work with Arrays

Where Explained: *Working with Arrays* (page 707)

SampleArray.java

SOURCE CODE: *http://java.sun.com/docs/books/tutorial/reflect/array/example-1dot1/SampleArray.java*

```
import java.lang.reflect.*;
import java.awt.*;

class SampleArray {

   public static void main(String[] args) {
```

```
        KeyPad target = new KeyPad();
        printArrayNames(target);
    }

    static void printArrayNames(Object target) {
        Class targetClass = target.getClass();
        Field[] publicFields = targetClass.getFields();
        for (int i = 0; i < publicFields.length; i++) {
            String fieldName = publicFields[i].getName();
            Class typeClass = publicFields[i].getType();
            String fieldType = typeClass.getName();
            if (typeClass.isArray()) {
                System.out.println("Name: " + fieldName +
                    ", Type: " + fieldType);
            }
        }
    }
}

class KeyPad {

    public boolean alive;
    public Button power;
    public Button[] letters;
    public int[] codes;
    public TextField[] rows;
    public boolean[] states;
}
```

SampleCreateArray.java

SOURCE CODE: *http://java.sun.com/docs/books/tutorial/reflect/array/example-1dot1/SampleCreateArray.java*

```
import java.lang.reflect.*;

class SampleCreateArray {

    public static void main(String[] args) {
        int[] originalArray =  {55, 66};
        int[] biggerArray = (int[]) doubleArray(originalArray);
        System.out.println("originalArray:");
        for (int k = 0; k < Array.getLength(originalArray); k++)
            System.out.println(originalArray[k]);
        System.out.println("biggerArray:");
        for (int k = 0; k < Array.getLength(biggerArray); k++)
            System.out.println(biggerArray[k]);
    }
```

```
    static Object doubleArray(Object source) {
        int sourceLength = Array.getLength(source);
        Class arrayClass = source.getClass();
        Class componentClass = arrayClass.getComponentType();
        Object result = Array.newInstance(componentClass,
                                          sourceLength * 2);
        System.arraycopy(source, 0, result, 0, sourceLength);
        return result;
    }
}
```

SampleGetArray.java

SOURCE CODE: *http://java.sun.com/docs/books/tutorial/reflect/array/example-1dot1/SampleGetArray.java*

```
import java.lang.reflect.*;

class SampleGetArray {

    public static void main(String[] args) {
        int[] sourceInts = {12, 78};
        int[] destInts = new int[2];
        copyArray(sourceInts, destInts);
        String[] sourceStrgs = {"Hello ", "there ","everybody"};
        String[] destStrgs = new String[3];
        copyArray(sourceStrgs, destStrgs);
    }

    public static void copyArray(Object source, Object dest) {
        for (int i = 0; i < Array.getLength(source); i++) {
            Array.set(dest, i, Array.get(source, i));
            System.out.println(Array.get(dest, i));
        }
    }
}
```

SampleMultiArray.java

SOURCE CODE: *http://java.sun.com/docs/books/tutorial/reflect/array/example-1dot1/SampleMultiArray.java*

```
import java.lang.reflect.*;

class SampleMultiArray {

    public static void main(String[] args) {

        // The oneDimA and oneDimB objects are one dimensional
        // int arrays  with 5 elements.
```

```
        int[] dim1 = {5};
        int[] oneDimA = (int[])
                            Array.newInstance(int.class, dim1);
        int[] oneDimB = (int[]) Array.newInstance(int.class, 5);

        // The twoDimStr object is a 5 X 10 array of
        // String objects.

        int[] dimStr = {5, 10};
        String[][] twoDimStr = (String[][])
                    Array.newInstance(String.class,dimStr);

        // The twoDimA object is an array of 12 int arrays. The
        // tail dimension is not defined. It is equivalent to
        // the array created as follows:
        //    int[][] ints = new int[12][];

        int[] dimA = {12};
        int[][] twoDimA = (int[][])
                              Array.newInstance(int[].class, dimA);
    }
}
```

SampleComponent.java

SOURCE CODE: *http://java.sun.com/docs/books/tutorial/reflect/array/example-1dot1/SampleComponent.java*

```
import java.lang.reflect.*;
import java.awt.*;

class SampleComponent {

   public static void main(String[] args) {
      int[] ints = new int[2];
      Button[]  buttons = new Button[6];
      String[][] twoDim = new String[4][5];

      printComponentType(ints);
      printComponentType(buttons);
      printComponentType(twoDim);
   }

   static void printComponentType(Object array) {
      Class arrayClass = array.getClass();
      String arrayName = arrayClass.getName();
      Class componentClass = arrayClass.getComponentType();
      String componentName = componentClass.getName();
```

```
        System.out.println("Array: " + arrayName +
            ", Component: " + componentName);
    }
}
```

KeyPad.java

SOURCE CODE: *http://java.sun.com/docs/books/tutorial/reflect/array/example-1dot1/KeyPad.java*

```
import java.awt.*;

class KeyPad {

    public boolean alive;
    public Button power;

    public Button[] letters;
    public int[] codes;
    public TextField[] rows;
    public boolean[] states;
}
```

APPENDIX **B**

Reference

THIS appendix contains the following reference information:

Number Format Pattern Syntax

This is a reference section for the trail, Internationalization (page 95). You can design your own format patterns for numbers by following the rules specified by the following Bachus-Naur Form (BNF) diagram:

```
pattern    := subpattern{;subpattern}
subpattern := {prefix}integer{.fraction}{suffix}
prefix     := '\u0000'..'\uFFFD' - specialCharacters
suffix     := '\u0000'..'\uFFFD' - specialCharacters
integer    := '#'* '0'* '0'
fraction    := '0'* '#'*
```

In the preceding BNF diagram, the first subpattern specifies the format for positive numbers. The second subpattern, which is optional, specifies the format for negative numbers. Although not noted in the BNF diagram, a comma can appear within the integer portion.

The notation used in the preceding diagram is explained in the following table:

Table 37 Notation Description

<table>
<tr><td>X*</td><td>0 or more instances of X</td></tr>
<tr><td>(X | Y)</td><td>either X or Y</td></tr>
<tr><td>X..Y</td><td>any character from X up to Y, inclusive</td></tr>
<tr><td>S - T</td><td>characters in S, except those in T</td></tr>
<tr><td>{X}</td><td>X is optional</td></tr>
</table>

Within the subpatterns, you specify formatting with special symbols. These symbols are described in the following table:

Table 38 Symbol Descriptions

0	a digit
#	a digit, zero shows as absent
.	placeholder for decimal separator
,	placeholder for grouping separator
E	separates mantissa and exponent for exponential formats
;	separates formats
-	default negative prefix
%	multiply by 100 and show as percentage
?	multiply by 1000 and show as per mille
¤	currency sign; replaced by currency symbol; if doubled, replaced by international currency symbol; if present in a pattern, the monetary decimal separator is used instead of the decimal separator
X	any other characters can be used in the prefix or suffix
'	used to quote special characters in a prefix or suffix

Date Format Pattern Syntax

This is a reference section for the trail, Internationalization (page 95). You can design your own format patterns for dates and times from the list of symbols in the following table:

Table 39 Date and Time Symbol List

Symbol	Meaning	Presentation	Example
`G`	era designator	Text	AD
`y`	year	Number	1996
`M`	month in year	Text & Number	July & 07
`d`	day in month	Number	10
`h`	hour in am/pm (1-12)	Number	12
`H`	hour in day (0-23)	Number	0
`m`	minute in hour	Number	30
`s`	second in minute	Number	55
`S`	millisecond	Number	978
`E`	day in week	Text	Tuesday
`D`	day in year	Number	189
`F`	day of week in month	Number	2 (2nd Wed in July)
`w`	week in year	Number	27
`W`	week in month	Number	2
`a`	am/pm marker	Text	PM
`k`	hour in day (1-24)	Number	24
`K`	hour in am/pm (0-11)	Number	0
`z`	time zone	Text	Pacific Standard Time
`'`	escape for text	Delimiter	(none)
`'`	single quote	Literal	'

Characters that are not letters are treated as quoted text. That is, they will appear in the formatted text even if they are not enclosed with single quotes.

The number of symbol letters you specify also determines thc format. For example, if "zz" pattern results in "PDT," then the "zzzz" pattern generates "Pacific Daylight Time."

The following table summarizes these pattern rules:

Table 40 Rules for Date Formats Patterns

Presentation	Number of Symbols	Result
Text	1 - 3	abbreviated form, if one exists
Text	>= 4	full form
Number	minimum number of digits is required	shorter numbers are padded with zeros (for a year, if the count of 'y' is 2, then the year is truncated to 2 digits)
Text & Number	1 - 2	text form
Text & Number	3	number form

Java IDL Glossary

attribute (IDL)

That part of an IDL interface that is similar to a public class field or C++ data member. The `idltojava` compiler maps an OMG IDL attribute to accessor and modifier methods in the Java programming language. For example, an interface `ball` might include the attribute `color`. The `idltojava` compiler would generate a Java programming language method to get the color, and unless the attribute is `readonly`, a method to set the color. CORBA attributes correspond closely to JavaBeans properties.

client

Any code which invokes an operation on a distributed object. A client might itself be a CORBA object, or it might be a non-object-oriented program, but while invoking a method on a CORBA object, it is said to be acting as client.

client stub

A Java programming language class generated by `idltojava` and used transparently by the client ORB during object invocation. The remote object reference held by the client points to the client stub. This stub is specific to the IDL interface from which it was generated, and it contains the information needed for the client to invoke a method on the CORBA object that was defined in the IDL interface.

client tier

The portion of a distributed application that requests services from the server tier. Typically, the client tier is characterized by a small local footprint, a graphical user interface, and simplified development and maintenance efforts.

Common Object Request Broker Architecture (CORBA)

An OMG-specified architecture that is the basis for the CORBA object model. The CORBA specification includes an interface definition language (IDL), which is a language-independent way of creating contracts between objects for implementation as distributed applications.

See also: *client tier*, *service tier*, *data store tier*

CORBA object

An entity which (1) is defined by an OMG IDL interface, and (2) for which an object reference is available. `Object` is the implicit common base type for object references of IDL interfaces.

data store tier

The portion of a distributed application that manages access to persistent data and its storage mechanisms, such as relational databases.

distributed application

A program designed to run on more than one computer, typically with functionality separated into tiers such as client, service, and data store.

distributed environment

A network of one or more computers that use CORBA objects. Objects are installed on the various machines and can communicate with each other.

Dynamic Invocation Interface (DII)

An API that allows a client to make dynamic invocations on remote CORBA objects. It is used when at compile time a client does not have knowledge about an object it wants to invoke. Once an object is discovered, the client program can obtain a definition of it, issue a parameterized call to it, and receive a reply from it, all without having a type-specific client stub for the remote object.

Dynamic Skeleton Interface (DSI)

An API that provides a way to deliver requests from an ORB to an object implementation when the type of the object implementation is not known at compile time. DSI, which is the server side analog to the client side DII, makes it possible for the application programmer to inspect the parameters of an incoming request to determine a target object and method.

exception (IDL)

An IDL construct that represents an exceptional condition that could be returned in response to an invocation. There are two categories of exceptions: (1) system exceptions, which inherit from `org.omg.CORBA.SystemException`(which is a `java.lang.RuntimeException`), and (2) user-defined exceptions, which inherit from `org.omg.CORBA.UserException` (which is a `java.lang.Exception`).

factory object

A CORBA object that is used to create new CORBA objects. Factory objects are themselves usually created at server installation time.

`idltojava` compiler

A tool that takes an interface written in OMG IDL and produces Java programming language interfaces and classes that represent the mapping from the IDL interface to the Java programming language. The resulting files are `.java` files.

implementation

A concrete class that defines the behavior for all of the operations and attributes of the IDL interface it supports. A servant object is an instance of an implementation. There may be many implementations of a single interface.

initial naming context

The `NamingContext` object returned by a call to the method `orb.resolve_initial_references("NameService")`. It is an object reference to the COS Naming Service registered with the ORB and can be used to create other `NamingContext` objects.

See also: *naming context*

Interface Definition Language (IDL)

The OMG-standard language for defining the interfaces for all CORBA objects. An IDL interface declares a set of operations, exceptions, and attributes. Each operation has a signature, which defines its name, parameters, result and exceptions. OMG IDL does not include implementations for operations; rather, as its name indicates, it is simply a language for defining interfaces.

Interface Repository (IFR)

A service that contains all the registered component interfaces, the methods they support, and the parameters they require. The IFR stores, updates, and manages object interface definitions. Programs may use the IFR APIs to access and update this information. An IFR is not necessary for normal client/server interactions.

Internet InterORB Protocol (IIOP)

The OMG-specified network protocol for communicating between ORBs. Java IDL conforms to IIOP version 1.0.

invocation

The process of performing a method call on a CORBA object, which can be done without knowledge of the object's location on the network. Static invocation, which uses a client stub for the invocation and a server skeleton for the service being invoked, is used when the interface of the object is known at compile time. If the interface is not known at compile time, dynamic invocation must be used.

Java IDL

The classes, libraries, and tools that make it possible to use CORBA objects from the Java programming language. The main components of Java IDL are an ORB, a naming service, and the `idltojava` compiler. The ORB and naming service are part of JDK1.2; the `idltojava` compiler can be downloaded from the Java Developer Connection (JDC) Web site.

name binding

The association of a name with an object reference. Name bindings are stored in a naming context.

namespace

A collection of naming contexts that are grouped together.

naming context

A CORBA object that supports the `NamingContext` interface and functions as a sort of directory which contains (points to) other naming contexts and/or simple names. Similar to a directory structure, where the last item is a file and preceding items are directories, in a naming context, the last item is an object reference name, and the preceding items are naming contexts.

naming service

A CORBA service that allows CORBA objects to be named by means of binding a name to an object reference. The name binding may be stored in the naming service, and a client may supply the name to obtain the desired object reference.

object

A computational grouping of operations and data into a modular unit. An object is defined by the interface it presents to others, its behavior when operations on its interface are invoked, and its state.

object implementation

See *implementation*.

Object Management Group (OMG)

An international organization with over 700 members that establishes industry guidelines and object management specifications in order to provide a common framework for object-oriented application development. Its members include platform vendors, object-oriented database vendors, software tool developers, corporate developers, and software application vendors. The OMG Common Object Request Broker Architecture specifies the CORBA object model. See `www.omg.org` for more information.

object reference

A construct containing the information needed to specify an object within an ORB. An object reference is used in method invocations to locate a CORBA object. Object references are the CORBA object equivalent to programming language-specific object pointers. They may be obtained from a factory object or from the Naming Service. An object reference, which is opaque (its internal structure is irrelevant to application developers), identifies the same CORBA object each time it is used. It is possible, however, for multiple object references to refer to the same CORBA object.

Object Request Broker (ORB)

The libraries, processes, and other infrastructure in a distributed environment that enable CORBA objects to communicate with each other. The ORB connects objects requesting services to the objects providing them.

operation (IDL)

The construct in an IDL interface that maps to a Java programming language method. For example, an interface `ball` might support the operation `bounce`. Operations may take parameters, return a result, or raise exceptions. IDL operations can be `oneway`, in which case they cannot return results (return values or out arguments) or raise exceptions.

parameter (IDL)

One or more objects the client passes to an IDL operation when it invokes the operation. Parameters may be declared as "in" (passed from client to server), "out" (passed from server to client), or "inout" (passed from client to server and then back from server to client).

PIDL (Pseudo-IDL)

The interface definition language for describing a CORBA pseudo-object. Each language mapping, including the mapping from IDL to the Java programming language, describes how pseudo objects are mapped to language-specific constructs. PIDL mappings may or may not follow the rules that apply to mapping regular CORBA objects.

pragma

A directive to the `idltojava` compiler to perform certain operations while compiling an IDL file. For example, the pragma "javaPackage" directs the `idltojava` compiler to put the Java programming language interfaces and classes it generates from the IDL interface into the Java programming language package specified.

pseudo-object

An object similar to a CORBA object in that it is described in IDL, but unlike a CORBA object, it cannot be passed around using its object reference, nor can it be narrowed or stringified. Examples of pseudo-objects include the Interface Repository and DII which, although implemented as libraries, are more clearly described in OMG specifications as pseudo-objects with IDL interfaces. The IDL for pseudo-objects is called "PIDL" to indicate that a pseudo-object is being defined.

servant object

An instance of an object implementation for an IDL interface. The servant object is registered with the ORB so that the ORB knows where to send invocations. It is the servant that performs the services requested when a CORBA object's method is invoked.

server

A program that contains the implementations of one or more IDL interfaces. For example, a desktop publishing server might implement a `Document` object type, a `ParagraphTag` object type, and other related object types. The server is required to register each implementation (servant object) with the ORB so that the ORB knows about the servant. Servers are sometimes referred to as object servers.

server skeleton

A public abstract class generated by the `idltojava` compiler that provides the ORB with information it needs in dispatching method invocations to the servant object(s). A server skeleton, like a client stub, is specific to the IDL interface from which it is generated. A server skeleton is the server side analog to a client stub, and these two classes are used by ORBs in static invocation.

service tier

The portion of a distributed application that contains the business logic and performs most of the computation. The service tier is typically located on a shared machine for optimum resource use.

static invocation

See *invocation*.

stringified object reference

An object reference that has been converted to a string so that it may be stored on disk in a text file (or stored in some other manner). Such strings should be treated as opaque because they are ORB-implementation independent. Standard `object_to_string` and `string_to_object` methods on `org.omg.CORBA.Object` make stringified references available to all CORBA Objects.

Security Glossary

Here are definitions and explanations of some general security and JDK security-specific terms and concepts you may have encountered in Security (page 477). Underlined words refer to other glossary entries.

Certificate

A certificate is a digitally-signed statement from one entity (person, company, etc.), saying that the public key of some other entity has some particular value. If you trust the signature on the certificate, you trust that the association in the certificate between the specified public key and the other entity is authentic.

Cryptography Algorithm

A cryptography algorithm is an algorithm used to help ensure one or more of the following:

- the confidentiality of data
- authentication of the data sender
- integrity of the data sent
- nonrepudiation; a sender cannot deny having sent a particular message

A digital signature algorithm provides some of these characteristics. Also see message digest algorithms. Digital signature and message digest algorithms have been available since JDK 1.1.

A separate release (Java Cryptography Extensions) provides APIs and algorithms related to encryption and decryption.

Decryption

Decryption is the inverse of encryption; it is the process of taking ciphertext (encrypted data) and a cryptographic key, and producing cleartext (the original unencrypted data).

Digital Signature

A digital signature is a string of bits that is computed from some data (the data being "signed") and the private key of an entity (person, company, etc.). The signature can be used to verify that the data came from the entity and was not modified in transit.

Like a handwritten signature, a digital signature has many useful characteristics:

1. Its authenticity can be verified, via a computation that uses the public key corresponding to the private key used to generate the signature.
2. It cannot be forged, assuming the private key is kept secret.

3. It is a function of the data signed and thus can't be claimed to be the signature for other data as well.
4. The signed data cannot be changed; if it is, the signature will no longer verify as being authentic.

Domain or Protection Domain

A protection domain ("domain" for short) encloses a set of classes whose instances are granted the same set of permissions.

In addition to a set of permissions, a domain is comprised of a `CodeSource`, which is a set of `PublicKeys` together with a URL. Thus, classes signed by the same keys and from the same URL are placed in the same domain. Classes that have the same permissions but are from different code sources belong to different domains.

Currently in JDK 1.2, protection domains are created "on demand" as a result of class loading.

Today all code shipped as part of the JDK is considered system code and runs inside the unique system domain, which has all permissions. Each applet or application runs in its appropriate domain, determined by its code source.

Encryption

Encryption is the process of taking data (called *cleartext*) and a cryptographic key and producing *ciphertext*, which is data meaningless to anybody who does not know the key.

Engine Class

An "engine class" defines a cryptographic service in an abstract fashion (without a concrete implementation).

API clients request and utilize instances of the engine classes to carry out corresponding operations. The following engine classes are defined in JDK 1.2:

1. `MessageDigest`: used to calculate the message digest (hash) of specified data.
2. `Signature`: used to sign data and verify digital signatures.
3. `KeyPairGenerator`: used to generate a pair of public and private keys suitable for a specified algorithm.
4. `KeyFactory`: used to convert opaque cryptographic keys of type Key into *key specifications* (transparent representations of the underlying key material), and vice versa.
5. `CertificateFactory`: used to create public key certificates and Certificate Revocation Lists (CRLs).

6. `KeyStore`: used to create and manage a *keystore*. A keystore is a database of keys. Private keys in a keystore have a chain of one or more certificates associated with them, which authenticates the corresponding public key. A keystore also contains certificates from trusted entities.
7. `AlgorithmParameters`: used to manage the parameters for a particular algorithm, including parameter encoding and decoding.
8. `AlgorithmParameterGenerator`: used to generate a set of parameters suitable for a specified algorithm.
9. `SecureRandom`: used to generate random or pseudo-random numbers.

An engine class defines API methods that allow applications to access the specific type of cryptographic service it provides. The actual implementations (from one or more providers) are those for specific algorithms. The `Signature` engine class, for example, provides access to the functionality of a digital signature algorithm. The actual implementation supplied in a `SignatureSpi` subclass (see next paragraph) would be that for a specific kind of signature algorithm, such as SHA1 with DSA, SHA1 with RSA, MD5 with RSA, or even some proprietary signature algorithm.

The application interfaces supplied by an engine class are implemented in terms of a "Service Provider Interface" (SPI). That is, for each engine class, there is a corresponding abstract SPI class, which defines the Service Provider Interface methods that providers must implement.

Message Digest Algorithm (or One-Way Hash Function)

A message digest is a function that takes arbitrary-sized input data (referred to as a message) and generates a fixed-size output, called a digest (or hash). A digest has the following properties:

1. It should be computationally infeasible to find another input string that will generate the same digest.
2. The digest does not reveal anything about the input that was used to generate it.

Message digest algorithms are used to produce unique and reliable identifiers of data. The digests are sometimes called the "digital fingerprints" of data.

Some digital signature algorithms use a message digest algorithm to compute the hash of the data that is being signed, and then digitally sign the hash value rather than the original data, since digitally signing the original data could be very expensive.

Opaque Key Representation

An *opaque* key representation is one in which you have no direct access to the key material that constitutes a key. In other words: "opaque" gives you limited access to the key—just the three methods defined by the `Key` interface: `getAlgorithm`, `getFormat`, and `getEncoded`.

This is in contrast to a transparent representation, in which you can access each key material value individually, through one of the `get` methods defined in the corresponding specification class.

Opaque Parameter Representation

An *opaque* parameter representation is one in which you have no direct access to the parameter fields; you can only get the name of the algorithm associated with the parameter set and some kind of encoding for the parameter set. This is in contrast to a transparent representation of parameters, in which you can access each value individually, through one of the `get` methods defined in the corresponding specification class.

Permission

A permission represents access to a system resource. In order for a resource access to be allowed for an applet (or an application running with a security manager), the corresponding permission must be explicitly granted the code attempting the access.

The policy in effect for a Java application environment specifies which permissions are available for code from various sources.

A permission typically has a name (often referred to as a "target name") and, in some cases, a comma-separated list of one or more actions.

The JDK has a number of built-in permission types (classes), and new types may be added by clients.

Policy

The policy in effect for a Java application environment specifies which permissions are available for code from various sources.

The source location for the policy information is up to the `Policy` implementation. JDK 1.2 has a default `Policy` implementation that obtains its information from static "policy configuration files," also known simply as "policy files."

Private Key

A private key is a number that is supposed to be known only to a particular entity (person, company, etc.). That is, private keys are always meant to be kept secret. They can be used to generate digital signatures. A private key is always associated with a single public key.

Protection Domain

See Domain.

Provider

Implementations for various cryptography algorithms are provided by *Cryptographic Service Providers*. Providers are essentially packages that implement one or more engine classes for specific algorithms. For example, the Java Development Kit's default provider, named "SUN," supplies implementations of various cryptography services and algorithms, including the DSA signature algorithm and the MD5 and SHA-1 message digest algorithms. Other providers may define their own implementations of these algorithms or of other algorithms, such as an implementation of an RSA-based signature algorithm or the MD2 message digest algorithm.

Public Key

A public key is a number associated with a particular entity (for example, an individual or an organization). A public key is intended to be known to everyone who needs to have trusted interactions with that entity. A public key is always associated with a single private key, and can be used to verify digital signatures generated using that private key.

Security Manager

Currently, all JDK system code invokes security manager methods to check the policy currently in effect and perform resource access control checks.

Most browsers install a security manager, so applets typically run under the scrutiny of a security manager. Each such applet is not allowed to access resources unless it is explicitly granted permission to do so by the security policy currently in effect. In Java platforms that are compatible with JDK 1.2, the permission must be granted by an entry in a policy file.

A security manager is *not* automatically installed when an *application* is running, and thus the application has full access to resources (as was always the case in JDK 1.1). To apply the same security policy to an application found on the local file system as to downloaded applets, either the user running the application must invoke the Java Virtual Machine with the new `-Djava.security.manager` command-line argument or the application itself must call the `setSecurityManager` method in the `java.lang.System` class to install a security manager.

Self-Signed Certificate

A self-signed certificate is one for which the issuer (signer) is the same as the subject (the entity whose public key is being authenticated by the certificate).

Signature

See Digital Signature.

Signed Code

An abbreviated way of saying "code in a class file that appears in a JAR file that was signed." See Digital Signature.

Transparent Key Representation

A *transparent* representation of keys means that you can access each key material value individually, through one of the `get` methods defined in the corresponding specification class. For example, `DSAPrivateKeySpec` defines `getX`, `getP`, `getQ`, and `getG` methods, to access the private key `x`, and the DSA algorithm parameters used to calculate the key: the prime `p`, the sub-prime `q`, and the base `g`.

This is in contrast to an opaque representation, as defined by the `Key` interface, in which you have no direct access to the key material fields.

Transparent Parameter Representation

A *transparent* representation of a set of parameters means that you can access each parameter value in the set individually, through one of the `get` methods defined in the corresponding specification class. For example, `DSAParameterSpec` defines `getP`, `getQ`, and `getG` methods, to access the DSA community parameters p, q, and g, respectively.

This is contrasted with an opaque representation, as supplied by the `AlgorithmParameters` class, in which you have no direct access to the parameter fields; you can only get the name of the algorithm associated with the parameter set (via `getAlgorithm`) and some kind of encoding for the parameter set (via `getEncoded`).

Java Native Interface Reference

This is the reference section for the trail, Java Native Interface (page 625).

Creating and Loading Shared Libraries

Procedures for creating and loading shared libraries are platform dependent. This section provides some answers regarding naming conventions for shared libraries and locating shared libraries.

Naming Conventions

Each Java Runtime Environment (JRE) provides a platform-dependent mechanism for mapping between the actual file name of a shared library and the name string that you pass as an argument to the `System.loadLibrary` method.

Solaris:

The shared library file name requires a `lib` prefix and a `.so` extension. Do not include the `lib` prefix or the `.so` extension for the argument that you pass to the `System.loadLibrary` method.

Win32:

The shared library file name requires a `.dll` extension. Do not include the `.dll` extension for the `System.loadLibrary` method argument.

Search Mechanisms

Each Java runtime environment provides its own mechanism that indicates where to find shared libraries for native method implementations. The platform-dependent wrapper script or application shell can use the appropriate mechanism to indicate where shared libraries are located.

Solaris:

The `LD_LIBRARY_PATH` environment variable defines a list of directories that the Solaris VM searches for shared libraries.

Win32:

The Win32 VM uses a search path that includes the current directory for the process or one of the directories listed in the `PATH` environment variable.

Avoiding Name Conflicts

To avoid file name conflicts, it is best to *prepend* directories or folders containing shared libraries to search paths, such as the `LD_LIBRARY_PATH` or `PATH` environment variables.

Supporting Multiple Platforms

Because a Java application with native methods may support multiple platforms, it helps to organize multiple shared libraries into subdirectories by platform, such as `<app-dir>/lib/<platform>`.

Modify Your Library Path

UNIX

```
% setenv LD_LIBRARY_PATH mylibrarypath:$\'7bLD_LIBRARY_PATH}
```

where *mylibrarypath* is the name of the directory containing `libhello.so`.

Win32

On Win32, the `loadLibrary` method searches for DLLs in the same manner as other language environments do.

Running javah

UNIX

```
% javah -jni HelloWorld
```

Win32

```
C:\'3e javah -jni HelloWorld
```

Set Your Library Path

UNIX

```
% setenv LD_LIBRARY_PATH mylibrarypath
```

where *mylibrarypath* is the name of the directory containing `libhello.so`.

Win32

On Win32, the `loadLibrary` method searches for DLLs in the same manner as other language environments do.

Index

Note: An italic *e* after a page number indicates an entry in Appendix A, Code Examples.

B

C

D

G

J

K

L

M

N

P

S

T

The Addison-Wesley Java™ Series

ISBN 0-201-31006-6

ISBN 0-201-31007-4

ISBN 0-201-48558-3

ISBN 0-201-43298-6

ISBN 0-201-31003-1

ISBN 0-201-31002-3

ISBN 0-201-48552-4

ISBN 0-201-63451-1

ISBN 0-201-63453-8

ISBN 0-201-63459-7

ISBN 0-201-30995-5

ISBN 0-201-63456-2

ISBN 0-201-69581-2

ISBN 0-201-63452-X

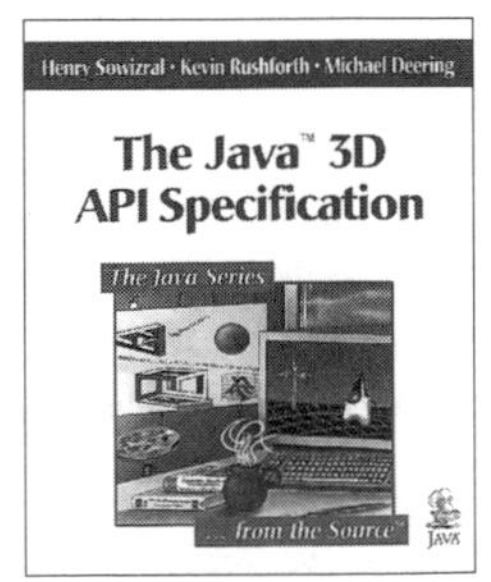

ISBN 0-201-32576-4

Please see our web site (http://www.awl.com/cseng/javaseries) for more information on these titles.

The Java Tutorial CD-ROM

The *Java Tutorial* CD-ROM that accompanies this book is loaded with development kits and documentation, including the content and code of all three books: *The Java Tutorial*, *The Java Tutorial Continued*, and *The JFC Swing Tutorial*. Where the release version is not noted, the most recent release at the time of printing is included.

Table 1 Development Kits on *The Java Tutorial* CD-ROM

Development Kits	Version(s)
Java Development Kit (JDK)	1.2, 1.1.7, 1.02
Java Runtime Environment (JRE)	1.2
Java Foundation Classes (JFC) *includes Swing 1.1*	1.1
Beans Development Kit (BDK)	1.0
JavaBeans Activation Framework (JAF)	1.0
Java Servlet Development Kit (JSDK)	2.0
Java Naming and Directory Interface (JNDI)	1.1

Table 2 Documentation on *The Java Tutorial* CD-ROM

Documentation	Version(s)
The Java Tutorial	
Java Programming Language API Documentation	1.2, 1.1, 1.02
JFC 1.1 API Documentation	1.1
The Swing Connection	
The Java Platform White Paper	

Table 3 Products on *The Java Tutorial* CD-ROM

Products	Version(s)
HotJava Browser	1.1.5
Java Plug-In	1.2, 1.1
`idltojava` Compiler	

Table 4 Specifications on *The Java Tutorial* CD-ROM

Specifications
Java 2D Specification
JavaBeans Specification
Servlet Specification
JDBC 1.2 and 2.0 Specifications
Security 1.2 Specification
Java Cryptography Architecture API Specification
Drag & Drop Specification

Table 5 Miscellaneous on *The Java Tutorial* CD-ROM

And more...
Java Code Conventions
Java Programming Language Glossary
100% Pure Java CookBook

The `README.html` file on the CD-ROM is the central HTML page that links you to all of its contents. To view this page, use the `Open Page` command or its equivalent in your Internet browser. On some platforms, you can simply double click on the HTML file to launch it in your browser.

You can check out the latest Sun Microsystems Java™ programming language product releases at: `http://java.sun.com/products/index.html`. If you sign up for the Java Developer Connection,[1] you will receive free, early access to such products, including the latest Java Development Kit (JDK).

See this book's Web page at: `http://java.sun.com/docs/books/tutorial/continued/index.html` for pointers to the latest versions of this content. The content is not supported and is provided as is, with no expressed or implied warranty.

---

[1] http://developer.javasoft.com/index.html